CHALICE INTRODUCTION TO Disciples Theology

CHALICE INTRODUCTION TO Disciples Theology

PETER GOODWIN HELTZEL, ED.

ST. LOUIS, MISSOURI

Cover art: Fotosearch
Cover and interior design: Elizabeth Wright

www.chalicepress.com

Print: 9780827205109 EPUB: 9780827205628 EPDF: 9780827205635

Library of Congress Cataloging–in–Publication Data

Heltzel, Peter.
Chalice introduction to Disciples theology / Peter Goodwin Heltzel, editor.
p. cm.
ISBN 978-0-8272-0510-9
1. Christian Church (Disciples of Christ)—Doctrines. 2. Theology, Doctrinal. I. Title. II. Title: Introduction to theology.

BX7321.3.H45 2008
230'.663—dc22

2007037291

Printed in the United States of America

Contents

Acknowledgments

This book began with a conversation with Trent Butler at the General Assembly in Portland, Oregon, in July 2005. During the Portland Assembly, I also had helpful conversations about the project with Rufus Burrow Jr., Kris Culp, Dennis Landon, Timothy Lee, Daisy Machado, Mark Miller-McLemore, Bill Tabbernee, Mark Toulouse, Keith Watkins, Sharon Watkins, and Newell Williams.

All the contributors have been a great support throughout the project, but I want to thank a few in particular. First, I thank Kris Culp for being a wise advisor and good friend throughout the project from beginning to end. I thank my colleagues on the writing team for the first two chapters—Jim Duke, Verity Jones, and Bill Nottingham. The four of us have had an ongoing theological correspondence through the past year that has helped to energize the project.

This project has benefited from five different forums in which its ideas were tested: Porto Alegre, Brazil; twice in Indianapolis; Chicago; and New York City. At the 9th Assembly of the World Council of Churches, I was able to discuss Disciples theology in context of the ecumenical movement with many fellow Disciples.

I thank Robert Welsh and the Council on Christian Unity for hosting a meeting at the Disciples Center in Indianapolis on Thursday, March 23, 2006. Several of the contributors met to discuss the project, including Sandra Gourdet, Richard Hamm, Verity A. Jones, Michael St. A. Miller, Bill Nottingham, Felix Ortiz, and Robert Welsh.

I thank Kris Culp for hosting a seminar for the project at the Disciples Divinity House of the University of Chicago, July 17–18, 2006. Several Disciples House Scholars participated in the seminar including: Garry Sparks, William Wright, Jordan Berry, and Santiago Piñón. Garry Sparks went out of his way to be a gracious host to the contributors, especially to our international guests, Bosela Eale from the Congo and Christobal Mareco Lird from Paraguay. I also thank the Oreon E. Scott Foundation for a grant to the Christian Board of Publication that helped fund contributors' travel to the Chicago seminar.

I am grateful to Rick Lowery for inviting me to present chapters 1, 2, 8, and 9 at the Association of Disciples for Theological Discussion on Saturday, October 15, 2006, at Christian Theological Seminary in Indianapolis, Indiana. At this meeting Serene Jones gave a thoughtful critique of these chapters. Kwok Pui-lan, Catherine Keller, Sharon Welch, members of the Theology and Empire group, also critiqued these chapters on Sunday, October 29, 2006, in New York City.

I thank Lawrence Burnley and Kenneth Henry for helping to deepen my understanding of the African American Disciples experience. I also thank

Rita Nakashima Brock and Brian Sarrazin for facilitating the writing of the final chapter.

I thank many Disciples around the country for their active theological friendship, including Rufus Burrow, Joan Brown Campbell, Wilson Dickinson, Chris Dorsey, Daniel Feliciano, Claudia Ann Highbaugh, Chris Hobgood, Tabitha Knerr, Lonnie Oates, Albert Pennybacker, Rafael Rivera Rosa, Richard Sturm, Darryl Trimiew, Jessica Vasquez, Raiford Wheeler, and Matthew Weiner.

Various congregations have also contributed to the development of this book, including First Christian Church, Vicksburg, Mississippi; La Hermosa Christian Church, Harlem, New York; and Third Christian Church, Harlem, New York.

New York Theological Seminary has supported this project in many ways. I thank my faculty colleagues for an ongoing conversation about contextual theological education in global urban centers, including Humberto Alfaro, Jin Hee Han, Obery M. Hendricks Jr., Edward L. Hunt, Dale T. Irvin, Michelle Lim Jones, Lowell W. Livezey, Lois Livezey, C. Vernon Mason, Eleanor Moody-Shepherd, Laura Pires-Hester, Rebecca M. Radillo, Jerry Reisig, Lester Edwin J. Ruiz, and George W. Webber.

It has been a joy to work with the staff at Chalice Press, including Russ White, Trent Butler, Pablo Jiménez, Pam Brown, and Wesley Bucheck.

I thank my family, Sam and Ann Heltzel, Rachel Rankin, Margie Heltzel, and Robert Heltzel. I also remember my grandparents, John and Marjorie Frazer who passed on the five generations of Disciples heritage in my family. Finally, I thank my wife, Sarah, for constant love and inspiring singing.

Finally, I thank Chloe Breyer, Ronald McKoy, Anthony Rivera, Henry Shaw, and Lilliam Vasquez for proofreading portions of the manuscript. I thank Rafael Reyes III for his invaluable assistance in preparing this manuscript for publication.

Preface

The *Chalice Introduction to Disciples Theology* could not have been published until now. It is not that the Stone–Campbell Movement, which early in its history shunned the word *theology,* has eschewed theology in practice. On the contrary, Barton W. Stone's *An Address to the Christian Churches in Kentucky, Tennessee and Ohio: On Several Important Doctrines of Religion* (1814) and Alexander Campbell's *The Christian System, in reference to the Union of Christians, and a restoration of Primitive Christianity as pled in the Current Reformation* (1835) both addressed theological topics—including the Trinity, Jesus Christ, atonement, the Holy Spirit, and faith—that were of particular interest to nineteenth-century North American Protestants. Neither is it that Disciples have never before published a multiauthor treatment of Disciples understandings of church teachings. In 1963 Bethany Press, an imprint of Christian Board of Publication, published the three-volume *The Panel of Scholars Reports,* with William B. Blakemore as general editor: volume 1, *The Reformation of Tradition;* volume 2, *The Reconstruction of Theology;* volume 3, *The Revival of the Churches.* The Panel, charged by the United Christian Missionary Society and the Board of Education of the Christian Churches (Disciples of Christ) to examine the doctrines and polity of the Disciples in light of contemporary scholarship, comprised fourteen educators affiliated with Disciples-related educational institutions and three ministers who were serving congregations during their membership on the panel. Rather than the subject—theology—or number of contributors, the global perspectives and the diversity of contributors sets this *Chalice Introduction to Disciples Theology* apart from any multiauthor Disciples introduction to theology that could have been published before now.

That Christian theology is coming of age in our increasingly globalized world is a fundamental premise of this introduction. The editor notes that as Christians from the Southern hemisphere confront the postcolonial realities associated with global capitalism, they provide important new challenges for contemporary North American theology. The Disciples theologies noted above assumed a universal theological context. In this twenty-first–century Disciples introduction to theology, the coverage of the five theological categories of The Task and Sources of Theology, God and Creation, The Church, Salvation, and Mission includes such topics as "Theology as Intercultural Conversation in an Age of Globalization," "Theological Reasoning in a Pluralistic Context," "Confessing Christ in Empire and Colony," "The Church as Sacrament of Human Wholeness," "Eschatology and Economy in Latin America and the Caribbean," "Mission in Africa: An African Disciple Perspective," "Mission in Pluralistic Contexts—A Caribbean Perspective," Ecumenism of Spirit and Mission: Disciples of Christ and Pentecostals in Venezuela," "Global Chalice of Blessing: A

Christological Reading in the Face of globalized Imperialism," "The Future of Christian Mission in an Age of World Christianity." A twenty-first–century Disciples embrace of Christian theology in a globalized world is reflected in the diversity of the contributors to this volume. Barton Stone, Alexander Campbell, and all seventeen members of the Panel of Scholars were white North American males. In contrast, ten of the thirty-four contributors to this introduction are women, ten are persons of color, and the book includes voices from the Southern hemisphere. Were it not for the increasing diversity of the Christian Church (Disciples of Christ) and the increasing theological openness to that diversity among Disciples, this *Chalice Introduction to Disciples Theology* could not have been published.

One further note: this introduction to theology *would* not have been published without the vision and commitment of Chalice Press, a publishing imprint of the Christian Board of Publication, and the volume's editor, Peter Goodwin Heltzel. Contemporary Christians and future historians of Disciples at the dawn of the twenty-first century will be grateful for their vision and commitment.

D. Newell Williams
Moderator, the Christian Church (Disciples of Christ)
in the United States and Canada
President and Professor of Modern and American Church History,
Brite Divinity School at Texas Christian University

Introduction

Christian theology is coming of age in our increasingly globalized world. Christianity is exploding in the Southern Hemisphere at the same time that global capitalism continues to extend its global reach. As Southern Christians confront postcolonial realities, they provide important new challenges for contemporary North American theology.

The *Chalice Introduction to Disciples Theology* is an engaging, contemporary introduction to theology that reflects Christian identity from the perspective of the Christian Church (Disciples of Christ), ecumenical generosity, and global scope. The text provides a critical introduction to the nature, sources, contexts, and major doctrines of Christian theology for pastors, theological students, and Christian leaders across the ecumenical spectrum.

The authors of the present volume all come from a common Disciples theological tradition, but speak to the whole church in the context of our contemporary global situation. Each author is in conversation with the tradition: the Disciples tradition, and the ecumenical tradition. Because of our ecumenical vision of an open table, Disciples theologians are well positioned today to speak to the wider church and culture.

While united by a common Christian heritage, the theological reflection in the volume is nourished by a variety of cultural settings and theological perspectives. Each doctrine is considered in light of theology's globally diverse and locally specific contexts. Some authors write from specific cultural contexts outside of North America, such as Paraguay, Puerto Rico, the Caribbean, and sub-Saharan Africa. Those in the European-American tradition write as if they are contributing to a larger conversation with the faith and practice of the worldwide church. The authors represent a broad perspective of cultural and gender perspectives so that together we embody the broader discussion of global theology.

Our new global situation calls for a prophetic, intercultural theology. Multicultural models of ministry and theology often do not go far enough in addressing the legacies of colonialism and white supremacy that continue to afflict communities of color. An intercultural theology acknowledges cultural particularity and embraces the conflict that emerges through the historic and hermeneutic struggles that inform our distinct cultural realities. Intercultural conversation becomes a vital model for expanding the possibilities of theological conversation, including the recentering of voices that have been—and continue to be—marginalized. Intercultural conversation holds out the hope of us singing new songs together as we join in the gospel struggle for peace, love, and justice.

This volume is divided into five sections. The first section discusses "The Task and Sources of Theology." In chapter 1, Peter Goodwin Heltzel, James O. Duke, Verity Jones, and William J. Nottingham describe globalization that has become a central and overriding force in contemporary political, cultural, economic, and religious practice and discourse. They analyze key concepts from postcolonial studies that will be helpful in the construction of an intercultural theology. They go on to argue in chapter 2 that the Disciples are well positioned to make a vital contribution to twenty-first–century global theology. They discuss five central themes in the tradition that play an important role in Disciples theological table-talk: restoration, unity, interpretation, mission, and eschatology.

In chapter 3, Hee An Choi argues that while the Bible remains the primary source of theology for Disciples, it is vital for Disciples to interpret it from a postcolonial perspective. This will ensure that we are sensitive to difference, while acknowledging that we are "all of one piece." In chapter 4, William Tabbernee argues that, despite the rhetoric of early Disciples leaders regarding "No creed but Christ" and "No book but the Bible," Disciples have, in practice, taken seriously (and continue to take seriously) both the apostolic tradition and, as it developed, Disciples tradition. The author argues that because of their strong commitment to the visible unity of the Christian Church, Disciples also understand the imperative to take "ecumenical tradition" seriously in order to incorporate the theological insights of others, especially where there is now an ecumenical consensus or, at least, a convergence on particular issues. It is recognized, however, that, equally, Disciples insights on Christian faith and practice can also enrich the Christianity of those in other ecclesial traditions. For Disciples living in postcolonial times, "doing theology" is not a matter of reading the Bible and taking a few notes. "Theologizing" is hard, meticulous work: understanding, sifting, and incorporating relevant data from the "sources" of theology—which include three interrelated types of tradition: apostolic, denominational, and ecumenical.

In his recent book *Identity and Violence,* Harvard University economist Amartya Sen observes that "many of the conflicts and barbarities in the world are sustained through the illusion of a unique and choiceless identity," derived from civilization or religion. A more adequate, less conflictive concept of identity, according to Sen, would recognize that identities are composites that draw together "plural affiliations" by making choices "about what relative importance to attach, in a particular context to the divergent loyalties"[1] that comprise human lives. Building from Sen's proposal that identity is a composite of plural affiliations, Clark Gilpin argues in chapter 5 that the tasks assigned to *reason* in modern theology have primarily involved interpreting the relation between religion and other features of personal identity or other communities of affiliation. The chapter proposes that the Christian's plural affiliations became a crucial theological issue for the founders of the Disciples of Christ in early nineteenth-century America. From this historical case study, the chapter elaborates three forms of theological reasoning and assesses their implications for religious identity in the contemporary pluralistic context.

In chapter 6, Kristine A. Culp argues that a living faith and a living theology will always be learning from experience. In our day this entails rendering learning from the experiences of generations of Disciples; being mindful of whose experience has been excluded and whose has been assumed to be normative; being suspicious of how "personal experience" is packaged and used in globalized consumer cultures; and being open to new testimonies of justice and truth that emerge from the balconies, borderlands, and margins of the Disciples of Christ and of the world.

In chapter 7, Peter Heltzel and Don Browning observe a convergence among many contemporary movements of theology around some of core concerns of practical theology. They argue for a contextual theological method in three moments: the gospel moment, the historical moment, and the constructive moment. They argue for a redefinition of restoration as reconciliation. Furthermore, they argue that the church should embody practices of reconciliation as a constructive response to intercultural challenges of globalization.

Section II contains essays on "God in Creation." Peter Heltzel argues in chapter 8 that Disciples should recover the doctrine of the Trinity in liturgical and social practice. Through analyzing Barton W. Stone's rejection of the Trinity in light of contemporary Disciples practice, he notes a resilient unitarianism within the denomination. However, the ecumenical theme that drives the movement has driven the denomination through ecumenical dialogue and the restructure process to develop a more fully Trinitarian doctrine. He sees the Trinity's emphasis on unity-in-diversity as supplying an important resource for intercultural theology today.

Clark Williamson's argument on christology in chapter 9 locates Jesus Christ and Paul's witness to him in the context of the Roman Empire and the varieties of Judaism at the time. It claims that this long-neglected but patently obvious context is crucial to understanding Jesus and Paul as well as the later Constantinian imperial subversion of their lives and witness. And it points out how the church was tempted by its establishment in the later empire to participate in this subversion as well. As an antidote to this subversion, both then and now in our American "imperium," it seeks to reclaim the early witness to Jesus and Paul's theology of the cross. In chapter 10, Rita Nakashima Brock writes a constructive christology. Building on her feminist critique of the atonement, she provides a postcolonial counter-genealogy to standard Western accounts of Christo-imperialism.

In chapter 11, Dyron Daughrity argues that we are witnessing a paradigm shift in the history of Christian theology. The Holy Spirit has made a radical comeback. Shortly after reaching its high point on Pentecost Sunday and in the lives of the earliest Christians, it soon became mired in controversy, particularly when adopted by Montanus, one of the better-known "heretics" of the second century. The Holy Spirit has since struggled to regain its rightful place as God. In recent decades, however, there has been a massive shift. Global Christianity is currently "under the influence" of the Holy Spirit in a profound way. Perhaps this great new fact of our time is not as evident in the West, but one thing is certain, the Southern churches have caught the winds of God—and they are on fire. This chapter provides an introduction to pneumatology by focusing on three contexts: biblical, historical, and the restoration tradition. Providing a backdrop for the chapter is the argument that pneumatology is making a radical comeback with the rise of non-Western Christianity. This will have major theological implications for the future of the Church.

In chapter 12, Victor Hunter argues for an approach to the doctrine of creation that explores the meaning of "eco-justice" and "creation-consciousness" in a world whose "life is under threat." The theological meanings of creation are illuminated in relationship to other biblical concerns such as world origins, anthropology, redemption, ecology, ethics, and eschatology. The doctrine of creation is then set in the context of the five historic themes in the theology of the Disciples of Christ.

Section III is simply on "the Church." In chapter 13, Sharon E. Watkins and Keith Watkins argue that the Christian Church (Disciples of Christ) [CCDC] has long sought to live in this world as though the reality of God's realm already applied. The desire to be a sign of a reality that only God can bring in its fullness can be described as sacramental. This sense of church joined with a passion for the unity of humankind suggests that for Disciples, church functions as a sacrament of human wholeness.

If the church is to be this kind of sacramental presence, it needs to move forward with clear purpose and strong resolve. The hard choice that churches are called upon to make is whether to live in ways that are consistent with and subservient to contemporary culture, or to live in ways that proclaim and exhibit a way of life that is more consistent with the realm of God that Jesus proclaimed. If the church is to be a sacrament of human wholeness, then the latter choice—difficult as it may be—is the one that must be taken.

In chapter 14, Thomas Best argues that in baptism Christ claims each of us for his own; and because we all belong to Christ, we all belong to one other, each of us members of Christ's one body, the church. Baptism is a sign of the *unity* of the church, and a challenge to our divisions. From their beginning Disciples have valued baptism, practiced by immersion on confessing believers ("adult" baptism), as the individual's response in faith to Christ's gracious gift of salvation. Disciples' experience in countries around the world, and within united and uniting churches, has led to a greater understanding of the intention behind "infant" baptism, and of some understandings of baptism other than our own.

Disciples have many opportunities for understanding of baptism to grow and develop. In worship we experience anew the saving events of our faith; we would do well as Disciples to practice remembering our baptism, as a way of renewing both the church and ourselves.

In Chapter 15, Belva Brown Jordan and Stephanie A. Paulsell reflect on spiritual and communal dimensions of the Lord's supper. In this chapter they reflect on our Disciples heritage, the stories of our faith, and our experiences of the Lord's supper to speak with gratitude about this central practice of Disciples life and with hope about how this meal—a meal that sets the standard for all our meals—teaches us to live with generosity and openness in a violent and troubled world.

In chapter 16, Kay Lynn Northcutt describes different operative theologies of Disciples preaching and applies them to the contemporary problem of cultural pluralism. With its righteous anger against church divisiveness and its distinctively modern insight that Protestant reform movements were themselves contributors to such divisions, the Disciples have not surprisingly birthed a wondrous variety of preaching, midwifed by a diverse chorus of preachers. This chapter explores the versatile voices, cultures, and operative theologies of preaching that emerged from the initial expressions of the Stone-Campbell movement up through its current global context as the Christian Church (Disciples of Christ).

In chapter 17, Mark Miller-McLemore argues that Disciples ministers understand themselves by what they do (their practices) rather than their pastoral office or doctrinal affirmations. Interviewing pastors from different racial-ethnic groups demonstrates that Disciples need to learn from other Disciples who do ministry differently.

Section IV turns to "Reconciliation." In chapter 18, Darryl Trimiew argues that Disciples need to embrace a doctrine of social sin. When it comes to controversial issues like race and gay-lesbian issues, Disciples have some very different understandings of what is sin. Trimiew argues that to be Disciples means to be willing to live with different understandings of sin. He sees this paradigm as providing a horizon of hope for communities that struggle with difference based on race and sexual orientation.

In chapter 19, Joe R. Jones argues that the heart of the Christian understanding of salvation is the incarnational narrative of the salvific work of Jesus Christ, which entails a trinitarian understanding of God and a sobering grasp of human sinfulness. Hence, the full range of salvation-talk is complex and multidimensional, and Jones proposes to map the deep interconnections in such talk. In the final analysis, Jones argues that the grace of God, as we know it in Jesus Christ, entitles and summons the church to trust in God's ultimate redemption of all creatures and the whole creation.

In chapter 20, Bosela Eale and William A. Wright take on the question, How and when do we make the transition from being lost to being saved? The authors engage in a dialogue between the experience of salvation within the Disciples of Christ Community in the Congo and the perspective on justification by faith within Euro-American theology, from the Reformation to Alexander Campbell and on to contemporary ecumenical breakthroughs. While the authors leave many questions open, they agree that the North American church should ask itself if it is taking seriously enough the difference salvation makes in our lives. Salvation, understood through justification by faith, cuts through the self-centering forces of our culture and opens us to a self-critical awareness of our global responsibilities.

In chapter 21, Karen Marie Yust argues that the early Disciples emphases on the Lord's supper and the importance of Bible study, coupled with reflection on our hymnody and the writings of Christian mystics, can help today's Disciples shape a contemporary understanding of holiness that fits the challenges of twenty-first–century life.

In chapter 22, Bonnie J. Miller-McLemore and Joseph D. Driskill argue that Disciples need to sanctify the ordinary through recovery of a spirituality of the everyday. In chapter 23, Angel Luis Rivera-Agosto presents eschatology in an earthy way that embraces the concrete struggles for economic justice in the Americas.

Section V focuses on "Mission." In chapter 24, Michael Kinnamon argues that prophetic witness is a vital part of the church's mission and witness. While the civil rights movement was a high watermark in the church's prophetic struggle, the struggle continues in an age of American empire. In chapter 25, Bosela Eale argues that African missiology is changing. There is no longer the thought of viewing mission as the work to be done by white men or women from Western nations. Africans are experiencing now the true sense of indigenous mission. In chapter 26 Michael Miller, a native of Jamaica, is critical of historic Christian mission ventures in the English-speaking Caribbean. He highlights the connection of these ventures with the colonizing project that included slavery and indentureship, and with the associated attempts to eclipse the religio-cultural foundations of non-European peoples. Miller takes the position that "the appropriate ethos for mission in the Caribbean is one in which religious and cultural diversity is engaged in critical, creative, and respectful ways for the deepening of insight, all-round refinement of thought, and strengthening of commitment to life-enhancing existence."

Miller identifies possible components for a broad conceptual framework from which can be derived tools of analysis and criteria for assessing relevant understandings of mission in the Caribbean context and elsewhere.

In chapter 27, Carmelo Alvarez argues that Disciples pneumatology should learn from the Pentecostals. He illustrates this through a case study of Disciples-Pentecostal dialogue in Venezuela. In chapter 28, Cristobal Mareco Lird explains the challenges of mission in Latin American, including the negative consequences of globalization. In chapter 29, Don Pittman provides a constructive Disciples theology of religions. Building on the Council on Christian Unity's 2006 report, "Disciples of Christ and Interreligious Engagement," Pittman argues that interreligious dialogue and cooperation should be important aspects of ministry.

In chapter 30, Carlos F. Cardoza-Orlandi argues that Disciples theology must continue to be transformed by developments in world Christianity. The demographic transformation of the Christian religion, with its growth and vitality in the Third World and its decline and stagnation among many Euro-American Christian communities, generates new agents of Christian mission, questions about the nature and character of mission practices and theologies, and the challenge of an intercultural and interreligious mission matrix, the lifeblood of historic Christianity. There is a significant challenge to reinterpret the movement of the Christian religion accentuating the reality of world Christianity and discovering how these changes become a catalyst for the renewal of theology, mission, and the practices of ministry in local congregations in any context.

SECTION 1

The Task and Sources of Theology

1

Theology as Intercultural Conversation in an Age of Globalization

Peter Goodwin Heltzel, James O. Duke,
Verity A. Jones, and William J. Nottingham

Christian theology in North America is at an impasse. At the moment when the U.S. nation-state as a superpower and the global hegemony of neo-liberal capitalism have coalesced, the church in the global South is experiencing dramatic growth; Europe is increasingly secularized; and North American historic Protestant churches are losing prominence. Not unrelated is the problem of global warming, as well as the growing gap between rich and poor that contributes to a crisis of hunger and violence worldwide. It is vital that contemporary Christian theology apply the gospel of Jesus Christ to these new global challenges. This chapter identifies critical elements of the current situation and suggests resources and directions for further theological reflection.

Globalization is one way of describing our new interconnected world. The term "globalization" can refer to a general system of social forces that presently function to bring our world together, including technology, telecommunications, urbanization, and democratic capitalism. Globalization has many dimensions, including economic, political, and cultural.

Economic globalization usually refers to a form of free-trade capitalism that has facilitated a transformation of national economies into regional and international trading blocks.[1] These new global economic networks have facilitated the flows of goods, services, and capital. Through digitalized money markets, investors are able to carry out massive global transfers of financial capital. The Asian financial crisis in the 1990s demonstrated the global economic risk of speculative money trading growing in influence over traditional production-oriented labor. Economic globalization has changed the way that we have done business, but it has also transformed politics and culture.

The tentacles of globalization have grown so vast and pervasive that some commentators have referred to economic globalization as new forces of "empire." They argue that the current challenges of empire lay far beyond the imperialism of the great European nation-states of old Europe in the eighteenth and nineteenth centuries. In our post-cold war, post-9/11 context, many commentators point to the United States as a superpower nation-state internalizing and enacting the self-regulatory myth of empire that animated these modern European nation-states.[2] Other commentators like Michael Hardt and Antonio Negri view empire as a more diffuse social force that now spans the globe through a neo-liberal form of economic globalization and cultural hegemony.[3]

In the current "empire" debate, the United States is in the hot seat. If we understand empire as referring to the sovereignty of the most dominant nation-state in any given epoch, then the United States is an empire (*political globalization*). Today the United States does exert political influence and control over the sovereignty of other political societies. We see an explicit example of this in the War in Iraq, where the United States is using its military might to help establish a democratic nation-state. When the War in Iraq is placed in the context of the broader neo-conservative foreign policy strategy in the Middle East, the United States's ambitions for empire are apparent. While the War in Iraq is an example of a certain form of political globalization, it also demonstrates some of the limits of this project when they are placed in the context of cultural and religious difference.

The U.S. confrontation with cultural difference in Iraq demonstrates that the forces of globalization have dimensions beyond politics and economic production, including the phenomena of *cultural globalization*. Global cities, while crossroads for the flows of capital and political discourses, are also at the matrix of multiple cultures and multiple religions. Global multiculturalism provides an opportunity for a new, multicultural, world Christianity to continue to grow. The expansion of churches in Africa, Asia, Latin America, and the islands of the Caribbean and the South Pacific challenges churches in the United States to develop new models of ministry and to rethink global mission. Theologians of the South are asking a new set of questions concerning global fairness, poverty, world hunger, so-called Third World debt, and interreligious living for justice and peace.

I. Globalization and Christian Identity

The challenges posed by globalization are confronting the U.S. churches precisely at a moment of great cultural accommodation among both evangelical churches and historic Protestant churches.[4] Many Evangelical churches in the United States have been quick to internalize the imperial logic of empire through a commodification of the gospel that is often individualist, consumerist, and nationalistic in its orientation. Regardless of their cultural and political excesses, these churches in the United States have been growing quickly since the 1970s.

The historic Protestant churches entered the twentieth century with their own version of internalized imperial logic, poised to provide intellectual, cultural, and political leadership to the nation, which they did through the 1960s. However, once the country emerged from the civil rights movement and the Vietnam War, the historic Protestant churches began to experience a period of intense disestablishment. Through the powerful cultural forces of secularization and disillusionment, many young people stopped going to church.

Christian theology thinks creatively and contextually about the implications of the "evangel." Evangel means gospel, the message of "God's good news" of redemptive love for creation. Jesus of Nazareth proclaimed this message. Christians then proclaimed it thereafter as supremely expressed in Jesus' person and work. Insistence on God's rule by redemptive love was an affront to worldly rulers everywhere, Jew and Gentile establishments alike. The early church struggled for its life under the hegemony of imperial Rome and its client states. Christians, as well as countless others routinely termed dissenters, traitors, and no-accounts, were martyred in Rome's Colosseum, and elsewhere throughout the Empire. Christian worship literally went underground into the catacombs. So vast, so pervasive, so inescapable and so terrible was the socio-political opposition to the message of God's sovereign rule by redemptive love that the church in its early period identified itself as the community "other" than empire, and in opposition to it.

With Constantine's Edict of Toleration in 313, which legalized Christian worship, and Theodosius's proclamation that Christianity would be the official religion of the Roman Empire, the church itself came to internalize a new imperial logic. Such logic continued in the West through the period of colonization from the sixteenth century to early twentieth century. Thus, Christianity and the logic of empire have often inhabited the same historic, ideological, political, cultural, and geographic space.

In the late twentieth century, discussions of empire focused on the modern nation-state, exploring how European colonization often exhibited a symbiotic relationship between imperial expansion and Christian evangelization. Interestingly, the United States's status as sole superpower nation-state has solidified at precisely the time when the Christian Right has gained an increasing amount of political capital. Images of a "Christian America" exporting "global freedom and democracy" dominate our culture. The Bush administration implemented a long-term international strategy and foreign policy similar to what Richard Falk called a "global domination project."[5] In order to understand the extent and complexities of this project and its use of religion, our purview must move beyond analyzing power at the level of the nation-state to critiquing economic globalization trends and the increased militarization of the world. We must begin to analyze the relationship between economic globalization and the political, military, social, and cultural inequities in power globally.

Michael Hardt and Antonio Negri, in their recent books *Empire* and *Multitude,* argue that the forces of empire lie even beyond the nation-state and superpowers, in the province of global neo-liberal capitalism.[6] They see empire as a complex, trans-institutional system of global capital flows, opening up an even more complex account of globalization.

In addition to its transformation of political economy, globalization has also ushered in a new multiculturalism. This cultural dimension of globalization includes "the interconnectedness of all areas of our world—ecological, animal, human—and of all the people in the world."[7] In contrast to forms of globalization that provide an infrastructure for empire, this new framework of global intercultural interaction provides a vocabulary and analytic framework that could help us see the positive features of our globalized world.

Global cities have become new crossroads of global migration and diverse cultural interactions. They are symbols of this new multiculturalism. Poor people flock to the cities as part of a growing transnational labor pool. Saskia Sassen writes, "Much of the multiculturalism in large cities is as much a part of globalization as is international finance."[8] Multiculturalism is a sign of hope for a world that is fractured and searching for peace. Respecting and extending hospitality to the cultural "other" becomes a new challenge for the social witness of Christian churches.

While many declining churches in the United States are trying to maintain prophetic witness and moral integrity in an age of empire, the churches in Africa, Asia, Latin America, and the Islands of the Caribbean and Pacific are exploding with life. Indigenous Christian communities dating from the time of the apostles and churches established by modern Western missionaries experience globalization very differently from churches in the North. The center of gravity of Christianity has shifted to the global South. Informed by mission studies, ecumenical theology, and church history, a new academic field, "world Christianity," appeared in the late twentieth century to study these new expressions of Christianity, particularly the ones that have been marginalized in the Eurocentric accounting of Christian history and theology.[9] Urban multiculturalism and world Christianity demonstrate not just that Christianity is a global, multicultural reality, but that it always has been and always will be.

Many expressions of non-Western Christianity stand in bold defiance to the fundamental assumptions and structures of Western Christianity, including its participation in the excesses of the United States, such as rampant consumerism and high rates of pollution. The rise of global Christianity intensifies the theological and ethical problems the U.S. church is facing: How is the church to bear prophetic witness today in the United States when we, as the church, are often in captivity to racism, materialism, and militarism? Will it ever be possible for the church in the United States to embody the radical, communitarian vision of Christianity of the early church that "held all things in common," when the forces of empire are so great? Do our models of church re-inscribe the logic of empire, or do they prophetically resist the forces of empire? How do our churches relate to "the other," be they a racial/ethnic other or a religious other? Will our churches be capable of a global consciousness for justice and peace in a suffering world?

As churches in the United States begin to confront honestly the numerous theological and ethical issues raised by these new global realities, new ways of doing theology open up. The recent recognition in religious studies of the emergence of Christianity as a global phenomenon, the status of the United States as the sole superpower in the world, the emergence of capitalism as the new global economic order, and the resistance of theologians in the South to Northern and Western models of faith create the conditions for the construction of a new, multicultural, North American Christian theology.

II. Theology's Postcolonial Context

In order for twenty-first–century theology to respond to its multicultural contexts, it must begin to answer questions raised by postcolonial studies. Postcolonialism is a political form of postmodernism. Postcolonial studies has an unflinching commitment to lifting up the voices of those who have been silenced through patterns and practices of colonialization.

Postcolonial studies has two primary strategies: deconstructing Western hegemony and reconstructing postcolonial identity. Because the focus of postcolonial studies is on culture, it is also referred to as "transnational cultural studies." As we reflect on Christianity's multicultural fabric, postcolonial studies provide important resources for addressing the collusions and contrasts between the empire and the evangel.

During the period of colonization, European nation-states "discovered" and "colonized" vast regions of land in Asia, Africa, and the Americas. The primary logic of national expansion was the imperial logic of empire. With roots in the civil theology of the Roman Empire, the logic of *imperium* compelled the empire toward expansion through conquest. This same colonial logic continued in the rise of the nation-states of Europe and in the current unilateral interventionism of the United States.

The postcolonial circumstance in the United States may be better described as *internal colonialism*.[10] The United States came into being through a violent and revolutionary break with the British Empire. However, as the young nation forged across the Western frontier—with religious groups like the Stone-Campbell followers moving with it—the young nation often implemented new forms of imperial logic.

American imperialism differed from the imperial projects of the British, French, and Dutch empires in Oceania, Africa, and Asia, whose colonial enterprises set the conditions for an eventual radical and rapid decolonization process through national independence movements. When the United States expanded across the frontier it did not form new colonized communities from its conquered territories; the European settlers simply moved in. Consequently, the conquered people experienced internal colonizing rather than overt colonizing. For example, Native Americans and Latino/as were treated as colonized people in their own land, while African American slaves were colonized through sustained violence and control.

As a result, colonization in the United States remained intentionally ambiguous. That Puerto Rico became a U.S. colony in 1898 even though other areas did not illustrates the ambiguous complexity of the American Empire's modes of colonization. While it became a commonwealth in 1948, Puerto Rico still exists in an "in-between" space between being a colony and being fully incorporated into the United States. Thus, internal oppression becomes a way of speaking about the neocolonial hegemonic structures that continue to legitimate racial and economic oppression in the dominating class in the United States and its "colonies" and "colonized people."

In addition to deconstructing Western hegemony, postcolonial studies provides three linguistic and symbolic resources for the construction of non-Western identity: *différance*, subaltern, and hybridity. Discussions in postcolonial studies often presuppose Jacques Derrida's French post-structural notion of *différance*.[11] *Différance* refers to the irreducible "otherness" that is constitutive of human identity. This thick sense of difference provides a counter-logic to the deceptively smooth sameness of empire by affirming otherness and particularity in the context of a common messianic longing among all humans and the earth.

Gayatri Spivak's concept, "subaltern," builds on Derrida's concept of *différance* in a manner that helps bring voice to the postcolonial identities of colonized peoples. "Subaltern" is based on two words: "sub," meaning below, refers to the people who are on the underside of colonization; "altern" refers to the unique "difference" in their subjectivity (their alterity). Subaltern describes the voices of those on the margins in an age of empire whose language and expression is defined by the empire.[12] Spivak's question is, in an age of empire is it even possible for subaltern voices to really speak?[13] Spivak warns that the process of subaltern voicing and the process of Westerners joining with subaltern voices is that these enterprises can veil new forms of neocolonial oppression.

One version of this form of neocolonization is the essentializing that goes on in the Western imagination relative to the rest of the world. For example, as Edward Said has pointed out in his classic *Orientalism*, "orientals" function as an imaginary "other" constructed by the West to implement discursive hegemony in the colonial enterprise in Asia.[14] The "Chinatowns" in U.S. cities become an example of the Western projection of "China" that lies hidden behind the hybrid, diasporic communities embodied in the Chinatowns of U.S. urban centers.[15] In these two examples, what is "Asian" is essentialized or reduced to an abstract essence in the terms "oriental" and "Chinatown."[16] When we essentialize a person or a racial/ethnic community, we imaginatively interpret people into our own image of who they are, instead of accepting them as they actually are. While Spivak warns people against being assimilated into dominant culture through acceptance of essentialized global ethnic identities, she also is against rejecting everything Western and adopting a purely "native" non-Western identity.

Solidarity becomes a mode of intimacy for subaltern voices and those outside. This solidarity can extend to all people who can acknowledge their difference and common human longings. Spivak argues that a genuine acknowledgment of *différance* creates the conditions for intimacy: "Solidarity comes from exchange of information and a bonding through acknowledgement of difference."[17] True solidarity provides a way for subaltern identity not to degenerate into individualism, particularism, or relativism. It provides the basis for true communication and a common human future. Spivak reminds us that multicultural solidarity can come about by moving beyond generalized notions of national identity to a posture of listening in which difference is accepted and respected.[18]

Spivak, like other postcolonial theorists, appeals to the concept of "hybridity" to frame this dialectic between solidarity and the subaltern. Hybridity refers to a multicultural identity that is not dominated by the hegemony of one race and ethnicity. The postcolonial language of hybridity provides another way of speaking about the difference and sameness that lies within the construction of all human identities. While modernity presented both interior and exterior space as a centered, unified whole, postcolonial spaces are "in-between" spaces on the borderlands. As Christian theology moves ahead in the twenty-first century, it will have to explore these "in-between" spaces on the borderlands of our world.

III. Theology as Intercultural Conversation

Globalization demonstrates that all of the different contexts of theology are interconnected. Postcolonial studies have lifted up cultural difference as an intellectual and ethical problem in light of the history of colonialism. Within modern theology, theologies of liberation have taken cultural context to be an important source of theology. In the 1950s and 1960s, many of these feminist and liberationist theologians conceived of themselves as functioning in unique and separate domains. However, postcolonial notions of culture challenge these contextual theologies to move beyond an identity-politics framework for theology that seeks to reflect theologically from one particular context. In contrast, we must now do theology through the interactions that occur at the borders of different contexts.

To respond theologically to the problem of globalization, we argue that theology should be conceived as an intercultural conversation. In the context of feminist theology, Kwok Pui-lan has argued that theology is an intercultural discourse.[19] Feminist theology began through Christian women theologizing on the basis of their experience of God as women. Postcolonial feminist theology has demonstrated that gender has different significations in different cultures. Thus, cultural context has become increasingly important in feminist theological method.

Early modern theorists of culture often thought about these groupings of ethnic people in categories of coherence and purity. However, postcolonial constructions of cultures as fluid and permeable have problematized these notions. The legacy of colonization has exposed that the cultural context of the colonized subject looks very different from the cultural context of the colonizing subject. The gap between these two experiences is caused largely by white supremacy. White supremacy has roots in the European Enlightenment and was exported through the whole process of colonization. David Theo Goldberg argued that general categories such as "exotic," "oriental," and "Jew" (as racial and not merely religious other)[20] originated during the Enlightenment. These European Enlightenment thinkers often thought of these racialized cultures as discrete (and pure) wholes. While many have noted the streams of racial "purity" in the signification of "whiteness," Renato Rosaldo argues that the white colonizers who were subject to "imperialist nostalgia" also conceived of the precolonial "native" cultures as pure.[21] Both of these two-way contrasts reinforced the power of the white colonizer. The colonizers, who were largely "whites" from Europe, took over territories that became their "colonies," and established institutions that benefited white power and privilege. Thus, in some sense the deconstruction of colonial institutions and mindsets is a dismantling of racist social structures and ideologies.

As the colonized subjects struggled for cultural autonomy through the process of decolonization, they were forced to account for the way in which local cultures shaped personal and collective identity, including one's religious identity. To become oneself was to move beyond the racialized and colonized constructions of selfhood. Postcolonial studies provide theologians with important resources to dismantle the ideas of white supremacy and empower communities of color to sing a new song in a foreign land. As Rita Nakashima Brock argues, the concept of "interstitial integrity" is a way to understand how people navigate their identity and allow them to exist in different and sometime conflicting cultures.[22]

Because of the struggle for postcolonial identity in light of the tortured history of colonization, contemporary theology needs to move from a multicultural framing to an intercultural framing. Kwok Pui-lan argues that feminist theology is:

> ...not only multicultural, rooted in multiple communities and cultural contexts, but is also intercultural because these different cultures are not isolated but intertwined with one another as a result of colonialism, slavery, and cultural hegemony of the West. By intercultural, I mean the interaction and juxtaposition, as well as tension and resistance when two or more cultures are brought together sometimes organically and sometimes through violent means in the modern period. This intercultural approach allows us to theorize identity, experience, agency, and justice through a cross-cultural lens.[23]

The intercultural approach to theology demands that we listen to and are shaped by different cultural others who have often been excluded.

We must also pay attention to the influence that cultures have on one another. Conversation provides the space of mutual listening and learning. Theology as intercultural conversation is a dialectical phenomenon. Robert J. Schreiter writes, "Dialectic is to be understood as a continuing attention to first one factor, and then another, leading to an ever-expanding awareness of the role and interaction of each of these factors."[24] Through conversation we gain recognition of the ways in which different cultures have shaped and continue to shape our theological thinking and practices. Practicing theology as an intercultural conversation demands new modes of historiography and new forms of constructive theology.[25]

Intercultural theology transforms church history. As we narrate Christian history, we must start with the voices that have been historically marginalized. Listening to and learning from each other in the context of trusting community is vital for our new horizon of theologizing. Listening to each person and community in their concrete cultural particularity is a form of loving the neighbor. While these interventions initially fragment traditional historical renderings, they also open up the space for new stories and new theologies to emerge. This historical transformation can be understood as moving from church history to world Christianity. Instead of thinking about Christian history in the Western categories of the Euro-American church, an intercultural theological approach considers Christianity from the vastly different cultural traditions that form it. In the context of North American Disciples theology, this will mean privileging African American, Asian American and Latino/a narratives.

Intercultural theology transforms our understanding of race. Intercultural theology provides new ways of thinking about race and the struggle for justice. Much of early Disciples progressive thinking on racial justice is indebted to embracing the African American freedom struggle. African American Disciples have struggled throughout Disciples history to help white Disciples understand this historic oppression. Through the Black Manifesto and the Anti-Racism/Pro-Reconciliation initiative, the African

American and white churches have grown closer, as well as deepened their interactions with Asian American and Latino/a Disciples. Intercultural theology as a postcolonial movement calls us to move beyond the construct of the liberation of people of one particular community. Robust intercultural transformation comes at the point of deepest interaction of intercultural conversation and solidarity. As all communities of color continue to grow together at the points of their deepest interactions, new liberating theologies will emerge. With the greatest insights from all cultural traditions, Disciples can contribute to the formation of ministries that are care-giving and justice-making in the face of the impact of globalization on church and community. It is only when all cultural communities have an equal place at our open table that we will be able to collectively actualize our subversive agency for the kingdom cause of love and justice in the world.

Finally, intercultural theology is also prophetic. By prophetic we refer to the tradition of ethical reflection embodied in the Hebrew prophets and embodied in the Messianic ministry of Jesus Christ (Lk. 4:16–18). Prophets proclaim a word of God's grace and judgment. In our contemporary context, this prophetic spirit includes denouncing evil and oppression while building subversive communities of peace, justice, and love that embody God's eschatological reign.[26] Thinking about theology as an intercultural conversation puts theology in conversation with new partners. The postcolonial and liberationist framing of this theology places the common struggle for justice in our globalized age at the fore. Therefore, a new coalitional social ethic often emerges through this conversation.

Conclusion

An increasing number of North American theologians are looking to postcolonial studies to provide a framework for constructive theology.[27] Postcolonial theology is able to build on models of contextual and local theology that emerged with identity theologies in the 1960s. Through a deeper consideration of the social location of particular theologies, including ethnic identity and socio-economic contexts, theology in North America has become more concrete in its expressions as well as more representative of the ethnic diversity of national and international Christianity.[28]

As we consider North American theology's different contexts, we notice several distinctions. First, the context of colonialism in the United States is different than that of Europe. Second, within North America, each ethnic group has a set of distinct contexts. Third, there is a difference between "white" European-Americans and people of color due to unjust power relations and community cultures. It is vital that historic Protestant churches navigate these complex postcolonial contexts and construct a new postcolonial theology that exhibits honest dialogue and solidarity between the colonizers and the colonized in matters of theology, ethnicity, and gender.

2

Disciples Theology in the Twenty-first Century

Peter Goodwin Heltzel, James O. Duke,
Verity A. Jones, and William J. Nottingham

Like all conscientious Christians, Disciples are called to respond in these times to the current theological challenges of the empire. A postcolonial analysis of empire poses "difference" as an issue for Disciples' reflection. The many dimensions of difference include gender, race/ethnicity, denomination/religion, income, and education. Difference makes human life worth living among unavoidable limitations and inherent contradictions. How are we as Disciples going to deal with difference within our church and around the world? How can we address problems of pluralism and critical reflection on assumed certainties that we confront today in new forms and with new force?

In this chapter we present five core themes of Disciples identity prominent in our churchwide discussions for many decades. They are, as phrased by Mark G. Toulouse, the *restoration* (or *apostolic*) theme, the *ecumenical* theme, the *interpretive* theme, the *mission* theme, and the *eschatological* theme.[1] It is vital at the threshold of the twenty-first century that Disciples attend to these theological themes of historic formative significance and reconsider them in light of today's global realities.

Disciples Theology in the Twenty-first Century

As we think creatively about Disciples theology in the twenty-first century, it is vital our constructive response be based on the wisdom of our Disciples past. Disciples' theological roots lie in reformatory movements on the American frontier led by Barton W. Stone, and Thomas and Alexander Campbell. Beginning with the Cane Ridge Revivals in Kentucky in 1801, churches of this movement grew quickly across the Western frontier. The Stone-Campbell movement emerged as a major Protestant presence at the turn of the twentieth century, but resisted calling itself a denomination, preferring to be a fellowship of churches called a "brotherhood." During the 1950s at the height of mainline Protestant establishment, the Disciples began conversations about "restructuring" as one "church."

The Christian Church (Disciples of Christ) [CCDC] constituted itself as a church in 1968 by adopting a document called *The Design of the Christian Church (Disciples of Christ)*, referred to as "the Design." We are a community of "congregations, regional and general ministries of the Christian Church (Disciples of Christ) bound by God's covenant of love."[2] The restructured church tried to achieve a balance between congregational integrity and covenantal fellowship in the regional and general manifestations. The creation of a delegate assembly at the general level provided the structure for Disciples to pursue Christian unity through ecumenical projects like the Consultation on Christian Union.

The founding constitution of the Disciples was a "provisional" Design for a variety of institutional and church-political reasons. During this period a vigorous debate ensued between those who favored restructure and those who did not. Disciples ecumenists who favored restructure hoped that the new denomination would dissolve into church union in the 1970s. For example, in 1969 Disciple Harold E. Fey anticipated the union of one-third of U.S. Protestants in ten years, specifically by 1979.[3] Since this ecumenical union has not taken place, the denomination has experienced an extended maturation process as it rethinks its theological and ecclesial identity amidst rapid cultural shifts.

This process of rethinking denominational identity and theology has intensified in the early twenty-first century, given the new public visibility of religion and politics. The "global trends" of American empire, economic globalization, multicultural interconnection, and world Christianity provide new contexts for Disciples to construct a new theological paradigm. Theology's task in an age of empire includes constructing a new intercultural vision of church that is faithful to the gospel, while extending interpretive freedom and embrace to those on the margins of our church and the world.

These are not issues we can dismiss as "not our business." On the contrary, they are challenges we face here and now because faithfulness to the gospel requires nothing less of us. The gospel's claim upon us in this regard is heightened and reinforced by the "blessed ties that bind" us to so many others around the world. Among these are Disciples in lands other than North America (e.g., Argentina, Paraguay, Mexico, Australia, New Zealand, both Congos, and Puerto Rico), Christians of Disciples heritage who are now integral constituents of United Churches (e.g., in Africa, Jamaica, Thailand, the Philippines, India, and Japan, or the United Reformed Church in the United Kingdom), our many ecclesial partners, and people of color in the United States and Canada.

Given theology's multicultural context today, we argue that theology conceived as "table-talk" is an important starting point for Disciples. From the basis of our common confession of Jesus Christ, we can hope to be reconciled in our difference at the table. Building on the work of the Forest Moss Institute, a collective of Disciples feminist theologians, we see Disciples theology as the kind of table-talk that extends hospitality to those who have been historically marginalized from God's open table.[4]

Engaging difference has been an important part of the Disciples heritage. It is reflected in our acceptance of diversity of opinion even on matters considered tests of faith in many church traditions. Indeed, to proclaim "No creed but Christ" was, and is, for Disciples an overture to open dialogue. It has signaled a faith in Christ of such depth and breadth that it embraces within the Christian community itself the plausibility of conscientious differences of opinion even on many contested issues of theology. In so doing, it opens up a space for the hope of overcoming divisions among Christians and thereby witnessing to the power of the gospel to foster reconciliation and peace in a world of conflict. This desire for unity could never die, but remains with us.

Yet Disciples have not always embraced difference. Our church's story includes group conflicts resulting in resentments and divisions. The founders relied a great deal on Enlightenment-era conceptions of universal truth and commonsense reasoning. Thereafter, each generation of Disciples taking on the task of updating or advancing beyond those conceptions has had to face a family quarrel as well as institutional inertia. Much the same can be expected today, especially since neither postcolonial thought nor ecumenical and interfaith discussions today turn on classical modern accounts of universal truth and reasoning. Here and now, it is well to recall that Christian unity is, as Disciples have often said, not uniformity but unity amid diversity.

A postcolonial approach would embrace the many different experiences of being Disciples, including differences of race and ethnicity, yet all within the context of Christian unity. Disciples theology provides themes reaching out toward a non-dogmatic universality (e.g., the ecumenical theme) that is not present in postcolonial thought and illustrates one of the gifts that Christian theology has for thinking pluralistically about community. When applied to theological concepts such as reconciliation and practices such as the open communion table, the ecumenical theme can also offer gifts for thinking pluralistically about community.

Yet confronting the church's postcolonial situation involves in some ways a difficult process for the CCDC in the United States and Canada. Its historic constituency base is, sociologically speaking, largely white, middle-class, and

Midwestern and Southern. Over history, its outreach to and the welcoming of African Americans, Asian Americans, Latinos, and other peoples of color have resulted in marginalization rather than a truly full measure of equality and participatory interdependence. Yet, Disciples are experiencing a new influx of ethnic churches, as are many denominations in the United States. The Disciples New Church Ministry project has helped plant more than four hundred new congregations in the United States since 2001, only 21 percent of which are predominantly Anglo or white congregations.

In this setting, older and newer members, congregations, and church leaders face a challenge. Can we together, in dialogue and solidarity, distinguish core commitments of faith from merely customary, comfortable habits and preferences of church and cultural life? One goal of theological renewal in a postcolonial context is an authentic multicultural solidarity that permeates Disciples church life.

The church expresses its reconciliation with God by working for reconciliation within itself. It fulfills its ministry of reconciliation by embodying the social as well as spiritual dimensions of reconciliation. We must fully accept each other and learn to live together under the gospel in such a way that the principle of mutual affirmation and admonition becomes the basis of a trusting relationship in which respect and love for the other will have a chance to thrive.

Confronting historic exclusions as an act of embracing each other is an important acknowledgment of the hybrid identity of Disciples. Why does hybridity seem such a natural fit for Disciples? Hybridity exists in the midst of cultural diversity. From an intercultural perspective, and given Disciples' presence across the world, our identity as a denomination is not culturally homogenous. The beauty of the Disciples rests within the different colors represented at a truly inclusive gathering. Therefore, the Disciples' vision of an open table is an important starting point in the process of embracing a hybrid theological identity.

Disciples are reconciled in difference at the table. The table has become a powerful metaphor for our denomination in many ways. The celebration of the Lord's supper is central to our worshiping life together. Theologizing together is best conceived as "table-talk."[5] A challenge for Disciples theology today is how to open the table more expansively, to allow those who have been on the margins of the denomination to talk at the table as the church listens to and learns from them.

In responding to this new multicultural situation from the strength and love of the table, Disciples committed to "faith seeking understanding" are called once again to give fresh thought—at once critical and constructive—to the signature themes of their church identity mentioned earlier: the *restoration* theme, the *ecumenical* theme, the *interpretation* theme, the *mission* theme, and the *eschatological* theme.[6] In fact, these themes function for Disciples less as predefined positions, but rather as "common places" in classical Protestant theologies. They are high-profile reminders of theological concerns deserving of serious, open-ended examination in any responsible account of Disciples understandings of faith and faithfulness.

The Restoration, or Apostolicity, Theme

The restoration theme refers to the Disciples' commitment of fidelity to God's good news in Jesus Christ as made known through the witness to the apostolic faith in the canonical scriptures. In the words of Thomas Campbell, Disciples seek to "restore unity, peace, and purity, to the whole church of God."[7] A reading of the faith and order of "New Testament Christianity," with particular focus on the Acts of the Apostles, became early on in the Stone-Campbell movement the paradigmatic "restorationist" ideal. Yet, disputes over properly defining the paradigm and applying it in ever-changing circumstances were frequent, and at times led to the breaking of fellowship.

In the process leading to the restructuring of the movement in 1968, there was an extended investigation into the soundness and relevance of the restoration theme for late-twentieth-century Disciples. The restoration theme's centrality as the theological motif providing a literal blueprint of the church was questioned for multiple biblical, historical, theological, and practical reasons. At the same time, the ecumenical theme was playing an increasingly important role in Disciples ecclesiological reflections. Taken together, the critique of restorationism and openness to Christianity's ecclesial bodies other than our own (both Catholic and Protestant) helped Disciples understand the restoration theme in terms of *apostolicity*.[8] This understanding takes note of the diversity of apostolic traditions embraced in early Christianity and the ongoing efforts of those faithful to the apostolic message of God's gospel in Jesus Christ to search for the most authentic and effective means for faithful witness to this gospel in changing times.

Following the restructure, varied Disciples' voices have sought to contribute to a growth in understanding among Disciples with regard to the meaning and means of faithful witness to the apostolic message in the context of today's world. A Commission on Theology under the auspices of the Council on Christian Unity e.g., offered—over the course of several decades—an entire series of theological reflections and resources dealing with the nature and the purpose of the church. The Commission sought as well to aid Disciples in undertaking serious theological reflection on controversial interfaith issues such as "no salvation without Christ alone" and Christian-Jewish relations.[9]

In these times, the restoration theme—understood as faithfulness to the apostolic message of God's gospel in Jesus Christ—is a vital theological "common place" of churchwide discussion reminding us, as Disciples, that we need to hear and proclaim the Word of the Lord. One of the central theological features of restorationism was its desire to hear the voice of

God above the din of all human voices, and their various human opinions. Restorationism sought a word of God that could make sense of life, the church, and their relationship to divine purposes. Disciples sought a way to submit both themselves and the church, and all their associated human tendencies, to equate their own particularities to God's way of doing things, to the judgment of divine authority. They ended up seeking divine authority through a misreading of history, but their goal was an essential and thoroughly theological one: to hear an authentic word from God.

Ecumenical Theme

The ecumenical theme of the Disciples refers to the church's commitment to seek the visible unity of the whole church. The prayer of Jesus for unity found in John 17 has been a touchstone of thought and work throughout Disciples history. Also known as the unity theme, the ecumenical theme is based on a common confession of apostolic faith shared by the Christian church universal. The implications of the unity theme include the willingness of Disciples to remain open to the leading of God's Spirit into ecumenical partnerships, mergers, and collaborations with other churches. Therefore, e.g., a partnership with the United Church of Christ (UCC) and commitment to uniting church movements such as Churches Uniting in Christ follow directly from the ecumenical theme. The most important theological principle associated with the ecumenical theme is that unity is God's doing, not ours. The church is "essentially" one, which makes the church accountable to reality: we are responsible to live in light of the reality that God makes us one in Christ. Unity is not a choice, or a human creation; it is a reality created by God to which all Christians and all expressions of church, whatever social location or ethnic, cultural, or racial identity, must be accountable.

Historically, church unity has been the "polar star" guiding Disciples' ecumenical witness. Christian unity is "our *raison d'etre,* our basic approach, our stance, our posture, our witness as a church and as our commitment as a community of God's people" writes Robert Welsh in his inaugural vision as President of the Council on Christian Unity.[10] Our ecumenical calling to church unity is based on our common reconciliation in Jesus Christ.

The ecumenical theme will play an important role in Disciples' theological renewal as it pursues multicultural solidarity. Though seeking visible unity among churches has been the primary impetus behind the ecumenical movement, ongoing efforts at unity have made it clear—and a matter of intense focus since the 1960s—that genuine ecumenism is inseparable from a unified struggle for peace and justice. Those in the ecumenical movement realized that conditions of poverty and systems of injustice separated the churches as effectively as doctrinal issues. Addressing injustice became essential to the ecumenical project beginning with the Geneva Church and Society Conference of the World Council of Churches in 1966. The Assemblies of Uppsala (1968) and Nairobi (1975), and the Commission for World Mission and Evangelism conferences of Bangkok (1972/3) and Melbourne (1980), moved further in that direction. The Vancouver WCC Assembly Report of 1983 names the understanding of the "Oikoumene" as the "One Household of Life," and the Canberra Assembly (1991) had as its theme "The Unity of the Church as Koinonia." Faith and Order Conferences at Santiago de Compostela (1993) and others gave theological support to this social justice and global solidarity orientation, as hopes for church union became less engaging.

This recognition of the relationship between church unity and the global struggle for justice symbolizes the universality of a Christian theological vision that is vital for pursuing multicultural solidarity. Disciples also embody an understanding of the church as a multicultural community of solidarity by thinking of the church as a "covenant communion." Thinking about church as communion is natural for Disciples, who celebrate the Lord's supper weekly. Disciples see the church as a eucharistic fellowship of love and justice. The open table demonstrates Disciples' focus on communion (both communion with God and communion with each other) as well as its spirit of inclusion.

Koinonia, meaning "fellowship" or "communion," is a Greek term that has infused ecumenical discussions of ecclesiology for decades.[11] The dialogue on the church as *koinonia* has more recently been transformed by the notion that this fellowship extends beyond the church into the global struggle for peace, justice, and the integrity of creation.[12] Christian theological reflection on the church has always acknowledged its communal dimension; however, in the late twentieth century *koinonia* has become one of the primary ways that theologians think about the nature, unity, and mission of the church beyond itself.[13]

Koinonia ecclesiology provides a vital framework for Disciples' concern about unity and justice. The Acts of the Apostles uses *koinonia* to describe the interaction or sharing of believers in the early church.[14] Through a common confession of faith and celebration of the sacraments, Christian churches seek to be in union and communion with each other, as Christ is in union and communion with the Father (John 17).

The meaning and implications of the term *koinonia* have been broadened and deepened through the Faith and Order movement of the World Council of Churches.[15] In particular, there has been a concerted effort in two ecumenical documents, *Church and World* and *Costly Unity,* to develop the social, political, and ethical dimensions of *koinonia.*[16] These documents attempt to articulate the role of the church in the moral formation of Christians in the context of community. They seek to expand the meaning of the term to include the work of peace and justice in and for the world. From the text of *Costly Unity*: "The community of disciples rather than the individual Christian is the bearer of the tradition and the form and matrix of the moral life."[17] The ethical implications of *koinonia* provide one way of calling the church to radical discipleship. The call of radical discipleship is a call of prophetic witness and action.

Disciples can live in this *koinonia* ecclesiology in the global age in two ways. First, through the church's commitment to combat racism through its Reconciliation Mission, we can live out our church life together in a more truly multicultural manner. This will mean dismantling the institutional racism that continues to marginalize people of color in the denomination and society. It will also mean growing together around an ever-expanding open table of communion, dialogue, and action. Globally, Disciples will need to be more intentional in their pursuit of solidarity with global partners, including Disciples around the world, partners of the Common Global Ministries Board that the Disciples share with the UCC, and fellow member communions of the World Council of Churches. As a result of these intentional interactions with theology's multicultural contexts, it will be necessary for Disciples to be open to a new hybrid identity emerging.

In terms of the macro forces of empire—the power of the U.S. nation-state and global capitalism—the Disciples should be a contrasting community of love and justice. One way would be to come to terms with how the early church held all things in common (Acts 2). Recapturing the theology of Jubilee that undergirds the Messianic ministry of Jesus Christ, Disciples can continue to incarnate God's reign of reconciliation, peace, justice, and love.

The Interpretation Theme

The interpretation theme refers to Disciples' commitment to the free inquiry of conscience and to intellectual integrity in the quest for understanding the message of God's good news in Jesus Christ, and its implications for the ministry of the church and Christian living.[18] Founders of the Stone-Campbell movement took this theme as a God-given, inalienable right of the people everywhere, and indispensable for true Christian liberty. They applied it in advocating their early nineteenth-century program of protest and reform. They protested against established churches, which were perceived to equate their *own* way with God's *only* way (this is the basis of the early Disciples belief in the necessity of the restoration theme) and to suppress conscientious questioning as if it were just bad faith. They urged people to examine the biblical message *anew* in order to discover and unite on the basis of apostolic Christianity's faith, order, life, and work. In some ways, the restoration theme operated as a check on the interpretation theme: individual interpretation was always accountable to something beyond itself. In this case, it is accountable to the New Testament articulation of expressed declarations and approved precedents; accountable to the clear meaning of the Bible that needs no interpretation—a problematic assumption, of course, that the Bible interprets itself.

Various slogans signaled commitment to the interpretation theme and its thrust. They included, among others, the right of private judgment, freedom of conscience, "No creed but Christ," true "Bibleism," New Testament Christianity, new Reformation, and Restoration of primitive Christianity. With the slogans came appeals for an intelligent, reasoned, and reasonable faith. In casting their message in such terms, the movement's most prominent first-generation leaders drew heavily on the resources of the moderate Enlightenment and Scots Common Sense thought. They distinguished their message from extremist rivals: authoritarian faith, emotional-mystical faith, and anti-religion. Urging followers to use sound and common rules of interpretation to discover the biblical norms for the church and for Christian living, they relied mainly on principles of grammatico-historical hermeneutics, often called "inductive" or "Baconian" methodology, which was at the time in widespread use among Protestant intellectuals.

The interpretation theme has remained a vital force in Disciples' history ever after, and into the present. Our history represents a "journey of faith" in which each succeeding generation has undertaken to apply and reapply the theme in faithfulness to the gospel. This aim has led Disciples, over the decades, to organize and then restructure their organizations for the sake of mission; to develop a wide variety of congregational, regional, and general ministries; to join in many ecumenical ventures; to respond to national and global issues; and to embrace healthy advances in learning and moral sensitivity. Enlightenment terms, Scots Common Sense philosophy, and grammatico-historical hermeneutics have long ago been augmented and in certain respects corrected by later inquiries, studies, and methods of interpretation that are still in common use among Disciples today.

The dawn of a new millennium marked by globalism, pluralism, and empire brings with it an urgent call to reapply the interpretation theme anew. Disciples can welcome such a call, perhaps more readily than a good many other churches, because reconsidering our customary ways is a right and responsibility that remains true to Disciples' heritage. It is altogether appropriate for Disciples to seek, once again, as Alexander Campbell put it, the proper "understanding distance" to the biblical message in these times. Disciples have good cause to encourage earnest, honest dialogue for mutual understanding and to venture into new forms of ecumenical and interfaith cooperation for the sake of worthy shared goals.

Reapplying the interpretation theme, however, is a demanding task. Disciples are called today, as are other Christians, to reconsider the adequacy of our dealings with the "other" in our midst. Provisions for "democratic, representative" church governance leading to wise collective theological decision-making and practical mid-course corrections of maximally persuasive effect are not yet fully in place. Insights to be gained from current critical and self-critical studies of scripture—especially but not only the postmodern and postcolonial initiatives—remain to be explored by the church at large.

The Mission Theme

The postcolonial challenge of mission is how to proclaim faith in Jesus Christ in a way that is culturally sensitive and acknowledges the unjust power relations between Western Christianity and those in the non-Western world. The church fulfills its global mission embracing its multicultural destiny as one gospel is translated into many languages and incarnated in many cultures for the whole people of God. This new hybrid theological vision has shaped Disciples' missiological practice. After a brief narrative of Disciples mission, we will apply several of these lessons to a contemporary vision of the church as a covenant communion in the United States and Canada.

A survey of Disciples mission reveals a movement toward a theology of reconciliation via a mid-century paradigm shift based on the *missio Dei.* While the American West was the great frontier for the Stone-Campbell movement in the early nineteenth century, today Christianity's great frontier lies outside of the borders of the United States, as the church grows in the global South and increasingly sends missionaries to evangelize *within* the United States. The whole notion of boundary and frontier is being challenged.

Disciples theology, often Americanist in orientation, is being recontextualized in a global setting. While all churches in the United States must deal with how to recontextualize in a global setting, it is particularly poignant for Disciples whose identity derives from a "new reformation" of the nineteenth century, referred to by many over the years as "restorationism." Yet its leaders, Stone and Campbell, were not only frontier revivalists, but also thoughtful theologians with a global perspective and a missiological understanding of the church. For example, Alexander Campbell wrote, "We shall, therefore, regard it as a fixed fact—*that the Church of Jesus Christ is, in her nature, spirit and position, necessarily and essentially a missionary institution.*"[19] Campbell's understanding of the church as a "missionary institution" was evangelical in intent and global in scope. As a result of the evangelical character of the early Stone-Campbell biblical theology of mission, their movement grew rapidly on the American frontier.

As the missionary movement emerged in the second half of the nineteenth century, Disciples were strategically placed to share their vision of restoring the spirit of the early church on "foreign mission field." This evangelical conception of mission led to a rapidly growing Disciples presence in places such as India, China, Congo, and Puerto Rico. During the nineteenth and twentieth century the Disciples sent more than 350 missionaries to the Belgian Congo, later Zaire, and now there are more Disciples in the Democratic Republic of Congo than in North America, reflecting current demographics in world Christianity.

In addition, the Disciples mission to Puerto Rico set the stage for a massive Disciples presence in that island. However, in the 1930s Disciples in Puerto Rico began to manifest practices of Pentecostalism, fueling conflict between Puerto Ricans and missionaries over Disciples identity and practice. As a result, the Disciples in Puerto Rico became an autonomous church in the 1960s. However, Puerto Rican immigration to the United States has contributed to the development of Disciples Hispanic congregations, a fast-growing constituency in the denomination.

The broad shifts in the ecumenical movement concerning mission forced the Disciples to rethink and reposition themselves from a more evangelical concept of *missions* (focused on evangelizing unchurched people and groups) to the more ecumenical understanding of *mission* (grounded in a recognition that this is God's "mission," not our "missions," and focused primarily on unity and justice).[20] After the Willingen Conference of the International Missionary Council in Germany in 1952, Virgil Sly, the Chair of the Division of World Mission of the United Christian Missionary Society (later the Division of Overseas Ministries), mediated a new vision of Christian mission and unity to the Disciples, a theological vision that was later championed by General Minister and President A. Dale Fiers.[21] This vision can best be embodied in the phrase *missio Dei,* Christian mission as participation in the mission of God through the Holy Spirit.[22]

This broader view of the church as focused on mission rather than missions is demonstrated in the *General Principles and Policies* that were approved at the Disciples General Assembly in 1981:

> The church is mission… The primary work of United States and Canadian churches is in their own countries, but no true witness and service is ever merely local. Without global concern, linkages and interactions, U.S. and Canadian churches will lose sight of the nature of the gospel and *the nature of the church*… The time for western domination of the church's life and witness around the world is past. Partnership and mutuality, servanthood and sharing are the words descriptive of mission today.[23]

This tradition is carried on today in the strategy of "critical presence" that animates the Common Global Ministries Board, the ministry that brings together the administration of world mission programs of the CCDC in the United States and Canada and the UCC. This missiological understanding of the church places global concern and solidarity at the forefront of our understanding of the gospel and the church. Sensitivity to the socio-cultural contexts of subaltern subjects reflects a Pauline affirmation of reconciliation in difference (Acts 14:17; Rom. 2:14–16). The socio-cultural awareness that we have learned from mission has taught us the importance of listening as a mode of practicing the ministry of reconciliation.

The Eschatological Theme

The eschatological theme is the expression in life and in death of the trust relation to the God of Israel—who creates the world with a covenantal purpose, and accomplishes within and beyond history—the divine will of justice, forgiveness, and love represented in the cross, resurrection, and glory of Jesus of Nazareth, which, in the Disciples of Christ tradition, has been experienced in many different ways and awaits new theological application. The title of Alexander Campbell's monthly journal *The Millennial Harbinger* proclaimed the centrality of eschatology as the meaning of history for the pre-Civil War community. Scholars and theologians of the twentieth century have neglected this in our denominational memory.[24] For virtually forty years, Revelation 14:6–7 was on the title page of *The Millennial Harbinger*: "I saw another messenger flying through the midst of heaven, having everlasting good news to proclaim to the inhabitants of the earth, even to every nation and tribe, and tongue, and people—saying with a loud voice, Fear God and give glory to him, for the hour of his judgments is come: and worship him who made heaven, and earth, and sea, and the fountains of water—JOHN. Great is the truth and mighty above all things, and will prevail."[25]

The eschatological theme and the mission theme were unified in the early thinking of the Stone-Campbell movement. The founding of the American Christian Missionary Society in 1849 cannot be separated from the millennialism of the period.[26] Barton W. Stone's eschatology was part and parcel of his expectation of Christian unity as a prelude to the return of Christ.[27] Evangelist Walter Scott drafted plans for a magazine to be called *The Millennial Herald*.[28]

This trend ended with Archibald McLean and the twentieth century.[29] Disciples no longer read the book of Revelation with the post-millennialist assumption of historical progress, but neither does the modern secular optimism of progress that followed reassure us. Apocalyptic scriptures reveal the tragic and self-destructive powers that dominate the world, and perhaps they will be more accessible to readers in the twenty-first century, as the moral ambiguity and inequities of globalization and the fatigue of war become more grievously apparent. The early days contained theological commitment to notions such as (1) an understanding that eschatology was linked to theological understandings of both creation and history—that all of history is meaningful and related to God's activity in both first things and last things; (2) an emphasis on "Emmanuel"—God with us—that enables Christians to affirm the presence of God, even when there seems to be no sign of God's presence whatsoever: the belief that God has entered our time, is with us, and is acting to redeem us; (3) an emphasis that the Disciples theology of church is rooted in an eschatological understanding, both in terms of the church's essential unity, and in terms of the church's mission—Disciples understood themselves and the church as active partakers in God's history of salvation and reconciliation.[30]

This retrospective of early Disciples eschatology lead us to reclaim theological engagement with the political, economic, cultural, and environmental dominions of the changing times. It requires repudiation of the anti-Catholicism, Jewish proselytism, and Euro-American chauvinism in the eschatology of those founders, along with the crude fundamentalism of popular millennialism at the start of the twentieth century. However, it also means taking seriously the pervasive apocalypticism of the New Testament. The founders had a high regard for the working of God's will in history: material progress for Campbell, the abolition of slavery for Stone, conversion and education for Scott. In *The Millennial Harbinger* of 1841, we read that all the conditions of society will be vastly improved, wars shall cease, and peace and good will among men will generally abound.[31] The *Brook Farm Harbinger,* published weekly from June 1845 to June 1847 by New England transcendentalists, could not have been more utopian, and it is not a coincidence that they both are called "harbingers" of a better world.

The importance of justice and peace in the new century of empire is not a moral exigency only but a corollary of the Holy Spirit. God's law and grace are the issue. It is not a matter of indifference that the demands of the Hebrew prophets for social justice are inseparable from their eschatological visions. Psalm 146 is both a reminiscence of ethical command and a celebration of hope in the Lord's eternal reign impinging on the present, typical of faith nourished by the Bible.

Both historical and global challenges call for fresh theological reflection by Disciples on eschatological hermeneutics and faith, which includes the personal and spiritual *koinonia* of the congregation. It is vital in this age of global insecurity that preachers proclaim a word of hope concerning the *parousia* of our Lord and Savior Jesus Christ. Old photographs at Cane Ridge and Bethany show the inscription, "In the hope of immortality, A. Campbell." The second half of the twentieth century in Disciples preaching was dominated by excessive modesty about the promise of life eternal, often even at memorial services. The coming reign of God, preached by Jesus, and experienced eschatologically by the early church, is both the realization of God's victory for humanity in the world and the meaning of paradise in death. Abundant life, eternal life, glorified life, are all relationships to the triune God and to our neighbor that bear interpreting in the expanding global reality of technology, violence, and exclusion. Boris Pasternak has a character in Doctor Zhivago say, on the brink of the Russian revolution, "We must remain faithful to immortality, faithful to Christ." So, too, must Disciples.

Conclusion

In conclusion, Disciples theology's task today is to create space for all of our members to dialogue together on the implications of the gospel of reconciliation in Jesus Christ. As Disciples move into the twenty-first century, we need to continue our eucharistic and theological practice around the open table. This will mean being more intentional in joining together with the voices that have been marginalized in our church. As we set the conditions for a new space for reconciliation, we will see a new hybrid identity emerge, one in which we can be unified in our diversity.

By emphasizing an open table in all areas of life, Disciples theology can confront the impact of colonialism and its aftermath on those from the global South, as well as the internal oppression of those in the United States. The open table means embracing both the marginalized in our midst as well as our own marginalized identity. A church at the margins is a de-centered communion. However, through this de-centering, we are poised to witness a new work of God emerging.

As the African American, Latino/a, Asian, and Pacific American churches continue to grow within the denomination, we experience localized contextual churches living in solidarity with one another as one church. Drawing on Disciples' experience in mission, we need to learn how to listen to each other with a special emphasis on the concrete particularity of our contexts. This will mean learning and accepting new "disjunctive narratives" in the way that we tell our Disciples story.[32] Our story will be more than a white, American story, but one that represents the true rainbow of color that paints the mosaic of Disciples in both the North American and global contexts.

A postcolonial Disciples theology provides a new space of differentiation and dialogue where diverse perspectives are both deconstructed and reconstructed through contact with one another. The church universal is in a difficult transitional period. A missiological theology of reconciliation with a *koinonia* ecclesiology is a vital new trajectory for Disciples to follow. It demonstrates once again the Protestant principle of *ecclesia reformata semper reformanda,* which points to the final reconciliation on "the day of our Lord." Seeing theology as ongoing table-talk in our postcolonial context opens a new horizon for the practice of an appropriately "catholic" or global Disciples theology. It provides the space for the biblical story to speak anew through the different cultural perspectives that we bring to the narratives and the world. It is vital that Disciples open up to the witness of Christians in other cultures both globally and at home. With this openness, we will truly be in a place to be the reconciling church we claim to be. Only through such openness to the Holy Spirit's presence in all God's children will North American Disciples be able to participate in the subversion of empire and bear faithful witness to the kingdom of God.

3

Theology and the Bible

CHOI HEE AN

Introduction

We live in a world that never stops changing, but at the same time contains consistent factors, probable changing factors, and interchanging factors. We live in between modern values and postmodern challenges. We believe what we have believed, but we renew and transform those beliefs. We have changed, but we have held on to what we had. The coexistence between modernity and postmodernity challenges our values, traditions, beliefs, cultures, and other things, but still they coexist.

As stated in the first chapter of this book, "Christian theology in North America is at an impasse," but world Christianity globally is exploding. The impasse of North American theology is demonstrated by its weakness in the face of racism, classism, sexism, heterosexism, ageism, body-ablism, colonialism/postcolonialism, imperialism, multiculturalism, and other ideologies. At the same time, the explosion of world Christian theologies encounters North American theology, bringing demands of modern and postmodern globalization in relations with other nations. The church in North America lives in the midst of these struggles. People in the church have watched their neighbors change. Some people left the church, and some churches were closed. However, many churches have remained and decided to open their doors to their new neighbors. They are ready to prepare themselves for the new challenges for the sake of their own survival. As a consequence, many churches have no choices but to seek justice and love in these situations of perpetuated unjust discriminations in which their own people live. These situations urge the church to create solutions deconstructing and recreating its own theology and its interpretations of the Bible.

The CCDC is no exception to this utterance of changes. The Disciples have to confront this unavoidable struggle. In this chapter I demonstrate how the Disciples have enacted this deconstructing and recreating process within their own context. In the first section, I introduce how the Disciples have struggled in the midst of these challenges and developed their understanding of the Bible and its hermeneutics through these challenges. From early Disciples history to the current context exploring their limits and possibilities, this section recapitulates the issues of multicultural biblical hermeneutics' necessities that the Disciples have faced.

In the second section, based on the "good Samaritan" story, I illustrate how our modern and postmodern theological constructions have reflected on the biblical hermeneutical consciousness and signified the reality of who we are. Corresponding to the modern and postmodern characters such as totality/particularity, unity/diversity, and purity/hybridity, this section will advance the multicultural identities and promote a new perspective of which we are a whole, as well as the pieces of that whole.

The Bible and Theology in the Christian Church (Disciples of Christ)

Since its official founding in 1968, the Disciples have been composed largely of middle-class Midwestern and Southern white Americans with the spirit of the American frontier. The denomination has pursued individuality and the personal revelation of Christ. This emphasis on individuality and the personal revelation of Christ also brought and embraced differences and diversities on the individual level that gave individuals freedom to interpret the Bible through their own eyes. Any individual could interpret the Bible using reason and conscience.[1] While Disciples agreed on "No creed but Christ," Christ has been interpreted and understood by them in numerous ways in relationship with the Bible.

As many Disciples had different understandings of the Bible, four qualities presented themselves as characteristic of the Disciples mind and acted as prescriptive guidelines for interpretation: reasonable, empirical, pragmatic, and ecumenical.[2] The Disciples gave the first priority to a combination of faith, the Bible, and rationality within the ecumenical context. Many Disciples believed that the Bible needed to be understood with a rational, or reasonable, mind. This reasonableness had a deep connection to the interpretation of Disciples theology. They believed that this reasonable mind and the interpretation theme provided the Disciples with the liberty to interpret the Bible with their own conscience and intellectual integrity. Even though historical interpretations of the Bible brought many conflicts and debates, because of being of a reasonable mind, the Disciples have maintained their diverse identities.

The pragmatic mind and the empirical mind added more openness to these diversities. They supported people in the application and adjustment of the biblical passages to their own times and in the prohibition of more literal interpretations. The Disciples agreed on the "law of expediency" to exercise common sense and relied on their own experience to understand life.[3] The ecumenical mind brought more attention to diversity in unity and played a significant role in relation to the ecumenical theme for Disciples. These different Disciples motifs implanted multicultural diversity in solidarity as the Disciples renewed their minds for the global struggle. Engaging in dialogue between the Bible and these principles, the Disciples undertook the task of following the path for creating a new faith life within their own belief in God in their own situation.

Some of the common hermeneutical principles familiar to Disciples were, "No creed but Christ," "No book but the Bible," and, "Where the Scriptures speak, we speak; where the Scriptures are silent, we are silent." These words of Thomas and Alexander Campbell were often used to describe Disciples' common attitudes toward scripture. However, as the Disciples allowed different interpretations on the individual level, several founders also demonstrated different attitudes about the Bible.

Barton W. Stone, who was born in America, insisted that anyone could read the Bible and understand the literal meaning with one condition: the help of the Holy Spirit. He did not have any need to learn a new method of interpretation, something advocated by other founders. He assumed that the text was clear in itself.[4] He disavowed any creeds or confessions, but followed the Bible as the truth.

For Thomas Campbell, his most characteristic hermeneutical principle was his distinction between the importance of the Old Testament and that of the New Testament, even though this principle was common to other founders as well. In his *Declaration and Address,* he described the Old Testament as a guide for the worship, discipline, and government of the Old Testament church and the particular duties of its members, and portrayed the New Testament as a perfect constitution for the worship, discipline, and government of the New Testament church.[5] Since his emphasis was on the early Christian church, he believed that the New Testament was perfect and offered more concrete ideas of the church than those found in the Old Testament. He adapted some rudimental literary and historical criticism methods that set out a list of questions such as, "Who is the writer or speaker of the portion read, or of any particular part of it?" "To whom is it written or spoken?" and "What historical facts are contained in it?"[6] Even though, like Stone, he read the Bible literally, he interpreted the Bible with some critical inferential methods that he created.

Alexander Campbell understood the Bible to be the life of the church and the minds of the people. In this understanding, he believed that people had to commit themselves to be followers of Christ, and strongly insisted on naming the denomination "Disciples."[7] However, he had a different attitude toward scripture. He would not believe the literal meaning of the biblical text.

Rather, he insisted on reading the Bible as he would read other texts and on opening the possibility of using non-Christian material to understand the Bible. He wanted to find the figurative meaning of the Bible. He even made seven rules to propose how to read the Bible.[8] He was willing to employ a critical methodology for his time despite his view of the Bible as "a book of facts."[9] However, he never fully exercised this method of interpreting the Bible freely, because he was also limited by his own traditions and culture.

As a preacher, Walter Scott read the Bible to discover Jesus Christ. Because of this emphasis, he viewed the Old Testament as a source of "types" of the New Testament. He acknowledged the Old Testament as "the shadow" and the New Testament as "the substance."[10] His interpretations of the texts deeply depended on the meaning of salvation, so that he employed some interpretive methods of other scholars for the purpose of preaching the gospel.

These four founders showed different but very similar interpretations and theologies of the Bible. They lived in-between liberal and conservative worlds. Even though they tried to open their thoughts to provide more possible methods that others could use, they limited themselves from using any other materials outside of the Bible. With their open minds and limits, they refined their faith though personal relationship with God and exercised their own personal interpretations of the Bible. Even though they denoted "No creed but Christ," they also created their own principles of how to interpret the Bible to persuade other followers.

This in-betweeness continues in the next generations. While the second-generation scholars such as Isaac Errett and Robert Milligan became custodians on the conservative side of the first generation's values, third-generation scholars such as John Walter McGarvey, Herbert Lockwood Willet, and others struggled with biblical criticism and theological liberalism on the liberal side as well as on the conservative side. As a result of the third generation's struggle, fourth-generation scholars such as Stephen J. England, J. Philip Hyatt, S. Vernon McCasland, and others developed an academic biblical competence and hermeneutical methods beyond denomination, becoming important leaders in the ecumenical movement.[11] Through continuous struggles in the history of the Disciples, the Bible has been the only authority that can be accepted in the Disciples of Christ. However, it has left the great legacy leading us to recreate our own interpretation of the Bible and our own theology.

Confronting the situation in the twenty-first century, the body of the Disciples has changed. The enormous growth among multi-ethnic churches challenges the Disciples identity and requires Disciples to alter their theology. Unlike other North American denominations that originated in Europe, immigrants in America founded the Disciples. Geunhee Yu, Executive Pastor for North American Pacific/Asian Disciples of the Christian Church (Disciples of Christ), proclaims that God has built the Disciples of Christ "by the immigrants, for the immigrants, and of the immigrants."[12] As many white congregations have closed and/or declined in church memberships, these immigrant churches have shown enormous growth and rapid development in the twentieth and twenty-first centuries. The Disciples have to learn how to coexist and live harmoniously together. The Disciples grow their own body and struggle to accept that "many of them became us."

Considering this shift, the interpretation of the Bible without considering current reality or discussing only an ancient text from the perspective of founders' theologies is "hiding its direct impact on the postcolonial [postmodern] world and maintains its (another Western ideological stance's) imperial domination of Two-Thirds World countries" and the hierarchical domination of North America itself.[13] Re-membering our own body requires remembering our multiple origins, cultures, and beliefs and reeducating our "Self." Now our question is how *we* understand *us*. How do we see our coexistence? What do we know about our own body in Christ? What does the Bible mean to us in our context? Using the story of the "good Samaritan" as an example, the next section grapples with the partial answers of who we are and how we see our coexistence in our own context. It will certainly also provide us with some glimpses of how we (can) understand the Bible from the different multicultural perspectives of our own members.

The Biblical Hermeneutics and Theological Constructions in Postmodern Contexts

> But wanting to justify himself, [the lawyer] asked Jesus, "And who is my neighbor?" Jesus replied, "A man was going down from Jerusalem to Jericho, and fell into the hands of robbers, who stripped him, beat him, and went away, leaving him half dead. Now by chance a priest was going down that road; and when he saw him, he passed by on the other side. So likewise a Levite, when he came to the place and saw him, passed by on the other side. But a Samaritan while traveling came near him; and when he saw him, he was moved with pity. He went to him and bandaged his wounds, having poured oil and wine on them. Then he put him on his own animal, brought him to an inn, and took care of him. The next day he took out two denarii, gave them to the inn-keeper, and said, 'Take care of him; and when I come back, I will repay you whatever more you spend." Which of these three, do you think, was a neighbor to the man who fell into the hands of the robbers?" He said, "The one who showed him mercy." Jesus said to him, "Go and do likewise." (Lk. 10:29–37)

The central character of this story, "a man," is undefined. Even though he is assumed to be a Jew, this story itself does not identify him with any nationality, race, religion, sexual orientation, age, or other categories.

"A man" is identified in this story not with these categories but by what happened to him—the violence and injuries. This man was robbed, stripped, beaten, and left half dead. The robbers left him with "nothing to identify his status except his desperate need."[14]

The central character of our history, "we" are also undefined. Actually, the renegotiation of the "we" is the main discursive focal point in our postmodern/modern society. The totalitarian tendency to define the "we" urges the unidentified we, "pieces of we," to demand knowledge of our "Self." We as a whole presumed that we already have knowledge of the pieces of we, but the dynamics between "we" as a whole and "we" as the pieces have created the complicity between the two groups and put all of us on hold amidst the memories of "epistemic violence" and historical injuries.[15] Many of our robbed, stripped, beaten, and unknown memories are caused from these traumas because "we" as a whole remotely devise to constitute the pieces of "we," not from proactively knowing, but from proactively controlling. Before we know who we are, "we" as a whole compels us to create who we should be. Power and desire of public institutions deny our particularity and demand the pieces of we to fit in a "stratification grid."[16]

This tendency can be best read in the table of race and ethnicity. "We" as a whole do not allow the pieces of "we" to identify with our nationality, race, religion, sexual orientation, or other categories, but our inclusion in these categories is the reason "we" as the pieces have been raided, stripped naked, crushed, and bloodied. The inscription/re-inscription of racism in the global context produced by imperial North American/Eurocentric Western culture disavows its impact on communal and individual constitutions of "we." It ravages our spiritual, social, and psychological self. It mocks the voices of the "pieces of we" and makes our various, particular, and unique histories invisible. The violence and historical injuries leave us with nothing to identify our statues except our desperate need of our "neighbor."

However, people whom we expect most to act as neighbor cannot understand our reality. In the parable of the good Samaritan, neither a priest nor a Levite helped the man who was hurting. They know that the unidentified man, the pieces of "we," exist, but decide to go on the other side and pass by. They cannot recognize the injuries of national, racial, religious, class, and other forms of violence. They who have preserved religious disciplines and doctrines cannot insist on anything but their own demands. They decide to go on *the other side.* Therefore they fail to save us. The pieces of "we" become fragmented and lost in institutional structures.

However, the unidentified man was not totally lost. He was found and saved by a Samaritan. There are many theories about the origin and early history of the Samaritans. They are seen either as an Israelite remnant; the captives from Babylon, Cuthah, Avva, Hamatah, and Sepharvaim; or a group created by intermarriage between the Assyrian and Israelite remnant.[17] Their existence itself is problematic. They are treated as either foreigners or as a mixed race. Because of their hybridity, particularity, and diversity, their existence is described as "unclean with the pollutions of the peoples of the lands, with their abominations" (Ezra 9:11b).[18]

One of the oldest temptations dreamed of in Christian history is unity. As we reflected above, historically and culturally the Disciples place an enormous emphasis on unity. The longing for unity has been a significant piece of the Disciples identity. However, in the North American/European context, this unitary discourse has brought serious injuries to the multicultural community. This discourse itself becomes possessiveness rather than an embraced vision. This obsessive representation fractures the meaning of unity itself. It suppresses varieties of the "pieces of we."

From the meganarrativization of "we," the notion of unity automatically is registered in the discourse of "intentionality" and "unidirectionality" to predicate the power of discursive domination.[19] The protocols of this engagement develop a unitary hegemonic formulation to disarticulate the dynamic of diversity and to suppress the multi-vocal, multidimensional "pieces of we" and turn them into a univocal, monolithic line. The hegemonic practices between white and black paradigm perpetuate prevailing racial order without allowing for the recognition of diverse racial, ethnic, and cultural identities. The emerging cultures of diversity are dismissed with manipulative stereotypes of classified images that later deprived them of their diversity as individual deviation. This process attempts to obliterate co-extensive provenances of the "pieces of we." The predominant construction of race interdicts the diversity of the "pieces of we."

However, salvation is from the Samaritan. Over racism, nationalism, colonialism, and other "isms," the Samaritan becomes a savior. The diversity, particularity, and hybridity of the Samaritan bring the healing of the unidentified one. The reality of diversity shakes unitary hegemony, which resorts to violence of mega-discourse. This attempted obliteration of diversity by the mega-discourse of unitary hegemony vehemently denies ample multicultural phenomena, but cannot erase its reality. A counter-hegemony force grows from the diverse cultures and historical memories that have been conceived and embraced by the pieces of our ethnic cultural identities. The collective memories of individual and communal experiences from the past historical enigmas and inspiration lead this counter-hegemonic discourse to signify a vigilant dynamic of variety and its flux. They demand the monologue to break its imperviousness to the richness of diverse reality and to adopt multicultural modifications. The multicultural reality redresses the monolithic vision of our society.

The subversive awareness of multicultural, multiethnic relationships is iterated in the case of Latino/a communities in the United States as an unavoidable example. The discourses between white and black and between racism and culture are challenged by the notion of Latinos'/as' self-understanding. They refuse to define their identity in a category between white and black and dispense with the representation of race as the first definition of their identity. From the perspective of the white and black American paradigm, Latinos/as are seen as one race despite their heterogeneity. However, their reality illustrates that they comprise many subgroups, such as Mexican, Puerto Rican, and Cuban in terms of national origin. People in these national origin subgroups also vary according to geographic distribution, immigration status, socio-economic status, languages used, political affiliation, nativity, generation in the United States, and other factors. "What makes Latinos a group is a combination of converging life situations, such as urban residency, disproportional poverty, and the experience of prejudice and discrimination, together with their treatment by the larger society and the large increase in their total number."[20] The stratification/categorization of black/white or white/not white has not easily explained the complexities of Latino/a life. Even though the bipolar system of racial categorization has a colossal impact on Latino/a identity formation, it does not prevent their diversity and racial flexibility. It cannot thwart their social mobility. The complexity of Latino/a identity dismisses the postulation of unitary discourse and enunciates the impossibility of unity without diversity. The critical enterprise of naming our unity in diversity cannot simply dissect its dialectical significance behind the pieces of our reality but should be seriously considered through the reality of us as the pieces, and imagine the possibility of we as a whole in-between unity and diversity.

The dynamics between Jews and Samaritans drive our attention to another domain: purity/hybridity. The premise of unity and purity requires the notion of "identical." It obliges identical features such as whiteness, maleness, and heterosexuality because it is believed that it "secures the 'pure' and original identity of authority" that we as a whole must obtain.[21] As a consequence, it demands a color line, gender line, sexuality line, nationality line, and others. As the bloodied Christian history has shown, "the Truth" does not allow for accepting other "truths." Not only medieval Christian history but also the current American religious history contains relentless debates between orthodoxy and heresy over numerous cases of Christian theological biblical interpretations, doctrines, disciplines, and other discourses. These countless battles have caused the separation of Christian churches into numerous denominations, and the Disciples have been a historical part of this process. The unidentified "we" has suffered from this power game.

However, the same bloodied history reveals the essential part of our identity: hybridity. The reason we have this history is that there have been continuous different pieces of our voices lifting up our "something different." Many of us have relentlessly challenged the purity, the authenticity, the origin, and the truth with which we have disagreed. The "in-betweenness"[22] of Asians/Asian Americans in global context is a symbol of this challenge.

Even though the dualistic, dichotic "color-blind"[23] approach excludes the visibility of the Asian/Asian American, the existence of Asians/Asian Americans themselves becomes a barrier in this racial color game. The presence of the hybrid color interrupts the defined relationship of who we should be, but it also devises the relationship between who we are and "where we're coming from."[24] Instead of entering into the toxic assimilation process that promotes white imperial values, their hybridity connects both worlds: Asia and America, white and black, native and foreign, and margin and center. Their in-betweenness de-centers the white superior values and re-centers the multicultural values from the margin. It concocts the "harmony of difference," and brings a new synthesis of the hermeneutics of centrality and marginality.[25] Our creativity demonstrates its product, something different: hybridity. Hybridity contrives to counter the existence of our whole body as a whole of the pieces and to discover new and boundless horizons of our "something different" identities. It is a fundamentally dialogical interaction with God. It understands and opens the actuality of the coexistence between purity and non-purity, totality and particularity, and unity and diversity.

However, the postmodern theological discourse does not stop here, because the salvation from the Samaritan is not the only answer that we can find. One of the Korean theologians, Suh Nam-dong,[26] challenged the paradigm of salvation in this story. His challenges start from the question, "Is the good Samaritan the only one who can be the savior?" He emphasizes the important role of the person who is robbed, because this unidentified person gives this Samaritan a chance to act on love. This person lets the Samaritan act humanely. This person's suffering and sighs awakens the goodness of the Samaritan's humane nature. The burden, pain, and suffering of the robbed person lead the Samaritan to save both of them. Who plays the role of savior? It is the person who is robbed, naked, thirsty, hungry, and abandoned. The act of saving this person is the act of being saved by God. Suh interprets it as the meaning of Jesus' suffering, cross, and death.[27]

The Samaritan is not the only savior. The unidentified one also brings salvation. In fact, the unidentified one has his/her own strength to bring the salvation. The development model that describes the formation of black identity is a good example of this transforming power. It illustrates how the "pieces of we" reclaim the process of narrating our particularity, resist the totalitarian discourse, and shift these dynamics in five stages: Naïve, Acceptance, Resistance, Redefinition, and Internalization.[28] In stage one, many black children become aware of their differences, but they do not have any concepts of inferior or superior in this stage. In the transition from the first stage, Naïve, to the second stage, Acceptance, they learn about power dynamic between white and black. In the second stage, they accept white values and reject/devalue blackness. However, they encounter the contradiction between their own self and social constructions of their selves. In stage three, Resistance, they acknowledge the existence of racism. They start to question its values, moral codes, and truths. They stop both their own victimization and passive acceptance. In the end of this stage, they seek to understand who they are. In the Redefinition stage, they do not concern themselves with rejecting or emulating whiteness or white culture. Rather, their consciousness opens to interact with other black people. They actively seek to redefine their selves and their social group membership. They begin to reclaim their heritage in a positive way. In the Internalization stage, beyond their survival, they nurture their selves in growth and development. While they use their power to be proactive in pursuit of self-defined goals, some of them open their hearts to adopt a multicultural perspective.[29]

This development model indicates how the "pieces of we" collect the memories of "epistemic violence" and historical injuries and transform themselves by creating new selves. This transformation provokes "a change of level addressing oneself to a layer of material which had hitherto had no pertinence for history and which had not been recognized as having any moral, aesthetic or historical value."[30] It envisages the healing of "we as a whole" rooted in the transforming "pieces of we." In this process, the pieces can represent a whole based on their difference. Our difference, the particularity, is accepted not as an ambivalent presage, but as a co-extensive provenance. Our imagination of irresistible desire for a weavable social fabric becomes real among our particularity in totality. This transforming particularity becomes the subject of salvation. From this practice, the unidentified one becomes the identified one, the savior who execrates the regeneration of an unjust social force that imposes an oppressive power circle not only on the individual level, but also on the communal level.

Still, salvation cannot happen from one race, culture, or person in this story. It cannot occur only in one person or one culture in this world. As the formation of African American identity development already implies, it requires bigger and broader multicultural perspectives. It demands solidarity. Solidarity between the Samaritan and the unidentified one make it possible for them to identify who they are, the saviors. The solidarity between them enables them to become saviors. The juxtaposition of their roles saved not only themselves, but also a priest and Levite who, in a different outcome, could have been guilty of negligent homicide rather than simple negligence. Their solidarity shakes the unidirectional tendency of the monologue about who we are. The questioner, a lawyer, asked Jesus, "Who is my neighbor?" However, the answer of Jesus was who his neighbor *could* be. The inquiry of the identification of the man's neighbor shifted from the Samarian to him. He has to become the neighbor and be united with the Samaritan. Again, the shift from another "I" to the neighbor, the unity of the "pieces of we," is required. The unity and solidarity are necessary to experience the salvation. However, these cannot exist without the particularity, diversity, and hybridity of the "pieces of we." We as the pieces and as a whole together create the salvation of this world.

Conclusion

The Bible is "a document of abundant histories of interpretation in the East, West, South, and North, as a reflection of past and present culture, political structures, and religions."[31] My approach to this story is an attempt to explore how my and our reality is constructed in the reflection of the Bible across time and space. In order to understand our Bible, we need to employ multidisciplinary, multicultural, and multidimensional sensibilities that mirror *who we are in front of God.*

The reality that the Disciples live in is the reality that the Disciples have inherited and created from many parts of the world. As in all of humanity, the Disciples live in the contingency of the past, in the creating process of the present, and in the envisioning hope of the future. The unity/diversity, totality/particularity, and purity/hybridity of coexistence have been part of the Disciples' spirits and identities. Therefore it is necessary that the biblical hermeneutics and theological constructions of the Disciples continuously reflect *who we are* and *where we go* and carefully recognize *how we do* in this world. Now, I know that *we* are taking a train in order to "go and do likewise."

4

Theology and Tradition

WILLIAM TABBERNEE

Introduction

Theology is not "created out of nothing." What we believe theologically about God, Christ, the Church, abortion, homosexuality, marriage, divorce, and a whole range of other issues is not based on what we think intuitively about these topics but on a careful and responsible examination of a number of "sources." Among the sources that inform and help to construct our theology are "scripture" and "tradition."

As explained previously, knowing what the Bible, especially the New Testament, says about a particular topic is vital to determining our own views about that topic. Knowing what Christians throughout the ages have traditionally thought about the same topics, however, is also crucially important. "Scripture" and "tradition" are much more interrelated than Protestants in general and Disciples in particular have often assumed. We do well to be reminded by our Roman Catholic and Orthodox friends that there was a "rule of faith" (i.e., an apostolic tradition about essential matters of Christian belief) before there was a "canon of scripture" (i.e., a final list of authorized books). The "rule of faith," sometimes called the "canon of truth," is referred to by Irenaeus of Lyons (ca. 130–200) and Tertullian of Carthage (ca. 160–220) and functioned as a summary of the content of the essence of apostolic teaching. Similarly, early baptismal confessions, made by the candidates at the time of their baptisms in response to questions asked of them by the persons baptizing them, developed into creeds such as the Apostles' Creed, which dates back to the second century. The Apostles' Creed and later creeds, such as those adopted at the First Council of Nicaea in 325 and ratified in slightly amended form at the First Council of Constantinople in 381, served as affirmations of faith on essential matters by those being initiated into the Christian Church. By way of contrast, not until Athanasius of Alexandria (ca. 296–373) published his Easter letter in 367 do we have the list of twenty-seven books now considered normative by Christians for the "New Testament." The total number of books comprising the Christian canon of scripture is, however, still not completely settled, as Protestants, Catholics, and various Orthodox communities include (or exclude) some books, such as, for example, the Wisdom of Solomon, considered by others as pseudepigraphal or apocryphal.

The Campbells and "Apostolic Tradition"

The first generation of Disciples theologians, similar to all Protestants of their era, privileged scripture over tradition. Thomas Campbell (1763–1854) and his son Alexander Campbell (1788–1866) went further than most of their contemporaries in additionally denouncing the use of creeds. Both Thomas and Alexander, at different times, expressed the view that, as Thomas Campbell put it:

> [N]othing should be made a term of communion in the Christian Church which is not as old as the New Testament; or that is not expressly revealed or enjoyed therein.[1]

Alexander's formulation of the same view shows that, while studying in Glasgow prior to joining his father in North America, he had reached the same conviction as that of Thomas Campbell:

> My faith in creeds and confessions of human device was considerably shaken while in Scotland, and I commenced my career in this country [the United States] under the conviction that nothing that was not as old as the New Testament should be made an article of faith, a rule of practice or a term of communion among Christians.[2]

Although Thomas and Alexander Campbell had come to their positions independently, the similarity of the way in which they expressed this joint position suggests that they discussed the matter frequently and communicated it to others in memorable language. Such language also included slogans like "No creed but Christ," "No book but the Bible," and "Where the Scriptures speak, we speak; where the Scriptures are silent, we are silent."

The rhetoric inherent in the Campbells' memorable language oversimplified and, to a certain extent, distorted what they really believed about the relationship between scripture and tradition. Martin Luther's *sola scriptura* ("the Bible alone") did not really mean "nothing but the Bible" but simply that the Bible should be taken as the final arbitrator of truth when ecclesiastical authorities, such as popes, bishops, or councils, promoted views which appeared to be in direct contradiction with what is revealed in scripture. Similarly, the Campbells did not totally reject everything that was not "as old as the New Testament." They only rejected post-New Testament "authorities," such as "creeds," if these were made "a term of communion." By "term of communion" the Campbells meant the criterion by which one was deemed to be deemed worthy to belong to a particular Christian denomination and/or receive the Lord's supper in that (or another) denomination. For the Campbells (and Disciples ever since), there is only one "term of communion," namely the "good confession" that "Jesus is the Christ, the Son of the Living God" (Mt. 16:16, paraphrased).[3] Neither Thomas nor Alexander Campbell believed that it was inappropriate to use creeds or other aspects of the "Apostolic Tradition" for educational, theological, or liturgical purposes—as long as they were not used to exclude Christians from fellowship! Indeed, the Campbells' most vehement attack on "creeds" was primarily directed not against the "ecumenical creeds" of the early church but against post-Reformation "confessions" such as the Westminster Confession of Faith (1647).[4]

A postscript to the *Declaration and Address*, one of the founding documents of the Disciples, makes clear that Thomas Campbell did not want to be misunderstood about the way he viewed and used creeds:

> As to creeds and confessions, although we may appear…to oppose them, yet this is to be understood only in *so far* as they oppose the unity of the church, by containing sentiments not expressly revealed in the word of God; or by the way of using them, become the instruments of a human or implicit faith; or, oppress the weak of God's heritage; where they are liable to none of those objections, we have nothing against them. It is the *abuse* and not the *lawful* use of such compilations that we oppose.[5]

Alexander Campbell frequently drew upon the early creeds, especially the Apostles' Creed—a statement that he considered "in every word true"[6]—in his teaching on christology and the Trinity.[7] Similarly, Alexander Campbell had a comprehensive knowledge of the writings of the so-called Fathers of the early church, which he used extensively in his discussion of a wide range of topics, including baptism,[8] the Lord's supper,[9] salvation,[10] and preaching.[11]

For the Campbells, what the post-apostolic writers said about a given subject was critically important in helping contemporary Christians determine what they should believe and practice. They did not always agree with the theological conclusions that the Church Fathers drew from the "facts" the Fathers passed on, and they saw the post-New Testament documents as of secondary rather than of primary significance for Christian faith and practice, but it is clear that, despite the rhetoric that might lead one to suppose otherwise, the "Apostolic Tradition" was extremely important to the Campbells—especially to Alexander.[12] The "Apostolic Tradition," as well as scripture, informed the Campbells' theology. For them, however, "nothing not as old as the New Testament" had the final word.

"Tradition" and "tradition(s)"

By privileging scripture over Tradition, the Campbells emphasized the point that Tradition, by itself, cannot be equated with apostolic faith. Tradition may be a vehicle by which the apostolic faith is passed on or by which it is clarified or articulated. Tradition, however, may also be the vehicle by which partial, inadequate, or even erroneous expressions of the apostolic faith are passed on or articulated. It is a common convention, at least in English-speaking circles,[13] to distinguish between "Tradition" with a capital "T" (meaning the "Apostolic Tradition") and "tradition(s)" with a lower case "t" (meaning the tradition[s] of particular Christian communities or churches). Consequently, one might (and should), for example, study the theology of the Disciples of Christ on topics such as the Lord's supper and baptism in the context of the "*Reformed* tradition" as well as the "Apostolic Tradition." In doing so, it is necessary to take into consideration both "continuity" and "discontinuity." For the Campbells, for instance, celebrating the Lord's supper *every* Sunday and baptizing "*believers by immersion*" meant a break in continuity with the (Reformed) tradition as they knew it from the context of the Presbyterian Church of their day in an attempt to "restore New Testament Christianity" as they saw it revealed in scripture and the "Apostolic Tradition." Continuity with the "Tradition" necessitated for the Campbells a painful discontinuity with Reformed "tradition."

Disciples "tradition"

Over time, the Disciples developed their own "tradition" of faith and practice. While emphasizing a minimalist approach in terms of what *must* be believed in order to be deemed a Christian, the founders were not against producing a coherent set of Christian beliefs and practices, which could serve as the theological undergirding of the new movement. For example, Thomas Campbell, in the postscript to the *Declaration and Address*, proposed the writing of:

> A catechetical exhibition...upon the entire subject of Christianity—an exhibition of that complete system of faith and duty expressly contained in the sacred oracles; respecting the doctrine, worship, discipline, and government of the Christian church.[14]

Alexander Campbell's *Christian System*, to a large extent, became the kind of "catechetical exposition" Thomas Campbell had envisaged and was very influential in shaping what may be called "Disciples theological tradition." In line with his minimalist approach, and influenced by the Enlightenment, Alexander Campbell distinguished between "facts" and "opinions." For him, the Bible contained "facts" that comprised the content of Christian doctrine—but which he preferred to call "The Christian System of Facts."[15] Campbell's summary of the "essential facts" about Jesus, "from his birth to his coronation in the heavens," ironically, reads very much like the christological section of an early Christian creed. Jesus "died for our sins—he was buried in the grave—he rose from the dead for our justification—and is ascended to the skies to prepare mansions for his disciples."[16]

Attempts at clarifying or explaining christological (and soteriological) facts, however, for Campbell, fall into the category of nonessential "human speculation"; that is, "opinions." For instance, while in Campbell's system the reality that Christ "died for our sins" is a biblically recorded "fact," the various theories of the atonement are fallible "opinions" about which, for the *sake of Christian unity*, there must be liberty and charity.[17] In the context of Christian education, however, such "human speculation" or "opinions" are neither out of place nor irrelevant. For Campbell and other early leaders, reason was very important in helping Christians to determine exactly what they believed beyond the bare bones of theological "facts." The early Disciples leaders were equally adamant, however, that there were real limits to human reasoning and that Christian unity was based on the "facts" of the faith—not on "opinions" about the "facts."

Subsequent generations of Disciples scholars recognized that the distinction between "facts" and "opinions" was somewhat artificial. They developed more comprehensive theological "systems," including the *Scheme of Redemption* by Robert Milligan (1814–1875)[18] and *Basic Truths of the Christian Faith* by Herbert L. Willett (1864–1944).[19] Such works, the various chapters in *The Renewal of the Church* by the "Panel of Scholars" (1957–1961),[20] *The Faith We Affirm* by Ronald Osborn,[21] and *The Church for Disciples of Christ*, edited by James Duke et al.,[22] are but a few examples of the publications that enable access to the rich tradition of Disciples theological thought.[23]

The "Preamble" to the Design of the CCDC, on which Osborn's book is based, is a beautifully crafted ("creedlike") "Affirmation of Faith."[24] This affirmation summarizes the essentials of Christian faith and practice in a way that accurately reflects the Disciples ethos. As this "Affirmation of Faith" is being used liturgically in more and more Disciples congregations on a regular basis during Sunday worship, it has the capacity of handing on ("traditioning") the Christian faith, as Disciples understand it, just as the "tradition" is also handed on verbally by the preachers and teachers of the faith, including Christian parents.

The process of "traditioning," of course, is culturally (as well as theologically) conditioned. In the post-Constantinian era, that which ultimately came to be adopted as the "Apostolic Tradition" was the Tradition deemed to be authentic by the "winners" in the theological controversies "settled" at councils such as those held at Nicaea (325), Constantinople, (381), and Chalcedon (451). As described clearly by Clark Williamson in chapter 9, powerful political considerations relating to empire were present at the Council of Nicaea. Similarly, given the cultural context of the time when "Disciples tradition" was being developed, the theological views and ecclesiological practices of white, male church leaders were predominant. It is also important to recognize that later generations of Disciples and especially the new ethnic congregations that are now so much a part of the Disciples of Christ have their own particular perspectives on Disciples tradition. It is more accurate, therefore, even in the context of one church or denomination, to speak of "traditions" rather than "tradition." Consequently, as in the case of reading scripture, one must interpret and utilize Tradition/tradition(s) by paying due attention to the cultural context(s) in which they developed and, where necessary, engage the Tradition/tradition(s) with a sense of appropriate "critical distance." Only by doing so can we both benefit from the Tradition/tradition(s) to which we are heirs and construct a relevant theology for our own situation.

The "Ecumenical Imperative"

Since the time of the Campbells, Disciples have also come to know that there was much more diversity within *early* Christianity than a simplistic reading of the New Testament or a post-Constantinian interpretation of the "Apostolic Tradition" would suggest. There were "Apostolic traditions" as well as "Apostolic churches" with a rich diversity of views and practices. The apostolic faith manifested itself in more than one way in the Christian communities of the first three centuries of Christianity—just as it has continued to do in more recent times. Hence, contemporary Disciples recognize even more than their forebears the importance of studying the (Apostolic) Tradition(s) and traditions(s) of the church(es), not so that they might restore the Church to its pristine (New Testament) state, but so that they may understand Christianity's theological heritage in the richness of its diversity.

The Disciples' emphasis on Christian unity demands not a naively conceived attempt at "restoration" but a joyful celebration of the additional theological gifts that other Christian communities can bring to the common enterprise of understanding and practicing the Christian faith. Disciples have an ecumenical imperative to understand the difference between unity and uniformity and to recognize that, while there are limits to acceptable diversity, it is our calling to draw the circle of ecumenical hospitality as widely as possible. In line with another early Disciples slogan, we implement theologically, as well as in other ways, the dictum: "In essentials unity; in nonessentials liberty; in all things charity." Disciples understand that no single Christian community possesses the whole of Christian truth. Each Christian tradition adds a dimension to the totality of theological insight on particular topics. Christian theology, as a whole, would be greatly impoverished if the rich diversity of Christian insights were to be reduced into a singular uniformity. Consequently, it is important for Disciples not only to be familiar with the Apostolic Tradition(s) and Disciples tradition(s) but also to understand and appreciate the traditions of other churches: Catholic, Orthodox, and Reformed.

"Ecumenical tradition"

In studying the theological traditions of other Christian communities, there is a danger of becoming involved in "comparative ecclesiology" rather than "ecumenical theology." That is, we may be tempted to ask, "How is this (or that) belief/doctrine/interpretation wrong because it does not agree with what I/my church/Disciples of Christ have always believed/taught/understood?" A more useful question is, "How can this (or that) belief/doctrine/interpretation enrich my/my church's/the Disciples of Christ's theological understanding?"[25] Asking such a question does not mean that all theological insights are of equal value or that theology is nothing but collecting together all the ways people have interpreted theologically particular topics throughout the ages. In working out one's own, or one's church's theology, choices need to be made regarding what can be taught about particular aspects of the faith with integrity so that one develops a consistent theology. The choices made, however, need to be *informed* choices, informed by the broadest possible range of theological traditions.

In making choices about particular theological interpretations—and a useful way of avoiding the traps of "comparative ecclesiology"—is to utilize the results of what Max Thurian, a former adviser to of the World Council of Churches' Commission on Faith and Order, has called the "ecumenical tradition."[26] Thurian rightly points out that, in addition to the "Apostolic Tradition" and the tradition(s) of individual churches or "families of churches," there is now, as the consequence of many years of official ecumenical engagement through bilateral and multilateral dialogues between churches, a shared "ecumenical tradition." This "ecumenical tradition" is seen most clearly in documents such as *Baptism, Eucharist and Ministry*, adopted by the member churches of the World Council of Churches at Lima, Peru, in 1982.[27] BEM is a "convergence document" produced through the collaboration of Christians from a wide range of distinctive "interpretative communities." It sets out clearly what the members of the various churches, with their own denominational identities and traditions, can say together and which issues need further discussion or will remain as distinct but complementary interpretations and insights. That which the churches can say together comprises the "ecumenical tradition," which, hopefully, will be "received" by Christians within their own traditions and which can function as a new standard by which the theologies of the churches and individual Christians may be informed and, where necessary, reinterpreted.[28]

Global and Interfaith Perspectives

One of the advantages of taking seriously the "ecumenical tradition" as well as the "Apostolic Tradition" and the "traditions" of various individual churches or "families of churches" is that the "ecumenical tradition" has incorporated the voices of Christian communities with whom—because of geographical distance and cultural factors—we may rarely engage personally. The World Council of Churches, for example, has been very intentional in ensuring that theologians from what is now often described as the "Majority World" (rather than the "Third World") have an equal voice at the theological table.

"Majority World" theologians bring to the discussion a global context, new methodologies, and insights that derive from those methodologies. Because they live in countries where other "Living Faiths" predominate, they also model the way in which Christian theology should be developed and articulated in the context of engagement with people of other Faiths. Majority World theologians help us to recognize the unity we share not only with fellow Christians but with all human beings created by the one God—whose worship the so-called Abrahamic Faiths (Judaism, Christianity, and Islam) have in common.

There is a difference between "ecumenical theology" and "interfaith engagement" in that the former has a Christian (and christological) focus whereas the latter deals more with mutual religious respect, human dignity, and common issues of justice and equity (often arising out of the effects of globalization). Nevertheless, there are important theological dimensions to all of the above-mentioned issues. For example, mutual religious respect means grappling with supersessionist tendencies within Christian theological traditions that, from the time of the early church onward, have erroneously taught that God's covenant with Israel has been replaced by God's new covenant in Christ.[29]

As "ecumenical tradition" arises out of the broadest possible spectrum of Christian voices, some of the potentially negative factors of the cultural conditioning of Tradition/traditions are minimized, although not eliminated altogether. Using "ecumenical tradition" as one of the sources of our "theologizing" means that we are utilizing a source that has already had to come to grips with working toward a consensus (or "convergence") in the context of a variety of social, political, ecclesiological, and cultural factors. Utilizing this source for constructing our own contemporary theology, however, does not mean accepting the whole content of "ecumenical tradition" naively or uncritically.

Conclusion

Engaging in sorting out what we really believe about Christian faith and practice in our "postcolonial," global world is hard work. It is, however, work that matters—work that determines what we as a church and as individual members of that church can affirm as essential to our lives as practicing Christians.

Constructing a theology relevant for our contemporary context is not to be equated with reading the Bible and/or reading theological texts. "Doing theology" involves engaging in both kinds of reading, but not as ends in themselves. Reading the Bible gives us access to the books that the early church considered to provide authoritative information about God's interaction with human beings, especially as revealed in the person of Jesus whom Christians confess as the Christ. Reading various kinds of theological texts, be they one-paragraph "affirmations of faith" or multivolume "systematic theologies," gives us access to the (Apostolic) "Tradition(s)," the "tradition(s)" of individual churches, and the (more recent) "ecumenical tradition." All these, the Bible and the three types of Tradition/tradition, are sources for our own theology—and provide necessary checks and balances for that theology.

Our theology needs to be informed both by a responsible approach to interpreting the Bible *and* by an equally responsible approach to understanding and integrating the three kinds of Tradition/tradition described above. For contemporary Disciples, this means (despite the earlier, often misunderstood rhetoric against "creeds") getting to know, and taking seriously, the Apostolic Tradition(s) *as well as* the Bible. It also means getting to know, and taking seriously, "Disciples tradition(s)"—recognizing that doing so is not confined to what the Campbells (and/or the other early leaders of the movement) said, but that it consists of Disciples theological scholarship and emphases up to and including the present time. Thirdly, in light of the Disciples commitment to visible Christian unity, doing theology for Disciples means getting to know, and taking seriously, what is now referred to as "ecumenical tradition." "Theologizing" is not carried out in an ecclesiastical vacuum. Other Christians, both those who as part of the "communion of saints" have gone before us and those who are our contemporaries in other ecclesial families, have grappled, or are grappling, with many of the same theological issues that confront us. The theological insights gained, for example, through "process theology," "liberation theology," or through "theologizing" that incorporates "feminist/womanist," "Black Church," "Asian," "Latino/Latina," and/or "postcolonial" perspectives both broaden and enrich our theological perspectives—whether through our own studies or brought to our attention by others.

As Disciples, we ultimately decide what we believe (i.e., "our theology") "*for* ourselves." However, as this chapter has shown, we do not decide what we believe "*by* ourselves." Three interrelated types of Tradition/tradition inform our theology: Apostolic, denominational, and ecumenical. Only by understanding and appropriately utilizing the insights handed on to us from these three types of Tradition/tradition (along with other sources such as scripture and experience) can we construct a meaningful and relevant theology for our contemporary situation.

5

Theological Reasoning in a Pluralistic Context

The Task of Reason in Theology

W. CLARK GILPIN

Introduction

In his recent book *Identity and Violence*, Harvard University economist Amartya Sen observes: "Many of the conflicts and barbarities in the world are sustained through the illusion of a unique and choiceless identity" that "drowns out other affiliations." Sen argues that this false attribution of a singular source for social identity occurs both among social theorists, such as those who hypothesize a "clash of civilizations," and among various fundamentalist movements who demand a single interpretation of religious identity. A more adequate view of identity, according to Sen, would recognize that identities are shaped by "plural affiliations" and that persons "make choices—explicitly or by implication—about what relative importance to attach, in a particular context, to the divergent loyalties" that comprise human lives. The task of interpreting religions is not to define the "all-engulfing identity" of Christianity, Islam, or Hinduism but, instead, to ask "how a religious Muslim (or Hindu or Christian) may combine his or her religious beliefs or practices with other features of personal identity and other commitments and values (such as attitudes to peace and war)."[1]

In the course of its development since the seventeenth century, modern theology has shown particular attentiveness to what Sen calls the "plural affiliations" of the person: to a profession, political party, friends, family, ethnic community, nation, moral ideals, and religion. Theologians saw that, despite the legitimate claims of these various affiliations, they frequently placed conflicting obligations on the individual, and they raised questions about the importance of the specifically religious dimension of identity. In response to these contending loyalties, many theologians argued that a sense of personal identity develops through prioritizing the communities with which one is affiliated. As a person's sense of self develops over time, certain loyalties become definitive of identity while others recede in importance. An adolescent faces a choice between loyalty to friends and obligations to family. Responding to some particular governmental policy, a minister is torn between a deeply held patriotism and a principled commitment to religious peacemaking. Such decisions are the practical and often difficult moments of identity formation. In the modern world in which identities represent the combination of many different affiliations, the theological question becomes the relationship between loyalty to God and the other loyalties that identify a self. Is fidelity to God one loyalty among many? Is it the comprehensive loyalty that orders the other, more proximate loyalties? This chapter argues that the tasks assigned to *reason* in modern theology have primarily involved interpreting the relation of the specifically religious dimension of identity to other features of personal identity and other communities of affiliation.

Language about *reason* appears in theological discussion when the theologian is interpreting the relationships among these communities of affiliation or thinking about the nature of the self who is making decisions that give one loyalty priority over another. Reasoning, thought of as a common human capacity, builds bridges between the specifically religious parts of life and other, secular domains in which the religious person collaborates with people of other religions, or of no religion. Reason becomes theologically important, in such cases, because it represents the process by which a religiously committed lawyer, for example, thinks about the relation between justice sought in the courtroom and justice as a religious principle. Reason also figures in Christian theology as an exercise of the faithful self; classically stated, it is "faith seeking understanding." Reason is the process by which a parent comes to understand the relation between the patience of God, "abounding in steadfast love," and the patience of family members one with another.

Theologians of early nineteenth-century America, such as the founders of the Disciples of Christ, present an especially interesting instance of the task of reason in modern theology. In that period of American history, the plural affiliations of the person became a crucial theological issue through the convergence of several social factors: the separation of church and state in the early republic, the separation of work and home in the industrial revolution, the emergent separation of education and religion in public schools and colleges, and the transit from one society to another in the first great wave of immigration to the United States. Theologians and church members in the early nineteenth century increasingly recognized that the church was one of many social domains in which they had obligations, and they had urgent questions about the relationship of religious membership to other social affiliations. Many Disciples were immigrants, recently arriving in Kentucky, Pennsylvania, and Ohio from Ireland, Scotland, or eastern parts of the United States, and they were establishing congregations in unfamiliar and unsettled societies. Many Disciples leaders were teachers and founders of schools, who had to think deeply about the relation of the Bible to science and history. Each of them had a direct experience of how difficult it is—to return to Amartya Sen's concept of identity—to "combine his or her religious beliefs or practices with other features of personal identity and other commitments and values." Not surprisingly, the reasoning human person played a "leading role" in books and sermons by early Disciples of Christ theologians. They quite frequently drew extended comparisons, for example, between the rights and responsibilities of the "citizen" of a republic and the "citizen" of the kingdom of God, in order to help church members think about the similarities and differences between membership in a nation and membership in a church.

The United States in the early nineteenth century thus offers a rich "historical laboratory" for analyzing the theological task of reason. The minister-theologians of this era thought deeply about the multiple sources of knowledge and intellectual authority in an increasingly pluralistic society, and they raised many questions of continuing importance about the role of reason in theology, even though some of their answers to these questions may be unsatisfactory in our contemporary context. After making some preliminary observations about reason, identity, and communities of affiliation, this chapter therefore illustrates the function of reason as a theological category by reviewing a significant book by one of the nineteenth-century founders of the Disciples of Christ: Walter Scott's *The Gospel Restored* (1836). From Scott's book, the chapter elaborates three forms of theological reasoning—narrative reason, systematic reason, and analogical reason—and assesses their implications for religious identity in the contemporary pluralistic context.

Reason, Personal Identity, and Communities of Affiliation

One striking feature of theological discourse about reason is that the term seldom functions independently. Instead, reason nearly always appears as one member of a pair of terms, and the relationship of the pair determines the theological task of reason. The nineteenth-century Disciples educator and theologian Robert Milligan explicitly identified one classic pair in the title of his book *Reason and Revelation* (1867). What, Milligan asked on the title page of his book, was "the *province* of reason" (my emphasis) in relation to the authority of the scriptural revelation?[2] In paired terms of this type, reason represents questions about the relation of religion to other domains ("provinces") of human thought and conduct: history, science, politics, and law.

Milligan and other early leaders of the Disciples of Christ, for instance, sought to demonstrate that Christianity was reasonable, in the sense of being compatible with the empirical reason of modern science, as it had developed since the time of Isaac Newton (1642–1727). According to the nineteenth-century Disciples theologians, the order of nature displayed the purposes of God, and the laws that guided the natural order could be observed through empirical scientific investigation. Analogously, the Bible also recorded facts attesting to the truth of religion, and Christians could apply scientific methods of study to these biblical facts. The biblical revelation presented facts not otherwise available to reason, but, expanding on the philosophy of John Locke (1632–1704), Alexander Campbell and other Disciples thinkers of the era argued that these revealed facts exceeded the capacity of unaided reason but were in no sense contrary to reason and that, once accepted in faith, they should be rigorously investigated.[3] In this fashion, Campbell and Milligan used the paired terms "reason" and "revelation" to make two claims about the nature and authority of Christianity in relation to the modern scientific world. First, the Bible was central and essential to Christianity because it revealed facts that were above, but not contrary to, the findings accessible to unaided reason. Second, religion was not simply a matter of feeling and emotion but of study and investigation that were parallel to the investigations of science. This dual commitment to the Bible and empirical reason became the guiding rationale for Disciples of Christ in the founding of schools and colleges throughout the nineteenth century. Indeed, not solely for the Disciples of Christ but for all religious groups in the United States, the study of religion at colleges and universities has become a crucial location for engaging questions about the relation between religious ways of knowing the world and other domains of knowledge ranging from the natural sciences to sociology and anthropology. Although approaches to the study of the Bible and conceptions of natural science have developed dramatically since the early nineteenth century, the underlying question about the relationship between religious reasoning and scientific reasoning continues to be a central task of theology.

As the example of reason and revelation suggests, theologians have used the term "reason" in their efforts to explain the relation of theology to other social domains or disciplines of knowledge that influence modern identity. But theologians have also used the term "reason" to interpret the human capacities of the individual who is responding to the claims of these various social domains on his or her life. The American theological ethicist H. Richard Niebuhr (1894–1962) fruitfully developed this way of thinking about the plural affiliations of the modern identity in his book *The Responsible Self* (published posthumously in 1963). According to Niebuhr, modern biology, sociology, and psychology "have taught us to regard ourselves as beings in the midst of a field of natural and social forces, acted upon and reacting, attracted and repelling." Responding to these various social forces can easily, of course, fragment the person's sense of self. With the tug of obligations in so many different directions, the human moral difficulty is to be responsible in responding and coherent in playing multiple social roles. Niebuhr asked, "What ties all these responsivities and responsibilities together and where is the responsible *self* among all these roles played by the individual being?"[4]

In a manner that effectively relates to Amartya Sen's views on identity, Niebuhr presented the self gradually emerging in a process of social dialogue and conversation. He thought that human actors were responsible when they appropriately interacted with others in a continuing society: "Personal responsibility implies the continuity of a self with a relatively consistent scheme of interpretations of what it is reacting to." This gradual working out of the self over the course of time and in the context of society led Niebuhr to advocate a broad conception of reason. Humans understand the world, he suggested, not only by logic and scientific experiment but also by story and symbol. The human "is a being who grasps and shapes reality, including the actuality of his own existence, with the aid of great images, metaphors, and analogies. These are partly in his conscious mind but so largely in his unconscious mind and in the social language that he tends to take them for granted as forms of pure reason. They are, indeed, forms of reason, but of historic reason." They are shaped by the person's choices and decisions in continuing interaction with the varied features of his or her social and natural environment.[5]

In sum, reasoning is relational. These examples from nineteenth- and twentieth-century American theology suggest that this relationality of reason takes two forms. In the example of scientific reason and biblical revelation drawn from the nineteenth century, reason interprets the relationship between different social domains in which the modern person participates. In the twentieth-century example of Niebuhr's "responsible self," the individual responds to these multiple social relations by a social process of decision making and symbolic reasoning that gives moral priority to certain of these relations and thereby gradually develops a coherent identity. Theological reasoning, in other words, concerns itself with interpreting the relationships among social institutions, and it thinks about the coherence of the person who simultaneously identifies him- or herself as a participating member in these various social domains. Theological reasoning addresses not only the relationship of religion to science but also the consistency of being both a Christian and a scientist. Equipped with these two points about the task of reason in modern theology, this chapter now turns to another historical example, which illustrates different modes or forms of theological reasoning.

The Theological Tasks of Reason in Scott's *Gospel Restored*

Born in Scotland in 1796, Walter Scott immigrated to the United States in 1818 and began teaching school in Pittsburgh. He met Alexander Campbell during the winter of 1821–22 and moved in 1826 to Ohio, where he was a traveling evangelist. Out of his preaching experience, Scott published *The Gospel Restored* in 1836. His primary purpose was to present "a connected discourse of the true gospel of Christ" for the work of evangelism, and the book exposited each of the main points of his famous, evangelistic "five-finger exercise": faith, repentance, baptism, the remission of sins, and the gift of the Holy Spirit. Although Scott primarily intended to present a biblically grounded "plan of preaching," his book's 128-page introduction laid out the general presuppositions on which the argument would proceed and, in particular, Scott's views on the theological task of "reason."[6] This should not surprise us. Preaching is an act of communication, and Scott recognized that, in order to establish new congregations out of persons from diverse backgrounds, his preaching had to create patterns of coherence that connected the diversities. Although contemporary theologians will doubtless disagree with particular conclusions that Scott reached, the formal issues he identified remain instructive with respect to the role of reason in theology, preaching, and the work of the ministry.

Most importantly, Scott thought that reason took different forms. He distinguished between three major modes of reasoning. The first I will call *narrative reason*. Scott thought that humans viewed the world as a "great drama," with "endless variety of under-plot and interlude, played off on a stage boundless as the great globe itself."[7] Scott therefore organized the introductory section of *The Gospel Restored* as a commentary on the Genesis narrative of creation and the garden of Eden. Moreover, he did not restrict his account to the Bible alone but interpreted it in conversation with John Milton's *Paradise Lost* (1667), sometimes agreeing and other times disagreeing with the great seventeenth-century poet's rendering of Genesis.[8] I take Scott's use of Milton to be a further illustration of the role of reason—in this case narrative reason—in drawing connections between religion and other aspects of culture, such as poetry and literature. Storytelling is a characteristic practice of cultures across the centuries, and it is surely among the most important cultural practices for shaping personal identity by relating the person to the larger stories of communities across generations. Narrative reason takes up the theological task of understanding Christian narrative in relation to other cultural narratives, thereby deepening and extending the person's capacity to tell Christian stories with formative power and insight.

But the main significance of the appearance of *Paradise Lost* in *The Gospel Restored* is that Scott thereby portrayed religious reasoning as participation in a historical community of interpretation, recognizing that he did not read the Bible in isolation but in dialogue with a long line of earlier interpreters. In *The Responsible Self,* Niebuhr explained that interpretive communities place a person not only in dialogue with "current companions" but also with past representatives of the community, and through responsiveness to this larger reference group the person "achieves a relative independence from his immediate associates."[9] Milton's way of retelling Genesis had interpretive points to make that have shaped modern readings of the Eden story but that also differ from modern interpretations. Participation in a historical community of interpretation, in other words, provides reason with the opportunity for a judicious distance from assumptions shared with the immediate, contemporary community. Christians cultivate a sophisticated capacity for narrative reason both by recognizing the extent to which each of us participates in larger narratives of self and community and by drawing critical comparisons among differing historical and contemporary narratives.

In addition to narrative reason, Scott was equally committed to a second style of reasoning, which I will call *systemic reason*. Like his friend and contemporary Alexander Campbell, Scott thought that human "rational life" exercised the power to perceive order, law, and design throughout nature, "distributed according to certain vital, mechanical, and mathematical laws of proportion, fitness, correspondence, contrast, contrariety and so forth."[10] In relation to the possibilities and limits of systemic reason, much of his introduction deliberated the relation between revealed religion and a natural theology accessible to any reasoning human, and he probed one of the great theological questions of the nineteenth century, the compatibility of science and theology. Systematic theological reason addresses the formal relationships among a society's ideas about the world in which humans live. Through systematic reasoning, the Christian seeks to understand how different Christian ideas are related to one another. In Scott's day, for instance, Christians struggled to make sense of believing in *both* the overarching providence of God *and* the freedom of the individual. Systematic theological reasoning also concerns itself with the relation of Christian ideas to other ideas about the setting of human life, such as psychological theories of the person or medical ideas about the beginning and end of a person's life. As the writings of Alexander Campbell, Robert Milligan, and Walter Scott make clear, Disciples of Christ minister-theologians of the nineteenth century considered systematic theological reasoning about the relation of theology and science to be crucial for developing a comprehensive Christian analysis of humanity's relationship with its environment.

Finally, Scott was a close student of a mode of reasoning I will term *analogical reason*. He pointed out, for instance, that most of the arguments of his time about the doctrine of the atonement mistakenly interpreted atonement through analogies to commercial justice, when, according to Scott, the proper analogies were to political justice, with its concepts of law, public safety, and the common good.[11] Reasoning of the analogical type recognizes similarity-in-difference. "The heart is a pump," one says. However, a quick visit to an oil field to see pumps with forty-foot rocker beams demonstrates that this analogical sentence is not completely accurate! But analogical reasoning has nonetheless drawn a connection, based on the capacity of the heart and the pump to move liquids through tubes. Analogical reasoning recognizes similarities across the space of difference.

Theologically, this analogical capacity also comes into play in the engagement of different persons one with another, especially in the process of questioning one another's assumptions and narratives. As the theologian David Tracy has observed, in these moments of difference one recognizes similarity: "We notice that to attend to the other as other, the different as different, is also to understand the different *as* possible. To recognize possibility is to sense some similarity to what we have already experienced or understood,"[12] even when the difference between persons seems as dramatic as the difference between the heart and the oil field pump. Walter Scott emphasized not only that such analogical reasoning was an indispensable tool of theological reflection but also that drawing appropriate analogies was crucial. Although Scott did not fully develop his point, he apparently thought that theologians should test their analogies by means of narrative and systematic reasoning. In the case of the atonement, for instance, he reached his judgment by asking about the consequences of a given analogy for wider understandings of the common good.

Conclusion

Throughout his introduction to *The Gospel Restored*, Walter Scott operated on the assumption that theological reasoning and concepts were fully interactive with reasoning and concepts drawn from literature, science, commerce, and politics. This is a far-reaching assumption about the task and sources of theology. Whether as a preacher or as a systematic theologian, the Christian scholar must be aware of different modes of reasoning—narrative, systemic, and analogical—and make choices about the appropriateness of a particular style of reason for the theological point that he or she wishes to make. Such theological choices about styles of reasoning have had and are continuing to have broad cultural effects, for example, in religious responses to the teaching of evolutionary biology in American public schools. Furthermore, it is not the case that Christians first understand theological ideas and then go to literature, science, commerce, and politics to find metaphors and analogies that convey their prior theological understanding. Instead, scientific concepts, literary narratives, and models of economic exchange stand in reciprocal relation to theological ideas, one constantly influencing and modifying another as humans seek to arrive at an understanding of their social and natural environment.

In the context of modernity, the Christian is constantly reasoning as simultaneously an economic person, a scientific person, and a political person, as well as a religious person. The diversity of modern society is not simply "out there," but inside each thinking individual who is striving for some relative coherence of thought and action. Hence, reasoning inescapably has a moral dimension. On this point, too, Walter Scott placed instructive emphasis. Notwithstanding humanity's "endless variety in art, his valour in war, and sublimity in science," Scott argued that human "mental powers" ultimately resolved into two classes of ideas: "ideas of what is, and ideas of what ought to be; in other words, ideas of knowledge, and duty." Scott therefore argued that the human reasoning capacity was, among other things, intrinsically ethical, and he, like the other Disciples founders, concerned himself to elaborate practical reason and the conduct, duties, and identity of the social self.

Scott's theme of the moral dimension to practical reason returns this chapter, of course, to the observations of Amartya Sen. Given the plural identities that characterize modern society, "the responsibilities of choice and reasoning" are central to leading a human life, which entails decisions "about what relative importance to attach, in a particular context, to the divergent loyalties and priorities that may compete for precedence."[13] Indeed, one of these ethical choices may be precisely the decision to think of oneself as combining plural affiliations rather than presenting a univocal religious identity. It may well be the case, as Sen proposes, that the univocal approach to religious identity promotes "a confrontational culture" in the name of a particular religion.[14] In this case, the cultivation of modes of theological reasoning that elaborate the plural dimensions of a Christian identity and that recognize similarity-in-difference may be one of the crucial steps toward Christian tolerance and peacemaking, both in the United States and around the globe.

6

What Do We Learn from Experience?

Lessons, Suspicions, and Testimony

KRISTINE A. CULP

We got on an airplane, the kind that is always pictured in fatal accidents involving people from rich countries in the process of experiencing the world as spectacle.

Jamaica Kincaid[1]

If any one thing in my experience, more than another, served to deepen my conviction of the infernal character of slavery, and to fill me with unutterable loathing of slaveholders, it was their base ingratitude to my poor old grandmother.

Frederick Douglass[2]

A living faith and a living theology will always be learning from experience. "Experience" does not simply provide raw data for theology, the portion of which can be adjusted according to one's preferred recipe for doing theology. Rather, we live out our faith—receiving and shaping and handing on what theological understanding we have—within vast moving fields of human experience. The task of this chapter is to consider "experience" or "experiences" as a medium for theological understanding and as a source and norm for theological reflection.

What do we learn from experience? Sometimes ways of experiencing the world hinder an adequate understanding of our place in the world in relation with others and before God. Persons may seek novel and intense experiences by boarding airplanes for far-flung places, in shopping or sports triumphs, or through food, sex, and religious practices. This kind of experience is something possessed and consumed rather than a means to understanding and relationship. The pursuit and consumption of novel or intense experiences can divert attention from other persons, the world, and God.

At other times experiences convict us of the most demanding truths. Frederick Douglass's abhorrence of slavery as an evil, dehumanizing system found its deepest root in the experience of the treatment of his enslaved grandmother. His autobiographical testimony, in turn, pointed beyond his own and his grandmother's experiences to the truth that slavery was "infernal"; it compelled others to reach a similar verdict. This kind of experience directs and demands, rather than diverts, attention. It causes us to confront the brutalities and glories of life; it draws us into profound matters of dignity, justice, goodness, truth, and God.

What do we learn from our own and others' experiences? What do we learn about God and about human plights and possibilities before God? To answer these questions involves sorting through which kind of experiences, whose they are and who is giving an account of them, and how experience itself is construed. The first part of this chapter takes up these considerations in relation to an 1891 essay, "Lessons from Our Past Experience," by James Harvey Garrison,the influential editor of the *Christian-Evangelist*.[3] His essay offers a useful case study in choices that Disciples make about the use of experience in thinking about their faith.

Experiences—whosever they are and whatever kind they are—are thick with cultural and theological assumptions and interpretations. Not all experiences demand the same attention or make the same claims. The relationship of theology and experience must be variegated, ranging from critique of some uses of experience to reliance upon what is gained in experience for a more adequate understanding of creaturely life in the world before God. The second and third parts of the chapter consider when appeals to experience ought to provoke suspicion and when experiences may give rise to compelling testimonies of truth and justice.

Lessons from Experience

Experience has been a multipurpose word. It is a noun with old linguistic connections to *experiment* and *attempt* and *adventure*. It is a verb, *to experience,* that moves its subject along without immediately raising the question of whether its subject is acting or being acted upon: he *undergoes,* she *meets with,* they *experience*. It can also be an adjective, *experienced,* that signals the wise accumulation of what has been undergone—or simply that there's been a whole lot of undergoing going on.[4]

Among these variations, one theme familiar to the Disciples of Christ has been experience as an edifying compilation of what has been undergone over time. An 1891 collection entitled *The Old Faith Restated* reviewed the first seventy-five years of Disciples teaching "in the Light of Experience and of Biblical Research." For this task, editor J.H. Garrison brought together a group of prominent Disciples intellectuals—"Representative Men," as the long subtitle presented them. His interest was with the accumulated—and still accumulating—collective experience of the Disciples of Christ and with the "lessons" in faith that "our past" could teach for his and the next generations.

The kind of experience to which Garrison turned was an accumulation of living, learning, attempting, failing, succeeding, and undergoing by a people called the Disciples of Christ. This amorphous accumulation, in turn, was collectively tested in relation to its usefulness and effectiveness, other experiences, common sense, the conviction of truth, and the teaching of the Bible. Garrison's approach to experience exuded an American spirit of experimentation and confidence in the ability of the Disciples movement—and, with the help of a vibrant Christianity, civilization in general—to progress through trial and error. His experimental, pragmatic tenor and his confidence in moral progress cohered with prevailing currents in late-nineteenth-century U.S. culture.[5] Garrison's assumption that experience could provide "light" also attested to his faith in a gracious, living God.[6] If saving knowledge of God is not a possession controlled by the institutions and dogmas of the ages, and God is not only known through the Bible but is met personally in Christ and is inspiring the church and bringing about the kingdom of God, then God in Christ will also be known in the experiences of present-day Christians.

Garrison depicted the Disciples as a dynamic, still changing movement united freely by their living faith in a personal Christ (and by their rejection of "religious tyranny"), who have a great mission relevant to the needs of the modern age. He evaluated the movement's past experiences with candor—analyzing problematic tendencies toward sectarianism, legalism, rationalism, "extreme individualism," and their "fondness for controversy." At the same time, he highlighted fifteen contributions that the movement was making to the common good and toward the advancement of the kingdom of God. Among these were denouncing divided Christianity, "free[ing] the human mind and conscience from the fetters forged by past generations," "lift[ing] the personal Christ above human creeds and dogmas," studying the Bible through the inductive method, reemphasizing the priesthood of all believers, and attending to the practical and ethical side of Christianity.

Garrison placed the Disciples of Christ in the flux of history and culture as agents of transformation. He rendered positive and negative lessons from what they have undergone. The rendering of experience produced a yet evolving body of practical wisdom.[7] This "sacred trust," in turn, must continue to impel outreach and mission, lest the Disciples cease to be a movement and become only a monument.

If we render the now nearly two hundred years of Disciples experience, its lessons still direct us toward agency in a changing world, albeit a world whose possibilities and perils differ from those of the late nineteenth century. Today we must disentangle a sense of the living God from the "progress" of our churches, cultures, and nations. Chastened by numerical decline in the United States and by failure in mission, as represented by the collapse of the National Benevolent Association but also by other failures, Disciples in the United States and Canada are rightly less sanguine about their future than were their late-nineteenth-century predecessors. Moreover, the lessons we have learned about the vulnerability of institutions echo lessons about ineffective, fallible, and sometimes corrupt institutions within the wider world. At the same time, Disciples have learned that we must rely upon organizations and collaborations, vulnerable and fallible as they may be, for effective engagement with a complex world—indeed, as means through which a gracious, living God is present in the midst of creaturely life. If anything, the changed situations of life and ministry make an experimental and pragmatic approach to experience more important rather than less so.

What we do with experience—including how we construe it—concerns how we are situated in the world before God and with others. Garrison's approach to experience situated the Disciples of Christ in a particular way in relation to faith, history, and culture. Two additional points elaborate the approach he took and the significance of his choices.

First, Garrison attended to the collective, ongoing, and cumulating experiences of a people of faith rather than to an intensely personal "religious experience" that the movement's founders had undergone. Had Garrison (or the Disciples of Christ themselves) appealed to the latter, then his essay (and the Disciples) might have focused on whether and how followers had replicated this experience and thus shared the same decisive insight into the saving reality of God.[8] But then the Disciples would have been a "monument," not a "movement," and their faith and its good works would cease to be "living" insofar as they would be oriented toward reproducing the past rather than working toward the coming kingdom of God. In our day, if we are to confront the world's pain and glory and to work toward the fullness of God's goodness, righteousness, and grace, then we must remain open to learning from fresh experiences. Moreover, we ought not limit God to special "religious" experiences, but rather anticipate that God's grace and transforming power may be manifest in every dimension of life.

Second, not all experience makes equal claims. The yield of truth and understanding from various experiences is not the same. Garrison's "past experience" is variegated enough to embrace a range of theological perspectives, yet it is a self-correcting accumulation that rejects some options.

He portrays a spirit of toleration that endures despite challenges from parties that aim for certainty through literalism and legalism and inspire "false confidence"; a right "proportion" of "head and heart" that emerges to correct overzealous rationalism; and reform in biblical teaching that satisfies "common sense" and helps ensure the accessibility of salvation and that prevails over those who would "shroud" the plan of salvation in "mystery."

Garrison depicts some perspectives as "extreme," as washing up outside the channel of the Disciples of Christ movement. Excessive enthusiasm and rationalism are set outside the bounds; both sentimental and authoritarian religion are rejected; cooperation is urged as the optimal mean between "extreme individualism" and "ecclesiastical despotism"; an equilibrium is sought between "habits of controversy" and "indifference to religious error." These channel markers in turn guide further assessment of experience. Although the terms may have shifted somewhat today, such markers remain useful for designating a way of faith and theology in which the "sacred trust" of cumulating experience—the *consensus fidelium*—contributes to toleration, common sense, and a collective head and heart that are well-balanced.

Suspicions about Experience

Garrison assured his readers "that most of the extremes...were never held by the representative men among us"[9]—surely a remark that today's readers hear differently than his contemporaries. We can imagine both that Garrison's lessons emerged from situations and conversations more diverse than the language of "representative men" suggests *and* that other varieties of Disciples' experiences were not fully taken into account. Confluences of region, race, gender, and theological perspectives that may have gone unnoted nevertheless shaped—altered, enhanced, limited—Disciples thought and practice as it moved through the next century.

When fresh and diverse experiences cannot enter the cumulating field of experiences and give rise to new expressions and affirmations of faith, then well-marked channels can become narrow ruts or stagnant ponds. If channel markers and boundaries come to limit genuine interactions with others, the wider world, and God, then faith and theology are deadened. Moreover, our expectations and conventions can effectively constrain the One we dare to name God.

In retrospect we can imagine lessons that Garrison did not observe. What of the experiences of the Chinese immigrants in Portland, Oregon, who under the leadership of Jeu Hawk became the first Asian American Disciples congregation, also in 1891? What of the experiences of Disciples who descended from Anglo-European immigrants and who first welcomed Chinese and Japanese American Disciples—and of those who within a few decades would spurn them? Or, what of the experiences of enslaved grandmothers who sat in the balcony at Cane Ridge, whose endurance of indignities and whose faith were part of the first generation Disciples of

Christ? What of the faith held and the indignities suffered by their great-grandchildren who were part of hundreds of Disciples congregations and who, in Garrison's day, were no doubt experiencing the rise of Jim Crow? Historians can reconstruct some gaps in knowledge; however, more than historical knowledge is at stake in these gaps. We can imagine other lessons that could have been rendered from experience—lessons about injustice and exclusion that went unobserved by "representative men" and most others; testimonies in faith that were not passed on to later generations in compilations of "Disciples experience."

These lessons from balconies, borderlands, and margins return us to the situations signaled in the chapter's epigraphs. Under economies of chattel slavery in which some owned others and some were owned, and under contemporary global political economies in which some consume and some are consumed, questions about what we learn from experience in doing theology are further complicated. Has "experience" been fashioned as a mode of diversion for privileged persons in a global consumer economy—"people from rich countries in the process of experiencing the world as spectacle"? Is our understanding of experience already warped by patterns of class and consumption, of race and ownership, of gender, sexuality, and possession? Does "experience" buttress modern tendencies to place the self in the center of the universe, to reduce freedom to the question of whether an individual can pursue what he or she wants? Or can "experience" break through the dull acceptance of everyday injustices and falsehoods to expose sturdier truths—"serve to deepen convictions about the infernal character of slavery," and of other tyrannies, inhumanities, and idolatries?

Elite and bourgeois westerners sometimes seem to board *en masse* the plane that Jamaica Kincaid describes with only the vaguest sense of peril, seeking satisfaction without entanglements. Experience becomes a consumer item, a possession to be acquired, and little regard is given to the privileges by which these experiences are created and acquired. Such production and consumption of experience fails to heed the economic, political, and cultural contexts out of which it is wrought. But the "exotic" and "unique" experiences of travelers often take place in the midst of someone else's daily routine[10]; experiences of care and relation may be ensured by someone's underpaid labor; "personal religious experience" may arise while someone else is segregated in the balconies and margins of religious communities. In such situations, theology's role is to be suspicious—to suspect the adequacy of what is learned about ourselves, others, and God when experience is acquired and consumed without attention to its contexts, connections, or consequences.

Most persons who read this chapter have a privileged place in the world, even if only relatively so by virtue of their citizenship and access to education and basic necessities. We who are relatively privileged must keep our suspicions engaged in order to be accountable and responsible for our place in the world. Experience must be more carefully attended to, not less. To take our place in the world responsibly, we must unwrap experience from its consumer packaging and understand it as something that connects us to others, something that situates us in the world before God, rather than something that we consume and possess. If we do not attend to experience as a connection to the wider world and to more expansive truths, then some political regime, cultural flow, religious dogmatism, or marketing strategy will step in to tell us what we have undergone and what to do with it.[11]

The Testimony of Experience

A relevant, living faith must cultivate a certain suspicion of the diversions of "personal experience" in a globalized consumer economy. It must also remain open to truth that is rendered from experience—albeit experiences that are already situated in and shaped by shifting intersections of meaning and power. After all, it is not cultural sensibilities, the teaching of the churches, or even the witness of the Bible to which Frederick Douglass points, but a conviction arising from experience. His experience of slavery as evil and of a contrasting sense of inviolable humanity of his enslaved grandmother exceeded the lessons in truth available from the cultural conventions and most churches of his day.

In 1839, just a few years before Douglass's narrative was published, Theodore Weld published *American Slavery as It Is: Testimony of a Thousand Witnesses*. It contained narratives by enslaved persons and accounts from newspapers, periodicals, and first-hand observers about the conditions, cruelty, and torture suffered by enslaved Americans. (The brutality of "upstanding" slaveholders—preachers, professors of religion, and public officials—received special attention.) Weld presented his material as evidence at a trial, starting with the testimony of witnesses—including "hostile witnesses," that is, slaveholders—and rebutting potential defenses. "Reader," he began, "you are empannelled as a juror to try a plain case and bring in an honest verdict."[12] Weld, like Douglass, believed that the testimony of experience could break through the dull acceptance of injustices and falsehoods to expose injustice and truth.

For Douglass and Weld, as for the early Disciples of Christ, the language of testimony would have had a biblical resonance as well as an association with empirical evidence and court trials. The gospel of John concludes, "This is the disciple who is testifying to these things and has written them, and we know that his testimony is true" (Jn. 21:24). Jesus' disciples were sent out to proclaim the good news and to heal; whenever a town did not welcome them, they were to "shake off the dust that is on your feet as a testimony against them" (Mk. 6:11; Lk. 9:5). Jesus and his disciples speak of immensities too vast to comprehend, but whose realities demand acceptance—a creation that overflows with the glory of God; life and love that rise beyond death; God's righteous and healing power now present and yet to reign. "Readers and listeners," these testimonies ask, "how will you judge these claims of truth, justice, and love? Will you believe this? Will you believe in Jesus as God's testimony of transforming love and justice?"

Testimony also resonates in our age, an era confronted by the monstrosities of human enslavement and also of death camps, killing fields, suicide bombers, and other modern genocides. These immensities, too, resist full comprehension and thus any narration creates a crisis of truth. When we are confronted with firsthand testimonies of enslaved persons or of survivors of death camps and killing fields, we encounter not only particular experiences, but also claims to abiding truths—about the depths of evil and inviolable dignity—that demand attention and action from us, their hearers.

According to the philosopher Paul Ricoeur, testimony in ordinary language involves a firsthand witness relating what has been seen or experienced and thus has at its basis a "quasi-empirical meaning."[13] It moves from a report of facts to a confession of what one believes to be true: "I was there...believe me." In a trial one doesn't simply tell true things or false things, one *is* a true witness or a false witness. The witness attests by assuming risks for the cause she or he defends, perhaps subjecting her- or himself to prosecution: "Are you truthful?" ("Are you the Christ?") To the extent that witnesses are accused and tried, their cause—say, the diminishment of life and God—is also tried, and they enter what Ricoeur called "the tragic destiny of truth."

The religious meaning of testimony involves an "irruption" of new meaning while also conserving the ordinary meaning of testimony. Particular testimonies and witnesses refer beyond themselves to make claims about God and the implication of all things in God. "What separates this new meaning of testimony from all its uses in ordinary language," Ricoeur notes, "is that the testimony does not belong to the witness."[14] Jesus' disciples were not just any witnesses, as the gospels tell us; they were those who were sent. Those who boycotted racially segregated buses in Montgomery, Alabama, in 1955–56 not only testified to the rights and dignity of all persons, they understood themselves to have a place in a divine destiny where "truth marches on" and justice cannot be denied.

All kinds of situations, mundane and extraordinary, may become occasions in which we are met, challenged, and changed by experiences of the grace and love, power and judgment of a living God.[15] In our day, theology must be especially attentive to the plight and dignity of persons who are commodified and constrained in globalized consumer political economies and to the testimonies that may arise from the world's balconies, borderlands, and margins.

Conclusion

"Experience is a teacher from whose school none are exempt, and there are some lessons which have to be learned in that school, and in no other,"

J.H. Garrison observed.[16] Among the hard-won and still emerging lessons of his day were tolerance; ecumenical generosity; openness to change and the future; reliance on the Bible, studied inductively and critically, as an orienting testimony of faith; the equal accessibility and accountability of all believers before God; a responsive, personal faith in Christ freed from authoritarian structures and dogmas; an intellectually credible faith balanced with sensibilities of the "heart"; resistance to religious demagoguery and tyranny; and the need for faith to have a moral, practical effect in the world. We still have lessons to learn about these very matters. Today any *consensus fidelium* formed among the Disciples of Christ must be subject both to ongoing revision and to ongoing suspicion.

If we do not learn well from experience, our faith and theology will fail to engage richly with life and history and to be accountable for our place in the world. Moreover, we will surrender the root of our ability to question false authority and to be agents of mercy and transformation. Experience will not offer us unambiguous perceptions, whole truths, or pure touch points of the holy. Nonetheless, it can disrupt what we have taken for granted about ourselves, others, and God; it can cause us to realign our affections, values, and ideas; and it can compel and shape our conviction of the fullness of justice, mercy, and truth that we name God.

7

Practicing Reconciliation

A Methodological Proposal

Peter Goodwin Heltzel and Don S. Browning

Multicultural fragmentation is an urgent problem for Christian theology. North America's recent recognition of diverse and colorful expressions of Christianity outside of the Euro-American orbit presents both problems and promise. Cultural plurality is one of the important challenges that world Christianity poses to theology. While the respectful engagement of cultural difference is a challenge, a diverse and inclusive open table of theological conversation holds great promise. If we can come to the table in loving, respectful conversation, the church may be able to model the beloved community that it is called to be.

To address the challenge of multiculturalism, Christian theology needs to cultivate a new way of being in the world. John Wesley's quadrilateral presents four sources of theology: the Bible, tradition, experience, and reason. In addition to these four sources, cultural context also needs to be taken into account.

In this chapter we argue that theology is fundamentally a conversation to and about the Triune God. Building on Hans-Georg Gadamer's argument for the centrality of conversation for integral hermeneutics, we develop the notion that theology is table-talk. Theology carries on a conversation with God that begins in baptism and is celebrated in the Lord's supper. Our vision is organized around three different forms of theology: gospel theology, historical theology, and constructive theology. Furthermore, we develop a postcolonial retrieval of Gadamer's notion of culture/tradition (*Bildung*) in order to engage the concrete differences of Christians from diverse cultural contexts.

Following the "practical turn" in twentieth-century philosophy, five recent theological movements have emerged that take cultural context as an important dimension of theological construction: (1) liberation theology (e.g., Gustavo Gutiérrez); (2) contextual theology (e.g., Robert Schreiter), (3) practical theology (e.g., Don S. Browning), (4) systematic theology appropriating cultural studies (e.g., Kathryn Tanner), and (5) postcolonial constructive theology (e.g., Catherine Keller). These five approaches are distinct in their methods, but all develop theologies that take cultural and social context seriously. Taken collectively, these five styles of Christian theology represent a breakthrough in academic theology, but they need to be translated into particular Christian communities.

A Christian theology of transformation provides a framework for moving our denomination from multicultural fragmentation toward intercultural solidarity. We identify our outcome as intercultural solidarity, in part, because the current rhetoric of multiculturalism cannot seem to get beyond a celebration of diversity. An intercultural approach to Disciples theology holds much promise when synthesized with the leading insights of practical theology in the hermeneutical tradition.[1]

Following the turn to culture and practice in contemporary theology, we argue for a theo-hermeneutical realism that can break some of the binaries of modernity and transform early twenty-first–century Disciples theology. We build on Don S. Browning's fundamental practical theology, condensing his four moments of theology (descriptive, historical, systematic, and strategic) to three (gospel, historical, and constructive).[2] In beginning with the gospel moment, we mean that the first act of practical-theological thinking and acting is simultaneously witnessing to the gospel while also describing our situation from its angle of vision. The social sciences can be useful in this act of description but only as subordinate to the interpretation of the situation from the perspective of the Christian tradition. The historical moment has to do with testing our initial witness and descriptions by a deeper and critical interpretation of elements in the tradition that are relevant to the questions emerging from our situation and the situations with which we dialogue. The constructive moment should be seen as further testing our beliefs and systematizing our practical response in light of the deeper historical-interpretive work of the second moment. The third step is also a matter of returning to the original context or situation with renewed and more faithful practices. All of these theological stages are practical in character.

Since "transformation" is the bridging concept in Browning's model of fundamental practical theology, we refer to this theological method for Disciples as a theology of transformation. We apply our method to the interpretation and restoration themes of Disciples theology. In both instances our concern is with developing practices of interpretation and reconciliation as concrete embodiments of the five themes of Disciples thought.

Multicultural Fragmentation

The CCDC provides a good case study for developing a theology of transformation because of its indigenous roots and multicultural future. Since the 1990s, the denomination has been infused by new churches, such as the Haitian Diaspora and Mexican American congregations, that are generally theologically conservative with a strong commitment to social justice. They are drawn to the theological simplicity of Disciples slogans such as, "No creed but Christ," and, "No book but the Bible," as well as our commitment to racial and economic justice. Since new congregations represent most of the major non-Anglo-European cultures—including African American, Hispanic American, Native American, and Asian American churches—Disciples are challenged to a deeper engagement with cultural complexity.

These different ethnic constituencies have often created serious theological and ethical dilemmas. One important manifestation of this problem is the way in which some of these churches, such as the African American churches, often feel marginalized from the broader church culture and from access to decision making at the regional and general levels of church life. In the case of the African American church, there is a very long history of "black suffering" with which, as James Cone reminds us, the white church has never come fully to terms.

A second example of multicultural fragmentation in our denomination is the "boundary" that separates many white Disciples from Mexican Americans in the South and the Southwest. Daisy L. Machado, in *Of Borders and Margins,* documents the ways that white Texan Disciples avoided interaction with Hispanic Disciples in the border region of Southern Texas during the period 1888–1945.[3] She utilizes concepts in postcolonial theory that suggest Disciples internalized a colonial logic that racialized and oppressed the Mexican other. Machado writes that "forces successfully combined theological concepts with ideologies of conquest, such as destined use of the land or the self-identification as a chosen people, which became rationalizations for creation of racial paradigms of inferiority and Otherness... The religion of the colonizers merged with concerns for domination; and in this process, the theology and theological identity of the Disciples would forever be altered."[4] Through a postcolonial lens, Machado lays out a stinging indictment of Disciples theology and theological identity as being permanently "altered" in a negative manner. However, postcolonial thought also provides categories for a horizon of hope, including border-crossing and hybridity, that can be used to build solidarity and community within our denomination.

Theology as Table-Talk: A Conversation with Hans-Georg Gadamer

As a result of the hermeneutical revolution in the twentieth century, theologians began to think more fully about the issue of cultural context. The practical theology movements outlined above have been influenced by this hermeneutical revolution. In the patristic and medieval periods, theology was undergirded by a hermeneutics of consent, while the European Enlightenment and its aftermath brought a hermeneutics of suspicion.[5] The German philosopher Hans-Georg Gadamer critiques the scientific method and historical-critical method because of their inability to interpret texts in religion and the humanities. Shifting away from modernist epistemology, he proposes a hermeneutics of conversation that focuses on personal and communal identity and situation.[6]

Gadamer, in his ground-breaking work *Truth and Method,* provides important resources for a practical Christian theological method concerned with culture, tradition, and action. Responding to the questions for the human sciences raised by the natural sciences, Gadamer develops a philosophy for the human sciences that is unique to human phenomena that cannot be reduced to positivist explanations. Human experiences of philosophy, art, history, and spirituality are "all modes of experience in which a truth is communicated that cannot be verified by the methodological means proper to science."[7] Gadamer rightly concludes that the scientific method is inadequate for the human sciences, including theology. This is why, in our method, we use the social sciences, but only as subordinate to what Gadamer calls *verstehen,* or understanding.

When thinking through how to speak about what goes on in the search for understanding or meaning in the humanities and theology, Gadamer hones in on the metaphor of conversation. The humanities often are enlivened through a dialogue about texts in the great wisdom traditions of various cultures. Thus, the humanities—including practical theology—demand a hermeneutical strategy that focuses on "a discipline of questioning and inquiring" embodied in conversation.[8] Gadamer's conversational approach is practical and oriented toward the other and the contexts of both self and other.[9] It is through *phronesis* (practical understanding realized through conversation) that the truth in action is apprehended. This hermeneutical tradition is an embodiment of practical wisdom.

Hermeneutics is focused on understanding texts. Gadamer draws an analogy between the conversation that two people have and the conversation a reader has with a text, acknowledging that the respective hermeneutics situations are not identical.[10] Gadamer writes, "Conversation is a process of coming to an understanding...each person opens himself to the other, truly accepts his point of view as valid and transposes himself into the other to such an extent that he understands not the particular individual but what he says."[11] Conversation with a text or a person is driven by the search for understanding. The desire to understand is impelled by a curiosity often expressed through the dialectic of question and answer.[12] As we seek understanding together we are always trying to negotiate different interpretations. "Interpretation belongs to the essential unity of understanding. Whatever is said to us must be so received by us that it speaks and finds a response in our own words and in our language."[13] This whole process of seeking human understanding through negotiating interpretations is the essence of the human search for meaning and applies to theology as well as other disciplines in the humanities.

Gadamer's hermeneutical theory is helpful in several ways for Disciples practical theology method. First, the theoretical underpinnings of the conversation metaphor deepen our notion of theology as table-talk. Part of the theo-retical underpinnings of conversation is God—a Divine Other—that is the basis of all others. Second, Gadamer's notion of *Bildung* helps us recover the importance of cultural context in the process of theologizing—i.e., in the process of asking theological questions and moving through the three steps of practical theological interpretation and action.

Theology is a practical discipline, an ongoing conversation between human others who worshipfully engage the Divine Other. Human truth entails going beyond a simple mechanistic account of human affairs. Gadamer notes: "According to Kierkegaard, it is the other who breaks into my ego-centeredness and gives me something to understand. This Kierkegaardian motif guided me from the beginning."[14] This transcendence is based on the Divine Other that breaks into human reality through the human other giving us a subject and context to understand. In order to understand the subject in front of us embodied in the face of the other, we need to have a conversation. The gospel moment in our three-step practical theology looks in two directions at once—first, trying to describe, interpret, and understand the human other in her or his context and, second, trying to describe, interpret, and understand the Divine Other, mediated in history, that is the foundation of both other and self. This threefold practical interpretive process is naïve and impressionistic in its first phase and must be tested and matured through historical theology and constructive-strategic amplification. This is why practical theology, in its first gospel step in both confessional and descriptive modes, should be humble. Faith's first impressions have not been tested.

For Christian theologians, this conversation begins with God's revelation in Jesus Christ and the interpretation of contexts from the angle of vision of our first grasp of Christ's meaning. As we have indicated, the social sciences can certainly assist us in this descriptive and interpretive task, but they always play a subordinate, though essential, role. This conversation with Jesus Christ and the prophets continues throughout the tradition of the church to the present. Gadamer's philosophy encourages Christian theologians to simultaneously listen to their own contexts *and* its questions, while also critically engaging their traditions. Today in our multicultural age this will entail engaging each other in conversation by not only interpreting our various present situations but also interpreting the Bible and Christian classics as they relate to these situations.

Tradition and Culture

Theology is concerned with understanding the God who is witnessed to in the text of scripture from the angle of the practical challenges of our contemporary contexts. Integral to the process of understanding is conversation. When we converse with each other, we must be prepared for a conflict of interpretations. Our situations will be different, the angle of interpretation of our theological classics will be different, and our practical responses may differ as well. Gadamer writes, "In human relations the important thing is, as we have seen, to experience the Thou truly as a Thou—i.e., not to overlook his claim but to let him really say something to us. Here is where openness belongs… Openness to the other, then, involves recognizing that I myself must accept some things that are against me, even though no one else forces me to do so."[15]

Gadamer's notion of *Bildung* helps Disciples to engage tradition and culture, two issues that have been difficult for us given the post-Enlightenment Scottish realism that undergirds our theology. It is particularly the issue of cultural "situatedness" in its great diversity that is the primary problem of this volume. Our various cultural situations are partially formed by our inherited religious meanings, but the unique conflicts of these situations in turn shape the questions we should bring to our struggles to deepen our understanding of the theological heritage that has formed us. To take anyone's culture seriously is to move into dialogue between our inherited meanings and emerging questions and the other's inherited meanings and emerging questions.

The search for understanding in the human sciences is unique because human phenomena are unique. We are creatures thrown into the world and into a particular cultural context that Gadamer calls our "situatedness." He writes, "The very idea of a situation means that we are not standing outside it."[16] While each person is bound by his or her hermeneutical situation, cultural context does not lead to relativism, but is rather the context for "*the concretion of the meaning itself.*"[17]

While the French deconstructionist philosopher Jacques Derrida argues: "There is nothing outside of the text,"[18] Christian doctrine amends this by believing in a God that is encountered both within and beyond the text, cutting through while also transcending the situatedness of the interpreter. Revelation, or God's self-disclosure to the world in the incarnation of Jesus Christ, is analogous to this divine ball thrown to us. God's revelation may be sudden or gradually mediated in history, but the whole process of catching this revelation is a form of empowerment that connects us in the deepest way with the fallen, but still fundamentally good, creation that with us groans and eagerly awaits the return of Jesus Christ. However, this divine pitch—this revelation—is always mediated to situations, and what the revelation means is partially shaped by these situations.

While, according to Gadamer, we as humans are thrown into life and into a *Bildung*, new conceptions of tradition and culture are acknowledging the cultural complexity in the process of receiving revelation. There is not a generic human culture. Jesus came in Jewish flesh, expressing the radical particularity of our context. Christian identity is an emerging process, where different cultural elements are marshaled in new ways through time. Kathryn Tanner writes, "Christian identity is therefore no longer a matter of unmixed purity, but a hybrid affair established through unusual uses of materials found elsewhere. Nor can Christian identity be understood from isolated attention to Christian practices *per se*; understanding it now requires the careful situating of Christian practices in the wider field of cultural life on which they are a commentary."[19] In contrast to a notion of tradition as "unmixed purity," the need to start thinking about Christianity as a "hybrid affair" opens up a new theological horizon that embraces the history of struggle in hermeneutics as well as among cultures.[20]

While theology begins with God's revelation, it is a human practice expressing the question-asking character of the whole process of practical theologizing. Chronologically, God's revelation in Jesus Christ is always prior to the act of theologizing. Theology assumes an initial naïve faith in Jesus Christ that propels the search for understanding (*fides quaerens intellectum*). Yet, from the standpoint of the theologian, the attempt to articulate theo-logos—the ordering of God—is always contextualized through our place in the world and the questions we are forming in that context. To repeat, theology follows three movements: the gospel movement that both listens to the gospel (confession) and interprets our context (description), historical theology that brings the questions of the first step to the retrieval of the central texts and norms of the tradition, and constructive theology that systematizes both belief and action. All three movements are practical all the way down. All three are products of a dialogue between practical questions and gospel answers.

Gospel Theology

Christian theology begins with confessing Jesus as the Christ, the Son of God, and, as nearly as possible, describes the situations of life from this perspective. Announced by the great Hebrew Prophets, the incarnation of Jesus Christ is a fulfillment of God's covenant with the people of Israel. Jesus' life and death do not just atone for humanity's sin but proleptically restore the whole creation. Through the Incarnation, God infiltrates all space and time. God's incarnational presence is manifest in the Holy Spirit, which continues to hover over, in, and through the earth, a promise of eternal dwelling with the Triune God. This is the gospel.

Gospel theology has a confessional mode and a descriptive mode. The confessional mode begins with our confession of faith as framed by the narratives of redemption in the Bible. The descriptive mode begins with social analysis of our current situation or context. The confessional and descriptive modes of gospel theology flow back and forth in a call and response structure. Like two jazz musicians following each other's lead, these two modes are interlaced throughout this primary stage of theologizing.

The Bible is the indispensable and incomparable source of the gospel. The Bible narrates stories of the redemption of humanity and the entire cosmos. We come to know ourselves through a lifelong conversation with the text of Holy Scripture. Paul Ricoeur writes, "To understand oneself is to understand oneself as one confronts the text and to receive from it the conditions for a self other than that which first undertakes the reading."[21] For Christians, the Bible sets the conditions for human selfhood. Gadamer writes that it is "the Word that needs to be believed and understood and by which we overcome the abysmal lack of self-knowledge in which we live."[22]

We enter gospel theology liturgically. "The proclamation of salvation, the content of the Christian gospel, is itself an event that takes place in sacrament and preaching, and yet it expresses only what took place in Christ's redemptive act. Hence it is one word that is proclaimed ever anew in preaching… The saving message preached in every sermon is the crucifixion and resurrection of Christ."[23] The sermon is "a call that impinges on each of us."[24] Through our hearing God's word preached and by our participating in the sacraments, our relationship with God is restored and nurtured.

Gaining salvation and self-knowledge through the biblical narratives of scripture demonstrates the power of the biblical horizon. As George Lindbeck says, theology's goal is to locate reality within the sacred texts, so that the text "absorbs the world, rather than the world the text."[25] The authors of this essay, however, understand this more as a fusion of horizons between text and our human questions, rather than an absorption that completely swallows our situated questions. The Stone-Campbell slogan, "No book but the Bible," emphasizes that it is the Bible and the Bible alone that provides the redemptive framework for our questions. But we also believe that there is much to learn about its meaning by studying and respecting the many centuries when the church struggled to interpret the Bible in its different cultures, contexts, and situations.

Newell Williams has argued that, because Disciples have largely internalized a historical-critical approach to the Bible, the gospel of love should be our primary theological norm.[26] Theology begins and ends with the gospel of Jesus Christ. The gospel provides a theological norm of love that can directly respond to contemporary cultural fragmentation. Williams recommends that Disciples follow Campbell's call for the gospel of Jesus Christ to be the theological basis of Christian union. Williams argues that proclaiming the gospel is our only hope because "the message that God is love, received in faith, alone has the spiritual power to reconcile people to God and to one another."[27] Gospel theology provides a reconciliation between the believer and God.

Gospel theology has the vertical dimension: "Anticipating through faith my justification in God, I change little by little from an *I-for-myself* into the *other* for God—I become naïve in God."[28] Through this reconciliation with God and becoming an "other for God" we are then in a position where we are "an other" for others, embodying a ministry of reconciliation.

Gospel theology in concerned with the revelation of Jesus' messianic identity as presented in the scriptures and lived in our context. "Then beginning with Moses and all the prophets, he interpreted to them the things about himself in all the scriptures" (Lk. 24:27). John Caputo argues that in this passage Jesus did some hermeneutics for his disciples. First, the disciples should be able to view the events in Jerusalem as a fulfillment of prophecy. Second, an intermediate stage occurs in which they understand the text, but not the person before their eyes as the one the scriptures were about or intended for. The third and final stage is the "final hermeneutic breakthrough" that recognizes Jesus when he breaks the bread.[29]

The Holy Spirit, through the process of illumination, plays a vital role in leading us to understanding as we hear the Word of God in scripture. The Holy Spirit helps us with interpretations (Jn. 14:16, 26; 15:26; 16:13). Roy Zuck writes that illumination is "the Spirit's work on the minds and hearts of believers that enables them not only to discern the truth but also to receive it, welcome it, and apply it."[30]

In addition to the creative insight drawn from the Holy Spirit, theological hermeneutics requires our common human experience in God's good creation and the Christian tradition, which is based on God's covenant faithfulness.[31] Kevin Vanhoozer argues that "Scripture in tradition" is the norm for two of the most viable post-positivist options in contemporary theology—the recent public theology developed at the University of Chicago and the new Yale post-liberalism. Kevin Vanhoozer argues, "Yale and Chicago now agree that what is normative for theology is 'Scripture in tradition.'" The phrase "Scripture in tradition" maintains the priority of the gospel in the Bible while also appreciating the unfolding of its meaning in subsequent interpretations through the ages. "Each affirms the priority of the biblical message, but Chicago wants to correlate it with what is intelligible in the contemporary context and Yale with what is appropriate in the context of the Christian community."[32] Both emphases are important.

Historical Theology

Gospel theology is followed by historical theology and proceeds by bringing the question arising from the situation into engagement with the Christian tradition. Historical theology can be conceived on one level as a commentary on scripture. Thus, Vanhoozer's term "Scripture in tradition" demonstrates that all scriptural interpretation is traditionalized. Gadamer writes, "Hermeneutical experience is concerned with *tradition.* This is what is to be experienced. But tradition is not simply a process that experience teaches us to know and govern; it is language—i.e., it expresses itself like a Thou... For tradition is a genuine partner in dialogue, and we belong to it, as does the I with a Thou."[33] Historicity and our historical consciousness is part of our humanity.

Each interpreter or group of interpreters brings a tradition of interpretation to the biblical text. The Christian tradition is vital for Christian theology's contemporary task because so many of the distinctive doctrines of Christianity have been formulated in different ecumenical councils and creeds. While historically members of the Stone-Campbell movement have been skeptical of the status of councils and creeds in theology, contemporary Disciples theology through its participation in the ecumenical movement has come to embrace many of these important theological articulations and the situations they were addressing without requiring ascent to them to become a test of fellowship.

When dealing with these sources of theology (the Bible and the classics of tradition), we seek to know the intended meaning of the authors of these texts. We seek this meaning as a form of loving and respecting these saints that have been custodians of the narratives of redemption through the ages as it has addressed different contexts and situations. We do not seek to romantically enter into the consciousness of the author as Schleiermacher sought, but attempt to explicate the meaning projected by the text as Gadamer recommends.[34] Understanding the text means, in part, understanding the situation addressed by the text—the biblical text as well as texts in the tradition that followed the founding texts.

As Protestants, Disciples theology continues a long tradition of privileging the Bible over the tradition. Our historic commitment to the restoration theme has fostered an interest in the biblical interpretation of the early church, including its practices of liturgy, preaching, teaching, and mission efforts. Yet the restoration theme has been modified in recent Disciples theology because of it historical naiveté. Both the process of history and the grandeur of the tradition demand a more nuanced appropriation of the past in Disciples thought. Different communities of readers will read a biblical text in different ways. It is precisely through the tradition that we Disciples can learn right reading and find true belonging. Gadamer writes, "Belonging is brought about by tradition's addressing us."[35] We are situated in tradition and must listen and learn from voices of the past.

Constructive Theology

Constructive theology seeks to creatively and comprehensively classify the central doctrines and practices of the Christian faith. These doctrines are not just abstract principles, but should be conceived as practices that address the original situation that stimulates the first two movements of practical theological reflection. Hence, for the purposes of this essay, we authors have collapsed some of the classical distinctions between constructive theology, theological ethics, and practical theology, or what Browning calls strategic theology.

Constructive theology is our unique statement of faith. As Christian theologians, we use our rationality to marshal the Bible and the tradition in a fresh confession of faith that draws on our experiential and cultural context. Critical to this task are the intellectual virtues of creativity and coherence. Constructive theology is not only a verbal confession of the faith, but is an embodiment of that confession. Constructive theology must acknowledge both its systematic and practical vocation.

Practices of Reconciliation: A Proposal

The practice of reconciliation provides an example of theology in practice. In this final section, we argue that the restoration theme should be reframed as reconciliation in our contemporary postcolonial context. In practical theology, we are also concerned about how this reconciliation theme will be practiced in the church. Practicing reconciliation is vital for the implementation of a truly intercultural Disciples theology.

For Disciples, a theology of reconciliation comes naturally. It is reflected in the Reconciliation Mission of our church, developed from a program authorized by the Disciples General Assembly in the 1960s to combat prejudice, injustice, and poverty in response to the civil rights push of 1963 and the urban crisis of 1968.

Reconciliation, as a theological category, affirms the restorationist theme's christocentric orientation, while giving it a more eschatological perspective. Faith in Jesus Christ can be said to be the foundation of Disciples theology. Alexander Campbell proclaimed:

> The principle which was inscribed on our banners when we withdrew from the ranks of the sects was, "Faith in Jesus as the true Messiah, and obedience to him as Lawgiver and King, the ONLY TEST of Christian character, and the ONLY BOND of Christian union, communion, and cooperation, irrespective of all creeds, opinions, commandments, and traditions of men.[36]

The church is called to proclaim and embody the gospel of Jesus Christ. Humanity's reconciliation with God in Christ, a restoration of communion, provides the basis for the reconciliation of persons within the church.

Reconciliation provides a vocabulary that is able to reinterpret the best of the restoration theme. While, in one soteriological sense, our communion has been "restored" in Christ, "restoration" as a metaphor for rejuvenating a past state is limited when viewed from the eschatological horizon of the New

Testament. Restoration emphasizes a paradise regained, while reconciliation implies an unfinished future.

Reconciliation provides a way to retrieve and reinterpret the restoration theme. Instead of a move backward to the early church, the move is forward toward the final reconciliation of all things in Christ Jesus, a reality that was inaugurated through the Incarnation and that will be fulfilled at the end of the age that the church eagerly awaits. Thus, reconciliation provides a way of bridging the restoration and eschatological theme, adding a dialectical dynamism to the process of theologizing.

"Reconciliation in Christ," then, provides a theological basis for the multicultural solidarity that we seek in our postcolonial context. According to 2 Corinthians 5, the church should be faithful to the evangelical "message of reconciliation" that is the gospel of Jesus Christ. The gospel or "good news" is that Jesus Christ, the unique Son of God, fully human and fully divine, has died for the sins of the world and been raised to new life, anticipating the resurrection of those who believe in him. Jesus Christ is the sole mediator between God and humanity (Acts 4:12). The confession of Jesus Christ as Lord and Savior is the firm foundation of the church and primary task of Christian mission. Missionaries are called to be "ambassadors of Christ" who proclaim "the reconciliation of the world accomplished in Him [Christ], heralds of His person and work."[37] Members of the church are to be heralds of the person and work of Jesus Christ.

This ministry of reconciliation is integral to God's call to every member of the church to be an ambassador and herald of Jesus Christ. It compels the church to reach beyond itself to the "other" in all its multilayered forms as the church moves with God toward the final reconciliation of all things in Christ.

As Christians, we have been called to the ministry of reconciliation. However, reconciliation is hard work; it is the result of justice. Working toward justice means being willing to listen to and respond lovingly to the cries of the stranger, widow, and orphan. The French moral philosopher Emmanuel Levinas writes:

> The presence of the face coming from beyond the world, but committing me to human fraternity, does not overwhelm me as a numinous essence arousing fear and trembling...To hear his destitution which cries out for justice is not to represent an image to oneself, but is to posit oneself as responsible, but as more and as less than the being that presents itself in the face... The Other who dominates me in his transcendence is thus the stranger, the widow, and the orphan, to whom I am obligated.[38]

Many of the strangers, widows, and orphans in our midst are people of color. Costly reconciliation demands a true forgiveness and love among enemies. Victims and perpetrators come together at the cross to be reconciled and join the struggle for peace and justice.

Within our own denomination, the segregation of black and white congregations in Mississippi, and white and Hispanic congregations in Texas, can only be overcome through practicing reconciliation. From the perspective of hermeneutic theory, we can expect conflict of interpretations given the different cultural contexts brought to the interpretive task. However, we have an ethical obligation to seek as a church to resolve and reconcile these differences in love. Because of sin and finitude in all situations, no one person or group will ever be in a position to have complete understanding. We need each other through conversation to arrive at meaning, self-understanding, and wholeness in Christ Jesus. Alexander Campbell saw this union of reconciled Christians as "essential to the conversion of the world."[39]

In conclusion, we believe that the Disciples tradition of theological practice is well suited to be formulated as table-talk, sensitive to the many contexts and special questions of the new cultural pluralism of both our society and our denomination. Disciples theology, hermeneutic theory, and the new practical theologies have a compatibility that opens new possibilities for America's most distinctive Christian movement.

SECTION II

God in Creation

8

Singing the Trinity

PETER GOODWIN HELTZEL

The doctrine of the Trinity is the heart of Christian theology. When the heart is strong, Christianity flourishes, but when it is weak, it languishes. Throughout theology's turbulent history, the doctrine of the Trinity has been hotly debated. The Arian controversy swept through the patristic world. It was perceptive and pugnacious Athanasius (298–373) who stood up to Arius (d. 336), arguing that the Father and the Son were of one essence. While Athanasius's argument for the consubstantial union between the Father and Son would be immortalized in the Nicene Creed, debates over the Trinity waged on. In nineteenth-century America, a passionate debate ensued between Barton W. Stone (1772–1844) and Alexander Campbell (1788–1866), founders of the CCDC. While Campbell affirmed the doctrine of the Trinity, Stone rejected it for a form of Unitarianism, representing a growing drift from classical Christian theology in American religious life.

In this essay, after explaining why the Trinity had been a theological problem in the patristic period, I explain this debate in relation to Barton W. Stone and Alexander Campbell's doctrines of the Trinity. Finally, I argue that contemporary Disciples theology needs to develop a more robust Trinitarian theology as a sound theological basis for our ecclesial life of mission and service. The doctrine of the Trinity provides the theological basis for the Disciples' theological principle of "unity in diversity." Since all Christians are unified by a common confession of Jesus Christ, we are free to embrace cultural differences that have become more apparent in the aftermath of colonialism. The difference between the three persons of the Trinity who are united in a communion of love provides a way of thinking about gender and cultural differences, while their shared unity provides an ontological basis for the unity of the church.

I. The Trinity as a Theology Problem

Throughout the history of Christian theology, many have viewed the doctrine of the Trinity as an irresolvable theoretical problem. How can three be one? This paradoxical question continues to confound even the best theological minds. Yet the Trinity is the foundation of Christian theology. The doctrine was refined through the many patristic debates, including the one between Arius and in Athanasius. It is enough to remind ourselves that Arius rejected the notion that the Son is of the same substance of the Father for the simple reason that it threatened the notion of the one God, one that is scripturally sound and that enjoyed wide support in Greek philosophical circles for more than a few centuries.

While Arius argued that there was a time when Christ was not, Athanasius in *On the Incarnation* persuasively argued that the Father and Son are of one substance with each (*homousion*). For Athanasius, Christ must be divine because our salvation requires him to be so. If salvation consists of freedom from death and corruption, as it does for Athanasius, then it must consist in the unity of the uncreated and the created.[1] The axioms that God "became man so that humans can become divine,"[2] and "only the uncreated can save the created"[3] are essential to understanding Athanasius's Trinitarian theology. If salvation is accomplished and given in Jesus Christ, and if salvation consists of freedom from death and corruption inherent in created nature and actualized because of sin, then Jesus Christ must be divine, otherwise there is no salvation.

The coequality between the Father and the Son provides the theological basis for a fuller Trinitarian theology that embraces the plurality within the Godhead. Plurality needs to be thought of in the very being of God and such plurality need not threaten the unity of God's being, i.e., the notion of the one God. Moreover, divine-human communion, the immanence and transcendence of God, require a mediator who is fully divine and human, who manifests a God who is above all yet in all, and who unites the uncreated and the created, the universal and the particular.[4] Athanasius forges a new, Trinitarian logic, one of divine-human communion against the monistic logic of the Greek philosophers. The Trinity is an expression of divine-human communion and the Christian response to the question of the transcendence and immanence of God, to the one and the many.

Classical Christian belief in the Trinity was based on a robust doctrine of revelation that was circumscribed by the boundaries of Holy Scripture and the living tradition of the church. Up through the sixteenth-century Reformation there was a strong consensus among the churches of both East and West that the Trinity was a non-negotiable part of the Christian Tradition, which had different particular expressions within each ecclesial tradition.[5] From the seventeenth century to the nineteenth century, Europe witnessed a gradual shift away from the church as the locus of religious authority to the mind of the human individual. Scripture and tradition had always been viewed as normative religious authorities in the Christian theology through the sixteenth century. These were the primary sources for the doctrine of the Trinity. However, in the seventeenth century a set of intellectual movements emerged in Europe that began to challenge some of the sacred doctrines of Christian orthodoxy.

II. The Trinity in the Stone-Campbell Movement

The European Enlightenment streams of rationalism, deism, and natural theology coalesced on the American frontier with a religious primitivism that emphasized biblicism, restoration, noncreedalism, and anti-Catholicism. These forces came together in Barton W. Stone's rejection of the classical doctrine of the Trinity and Alexander Campbell's embrace of the Trinity. Stone and Campbell's disagreement expressed a larger debate about the Trinity that was carried on across the religious spectrum of the day, which included Deists, evangelicals, and Unitarians. While Stone and Campbell reached two different conclusions on the doctrine of God, their different interpretations of the doctrine of the Trinity did not prevent their movements from uniting in 1832.

Barton W. Stone's Rejection of the Trinity

While Stone accepted Father, Son, and Holy Spirit as a name of God, his own position resembles Unitarianism. From his earliest theological studies, Stone had intellectual problems with the doctrine of the Trinity. From Dutch theologian Herman Witsius's defense of the Trinity to the affirmations of the Trinity in the Westminster Confession, the rigidity of the Reformed confessional tradition of Trinitarian theology was perplexing to Stone. From the early days of America to the passing of the frontier, Unitarianism became an increasingly powerful viable option. Thomas Jefferson wrote, "I trust there is not a *young man* now living in the United States who will not die an Unitarian."[6]

In his *Address to the Churches,* Stone explains his views on the Trinity. He begins with the claim, "That there is but one living and true God."[7] Entailed in this claim for Stone is a rejection that there is any plurality within the Godhead, including the notion that Jesus Christ is eternally divine. The word *Trinity* is not a biblical term and the concept is rationally incoherent.[8] Stone found the idea that God is one in three persons unbiblical and irrational.[9] The Trinity became an illustration of the type of "human opinion" that unnecessarily divides the church.

Stone's rejection of the Trinity began with a debate over biblical interpretation concerning the identity of Jesus Christ. Some passages within John's gospel indicate a unity between Father and Son ("The Father and I are one;" Jn. 10:30). Other passages show a subordination of the Son to the Father (Jesus' statement, "The Father is greater than I;" Jn. 14:28). For Stone, affirming the coequality between the Father and the Son implies a plurality that is logically impossible for the divine unity.[10] Commenting on John 14:28, Stone writes of the Father being "greater" than Jesus, "If they were one substance, or one being, there could be no comparison; as *one* can not be greater or less than itself."[11] Thus, Stone argues that Jesus' argument that the Father is greater implies the Father's ontological superiority.

For Stone, the ontological superiority of the Father is based on the Father's eternal nature, while the Son, as "first born" of the Father, is not eternal. Stone rejects the eternity of the Son based on his interpretation of Jesus Christ as the original first-born creature.[12] He emphasizes that Jesus Christ is the "the only begotten Son of God—begotten *by* and *of* the Father himself."[13] He argues that Jesus Christ as the "Son of God" is preexistent; however, the "was a time when he was not," since he was literally the "first born" Son of God.

Rejecting the eternity of the Son ("eternal begetting") and that Jesus is only a human being, Stone believes that Jesus' soul did exist before the Incarnation.[14] Stone writes, "My own views of the Son of God are that he did not begin to exist 1820 years ago, nor did he exist from eternity; but was the first begotten of the Father before time or creation began—that he was sent by the Father 1820 years ago into the world, and united with a body, prepared for him."[15] So Jesus' preexistence is before the existence of the world, but comes "after" the eternal existence of the Father.

It is the rejection of the eternity of the Son that is the basis of Stone's revision of the deity of Christ. Stone accepts that the Father begets the Son, but rejects the idea of "eternal begetting." Stone writes, "That the Son of God was very and eternal God, and yet eternally begotten, is a doctrine to which I can not subscribe; because the terms eternal Son, eternally begotten, are not found in the Bible. As they are human inventions, by human reason they may be tried, without the imputation of impiety."[16] Stone's construction of the Sonship of God is an explicit denial that Jesus Christ was "very God" or "eternal God."[17]

For Stone, Jesus shares a functional divinity with God in the history of redemption, but not an ontological divinity in eternity. Stone writes, "He is not equal in essence, being or eternity; else he could never be subject to the Father—and such an equality would destroy the unity of God. But he is equal in the great work of redemption; all power in heaven and earth being delivered to him, and all things in heaven, as principalities, powers, etc., being put under him, to accomplish the work, for which he was sent."[18] Jesus Christ is not equal to God in essence, but his divinity expresses itself in his essential role in redemptive history.

One of the problems with Stone's theological method is that he often begins with a human analogy of the differentiation between persons and then applies this distinction to the divine persons to refute the idea of a God being a unified communion of persons. For example, Stone writes, "Nor is it correct to say, these three are one being; for Paul and Apolos [*sic*] are said to be one—I Cor. iii: 8. 'Now he that planteth and he that waterth are (*then*) *one*.' No one imagines that they were one being; but agree, that they were two distinct men engaged in one work, in one spirit."[19] Stone draws from biblical examples of human oneness to argue that the Father and Son are distinct like two human beings, but are united in a common purpose. Thus, Stone rejects the Council of Nicaea's (325) claim that the Father and Son are *homoousios*, or share one essence. For Stone, the oneness that the Father and Son share is a oneness of "spirit, purpose, and mind," not of substance.[20]

In summary, Stone rejects the Trinity on christological grounds. This decision produces a monistic conception of God. He reduces the Christian doctrine of God to a single principle and relativizes the differences between the three triune Persons. Thus, we have a strong affirmation of the Disciples' unity principle, but a construction of it that cannot deal with difference. One implication of this monistic notion of God is that when it is translated into ecclesial and social terms it promotes a notion of life together that is as a loose affiliation of individuals, reinforcing problematic themes in the tradition like radical individualism, "private interpretation," radical democracy, and congregational autonomy. Monist notions of God such as Stone's can easily be enlisted to support the culture of autonomy that we Disciples continue to be plagued with. While Stone's monist notion reinforces Disciple's individualism, the promise of Stone's doctrine of God is his strong affirmation of love as the primary character of the divine nature and the basis of the divine-human communion. When we embrace the Nicene contours of Trinitarian orthodoxy, Disciples have a much stronger theological basis for developing the love of God theme.

Alexander Campbell's Doctrine of the Trinity

Stone's colleague in the restoration movement, Alexander Campbell, affirmed the orthodox doctrine of the Trinity. Influenced by his father Thomas Campbell, who became Scottish Presbyterian after spending his first twenty-nine years as an Anglican, Alexander Campbell embodied a more robust Trinitarian impulse within Disciples theology. The tradition of Reformed Christian systematic theology that Campbell embarks upon is based on a Calvinist "scheme" or "pattern of redemption" that includes interpreting God's action in the economy of salvation through the unified action of the three persons of the Trinity.

Campbell begins and frames his *Christian System* around the doctrine of the Trinity. In this work, Campbell grounds the history of redemption in God's triune nature. God's triune being and perfections are revealed in the divine word and works of God in three manifestations: "Creator, Lawgiver, and Redeemer."[21] The threefold works of God express the Trinity's internal plurality as three persons.

While Campbell affirms with Stone that God is one, he argues that God is "certainly plural in its personal manifestations. Hence we have the Father, Son and Holy Spirit equally divine, though personally distinct from each other."[22] Campbell affirms the coequality of the divine persons, each maintaining a significant degree of personal distinctiveness: "Each name of the sacred three has its own peculiar work and glory in the three great works of Creation, Government, and Redemption. Hence we are, by divine authority, immersed into the name of the FATHER, the SON, and the HOLY SPIRIT, in coming into the Kingdom of God; and in the kingdom the supreme benediction is, 'The *grace* of the LORD JESUS CHRIST, and the *love* of GOD, and the *communion* of the HOLY SPIRIT, be with you!'"[23] Campbell's doctrine of the Trinity has an understanding of persona that allows for a true Trinitarian pluralism. For Campbell, Trinitarian pluralism is expressed in the redemptive economy. Thus, we see God revealed in three persons through their distinct role in redemptive history. The three persons are united in one essence in both their immanent and economic manifestation; however, as they appear to us in the economy of redemption, Trinitarian difference is disclosed in human history.

Campbell sees this plurality of manifestations in the divine nature as providing a basis for the communitarian nature of human and angelic life. He draws an analogy between God's community and the community experienced in the first human family, Adam, Eve and their firstborn, Cain.[24] While there is a radical dissimilarity between the divine and human community at the level of essence, the analogy helps us to see that human community has ontological grounding in the community experienced in the immanent Trinity.

With Athanasius, Campbell sees the Father and Son as sharing one eternal essence. He answers Stone's objection to the eternal begetting of the Son by arguing that Jesus Christ did exist as the Word of God from all eternity. Campbell writes, "An idea cannot be without an image or a word to represent it; and therefore God was never without his word, nor was his word without him…While, then, the phrase "Son of God" denotes a temporal relation, the phrase "the Word of God" denotes an eternal, unoriginated relation. There was a Word of God from eternity, but the Son of God began to be in the days of August Caesar."[25] Jesus Christ as the Word is with the Father from eternity and they are never without each other, implying a mutual interdependence. Campbell makes a sharp distinction between Jesus Christ as Son of God (temporal) and Jesus as Word of God (eternal). This distinction between the temporal earthly sonship of Jesus and his eternal existence as the preexistent *Logos, for* Campbell, becomes the christological grounding of the broader Trinitarian doctrine.

In summary, Alexander Campbell affirms the Nicene doctrine of the Trinity. His *Christian System* is based on this Trinitarian foundation. Through his dramatic retelling of redemptive history through the unified action of three distinct persons of the Trinity, Campbell is able to demonstrate that it is salvation itself that is at stake in God's triune revelation in the redemptive economy. Campbell argues that without understanding the "holy and incomprehensible relations in the divinity" it is impossible to achieve "any real and divine proficiency in the true knowledge of God" and the major Christian doctrines and practices.[26] This embrace of the incomprehensible mystery of the Trinity is a welcomed contrast to Stone's rational repudiation of the importance of mystery in theology, calling mystery "one of the names of the whore of Babylon, written in large letters on her forehead."[27] While Stone's monistic conception of God promotes an individualism that is a perennial problem in American religious life, Campbell's Trinitarianism allows for a clear account of the communion between the Divine and the human, and holds great promise for a postcolonial Disciples theology of interdependence within our global, ecumenical horizon.

III. Singing the Trinity: Toward a New Disciples Theology

As Disciples of Christ, we sing the Trinity. As postcolonial Disciples, we sing the Trinity in different languages. This singing the Trinity together with global voices is a new Pentecost. It is the Holy Spirit that gives birth to our faith and gives life to the Church. Through our common confession of Jesus Christ and communion of the Holy Spirit, we are united with our fellow Disciples and our brothers and sisters in the whole church.

We sing the Trinity first and foremost in Holy Baptism. Following Jesus' call in Matthew's gospel to "Go therefore and make disciples of all nations, baptizing them in the name of the Father and of the Son and of the Holy Spirit" (Mt. 28:19), Disciples have lived out Trinitarian theology in our practice of Trinitarian baptism by immersion through our church's mission and service in the world. The Trinity is a song of baptismal celebration! The heavens rejoice each time a lost lamb is brought back into the flock.

We have been singing the Trinity for years as we celebrate the baptisms of new Christians and congregants into our movement. The doctrine of the Trinity was given liturgical form in the great baptismal formulas of the New Testament. We continue this tradition liturgically in our service of Christian baptism. From the baptismal collect ("Creator Spirit...Father and the Son") to the confession of faith ("Looking to your baptism in the name of the Father, Son, and Holy Spirit, do you, in the company of all Christians, believe and trust in God the Father, who made the world; and in his Son Jesus Christ, who redeemed humankind; and in the Holy Spirit, who gives life to the people of God?") to the baptism ("By the authority of Jesus Christ, I baptize you, *[Name]*, in the name of the Father and of the Son and of the Holy Spirit"), we sing the Trinity in the baptism liturgy.[28]

Reclaiming this doctrine of the Trinity liturgically will continue to benefit our ecumenical theology through our works for visible unity and ongoing ecumenical dialogue. It is through our deep engagement with the ecumenical tradition in the twentieth century that we have deepened our Trinitarian faith as Disciples. Disciple leaders shared a great enthusiasm for the Evangelical

Alliance, which convened in London, England, in 1846.[29] The theological basis had nine articles that included an affirmation of the "unity of the Godhead and the Trinity of persons therein."[30] The second article of the Chicago/Lambeth Quadrilateral, which was ratified at the Lambeth Conference of 1888, affirmed "The Apostles' Creed as the Baptismal Symbol; and the Nicene Creed as the sufficient statement of Christian faith." Disciples accepted this second article on the Trinitarian creeds as well as the first article (that Holy Scripture is the rule and ultimate standard of faith) and the third article (that baptism and the Lord's supper are the two sacraments instituted by Christ), but rejected the fourth article (on the necessity of the historic episcopacy). For example, George Plattenburgh writes in response to article four: "It is wholly inconsistent with the nature of Christianity to condition unity upon a mere ministerial function."[31] So even back in the late nineteenth century, in our ecumenical theology, Disciples were living into the Trinity.

Disciples' directionality toward a fuller Trinitarianism intensified in the twentieth century. We see this in the Trinitarian theological basis of both the National Council of Churches and the World Council of Churches, both councils coming into existence through generous financial, staff, and theological resources given through our denomination, as well as others. This ecumenical tradition of Trinitarian reflection reaches late-twentieth-century apex in the Faith and Order document, *Baptism, Eucharist and Ministry* (BEM), as well as contemporary discussion of *koinonia* ecclesiology.

In addition to the Trinity being a basis for our being member churches in conciliar ecumenism, it is the theological basis of the bilateral and multilateral theological dialogues that we participate in. For example, our current bilateral dialogue with the Roman Catholic Church reflects this common Trinitarian basis and the renewed and rigorous ecumenical theological dialogue that emerged in the wake of Vatican II. One of the important developments in this regard is *koinonia* ecclesiology. It is with this notion of communion that we are able to relate the nature of God with the nature of the church. God as one in three persons is fundamentally a communion of love.

As John Zizioulas argues, the Trinity as a communion of love provides the onto-mimetic foundation for the church as a communion of love.[32] What is unique about a postcolonial interpretation of the Trinity is its emphasis on difference and diversity. This emphasis on difference provides us with a way into the complexities of contemporary multicultural fragmentation both within the church and outside of it.

One way that we can think in Trinitarian terms about cultural difference is to think in the categories of music and song. Of all the musical instruments that may be employed in the praise of God, the human voice has priority. Other instruments are to be used primarily in the service of the singing of God's people. Reformed theologian Karl Barth points out that singing is not an option for the people of God; it is one of the essential ministries of the church:

> The Christian church sings. It is not a choral society. Its singing is not a concert. But from inner, material necessity it sings. Singing is the highest form of human expression... What we can and must say quite confidently is that the church which does not sing is not the church. And where...it does not really sing but sighs and mumbles spasmodically, shamefacedly and with an ill grace, it can be at best only a troubled community which is not sure of its cause and of whose ministry and witness there can be no great expectation...The praise of God which finds its concrete culmination in the singing of the community is one of the indispensable forms of the ministry of the church.[33]

As Disciples, throughout our history we have sung the Trinity through our hymnody, from "Holy, Holy, Holy! Lord God Almighty" to "Dios Padre, Dios Hijo (Father God, Father Son)."[34]

Singing the Trinity is also a corporate activity, an embodied expression of our interdependence. Singing together and being open to others' songs, melodies, and chordal structures exhibit the dialectic of unity in diversity that reflects the unity dialectic of the Trinity. Sergei Bulgakov writes, "God is love: and this love is not a quality or property, not a predicate, but the very essence of Godhead. And in this divine love, each hypostasis, surrendering itself in love, finds itself in the other hypostases and thus actualizes the unity of the Godhead. In the Trinity, the absolutely personal character of the Godhead, its *hypostatic* nature, is united with the absolutely *transpersonal* character of its threefoldness—'trinity in unity and unity in trinity.'"[35] Thus, to be unified in difference is truly to love the other in their difference, without absorbing or being absorbed by them.

Of all the art forms that may be employed in worship, singing is especially corporate. Indeed, it is the art form most suited to expressing the church's unity in the body of Christ. Different voices, different instruments, different parts are blended to offer a single, living, and unified work of beauty. John Calvin recognized the power of congregational singing and unison prayer in helping the church express and experience the unity of the body of Christ. Asserting that the human tongue was especially created to proclaim the praise of God, both through singing and speaking, he noted that "the chief use of the tongue is in public prayers, which are offered in the assembly of the believers, by which it comes about that with one common voice, and as it were, with the same mouth, we all glorify God together, worshiping him with one spirit and the same faith."[36] As we are open to making a joyful noise together, we can musically find each other. Hans Urs von Balthasar argues that the purpose of pluralism is "not to refuse to enter into the unity that lies in God and is imparted by God, but symphonically to get in tune with one another and give allegiance to the transcendent unity."[37] It is only when we sing together that we can get in tune with each other, and corporately worship the Trinity as a great symphony with many different instrumental sections and choruses.

Embracing a theology of singing the Trinity, drawing on the deep Trinitarian streams of the ecumenical tradition of twentieth-century ecumenism, provides a way for Disciples to continue to embrace and live into the doctrine of the Trinity. As we sing the Trinity together we perform "unity in diversity" in our new postcolonial age. A postcolonial Disciples theology provides a new space of differentiation and dialogue where different perspectives are both deconstructed and reconstructed through contact with one another. The notion of hybridity expresses the Christian paradox of difference in unity that is expressed in our confession of God as Triune, three in one. Life in the postcolonial church is life together-in-difference. Thus, we can be nurtured by the differences of otherness, instead of demanding that all be assimilated into a hegemonic space of sameness. Our difference and diversity is our greatest strength in an age of multicultural interconnection.

9

Confessing Christ in Empire and Colony

Clark M. Williamson

Deeply embedded in the hearts of many Disciples is affection for the early church and its witness to Jesus Christ. This essay revisits the early church in the light of today's concern with empire and postcolonial theology.

N.T. Wright says of the land of Israel: "Empires have fought over it. Every forty-four years out of the last four thousand, on average, an army has marched through it."[1] The early churches lived in the Roman Empire and in its colonies. New Testament texts have contexts, are involved with politics, and are written from the peripheries of the Empire. They can no more be understood apart from their interactions with the Roman Empire than reduced to an understanding of those interactions.

Two assumptions about the early church need to be set aside. One is that politics, economics, and religion have nothing to do with each other. Another is individualism, in which the individual is the end or purpose of all social and political arrangements. Both are fundamentally misleading. It is not viable to separate faith from political and economic life in any traditional society, and particularly in first-century Jewish life. The biblical tradition was about how these dimensions are to be held together so that life and well-being can be available to all, particularly to the most vulnerable members of society: widows, orphans, and strangers. Individualism is an illusion. Personal identity, beliefs, and behavior cannot be disconnected from the network of relations, traditions, and institutions in which we are embedded and by which we are shaped.

We need to unlearn our habit of seeing Jesus and Paul in conflict with other religious leaders over essentially religious issues. They were concerned, in Jesus' case, with the rule ("kingdom") of God over all aspects of human life, and in Paul's with the soon-to-come *parousia* of Jesus, which Paul expected would put an end to "the sufferings of this present time" (Rom. 8:18).

We first look at a text from Mark and its setting in Romanized Galilee.

Mark 6:17–29; 30–43 (// Matthew 14:3–12; 13–21)

Mark links together the stories of Herod's banquet and Jesus' feeding of the five thousand together, indicating that they are to be understood in relation to each other. Jesus' banquet is a mirror image of Herod's, in which each detail is the diametrical opposite of its counterpart in the story of Herod's banquet. The story of the feeding of the five thousand is not simply a claim; it is a counterclaim. To understand it in its literary context is to grasp its historical, moral, and theological significance for the life of faith. This is a good place to remember the hermeneutical principle that a text without a context is merely a pretext.

The Context of Herod's Banquet

Herod's banquet is a microcosm of its society. Herod Antipas, ruler of Galilee, was a Roman puppet king, deeply enmeshed in the Roman imperial system. When Herod the Great died about 5 B.C.E., Rome installed his son Antipas in Galilee as its king. Antipas had been educated in Rome and knew well the benefits and demands of the Empire—benefits for the Empire, demands imposed on provincial peasants.

As soon as Herod was appointed, Judas, son of Hezekiah, led an army of revolutionaries in Sepphoris, the Roman provincial capital of Galilee, three miles from Nazareth. The Roman army responded quickly, captured Sepphoris and sold into slavery all its residents whom it did not massacre. Then it burned the city to the ground. Varus, the Roman legate, moved with his army on Jerusalem, where another revolt against Roman rule was taking place, and crucified two thousand revolutionaries as he restored what Rome called "peace." "Peace through victory" was Rome's motto.[2]

Antipas then reconstructed Sepphoris as the capital of Galilee, providing it with a combination palace and fortress, a Roman colonnaded avenue and a three-thousand seat theater. Roman baths, circuses, and brothels were also built and the town named Autocratoris (the Greek for Imperatoria) out of reverence for Rome.

Shortly thereafter, he built Tiberias on the western edge of the Sea of Galilee in honor of his patron Tiberius, who had followed Augustus as Caesar; soon Tiberias replaced Sepphoris as the provincial capital. He built the castle (along with a stadium, baths, and forum) that is the setting for the banquet of which Mark tells us.[3]

All this building subjected Galilean peasants to great economic hardship. In addition to tribute to Rome, taxes to Herod, and tithes and offerings to the temple, Antipas needed to fund his building projects. This further exhausted the people economically, hence the many references to debt and hunger in the gospels.

The purpose of empire was economic: wealth from the provinces flowed to the center in Rome to serve its well-being. The military saw to it that this system worked. The system created the "glory that was Rome," a glory built on the backs of provincial peasants. In Galilee and Judea, where one percent of the people owned fifty percent of the land, wealth existed in an upside-down pyramid mostly distributed at the top to the fewest people. The system profited local plantation owners, members of the court, military big shots, and the Temple oligarchy through whom Rome ruled. Jesus lived in a time of economic subjugation, military occupation, oppression, and the threat of idolatry.

The land of Israel was to be the place where the people Israel were so to live that they could be "a light to the Gentiles." Under Roman occupation, how could this be possible? In these two stories we see Mark's view of an aspect of Jesus' response.

A word about Roman dining patterns in the land of Israel is pertinent. Roman dining rooms were called *triclinia*. A remarkable one is at Sepphoris (the Dionysos Villa). A triclinium had three couches on which the host and his guests reclined (*tri-*, "three," *clinium*, "recline," says just this). Royal and wealthy Romans reclined to eat. Roman dining emphasized the social standing of the host at the peak of a stratified pyramid of power and rank. Antipas brought this Roman emphasis on social and economic class and hierarchy to Galilee.[4]

Antipas's Banquet

Herod Antipas's birthday party was a Hellenistic banquet; it was a Hellenistic custom to invite friends to one's birthday celebration. It took place in Herod Antipas's palace in Tiberias. The guests were the "chief men of Galilee" (the large plantation owners), members of Herod's court, and his military leaders.[5] Antipas and his high-ranking guests reclined at dinner, standard behavior at a Roman or Hellenistic banquet. Women and other slaves served dinner to the wealthy and powerful. The evening's entertainment featured one dancing girl, and John the Baptist was executed. Antipas's banquet ends on the note of death and curse.

Mark leaves the impression that Antipas reluctantly had John executed. Yet, he had already thrown John in prison because John had condemned his marriage to Herodias (cf. Luke 3:20) as immoral (Lev. 18:16, 25). This politically charged condemnation meant that Antipas's rule was illegitimate, that he was in violation of fundamental moral principles. In all probability, Antipas was eager to get rid of John and squash his movement. Josephus claims that Antipas executed John because he attracted crowds and hence might foster sedition.[6]

Jesus' Banquet

Mark 6:34 links these stories: Jesus "had compassion for them, because they were like sheep without a shepherd." This taps into the prophetic criticism of kings who are supposed to be the shepherds of the people but who feed themselves and let the sheep go hungry: "Should not shepherds feed the sheep?" (Ezek. 34:2). "The people wander like sheep; / they suffer for lack of a shepherd" (Zech. 10:2).[7] Mark lets us know that the story of Jesus feeding the hungry crowd is an acerbic comment on Antipas's self-indulgent birthday party celebrated with the "haves" while the "have-nots" went hungry.

Mark's banquet takes place not in a palace but in the desert (7:31, 32, 35). We are to remember another time when God graciously fed desperately hungry people in the desert.

The guests at Jesus' banquet were not courtiers, owners of large estates, and military leaders. They were the destitute (*ptōchoi*), the hungry, and those who mourn. The realities of Roman occupation and brutality explain why there were so many of them.

Then, Jesus' disciples succumb to a temptation to which we too readily yield: we want to duck our responsibilities, to send the destitute away to buy food, an unlikely prospect, even if they had the ready cash, which the destitute did not. Jesus responds to them with a simple imperative: "give them something to eat" (6:37). They did, and Mark reports that it was more than enough. The exuberant grace of God is witnessed to with this excess of the staff of life and well-being. In contrast to Antipas's banquet, Jesus' dinner ends with the means of life and well-being overflowing.

The disciples served the meal. They did the work that the slaves and women did at Herod's banquet. In a reversal, the nobodies were served. Also, Jesus instructed the poor, the hungry, and the mourners to *lie down*. The NRSV says "sit down," but the Greek *anaklinai* means "lie down." Jesus treats the destitute and the hungry like royalty!

So we have stories about two kinds of kings, two kinds of kingdoms, two kinds of meals, each the mirror image of the other. In that contrast and the way in which this movement called the "kingdom of God" went about its task, we see Jesus of Nazareth, the wandering teacher in Israel, responding to the realities of Roman occupation and the real needs of hungry, destitute people. His response openly contradicts Roman ways in Galilee. His movement was in the service of the way of life and well-being instead of the way of death and curse, in an economy of scarcity. It was a movement in which whoever would be first of all must be servant of all—a point that the disciples act out in this story. It is a movement that proclaims that only God is King, contradicting the claim that the king (Caesar) is God. This is social and political (in the large sense of the word). In no sense a military response to Roman occupation, it was a revolt of the colonized. These historical parables from an early church speak about an oppressive, rapacious government and how we should, instead, live. They question whether Herod Antipas defines what we mean by terms like king and kingdom, or whether the Jesus-story does. "[A]mong the Gentiles those whom they recognize as their rulers lord it over them...it is not so among you...whoever wishes to be first among you must be slave of all" (Mk. 10:42–44//Mt. 20: 25-27//Lk. 22:25-26).

Herod Antipas and Constantine

Three hundred years after Jesus' banquet for the destitute, in the year 325, the Emperor Constantine threw a banquet for the bishops of the church at the conclusion of the Council of Nicaea. The church historian, Eusebius, unaware of the irony of his words, described it: "Detachments of the body-guard and troops surrounded the entrance of the palace with drawn swords [keeping at a safe distance the destitute, the smelly, and the scruffy], and through the midst of them the men of God proceeded without fear into the innermost of the Imperial apartments, in which some were the Emperor's companions at table, while others reclined on couches arranged on either side. One might have thought that a picture of Christ's kingdom was thus shadowed forth, and a dream rather than reality."[8]

Jesus' banquet for the poor has been forgotten; the bishops now dine with Herod Antipas. A betrayal has taken place. We would like to believe that these bishops had second thoughts about being treated like royalty while the destitute served them.

Constantine's embrace of the church, and its subsequent establishment by Theodosius, were not happy developments for authentic Christian faith. Consequently we learn more about how Christians were taught that they should eat and conduct themselves. A local council of the church passed four canon laws banning Christians from intermarriage with Jews, from eating with Jews, from having Jews bless their crops, and banning Christian men from committing adultery with Jewish women.[9] Laws passed against certain behaviors are designed to put a stop to them. Christian and Jewish laypeople seemed to relate to each other in all kinds of ways, but Christian leaders tried to effect a separation between the two communities. Note that the church turns toward the empire and against "the Jews" who now serve Christian discourse in their three roles of prologue, antithesis, and scapegoat.[10] They are the objectified other about whom Christians talk but whom they pointedly do not invite to an open table of conversation.

The church largely lost both the Pauline view of the relation of Gentile believers in Jesus Christ to Jews and Jesus' commitment to all "the lost sheep of the house of Israel" (Mt. 10:6). "You Gentiles," says the letter to the Ephesians, "were...without Christ, being aliens from the commonwealth of Israel, and strangers to the covenants of promise, having no hope and without God [*atheoi*] in the world." He has brought peace, breaking down the wall of hostility between us. We are "no longer strangers and aliens, but...

citizens with the saints and also members [*sympolitai*] of the household of God" (2:11–22). "Also members" does not mean the "only members." We "also members" now made the people Israel "strangers and aliens" to us, "aliens of the evil imaginings of the heart."

Paul and the Theology of Empire

We look at Paul's letters, not the Paul of the book of Acts. Disciples have long regarded Acts as describing the universal practices of the early church. The Paul of Acts, in his speeches, sounds like Peter and Stephen (Acts 2:14–31; 7:2–50; 13:17–37). Like Peter, he preaches "forgiveness of sins" (13:38; 26:18). This vocabulary is absent from Paul's letters, where he speaks of sin in the singular as a power (Rom. 5:12, e.g.). Also, in Acts Paul is opposed by "the Jews" and rescued by Roman officials (e.g., 17:12–17), whereas in his letters Paul's opponents are mostly his fellow missionaries. In his letters, Paul also claims to have been beaten three times "with rods" (2 Cor. 11:25), a Roman punishment. Nor does Acts tell us of Paul's execution in Rome. That Acts presents Roman officials as friendly to the young church discloses its concern to assure its readers that the church was no threat to the Empire.[11]

Paul could not have been unaware of Roman domination or of the theology and cult of the empire. In the Julian basilica in Corinth, archaeologists have found numerous statues to Julius and Claudius Caesar and one of the first public inscriptions to the divine Julius. There was a shrine to Apollo Augustus, the divine Augustus Caesar; temples to various emperors and one to Venus built by Augustus to honor her as his divine ancestress and mother of Rome.[12]

Paul opens his correspondence with the Corinthians by proclaiming "Christ crucified...Christ the power of God and the wisdom of God" (1 Cor. 1:23–24). Paul declares the foolishness of God (1:25), God's true wisdom, which is not "a wisdom of this age or of the rulers of this age [*tōn archontōn tou aiōnos*], who are doomed to perish" (2:6). Christ crucified is set in opposition by Paul to certain mortal rulers. Christ's work will be completed when "he hands over the kingdom to God the Father, after he has destroyed every ruler and every authority and power" (1 Cor. 15:24). God puts "all things in subjection under his feet" (15:27). Paul's theology is rooted in Jewish apocalyptic thinking, which conceived of contemporary historical conflicts as involved in God's struggle against superhuman forces. That is not an evasion of concrete historical struggles; it is a theological interpretation of them.

The Roman Empire's "theology" expressed the Roman right to victory and domination. Empire has its theology; theologians critical of empire are not importing theology into a situation to which it is alien. Imperial theology is ripe for criticism.

An inscription from 9 B.C.E. discovered at Priene, south of Ephesus, proclaims the gospel of Augustus Caesar:

> Since the providence that has divinely ordered our existence has applied her energy and zeal and has brought to life the most perfect good in Augustus, whom she filled with virtues for the benefit of mankind, bestowing him upon us and our descendants as a *saviour*—he who put an end to war and will order *peace,* Caesar who by his *epiphany* exceeded the hopes of those who prophesied *good tidings* [*euaggelia*], not only outdoing benefactors of the past, but also allowing no hope of greater benefactions in the future; and since the birthday of the *god* first brought to the world the *good tidings* [*euaggelia*] residing in him... For that reason, with good fortune and safety, the Greeks of Asia have decided that the New Year in all the cities should begin on 23rd September, the birthday of Augustus[13]

Dieter Georgi argues that Paul deliberately evoked associations between his theology and Rome's "political theology."[14] Terms such as "gospel" (*euaggelion*), "faith" (*pistis*), "justice" (*dikaiosynē*), and "peace" (*eirēnē*) play central roles in Roman political theology. Caesar is proclaimed as the savior (*sōtēr*) who brings peace (*eirēnē*) and justice (*dikaiosynē*) to the whole world. These are the *euaggelia,* good news that Caesar provides. Caesar is celebrated for his faithfulness (*pistis*). In Paul, faith refers to God's faithfulness or Christ's faithfulness more often than faith in God or Christ. "Peace through victory" was a standard Roman motto. "Grace to you and peace from God" is a standard Pauline greeting (2 Cor. 1:2; Gal. 1:3). Every key term in Paul's theology is a key term in the Caesar-theology, but as applied to Christ it contradicts Roman state theology.

The conflict between Roman and Pauline theology focuses primarily on differing ways of speaking of God. The clash is between the imperial understanding of divinity and God as disclosed in Jesus Christ. Christ, as Paul saw him,

> did not regard equality with God
>   as something to be exploited,
> but emptied himself,
>   taking the form of a slave,
>   being born in human likeness.
> And being found in human form,
>   he humbled himself
>   and became obedient to the point of death—
>   even death on a cross. (Phil. 2: 6–8)

The theological conflict is between divinity understood as being in control—dominant, absolute power—control exercised in violence and death-dealing and Paul's view of Christ's having become "obedient to the point of death—even death on a cross" (Phil. 2:8). The cross was a Roman instrument of warfare and oppression; Rome crucified enemies and rebels in massive numbers. Paul turned the cross into its antithesis and made it a symbol of peace through the faithfulness of God and Christ.

The theology of glory and victory has long been a temptation for the church. Yet we can find in the early church's witness to Jesus Christ clear indication that it is alert to the risks involved in divinizing such power. In countless ways the gospels and letters engage in a prophetic critique of power—in Matthew's story of Herod the Great's attempt to kill the infant Jesus (Mt. 2:16); in Paul's declaration to the Philippians that "our citizenship is in heaven" (Phil. 3:20); in Jesus' casting out the demon Legion from the Gerasene demoniac and sending it into the pigs who drowned in the sea, particularly when we remember that the pig was the symbol of the Tenth Legion (Lk. 8:26–39); in Jesus' triumphal entry into Jerusalem, mounted on a donkey, under the watchful eye of the Tenth Legion, which it is tempting to read as a parody on the victorious entry that Pilate made into Jerusalem every Passover from Caesarea Maritima with the Tenth Legion; in Paul's transvaluation of values when he reminded the Corinthians that "God chose what is weak in the world to shame the strong" (1 Cor. 1:27b).

Paul refuses to identify God with imperial power and victory and to confuse the church with the rule of God that he ardently anticipated in Christ's yet-to-occur *parousia*. The later church, in its lust for power and its heightened negativity toward Jews and Judaism, began to understand itself in terms of the theology of triumph. It was seduced by Constantine and its own establishment as the official religion of empire. Constantine had a vision of the cross on the eve of the battle of the Milvian bridge: "He saw with his own eyes the trophy of a cross of light in the heavens…bearing the inscription 'conquer by this.'"[15] Later the church would use the figures of two women to express the theology of triumph. They face each other across the central door into Notre Dame in Paris. On the left is the figure of the church, standing erect, a crown on her head and a shepherd's staff in one hand, a chalice in the other. She gazes confidently at the other woman, the synagogue, who leans on a broken spear with which she has just pierced the side of Christ, holds in one hand (or has dropped on the ground in other versions) the five books of Torah, and wears a blindfold around her head.[16] The church is victorious! Behind Notre Dame, little visited, is a memorial to all the Jews deported from Paris during the Nazi occupation. There is a relation between the statues on the front of the Cathedral and the memorial out back.

The theology of victory is what Luther called a *theologia gloriae*, a theology that sustains itself by lying about the human situation. "A theology of glory," said Luther, "calls evil good and good evil. A theology of the cross calls the thing what it actually is."[17] Luther's quarrel with the medieval church was as much over its inadequate gospel as over its authoritarianism. He knew that the church could easily get Christ down off the cross, but that it was an altogether different thing to remove the cross from human existence, which is the mission of the church, one awaiting its consummation. Luther uncovered a stark alternative to the theology that glorified the church at the expense of truth about the human situation. The triumph of Caesar may be realized; many of his triumphs were. But the triumph of the Christ is not yet fully realized; in this world it is seen only by faith and in hope, "hidden beneath its opposite," the cross, the suffering of human beings.

The soteriological stress in the theology of the cross is on the cross as symbol and means of solidarity with suffering humanity, God's solidarity with suffering humanity and the solidarity with suffering humanity of Christians who follow Christ. The doctrine of the church needs to be decentered. Suffering humanity is at the center of the story. Christ goes to the cross not to placate God's wrath but because that is where human beings are.

The theology of the cross interprets the resurrection in a way that differs from that of the theology of glory. It rejects the idea that after the first Easter the human condition is no longer that of the cross. Rome was just as murderous on Easter Monday as it had been on Good Friday; evil still stalked the streets of Alexandria, just as it still stalks our streets today. Empires still wage war.

Amid its inexhaustible range of meaning, the resurrection refers to the mystery of the courage to engage evil, a courage given wherever the Spirit wrestles with human spirits, of that faith that dares to take on principalities and powers because it believes that they have already been taken on by One who suffered under their dominion and has broken that power from within, proleptically.

The early church was born in an age of empire and made its witness in the colonies and the capitol of that empire. It often, if not always, spoke courageously and directly to the reality and abuse of imperial power and contradicted the empire in its parables of Jesus' acted-out ministry of the rule of God in which the Roman ways of organizing society were turned upside down, and in its gospel of the power and wisdom of God disclosed in weakness and crucifixion. Today's church, looking to scripture and tradition, should think just as critically in a new age of empire and postcolonialism.

10

Who Do We Say He Is?

Rita Nakashima Brock

Jesus went on with his disciples to the villages of Caesarea Philippi; and on the way he asked his disciples, "Who do people say that I am?" (Mk. 8:27)

The question every generation of Christians must answer is, Who is Jesus Christ for us and for our world? This task is both rewarding and difficult: rewarding because faith must be constantly renewed, and difficult because every answer has important implications. The greatest danger we face is not that our reflection is obscured or limited but that we are tempted to pretend our answers are timeless or universal, as if we did not live in space and time. We always see the past through the lens of our own rich cultures, language systems, and life experiences; this is the value and limitation of what it means to be human.

To answer the question, I want to disrupt three commonly understood assumptions about Christian faith. First, Christianity is not other-worldly. It is a life-affirming faith concerned about human life in the present, not about personal salvation in the afterlife. Second, Constantine did not accomplish the imperial takeover of the church. Instead, that achievement belongs to the reign of Charlemagne in the ninth century, and with the emergence of atonement theology, used to sanctify war and state terrorism. Third, focusing on the crucified Christ does not enable us to resist the vast forces of colonialism and economic exploitation that harm so many in our world. With these disruptions, I believe a new christology is not only possible, but necessary to sustain Christianity's life-giving possibilities in an age of globalization.[1]

Salvation Here and Now

Genesis 1 tells the story of God's creation. Genesis 2 is about paradise, a garden called Eden, which God created to be humanity's home on earth. Adam and Eve were banished from it because they listened to the empire-centered serpent instead of God. Among the curses visited upon them were gender inequality, endless toil, and death. Some biblical scholars, such as Phyllis Trible, suggest that the Song of Solomon (or the Song of Songs) is the story of humanity's return to the paradise garden.[2]

The New Testament draws on this Hebrew tradition. It proclaims that Jesus Christ overcame the curse of sin. The gospel of John begins by recapitulating creation, and it casts Jesus in the role of a prophet like Moses who brings the life-giving Word to the people. John affirms that this *kosmos,* this world, is the dwelling place of God. Like paradise, with its great river, and the stories of Moses and water, Jesus' story is bathed in living water. It poured forth from paradise, and early Christian baptismal rituals were littered with phrases from the Song of Songs like pink rose petals at a wedding—the newly baptized, male and female, were called "brides of Christ." At the end of John's gospel, Jesus first appears to Mary in a garden, as if they were the new Adam and Eve. Creation had been re-booted.[3]

Christian understandings of paradise were not utopian nor naïve. Struggles against the many forces that inhibited the fullness of life dominated the politics and spirituality of early Christianity. The second-century church in Rome personified Satan in their baptismal liturgy as the goddess Roma. People were often plagued by personal demons and subject to the oppressions of imperial domination, so baptism was designed to transform them and free them. When the waters washed over them, the Holy Spirit, left in the Jordan by Jesus at his baptism, entered their flesh. With baptism, Christians were restored to life in paradise, captured by the affirmation of earth as humanity's home.[4]

Under Rome, life expectancy was 25, two-thirds of infants and children died, and fewer than 5 percent of people lived beyond the age of 50, not a context in which one would expect people to find paradise.[5] Nonetheless, under these conditions and during nearly three centuries of periodic persecutions, Christians affirmed that paradise was this life, salvation here and now. Today, paradise no longer means earth. It is often confused with heaven, even among scholars and skeptics, so that paradise has become associated only with the afterlife.[6] Since 9/11, many think of it as the reward sought by suicide bombers who will, perhaps, find themselves in a neighborhood near Christian fundamentalists. In popular culture, paradise carries the allure of affluence—of exotic fashions and tourist destinations with tropical beaches.

The New Testament insists Jesus offered a life better than anything Rome and its local lackeys could provide. For example, the Roman emperors regularly pacified popular uprisings by distributing wheat from Egypt. The gospels' story of the feeding of the multitude occurs six times, the most of any miracle, as if to emphasize Christian generosity over the measly imperial dole. The feeding of the multitude defined the meaning of the early church eucharist.[7] The prayer of blessing called down the Holy Spirit to lift up the entire community to feast with the incarnate Christ—this was salvation here and now, not promised, but already real. At the feast, they communed with each other, the heavenly hosts, and all the beloved departed saints who visited during the eucharist and comforted the living in dreams and visions.[8]

Christians belonged to the body of Christ, which drew its life from the Holy Spirit. This meant that salvation was never individual, but came through communities organized to take care of their members. The church's leaders, men and women, enacted power and leadership distinct from the military authority of Roman emperors or the sacerdotal roles of pagan priests. They were shepherds, modeled on Jesus, who cared for their community's troubles, settled disputes, healed the sick, defended the faith, taught its tenets, and conducted the church's rituals.

Constantine and Christ

Constantine's predecessor Diocletian had created an innovative administrative structure that led to the most effective and devastating of the empire-wide persecutions of Christians. After Constantine decriminalized Christianity in 313 and became the Emperor of both West and East in 324, he invited all 1800 Christian bishops to Diocletian's former capital, Nicaea. He pressured them to settle an intense theological dispute about Jesus' divinity that had erupted into serious conflicts.[9]

Eusebius of Caesarea was there. He later became Constantine's religious advisor, and later, long after he had been suspected of heresy, he wrote his version of the events. His life of Constantine and his history of the church are suspect as hagiographies and reputation-restoring propaganda. Eusebius claimed that Constantine defeated his rival in Rome under the sign of the cross. While this legend became the standard understanding of the imperial co-optation of Christianity, it is too simplistic a picture of a contested process. For a millennium, empire and church mutually influenced each other while also remaining distinct.[10]

The Nicene Creed affirmed that Jesus Christ was equal to God. This theology was not invented on the spot. It was based on several creeds formed during Christian resistance to the Roman Empire and echoes Philippians 2:5–11. In Greek and Roman culture, powerful humans could become divinities, and Christianity competed for followers in that context. Clement of Alexandria (c. 150–215) likened Jesus to Apollo, and the original third-century St. Peter's in Rome has an image of Jesus riding a chariot into the sky with rays of light radiating from his head. Rome had declared its deceased emperors divine—coins showed them riding a chariot to the heavens. The empire tolerated the religions of its subject peoples, as long as they also respected the cult of the emperor. For Christians to claim Jesus was Lord instead of Caesar was an act of treason.[11]

The bishops at Nicaea did not equate Jesus with the emperor. They put him above the emperor. This theology put the church in tension with the political power of the empire. It also placed emperors in a double bind. If the emperor was a Christian, he would be subject to the church and under the moral authority of its leaders. Most emperors made a practice of deferring baptism until their deathbeds. As catechumens, they could sin and avoid penance. Catechumens, however, lacked the moral authority and spiritual power of baptized Christians.

In post-Constantine church images until the tenth century, Jesus is always depicted in his Incarnation and resurrection, never in death.[12] In the earliest existing apse image of Christ, Rome's fifth-century Saint Pudenziana, Jesus is seated on Jupiter's throne, not the emperor's throne. His toga-clad apostles sit like a council of gods, but even senators were not allowed to sit in the presence of the emperor. Christ holds a book, not a scepter. A large golden cross of resurrection floats directly above his nimbus. Below Christ, the original image depicted the meadows and rivers of paradise. The bishop's seat would have been positioned directly under this apse to indicate the divinity of the church, which received its authority directly from Christ.[13]

The Nicene Christ reflected a tension between the power of his church and imperial domination, especially around bloodshed, which the church regarded as sin. The greatest mark of imperial power was the military. When the fifth-century Theodosian Code required all soldiers to be Christian, the church prohibited its servants from taking up arms or shedding human blood. Christians who killed for any reason, including soldiers, were expected to undergo some form of penance before partaking of the eucharist.

In the face of imperial might, the church defined its spiritual power as creating just community, loving wisdom, appreciating beauty and truth, and cultivating the ethics of love and care for all. In other words, it valued the right use of power and expected Christians to become self-critical and astute about its uses. Even the lowest in social status were part of the body of Christ and contributed to it. While often failing at its mission and cooperating with political powers, it held to its historic tension with imperial domination until the ninth century.

Nicaea did not result in a simple collusion of church and empire. It established a conciliar model of church that mimicked Diocletian's administrative innovations, but it did not create a theology that supported imperial power. Constantine's attempt to quell religious conflict actually increased it among Christians, pagans, and Jews, with conflicts between Nicene and Arian Christians erupting into riots. The church's moral stand against shedding human blood, while never lived out adequately, also did not end suddenly with Constantine. As late as the Norman invasion of England in 1066, warriors went to monasteries to do penance for their sins.[14]

Crucifixion and Empire

Charlemagne conquered the church for the empire by making bloodshed sacred. He sought to expand and solidify his empire by enforcing a single form of Christianity on subject peoples. His most protracted and bitter wars were against the Saxons, a thirty-year campaign that also stands as the most brutal page in Christian missionary efforts in Europe. He instituted the death penalty for any Saxon who refused baptism. In addition, he chopped down their sacred forests, which began the deforestation of much of northern Europe.[15]

Christian bishops objected to Charlemagne's policies. His court theologians, however, looked back to Eusebius's Constantine as the model Christian emperor. They insisted Charlemagne used the cross in the same way, to sanction the Empire's victories over the forces of evil. Charlemagne's theologians also introduced innovations in ritual that worshiped violence. They pressed major changes in the meaning of the eucharist on the Saxons. In 831, the Carolingian theologian Paschasius Radbertus (786–860) propagated the idea that the eucharistic bread and cup represented the *crucified* blood and flesh of the Lord. He wanted the Saxons to see their sins as killing Christ, who became the terrible and terrifying judge of sinners. The corpse on their eucharistic table judged them for their resistance to imperial domination and Latin Christianity.

The Carolingian eucharist put Saxon Christians in a double bind. The Empire forced them to convert and then taught them to regard imperial violence as justified to save them. They would be forever condemned unless they repented and performed sufficient penance by acquiescing to the Empire. Actual victims of bloodshed were forced to see themselves as sinners against a symbolic and ritual corpse of Jesus that the Empire inflicted on them. The divine Christ became a punitive judge while humanity lost its divinity and became sinful and helpless. Archbishop Hincmar (806–882) further elaborated Paschasius's ideas, instructing that priests should "'declare him killed and offer him to be sacrificed in his mystery,'...'Kill! That is, believe him dead for sinners!'"[16]

Theologians in Saxony and elsewhere countered with the traditional doctrine: the resurrected body—not the crucified body—was present in the ritual. The eucharistic elements represented the heavenly, living Christ transferred to earth, making the eternal present in the ritual of life. Christ's death, a past event, could not be repeated and was not present. The Saxon version of the gospels, *The Heliand,* written around this time, equates Charlemagne with Herod (Herod marches from Ft. Rome) and affirms this world as paradise and Jesus as companion, friend, and leader of resistance to Herod.[17]

The Carolingian eucharist also created confusion about the shedding of Saxon blood. Was it virtue to kill the enemies of God, or did the blood of their victims cry out against them, like Christ's blood on the cross? This conflict, enacted in a eucharist focused on a bloody corpse, trapped warriors and their victims in unending, unmitigated guilt. The crucified body made everyone sinful and blameworthy. Carolingian soldiers still faced judgment because shedding human blood continued to be regarded as a sin. The night before a battle, priests prepared soldiers to kill by absolving their sins ahead of time.[18]

Carolingian innovations placed the execution of Jesus—rather than his resurrection—at the center of the eucharist. Instead of being the loving host of the table and the symbol of life's victories over death, Christ became the perpetually dying, terrifying judge. Clergy were forbidden to kill in war, but they enacted ritual "murder" in the church's most sacred ritual and policed access to it. All murders committed by sinful humanity became fused into the one great murder of Christ, the consummate victim of every sin, the only "murder" priests were allowed to commit. The priests were also the sole source of penance and absolution for the murder. This eucharistic system placed enormous control in the hands of the clergy and made humanity into helpless victims of their own sin.

Though the Carolingian Empire collapsed within a half century, its view of the eucharist triumphed. Pope Sylvester II (c. 940–1003) declared Paschasius's views correct, and death achieved a new ontological status, along with the past. Whereas in the traditional eucharist Jesus had overcome death, never to die again, the new ritual transformed the historical crucifixion into an ever-repeated state of dying. The death that defeated death became an eternal and narrow gateway to salvation promised somewhere beyond this world. His resurrection nearly disappeared from the ritual and from theologies of salvation. Crucifixion became eternal, forever available to haunt the Western imagination in rituals, prayers, images, and theology, and it perpetually justified violence, especially against pagans, Jews, heretics, and infidels.

In 1095, with the momentum of these shifts, Pope Urban II launched the First Crusade. He promised that all who joined the holy war could count their duty as penance for their sins, a ritual of pilgrimage to, and pillage of, Jerusalem. He also promised that if the crusaders died, they would immediately gain salvation, which he displaced from life here and now into the afterlife. Shedding human blood became absolution for sin and the fastest route to salvation. Salvation became increasingly individual.[19]

With Urban's call to take the cross of the crucified Christ, Christian constraints against bloodshed ended. In their first act, crusaders killed nearly 30,000 Jews in the Rhineland—the first large-scale Christian massacre of Jews. Then the crusaders turned toward the Middle East, and were massacred in Eastern Europe. The next wave of crusaders took Jerusalem and slaughtered Muslims without mercy. The wealth they pillaged funded Europe's economic flowering and set a pattern for conquest and colonization that lasted for centuries.

Anselm of Canterbury (c. 1033–1109), Urban's friend, provided the theological fuel for holy war. He underscored Jesus' death as penance for sin. *Cur Deus Homo?* written three years into the First Crusade, exhorted Christians to imitate Christ's gift of death. "There is nothing more bitter or more difficult for man to suffer for the honor of God voluntarily and without obligation, than death, and man absolutely cannot give himself more fully to God than when he commits himself to death for God's honor."[20] To kill or be killed for God redeemed all sin. Anthony Bartlett and James Carroll show how Anselm's theory was an ideological basis for genocide and propose the work of Peter Abelard as an alternative. [21]

Abelard (1079–1142) opposed the Crusades and lived during a renaissance of thinking in twelfth-century France, influenced by its proximity to Muslim scholars and libraries in Spain. He proposed that Jesus was crucified not because God's justice required it, but because, through his suffering and dying, Christ proved the extent of divine love as self-sacrifice by forgiving sinners. This sacrifice indicted all sinners and asked them to recognize their sinfulness. In this self-recognition and the response of contrition, human beings were bound to God by love. Submitting to crucifixion demonstrated love for Christ as the supreme example of love. The crucifixion, thus, became the deepest bonding in love between Christ and sinners. [22]

By reducing salvation to an inner subjective process, Abelard individualized it, narrowing faith to an internal consciousness, unmediated by relationships except to Christ as the innocent, dead victim. Abelard placed an enormous burden on purity of feeling, on self-knowledge, and on the ability of human beings to will one pure thing. He had little means for understanding self-deception or the complex motivations that prompt most human acts. He also provided no means to assess conflicting moral choices, as if loving God produced self-evidently ethical actions, if one felt guilty enough.[23]

Abelard's selfless love was powerlessness. As he notes:

> There are two things that render us subject to God: fear and love. Power and wisdom produce fear, since we know that God is both able to punish and also that nothing is hid from Him. But love has its origin in goodness. If we hold that God is most good, then we have reason for offering Him the greatest love… Goodness, in fact, is not power or wisdom, and to be good is not to be wise or powerful. [24]

Bernard of Clairvaux (1090–1153) had Abelard excommunicated. Bernard advocated crusading as an act of love and wrote a defense of the "new knighthood" that merged the warrior with the monk. He called crusaders "God's ministers" and described their killing as glorious service to God. He coined a new term, *malecide,* killing an evildoer, rather than *homicide,* killing a human being.[25] Bernard's erotic mysticism fused the nuptial bliss of the Song of Songs with Christ's crucifixion.

By the time of Anselm, Abelard, and Bernard, resurrection had become unimportant—Anselm fails even to mention it in *Why God Became Human*. Salvation eventually disappeared into purgatorial penalties and the ever-delayed hope of a post-apocalyptic new heaven and earth.[26] Western atonement theology created an idol of execution, bowed down at its bloody feet, and sacrificed the living Christ on its altar, partaking in the body of death. Whereas the incarnate, risen Christ had once been the comforter and healer of the afflicted and the forerunner of Christians' own journey to divinity and wisdom, the dead Christ became the judge of their failure and helplessness. Whereas the cross had symbolized victory over death and salvation in this world, it came to symbolize death both as the killing of Jesus and as malecide. Rather than drawing Christ and humanity together into communities committed to moral virtue, love, and care for each other, atonement theology both fused them through violence as sinners and separated them through individual judgment.

Atonement theology is useful to imperial power. It is built on innocent, powerless victims who perpetually haunt the present and are required for the repentance of sinners. It leans toward an imaginary future of salvation. Instead of encouraging acute attunement to the present, astute judgment, and wise uses of power, it teaches suspicion of the present as the realm of conflict and death and valorizes the helpless. It also perpetuates structures of benevolent paternalism. Renato Rosaldo called such paternalism "imperialist nostalgia." Faced with what imperial conquest destroyed, and anguished by guilt about their own savage behavior, imperialists attempt to retrieve their own lost sense of goodness by idealizing their victims and loving and admiring them in what they imagine as their innocent pre-conquest state. They seek to assuage their guilty consciences and moral failures by seeking absolution from token members of such groups who are willing to befriend them and appear grateful for their help. Imperialists trapped in nostalgia do not form actual relationships to living people who are neither helpless nor innocent. To do so would be to abandon their innocence and to face honestly into the ambiguous past.[27]

Atonement theology lacks ways to understand human agency as moral because it places morality in being powerless, and it does not understand love as the wise use of power. To regard the poor, oppressed, and victimized as innocent and good reinforces the structures of benevolent paternalism, whereby helpless victims can be admired and their champions can maintain power by denouncing evil on their behalf. That Christians with education, privilege, and affluence in developed countries often feel helpless to combat racism, violence, poverty, and oppression is a luxury the world cannot afford. It is a retreat into a pretense of innocence, based in narcissistic self-preoccupations. Feeling helpless, and therefore moral, is encouraged by the Abelardian atonement, which asks us to identify with victims, rather than to take responsibility for the great power that we have and to learn to use it justly and lovingly.

Faith in an Age of Globalization

Early church christology offers guideposts for an answer to Jesus' original question, "Who do you say I am?" We live in a world driven by injustice, war, and economic exploitation. Though many people in the world now live in democratic societies, the will to pursue power and domination, the quest for wealth and status, the denial of knowledge and truth, the reliance on bloodshed and terror, and the scarcities and betrayal of love remain unabated since Roman times. In our world, these sins have been given greater reach and control through technological advances that now threaten not only individual societies or nations, but the interdependent web of life.

Our answer to Jesus' question defines what kind of church we are. We claim to be disciples of the Jesus Christ of the New Testament. He taught resistance to the unjust principalities and powers of the world, declared that we must be friends of God and each other, and organized a movement to enable the least respected and most oppressed a place at the table of life and leadership in his community—women, poor peasants, slaves, paupers, prisoners, the homeless, and the disabled and sick. He was tortured and murdered for resisting injustice and challenging authorities. He lives still among those who love him and each other.

Jesus Christ lives because the truths he taught and the God he revealed have not vanished from the earth. This God is the breath of life in all creation, and still calls to the Spirit in us. Our lives depend on this world. We are asked to love it and to struggle to mend it. What we do not know or cannot love, God loves. Our salvation comes through that love and our ability to live on this earth and in the church, here and now. Salvation brings the whole world along with it, into our very midst. And in loving it, we discover the meaning of eucharist: *thanksgiving*. When we gather around the communion table, we celebrate the gift of creation, recommit ourselves to be the bread of life to the world, and remember all whom we love and have loved. We must give thanks for the blessings that give us respite from the daily struggles of life.

We must learn to tell the truth about violence. Violence and oppression invade human communities, destroying defenses and burying emotional scars deep into perpetrators and survivors. Survivors may try to suppress trauma through denial or uproot it furiously with anger, hate, a need for revenge, or a desire to punish. Negative feelings toward another are intense forms of emotional possession, trapped in unhealed memory, like larvae in amber. Unleashed, they betray people's moral ideals and lead to cycles of violence. We tell the story of the crucifixion of Jesus because oppression, injustice, and bloodshed continue, and, as we mourn their victims, we hold fast to the courage to do what we must to resist death-dealing powers.

Good and evil live side by side in our world, in our communities, and in ourselves, and our life in the body of Christ is a commitment to struggle to know the difference, an understanding the church called wisdom, Sophia. Sophia's fruits are works of love, a passion for justice, care for the sick and the poor, an appreciation of beauty, the discernment of the spirit in the world, and the embrace of this world as good, as blessed, and as beloved by God. We seek to use our power wisely for the well-being of the whole world in all its diversities—for loving sameness requires no wisdom or courage. Living in unjust systems, many risk crucifixion to restore life. The courage to take such risks is grounded in our knowledge that we stand in solidarity with all who seek justice, and we are part of a very old legacy of such work.

One of the greatest confusions about the death of Jesus is the meaning of forgiveness, which has been turned into self-sacrifice as love that bonds perpetrators and victims. Forgiveness is valorized as the absorbing of violence through love. This distorts the meaning of love. Pumla Gobodo-Madikizela, a Black South African, served on the Truth and Reconciliation Commission (TRC). As part of her work, she screened all testimonies in the Western Cape, including Capetown, to determine which should be presented to the TRC. A social psychologist and a Christian, she also wanted to understand what she observed about forgiveness. Survivors of violence and families of victims forgave perpetrators, including some who forgave unrepentant, unapologetic perpetrators. She concluded that forgiveness was not about love for perpetrators, but about freedom for their survivors. Once perpetrators no longer had any power to hurt them, the survivors chose to change their relationships to them and to the harm done to them.[28]

Gobodo-Madikizela observed that survivors who pronounced forgiveness were freed. They relinquished the anger or hate that had dominated their lives, not because they loved the perpetrators, but because they loved each other too much to let what happened hold them captive to the past and destroy their future. They had decided that what the perpetrator did or did not do would no longer determine their responses and that evil would no longer haunt them. In this decision, they achieved greater freedom by laying the burden of violence down. They stepped into a future with possibilities for a new life. Though they did not expect or require it, they unlocked a door to love between enemies.

We take risks, we make sacrifices, but those who choose to harm others are morally responsible for their choices. Those who survive violence must repair what is broken and struggle to "make and make again where such unmaking reigns," as Adrienne Rich says,[29] and the eucharist is where we make and make again whenever we come together. Through it we maintain our love for each other and widen the possibilities for more love beyond our imagining.

Whatever the principalities and powers of human societies try to do, resurrection affirms that they cannot destroy love. The Spirit of God in our communities sustains human beings through even the worst tragedy. To see salvation in the Incarnation and resurrection is to know that life in community is stronger than the forces of death and destruction, that violence has no place in the community and must be addressed when it appears. Communities of life help us to survive violence. The torn network of love must be mended. Beauty must return to the world. Resurrection is essential. To have Christianity without resurrection is the Christian heresy. Death is a part of life, love brings resurrection, and life is eternal.

The Thanksgiving Prayer of the Gallican Eucharist Rite, used throughout Europe until the ninth century, said:

> Eternal God…you gave wonderful forms to the amazed elements: the tender world blushed at the fires of the sun, and the rude earth wondered at dealings of the moon… Your hands made from clay a more excellent likeness, which a holy fire quickened within, and a lively soul brought to life throughout its idle parts… To you alone is known the majesty of your work: what there is in humanity, that the blood held in the veins washes the fearful limbs and the living earth; that the loose appearances of bodies are held together by tightening nerves, and the individual bones gain strength from the organs within… Whence comes so great a bounty…that we should be formed in the likeness of you and your Son, that an earthly thing should be eternal.[30]

11

Under the Influence

Pneumatology in Global, Historical Perspective

DYRON DAUGHRITY

Introduction: The Spirit's Comeback

You and I are witnesses to one of the great turns in the history of Christian theology. The Holy Spirit has made a radical comeback. Shortly after reaching its high point on Pentecost Sunday and in the lives of the earliest Christians, it soon became mired in controversy, particularly when adopted by Montanus, one of the "heretics" of the second century. The Holy Spirit has since struggled to regain its rightful place as God.

For years it has been conventional to begin an essay of this nature with a disclaimer. For example, "The doctrine of the Holy Spirit has seldom received the attention given to other doctrines of the faith such as Christology and the authority of Scripture."[1] Things have changed—in a radical way. Probably not since the filioque controversies of medieval times has pneumatology been at the forefront of Christian thinking. The Holy Spirit is, arguably, *the* most prolific member of the Holy Trinity today! This is due largely to global Pentecostalism's rapid growth and potential majority status in several key places in world Christianity. If the Azusa Street revival of 1906 is accepted as the dawn of modern Pentecostalism, then this movement is mesmerizing in its rapidity of growth. If we ask a Pentecostal what discharged this dazzling growth rate, it is likely the answer will revolve around a discussion of pneumatology. Perhaps as many as 500 million people in the world today are "under the influence" of Pentecostalism—and its highly pneumatological complexion.

What is pneumatology? The word *pneuma* is the Greek word usually translated "spirit." Thus, pneumatology is that field of study concerned with spirits, phenomena, and, most importantly for Christian theology, the study of the Holy Ghost. This article discusses the doctrine of the Holy Spirit within three distinct contexts: biblical, historical, and Restoration.

The Biblical Context

The Hebrew word for spirit is *ruach,* a feminine term that can also be translated "wind" or "breath." This is an important point because in the New Testament (NT), the word for spirit is *pneuma,* a neuter term. To further complicate matters, the Western, Latin Church preferred to make spirit a masculine noun, *spiritus.* Nonetheless, the earlier, feminine understanding of *ruach* in the Hebrew Bible lived on in the NT, such as when Jesus speaks to Nicodemus about being birthed of water and the Spirit (Jn. 3:5–6).

Precisely what is the Holy Spirit? Perhaps it is fitting that the notion of God's Holy Spirit is so rich that it defies any attempt to rationalize or define it. Any rudimentary word search of "spirit" in the Bible reveals that biblical writers understood the concept in manifold ways. What follows are brief discussions of the Holy Spirit in both testaments.

The Spirit of God makes its entrance in Genesis 1:2: "Now the earth was formless and empty, darkness was over the surface of the deep, and the Spirit of God was hovering over the waters."[2] Impressive as it is, this text is also confounding. Is the Spirit of God a distinct being, such as the third person of the Trinity? Is it a ghost? Is it God's breath? Or is it simply wind?

The Hebrew Bible generally discusses the concept of the Spirit as a power emanating from God. Frequently we read the Spirit of God "came upon" someone. This often occurs in the context of prophecy. One vivid account is 1 Samuel 19. Not only does the Spirit cause prophecy within Samuel and his band of prophets, but Saul's men seem unable to stop prophesying while under its influence. What is even more puzzling about this text is the section about how "an evil spirit from the LORD came upon Saul," causing him to attempt to murder David while he was practicing his harp. The chapter ends bizarrely with Saul naked, lying on the ground, prophesying in the presence of Samuel.

The Spirit of God is also seen as a power emanating from God in the context of leadership. Israel's judges are identified as having the Spirit of the Lord coming upon them. David seemed to be aware of the threat of God's Spirit being withdrawn from him, writing, "Do not cast me from your presence / or take your Holy Spirit from me" (Ps. 51:11).

Most captivating in the Old Testament (OT) however, is the Spirit of God's activity in the Messianic age, most clearly put forth by the prophets. Joel tells of a time when God will "pour out" God's Spirit on all people, a text that the early church eagerly embraced (Acts 2). Perhaps the most Spirit-filled passage in all of the OT is Isaiah 11. This anticipatory text tells us of a Messiah figure who will be especially ordained by God's Spirit in all respects. "The Spirit of the LORD will rest on him... With righteousness he will judge... With the breath of his lips he will slay the wicked." Jesus was also drawn to Isaiah's discussion of the Holy Spirit in chapter 61, referring to Isaiah's words when he launched his ministry with

> "The Spirit of the Lord is on me,
> because he has anointed me
> to preach good news to the poor.
> He has sent me to proclaim freedom for the prisoners...
> to release the oppressed,
> to proclaim the year of the Lord's favor." (Lk. 4:18–19)

"The NT teaching on the Spirit is rich and complex in comparison with OT materials."[3] There is, however, unmistakable continuity from the OT to the NT. For example, the term itself, *pneuma,* like *ruach,* has at its root the constitutional elements of air, breath, and wind. Similarly, NT understandings of Spirit have much to do with prophecy, evinced early in Luke (1:39–45) when Elizabeth, under the influence, pronounces a blessing on Mary because of her faith. Luke is particularly concerned with the Holy Spirit, a fact likely having something to do with his Pauline connection. For Luke, the age of the Spirit was at hand with the arrival of Jesus. Jesus' birth in Luke's narrative is inundated with Spirit. Every major figure in that text speaks with prophetic authority from the Holy Spirit of God: Elizabeth, Mary, Zechariah (1:67), Simeon (2:25), and Anna (2:36).

Luke's prominent *pneuma* theme is key in distinguishing between two seemingly similar figures: Jesus and John the Baptist. While John was prophetic and full of charisma, Jesus was uniquely under the influence of God's Spirit. John merely baptized with water, Jesus "will baptize you with the Holy Spirit and with fire" (Lk. 3:16). Luke saturates Jesus' early ministry with *pneuma*: Heaven opens and the Holy Spirit falls upon Jesus at his baptism (Lk. 3:21–22). The Spirit leads him into a period of fasting and temptation (Lk. 4). He launches his ministry in the synagogue with haunting, recognizable words, "The Spirit of the Lord is on me" (Lk. 4:18). Spirit-power exudes from him as he confronts and exorcizes lesser spirits, heals the sick, preaches boldly in the synagogues and streets, and attracts a following that is utterly in awe of him (Lk. 5:1–11).

Luke makes it clear in Acts that this Spirit-power would continue in the lives of the apostles (Acts 1:8). With these words, "And you will be my witnesses," Luke makes a strong connection between the missionary efforts of the apostles and the Holy Spirit (Acts 2; 5:32; 9:31; 10:44; 19:6).

While the other synoptic gospels deviate little from Luke's pneumatology, there is one compelling pneumatological passage that deserves mention because of its appearance in all three: the blasphemy of the Holy Spirit, or, the unforgivable sin of Christianity. What do we make of these passages (Mt. 12:24–32; Mk. 3:19–30; Lk. 12:8–12)? The story seems to indicate that some were attributing Jesus' miracles to the work of Beelzebub. Scholarly consensus gravitates towards the idea that "blasphemy of the Holy Spirit" was a willful, determined opposition to Jesus' miracles and ministry. This seems a sensible enough idea. How can one be forgiven if one attributes the salvific, miraculous work of Jesus to Satan?

John's pneumatology is unique. Not only does John introduce the concept of the "*paraclete*" (Spirit as comforter, helper, and advocate), but he also draws liberally from OT imagery: water, wind, and breath. John links the Spirit to rebirth and wind in chapter 3. In chapter 20 Jesus breathes the Holy Spirit on his apostles.

Pauline pneumatology is rooted in his christology. One is hard-pressed to divorce Paul's pneumatology from his larger Trinitarian perspective. For Paul, the Holy Spirit is the Spirit of Christ (Rom. 8:9; Gal. 4:6; Phil. 1:19), confession of Christ is made possible by the Spirit (1 Cor. 12:3), all members of the body of Christ were baptized in the Spirit (1 Cor. 12:13), and the Spirit is the only one who knows the "deep things of God" (1 Cor. 2:10–13). Paul's understanding of the "gifts of the Spirit" (Rom. 12; 1 Cor. 12) in the individual life parallels certain passages in the gospels, for example, John 14:12, "I tell you the truth, anyone who has faith in me will do what I have been doing. He will do even greater things than these, because I am going to the Father."

The Historical Context

Not only did the Holy Spirit suffer neglect throughout the centuries, one could even argue that it tended to arouse suspicion—if not open hostility. Montanus, one of the more notable early Christian personalities, challenged the mainstream around the year 170 with his ecstatic prophesying and distinct form of Christianity that even allowed full, feminine participation in the clergy! For a time, the movement was known as "the Phrygian heresy." Joined by prophetesses Maximilla and Priscilla, Montanus founded a movement based on Jesus' promise in the gospel of John, "Unless I go away, the Counselor will not come to you; but if I go, I will send him to you" (Jn. 16:7). While Montanus was excommunicated by the Roman bishop Eleutherus in 177, Montanism continued to attract converts, some of them important, such as Tertullian, "the first significant Christian author to write in Latin."[4] The underdeveloped pneumatology of the Nicene Creed (325) is illustrative of the continuing suspicion of the Spirit in Christian theology. After extensive explanation of the nature of Christ and his relationship to God, we are left with that meager phrase, "And [we believe] in the Holy Spirit."[5] Immediately following that exiguous sentence, we have a condemnation of Arius that is about six times the length of the pneumatological affirmation!

Shortly after the Council of Nicaea in 325, the Eastern Fathers began devoting their outstanding intellectual energies to the paltry pneumatology evinced in the Creed. Three men from the Cappadocian region corrected this problem. Basil the Great, his brother Gregory of Nyssa, and Gregory of Nazianzus, known today as the Cappadocian Fathers, "helped convince the church that the Spirit belonged, both in equality and in dignity, to the holy Trinity." In fact, an important theologian has recently argued that it was the Cappadocians who essentially "deified the Spirit."[6] This new wave of critical thinking on the nature of the Trinity led to a far more sophisticated pneumatology later that century.

The Constantinopolitan Creed of 381 represents a significant improvement. In that creed, the Holy Spirit is fully deified with the famous words:

> And [we believe] in the Holy Spirit, the Lord and life-giver,
>
> Who proceeds from the Father, Who is worshiped and glorified together with the Father and the Son, Who spoke through the prophets.[7]

The importance attached to the Spirit in those words proved bittersweet. This creed represents something of a turning point in Christian history and theology. One short, seemingly insignificant clause eventually played a major part in ripping the global Church into two fragments, "Who proceeds from the Father." The biblical verse informing the entire affair was John 15:26, "When the Counselor comes, whom I will send to you from the Father, the Spirit of truth who goes out from the Father, he will testify about me." At issue was whether or not the Holy Spirit proceeds only "from the Father," or "from the Father *and the Son*." In Latin, the word *filioque* translates "and the son." The ensuing controversy is often known in Church history as "the filioque controversy." The crux of the matter was whether or not the filioque clause should be added to the historic creed. In time, the Western, Latin Church insisted the filioque should be added, and it was. The Eastern Churches were reluctant, firmly opposing any alterations to the historic creed.

The history of the filioque controversy is long and complex. The problems began early in the fifth century when Christians ruminated whether the Holy Spirit proceeds from the Father or from the Father *and the Son*. The filioque controversies were at least as much an issue of authority as they were theology. Rome and the Eastern Churches had an involved history of just who was the authority in ecclesiastical affairs: Rome, or the historic Councils such as Nicaea, Constantinople, and Chalcedon. The Eastern Churches believed the councils to be the highest authority, while the Western Church viewed the council's decisions binding only if ratified by the bishop of Rome, their Pope.

After centuries of tit-for-tat, the Eastern Orthodox Churches and the Western Roman Catholic Church split in 1054. While the filioque controversy certainly played a large role in the Great Schism, there were other issues involved: language barriers (Greek and Latin), cultural misunderstandings, personality clashes, and constant misinformation at a time when long-distance communication was not easy. The breach between Eastern and

Western Christianity continues, although attempts at reconciliation have occurred sporadically since 1054.

We would be remiss to limit our historical analysis of pneumatology to the Great Schism, as it represents one of the more lamentable episodes in Church history. A cursory look at some of the significant figures and events in the development of pneumatology will only touch on the rich legacy we have inherited.[8] Shortly after the Cappadocian Fathers, Augustine's masterpiece *The Trinity* appeared. Augustine's primary contention was that the Spirit is what links together the Father and the Son in a bond of love. Augustine's love-bond idea precipitated later medieval pneumatological reflection.

Hildegard of Bingen (twelfth century) conceived of the Spirit in botanical terms. She believed that God's Spirit flows on humans as water on plants—in order to sustain and enliven them. Bernard of Clairvaux (twelfth century) compared the Spirit to a kiss coming from the Father and Son to the "bride," or the believer. In other words, the Spirit is the intimate link that connects humans to the Trinity itself. Catherine of Siena (fourteenth century) located the Spirit in the form of a waiter, bringing food to the believer. In her typically poetic vividness, the Father is compared to the table, the Son is the food, and the Spirit is the servant lovingly bringing food to the Christian—who feasts upon every divine morsel.

According to Yves Congar's important survey of pneumatological history, Luther and Calvin "both kept to the classical teaching of Nicaea and Constantinople...with regard to the Trinity."[9] However, both faced challenges from more radical reformers who appealed to the Holy Spirit as their source of authority. Luther fiercely denounced the Anabaptists, led by Thomas Muntzer, because of their belief that the Spirit is operative in the united voice of the Church. Luther also loathed their understanding that God's Word requires no intermediary to communicate to people—this process can simply occur in the Spirit. Luther's devaluation of the clergy never went this far. Luther wrote, "Muntzer claimed us to be learned in Scripture, while he himself claimed to be learned in the Spirit."[10]

The Anabaptist position reached new heights with George Fox (seventeenth century) and the Quakers. Fox disdained a formal clergy, the sacraments, church buildings, and even external worship. For Fox, "There was no other principle of worship and no other rule than the Holy Spirit."[11] The Pietist movement also went in a heavily subjective direction, without jettisoning the institutional church. Philip Jakob Spener's classic work *Pia Desideria* (1675) emphasized the Spirit's activity in the individual's life as well as in the life of the spiritual small groups that the Pietists became so famous for. It was Zinzendorf (eighteenth century) who was largely responsible for sending this message all over the world with his Herrnhut missionaries. Moravian missionaries from Herrnhut influenced John Wesley (eighteenth century). Their influence on later developments—in particular the Azusa Street Revival of 1906—is well-known.

The Restoration Context

"Except for polemical purposes, leaders of the Stone-Campbell Movement have devoted little time to the doctrine of the Holy Spirit."[12] There are several reasons for this. First, it is clear that from the earliest days of the Restoration revivals that the Campbells disagreed with Stone on the gifts of the Spirit. Stone seemed pleased with the "exercises" in the Spirit, which were so pronounced at the Cane Ridge Revival in 1801, although he was reluctant to promote this behavior once his movement began to cohere. The Campbells, on the other hand, "were appalled by the 'exercises.'"[13]

Another reason has to do with hermeneutics. Alexander Campbell in particular was prone to a heavy rationalism that pervaded his system of thought. Leonard Allen has written that this "enormous confidence in human reason" made "the Holy Spirit nearly indistinguishable from the Bible."[14] Allen goes on to argue that this interpretation leaves little room for the supernatural and prefers to understand the Bible as a collection of facts. God has given us his guidebook and has left it to us to use our reason to interpret it accurately.

Third, our faith tradition has engaged in vociferous debates regarding the activity of the Holy Spirit in conversion. Byron Lambert has excellently organized the various and arduous views, demonstrating just how cumbersome the debates could get in early Restoration history. Essentially, the debates revolved around these questions: Does the Holy Spirit operate exclusively through the written Bible? Or does the Holy Spirit indwell the individual and operate separate and apart from the Bible? Alexander Campbell tended toward the first of these views; however, this was not always the case. There is evidence that later on in his career he began to ease up on his strict view that the Holy Spirit was exclusively found in the Bible words and facts. Walter Scott attempted to steer Restoration preaching away from the "Word-alone" interpretation. Scott argued that by obeying the Bible, one could experience the fruit of the Spirit. It was Robert Richardson, however, who worked to rescue the Stone-Campbell movement from what he viewed as spiritual aridity. His treatise *A Scriptural View of the Office of the Holy Spirit* (1872) argued that it was a mistake to speculate on theories unknown in apostolic times. Thus, the evangelist's duty was to "preach the gospel and leave the results to the Holy Spirit."[15] J.H. Garrison's *The Holy Spirit: His Personality, Mission, and Modes of Activity* (1905) continued to dispel the "Word-alone" interpretation.

Alexander Campbell's equivalency of the Bible and the Holy Spirit is a view that never completely died, in spite of its detractors. The twentieth century witnessed some controversy in the Restoration on the issue, notably among J. D. Thomas, who taught a "literal indwelling," and Foy E. Wallace Jr., who identified with the "Word-alone" camp. More irenic Restoration scholars such as Carl Ketcherside and Leroy Garrett worked toward reconciliation throughout the century. The Restoration movement is undergoing something of a pneumatological awakening today.[16]

Conclusion: Under the Influence...Again

Around the year 2000, Pentecostalism quietly surpassed the Eastern Orthodox family of Churches as the second largest grouping in Christianity, second only to the Roman Catholic tradition. Pentecostalism could reach majority status if trends continue. By all accounts, global Christianity is "under the influence" of the Holy Spirit. Perhaps this great new fact of our time is not as evident in the West, but one thing is certain: the Southern churches have caught the winds of God—and they are on fire.

Historians Philip Jenkins and Harvey Cox have brought this somewhat unexpected reality to light. Jenkins' widely celebrated *The Next Christendom* continues to raise eyebrows among historians:

> By most accounts, membership in Pentecostal and independent Churches already runs into the hundreds of millions, and congregations are located in precisely the regions of fastest population growth. Within a few decades, such denominations will represent a far larger segment of global Christianity, and just conceivably a majority.[17]

It was Harvey Cox, however, one of the great proponents of the 1960s secularization thesis, who first clued in to this revolution in Christian demographics in 1995 with his *Fire from Heaven: The Rise of Pentecostal Spirituality and the Reshaping of Religion in the Twenty-First Century*. Cox, formerly known for his landmark *Secular City* thesis, had made an about-face: "The Pentecostal movement is thriving."[18] Cox's earlier estimation that Christianity in the West was on the decline is still helpful, particularly when understanding Western European trends. However, in terms of global Christianity, he and the sociologists could not have missed the mark more flagrantly. As Jenkins writes, "Christianity is flourishing wonderfully among the poor and persecuted, while it atrophies among the rich and secure."[19]

What implications does this have for our movement? For the time being, as Disciples, we must appeal to our "table" metaphor. If we imagine the world as our eucharistic table, Disciples in the twenty-first century must come together, commune, and celebrate our fellowship—as a global, diverse body. More importantly, we must listen to one another. We in the West must invite unfamiliar guests to our table, particularly those who are breathing the breath of God. We must learn from them. Some Disciples in Latin America, Africa, Asia—and even in the United States—*practice* pneumatology, rather than merely reflect. Perhaps those are the ones who should guide us, direct our conversations, and teach us about the Holy Spirit. Southern Christians seem to understand this topic best.[20]

12

Creation

Victor L. Hunter

The doctrine of creation in the Bible and in Christian tradition affirms God as Creator of the world, the whole of creation as good, and the created order as the object of God's loving attention from its inception to its consummation. The thesis of this chapter is that Creation is to be understood as both act and process, and that human beings, as God-imaged creatures, are invited into and commanded to be a part of the care of the integrity of creation. Furthermore, a constructive theology of creation in an age of empire and postcolonial critiques of power at the beginning of the third millennium must address the current threat to the life of the world—"world" meaning the cosmos, the creation, the whole of God's created order and its resources, including both sustainable, life-engendering natural systems and just human communities. The theological principles of eco-justice and creation-consciousness discussed in this chapter challenge us as the created and called people of God to seek the well-being of all humanity on a thriving earth.

Even a cursory look at our planet under current political, economic, and ecological conditions and policies reveals creation under threat. Affluent and powerful human societies devastate the earth with the wastefulness of consumer culture, acting out of a spiritually impoverished and distorted materialism based on the glutted blindness of a theology of scarcity. The paranoid conviction, "there is not enough," gives way to a hoarding mentality that believes, "enough is not enough." In the poorest areas of the world, devastation of resources can take place in the very struggle for survival. The widespread use of herbicides and pesticides poison people and places, with toxic impacts far beyond their intended targets. Rainforests are denuded by unsustainable timber harvests and inappropriate agriculture, destroying the homelands of indigenous peoples while driving species of animal and plant life into extinction. Pollution, destructive fishing practices, and warming seas are destroying the world's coral reefs—fragile and fertile nurseries for large portions of ocean life. Freshwater resources are becoming increasingly scarce around the world, with devastating effects on both natural systems and human societies. The insatiable appetite for cheap energy spews pollution, ruins landscapes, and releases gases (which drive the catastrophe of global climate change), and, in the process, spawns war and conflict. Willful ignorance and callous inattention to humanity's reckless impact on the environment and the integrity of creation itself are unraveling the complex fabric of life on earth.

A theology of creation speaks directly to "all that is and all who are" in God's economy. Eco-justice and creation-consciousness bind together Christian theology's concern with peace and justice, salvation and wholeness, sin and redemption, ecology and economy, power and poverty. A theology of creation allows for no bifurcation of the spiritual and the natural, the environment and the redemption of the world, the creation and the new creation, the origin of the world and the consummation of the world within the creator God's loving purposes. When environmental degradation creates human suffering, and the technology of the powerful ignores the ethical mandate of care of the earth, Disciples of Christ must address these realities as "matters of faith" that "matter to the faithful."

I. Foundations: Biblical Texts and Christian Confessions Regarding Creation

The core creation biblical texts informing these theological reflections are: Genesis 1 and 2 (especially 1:1, 26, 27, 31a); Psalm 24:1; John 1:1-4a; Romans 8:18–25; 1 Corinthians 5:17; Colossians 1:1–15; and Revelation 21:1–5. The Nicene Creed, the Apostles Creed, and the Disciples of Christ Affirmation of Faith all confess belief in God as maker of heaven and earth, creator of all things seen and unseen. The biblical texts and the creeds taken together proclaim the church's confession that God's creative Word called the world and the church into being. Both the natural world and witnessing community are responses to the creator God who calls them into being by the creative Word. Both originate in God's Word, both belong to God, and both are gifts of God.

The Hebrew texts reflect that God is God, creation is creation, creature is creature. God lives, creatures die. Yet Creator and creation are relational. The beginning of creation is good. The world is loved. The world is not abandoned. The world is invited into response, not scorned. The created world is understood only in relationship to a transcendent referent, the creator God. It is contingent but free to respond. It is neither tyrannized by a despotic ruler nor left to its own devices. There is purpose and there is promise. The Creator values creation. The "meaning" of creation is found in the love and will of the Creator. The creatures of the creation are commanded, invited, and wooed into valuing the creation that has been entrusted to them.[1]

The New Testament texts reflect the Hebrew "in the beginning" and God as creator of the universe, affirming the role of Christ in this creation as the preexistent, creative Word of God who speaks the world into being. As such, the creation is again affirmed as "good." The same Christ is both life-engendering and life-illuminating in creation. Christ is the image of God, and the means of creation in the past *and* continuing creation in the present. Christ is the coherence of creation. Christ is the cosmic reality of the new creation. This soteriology is not simply a personal message of salvation for individuals or a psychological message of inner change or a sense of private well-being. Creation and new creation belong together within the continuing love of God in Christ. It is the world, the creation, which is being redeemed, renewed, and saved.[2]

Undergirding these stories of creation and their implications for Creator/creation relationships is the concept of covenant. This is born out in the Affirmation of Faith in The Design of the CCDC: "rejoicing in the covenant of love which binds us to God and one another." The biblical concept of covenants between God and creation reveals that God initiated the means of living in right relationships for the well-being of all of creation. God is both "creator God" and "covenantal God." The covenants are, from the beginning, signs of God's gracious relational love for God's world and the moral responsibility of God's covenanted partners in life lived "before God" within creation. The covenantal relationships encompass the connectedness between people, the whole of the environment, and God. Theology today must recapture this scriptural insight regarding creation and covenant in regard to the environmental crisis, thus freeing us from a restricting and destructive anthropocentric obsession and enabling us to see the "wholeness" of God's redemptive work. The everlasting rainbow covenant with Noah and his descendants and *"every living creature...the birds, the livestock and all the wild animals...a covenant for all generations to come"* (Gen. 9:8–17 NIV) is an example of what Clark M. Williamson calls a "covenantal ecology" rooted in the life of "Israel and its re-presentation in the New Testament."[3]

II. Faith in Search of Understandings: Five Core Theological Meanings of the Doctrine of Creation in the Current World Context

What do we as Christians profess about the doctrine of creation? What informs us theologically as Disciples as we attempt to live responsibly (faithfully and ethically) in relation to God and the created order? The world as both "created" and "fallen" sounds a warning for our reflections: we cannot be "overly pessimistic or nihilistic" about the world because it is created; we cannot be "overly optimistic" about the world because it is fallen. Christian theological interpretation of creation is rooted in a kind of Christian realism that encompasses both history and hope within and beyond history.

The Significance of God as Creator

The Bible assumes that God is the ultimate source and sovereign of the world. As Christians, we understand the world in light of the Creator. This source is love, not simply power. This is a critical beginning point in a context of empire, in which power itself has become a supreme value. The story of creation challenges our bewitchment by the Western or Greek conception of the attributes of God as being omnipotence, omniscience, and impassability. The Hebrew tradition and the Jesus story reveal God the creator as One who exercises, even in the acts of creation, self-limiting, other-affirming, and future-opening power.[4] This is the God, not of unrestricted and static powerful "god almightiness," which resulted in empire's worship of "power itself," but the social and relational God, the Trinitarian narrative God, the vulnerable God, the God of covenantal invitation and participation—in short, the God of the power of love. The creator God of love is by nature relational and is therefore self-limiting, other-affirming, and future-opening. These are the very dynamics of loving relationships. The creator God of the Bible by nature says "No" to unlimited power, a self-centeredness that denies the integrity of the "other," and all closed systems that do not make room for life.

The whole of creation, the cosmos, is the object of God's love (Jn. 3:16), de-centering our restricted anthropocentric focus. The world is God's, not ours. Human beings are not to abuse creation, for, as creatures in "the image of God," we befriend the world. Our "dominion" includes authority over our own abuses of power, consumption, and degradation of the God-created and God-loved world.

Human dominion implies the loving power of the stewardship of creation, not unlimited power for greedy and selfish abuse of creation. God creates "in the beginning," but the beginning is the alpha of a creation that continues to its omega. God is the continuing creator in the process of new beginnings, new future-opening possibilities, new events even to the hope of a new heaven and a new earth (Rev. 21.) God as creator focuses not on "how," but "who" and "why." God, as creator and source, indicates divine transcendence, freedom, and otherness from creation. The Creator and source, as love, indicates God's involvement in, with, and on behalf of the creation, or God's immanence.

The Significance of Creation as Good

Everything in the created world is good. Richard H. Lowery rather whimsically says that the phrase "everything is good" does not convey the intensity of God's pleasure in creation. He speaks of the creation as "delightful" and calls this phrase "God's cosmic Wow!"[5] The good creation allows for no dualism, no belief in matter as being evil or the body as being bad. Bodily life is good. Earthly life is good. We value the goodness of God's creation, respecting it, protecting it, and nurturing it for the good of all. It is a truly ecumenical goodness—all peoples, all of nature, everything and everyone. The church is committed to this cosmos of God's love, not to the "extraction of souls from a bad world."

The Significance of the Distinction between Creator and Creation

Creation is good, but it is not God.[6] This means we are liberated from paralyzing fear before the whole of creation for creation is neither ultimate nor omnipotent before the creator God. Nor is anything (any person, structure, ideology, nation, race, empire, economic system, political perspective, i.e., *anything created*—to command our worship, demand our ultimate loyalty, or control our destiny. All is relativized before the creator God. "This means at once freedom *from* the world (as the home of enslaving idols) and freedom *for* the world (as God's good creation)."[7]

The Significance of Human Beings as "God-imaged" Creatures among Creatures

The doctrine of creation affirms that God created male and female in God's own image. What is the "own image of God?" From the Old Testament creation stories, "...humans, by virtue of their creation in the image of God to rule and master the earth, have a special responsibility for the welfare of all living creatures, especially the most vulnerable. By portraying God's sovereign rule as fundamentally benevolent, Genesis 1 authorizes God-resembling humans to exercise power in the world with responsibility and generosity."[8] Humans, created in the image of God, in relationship to the rest of creation, are to exercise beneficence, responsibility, and generosity to the whole of the created world. The creation texts we have pointed to in the New Testament confess: "Christ is the image of the invisible God." From a Christian perspective, the image of God is Christ-shaped and Christ-formed, a lover of God's cosmos. It should be noted yet again that this moves us beyond anthropocentrism, not only in our understanding of creation, but in our understanding of redemption. Redemption occurs for the whole created order, thus expanding our understanding of redemption rather than limiting it.

Human beings as God-imaged creatures among other creatures also has profound implications for Christian anthropology and for our "point of view"—how we see the rest of creation. Simply put, humans are primarily worshipers, not consumers; stewards, not predators; covenantal partners, not dominating exploiters; blessers, not devourers; lovers, not rapists; creators, not destroyers; life engenderers, not life threateners; protectors, not pillagers.

The Significance of Abundance with Limitation in Creation

Professor Lowery's reading of the Genesis creation stories and Sabbath stories emphasizes the themes of natural abundance and human self-restraint. The creation story "portrays a world fundamentally benevolent and able to produce enough to sustain prosperous human life. This theme of natural abundance is coupled, however, with a theme of self-restraint. Rest is woven into the fabric of the universe. Periodic self-limitation, deliberate relinquishment of power to work the world and control it, is by Sabbath example a cosmic principle."[9]

God rests. God-imaged humans rest. Self-restraint in work, power, and consumption in the human community is the reflection of the creator God's self-limiting, other-affirming, future-opening power and a reminder that infinite growth on a finite planet is not possible. There is abundance, but not for greed. Power limited is power shared, and abundance shared is abundance limited.

III. Interpretive Principles in Search of Applications: Disciples Historic Theological Themes and the Doctrine of Creation

Free inquiry and intellectual integrity are at the heart of Disciples theological work. Disciples "think the faith" with a "mind" that is concerned with being *biblical, reasonable, empirical, pragmatic, and ecumenical.*[10] This book has been concerned with connecting a new constructive theological paradigm with the five core themes at the heart of our historical movement and hermeneutical reflections. These themes will help keep us biblically based, epistemologically sound, scientifically legitimate, confessionally appropriate, anthropologically de-centered, and *shalom* focused: justice and "other" oriented. It is now my purpose to examine these core themes as they relate to the "Disciples mind" and our theology of creation.

The Interpretive Theme

It is the *reasonable and empirical* aspects of the "Disciples mind" that concern us regarding the *interpretive* theme in relationship to the doctrine of creation.

Rationally and empirically, different universes of discourse for understanding and interpreting life exist. Different kinds of questions require different categories of understanding in relationship to truthful knowledge. This is certainly true in theological discourse as opposed to scientific discourse. The Bible is not a science book.

For example, to speak of a "heart attack" is different than speaking of a "broken heart." To speak of a "heart transplant" is not the same as speaking of a "change of heart." When we attempt to force one universe of discourse upon a different universe of discourse, we violate the reasonable and empirical aspects of the interpretive theme. We make a categorical mistake. Attempts to speak of "creationism" as a kind of science reduces and trivializes the theology of creation. It is a categorical mistake that actually distorts the doctrine of creation rather than illuminating it. We need to free ourselves from the falsity of the "science verses religion" debate and the misleading work of "harmonizing the Bible with science." The reasonable and empirical aspects of our interpretive theme help us avoid a fundamental category mistake and give us back the integrity of both science and religion.

The Restoration Theme and the Eschatological Theme

The "*biblical*" aspect of the "Disciples mind" concerns us in relationship to the themes of restoration and eschatology. The restoration theme addresses our concern with being biblical and paying attention to the centrality of scripture. The eschatological theme is concerned with the end and consummation of things. Eschatology is future-oriented and apocalyptically informed. Both the restoration theme and the eschatological theme are concerned with revelation and the biblical vision of origins and endings. In terms of the doctrine of creation, they deal with its alpha and omega.

Rejecting the "literalist" or "patternist" version of the restoration theme, the Disciples hermeneutic emphasized the dynamic dimension of restoration: being restored to relationship with God (reconciliation) and being restored to the image of God (new creation). Reconciliation and new creation call us to participation in beneficence, responsibility, and generosity to the whole of the created world. It is a restoration to the image of the God who exercises power in self-limiting, other-affirming and future-opening ways. This restoration is forward looking (eschatological), not backward looking, and lives toward the restoration of all things in Christ in the consummation and completion of God's creation. Restoration and eschatology are linked and are future in orientation and global in scope.

In the creation story, "God promises well-being that includes all of life (peace, economic sufficiency, health, safety, fertility, God's loving presence) and makes for the fullness of human life [life restored]. The fullness of human life is a gift from the fullness of God's life.[11] Likewise, the fulfillment of creation in consummation and completion is a gift from the fullness of God's life. God's creativity is not a "once upon a time" event, but a continuing process of creativity and new creativity, leading to redemptive and consummating creativity in the new heaven and new earth.[12]

The Ecumenical Theme and the Mission Theme

It is the *ecumenical* and *practical* aspects of the "Disciples mind" that concern us here. The ecumenical principle has grown in the church's understanding, not only to include Christian unity, but also to include solidarity in the struggle for peace and justice and the integrity of creation—what we have called eco-justice and creation-consciousness. The Institute for Ecumenical Research in Strasbourg, France, launched a project in 1982 to relate the studies of the doctrine of creation and ecumenism.[13] The ecumenical principle has been articulated in the World Council of Churches in its assemblies and documents to recapture the original meaning of *oikumene*—"the whole inhabited earth" or "the one household of life." The ecumenical principle central to the Disciples of Christ history and theology holds tremendous promise for bringing together our social justice, peace, and environmental concerns as being inextricably interrelated with the church's mission concerns in terms of both proclamation of the good news of Jesus and the ethics of the good news of Jesus. As has been made clear, the doctrines of creation and redemption are concerned with "all that is and all who are"—a truly ecumenical vision.

The ecumenical principle has always been connected to the mission principle in the Disciples of Christ. Today, the mission principle, especially in North American churches, must concern itself with stepping down from prominence and a self-centered worldview in terms of power, economics, and environmental resources in order to step forward in solidarity with the marginalized in a self-limiting, other-affirming, and future-opening vision. Mission and ecumenism both involve coalitions—what has been referred to in this book as hybridity. The mission of the church, especially in North America, will involve renewed commitment to prophetic witness—speaking truth to power.

The doctrine of creation calls us to repentance and action in terms of ecumenics and mission. Have we not denied the creator God in very practical ways by restricting our concept of mission to issues of personal salvation and individual peace and fulfillment, forgetting the whole household of God and all of creation? Have we not in practical ways ignored the degradation of creation and what this means for others' economic, social, and spiritual well-being, all for the purposes of greed? Have we not in practical ways forgotten what it means to be in relationship with creation as well as with the Creator? Does this not deny that the cosmos is God's? Have we forsaken the essential prophetic requirement: "to do justice, and to love kindness, / and to walk humbly with your God" (Mic. 6:8)? These issues concern not minor infractions of moral law, but essential unbelief in the creative and abundant, trustworthy and caring, relational and covenantal God.[14] These are theological sins contributing to ethical transgression. They must be addressed at the theological level.

Martin Luther King Jr. captured something of the true meaning of *oikumene* in an essay called "The World House."

> Some years ago a famous novelist died. Among his papers was found a list of suggested plots for future stories, the most prominently underscored being this one: "A widely separated family inherits a house in which they have to live together." This is the great new problem of mankind. We have inherited a large "world house" in

> which we have to live together...a family unduly separated in ideas, culture, and interest, who because we can never again live apart, must learn somehow to live with each other in peace.[15]

The new world house demands an ecumenical vision in which peace, justice, and the ecological integrity of creation are woven together in a tapestry of creation-consciousness and eco-justice.

IV. Affirmations in Search of Practical Actions: Eco-Justice and Creation-Consciousness for the Future of Disciples Theology and Practice

The doctrine of creation affirms that God's work of creation is a work of love and that God will bring that work to completion and fulfillment. Creation and new creation come together in eschatological hope for Christian faith. Jesus, the creative Word and image of the invisible God, loves the world of God's love. Disciples of Jesus love the world of God's love. Recognizing the distortions in the created order, Disciples of Jesus work on behalf of the goodness of God's created order—economically, ecologically, relationally. They do this in the mode of faith and trust in the God who is maker of heaven and earth. They do this in the belief and trust that the redemption of God's creation through Jesus Christ is cosmic as well as human. They do this in the belief and trust that the God who "in the beginning created" and saw that it was "very good" maintains that commitment to creation and will see it through to its consummation and fulfillment in the creation of a new heaven and a new earth, which will be very good. They do this in the belief and trust that leaves the "how" of the eschatological fulfillment to the mysteries of God, just as they leave the "how" of the creation "in the beginning" to the mysteries of God. Knowing that the "why" and "wherefore" of creation belong to the journey of faith, they, as God-imaged and God-reconciled creatures, will not abandon the creation but will love it with self-limiting, other-affirming, and future-opening power. Disciples of Jesus will delight in the creation, will learn to live in relationship with it in humility, and will seek to live with the whole inhabited world in a just, restrained, and loving way. They will renew their commitment to the Hebrew prophetic tradition and the power-subversive vision of Jesus.

Why the Creator? Why the creation? Why the response of faith and hope? Christian faith answers: "Love. We live in a God-created, God-loved, God-visited, God-purposed, God-redeemed, God-with-us-to-consummation world."

SECTION III

The Church

13

The Church as Sacrament of Human Wholeness

Sharon E. Watkins and Harold Keith Watkins

The Context for a Practical Ecclesiology

The early years of the twenty-first century provide a challenging context for describing the religious community that understands itself to be the body of Christ. Religions around the world have taken on new life as strong, partisan communities, determined to establish their respective ways of life as normative not only for their own adherents but for the larger society within which these communities exist. In the United States, this tendency is evident among some segments of conservative Christianity that are prepared to do everything possible, including revising the United States Constitution, in order to require all citizens of the nation to live according to a certain understanding of biblical law. In other parts of the world, a similar purpose is expressed by the determination of some to establish Islamic religious law as the one guide to life in every aspect of a nation's culture. Ironically, the strong move toward uniformity results in division and conflict.

In this larger context, that particular part of the body of Christ known as the Christian Church, (Disciples of Christ), discovers its own challenges. A church whose very roots include championing Christian unity for the sake of mission finds that successful mission, in the form of a new church movement, challenges the very sense of unity. Having discerned a calling to welcome new congregations and having faithfully pursued that goal, Disciples in the early years of the twenty–first century find themselves an increasingly diverse community. North American Disciples now speak Spanish and Korean, Samoan and French Creole, as well as English. Many worship in a distinctly charismatic manner compared to the reserve that has been characteristic of the community in its majority Anglo manifestation for over a century. The greater diversity leads to questions about the true nature of Disciples identity. Concern is expressed about how to maintain a vision of wholeness and oneness in the midst of such diverse expressions of faith. As in the larger context, a desire for consistency, order, and truth compete with a lived experience of randomness, radical diversity, and relativity.

This struggle—both for the CCDC and for people of faith around the world—to find the appropriate interweaving of unity and diversity, of oneness and particularity, at times threatens the very fabric of the communities involved.

The Vision of a New Humanity

Though Christian communities sometimes participate in the world's brokenness, surely this is not God's intent. One of the major themes in the biblical prophets is that God is bringing the nations together in a new world of peace and justice. A similar vision has inspired prophets throughout Christian history. Reform movements of earlier eras often have included the intention of working to complete the transformation of the world through the good news of Jesus Christ.

This passion was one of the inspirations of early leaders of the Disciples movement. Alexander Campbell's journal, *The Millennial Harbinger,* had two purposes: to destroy sectarianism, and to introduce "that political and religious order of society called THE MILLENNIUM, which will be the consummation of that ultimate amelioration of society proposed in the Christian Scriptures."[1] The restoration of the church in its apostolic and united form was, in Campbell's understanding, the final step in the completion of God's design, and his movement and new journal would be dedicated to accomplishing this purpose.

Through the early use of the metaphor "citizens of God's kingdom" and the later use of the term "brotherhood," Disciples have identified their movement as part of a renewal of God's purposes for humankind. They have sought to express their calling to live in this world as though the reality of God's world already applied. They have endeavored to embody a message of liberty, health, opportunity, and fulfillment—for individuals and society at large. This desire to participate in and be a sign of a reality that only God can bring in its fullness can be described as sacramental. This sense of church joined with a passion for the unity of humankind suggests that, for Disciples, church functions as a sacrament of human wholeness.

Biblical Foundations

A concern for human wholeness appears throughout the scriptures. Its foundation is the vision of well-being expressed by the Hebrew word *shalom* and its Greek equivalent *eirene.* Both are commonly translated as "peace," but their meaning is more complex than our English word indicates. These terms refer to completeness, fullness, health, well-being, and prosperity.[2] They are perhaps best translated by the English word *wholeness*. In many biblical passages, these words describe a covenantal relationship that results in harmony with God, with other people, and with creation itself—a world filled with the intimate knowledge of God, where even the wolf and the lamb can live together; the leopard can lie down with the kid;...and they will not hurt or destroy (Isa. 11:6, 9).

Visionaries, the biblical prophets do not look at the world through rose-colored glasses. They are hopeful realists. They understand that the world is broken, in need of repentance and repair. Yet they hope that, by God's power, the world can mend. "The LORD has anointed me; / he has sent me to bring good news to the oppressed, / to bind up the brokenhearted, / to proclaim liberty to the captives, / and release to the prisoners; / to proclaim the year of the LORD's favor,... / to comfort all who mourn" (Isa. 61:1–2). The world is broken and sick, but God is at work to heal and restore.

This prophetic witness lies at the heart of Jesus' message and ministry as portrayed in the gospels. According to Luke, Jesus began his ministry by proclaiming Isaiah's ancient vision of wholeness. In his home synagogue, Jesus preached Isaiah 61 and said that he had come to free people from the political oppression and physical distress keeping them captive to fear and poverty and condemning them to a life of mistrust and separation (Lk. 4:17–19). The combined witness of the synoptic gospels is that Jesus built his movement on the conviction that the reign, the commonwealth, of God was springing forth into history precisely in the midst of a people beaten down and torn apart by the unrelenting pressures of economic and political globalization. Healing the sick and exorcising the demonized, Jesus restored fearful and marginalized people to full participation in community. Marshaling the seemingly meager resources of the community gathered, he showed his disciples that when the community shares its resources, everyone can be fed, with fish and loaves to spare. The logic of sharing, of community, of the commonwealth of God, stood in stark contrast to the logic of Roman imperial power built on military might, social status, and economic concentration in the hands of an elite few. The reign, the commonwealth, of God would transform the political, economic, and spiritual structures of the world, giving the vast numbers at the bottom of society hope, an opportunity to live life abundantly, to become the complete, whole people God intended them to be.

As recent scholarship has shown,[3] Paul and others in the early Christian movement kept faith with Jesus' prophetic vision of human wholeness. In one of the boldest statements in the New Testament letters, Paul discusses the connection of Jews and the Law with Christians and the gospel. After asserting that the foundation for both communities is faith in God, Paul claims that Christ has broken down the wall that divides people according to class, gender, social status, and political condition (Eph. 2:11–14, Gal. 3:28). The Christians reflected in the letters were struggling to build and maintain communities that overcame the fracturing, death-dealing pressures of everyday life in the Roman Empire, to realize the different kind of life that was possible by the power of God that raised Jesus from the dead, a life consistent with the teachings of Jesus who had organized everything around love of God and neighbor.

God's intention expressed in the prophetic search for shalom, Jesus' proclamation and the apostles' teaching, is that the human community, indeed the cosmos, though broken and dying, can and should live in peace, in wholeness.

The Church as Sacrament of Human Wholeness

Much of the Bible is focused on life in community. In the ancient world, personhood was held in a tight web of social connections defined by family and kin group, understood to stretch into the indefinite past and future. To be a person was to be fully integrated into the family and the community. This communal understanding of personhood accounts for the significance of the promise to Abraham that lies at the heart of much biblical tradition. God's promise in Genesis 12—"I will make of you a great nation"—is simultaneously personal and national. God's covenantal relationship with Abraham will be fully realized in the "great nation" that his family will become. Finally, however, the covenantal promise will transcend the boundaries of individual, family, and nation. "I will bless you…so that you will be a blessing… In you all the families of the earth shall be blessed" (Gen. 12:2–3). By the surprising logic of God, the promise to this man and his family will finally have universal implications. The purpose of the promise to the family of Abraham is the blessing of the nations.[4]

By the time of Jesus, Abraham's descendants had spread throughout the Mediterranean world. The name of the place where these local communities practiced their shared religious activities was the synagogue, "the coming together." Though Christians eventually came to distinguish their religious actions from those conducted by the synagogue, they kept the corporate character, simply adopting a different Greek word, *ekklesia,* "gathering," to replace the word *synagogue.*

For Christians, the *ekklesia* is the religious sphere where people meet God through Jesus Christ, are formed in their faith, and move toward the "measure of the stature of the fullness of Christ." As with Abraham's family, the very human community of the church has implications for the larger human community. The word *sacrament* helps express the church's role in signaling the fullness of life that is possible through faith in Christ.

Sacraments are of the same genre as symbols. They are enacted words or highly stylized processes with these qualities: (1) They refer to and affirm a reality that is greater than themselves and usually beyond our full access;

(2) they convey a portion of that greater reality so that people involved in the sacramental event experience something of that toward which the sacrament points; (3) they provide a way for transforming ordinary reality so that it conforms to the greater reality.

To speak of the church as a sacrament means that its concreteness as a social form allows us to perceive a reality that is greater than the world we experience now. That reality is the new order, which is trans-historical, but at the same time is a pattern of life that breaks into our world. The Jesus movement itself was the beginning of the church as sacrament, but on Pentecost Sunday it came into fuller form. People experienced forgiveness and received a new spiritual power. Ethnic separations were overcome as people heard the gospel in their own languages. New communities were formed in which participants experienced great joy. A new spirit of generosity emerged that bound people together despite the fact that they represented different social classes. For a while, at least, the people "who were being saved" could believe that the holy commonwealth, God's empire, had already broken in upon them. Through the church, it was God's government, not Rome, that now ordered their lives and gave them a foretaste of so much more.

The Fragility of the Church as Sacrament

Beginning in the New Testament, and continuing throughout history, the sacramental character of the church has often been obscured by its social character as a human community. Someone once said that the church consists not of two qualities but three: the divine, the human, and the all-too-human, with the last one usually predominating. Much of the New Testament was written to address the practices that diminished the clarity of the church's function as a foretaste of the holy commonwealth in which all people would come to the fullness of life. These destructive qualities can be summarized as follows: (1) the loss of the divine point of reference; (2) contradictions within the community's life; and (3) and false relations with the larger society.

Disciples have struggled with the first. In order for the church to be the sacrament it was meant to be, the vision of God's new order needs to remain clear. It needs to remain clear that it is, in fact, God's commonwealth that should be represented in the all-too-human community of the church.

Disciples, seeking an image of church that would honor both divine and human characteristics, chose "covenant." In biblical covenant, God initiates. The people respond. They either accept God's terms or they are out of covenant. The people are in covenant with each other as they attempt to honor in community their mutual allegiance to God.

For twentieth–century Disciples, the notion of covenant was appealing. They were just learning to think of themselves as one "church" consisting of many congregations. They needed a way of understanding themselves that honored their common life as "church" under God's authority without forcing them into a model of church that would require obedience to human hierarchy. So the Preamble to the Design of the CCDC says: "We rejoice in God, maker of heaven and earth, and in the covenant of love which binds us to God and one another."

In the paragraphs that followed, the Design (until the amendments adopted in 2005)[5] spelled out the relationship between the connecting tissue of covenant and the important counterweight of the free and voluntary manner in which the various expressions of the church join together in this covenant. However, as Joe Jones observed in his 1980 theological analysis of the Design[6], the emphasis on "free and voluntary" led to a distinctly unbiblical notion of covenant as fundamentally a human choice about belonging. The sense that the covenant was God's was missing. The understanding that we are together because God first reached out to us offering us the opportunity to be a foretaste of God's commonwealth in the world faded behind an insistence on the primacy of human freedom and agency.

The second breakdown in the sacramental character of the church is the maintenance of a way of life that violates the reality the church, as sacrament, is called to represent. Too often churches become toxic institutions instead of being places where people experience the wholeness of the transforming love of God and the emergence of hope and acceptance with one another.

In the New Testament, the Corinthian community compromised its sacramental character by bringing divisions of class, wealth, and social status into their life together as church. Corinthian Christians shunned the egalitarian sacred reality to which their sacramental community should have pointed, and instead brought the divisions and hierarchies of the imperial world into their gatherings. The way of life they maintained violated the divine reality they were called to express: "When you come together as a church (*ekklesia*), I hear that there are divisions among you... When you come together, it is not really to eat the Lord's supper... For all who eat and drink without discerning the body [i.e., the commonwealth community], eat and drink judgment against themselves" (1 Cor. 11:18, 20, 29).

With New Testament teachings such as these firmly in mind, Disciples have had a deep-seated passion to embody Christian unity within their expressions of church. As Disciples' European forebears came across the Atlantic Ocean to establish communities in North America, they became aware that doctrinal divisions among them seemed less relevant than they had on European shores. Their plea was to be "Christians only."

Yet, Disciples have been unable to maintain unity. Two major splits and other minor ones have marked the brief history of our movement. Disciples, desiring to be a sacrament of human wholeness, a sign of God's commonwealth already breaking into this world, often have not participated well in the divine reality we seek to represent. Moreover, new challenges keep appearing. In the early days of the twenty-first century, one of our greatest challenges is to maintain a deep sense of unity and community as ethnic and cultural diversity increases among us.

Third, the church can compromise its sacramental character by allying itself too closely with an ethnic, racial, political, or economic entity. From slavery, to European colonialism in Africa and Asia, to Nazism, to apartheid and ethnic cleansing, church leaders have legitimated regimes that give political and economic power and privilege to some at the expense of others. Less dramatically, but no less importantly, participation in twenty-first–century North American structures of white privilege continues to distort the church's character as sacrament of human wholeness. Additionally, North American Christians face a particularly dangerous temptation to bless, implicitly or explicitly, the values of economic globalization and consumerist culture.

Silence in the face of injustice and active support of destructive ideologies compromise the sacramental character of the church as sign of God's commonwealth. Either one mars the gospel vision of unity in diversity, of a common table where all are welcome.

Disciples have always understood the tight connection between internal life and external witness. Indeed, the longing for Christian unity has not been for the sake of unity alone, but for the sake of mission and witness. Disciples have appealed to John 17:20–21, in which Jesus prays for the unity of generations of followers "that the world may believe." When the church is divided, its witness is divided. The sacramental character of participating already in God's new reality and being an inviting sign of that reality to the world is lost. The church becomes just one more human institution seeking its own survival instead of a seeking to offer a joyful foretaste of universal shalom.

Recovering the Church as Sacrament

The challenges to the church's sacramental nature also point the way to recovering the church's capacity to function as a sacrament of human wholeness. A first element of renewal will be to claim a strong theological foundation for the church's work in the world. The church today needs to recover its awareness of God's sacred presence in all of life. It needs to craft its proclamation and action to counteract the divisive ideologies of our time. It needs to proclaim a vision of human life that allows individuals to mature, communities to be humane and health-giving, and nations to live together constructively. For Disciples this means continuing to work on an understanding of God's initiating role in the covenant shared within the church. A small move in the right direction came with changes to the Design adopted by the General Assembly in 2005, which reinforce "covenant" language and drop the phrase "free and voluntary" in at least two instances.[7] The ongoing challenge to Disciples will be to live into the consequences of knowing that our ecclesial freedom is tempered by a responsibility to shape our church life so that it intentionally begins to embody a foretaste of God's new order.

Second, the renewal of the sacramental life of our church includes congregations once again becoming places where people actually expect an encounter with the living God, where church-goers experience the wholeness of forgiveness, healing, renewal of hope, and power for life. This emphasis on congregations as places where people experience wholeness is especially important in a time when human life and human society are so fractured. People need to experience a love that affirms their being even as it offers them the possibility of new life and forgiveness for all that needs to be put aside.

Furthering the recovery of church as sacrament of human wholeness will involve congregations and other expressions of the church developing ways to work through their own internal conflicts. Christians cannot claim to represent the redeemed and reconciled people of God when they divide over matters of faith, ecclesial practice, morality, and public policy. The point is not that Christians should never disagree, but that the church should model for the world how to disagree on important matters and still come to a common table for shared sustenance, a celebration now of God's commonwealth that we seek to represent.

To address the third challenge, it will be necessary to develop theologically appropriate ways for the covenanted body of Christ to be connected with the larger processes and structures of society. For Disciples, this represents a considerable challenge. Growing theological, cultural, and generational diversity makes it increasingly difficult to know how to relate to the larger community and world. A tradition, shared with other mainline denominations, of being "in sync" with the larger culture, is no longer the experience in the early twenty-first–century church. There is no consensus on what stance to take with regard to social and political issues of the day.

Yet, Disciples declare that their vision is to be a church marked by its passion for justice. They list among their early twenty-first–century priorities the dismantling of systemic racism within the church. From within the Hispanic community come calls for the church to walk in solidarity with undocumented workers. A discernment process on the proper role of lesbians and gays in church leadership in the light of the gospel continues with great passion. There is a strong desire for consensus to be reached on these and other issues; however, the sacramental character of the church will be determined less by the opinion finally reached than on the manner in which the church carries out its discernment.

Being a place of wholeness even in the midst of disagreement best represents the Disciples original sense that unity is for the sake of mission. It best represents the way to already embody a taste of God's emerging reality of wholeness so the world may see and believe.

On the way toward consensus, churches will need to further correct their relationship with the world around them by looking beyond their own walls and concerns, by including the entire world and all of its concerns in their prayers, including the prayers at the communion table. In sermons, healing services, and the offering of the peace of Christ to one another in worship, Christians minister to the world.

Churches can begin to express wholeness by becoming communities in which people study and debate the ethical and moral issues of our time, seeking at all times to discover points of view that transcend the political and cultural divisions that often inhibit discussion and understanding.

Churches can advocate the values that they believe to be critical to the well-being of people and the world, and at the same time they can identify those aspects of life both within and outside of the church that fall short of those ideals.

Churches can encourage their members to become active participants in public life, using their energies and professional capabilities to bring this world into closer conformity with the holy commonwealth that Jesus proclaimed.

Churches can develop ministries of their own that address the needs of people in the world today.

Churches can stand with their members who take public leadership.

Churches can witness against the ephemeral values of consumer culture and call our members to primary allegiance to the communal, long-term values of God's commonwealth.

The Hard Choice

Churches, including the CCDC, have a constructive role to play in the world. Churches are to be places where people experience, at least for brief moments, the world that God intends for all people to enjoy. If the church is to be this kind of sacramental presence, it needs to move forward with clear purpose and strong resolve. Writing about the decline of mainline Protestantism a generation ago, Dean M. Kelley noted that in times past churches had often been "independent variables," able to determine or modify the cultural climate and value system within which they existed. Again in our generation, the churches have to decide whether they are dependent or independent variables. Do they respond and react to what is going on around them, always in a defensive posture? Or are churches capable of acting on their own?

The hard choice that churches are called upon to make is whether to live in ways that are consistent with and subservient to contemporary culture, or to live in ways that proclaim and exhibit a way of life that conforms to the holy commonwealth that Jesus proclaimed. If the church is to be a sacrament of human wholeness, then the latter choice—difficult as it may be—is the one that must be taken.

14

Baptism and the Disciples of Christ

THOMAS F. BEST

Introduction

Baptism is central to the life of the churches and to the ecumenical movement. The "mutual recognition of baptism" is often identified as the basis on which churches, even when they have serious differences, can still work together toward visible unity and offer common witness and service in the world. Thus it is baptism, however differently it is understood and practiced by different churches, that enables the quest for Christian unity.

The term "mutual recognition" has become so familiar that many forget the profound truth that lies behind it: in baptism God, through Christ and in the power of the Spirit, calls men and women who respond in faith into Christ's one body, the church. *Christ's* action is primal, and prior to any claim or action of any church. We are baptized in a church, but into Christ; we belong to Christ, we are his and no other's. This has consequences: churches that reject baptism performed in another church are rejecting not only that church, but Christ himself. In recognizing baptism churches admit Christ's prior claim upon every believer; they limit their own sovereignty in recognition of Christ's action in baptism, even baptism done in ways other than their own. Baptism is *actively subversive* of the divisions among the churches.

But baptism itself is being actively discussed today. One focus among Disciples is the admission of children, not yet baptized, to the Lord's table. Other discussions are taking place in other churches. As "cultural Christianity" gives way to intentional faith commitment and church membership, a seismic shift is taking place in baptismal theology and practice, with adult baptism emerging as the dominant practice, of a surprisingly wide range of churches.[1]

Some churches are testing the current baptismal consensus: the Coptic Orthodox Church has been known to "re"baptize even other Orthodox Christians; Quakers and Kimbanguists, for very different reasons, do not use water; some churches follow one New Testament practice and baptize "in the name of Jesus" only; some persons in many churches ask whether the classic biblical language of "Father, Son and Holy Spirit" is necessary today.

Thus baptism is an area of growth for Disciples and ecumenically today. In what follows I review the understanding and practice of baptism among Disciples, noting especially what we have gained from our encounters with the liturgical and ecumenical movements, and then consider several areas for future growth in our baptismal understanding and practice.

Baptism and the Disciples of Christ

Early Convictions

Disciples have always considered baptism central to the faith and the church. For Alexander Campbell, baptism belonged to the "ecumenical consensus" of his day on the core "commemorative institutions" of the faith: "These are Christian Baptism, the Lord's Day, and the Lord's Supper."[2] Walter Scott is said to have baptized more than ten thousand persons in the Western Reserve.

Baptism was to be done by immersion, as Jesus was baptized "in" the Jordan by John the Baptist (Alexander Campbell, in his edition of the New Testament, famously translated the Greek *baptizein* as "immerse"). As Restorationists, Disciples knew that baptism was for the remission of sins—and thus only for penitent, professing believers, "adults" old enough "to know what they are doing." It denoted justification by grace alone: for all the emotion of the frontier Revivals, Campbell nevertheless insisted that "in baptism we are passive in everything but in giving our consent." For those who associated infant baptism with the "state churches" of Europe, adult baptism was also a way of distinguishing the new church, in the new world, from both the state and most of the surrounding churches.

"Re"-baptism prevailed in the early generations (though Barton W. Stone had not insisted upon it as the sole possible mode of baptism) as a way of "completing one's obedience to Christ." This contrasted with Disciples' practice of open admission to the Lord's table (which was sometimes extended to persons not baptized by immersion). This spirit of ecumenical generosity limited our early preference for "re"-baptism, and by about 1900 most Disciples readily admitted Christ's action in forms of baptism other than our own.

Current Perspectives

Disciples today hold a range of views about baptism—as about almost everything else—but the following reflects, I believe, a current consensus.

Baptism is a public act of the church in which a believer, confessing his or her sin, responds to God's initiative for salvation through Jesus Christ and is brought into the church. Following instruction, and normally during Sunday worship, the believer is immersed once in water in the name of the Father, Son, and Holy Spirit. Baptism is performed before the congregation in a baptistry in the church building (exceptionally the "baptistry" may be a flowing stream or lake); following baptism the believer member is introduced to the church as a new member.

Theologically baptism involves participation in the death of Christ, a washing for regeneration, forgiveness of sins, receiving of the Holy Spirit, incorporation into the body of Christ, and it is a sign of God's sovereignty in the world.[3] It is a sacrament, in that the water is a physical sign and expression of God's grace for the believer, the church, and the world. Baptism is into the whole church and not just the Disciples "part" of it. Its consequences are personal and social: through baptism the believer is incorporated into the church, and called to a life of witness and service. Disciples' "adult" baptism has been done starting at about age thirteen. Many congregations practice a dedication of young children to inspire their parents to raise them within the faith and to embed them within the life of the church.

Disciples baptismal *practice* usually includes the following: proclamation of scripture; personal repentance; personal profession of faith in Jesus Christ as Lord and Savior; an invocation of the Holy Spirit; submersion in water; a Trinitarian reference (see Mt. 28:19); and a welcome into the church universal, the Christian Church (Disciples of Christ), and the congregation. Ordained clergy normally perform Disciples' baptisms (and thus is not as distinctive liturgically as communion, with its prominent role also for elders).

Disciples owe much to the liturgical renewal movement, with its recovery of classic patterns of baptismal thought and practice. Since 1960 we have grown into a more careful preparation of candidates, more stress upon the believer's entry into the faith community of "Christians of every time and place";[4] modest expansions of the service, for example by a blessing of the water; a stronger expression of the Spirit's role both in baptism and as the believer continues to grow "into the likeness of Christ"; and renewed interest in baptismal "sponsors," to set the believer within a stronger framework of spiritual support. And not least, there is a fresh interest in the remembrance and renewal of baptism, within regular worship or in connection with special worship events.

Disciples are also indebted to the ecumenical movement, with its sharing of baptismal thought and practice across confessional divides. Churches Uniting in Christ (formerly the Consultation on Church Union) encourages Disciples to explore new baptismal options.[5] The WCC Faith and Order text *Baptism, Eucharist and Ministry* (BEM) has reminded us of baptism's strong social as well as personal dimension,[6] and that baptism, as a sacrament of unity, is unrepeatable. This view was affirmed in the Disciples' official response to BEM, which has consolidated our official rejection of "re"-baptism (though exceptions have been known, for pastoral rather than theological reasons).

Global Perspectives

Disciples too were stirred by the missionary impulses of the nineteenth century, and planted new churches around the world. The Congo, South Africa, Argentina, Paraguay, Puerto Rico, Mexico, New Zealand, Australia, the Philippines, India, Thailand: all received the Restorationist gospel, with its baptismal understanding and practice.

In many places these churches have retained their earlier identity and baptismal practice. But the elements of this are configured differently: the Church of Christ in New Zealand combines a baptismal theology stressing personal salvation, with Praise worship practices; the Church of Christ in Australia combines Praise services with a nuanced stress on adult baptism and a lively sense of the church's social witness.[7] Baptism for Central and Latin American churches (Argentina, Paraguay, Puerto Rico, Mexico) stresses individual salvation and a fervent confession of sin, often leading to a prophetic social witness.

Perspectives from United Churches

Other Disciples, exercising their "ecumenical principle" in a radical way, have entered church unions—again, with varying results for baptism. In the Congo, where the Disciples form a distinct *Communauté* within the *Eglise du Christ au Congo,* the original pattern of adult baptism remains. Elsewhere union has meant the integration of divided churches to form a single, new church.[8] Such unions unite baptismal practices too; since church unions embrace diversity,[9] many unions (for example, with Disciples and Presbyterians) include both adult and infant baptism as norms. Disciples now within the United Reformed Church (in the UK) experience this diversity as part of *normal* church life. (Many feel that "their" way of baptism is "better" but no longer reject other forms, having seen them practiced regularly in their own congregation.)

This has put the rite of baptism, whether adult or infant, within the context of the believer's *lifelong growth into Christ,* and thus encouraged the reconciliation of diverse baptismal theologies and practices. Within the Church of North India, Disciples could accept infant baptism because the Confirmation Service, at age thirteen, stresses so clearly the believer's personal confession of sin and acceptance of the Lordship of Christ. The reconciliation of baptismal practices happens also in united congregations, formed by members of still-separated denominations. The United Reformed Church is involved in some four hundred such "Local Ecumenical Partnerships" in England, and this too forms part of Disciples' experience of baptism.

In summary, Disciples have a close relationship to baptism. Adult baptism is strongly our norm, but we were early in our reluctance to "re"-baptize and through united churches and united congregations many Disciples worldwide have gained a greater understanding of infant baptism.

Baptism and the Disciples' Ecumenical Future

Let us look now toward the future: What challenges confront us through baptism today? How will new currents and convictions in theology, liturgy, ethics, psychology, pedagogy, and our ecumenical experience affect our baptismal life? What questions do these pose to our baptismal understanding and practice?

The Liturgical Dimension: Memory and Meaning

A first point relates to the liturgical dimension of Disciples' identity.[10] Our relationship to baptism can be enriched by recent liturgical work on the themes of memory and meaning.[11] This has identified a three-fold structure for significant human experiences: they are *anticipated,* when they lie in our future; *experienced,* as they are happening in our present; and *remembered,* once they lie in our past. We move from anticipation, through experience, into remembering. Experience is the process of converting anticipation into memories; the present is the point at which the future becomes the past, when what is anticipated becomes what is remembered.

In this process we are active participants in our own experience: in anticipating an event, we participate through expectation and hope; in experiencing it, we participate through direct engagement with what is happening; in remembering it, we participate through memory. As much as touch and taste, memory is a *sense;* unlike those senses, it relates us not to the present but to our past, to our own experience. Through memory, we bring past events again into the present, making them effective once again.

Let us consider liturgy as the *memory* of the Christian community, the "sense" through which the church, week by week, grasps the events on which it is founded and experiences them ever anew. In worship we read the scriptures, testifying to the mighty facts of Christ's life, teaching, death, and resurrection; we pray prayers as Jesus taught us, bringing to God our praise and our intercessions; we act most explicitly "in remembrance of him" in the breaking of bread and the pouring out of the fruit of the vine.

In baptism, women and men are brought into new life in Christ and into Christ's body, the church. But baptism is related to memory in a special way, for baptism is one of the few liturgical acts that one does not personally repeat: the power of the Lord's supper lies in its repetition each Lord's Day (as Disciples well know); the power of baptism lies in its uniqueness, its happening for each of us once for all. Yet faith lives from repetition, as in worship we remember and reinforce Christ's saving acts. Thus it is imperative that, from time to time, we actively remember our own baptism, allowing the memory of that unique event to bring it again into the present, affirming our belonging to Christ and to his one body, the church.

This can be done whenever a baptism occurs, but also when a new member joins the congregation by transfer, or on other occasions. Most powerfully, it can be done in the service at the Lord's table, thus linking the two great sacraments of salvation. (Here the Lutherans especially have much to teach us.) The question to our Disciples baptismal services is clear: Do they encourage such remembering of our own baptism, and develop it as a creative force for renewal within our church?

The Ecumenical Dimension: Koinonia

A second point is the *ecumenical dimension* of Disciples identity, meaning both our historic drive to seek the unity of the church, and what we have learned through encounters with other churches. Especially significant for baptism is the ecumenical notion of *koinonia ecclesiology.*

Here the New Testament background is foundational. In wider Greco-Roman culture, *koinonia* indicated sharing or participating in a social group or set of values; the early Christian community adopted the term to denote their belonging to Christ, and therefore to one another.[12] In the New Testament, *koinonia* and its cognates *koinoneo* and *koinonos* are used some thirty-five times. The terms often refer to sharing or participating in *spiritual things* (the gospel, Phil. 1:15; faith, Philem. 6; Christ's body and blood, 1 Cor. 10.16; "the fellowship of his Son," 1 Cor. 1:9; the "communion of the Holy Spirit," 2 Cor. 13:13; the divine nature, 2 Pet. 1:4; "the glory to be revealed," 1 Pet. 5:1; sufferings, either those of other Christians, 2 Cor. 1:7, Heb. 10:33, or, strikingly, of Christ, Phil. 3:10, 1 Pet. 4:13). But they also refer to sharing in *material things*: Paul employs the term in speaking of his collection for the "saints" in Jerusalem (Rom. 12:13; 15:26–27; 2 Cor. 8:4; 9:13; also 1 Tim. 6:18); and more generally to sharing (cf. Gal. 6:6; Phil. 4:15; Heb. 2:14; 13:16).[13]

Koinonia, then, points both to common faith and participation in Christ, and to prophetic witness and service to other Christians and to the world. Thus it has helped to integrate Faith and Order (and other ecumenical) work against the classical *theological* issues dividing the church, with work on *social* sources of division among the churches.[14] It has encouraged joint work between Faith and Order and other forces, such as the WCC's program on Justice, Peace, and Creation, which addresses issues of justice from a Christian ecumenical perspective.[15] Ecumenically it points to the *quality of relationships* among Christians and churches, calling for these to reflect our common participation in Christ and our mutual support in situations of spiritual and material need.

In relation to baptism, *koinonia* says: the Christian community entered through baptism is marked by sharing in spiritual, but equally in material, things a community that both prays together and does not rest until justice is done and all have enough to eat. This poses questions to Disciples baptism: Do our baptismal services say enough about the *kind* of community we are entering through baptism, about its social and justice dimensions as well as its personal "benefits" for the believer?

A further point in this connection: despite the affirmations of koinonia ecclesiology, we are still divided. The painful paradox of baptism is that it brings us into the one church, but also into *one of* the churches, into a particular denomination with all its relationships (some functional, some dysfunctional) with other churches. We are baptized into the unity of the church but also into the divisions of the churches.[16] Do our baptismal liturgies dare to reveal this irony, and remind us also of the scandal of division? Do they show how baptism is a resistance movement against the divisions of the churches? Do they include an appeal for the newly baptized, as part of their Christian vocation, to do everything possible to work against the separation of the churches?

The Ecumenical Dimension: Baptism and Lifelong Growth into Christ

A third point arises from the recent ecumenical emphasis on baptism, whether adult or infant, as a decisive moment within a process of lifelong growth into Christ. Already present in BEM,[17] and experienced especially in church unions incorporating both forms of baptismal practice, this notion has helped a wide range of churches recognize a similar *intention* in the practice of other churches, even if baptismal events happen there at a different age and stage of life.[18] This in turn has encouraged a wider mutual recognition of divided baptismal theologies and practices. Let us look more closely at four consequences of seeing baptism as a decisive moment within the life of the believer as a whole.

Baptism and Faith

First, this enriches Disciples' understanding of the relation between *individual faith* (as expressed in the baptism of adults or professing believers) and the *faith of the Christian community* (as expressed in the baptism of infants). Recent ecumenical work stresses that the believer, however personal his faith may be, lives within a faith community:

> As Christians mature, their faith grows into deeper participation in the faith confessed, celebrated and witnessed to by the Christian community, both locally and worldwide, both now and through the ages. The believer's faith grows and deepens...and that faith discovers its congruence with the faith professed by the whole church throughout the ages... The faith which the believer comes to confess as his or her own is *that* faith and no other... The "we believe" of the Christian community and the "I believe" of personal commitment become one.[19]

Do our baptismal liturgies make plain this interaction between the faith of the believer and the faith of the community? Do they convey not only that the believer is responsible for his or her own faith, but also that the believer is embedded within a community of faith that tests and enriches the believer's faith?

Baptism and Eschatology

Second, this perspective reminds us of the *eschatological* aspect of baptism, which points toward a final goal. Baptism follows instruction in the faith but it is a beginning, not an end. It looks forward to personal growth in Christ (cf. 2 Cor. 3:18), and into the Christian community. In baptism Christ claims us for his own, bringing us "into Christ" and into the church; it holds the seed for our growth in this life, just as death, seen in the light of Christ's resurrection, holds the seed for our growth after this life. In baptism we remember our future,[20] learning who—and whose—we are.

This perspective also raises questions for Disciples baptism: Is its eschatological dimension sounded strongly enough in our baptismal services? Do they make plain the goal of the baptismal life: living all of life, for as long as we may live, under Christ's lordship and within his one body, the church? Do they point clearly enough to our final destiny in Christ when, after this life, we shall be united fully with him?

Baptism and Pedagogy

A third point is that of Christian education or *pedagogy*. Our focus on baptism as final, "once for all," may lead us to undervalue the lifelong growth into Christ that should follow. Perhaps we could learn from churches that speak of the *baptismal life* as a series of stages. If "infant baptism" churches practice confirmation at age thirteen, marking the passage into adolescence, could "adult baptism" churches practice baptismal renewal, marking the transition to a next stage of life, say at middle-age? (This would not seem so strange it if were set within a more regular liturgical practice of remembering and renewing baptism.)

The questions are clear: Do our baptismal liturgies take this pedagogical aspect seriously enough? Could they announce more clearly the baptismal goal of lifelong growth into Christ, and introduce the believer into a life of continuing Christian formation within the life of the church?

Baptism and Ethics

A fourth point arises from the relation of baptism to *ethics*. BEM has stressed that baptism motivates Christians "to strive for the realization of the will of God in all realms of life (Rom. 6:9ff.; Gal. 3:27–28; 1 Pet. 2:21–4:6)."[21] Recent ecumenical work has put this in a more radical way:

> It is not only that baptism has certain ethical implications for both personal and social life. More fundamentally, the meaning of

> Christian baptism and the nature of the ritual acts associated with it are *normative for Christian ethics itself,* and this in two ways. First, baptism as a life-long process of incorporation into Christ leads inevitably to an ethic rooted in and oriented towards life within community. Second, baptism as focused in the ritual action of dying and rising again leads inevitably to an ethic rooted in and oriented to a life of self-giving service. What does it mean that baptism is a process of initiation into a *community of faith*? And what does it mean that the metaphor for the central ritual act of baptism is that of *dying and rising to new life*? These questions point the way to understanding the basic nature and quality of Christian ethics.[22]

Again, this raises questions: Do Disciples' baptismal liturgies reveal the fundamentally social quality of the Christian life? Do they show that our "dying" in baptism is also a dying to self, a *kenosis* or self-giving, in order to rise again in service to others and the world? Are our *ethical* reflections grounded in the unique quality of the Christian life as rooted in a community entered into by an act of dying to self?

Finally, we might ask: What does baptism, as an act of dying and rising to new life, say about the church itself? Dare we speak of a *kenotic ecclesiology,* with the church judging its own behavior against the measure of Christ Jesus, who emptied himself that others might live? What if the church took that as its standard, rather than its own preservation as an institution? What would a *kenotic* ecclesiology look like?

Conclusion

Baptism is central to the faith and life of the Disciples of Christ, as to all churches. We have seen some examples of how baptism empowers and challenges us today. More than any other single thing, the frequent remembrance and renewal of baptism could strengthen our life as a church today, illumining it from within. In baptism Christ claims us for himself and for his church. May we claim baptism as a sacrament and source of unity, a blessing upon ourselves, our church, and our world.

15

The Lord's Supper

BELVA BROWN JORDAN AND STEPHANIE A. PAULSELL

As lifelong Disciples, the Lord's supper has shaped us, sometimes in ways we did not fully understand until we began talking to each other about this essay. Similar to many Disciples, we are full of memories of the Lord's supper: our childhood puzzlement over those hard little pellets that we passed on trays from hand to hand; communion meditations and invitations to the table we heard years ago in church or at camp or in a CWF circle meeting that we have carried in our hearts ever since; moments when the welcome we received at the table, as strangers in unfamiliar places, took our breath away. In this essay, we have tried to think with our Disciples ancestors about the stories of our faith, and our experiences of the Lord's supper in order to speak with gratitude about this central practice of Disciples life and with hope about how this meal—a meal that sets the standard for all our meals—teaches us to live with generosity and openness in a violent and troubled world.

Stephanie's first job in ordained ministry was as an associate minister in a university chapel, working with an Episcopal priest. He had created, from *The Book of Common Prayer,* an ecumenical Christian service of worship that gathered a community of students, faculty, staff, and people who lived in the surrounding neighborhood. Every Sunday, he celebrated the eucharist at an enormous, ornate altar that sat in the middle of a vast chancel. She assisted him, receiving the bread and wine from the people who brought it forth from the congregation, handing him neatly pressed linen napkins to wipe the lip of the cup, taking the leftover consecrated wine outside to pour on the ground, spreading out the bread for the birds. After a few weeks, once she had gotten the hang of things, the priest asked her to serve as the celebrant, the one who would lift the bread and cup toward heaven and offer God's gifts back to God.

The service was beautiful, the words at once simple and profound, and the gestures took account of the body in ways she found startling and moving. But she looked at that enormous altar and felt her Disciples ancestors rear up inside her. *Should I do this?* she wondered. Can *I do this?*

She went to her colleague and said, "In my tradition, we share a meal around a table, not a sacrifice at an altar. I don't know if I can lead the community in this ritual, because I don't really know what it means."

And he replied, in words she's never forgotten, words that set her Disciple soul at ease: "We don't do this because we know what it means. We do it in order to find out what it means."

True to our interpretive principle, Disciples have been finding out what the Lord's supper means, week in and week out, from our earliest beginnings. When the earliest Disciples read the New Testament, they heard an invitation to gather at the Lord's table every week. That invitation made a claim on them. While other Protestant communities held the Lord's supper only a few times a year, Disciples set the table every time they met for worship. Sharing the bread and cup each week, early Disciples believed they had lowered themselves through centuries of liturgical accretions and touched down on bedrock. The Lord's supper is a golden thread running through our history, linking us to one another across the boundaries of time and place.

If we could listen in on invitations to the table, communion meditations, and prayers over the bread and cup offered by countless lay leaders and ministers throughout our history, we would hear what the Lord's supper has meant in times of war and times of peace, times of fear and times of hope, on the frontier and in the city, and in communities around the world. Some themes would remain constant: "This is my body"; "This is my blood"; and, "Remember me." We would also hear some changes, perhaps especially in the way lay leaders and ministers extended the invitation to the table. In the early days, we might hear an invitation extended only to those who had received believer's baptism. In our day, we might hear an invitation to anyone seeking the presence of God. In the years in between, we would hear Disciples testing ways of articulating God's openness, God's hospitality. As Disciples moved out across the American frontier, and then out across the world, we would hear the invitation widening and widening.

What are we learning through gathering for the Lord's supper today? We live in a world the Disciples founders might have had a hard time imagining. Disciples are to be found, not only in the Southern and Midwestern United States, but also in Argentina, Paraguay, Mexico, Australia, New Zealand, the Congo, and Puerto Rico. Disciples are partners in United Churches in South Africa, Jamaica, Thailand, the Philippines, India, and Japan. Women ministers lead congregations; women elders invite the community to the table, say the words of institution, offer prayers over the bread and the cup.

Feminist theologians critique the notions of sacrifice undergirding many of our interpretations of the Lord's supper. Liberation theologians point to the table as a place of resistance to oppression and violence.

There are other, less promising differences between our world and the world in which our Disciples ancestors placed the Lord's supper at the center of their religious practice. The world in which we gather at the Lord's table is a world in which the birthplace of the CCDC has become the world's sole superpower, with the potential to do good, but also to inflict incredible harm. The forces of globalization have created lively communities in which people from many cultural and religious backgrounds intersect daily and in which Christianity has flourished in diverse forms. But these same forces have driven the wedge between rich and poor even deeper, benefiting some and leaving others far behind. The world in which we gather for the Lord's supper each week is a world marked by a crisis of hunger and violence.

Hunger. Violence. Community. Hope. The Lord's supper has everything to do with the embodied realities of our world. What can we learn from celebrating the Lord's supper in these days?

The Lord's Supper as Ordinance

Alexander Campbell and Barton Stone both understood the Lord's supper as an ordinance, a practice instituted by Jesus and faithfully continued—weekly, according to Campbell's exegesis of Acts 2:42; Acts 20:7; 1 Corinthians 6:20; and 1 Corinthians 16:1–2—by the earliest Christians. We gather for the Lord's supper each week, Campbell insisted, because God desires it. We are obliged to celebrate the Lord's supper each week, Campbell wrote, "not in such a manner as our own inventions suggest, but by such means as Christ himself has prescribed to us."[1]

According to Campbell and Stone, what did Christ prescribe? That only one loaf should be used for the supper; that it be unleavened; that his followers shape their weekly worship around this shared meal. For Barton Stone, the single, unleavened loaf was non-negotiable, not only because that was what Jesus used at the Last supper, but because of the emblematic meanings attached to the single, unleavened loaf. For Stone, using more than one loaf at the supper would obscure our view of Jesus' one, single body, suffering on the cross; and a leavened loaf would allow us to forget the roots of the Lord's supper in the Passover, during which only unleavened bread can be eaten. If Christ is *our* Passover, sacrificed for us, Stone reasoned, the bread we break at the Lord's table should reflect that truth. For Stone, too, leaven is emblematic in scripture of sincerity and truth. "How preposterous, then, to have the one loaf, which is to represent the body of Christ, leavened as if he were malicious and insincere!"[2]

Campbell and Stone's strict adherence to scriptural precedent for when and how the church should gather for the Lord's supper may strike us as literalistic, and their insistence on communion as an ordinance may seem dry. But their willingness to argue vigorously that the Lord's supper should be the center of the church's life, that Christians should participate in the supper when they gathered each week, and that the elements of the supper should reflect and reinforce the basic truths of the Christian faith has meant that we have inherited a powerful practice that has shaped our church and continues to shape us. Campbell and Stone's insistence on the Lord's supper as an ordinance we are obligated to observe every week has made it possible for us to find out what the Lord's supper means in times of plenty and times of want, in times of joy and times of fear, in all of the ordinary and extraordinary circumstances of our lives.

It is not enough to theorize about how Jesus Christ creates one body out of many, our Disciples ancestors insist. We must experience it, week after week, at the table to which he invites us; we must learn what communion has to teach us not only in the form of reasoned propositions but in our bodies. "Each disciple," Campbell wrote, "in handing the symbols to his fellow disciple, says, in effect, "You, my brother, once an alien, are now a citizen of heaven; once a stranger, are now brought home to the family of God. You have owned my Lord as your Lord, my people as your people. Under Jesus the Messiah we are one."[3] Sharing the Lord's supper, we acknowledge that God has placed us in each other's care. Passing the bread and the cup, we nurture our allegiance to all who eat and drink at the Lord's table the world over.

Belva remembers being taught by her parents that "handing the symbols" to her fellow disciples, even when she was too young to partake herself, was a form of participation in the Lord's supper, a ministry even a child can perform:

> Communion to me is an equalizing event that connects each of us with our diverse gifts. We go to the Table and serve each other. It is important to me to pass the trays. As a child before I was baptized and could take communion, my mother and father taught me that the way I participated was to serve the person next to me. I always felt I was a part of the event. Sharing was equalizing because we are welcome as we are and bring what we have as we partake of the holy meal.[4]

The practice of communion imparted to Belva a sense of the way the Lord's supper invites us all into the ministry of the church. Campbell and Stone knew that the practice of the Lord's supper was powerful in this way; they knew that the ritual bore knowledge about our relationship to one another and our relationship to God. Belva's childhood insight captures the way the riches of the Lord's supper unfold over time in and through our participation in it.

What Belva experienced as a child passing communion trays down the pew also reflects another key conviction of our Disciples ancestors, which

Alexander Campbell expressed in the form of a proposition: "All Christians are members of the house or family of God, are called and constituted a holy and royal priesthood, and may, therefore, bless God for the Lord's table, its loaf, and cup."[5] Serving at the table required simplicity and dignity, but it did not require an ordained minister. The "royal priesthood" of Christians, Campbell emphatically insisted, "may approach the Lord's table *without fear*."[6]

Disciples' commitment to the priesthood of all believers is a precious inheritance. There are a few Disciples churches that still practice a radical form of this commitment in relation to the Lord's supper. When it comes time for communion, the minister sits down in the congregation while lay leaders set the table, offer communion meditations, speak the words of institutions, and break the bread. In most congregations, the minister presides at the table along with elders who pray over the elements. Because of Disciples' commitment to the priesthood of all believers, insisted upon by Alexander Campbell and still embodied today in the meditations and prayers of our lay leaders, the Lord's table is one of the places in our church where a range of voices can be heard. It is a place where we cultivate our theological voices and struggle to find the right words to express what we have found out through gathering at the table week after week.

Seeking God's Presence at the Open Table

"Every time the disciples assemble around the Lord's table," Campbell wrote, "they are furnished with a new argument also against sin, as well as with a new proof of the love of God."[7]

Argument, proof: this is the language Alexander Campbell loved. He loved to argue his points from scripture and from philosophy, to pile up argument upon argument until he had built an edifice of reason in which to house the practices of the church. For Campbell, faith was "belief in testimony, specifically the apostolic testimony of the apostles,"[8] and he was at his most passionate when he was arguing for the substance of that testimony. Certainly, for Campbell, the Lord's supper was intended to "quicken us to God" and "to diffuse his love within us,"[9] but Campbell's intellectual, spiritual energies were most often marshaled toward arguments for the apostolic origins of the ordinance.

Other Disciples close to Campbell used a more intimate language when speaking of the Lord's supper. Robert Richardson, a confidante of Campbell's, a physician who taught science and served as an administrator at Bethany College, worried that his fellow Christians in the Restoration Movement overemphasized reason at the expense of mystery. "The mysteries of faith," he wrote in the *Millennial Harbinger*, "are more sublime than those of reason."[10] When Richardson spoke of the Lord's supper, he used the language of bliss, of love, of relationship. For Richardson, intimate communion with God "is the great end of religion."[11]

At the Christian Church in Bethany, Richardson, a layman, was known for his communion meditations, which he often based on passages from the Psalms. It is here at the table that Richardson said to the congregation, "that truths concentrate; that extremes meet, and the first and the last, the beginning and the end, are one."[12] He invited the congregation to the table "to approach the fountain of being and of blessedness, to drink of its ever-flowing streams of eternal life and joy,"[13] to deepen their life with God.

Richardson's words capture what we go to the table seeking, and what we find there, week after week: the presence of God, a God who knows our hungers and within whose economy there is enough for everyone to eat. We find there the generous presence of Jesus, who saw and met the hunger of the crowds who gathered around him and who knows that we also need to be fed in order to follow him into the places he would have us go. We find there Jesus' desire to meet all our hungers, physical and spiritual, and his confidence that these hungers can be met. We sense at the table the holiness of our most basic needs, and we remember that the God we seek is the God who sustains our lives in every moment of every day.

We Disciples often speak of the Lord's supper as a gathering of family. But "family" is never a closed circle at the table set by Jesus. Reading the gospels, it is impossible not to notice that whenever Jesus sits down to eat, he often does so with people others say should not be at the table—tax collectors, sinners— and he welcomes the woman who weeps over his feet at dinner and dries them with her hair. Jesus scandalizes others by sitting down to eat with the unwelcome. If we are to encounter Jesus at our communion tables, we must set tables from which no one is turned away. Ours is a family gathering that must always hope to be interrupted; a family gathering that must always *look* for ways of interrupting itself and making room for others. We must always be scooting down the pew, squeezing close to make room for new participants. We must always be ready to enlarge our circle. When we make room for everyone, we will find we have made room for God.

A Body Broken, a Body Restored

Barton Stone insisted on one loaf because he wanted the suffering body of Christ to be visible when we commune with one another and with God at the table. The one loaf representing Christ's one suffering body does not obscure that other bodies also suffer; in fact, it is a symbol that points us to the suffering of the world. We have found that those with firsthand, embodied knowledge of violence—survivors of rape and torture, human rights workers, those living in the midst of war-making—often cherish this Lord's supper for this very reason: it doesn't lie about the world. It tells the truth about the cruelty that is visited upon human bodies every day. We encounter that truth at the table in the presence of Jesus, who touches our hearts and makes them tender, as he did when he fell into step with the disciples on the road to Emmaus. When Jesus gathers us at his table, he places us in one another's care. He opens our eyes to the pain of others, and he nourishes us for the work of discipleship.

The Lord's supper makes visible the world's broken bodies and makes tangible their claim on us. There is no brokenness in our lives or in our world that cannot be placed on the table, alongside the bread and the cup. "In the awful mysteries of life and death," Robert Richardson said to the Christian Church in Bethany, "we hold communion."[14]

But the Lord's supper is not only about brokenness. Claudia Camp reminds us that the Lord's supper is also about the creation of the body, the gathering together from the north and south and east and west the body of Christ that is the church. "One of my wishes for communion," she remarks in a conversation about the Lord's supper with Disciples women, "is more language at the Table that affirms that the body is created by communion."[15]

This is our wish, too. An early Christian communion liturgy offers this prayer: "Just as this broken [loaf] was scattered over the hills [as grain], and, having been gathered together, became one; in like fashion may your church be gathered together from the ends of the earth into your kingdom."[16] The Lord's table gathers us, brings us into proximity with one another. The Disciples passing trays down the pews in Texas are being knit into one body with Disciples sharing the bread and the cup in the Congo. When we make Jesus' desire to gather us from every corner of the world more visible in our invitations to the table, our communion meditations, and our prayers, the Lord's supper nourishes us with the desire to be in closer communion with each other. The table becomes a bridge from which we reach out to one another. At the table, we remember a body broken. At the table, we create, week after week, a new body, the body of Christ, the church.

The power of the Lord's supper is to create wholeness from brokenness; its power to create a new body can be experienced on a global scale. It can also be experienced on a very local level, the level of the circumstances of our lives. When Belva served on the faculty of Lancaster Theological Seminary, she lived in a house on campus that she intentionally opened to the community as a convivial place for meals and good conversation. During Advent one year, the house was burglarized—and not just burglarized, but invaded, torn apart. Every closet and drawer wrenched open, every room ransacked.

Belva and a friend reordered and cleaned each room. It took hours and hours to reclaim those rooms. When they had finished, Belva knew what to do. Calling upon the Holy Spirit to help in the work of reclaiming her living space, she brought out her grandmother's worn and patched cotton tablecloth, a tablecloth at least seventy-five years old. She and her friend spread it out on the kitchen table, laid out napkins and silverware, and ordered in a meal of Chinese food. When the food arrived, they prayed together, "broke bread" together, and experienced together the healing spirit of Christ. In the presence of God, Belva's grandmother, and every woman who had touched that tablecloth, they knew God's mending mercy. They prayed for all who needed healing, including the one who had violated their home.

We come to the table each week to encounter that healing spirit. We spread out the tablecloth, we set out the bread and the wine, we hand one another simple elements that have, for us, as Stephanie's father puts it, "eternal importance." This is where we encounter Christ and remember his terrible death; and where we remember his resurrection. This is where the brokenness and pain of the world is made visible, and this is where we rekindle our hope, week after week. This is where our bodies are shaped for service and solidarity. This is where we learn to make room for others. This is where we encounter the living God, "the fountain," as Robert Richardson put it, "of being and blessedness." This is where we can see each other as we really are, as children of the living God, made in God's image. This is where we learn to risk living within God's economy, where all God's children eat together and there is enough for all.

Thanks be to God.

16

Operative Theologies of Disciples Preaching

KAY LYNN NORTHCUTT

Introduction

This amazing amalgam of a church, the Christian Church (Disciples of Christ)—with its righteous anger against church divisiveness and its distinctively modern insight that Protestant reform movements were themselves contributors to such divisions—has, not surprisingly, birthed a wondrous variety of preaching, midwifed by a diverse chorus of preachers.

While our founders intended to "revive the religion of...union taught by Jesus and his apostles,"[1] the aspect of the early church we, the CCDC, most aptly restored is that of spending our first century in disputes and sufferings over the basics of what constitutes *church.* We, like the early church, have spent our second century sorting out those aspects of diversity that we could hospitably engage from those that we could *not,* examples of which surfaced during the split with the noninstrumental Churches of Christ and the Independent Christians. It is no small paradox that our founders' intentions to restore the modern church to the New Testament church's presumed Golden Age has, by contrast, rather imitated the early church's ambiguities and insecurities. Though such a fluid situation might elicit frustration among church historians and theologians, one can scarcely imagine a more fruitful catalyst for preaching! "For wisdom is more mobile than any motion" (Wis. 7:24). Surely God has been at work among us in our over one hundred and fifty years of versatile, contextually rich preaching!

Though our founders spoke of the early church, it is more astute to speak of the early *churches.* It follows that the CCDC is not singular so much as it is plural. We are not so much the Christian *Church* (Disciples of Christ) as we are the Christian *Churches*[2] (Disciples of Christ), taking our shape from a breathtakingly nonunified and diverse set of foundational leaders, geographies, theologies, and peoples. Consequently, positing "an operative theology" of Disciples preaching is as artificial (and naïve) a concept for *our* era as our founders' notion that within the pages of the New Testament there was *a* church to be restored. It follows that we are not in possession of an operative theology of preaching for the CCDC so much as many operative theolog*ies* of Disciples preaching.

That being said, each of those earliest, unique "New Testament" churches held broad characteristics in common, such as, for example, practices of hymn singing, praying, prophesying, and table fellowship. Even within the almost chaotically diverse traditions of the current CCDC, from Park Avenue Christian Church in New York City, to First Christian Church in Sand Springs, Oklahoma, to Primera Iglesia Cristiana de Orlando in Florida, to Atlanta's mega-church Ray of Hope, to Communauté des Disciples du Christ au Congo-Poste Ecclesial de Kinshasa, Congo, we parallel the development of early churches, holding certain broad characteristics in common, preaching being central among them. In fact, the cherishing of preaching is among the very few essentials *all* Disciples revere. The encouragement of great preaching—as well as the *teaching* of preaching—reaches like a plumb line through all our theological diversity as well as cultural, gender, and racial differences; privileging the Word and its effective proclamation.

Letty Russell uses the image of a round table as a metaphor for what Christian faith should ideally be: utterly inclusive, *without* exclusionary corners.[3] A "not-quite-round table,"[4] however, provides a more apt metaphor for Disciples preaching. While a variety of voices, cultures, and homiletic approaches have, in fact, been present since the movement's inception, the diversity has not always been fully acknowledged.

I. Preaching as Restoring: The Initial Proclaimers

Even a quick glimpse at the writings of Barton Stone (1772–1844) and Alexander Campbell (1788–1866) reveals two diverse approaches to preaching. Stone's homiletic is heartfelt, Spirit-driven, God-centered, biblical preaching. Stone advises preachers: "Be careful that you live and walk in the spirit everyday. Your preaching will then be spiritual and profitable to your hearers. A…spiritless ministry is a…ministry of death."[5] Stone further advises that preachers who "address the hearts of their hearers" are preachers whose hearts themselves are filled with "the love of God."[6] For Stone, "The successful preacher is the feeling preacher, and the feeling preacher is one who converses much with his own heart, and is often on his knees conversing with God…"[7]

Campbell's homiletic, though intentionally biblical, was driven by the philosophy of John Locke. Robert Richardson, Campbell's first biographer, noted that Campbell maintained a perfectly motionless stance—one arm extended on a cane—while preaching.[8] Campbell's physical restraint while preaching symbolically represented his disagreement with the "excited feeling—of sympathy with tones, and attitudes, and gestures—of the noise, and tumult, and shoutings of enthusiasm" exhibited in the evangelistic preaching of the Great Awakening. Campbell was convinced that people could not "get religion on the spot."[9] Consequently, Campbell argued that preaching's task must be that of substantively *shaping* Christians. Because preaching must shape human persons into Christians, Campbell, in 1862, expressed "a view which he had held for at least forty years,"[10] namely, that the teaching function of preaching be separated from its evangelical function of persuasion to decision:

> A *preacher* proclaims *facts* and then proves them by *witnesses;* a *teacher* ascertains and develops *truth,* and supports it by *arguments;* an *exhorter* selects *duties,* and recommends and enforces them by *motives.*[11] (emphasis Campbell's)

While Campbell and Stone exhibited diverse approaches to preaching—the driving force of *uniting,* which primarily motivated both of them, muted the sometimes daunting theological and homiletic differences between them. As Mark Toulouse points out, both of them sought "Simple and reasonable preaching about how God acted in Christ to save human beings."[12]

Women were essentially silenced during the initial expressions of our movement's homiletic—if by homiletic we insist upon an exclusively narrow definition such as *pulpit* preaching. If, on the other hand, a broader understanding of homiletic is adopted, such as a homiletic of activity as well as a homiletic of public, non-ordained preaching—we have a very rich heritage to explore.

Many Disciples women during this era imitated the women of the earliest churches—such as Lydia and Phoebe—becoming philanthropists and leaders. Benefactress Emily Tubman (1794–1885) gave tens of thousands of dollars supporting "causes of the Stone-Campbell movement." Tubman's will included "charitable bequests totaling $195,800," much of it endowing educational institutions, for example Bethany College, where preachers and evangelists were educated.[13] But also, several late eighteenth-century and early nineteenth-century kairotic developments, both within the United States and the "Christian" movement, initiated an era of liberty and egalitarianism resulting in a small cascade of non-ordained, itinerant women preachers!

Nancy Gove Cram (1766–1815), a Freewill Baptist, became swept up in the ideals of the "Christians."[14] In 1812, following a prayer she prayed publicly (uninvited!) at a Baptist funeral in Charleston, New York, moving many to tears, Cram was invited to conduct revival meetings, preaching to large crowds. Tragically, Cram died at forty years of age, but not before she founded and organized a church for her converts. Not being an ordained minister, Cram borrowed ordained "Christian" ministers from Vermont to do so. Cram converted at least seven future "Christian" male ministers,[15] as well as Abigail Roberts (1791–1841), a former Quaker, who, like Cram, became a powerful preacher, founding at least four churches in her twelve-year ministry (1816-1828).[16]

Nancy Towle (1796–1876), converted in 1818 under the preaching of "Christian" exhorter Clarissa H. Danforth, was a "bold...relentless preacher on the move" who covered "fifteen thousand miles in a decade of preaching."[17] Both Towle's family and her community so fiercely rejected her call to preach that when finally she took up her itinerancy it required turning her "back on country and kindred as Abram did."[18]

Historical records "of 1820 list African Americans as members of the two earliest congregations at Cane Ridge, Kentucky, and Brush Run, Pennsylvania."[19] African Americans "[t]hough most often as slaves... were nevertheless charter members" in the American-born religious body eventually known as CCDC.[20] The institution of slavery kept masters and slaves separate from one another during worship, with slaves "sequestered" in slave galleries. The Lord's supper, too, was divided by race.

Within mixed congregations, African Americans served as exhorters, deacons, and custodians. But soon black preachers arose and with them the early black congregations of the CCDC.[21] Records concerning early African American leaders are woefully "sketchy"[22] but those mentioned are: "Alexander Campbell of Cane Ridge, Samuel Buckner, Isaac Scott, Abram Williams, Thomas Phillips, J.D. Smith, Henry Newson, Peter Lowery, and Hesiker Hinkel."[23]

From our movement's inception, the voices engaged in preaching were varied not only in race, gender, social status, and class but in diverse theologies and homiletic approaches as well. The compelling theme of *uniting* served as fulcrum and balance amidst such diversity. The initial proclaimers of the Stone-Campbell movement were preoccupied with preaching the restoration of New Testament Christianity through which they believed Christian unity would be achieved. Such restored unity, they proclaimed, was based on God's saving works through Christ. Soteriology, therefore, not the particularities of any program of restoration, formed the basis of the Disciples' nascent operative theology of preaching.

II. Preaching as Persuading: The Itinerant Evangelists

The evangelists—like the preachers who gave initial homiletic expression to the movement—proved "more mobile than any motion," bringing diverse theologies and unique homiletic approaches to bear upon their work. Unity remained a commitment held in common.

Well-known for his "five-finger exercise" of salvation, Walter Scott (1796–1861) is credited with bringing over three thousand converts into the Stone-Campbell movement and stabilizing what would become the

CCDC. Not surprisingly, the complex question "What must a person do to be saved?" drove Scott's operative theology of preaching though he held a unique position (in conflict with Calvinists and other revivalists of that era) regarding the Holy Spirit.[24] Scott insisted the Spirit works through *external* testimonies such as preaching and the Bible, prompting a rational assent to faith—rather than an internal working within the soul.[25] Though Scott's overriding homiletic of *persuasion* was typical of the evangelists, his distinctive take on the Spirit is representative of the diverse theological approaches found among Disciples preachers.

John Smith (1784–1868) practically "single-handedly spread the message of reform over much of the state of Kentucky."[26] People loved not only to hear Smith's sermons—they loved to *listen* to them. Smith possessed a sonorous voice, and reportedly the aural cunning of his sermon delivery was captivating. Though Smith evangelized for the Disciples of Christ, he worked for unity among all Christians, inaugurating an effective method upon which later homileticians could model their ecumenical preaching.

By 1861 there were over 1500 African American churches in Georgia, Kentucky, North Carolina, Ohio, and Tennessee.[27] One can only imagine the magnificent preaching that so dynamically evangelized and supported these churches. This tangible accomplishment elicits not only admiration but also grief for the absent (perhaps yet undiscovered) written records of such powerful African American (CCDC) preaching. The absence of written documentation of such voices—and the activities of African American women—tragically diminishes our known homiletic heritage.[28]

Melissa Terrell (1834-1899) was, on March 7, 1867, the first woman ordained as an *elder* and licensed to preach as "an ordained minister of good standing" by the Southern Ohio Christian Conference—having also preached the conference sermon.[29] The first woman to be ordained from within the "Campbellite" branch of the "Christian Church" movement, however, was Clara Celestia Hale Babcock (1850–1924). Among the evangelists, Hale Babcock was exceptional, reported to have converted over fourteen hundred people, baptizing a thousand of them personally.[30]

Scott's unique view of the Spirit—and Smith's evangelizing for the Stone-Campbell movement while simultaneously championing unity—along with the ordination of the first women preachers, and the dramatic increase of African American congregations, demonstrate the rapidly expanding and diverse preaching of the evangelists. But a unifying theme among them can be found within the operative theology of an economics of exchange—one's confession of Christ in exchange for salvation.

III. Preaching as Explaining: The Settled Pastorate

When Disciples moved to weekly preaching in settled pastorates it became necessary to re-imagine preaching's primary aim. Since most of those filling the pews in established Disciples congregations were already "saved," the previous theology of transaction proved to be not fully adequate. About this gradual shift, historian and homiletician Joseph R. Jeter observes, "*Theologically speaking* in terms of sermon content (in moving away from thinking of salvation as a transaction to that of a relationship *with* God) many modern preachers weren't certain what to do."[31] Disciples historian Ronald Edwin Osborn (1917–1998) too, observed "a shift from theological understanding having to do with the biblical concept of salvation—[to] thinkers of our time [who] emphasize salvation as a relationship."[32] That is to say, once Disciples preachers inhabited settled pastorates, they asked not so much, "What does it mean to be saved?" as, "What does it mean to be Disciples of Christ, a people of faith, in relationship to God who saved us?" Many Disciples preachers resolved the latter question regarding the meaning of faith through ethical categories such as duty, fidelity, and self-sacrifice, but also in existential categories including risk and self-disclosure. Reinhold Niebuhr, in his *Nature and Destiny of Man*,[33] invoked the language of relationship to interpret revelation, but remained deeply skeptical of anything that hinted of Roman Catholic mysticism in seeking God. Similarly, many Disciples preachers adopted an ethical/existential theology while remaining wary of Roman Catholic sacramental (or monastic) understandings of the spiritual life.[34]

The paradigm shift with respect to preaching within settled pastorates was not limited to the theological shift from transactional to relational theology. Homiletic theory itself shifted emphasis, during this era, from persuasion to explanation. An influential textbook by John Broadus (1827–1895) proved pivotal in this homiletic shift. Broadus's text, *A Treatise on the Preparation and Delivery of Sermons*,[35] was "widely considered to be the most successful American textbook on preaching of all time with forty editions published from 1870 to 1896 alone."[36] As homiletician Thomas Long notes, "The preacher as persuader was being replaced by the preacher as explainer."[37] North American sermons became informational, propositional, and content-driven, with multiple illustrations and "proofs." The purpose of such preaching was "the clear, logical, and rational presentation of ideas derived from the gospel."[38] Many Disciples preachers scaled with mastery and power the heights of the modern homiletic's content-driven, rational sermon.[39]

Other Disciples preachers adopted the "counseling model of preaching" profoundly influenced by Harry Emerson Fosdick (1878–1969), whose weekly sermon broadcast on The National Vespers Radio Hour reached "millions of people."[40] Fosdick pioneered and nurtured the notion of preaching as "counseling" in 1928 with an article called "What Is the Matter with Preaching?"

> Every sermon should have as its main business the solving of some problem—a vital, important problem, puzzling minds, burdening

> consciences, distracting lives—and any sermon which thus does tackle a real problem, throw even a little light on it and help some individuals practically to find their way through it cannot be altogether uninteresting.[41]

Invariably these sermons focus upon individual problem-solving, and the wisdom sources cited in preaching-as-counseling are those of modernity's disciplines: psychology, science, and sociology.[42]

Given the prominence of these discourses in modern preaching, the distinctive voices of classical Christian wisdom, exegetically driven biblical preaching, and the congregational aspects of community formation, as well as the religious authority and identity of the preacher, were relatively obscured by the assumption that *all* of us faced a new, common situation: modernity.[43]

By the late 1950s and throughout the 1960s, however, new voices arose to challenge the assumptions of both the liberal "explanation" *and* Fosdickian "therapeutic" models of preaching—both of which privileged primarily Caucasian, male, middle-class experience, and both of which had assumed incorrectly (and somewhat naively) the "commonality" of modern life—that sense that we were "all in the same boat together." The civil rights and feminist movements sounded the alarm on behalf of economic and political equality for African Americans and women. These calls for justice, which interpreted the theological notion of *imago Dei* through the modern lens of political equality and, simultaneously, challenged the implicit racial and patriarchal assumptions of Christian God–language, shifted the language of salvation from divine reward to this-worldly transformation, and the terms of authority from the religious tradition to that of social experience of injustice.

Many African American preachers of this era greatly utilized the "relational theology" or the "feeling" track of Disciples preaching, exhorting their congregations to keep the faith and stay together—close to the cross of Jesus—in the face of the Klan,[44] Jim Crow segregation, and a thousand other daily forms of racism. The emergence of the civil rights movement, however, also united with the black churches' deep identification with the suffering of Jesus. Prophetic, activist, black preachers exhorted their congregants to participate in the civil rights movement's prophetic critique of racial injustice.[45]

Previously silenced voices—of feminists, Latinos/as, Hispanics, and African Americans—asked of their congregations both political and social commitments resulting in theological and cultural tensions with primarily middle-class, male, Caucasian voices.[46] Denominational publications, such as *The Disciple,* took a leading role in attempting to educate and persuade their readers of the importance of social justice concerns. In the mid-to-late-1970s, *The Disciple* magazine was consistently recognized as the leading social justice publication by The Associated Church Press.

These previously silenced voices informed a new generation of preachers with theological and moral convictions that did not always square with either the modern therapeutic or the more traditional other-worldly salvation model of Christian preaching. The result has been a further diversification of theological perspectives as Disciples enter the postmodern era of proliferating voices and an often-confused sense of congregational orientation and denominational identity.

IV. Preaching as Formation: The Postmodern Preachers

Paradoxically, the twenty-first century for Disciples mirrors the nineteenth century from which Disciples emerged; the "new" global reality uncannily replaying anxieties and concerns of that earlier so-called "unsettled frontier."[47] What began as a minuscule regional movement has become an international denomination currently rapidly expanding in Africa.[48] Remarkably, a religious movement founded upon difference and unity has flourished into phenomenal difference with an *unsettled* unity that contemporary Disciples preaching—throughout the United States, Canada, Africa, Puerto Rico, Australia, New Zealand, and the rest of world—reflects.

Among Disciples preachers in the Congo, sermons are not expository but rather topical. Almost all preaching is focused on *hope*. Since the Congo's great sufferings—both prior to and following independence in 1960—the country and its people have encountered heart-wrenching and life-endangering struggles. It is no surprise that Disciples preachers in the Congo focus on hope and *faith,* with Romans 8:28 serving as a principal, privileged text. Congolese preachers form their sermons toward an eschatological theology.[49]

By way of theological contrast, a great many Disciples Latino/a preachers in the United States rely on liberation theology. Interestingly enough, "the most influential manual of homiletics in Latin America" was *Tratado sobre la predicación,* a Spanish translation of John Broadus's treatise (also profoundly influential in Caucasian preaching in the United States), which presumes preaching's purpose is to instruct and persuade.[50] Disciples homiletician Pablo Jiménez notes that in contemporary Hispanic preaching the emphasis is shifting from form and content to "the theological interpretation of Latino and Latina experience"[51] and that maintaining Hispanic cultural identity is central to the purpose of Hispanic preaching. Ultimately Hispanic preaching is formational, empowering Hispanics "to persevere and prevail in their *lucha por la vida,* their struggle for life."[52]

African American Disciples' sermons convict, convert, and celebrate with breathtaking power. Though African American preachers cover the gamut of theological perspectives—from that of the God of providence to those of womanist and liberation—African American preachers display masterful skill. Campbell's suspicion of Revival "emotionalism" would, little doubt, be humbled by the emotional power of Disciples African American preaching in the United States,[53] especially in light of the fact that Disciples

Black preachers faithfully perform what for Campbell was preaching's most basic purpose: the *formation* of Christians.[54]

North American Pacific Asian Disciples (formerly the Fellowship of Asian American Disciples) currently represent twelve different language groups. In 1992 there were only eight Asian American Disciples congregations. Consequently, Geunhee Yu was appointed to "develop and grow Asian ministries," resulting today in over seventy Asian American congregations "consisting primarily of seven different ethnic groups: Chinese, Japanese, Filipino, Korean, Vietnamese, Indonesian, and Samoan…though Korean Disciples represent about seventy-five percent of all NAPAD congregations."[55] Currently there are over one hundred Korean Disciples ministers in the United States. Though as of yet there are no published books of Disciples Korean sermons or about the history of Disciples Korean preaching, United Methodist homiletician Jung Young Lee notes the "most popular [Korean American] sermons are uncritically exegetical and uncompromisingly doctrinal,"[56] "stressing the witness of the Holy Spirit"[57] with a "continued nineteenth-century missionary emphasis on conversion."[58]

Global Disciples are separated by theology, location, culture, race, class, identity, and gender.[59] In the rapidly escalating Disciples population in Africa, for instance, issues of feminism and womanism are virtually silenced as irrelevant—while in the United States feminist and womanist views are representative of most women Disciples preachers.[60] In the Caucasian, middle-class churches of North America, issues of liberation theology are relatively unknown and unemphasized, while in the Disciples Hispanic churches daily survival depends upon a liberating God. That being said, Disciples persist in holding certain broad characteristics in common. These include not only prayer, table fellowship, and singing, but also the cherishing of the Word and the formation of Christians, individually and congregationally.

Conclusion

An amazing array of voices, cultures, and homiletic approaches have been present from our very beginning,[61] though it has taken the greater part of almost two hundred years to *see* and to claim the diversity, differences, and richness within the past and present operative theolog*ies* of Disciples preaching.

17

Ministry

How Disciples Understand It

MARK MILLER-MCLEMORE

How Do Disciples Understand Ministry?

At least one path to understanding is to look at official documents. Therefore, I intend to review what the church has said more explicitly about ministry, through its historians and theologians and formal channels and statements. A second important way to discern Disciples understandings of ministry is to look at the documents used most often by the church and its ministers in their practice. How do these documents implicitly embody theologies of ministry, and how do they fit with the more explicit ways we discuss it? And, finally, a third path to pursue is to talk to Disciples ministers. In an expanding Disciples world, and in changing Disciples communities, how do ministers understand themselves and their ministry? Finally, I want to ask how these three sources of understanding fit with each other.

I enter this conversation with a thesis formed from "reading" my own experiences in ministry in congregational and educational settings, as well as conversations with others in ministry. I served for fifteen years as a pastor in a small, largely blue-collar, inner-city church. I have now been teaching leadership and ministry for eleven years at a university-based divinity school. My overriding impression is that our implicit theological documents, as well as Disciples ministers in practice, see ministry more through a functional lens, rather than through the lens of "office" or person. In other words, "ministry" for Disciples ministers is "what a minister does" more than the person a minister is or the role or office a minister fills. This approach may be in significant tension with our explicit theological documents, which reflect such a functional approach to a much lesser degree.

I also explore a sub-thesis: that the pragmatism that marks us "on the ground" may be something to lament, a nontheological understanding of ministry that many find trivial and troubling; or it may come out of a distinctive theological tradition, itself to be described, owned, and celebrated. If so, how might we do it better?

The Question of Norms

We first must ask: How do Disciples answer such a question? It is "notoriously difficult" to do normative theology among the Disciples.[1]

Ministry students frequently are assigned the task of reporting their denomination's position on a theological question, and the Disciples students often have a tough time. Where do they turn?

Disciples intentionally use a minimal test of fellowship, and come from a heritage of creedal and theological suspicion, leading to a lack of doctrinal positions for reference. We are nonhierarchical in structure. We have rightly rejected the early Restorationist hermeneutic authority that initially guided our efforts and thought, creating a historical trajectory that twists and turns, at best. We have no teaching authority or magisterium to define the faith, and we show a pattern of stances and actions highly susceptible to uncritically received influence from our surrounding culture. We share no clear consensus about positional authority to define or teach or even speak theologically for our church. Do we rely on teaching faculty in seminaries, commissions on theology, ecumenical statements, local pastors, regional and denominational leadership, laypersons, bureaucrats, boards?[2] In terms of norms and sources and authority, we are undefined, open, even confused. Yet we rightly and necessarily continue to theologize, despite the likelihood that, all too often, few are listening.

Given this lack of shared norms, much Disciples theological work takes the shape of description, telling us who we are at a particular point, or where historically we once were. Other Disciples theology takes on an exhortatory, persuasive tone, explicit or not, sometimes in the guise of description, telling us who we ought to be. Still other statements embodying theological reflection are not rigorously rooted in either of these approaches. Consensus is lacking, and we are becoming more diverse, which challenges our lack of clarity even more.

Perhaps the biggest change in the larger theological world in the last fifty years has been the explicit turn to experience as a primary source and norm for theological reflection. The source of the experiences serving as a base for theological reflection has shifted from its predominantly male, white, Anglo-European character to incorporate the experiences of women and people of color of vastly different origin and home. Most recent theologies simply start from a different place than the Panel of Scholars did in mid-century. New Disciples with new experiences have led to new thinking. Authority in theological reflection is becoming even harder for us to pin down.

However, one could argue that Disciples have always been more characterized by this kind of experience-oriented theological approach. If theological thinking among us arose in an attempt to understand the best ways to live the Christian life, individually and together, then as the Disciples community expands and changes, our understandings will reflect new light as well.

Questions of theology for Disciples seem both to arise from and inform the questions posed by a living experience of faith. As W. Barnett Blakemore notes in his essay on "The Christian Task and the Church's Ministry," "It is only at the junction point of these two approaches (the 'theological,' or conceptual, and the 'practical,' or lived) that there is enlightenment."[3] It seems rare, however, that we do this kind of theological thinking well.

Explicit Theological Documents

Disciples of late seem to write on ministry about every ten years.[4] Newell Williams's monograph *Ministry Among Disciples: Past, Present, Future*[5] offers a helpful overview of the development of practice and understanding of ministry among Disciples over the last two hundred years. What emerges clearly from this review is the wide diversity of terms used for ministry, the changing of related functions, and an ongoing development to meet changing demands. Evolving practice and competing justifications mark our tradition from the merger of the Christians with the Disciples in 1832, in which Stone's and Campbell's understandings differed in significant ways. Disciples have been both anticlerical (Campbell) and more accepting of "hired clergy" (Stone); have stressed ministry by laity (in the tradition of the priesthood of all believers) as well as a set-apart ministry; have ordained both elders and ministers; and have used a plurality of terms for ministers in a variety of settings.

Campbell's early anticlerical teachings attacked what we would call the "profession of ministry." He clearly upheld a set-apart ministry but focused on it as related to the needs of congregational life. Elders and deacons served within established churches; evangelists from established churches started new congregations and served until elders were ready to take on their role of leadership. Ordination of elders, who served as leaders called from and representative of the congregation, was of local effect only. Early Disciples stressed the ministry of the laity, but not perhaps as Disciples understand that notion of ministry today when we speak of "the priesthood of all believers." Despite anticlericalism, even elders were called, set apart, and ordained to serve.

Later moves toward the "one man" or "settled" system, with its higher expectations in education, were based on the changing needs and resources of congregations. These moves represented an expedience-based,[6] only-partial affirmation of a "set apart ministry" and happened gradually, congregation by congregation, not in a unified manner, creating tension with the established system of elders as ministers. The development of cooperative mission work beyond the purview of single congregations demanded leadership to carry out wider cooperative functions—again, a response to changing needs. The rise among Disciples of the "functional committee system" of ordering congregational work further displaced the ministry of elders in congregations and solidified the role of a set-apart, ordained, full-time, paid ministry in congregations—in part, to direct the congregation's programming.[7]

Disciples have struggled subsequently to legitimize and name their ministries, lay and ordained, both in and beyond the congregation, in cooperative work, and in work with the wider church, as we have moved toward new understandings of its life together following restructure in 1968, and in ecumenical conversations.

Ministry Among Disciples concludes with a report from the Commission on Theology called "A Word to the Church on Ministry," received by the 1985 General Assembly of the Christian Church. This study document proposes that Disciples move to an ecumenical understanding of a three-fold order of ministry, "one order in three offices":

1. The ministry of service to church and world (the diakonate, or deacons)
2. The ministry of proclamation by Word and Sacrament (the presbyterate, or pastors and ministers)
3. The ministry of oversight (the episcopate, or bishops)[8]

This study document argues that such an approach is more in keeping with predominant understandings among other traditions, as well as within contemporary discussions in the (then) Consultation on Church Union. It also notes difficulties from such an approach with current Disciples practices and traditions, especially the long-standing Disciples practice of the ministry of congregational elders and deacons, in addition to pastors, as well as the ongoing existence of licensed (or commissioned) ministers.[9]

It is almost impossible not to note the tension between the recommendations of the Commission for discussion by the Church and the widely divergent practices and understandings described in our historical development. As Richard Harrison notes, the Disciples' understanding of "the office of elder, and the understanding of church and ministry that lies behind this office...may well be one of the most significant offerings of the Disciples tradition to the larger church."[10] Yet the three-fold delineation above makes no place for Disciples elders, as the document acknowledges.

Only twenty years earlier, an essay by W. Barnett Blakemore showed little trace of this ecumenical understanding of ministry for Disciples. In fact, Blakemore suggested that Disciples had forgotten their own distinctive heritage of a three-fold order of ministry within congregations as deacons, elders, and pastors or evangelists. He claimed Disciples had collapsed all three into the single congregational office of pastor, and that we had increasingly rendered the ministry of elders and deacons symbolic and shallow.[11] Blakemore also called for a renewal of three ministerial offices. But they are contained *within* the congregation, not beyond.

The restructured church's first formal document on ministry (1971) has since gone through several versions. "The Order of Ministry for the Christian Church (Disciples of Christ)" (2003) currently is in another revision process under the auspices of the General Commission on Ministry.[12]

The document notes at its outset the constitutive ministry of Jesus; the foundational corporate ministry of the whole church; and, third, a representative "Order of Ministry" consisting of two offices, ordained and licensed, each authorized by the church. Licensed ministry seems intended as authorization for persons who feel a call to serve and have a context in which to do so, but who are unable to seek the kind of educational preparation required of ordained ministers. The document offers, for both kinds of ministers, procedures and qualifications for candidacy; describes individual and institutional rights, responsibilities, authorization, and appropriate liturgical services; sets forth where accountability is lodged for ongoing recognition ("standing"); lays out the processes whereby ministers may secure employment; and describes professional misconduct. These latter two functional sections comprise more than half the document's length.

The most recent draft document[13] seeks to advance much more explicitly as normative for Disciples the understanding of three offices within one representative and set apart order of ministry, as set forth by the Commission on Theology in its 1985 report. It is, like its predecessors, a mixture of theology and practice. It blends theological assertions as to the nature of ministry and vocation with institutional processes and procedures—even requirements specific to the service of consecration proposed for regional ministers, or the signing of the "Ministerial Code of Ethics" in the ordination service.

This is a draft in process, in no way yet official policy, but with plans to present it to General Assembly for action in 2007. The major change in the draft's emphasis is its attempt to move Disciples' stated and official understanding of ministry into accord with the ecumenical document *Baptism, Eucharist and Ministry* (BEM).[14] The document lays out the "three offices" of ministry as "commissioned minister, ordained minister, and minister of oversight," which "correspond to the offices of deacon, presbyter, and bishop in other traditions." It attempts to offer theological warrants for this change through reference to, first, "Apostolic Tradition," second, "Disciples Perspectives" and "the Stone-Campbell tradition," and, third, "Ecumenical Perspectives." It also adduces various scriptural verses and a quotation from Alexander Campbell in support. But it gives little attention to the historical trajectory of development and change within Disciples understandings, such as Williams's work provides. (For example, does Campbell's use of three offices map easily onto the BEM understandings?) It does not explore why a Disciples theological method should begin with

"Apostolic Tradition." Nor does the document offer explanations of the strategic and political issues involved in this change. The gains and losses are not counted. It gives no explicit warrant for why such changes might therefore be compelling to Disciples today.[15]

Recent writers have seriously questioned the wisdom and appropriateness of Disciples understandings moving in such directions without careful, broad, and lengthy discussion. Harrison worries about whether our lack of theological clarity "implies that clergy especially have a special claim and authority," leading us away from our historic understanding: that the authority for ministry belongs to the whole church and is conferred by the church on its representatives for servanthood in the church.[16] "When the language of 'word and sacrament'...is joined together with stated oversight authority, traditional Disciples understandings of ministry are being seriously undermined."[17]

In an abstract for an article unfinished at his death, Anthony Dunnavant suggests:

> From the middle twentieth century forward Disciples ecumenical involvement, which increasingly favored communions with highly clerical traditions of ministry, exacerbated the negative effects of the adoption of the functional church organization. Cut off from their own roots, Disciples have recently tended to order their ministry, to too great a degree, by imitation—by the superficial appropriation of symbols and practices adopted from admired ecumenical conversation partners.[18]

This is a serious indictment. If our tradition has different understandings and ways, grafting another theological branch will only serve to confuse.

Implicit Theological Documents

The Disciples "Ministerial Code of Ethics," appended to the "Order of Ministry," is often affirmed in ordination services for Disciples. As one might expect in a code of professional ethics, it deals with actions and their morality: what is right and what is not right for ministers to do. "Do not perform pastoral services in a former pastorate without the invitation of your successor," for example.[19] The document is organized under the headings "Personal Conduct," "Relationships to the Church I Serve," "Relationships to Ministry Colleagues," and "Relationships to the Community and the Wider Church."

Another theological "text" to examine is perhaps the single most prevalent and widely used document about ministry by Disciples ministers and congregations. The "Search and Call" process requires every Disciples pastor seeking a congregational ministry and every Disciples congregation seeking a pastor to complete a form indicating their "ministerial emphases."[20]

In this document (approved by the General Commission on Ministry in 2005), ministers and congregations are requested to rate the areas of pastoral ministry they think to be most important to the gifts and interests they bring or to the demands of a particular setting. The document lists twenty different pastoral activities, and the activities listed are divided into three major areas: Outreach/Teaching Ministries, Membership Development/ Administrative Activities, and Pastoral/Worship Ministries. Obviously, the collection of ministerial activities from which to choose is clearly function-oriented as well as overwhelmingly congregational: "Proclamation of the Word," "Congregational Home Visitation," "Involvement in Mission Beyond the Local Community," "Educational Program," "Responsibilities and Relationships with the Christian Church Disciples of Christ, both Regional and General," and "Planning Congregational Life" are a half-dozen.

Our ministers and churches deal with these documents on a regular and frequent basis. They have inevitable impact. What do they reveal? A context-based, congregation-centered orientation to ministry is predominant.

As Winfred Ernest Garrison and Alfred T. DeGroot note about Disciples in their early years among the Baptists, "whereas other denominations considered the Baptist view of the ministerial office sadly loose and low, the Baptists thought the Reformers' view looser and lower."[21] Even if we do not fall quite so far as that, it is clear that we have among us widely divergent views of ministry.

What Ministers Say

What can we learn about ministry from those Disciples engaged in its practice?

My question arises in part from reading an article in a church newsletter by a recent outstanding Divinity graduate, answering the question, "What do you ministers do?" I was struck by her beautiful account of the complexity and challenge found in a typical minister's week.

I am part of a pastoral colleague group that has met now for nineteen consecutive years to read, write, and talk theology about ministry. I am amazed at the longevity of commitment of my colleagues to this group, as well as to its task of thinking theologically about ministry. These are fine pastors from widely separated places and churches, but they share a quality of life and reflection that is wise and life-giving, centered on faithfulness to Christ, nurturing to their congregations, and good.

These ministers are theologians. But "the closer one is to practice, the less time one has to theorize about it."[22] Ministers' theologizing is done not in articles for journals and books for libraries so much as it is done in sermons and weekly columns and reports and eulogies, at the hospital bed and in the office or in a church meeting. This theology is highly situation-specific, not easily transferable, and develops over time in relationship; but, for just those reasons, often it is profoundly meaningful and faithful to the quest for understanding of life lived in the light of God. It is important theology, and I think it is disclosive to look at theological documents of this sort as well.

I spoke with seven Disciples ministers[23] with the goal of seeking out their understanding of who they are and what they do. What do they understand to be distinctive about Disciples ministry?

All seven ministers were deeply related to and *invested in their place and context* of ministry. Specific activities and people and settings were crucial to their understanding, and the more thematic understandings that guided their work emerged in connection with a specific congregation. Ministry for Disciples is not done in the abstract. It is concrete.

All remarked on the importance in the Disciples tradition of the sense of *hospitality and welcome* inherent in an open communion table, as well as in the freedom from creeds as tests of fellowship disclosed in our minimal confession. They valued the way that people of great diversity of opinion can come together in our churches, when at their best, to live and love in the name of the same Christ. There is a yearning for that diversity to be more than theological. There is a sense of "ecumenism turned inward," in which all Disciples of Christ, lay and ordained, have access to the holy together: in ministry, the sacraments, in understanding God's word, in practices of faith, and through service, all in the church.

Yet they also have come to see their role in ministry as different from others. This dimension of their understandings stood out as they discussed the importance of a strong inner sense of *special calling,* affirmed by the church, which shapes their various ministries, impacts their experience every day, and sustains them in the face of incredible challenge with "enthusiasm and unwavering passion" for their work. They feel and affirm the leadership role they have in ministry: *modeling* a life lived before God and toward Jesus Christ, through the use of their gifts in many contexts: immersion in scripture and *spiritual practices; offering welcome* on behalf of God in Christ, and people, and church; seeking to *make sense* of life and faith through preaching and teaching and living the Gospel; living willingly to a *different standard,* even one demanding sacrifice; experiencing the joyful burden of *access to sacred moments* in the lives of those to whom they minister, in Christ's place.

These theological documents are worth examining at more length, but here we ask: How do they relate to other Disciples understandings? The focus and orientation and tone of these ministers' comments are quite different: more context- and person-related, and more embodied in function or act, more "ground up" and less "top down." Certainly, they are closer to the "feel" (but with much more beauty and depth) of the "Search and Call" form than to the latest draft document of "The Order of Ministry."

Conclusion

How do these diverse sources of understanding ministry work together to help us understand Disciples?

It seems clear that our understandings are all over the map. Some things we say are strictly and shallowly functional, while others are profoundly contextual, while others are at odds with our past. We cannot be said to have a single theology of ministry. No consensus has emerged, and I do not think it is evident that it ever will. In fact, significant tensions exist in our historical development, between our explicit and implicit theological positions, and with new proposals and pastoral reflections. However, if we can be said to exhibit commonality, it is around the way in which our reflection is drawn forth from context and experience.

It is probably unwise to attempt to impose on such a mixed, experience-based, contextually centered, grassroots tradition a singular model, uncritically appropriated from other traditions, without more compelling reasons than have been offered as yet. Such a change is unlikely to "take" in our odd and distinctive culture, and would likely only further confuse an already confused sense of who we are as a special people of God within the whole people of God. In particular, the "three-fold order of ministry" proposal in "The Order of Ministry" in draft form seems to strain against our more "bottom-up" way of evolving understandings of ministry in light of changing circumstance. Dunnavant's critique, that this proposal is a form of imitation that ironically does not legitimate us in the eyes of our ecumenical conversation partners, is important.[24] What compelling reasons exist to move us from our other ways of understanding? Do we see ourselves as evolving toward a single understanding or order, or is a lack of conformity more characteristic of who we are? Should we rather celebrate our theological diversity?

Blakemore's famous essay, "Reasonable, Empirical, Pragmatic," characterizes us more "as a practical than a speculative people."[25] Clark Williamson has characterized us as a people more concerned with right behaviors than right thinking and has noted how our behaviors may offer a truer window upon our theological souls than our more formal statements and explicit theologies.[26]

If they are correct in their characterizations—and I believe they are—then it will be the case that a different, "bottom-up," occasional style of theologizing will be more appropriate to an emerging Disciples understanding of ministry. What might be the implications of such a style for a Disciples theology of ministry?

We should encourage our ministers to reflect in writing on their ministry, lived in the light of the gospel of Jesus Christ where they are. What they think and write can be beautiful, faithful, and true to the acts of ministry. It contributes to a fuller sense of who we are, and it has value that preservation and dissemination would sustain over time. Such thinking would also contribute to a growing body of faithful work that could feed deeper, more grounded reflection on ministry among us.

Some of our documents implicitly showing theology, especially the "Search and Call" document, need serious attention and greater theological care, because they prominently reinforce shallowly functional understandings of ministry that are important but misleading. While we would affirm that ministry is embodied in its actions, we would also wish to connect those actions to a larger horizon of meaning and value in the church and in the world than the current documents exhibit. These are the theological pictures of ministry most used by churches and pastors. We can do this part of our theologizing much better.

Given the legacy of our tradition, in which ministries evolved in response to the churches' needs, we should think carefully and much longer about "The Order of Ministry." Our varied expressions are complex and valid and should not be abandoned lightly. In particular, our understanding and practice of the lay eldership deserves attention and honor in our constructive thinking. It should not be abandoned or neglected, but incorporated in our best thinking about who we are.

And last, as we learn better to think theologically in these context-centered, grassroots ways, we will be more open to the appropriate gifts that a new diversity among us can bring. We have been a people whose understandings and practices change in relation to the demands of the times and context. In terms of understandings of ministry, we have made many beginnings, but we clearly have unfinished business.

SECTION IV

Reconciliation

18

The Problem of Social Sin for Twenty-first–Century Christians

DARRYL TRIMIEW

To be human is to be self-deceived.
Roger Betsworth, *Social Ethics*[1]

Social sin is a ubiquitous term, one that does not lend itself to an easy definition. We Disciples have no one simple understanding of this term. This chapter explains why in a two-step process. First we examine how one of our founders, Alexander Campbell, looked at one "social sin" issue: namely, slavery. Second, our examination of his views on this subject and our discussion of a modern problem, the theological assessment of ordaining gay clergy, help to explain the diversity of social sin assessments of Disciples as well as the problematic nature of such assessments. Prior to these examinations we must briefly address what is meant by the term "social sin" from a theologically ethical point of view.

One prominent ethicist, Stephen Charles Mott, explains this term by first characterizing the wider moral universe. For Mott the created world is not the reign of God, which is sinless, but the sinful created order that God has redeemed. By sinful created order, Mott is recognizing not so much the phenomenon of natural evil, but the evil of every social system. Thus he writes:

> Our social systems are not eternal or absolute but reflect the ambiguous nature of humankind and the angelic guardians of culture. Our institutions are not just a constraint on sin (a conservative attitude toward institutions); they themselves are full of sin. The structures

> of social life contain both good and bad. Because of the hold of self-interest we will tend to see only the good in those social forms which favor our interests unless we have a strong theology of sin. Our social life is fallen with us, and no social system is beyond the need of reform or perhaps even of reconstitution.[2]

Mott goes on to note that:

> Dealing with the evil of the social order and the worldly powers involves social action, action in the world. Christian social reform has been effective when there has been a sense of a stronghold of evil in society which must be resisted. The discovery that evil resides in the social order as well as in our personal life confounds the common inventory of besetting sins. "Stealing, gambling, profanity, desecrating of Sunday, murder, lasciviousness, or whatever is eternally wrong is a typical list of what is often considered public unrighteousness. The biblical sins of economic exploitation or oppression or of hoarding of wealth from the poor have vanished. But the prophets spoke out not only against sinful personal relationships but also against breakdown of social relationships between groups with unequal shares of power. Thus they attacked broad economic patterns, such as the consolidation of the holdings of peasants into vast estates of the rich (Isa. 5:7–8.) In Scripture, sin includes participation in social injustices or failure to correct them.[3]

Social sin is simply one form of evil that is a permanent feature in human life and community; it is an evil that must constantly be resisted and overthrown.

Similarly, E. Clinton Gardner has noted:

> Human nature°nder sin, then, is perverted or distorted. The ultimate harmony of man with God and his fellows is broken in all of its aspects. Man himself—not just his reason or his physical nature or some one relationship—is affected at his very core. Moreover, since man is so inescapably social in nature, not only is the whole self (ego totus) affected by sin but the entire community of men (nos toti) is thrown out of harmony and runs counter to its true good. One of the enduring insights in the Augustinian concept of the fall of the entire human race in Adam is this insight into the communal nature of man. It is the fate of man to live in a community of men whose destinies are bound up together. No man sinneth unto himself alone, and no man doeth good unto himself alone. God has created each man, but He has created each for community with others, and this means with responsibilities for others. Whether he wills it or not, each man is his brother's keeper, and each shares the responsibility for the sin of the group.[4]

These quotes characterize social sin as a manifestation of corporate human behavior rather than the evil eccentric acts of isolated individuals. In the Bible it is best illustrated not by acts of evil—by David, for instance, committing adultery with Bathsheba and murdering her husband by proxy. Rather, the best example of social sin is manifested in the actions of the wealthy in Micah and Jeremiah, who act in concert to gobble up the poor through economic exploitation. Social sin is the instantiation of certain widespread practices, arrangements, distributions, and processes, wherein some groups of people are either treated solely as means to another end, or simply left out of the decision-making processes in community, or the corporate processes, within which the life of the group is discussed, charted, and implemented. Social sin is a breaking of the covenant with God—a refusal to act in favor of the widow, orphan, and sojourner in the land, who are as a consequence systematically abandoned to their own devices and fates. Social sin violates God's command for Israel and for other peoples of God to intervene on behalf of the downtrodden. Social sin has a vertical component, but its primary victims are those around us who are not treated fairly and loved as they ought to be. At least this is how I understand social sin.

Turning to the distinct question of the Disciples of Christ position on social sin, the two main ecclesiastical streams from which the Disciples of Christ emerged, namely Presbyterians and Baptists, come into play. Both are reformed traditions that have historically understood themselves to be seriously concerned about the problem of sin. As noted elsewhere, John Calvin, the founder of the Presbyterians, was aware of the seriousness of this problem.[5]

Early Disciples carried on that tradition, but our ecclesiology and non-creedalism make such concerns more difficult both to discern and address than it once did for our source denominations. The hierarchical structure of other denominations, along with their reliance on creedalism, further complicate this picture. Our commitment to "no creed but Christ," to intensive examination of as well as commitment to the New Testament as both a source and a controlling guide to a variety of practices, commits us to a very adaptive process of interpreting theology, ethics, scripture, and church traditions in ways never dreamed of by nineteenth-century exegetes and ministers.

Alexander Campbell's historic position on slavery is, for example, a good case study of this problem.[6] While Presbyterians, Methodists, and others split over the question of slavery along regional, political, and economic lines, Disciples, following Campbell, interpreted the question of slavery as a social rather than a theological question. Hence, we are left with Campbell's insistence that the retention of slaves could not be a sole reason for disfellowship from a Disciples congregation. Like Presbyterians and Baptists, Disciples fought for the South *and* the North, but did so without the explicit schisms into separate denominations that occurred in our fellow denominations over the question of slavery.

Accordingly, since we were not pacifists, Yankee Disciples fought for and killed Confederate Disciples over the issue of slavery and vice versa, without either side having committed (in their respective minds, at least) any sinful acts.

In the early nineteenth century, this flexibility in theology, this true commitment to the freedom of the individual's conscience and in his/her interpretation of scripture, made the determination of sin in the uncontroversial sense limited to cases of direct violations of the Ten Commandments and/or the promotion of ecclesiastical discord and schism. Indeed, historically speaking, the only social sin that Disciples have always agreed upon as constituting social sin is the sectarianism and schismatic discord that Christians have engaged in that Disciples came into being to try to eliminate. Accordingly, other notions of sin had to be argued for from scripture in ways that did not allow for the achievement of consensus in absolute and clear categorizations of human actions and/or states of being, or systemic failures to intervene.

Ironically, if most Disciples of Christ were now polled as to whether or not slavery is a theological issue or a social one, doubtless most would now say theological, thus rejecting Campbell's historic stance. Similarly, most if not all would say that the practice of slavery is and always was sinful. This post-Civil War consensus is now seen as a kind of Christian "common sense." Accordingly, Campbell and others, especially Disciples slaveholders, must be viewed, by modern Disciples, as people who were committed to errant interpretations of scripture and, in addition, slaveholders must be considered carriers of sinful practices and traditions. At this time in history, such an ethical assessment does not seem to be very controversial, but our process of interpreting scripture and determining Christian truths and doctrines is still mired in a process that is difficult, if not impossible. While slavery is now judged by nearly all as sinful, other forms of human action and behavior are much more open to controversy and debate. Take for instance the issue of sexual orientation and sexual ethical practices.

For some Disciples, their reading of scripture leads them to a clear conclusion that engaging in acts of same sex intercourse and marrying two people of the same sex are sinful. For other Disciples such matters demand that the compassionate believer should refrain from interpreting scripture in ways in which the aforementioned practices are routinely and summarily condemned as sinful. For these latter Disciples, the reliance upon the individual's efficacy in judging for himself/herself is paramount. Thus some Disciples are "open and affirming." Many of these Disciples insist that all Disciples come to that conclusion and that the failure to do so smacks of the sin of heterosexism. Many Disciples do not arrive at either pole of interpretation of sexual ethics and can be found wandering (and sometimes being highly confused) somewhere between these opposites. Can everyone be right on this issue? Logic would suggest that this is not possible, yet Disciples have remained faithful to not demanding that people pick sides; at least we have not done so publicly. What many of us have done is pick sides privately or leave the denomination for the more liberal pastures of the UCC, or the more conservative pastures of the Churches of Christ.

Yet leaving the Disciples for another denomination that more easily suits our interpretations of doctrine and scripture is precisely a rejection of the fight against ecclesiastical schism and controversy that brought the Disciples of Christ into being. *To be Disciples is to live together with a variety of understandings of what constitutes* sin, *including social sin.* Again we must ask, is such a way of Christian life possible?

Some Disciples maintain that it is not. Thus they continue on as Disciples but only while they are waging a never-ending battle against holders of bad theological doctrines and practitioners of sin.

It is clear that slavery was always sinful, that Campbell was wrong on that point, and that the wages of the sins of slavery continue to pay off in death. Noncryptically speaking, the racism that justified slavery was not disavowed in the triumph of abolitionism. I have written on racism manifesting itself in a variety of denominations and movements elsewhere.[7]

What is necessary is an examination of what can be done with such an assessment and how what is done may further a Disciples approach to the Christian moral life while still attempting to advance antiracist practices.

First, it is not apparent that one can be antiracist and not call racist practices sinful. In doing this, practitioners of racist practices are implicitly categorized as sinners. For some this conclusion is uncontroversial, but for others it is an indulgence in hubris and sin. Yet, we can live together and possibly even worship together if we will forgive each other.[8]

Such "living" and "worshiping" "together" is fraught with practical difficulties. First, in America, *de facto* segregation has replaced *de jure* segregation.[9] The public schools of Newark, New Jersey, in which I was educated well in an integrated setting in the 1950s and 1960s, have been replaced with highly segregated, white-student-free receptacles for the abandoned poor—Blacks, Hispanics, and other poor non-whites. These students are not being well educated and many Blacks of middle-class and above status have abandoned our former historic commitment to "lifting as we climb" covenants, and have moved to integrated suburbs or even all-Black, all-middle-class suburbs. What I am pointing out here is that in the modern global setting the problems of biblical interpretation, interpretation of the world, and the moral interpretation of human practices have been exponentially compounded. Frequently we Disciples are denominational co-members, but experientially strangers.

We come together at General Assembly from different worlds. At the table of the Lord we celebrate the saving acts and presence of Christ.[10] There is the presence of Jesus Christ there and, for a time, there is liminality, unity, and worship. All of this is good. But *this experiential consensus does nothing to clarify what constitutes social sin.* The Lord's supper is a blessed ordinance, but it does not allow for debate and clarification of different points of view during its observance. Thus after we have given thanks and broken the body of Christ and drunk the blood of the new covenant, we dismiss ourselves from each other without repenting from practices that we have *not* jointly understood to be "sinful."

For example, while it is now uncontroversial to say that slavery is and was sinful, and was a seventeenth and eighteenth century manifestation of racism, what practices now constitute racism and "sin" in the twenty-first century? I would suggest that the white Disciple who sells his home in a town, city, or suburb because the neighborhood is changing, i.e., becoming too Black or too Hispanic, is racist and is sinning. Some readers of this essay probably agree with me, surely others do not, especially those who are selling their homes in the haste of "white flight." But am I correct? Such an assessment comports with my reading of scripture, my understanding of Christian theology, and my experiences with the Holy Spirit and with "white flight." But I must admit that the very freedom of conscience and interpretation of scripture that I hold to be my Disciples heritage and joy allows others to differ from me in the extreme. This then is the ongoing problem of understanding and interpreting sin in this century.

Lest we feel sorry for ourselves, such a problem of interpretation was always an aspect of Disciples worship and life. In our founding congregations, including Cane Ridge, slaves worshiped in chains in the slave galleries. Being kept there in chains was sinful, yet white masters did not perceive such practices as sinful. In a similar fashion a variety of oppressors and masters act with untrammeled consciences even to this day.

For Roger Betsworth, *to be human is to be self-deceived,* and one way of interpreting racist practitioners is to say that they fit into this category. But self-deception cannot be limited to the sin of racism. There are a host of social practices that are sinful, let alone the customary vices that have been historically judged as sinful.[11]

Our discussion should return to one group of practices for further clarification. In the Northeastern region of our church, disputed opinions have raged over the issue of sexual ethics in relationship to Christian practices as well as ordination. Just a few years ago, in the Northeastern region (my current region), ministerial candidates could appear before the committee on ministry and, assuming they had the requisite gifts and graces, education, and calling for ministry, they would be approved for ordination. This determination would be made even if the candidate admitted, or was known, to be a gay man or a lesbian. In those days, one's sexual orientation was not a bar to ordination. This state of affairs did not persist. At a subsequent regional assembly the issue was properly raised, debated, and settled by vote that this practice would be held under a moratorium. No vote was taken that gay candidates were "sinful," yet the practical implicit result of the change characterizes them as such. No vote was taken to maintain that those who disagreed with the moratorium on gay ordinations were wrong or sinful. In other words, those who were in the voting minority were not condemned nor corrected; to have done that would have deeply breached our understanding of ourselves and our polity, discipline, and theology. Yet at the end of the day, a number of Disciples were outraged about the outcome of the vote. For them the assembly was enmeshed in sin.

For the voting victors, a bad, perhaps even sinful practice had finally been brought to a halt, namely the ordination of gay ministers. For them, the Church had been stopped from moving on what was to be a downward slope. For the gay ministerial candidate, such a vote was a disaster. For some "conservative" congregations the vote was a last act of cleansing, a life preserver that allowed the congregation to remain true to Christ. Whose interpretation of sin is right?

We Disciples are caught in a trap of our own making; the issue of the ordination of gay ministerial candidates is merely one example. Our desire to allow for extensive individual interpretation of scripture, tradition, social practices, and theology mandate that in every generation there is at least one social practice that can be interpreted by at least some (with substantial opposition and disagreement from others) of us as "sinful."

Yet this same trap also blesses us Disciples, acting as an escape hatch that allows us to worship, work, and live together despite widespread disagreement and controversy over important issues. We do not excommunicate anyone, and such tolerance has its merits. Some who have been excommunicated by others join our folds. However, some who have been with us from the beginning leave for narrower gates and higher fences.

Finally, then, what does this approach have to say about our understanding of sin? Implicitly we accept, perhaps even unintentionally, Betsworth's understanding of human nature: to be human is to be self-deceived. *Yet we uphold the right to differ on what constitutes sin.* This approach does not directly correct the "sinner." Such a person must find correction from God or the scriptures or their own imperfect conscience. This is why we practice an open table, holding to Paul's admonition that each should judge himself/herself. This is also why, probably (aside from our liturgical tradition), we take the Lord's supper frequently: we are all in need of a lot of opportunities to search our hearts, minds, and practices. With a church that does not speak with one voice, a church that does not have a Pope or a Sanhedrin, let alone an Inquisition, we search our hearts and the scriptures and the Holy Spirit for guidance. And the Holy Spirit also searches each and every one of us. *Doctrinally speaking, we have chosen the least clear path.* In a way, Jesus Christ our Great Shepherd has the proverbial task of "herding cats." Yet Jesus is up to the task. I close with some observations about our historical affirmation and our recent affirmations.

Our Affirmation of Faith is a confession and is not generally characterized as a creed.[12] What is striking about our affirmation is that it does not ask for us to repent from anything. The verbs used in our affirmation are "proclaimed," "accept," "witness," "serve," "rejoice," "enter," (to be) "joined together," "celebrate," "receive," and "yield." Never in our affirmation do we claim to repent. That we are sinners is implicit in our confession that Jesus is the Savior of the world. This confession at least implies that the world is lost and that we are saved because of the saving acts and presence of Christ. Even our confession that we yield ourselves to God focuses on the present and the future. In our present existence we yield ourselves to God. And, in the future, we yield ourselves to God that we may serve the one whose kingdom has no end. Our affirmation does not dwell on the past. Without a call to reflect on our past evil actions, it is an affirmation that does not directly call for repentance. Furthermore, without a call to repentance, there is no active call to discern what actions we may have taken that were sinful, individually *or* collectively. With this kind of affirmation, confessed weekly (sometimes very "*weakly*"), we *are not explicitly encouraged to contemplate the meaning of sin in any sense.* Lest some think that I am glossing over our affirmation, let us also consider our recently affirmed mission covenant.

This new covenant has many fine goals and strategies, but none of them explicitly confess that we have done anything wrong and need to repent. Accordingly, it is a statement much like our affirmation; it does not explicitly explain what sin is and who has been committing it. In summation, we Disciples have nearly as many understandings of the concept of social sin as we do Disciples. We serve God as a group of believers who understand ourselves to be saved and therefore at some level as being sinners or having been sinners. The affirmation commits us to practice "deep Christian spirituality," but does not make it clear to anyone what exactly that phrase means and whether it requires us to repent from sin, to be sanctified from sin, or how to avoid it. It is also unclear how we are to oppose or repent from our "social sins." With our passion for "justice" we move forward in our service, but to have a strong understanding of justice, one must have some clear understanding of injustice. Unfortunately, neither justice nor injustice is spelled out. The aforementioned covenant suggests clearly that racism is wrong and hence, assumedly, "sinful," but nowhere is it suggested that racists should be disciplined or removed from the church. This refusal to patrol our borders is as it should be; we need no Inquisition to purge racists from our midst. On the other hand, this covenant does not even call for those who are racist to desist voluntarily from racism or to repent from the past. Our refusal to even discuss among ourselves the need to repent leaves us helpless to even suggest a clear understanding of sin. Somehow, I suggest that such a stance is mistaken, erroneous, and (dare we say it?) perhaps even sinful. Disagreement with this essay and discussion of it is encouraged, as that is the Disciples way of doing theology and ethics.

Recapping the beginning of this essay, Disciples formed in this country a restoration movement that was deeply concerned with sin. One of the founders of the movement was Walter Scott, the preeminent Disciples evangelist.[13] As a mnemonic device Scott devised the five-finger exercise; two of the fingers explicitly referred to repentance and the remission of sins. Clearly then, our roots acknowledged a deeply held resistance to sin. This early theological position was never clear on the issue of social sin and, accordingly, we remain in the theological morass of such imprecision to this day.

How then are we to live together today? If we are willing to forgive each other, we can as a body of Christ (in our individual camps) fight against social sin as we strive to understand it. On one level, as a liberationist, I am obligated to engage in extensive social critical analysis, ethical reflection, and revolutionary praxis. Part of my calling is to call oppression oppression. This practice I can do without violating Disciples practices. I can march for peace, march against sexism, protest against racism, and work in prisons. I can help build houses for the homeless, and I can write critical essays. What I cannot be is infallible in any of these endeavors. Sometimes I will simply be wrong. Those who are promoting or tolerating what I understand to be social sin, will, at least on some occasion, actually be closer to the truth or the will of God than I am. I must accept our own fallibility. I will continue to try to convert others to my understanding of theology and ethics and social sin. Yet, I must hold open the reality that we can best convert and be converted when we are unwilling to excommunicate the other, especially when the other is at least trying to act in good faith.

Social sin will not go away. Betsworth, Mott, Gardner, Cone, Miguez-Bonino, and others make it clear that social evil must be resisted. We are all fallible. Reinhold Niebuhr, a great ethicist who wrote extensively on the intractability of social sin, was himself quite imperialistic and xenophobic with relation to his understanding of the third world and the relationship of American power to it.[14] He was not unaware of the problem and we must be equally sophisticated. We must be wise as serpents and harmless as doves. In fighting against social sin, we must not call for a *jihad,* or for a crusade. We can never effectively oppose social sin by engaging in the social sin of dehumanizing our enemies: Christ died for them also. Without resort to creeds we must wrestle with each other as Jacob wrestled with the angel at Peniel. It is only in doing so that we can receive a blessing and a new name.

In closing, we must confess that our understanding of social sin is itself imperfect and subject to the influences of social sin itself. But if we talk to each other, listen to each other, pray together, work together, and on occasion lovingly oppose each other, social sin can be vanquished as we serve the One whose kingdom has no end. The aforesaid Niebuhr, enmeshed in a commitment to social sin in support of American hegemony, once wrote sanguinely:

> Nothing that is worth doing can be achieved in our lifetime; therefore we must be saved by hope. Nothing that is true or beautiful or good makes complete sense in any immediate context of history; therefore we must be saved by faith. Nothing we do, however virtuous, can be accomplished alone; therefore we are saved by love. No virtuous act is quite as virtuous from the standpoint of our friend or foe as it is from our standpoint. Therefore we must be saved by the final form of love which is forgiveness... The irony of America's quest for happiness lies in the fact that she succeeded more obviously than any other nation in making life "comfortable," only finally to run into larger incongruities of human destiny by the same achievements by which it escaped the smaller ones.[15]

Niebuhr reminds us that the human heart is desperately wicked and the earthly institutions that sinful humans build continue to bear the irony of humanity's sinful condition. While the American project of freedom has been made manifest in the lives of some American citizens, it has also exposed "larger incongruities" of the American empire. In our post–cold war age of global capitalism, these ironies have become more pronounced.

Finally, we must never forget that God has defeated even social sin. As reminded by Mary in the gospel of Luke 1:51–54:

> He has performed mighty deeds with his arm;
> he has scattered those who are proud in their inmost thoughts.
> He has brought down rulers from their thrones
> but has lifted up the humble.
> He has filled the hungry with good things
> but has sent the rich away empty.
> He has helped his servant Israel,
> remembering to be merciful. (NIV)

So, as we go about opposing social sin, we must entreat God for awareness when we have "crossed the line." For, when we have crossed the line, not only is God not on our side; terrifyingly, God is about to scatter us, the unknowingly sinful to the four winds. Is it not great that we serve a great God?

19

Salvation

Mapping the Salvific Themes in Christian Faith

Joe R. Jones

From biblical times to the present, the discourses and practices of the Christian church have pivoted around the central conviction that the God of Israel, the Creator of the world, became incarnate in the life, death, and resurrection of the Jew Jesus of Nazareth for the salvation of the world. It is this central conviction that gave content to the joyful belief that there was a *Gospel*—good news about the salvation of the world. Drop out this conviction and this Gospel and the discourses and practices of the church lose their coherence and continuity. But having firmly said this, I must acknowledge that the meaning of the word *salvation* has been more variegated and multidimensional than the church has often been willing to admit.

The purpose of this chapter is to explore the various uses of salvation language in the life of the church, identifying some differentiated uses and their interconnection with other doctrines or teachings, and to propose some ways of understanding how the church might understand salvation in relation to who God is, what it means to be human and sinful, and how the church is to witness to the salvific work of God.[1] I am hopeful that this chapter will provide a diagnostic and constructive map of how salvation language properly should work in the discourses and practices of the church's life and witness.[2]

Some Orienting Remarks and Distinctions

While the church, even in biblical times, talks much about *salvation*, that word is related to other words and uses, such as deliverance, liberation/freedom, redemption, reconciliation, atonement, sacrifice, rescue, justification, righteousness, forgiveness, sanctification, regeneration, justice, restoration, and healing.[3] All of these words play differentiated and interconnected roles in the church's discourses about salvation, or what we might now call *soteriology*: how is it that persons and communities come to be saved. And none of this could be discussed without reference to God's love, grace, judgment, and forgiveness.

To gain some traction on these matters, let us recall how biblical words in Hebrew and Greek are initially rooted in ordinary language. In such ordinary language we can discern that salvation-type words have their meaning in relation to a presupposed contrasting condition. To be saved is to be *saved from* some perilous and threatening condition and thereby *saved to* or *saved for* some safer or more hopeful condition. It should be lucid to us as well how such words as *liberation* and *freedom* have similar contrasting conditions: to be liberated or freed is to be liberated or freed *from* some oppressive or restraining condition. Notice also how *deliverance* language fits neatly into salvation language: a person or a community of persons is delivered *from* a perilous situation *to* a safer situation. We can carry these diagnostic comments further by imagining the contrastive conditions that make reconciliation and redemption intelligible to us.

It will be helpful in our further discussion to keep this contrastive character of the many types of salvation language in mind. Of course, in ordinary language the characteristics of the contrasts are so numerous as to defy exhaustive definition. However, in the church's discourse we can gain some leverage on the nature of the contrasts by recognizing that they pivot around the many ways in which humans are being *saved from sin and the consequences of sin*. We need, therefore, to have some grasp of sin and its consequences in order to understand the sort of salvation themes that are central to Christian faith. We must understand that the relevant concept of sin is a *theological concept*, which means that it cannot be articulated without identifying who God is and what it means to be a human being living before God.

Identifying God, Human Being, and Sin

It is a basic Christian confession that God the Creator of all things has been normatively self-revealing and self-manifesting in the election and liberation of Israel, in the life, death, and resurrection of Jesus of Nazareth, and in the empowering work of the Holy Spirit in the summoning of the church into life. It is this understanding of God as having an interactive Life with the world that has entailed for the church identifying God in triune ways: God the Creator of the world; God the incarnate Reconciler in Jesus Christ; God the Redeeming Spirit. It is this triune God that the church has always confessed is the *Savior of human beings otherwise lost in sin.*[4]

What sort of being, then, is the human being? I propose that Christian discourse's understanding of human being can be usefully understood in these interrelated ways. First, human being is *creaturely being,* created by God as a creature among countless other creatures. To be a creature is to be interdependent with other finite, embodied creatures under the temporal and spatial conditions of life: no human exists without this interdependence upon other creatures. Further, to be a creature means that human being is not God.[5]

Second, human being is a peculiarly *personal being,* but intimately formed by social interdependence with other persons. As a person, human being is an *I*—a subject, a self—that can construe a world through language and is thereby capacitated to speak to and listen to other persons. Personal being is endowed with the gift of finite freedom to make decisions and can encounter other persons as subjects who also can make decisions. While no person is simply reducible to relations to other persons and creatures, no person exists without some interdependence with other persons and creatures.[6]

Third, human being is *spiritual being,* that sort of creaturely embodied person who is made in the *image of God* and thereby summoned by God to live in obedient relationship with God and in loving mutuality with other humans, now construed as *thous.* It is the human spirit, as originally endowed by grace, that can discern and hear God's summons into authentic community, in which mutual flourishing is possible and the plentiful creation is the scene of joyful and peaceful begetting, laboring, sharing, and friendship. As spiritual being, a human can grasp her or his life as a gift from God and therefore as one loved by God. In short, human spirits are created and summoned to enjoy life together in the kingdom of God as friends of God.[7]

While these points are only briefly noted here, they are deeply encoded in the distinctive discourses and practices of Christian communities. We should not suppose, however, that these concepts are the common property of the secular discourses today that propose to tell us what it means to be human. Christians construe human being in ways often different from—sometimes in conflict with—the regnant theories and opinions of the secular world.

We are now ready to identify the characteristic respects in which humans are sinners in need of God's salvific interaction. Sin is that absurd corruption of God's purposes in creating a world of creatures, of persons, and of spirits. Sin is that disruption and disorder that penetrates into the human individual and social life and thwarts those conditions of fulfillment and gladness ordained by God. Sin disrupts the human relationships to God, to other creatures and persons, and to oneself that were intended by God in creating human being.

At the heart of human sin is *unbelief*—that devastating practical refusal to believe in God in which humans rebelliously want life on their own terms, utterly unbeholden to God. From this basic rebellion and unbelief, Christian discourse has identified the following faces of sin: (1) *pride* or *hubris*—that incessant self-centeredness and selfishness in which the individual and/or the individual's social group are the center of all valuing of life and death; (2) *concupiscence*—that disordering of desire in which the goods that can confer blessing and peace are rejected under the urgency and compulsion of the quest for immediate sensual satisfaction; (3) *sloth*—that unwillingness, that despair about being a self accountable to God and summoned into a future of responsibility; (4) *lying*—that refusal to care about the truth and that willful telling of lies about others and oneself.

The consequences of sin—the sin that individuals enact and the sins of others that are enacted against them—are in their multiple forms and faces *socially systemic* and corruptive of human life. Humans are incessantly stalked by their own alienation from God, their alienation from their own created nature, and their alienation from other creatures and especially other person-spirits. Rivalry for goods thought too scarce to be shared provokes enmity, violence, and deadly conflicts, resulting in much subjugation and oppression of others. Fear of death and the consequential fear of others who might harm or kill become the dominating dispositions and passions of human life in its individual and social forms.[8]

It is this shabby and frightful life that Christian discourse identifies as life under sin and its consequences, which stands under the *judgment* of God as that condition that is powerless to confer the goodness and blessing the Creator intended from the beginning. This is *not* how life was created to be, and it is a life that, left to its own devices, is a living hell. God says "no" to sin as that human quest to determine on its own what creaturely powers are the real keys to life and death and therefore are worthy of their loyalty and obedience. Idolatry is the irrepressible urge of human life in and under the powers of sin.

What is God to do about humans who live in such a way that they *deserve* the alienating consequences of their lives together? Enmity and violence, despair and fear, pain and suffering, and the unrelenting dominance of death over life emerge as the sad tale of human life under sin. Does the just God simply accept that the order of *justice* requires these devastating consequences of human sin: a destiny of the futile human efforts to attain peace and fulfillment? Is it simply the case that humans either get their act together by their own free striving and live in peace or they face endless conflict and alienation? Having created and summoned human spirits into relationship with Godself and fruitful fellowship with others, does God simply leave it all up to humans to achieve whatever relief or salvation might be achieved? How, then, shall we construe the salvific acts of God in Israel, in the life, death, and resurrection of Jesus Christ, and in the movements of the Holy Spirit?

The Enactment of Salvation in Jesus Christ as the Incarnate Life of God

The Bible is the primitive narrative of how the God who creates all things acts upon and in the created world to save the world, especially humans but not only humans, from sin and the consequences of sin.

In brief, we can identify the basic salvific acts of God—all of which are the acts of God's grace—as the election of and covenanting with Israel, the incarnation of God in Jesus the Jew, and the empowering work of the Holy Spirit in calling the church as an alternative community witnessing to and living under the summons of God's grace.

The primacy of the life, death, and resurrection of Jesus of Nazareth must be understood as the fundamental self-revelation of God's work of salvation. It is in Jesus that the God of Israel decisively takes up the human peril under sin and enacts that gracious work that limits the effects of sin and opens up a new future. Essential to Jesus' salvific work is that the reality of his life, crucified death, and glorious resurrection from the dead are understood as also the work of God. Affirming that Jesus is both human and divine means that God has become active in and vulnerable under the conditions of the humanity of Jesus' life. God, living as a Jewish human being, is taking up the cause of humans living under those conditions that are the consequences of human individual and social sin. In affirming these claims about Jesus, we are affirming that the *Person* of Jesus is both human and divine.[9]

But merely to say "Jesus is God incarnate" is not yet to characterize what he does that is salvific for humans, which the traditions have called the *Work* of Jesus. Yet the Person and Work cannot be separated: *Jesus is who he is as the one who does what he does.* What then does Jesus do that is salvific? I will use a reworked understanding of the three-fold offices of Jesus as *Prophet, Priest,* and *Victor*. In performing all of these offices Jesus is that human being loving God and loving other humans in the ways summoned by God in creating human life, and he is God loving humans in those reconciling ways of forgiveness and grace.[10]

As *Prophet* Jesus proclaims the coming kingdom of God as that community of peacefulness and mutuality, not torn by enmity, jealousy, violence, and oppressive domination of one human by another. Since it is God who is bringing the kingdom, Jesus does not summon folk to bring in the kingdom by their own earnest efforts, though he does counsel folk about the sort of responses appropriate to the kingdom's imminence: loving the enemy and the neighbor, renouncing violence, turning the other cheek, forgiving one another, refusing that exercise of power that intends to dominate and coerce others. Those who so respond to Jesus' prophetic invitation become his disciples and the vanguard of the kingdom.

As *Priest* Jesus is the one who submits to the exercise of coercive and subjugating power by those principalities that rule in human empires perpetuating human oppression and domination. These powers claim to be the rulers that determine life and death and under what conditions humans are allowed to live. In the name of orderly peace and security against enemies, these powers enslave their subjects and murder unruly enemies. These powers murder Jesus on a brutal cross as a sign of his criminal status—he is an enemy of and a threat to the empire's "peace and security."

To his disciples Jesus' crucifixion initially appears as a sure sign that the kingdom he proclaimed and lived is an illusory hoax brutally cancelled by the powers of human empire. Only in their encounter with the resurrected Jesus do the disciples come to understand that Jesus is the Priest who lays down his life, like the sacrificial lambs of the temple, for the sake of reconciliation. Jesus is the Christ, the divine/human reality that takes the full brunt of the powers of sin—as they presume to administer life and death—upon and into the divine Life itself, thereby depriving those powers of their claim to be the determiners of human life and destiny. The human pretence to live life in repudiation of the summons of their Creator—to live life on their own terms—is exposed as a lie. It is in Jesus' resurrection from the dead that his followers understand that he is indeed the *Victor* who finally and truthfully lives without sin and has overcome the consequences of sin, thereby ruling over life and death, over sin and the forgiveness of sin. Jesus is the one who enacts and reveals God's salvific grace in overcoming God's own alienation from the alienating lives of sinners.

Jesus' faithfulness, his love, his unwillingness to seize the sword against enemies, and his forgiving of enemies as they crucified him become that pattern of life that can repudiate sin as that way of life that is unavoidable and necessary to human beings in their sociality. Jesus' followers are summoned by the Spirit into a community of faith, love, and hope, living an alternative way of life to the ways of life of the world still bedeviled by sin—that is the summons of the Holy Spirit, as the Spirit of Christ, to be the church as the body of Christ in and for the world.

For Christians, then, talk of salvation will pivot around what God has done in Jesus Christ for the salvation of a world caught up in and being torn apart by the doing of sin and the being undone by sin. What we might call the *Way of Salvation* is intimately related to the life, death, and resurrection of Jesus and the calling of the church.

The Shadow of Dual Destiny

Before proceeding further to examine the way of salvation, we must acknowledge what I will call a shadow that looms heavily over much of the past discourses of the church. As we have seen earlier in our discussion, salvation-type words always have a contrasting condition. This clearly implies that there is a crucial conceptual distinction between "being saved" and "not being saved." If we further assume that there must be persons who are in each category of saved and not-saved, we seem confronted with the conclusion that there is a *dual destiny* among humans: some persons are saved and some are not-saved, or are damned. Dual destiny language then forces us to inquire about how it comes about that some persons are saved and some are damned.

Along this line of inquiry, the church invoked the language of God's justice wherein such justice is understood to be *retributive* in character: God administers to humans what they justly deserve, whether that be reward and blessings or punishment and rejection. This is justice as *just deserts*.[11] When these concepts structure salvation language, it inevitably appears that those who are saved in some sense *deserved* their salvation, just as those who are damned deserved their damnation. This sort of salvation language is deeply hedged in by such concepts as *earning* or *winning* or *achieving* one's salvation. Yet what is it that the saved *do* that deserves or earns their being saved? It would appear, then, that this logic of salvation is veering in the direction of that sort of *works righteousness* that Paul and others thought denied that persons are saved by the *grace of God*.[12]

Not wanting to openly embrace a works righteousness understanding of salvation, we might retrieve some sense of grace by saying that Jesus met the just demands of God and satisfied God's judgment against sinners.[13] Hence, sinners no longer have to meet God's just demands in order to be saved. But, how then do we avoid slipping into saying that all persons are saved by the grace of God in Jesus Christ because Jesus took the place of sinners before God and met God's just demands? Dual destiny thinkers, finding that belief abhorrent and presumptuous, rush in to reestablish dual destiny by saying that persons must do or feel or have an attitude that accepts Jesus as one's Savior in order thereby to be saved. It is almost impossible for this line of thinking to avoid the subtle belief that salvation is finally up to the individual: either one accepts Jesus as Savior and thereby *earns* being saved or one refuses to accept Jesus—or just remains in ignorance of Jesus—and therefore *deserves* damnation. However this view twists and turns, the retributive justice image of God remains dominant and somehow something persons do determines their salvation. It remains obscure, then, just what it might mean to say one is saved by the grace of God. If grace is a free gift, then how could one also be said to have earned the gift? One earns rewards, not free gifts.

It is no accident that popular Christianity embraces a dual destiny view something like this: human life in time is a trial—pivoting around accepting Jesus as Savior—that will determine whether one is saved to a life beyond death or is damned to a life in hell.

Assuming, however, that we are committed to the dual destiny language but want to avoid a just deserts understanding of salvation, we could, with Augustine and Calvin, affirm that anyone who is saved is saved only by the grace of God. Since everyone already deserves the damnation inherent in sin, anyone actually saved from this damnation is saved only by the gracious and inexplicable decree of God. To try to explain why this person is saved and that person is not is impossible by appeal to any criterion of just deserts. But this view that salvation and damnation are already dually determined in God's eternal predestination seems strangely detached from any understanding of salvation being brought by Jesus Christ. The singular virtue of this view of salvation is its firm grasp that salvation is first and last the work of God's grace. Perhaps the conundrum we are facing here is rooted in the attachment to retributive justice, just deserts, and dual destiny as the baseline concepts for understanding salvation.[14]

On Resisting Some Recent Temptations

In the last two hundred years—a period of wrenching critiques and disagreements within the theological discourses of churches—there has been a tendency to focus on one aspect of salvation language at the expense of other aspects. Hence, the rich diversity and interconnected language of salvation gets reduced to one defining image of what salvation really is. It will be instructive, I hope, to review briefly some of these temptations to reduce salvation to a single defining image.

Salvation as Existential Authenticity: Claiming that the eschatological vision of salvation as eternal life beyond death has been devastated by modern thought, Christian faith can still identify that feature of human existence that is determinative of the meaning of salvation, namely, the deep existential *how* of a person's life in time. Interpreting sin as inauthentic life manifesting itself in the all-consuming fear of death, the sinful *how* of a person's life results in much lying, self-deception, and deep despair. But in Jesus' call to faith and in the gracious bestowing of faith, persons come to live authentically, accepting God's forgiving grace as proclaimed in the gospel and candidly facing their own deaths without resort to the myths of immortality. Eternal life is, therefore, not some future life after death; rather it is that state or event in some individual's life in which authentic response to God's grace is realized. Salvation is to be identified precisely in this qualitative way in which a person puts his or her life together. Obviously, there is still a dual destiny, though not perhaps of just deserts: some receive the grace and are transformed and some do not receive and therefore are not transformed. This view of salvation is similar to all those views that collapse the whole meaning of salvation into a primary concern with the transformation in time of the individual's relationship to God. Yet this view lacks a vivid sense for the restoration of human community and the way in which the Gospel summons persons to live in liberating ways on behalf of their neighbors. Further, it too cavalierly repudiates life beyond death.[15]

Salvation as Social Liberation: Largely as a critique of existential individualism, the liberation theme emphasizes that Christian life is the liberation of persons from social oppression to a situation of justice and freedom. Where the powers of the world enslave persons and deprive them of their just share of society's goods, there is no justice and therefore no liberation and no meaningful sense of salvation. Liberation thinkers have helpfully discerned the many ways in which sin is a socially systemic problem and that political/economic realities must be engaged if there is to be actual social salvation for the oppressed. While this is a word that is needed by the church, it does seem to imply, when it is understood as the only or primary meaning of salvation, that the socially oppressed are simply in all respects determined by their oppression and therefore lacking any meaningful sense of salvation. This also implies that the oppressed of the past—who never knew liberation from social oppression—have somehow missed the saving work of God in the world. As a necessary theme in Christian faith, liberation from social oppression is uneliminable; yet, as the primary or defining theme of salvation, it is devastating to our understanding of the limits of God's salvation. It needs an appreciation of how Paul in jail and a host of oppressed Christians of the past felt also liberated by God's grace with a hope in God that transcends any particular conditions of human life in time.[16]

Millennial Salvation: This theme emerges out of the book of Revelation (20:4–6) in which a thousand-year reign of Christ seems to be prophesied. While that notion itself seemed misleading to many in the first centuries of the church's life and even threatened the final inclusion of Revelation in the New Testament canon, it does reappear time and again in the life of the church. The central point of the millennial theme is that there will be a thousand-year reign of Jesus in *human history*. It is a vision of peace and well-being actually being lived out by humanity under the gracious reign of Jesus. Pre-millennialists believe that Christ will return and usher in the reign of peace, at the end of which the final judgment of all things will be rendered. Post-millennialists believe Christ will come at the end of the thousand years and judge all things. We should appreciate the emphasis of the millennialists on the concreteness of the kingdom in history, which is similar to the liberationists concern for tangible social justice. However, two perils lurk in millennialism: (1) it can devolve into emphasizing that the Christians must themselves bring in the kingdom by their righteous efforts or at least their righteous efforts will be the precondition for Jesus bringing in the kingdom; or (2) the beginning or the ending of the millennium becomes bathed in violence, either the violence of slaughtering the evildoers in order to bring in the kingdom or the violence of slaughtering at the end. This violence language seems inevitable when this vision of salvation rests primarily on the book of Revelation, which is replete with violent language about the conflict between good and evil.[17]

All of these views, in their tendency to insist that the center of the church's understanding of salvation is defined by their particular emphasis, can mislead the church about the differentiated and interconnected range of meanings available in a full-orbed understanding of the salvific work of the triune God. The following section proposes a map of salvation issues and concerns that comprehensively fit together without obvious self-contradiction.

The Spheres of the Way of Salvation: A Proposal

In the gospel narratives, a rich young man confronts Jesus, asking: "Teacher, what good deed must I do to have eternal life?" After the young man avers that he has kept "the commandments," Jesus summons him to sell his "possessions, and give the money to the poor…then come, follow me," to which the man responds by going away "grieving, for he had many possessions." The puzzled disciples ask: "Then who can be saved?" to which Jesus replies: "For mortals it is impossible, but for God all things are possible." (See Mt. 19:16–27; Mk. 10:17–27; Lk. 18:18-27.)

In great proximity to this text, it is often asked: "What must I do to be saved?" The accent is on *what must be done* in order to gain salvation, here understood as "eternal life." This picture of salvation and the earning-of-salvation has exercised a tight grip on much Christian imagination for centuries. That same picture, of course, ignores the further words of Jesus: "For mortals it [viz. inheriting eternal life] is impossible, but for God all things are possible." Salvation, inheriting eternal life, is impossible for mortals by the powers of their own actions? Many are the issues lurking in this passage, which we will now try to unfold.

To make sense out of this passage and to overcome some of the unsatisfying lacunae in the just deserts/dual destiny language, I propose to differentiate the language of salvation among the following spheres of salvation issues, while still grasping the deep interconnections of the theme of the triune God's gracious salvation in Jesus Christ and the summoning of the church through the Spirit. It is through the language and realities of the spheres that we will be able to appreciate the complex and differentiated ways in which the church can talk about salvation.

The ***first sphere***, in the language of *incarnation, atonement, reconciliation,* and *justification,* emphasizes what was done—what was achieved—in the life, death, and resurrection of Jesus Christ. Something happened in this particular human's historical career—what he did and what was done to him—that has a sovereign reality not simply dependent on the response of believers or followers. Indeed, who Jesus was and what he did—as have been identified in our previous discussion—are the fundaments of whatever else the church might say about God, human life, and salvation.[18]

However, this sphere can fall into disarray if we do not hold together and appreciate the interpenetration of Jesus' work as Prophet, Priest, and Victor. He is the Prophet of the Kingdom that is crucified on the cross and raised as the Victor over life and death. He is the vulnerable Priest who proclaims a Kingdom of peace and nonviolence and was murdered by the principalities and powers—imperial political and religious leaders—that murder in order to dominate and subjugate. He is the Victor raised from the dead who is the presence of and the forerunner of a Kingdom of peace. In all these offices, Jesus is the incarnate life of God graciously taking the sins of the world upon and into the divine Life and thus disarming them of their power to determine human meaning and destiny *before God*.

So, who is saved in this sphere? All humans are saved from the condition of being condemned by their sins before God to the condition of being graciously forgiven and justified in ways beyond their deserts. This gracious forgiveness stands there just on its own, independent of its acceptance and appropriation by any person, though its acceptance and appropriation bring the forgiveness and justification home to the believers.

The ***second sphere*** of salvation language pertains to the actual ways in which persons subject to sin find their lives forgiven, graced, healed, and transformed by the Spirit of Christ. The centering focus of this transformation is how persons *appropriate* in their lives and communities *what* Jesus revealed and accomplished for them. This is the sphere in which life in the church and the discipleship to Jesus become decisive themes. This sphere we will call *historic redemption* as what is taking place in what I will also call *historic destiny*: how life unfolds in the spatiality and temporality of human history. The special role of the church in historic redemption is that it is the body of Christ in the world and the bearer of the *means of grace*—embodied in its distinctive discourses and practices—by way of which persons come to know and appropriate the grace of God revealed and enacted in Jesus Christ. Distinctive Christian life becomes an *ethics of grace*: given what God has done in Jesus Christ, Christians live under the summons to be peacemakers and forgivers, lovers of neighbors, strangers, and enemies. This is not an ethics of how to earn God's grace but an ethics of how to live in conformity to grace freely given and freedom conferring. Indeed, being liberated from the destiny-determining power of sin, Christians can live for others without fear of death or the threat of death.

Hence, in its distinctive discourses and practices, the church bears a witness to the gracious salvific acts of the triune God, intending in every way to be a alternative community of faith, love, and hope living for the benefit of the world otherwise entangled in sin. The church's life unfolds amidst the dynamic interaction of its *nurturing practices*—worship, communal care, and educational formation in faith—and in its *outreach practices*—evangelism, prophetic critique of the worldly powers of domination and oppression, and the actual engagement in works of love on behalf of the world. It is in these outreach practices that the church enacts a liberating dismantling of the many individual and social forms of sin in the world. It should be apparent that *all of these works of the church in historic redemption are from beginning to end salvific in character and purpose.*[19]

Having now affirmed this work of God in historic destiny, we must also admit that many are the individuals and the socio-political arrangements and communities that never respond to the work of forgiveness in Jesus and the work of transformation in the Spirit. In some sense, then, we must admit that in historic destiny, some folk know no healing and loving God of grace. If historic destiny is the complete *scope* of human life before God, we would have to admit that many are they who die in time having lived lives ravaged by sin—their own sin and the sins of others against them—without any apparent experience of God's salvific grace. Because the church believes that Jesus was raised from the dead and reigns as Victor over life and death, it also believes that historic destiny is neither the full scope of life nor the final determiner of life before God.

The ***third sphere*** of salvation language pertains to how we identify issues of *ultimate human destiny*. To ask about ultimate human destiny is to ask about the ultimate *end* of human life, meaning both end as *telos,* or goal, and end as *finis,* or finality and conclusion. In discussing these issues we are entering the doctrinal theme of *eschatology*: God's ultimate determination of the meaning, reality, and scope of human life, indeed of the life of the whole cosmos. Is death simply what is final about human life, and now death under the shadow of sin? Or are there *transhistorical* possibilities and realities? In traditional language, notions of heaven and hell emerge in this sphere.

The center of ultimate destiny language is the reality of the triune God: Creator, Reconciler, and Redeemer. We have affirmed that much pivots around what God did in Jesus Christ and its *benefits* for humanity. Not only does the incarnational narrative of Jesus' work include the cross as manifesting the vulnerable power of the divine Life in taking the destined consequences of sin upon and into God's Life and thereby depriving them of their power to be the *determiners of human destiny,* but the resurrection of Jesus is the gracious opening up of life beyond death. But for whom is this life beyond death—what I am calling *transhistorical life*—made possible? Only for those who have faithfully followed Jesus and thereby *earned* the right to dwell eternally in God's grace? Were this the logic of life beyond death, then only the faithful will be ultimately redeemed and the unfaithful will be absent, either in absolute annihilation in death or in being raised to an everlasting life in hell! Is it possible that the crucified Jesus descended into hell—as that stark and devastating extremity of human alienation from God—and thereby emptied hell as the ultimate destiny of any human being?[20]

I am proposing that the Life of the triune God with the world is from beginning to end—as the Alpha and Omega of life and being—the life of a gracious Creator in search of the redemption of rebellious creatures and therefore precisely as Omega has, is, and will be the *Ultimate Companion and*

Redeemer of all creatures. Hence, rather than being saved by their merits or condemned by their demerits, in this sphere of ultimate destiny, all will finally be saved by the grace of God. Being raised to life beyond death is a gift of God and is neither a natural attribute of being human nor an earned reward for righteous life. Christians, above all, not only know the grace of God, they also are keenly aware of the repetitious ways in which sin clings to their own acts and feelings. This awareness thus disabuses Christians of trusting that the presumed stalwartness and extent of their faithfulness could earn them such eternal life. Christians are those who deeply and passionately encounter death—their own and the deaths of the many others—as a dying unto the sheer gracious love of God. Bluntly, Christians trust and hope in the grace of God, not in their own presumed achieved righteousness! When all things are subjected to the work of Jesus Christ, they will be subjected by the transforming power of the triune God who incarnately and ultimately refuses to count the sins of the world against it and who graciously redeems all creatures. Joyfully, God's power and grace are the final and ultimate determiners of the meaning and destiny of human life. God speaks and enacts an unceasing triumphant *yes* to the world.

Yet God's ultimate redemption is not only the destiny of human life; it is also the destiny of the whole creation, including all creaturely beings and powers. Affirming that the created world as created is finite with a beginning—which is the beginning of time and temporality—the world also has an end, both as goal and conclusion. At some point in the future, God will consummate the whole creation as a redemptive kingdom in which nothing good is lost and all creatures cease conflict and rest in peace. It is the ultimate *yes* of God that subverts every doctrine that claims God will ultimately *destroy* the world in a final act of violence.

The church must never forget nor neglect the belief that the triune God, who lives in freedom and love, is the Alpha and the Omega—the beginning and the end—of all creatures and all principalities and powers.

20

Faith and Justification

Commencing Salvation

BOSELA EALE AND WILLIAM A. WRIGHT

This chapter takes the form of a conversation between a Congolese theologian who is Regional Minister of Kinshasa and an American Disciples theologian trained in academic theology. We aspire to fulfill the mandate that theology take place today in mutual accountability and conversation across the world's dividing lines, out of love and a shared faith in the one God. The topic is what faith and justification mean for the Christian and the church. The ultimate seriousness of this topic prohibits us from being satisfied with a mere "*my* theology." Because of both changing global demographics within the church and a historical North American ethnocentrism, we begin by listening to the meaning of salvation in the Congolese situation, as described by Rev. Eale.

Reverend Bosela Eale: Faith and Salvation in the Congo

During a recent visit to the U.S., I was discussing the issue of faith with one of my American Disciples minister colleagues. She told me that some day she hoped to come to Africa for mission work. She wanted to come especially to teach about faith, because she believes that Africans need to grow in their faith. Then I asked her, do you have a bank account? She said, yes. I asked again, you have a car, don't you? She responded, yes I do. I then asked her again, you have food in the fridge and in the pantry, don't you? She said, yes of course. Then I asked her, if you did not have all these things, would you go to church on Sunday and praise God and thank Him that you lack what you are accustomed to having? She said no. And I asked her, where is your faith?

In the Bible, "salvation" is a broad term that means deliverance from all the threats to life, both now and in the time to come. It is also used as the equivalent of "life" and entering the kingdom of God. As Africans, we strongly believe in God as the source of life and salvation. It is unfair to give a statement such as, "Africans do not know God." Africans know very well what salvation and faith stand for. God is the ultimate receiver of all prayers, so all offerings begin with calling upon God. This God has been with Africans from the beginning and is featured in prayers and greetings, blessings and curses. The saying, "God will pay you back," is feared as a most potent curse. This saying shows how African people strongly believe that God has the power to do whatever God wants. All over Africa, people generally assume that God created the heaven and the earth and all their contents. Heaven is the counterpart of the earth.[1] This is to say that God is not unknown to Africans. The main issue here is how to relate to that God.

Africans are aware of the divine presence in such a vivid way that oftentimes the fear of the spirit world manifests itself as a dominant factor in the shaping of African life. Since the time when missionaries brought the Gospel to Africa, however, African Christians began to change their mind. Ancestors who formerly played the role of "mediators" between God and the community are no longer being considered as such. Today, the Disciples in the Congo consider Jesus to be the mediator through whom God blesses his people.[2] Jesus, who is the only way to God, has bridged the gap between the Supreme Being and the people.[3]

While I truly believe this, I do have a lot of respect for people of other religions and faiths and I also enjoy meeting and talking with them. But the mutual understanding we share does not gainsay the truth that Jesus died for the sins of all humanity. Some people believe that all religions are generically the same. Byang H. Kato observes:

> This type of "mutual understanding" that is a weapon for the *coup de grace* (the death of) of evangelism is evidently contrary to the mission of rescuing the perishing souls steeped in sin, whether they are religious or not. This is the mission committed to the Disciples of Christ (Mt. 28:19; Acts 1:8). Although conflict with other religions may be the outcome (2 Cor. 11:23–33), the servant is not greater than his Master (Jn. 15:20).
>
> The Christian understanding of men of other religions can only be that once he too, like them, was blind, trying in vain as a drawing person, to secure a broken reed. But now the grace of God has rescued him so he should be burdened for those still groping in darkness (and not ridicule them)—burdened enough to want to share the bread of life with them, just as a fortunate mendicant lovingly shares a bowl of rice with his former colleagues![4]

When we talk about faith and salvation, it is very important to stress the object of our faith and the one who accomplishes salvation. God is at the center of both salvation and faith. Yet the knowledge of God available to humankind is limited. As quoted by Tokunboh Adeyemo, Bolaji Idowu asserts that no nation or race can claim an absolute knowledge of God, because, despite his intellectual acumen, while man remains finite, God is infinite.[5]

Still, God has shown himself through the sacrificing gift of Jesus Christ. Members of the Disciples of Christ Community in the Congo believe that salvation is individual, not universal, and that Jesus is the only way to God. Jesus plays a key role in the faith of the Disciples. Faith has an object—Jesus Christ—and God only asks us to put our faith in Him who incarnates salvation. The teachings that hold the view that all people will eventually be saved through the atonement of Christ—even those who have openly rejected Jesus, even those who have willingly committed horrible crimes and died without repentance and without the covering of Christ's blood, that even they will enjoy a future with God—these teachings seem dangerous to me.

We all know that God is sovereign. God can save anybody. But I want just to limit myself to what I believe is biblical truth. In John 8:24 (NIV), Jesus said, "If you do not believe that I am the one I claim to be, you will indeed die in your sins." I do not see how one can talk about salvation and not put Jesus in the center of his or her belief. From faith in Christ comes the logical consequence of justification, according to which we say: "I am what I am because of what I have believed in." Faith makes things happen.

Contrary to the universalist views of some, salvation in the African context today is understood to apply to some individuals and not others. This is a lesson I have learned throughout my life. Born and raised in the Disciples of Christ Community in the Congo, I thought that this alone was enough for me to claim to be saved. Again, when I was baptized by immersion in the Missionary Station of Monieka in 1968, baptism was something that I thought gave me salvation. This was the view according to the teaching I received at that time, something that continues to be taught in some places among the Disciples in the Congo. In all this, I do not see how and when the Gospel was explained clearly to me in such a way that I could have made a decision that would change my life. I do not mean to say that the change of life would come through my own effort, but this change indeed did come later, when I made the decision to commit my sinful life to Jesus Christ. He then transformed my life by the power of the Holy Spirit. I did not sense something that day when I committed my life to Jesus Christ, but I cried seriously when I realized how pitiful and wretched I was. I knew that Jesus was the only one who could rescue me from the eternal judgment and punishment that was waiting for me.

What does Jesus save us from? Does he save us from our actions, our temperament, our thoughts, and ourselves? I do not believe so. Rather, he saves us from the wrathful judgment of God upon us because of our sinfulness. There is a natural consequence to being a sinner: God's judgment. If a person rejects Jesus, he or she does not have a covering for sin, does not have forgiveness of sins, and therefore the wrath of God abides upon him or her: "Whoever believes in the Son has eternal life; whoever disobeys the Son will not see life, but must endure God's wrath" (Jn. 3:36). Jesus saves all those who receive him so that they can escape the judgment to come. In several places in the Bible he warned his hearers about hell (Mt. 5:29–30; 32:33; Mk. 9:45; Lk. 12:5). If there is no eternal fiery hell, no dread of being cast into it, no wrath to come, where is the power in Jesus' warning?

Salvation comes through justification and faith. As stated in the Bible, it is not a result of human efforts: "For by grace you have been saved through faith, and this is not your own doing; it is the gift of God—not the result of works, so that no one may boast" (Eph. 2:8–9). Salvation is God's business, a matter of God's love and grace; it is not a matter of human merit or achievement. I trust in God's mercy and faithfulness revealed in Jesus Christ.

Salvation is in God's hands, but we cannot neglect the importance of faith and human decision. God has put before us two ways, the way of life and the way of death. God urges people to choose the way of life. We are human beings; God does not treat us like robots. We have to make a choice. Each of us must make a choice that determines our eternity, either with God or in hell.

But, of course, the ability to survive the struggles that each day presents also depends on choosing the way of life. In my ministry, I see testimony to the power of God's grace every day in the life of the faithful. Parents rejoice when their children decide to come back to Jesus. Families living in poverty unimaginable to most North Americans sing God's praises. Women who believe that their inability to conceive is God's punishment for a previous abortion receive forgiveness. There are many stories to tell of grace in the midst of suffering, and we should share each other's stories, like we share the stories of the Bible. By reading together books like Job and others, we arrive at a common agreement that suffering and hardship can be a tool for measuring faith in God. How can someone live in a situation of hardship and still consider God to be merciful unless he or she has a personal relationship with God? I think again of the story about the conversation with my North American ministry colleague. Hardship accentuates faith.

When people are looking for miracles, I can say that in the Congo, our daily life is a miracle. How else can a family with six children live on twenty dollars a month? Yet somehow the rent gets paid. Then there's the health care that the family cannot afford, but still they are alive. On Sunday, one will see the same suffering and believing Christian family in the church praising God and shouting, "Alleluia!" Isn't this a sign of faith in God? For the people of the Congo, salvation is both spiritual and physical. It is in the present, the past, and the future. This is why Congolese people and most of Africa believe in God not just with the intellect but also with faith, and in communion with each other. The church has become the center of life.

It is possible for everyone to know, starting today, whether salvation is meaningful in one's life. It is possible for each to decide. But there is no decision about what will happen if we hold on to universal salvation. Why should we not stay with what is available now, salvation through faith in Jesus Christ, before we jump ahead to when God will redeem the whole creation in God's sovereignty?

William Wright: Disciples Doctrine of Justification in Historical and Ecumenical Context

Rev. Eale's description of being saved from God's wrath by faith in Jesus will resonate with some North American Disciples; others will associate his language with a seemingly familiar evangelical message. Our reactions will vary depending on social location and personal conviction. I could raise many questions about the role of faith as a decision, the tension between God's mercy and wrath, and the working of God's Spirit in those who do not acknowledge the name of Jesus; these are the questions I generally pose to evangelical theology. But these questions would not do justice to the richness of Rev. Eale's faith as lived in its context.[6] What I find strikingly unfamiliar about Rev. Eale's portrait of salvation, what makes it distinctive among the evangelical theology I know, is the conjunction of strong Jesus-centered piety with a sense of God's justice on the side of the poor—indeed, a level of poverty few North Americans will likely ever know. For Rev. Eale's flock, God's justice for the poor is the ligature of the people of God, and their individual decisions for Christ confirm upon this bond personal agency. His testimony offers a unique opportunity to challenge the North American theological framework of both evangelicals and non-evangelicals, but I will focus on the latter, which includes the majority of North American Disciples and established Protestant churches. In response to Rev. Eale's description of salvation, this is the challenging question I hear posed to us: have we lost the seriousness of what it means to be saved?

A brief look at Disciples history shows that, at the beginning of our movement, making the transition from perdition to salvation was a serious matter, often accompanied by vivid personal experience. We have preserved a space for the decision to commit oneself to Christ in our continued use of the invitation and practice of adult baptism. Yet there is no doubt that North American Disciples theology has changed over these many years, first of all in reaction to modern Euro-American scholarship in science, biblical studies, history, and theology. Second, with regard to the twentieth-century ecumenical movement, Disciples theology has been shaped by a growing sense of accountability to a larger Church tradition. In this regard, I will review the momentous yet quiet milestone marked by the signing of the *Joint Declaration on the Doctrine of Justification* (JDDJ) by Catholics and Lutherans in 1999. Third, Euro-American Disciples are finally beginning to recognize their accountability to communities of color within the Disciples and throughout the world, particularly in the expanding church of the Southern Hemisphere. After a brief review of Disciples history, I explore the contemporary significance and ecumenical standing of the doctrine of justification, or how the Christian acquires faith, receives forgiveness, and is brought into Christ's salvation. Finally, Rev. Eale and I will explore together what consensus is possible when the resources of North American Disciples theology are informed *by* and become responsible *to* the witness of Congolese Christians.

The doctrine of salvation, or soteriology, remains a vital issue for the church in the Congo. Yet many Disciples churches in North America may not describe themselves first of all as a place where people come to get saved. Truth be told, the early Disciples were much more like Rev. Eale than like many current Disciples congregations in North America when it comes to their passionate understanding of salvation. Why are so many Disciples often underwhelmed by the idea of salvation?

There are no doubt some false reasons—that is, reasons without theological legitimacy. It may be that churches regard themselves more as a social club or community center than as the body of Christ here to serve God. This reason is indefensible theologically. It may also be that, particularly for those living in relative comfort and ease, life is not under an obvious threat from which could arise a powerful desire to be saved. Life is full of abundance; death is remote and deferred until old age; opportunities are promising for oneself and one's descendents. Many of us begin with Job's prosperity and never know anything different. While North American comfort and prosperity is an understandable source for soteriological apathy, it is no excuse, since it depends upon our willful ignorance of those less "fortunate," indeed, those who are even the suffering survivors of our comfort.

Yet it could also be that some North American Disciples forsake the early Stone-Campbell emphasis on salvation because they no longer find that sense of salvation theologically plausible. They could offer the rationale that the founders concentrated on avoiding hell and gaining the ultimate reward of heaven. The concept of hell, they might continue, saddles God with willing eternal punishment and is impossible to reconcile with affirmations of God's love. Little better, the idea of being motivated by a heavenly reward reduces religion to little more than extended self-interest, belying the powerful calling of Christ to serve God selflessly. Furthermore, the Disciples founders were arguably too focused on *individual* salvation, and thereby obscured the biblical message of being made a people of God, and of seeking the kingdom of God. Some present-day Disciples may be seeking a more communal instantiation of God's presence and power, one they feel the early Disciples did not articulate. These are indeed legitimate theological concerns that need to be addressed. One can only hope that these are the more prevalent reasons for a lack of passion about being saved, rather than the contented apathy that is a product of North American affluence.

I know from my conversations with Rev. Eale that the Disciples of Christ Community in the Congo lives out its faith with both a lively expectation of (eternal) salvation and also an active, mutually supportive community life. In their context, the question asked by Paul's jailor in Acts 16 ("What must I do to be saved?") expresses a deep yearning and carries tremendous power. Their response is to proclaim faith in Jesus Christ as Lord and Savior and present themselves for baptism. Among the rich variety of biblical meanings of salvation outlined by Joe Jones in his essay in this volume, why does this sense of salvation as a personal transference from being lost to being safe with Jesus carry such personal and communal power for Rev. Eale's flock? And for us Disciples who, like the Congolese church, typically practice the "invitation" after the sermon and adult baptism, should this personal dimension of salvation still carry the same urgent concern and transformative power? Addressing this question requires a broader theological perspective.

Behind the questions of becoming a Christian, conversion, professing faith, and baptism, lies the classical theological topic of justification by faith. The language of justification by faith received its biblical stamp in Paul's letters, and was reaffirmed at crucial junctures in the theological tradition by Augustine, Luther, and most recently in the JDDJ, issued by the Roman Catholic Church and the Lutheran World Federation in 1999. In the sixteenth century, justification by faith was the rallying cry for the Protestant Reformation that split the Western church. The Disciples of Christ, as a movement, bear a twofold inheritance from the Reformation:[7] on the one hand, we carry forward the Protestant beliefs about the integrity of individual conscience, the equality (or "priesthood") of believers before God, the centrality of personal commitment to Christ, and earnest commitment to scripture; on the other hand, we uphold a "Catholic" dedication to Christian unity and yearn to heal the divisions that grew out of the Reformation. Remarkably, these two Disciples inheritances from the Reformation have recently come closer together with the aforementioned JDDJ, in which Catholic and Lutheran theologians have announced a significant consensus on the very issue that for so long was thought to divide them irrevocably.

Just what is justification by faith? For Paul, justification by faith is contrasted to works of the law. While interpretations of Paul are contested, the main point seems clear: in the context of his struggles, justification meant affirming the inclusion of Gentiles into the church without requiring them to adopt the obligations of the Torah, e.g., circumcision and dietary restrictions.[8] The Reformers read Paul's language from their own context, finding in Paul novel theological applications for their disenchantment with Catholic theology and practice of the day. For the Reformers, justification by faith principally stands for the experience of God's forgiveness and the acceptance of the sinner as beloved by God; salvation begins here. The Reformers encouraged believers to picture themselves before God's judgment seat, submitting themselves to God's verdict. Face to face with God's holy majesty, how could we not feel condemned by even our smallest flaw (cf. Isa. 6:1–7)? In presenting ourselves before God, we believers find peace only by letting Jesus Christ be our Mediator before God. Christ has shown God to be merciful both by his ministry of forgiveness and by dying as the once-for-all sacrifice to make us acceptable before God.[9] Accordingly, to determine whether we are acceptable to God or not, and thus saved, we should not look to ourselves nor to anything we do. For the Reformers, looking only to God's grace (*sola gratia*) was the antidote to much Catholic theology of the day that had a hard time not thinking of salvation as something we must in some way "merit" through good works. Rather, the Reformers preached that one should look only to God's verdict in Christ. For that reason, Calvin preferred to speak of "justification in Christ" rather than "justification by faith." Too much stress on the "by faith" will make justification seem like a work that we do; rather, Christ accomplishes justification for us and thus our new life is in him.

By placing faith and the personal relationship between the individual and God at the center of soteriology, the Reformers accentuated the individual reality of salvation. Yet they should not be accused of restricting salvation to the subjective and introspective realm of the single individual. In a peculiar way, the Reformers' doctrine of justification by faith speaks deeply to our individuality and acknowledges it, but toward the goal of surpassing and overcoming our personal subjectivity. Justification transcends mere personal opinion or egotistical concern. Justification by faith means looking to Christ alone, and indeed is precisely the opposite of looking to ourselves. We are to "forget about ourselves."[10] The goal is to have certainty and assurance in Christ, so as to no longer to worry obsessively about our individual salvation. The faith that justifies takes us "out of ourselves,"[11] opening us to receive who and what we are from God. Faith is just this way of being an open and receiving self. When we think of it that way, it is easy to see how faith equips us to love our neighbor.[12]

Introspection and attending to oneself, if indeed these were ever overcome, returned to Protestantism with a vengeance after the first generation of Reformers. In America, the Presbyterianism that nurtured Barton Stone and Alexander Campbell encouraged an anxious investigation of one's inner state for signs of grace and election. Certainly, both Lutheran Pietism and the increasing attention paid to signs of individual election in Calvinism are partly to blame. Perhaps behind this return is the Reformers' own insistence on judging those Christians who disagreed with them as condemned and destined to hell, what early Disciples called having a "party spirit." While Disciples arguably offered a less divisive and more communal understanding of salvation than their contemporaries (see below for Clark Gilpin's argument to this effect), they nonetheless, like other Christians of the era, put the individual's conversion at the center of the drama of salvation. Stone writes movingly of his own quest for assurance of salvation, finally being converted after hearing the preaching of William Hodge on God's love.[13]

Campbell was more ambivalent about the centrality of having a certain kind of conversion experience, which was a common feature of revivalism. Like the early Reformers, he preferred to focus on God's scriptural testimony, rather than the individual's inner experience:

> There is a prevailing idea that persons are pardoned by means of, or in consequence of, a thought or a feeling. Hence we often hear persons, in relating their experience, date all their joys and their hopes of heaven from some idea which they formed, or from some impression made upon their minds, at a certain time.[14]

Campbell's description could fit many modern-day evangelicals who are keen to pin an exact date on their conversion. Relying too heavily on personal impressions, argues Campbell, entails that the sense of being pardoned can vary with one's changing emotional state. Echoing the Reformers, he counters: "The foundation of this assurance [of pardon] with the ancient converts was the *testimony* of God."[15]

While Campbell directed the individual Christian to scriptural testimony of God's pardon through Christ, he also emphasized the importance of the individual's free acceptance of that testimony based on the power of reason. He believed that a theology acknowledging the role of an individual's own will and intellect was "more honorable."[16] Thus justification by faith, the commencement of salvation, ought to involve something we ourselves do, if is to really be our salvation. Similarly, Rev. Eale has stressed the importance of the individual's decision, although noting that the individual does not accomplish salvation.

For Campbell, the commencement of salvation was the knowledge and acceptance of God's forgiving nature, or faith. Walter Scott famously and perhaps too methodically drew out the rest of the sequence that followed for a full account of salvation: faith, repentance (sorrow for sins and mending one's ways), baptism, remission of sins (or reconciliation with God, the completion of justification), the gift of the Holy Spirit and the promise of eternal life. On the one hand, as Clark Gilpin has argued, this order keeps the remission of sins within the communal, sacramental practice of the church. Campbell and Scott thereby intentionally reversed the order of salvation typical of revivalists in their day, according to which salvation is manifested individually in certain charismatic experiences.[17] In other words, for Campbell and Scott individuals do not experience salvation first, only to seek a church later; rather, salvation is a communal reality from the beginning. Yet on the other hand, this "five finger exercise" appears to consist in, first, the three steps we do, and second, the three promises God fulfills. (A sixth finger seems in order.) As a theological statement, it thus left itself open to the interpretation that salvation consisted in God's rewarding human endeavor.

Toward the end of the nineteenth century, a general cultural optimism about human self-improvement, combined with a growing awareness of the historicity of all expressions of faith, including the New Testament, led to the flowering of theological liberalism. Disciples scholars like W.E. Garrison (1874–1969) no longer found meaningful the gravity of sinful humanity before a just God, with humanity suspended between heaven and hell. Not until his later, more ecumenical writings did Garrison find value in the Protestant doctrine of justification.[18] Reflecting upon the influence of the related Social Gospel movement, as well as a traditional Disciples pragmatism, Clark Williamson suspects that the real theology behind Disciples' active life is a theology of sanctification. He sees striving toward the kingdom of God through social action to be more important for Disciples than matters of justification, such as the problem of original sin and the redemptive answer found in Christ's death.[19]

Williamson's characterization of the Disciples applies also to segments of other established Protestant churches in North America. That is what makes so surprising the achievement of the *Joint Declaration on the Doctrine of Justification* (JDDJ) in 1999. While the agreement over most of the central issues that split the Western church sounds momentous, it may be that the agreement became possible just because the doctrine of justification had ceased to seem relevant. Indeed, the announcement of the agreement was far from earth-shattering. Yet behind the agreement lies the remarkable theological breakthrough of Karl Barth (1886–1968) in the early and mid twentieth century, and the surprisingly warm reception of Barth by major Catholic theologians as different as Hans Küng and Hans Uhrs von Balthasar.[20] Barth rediscovered and even sharpened the *sola gratia* (by grace alone) edge of classical Protestant theology, repudiating the subjectivism that previous Protestants were never able to expunge. Salvation, according to Barth, is not a story about how one personally experiences transformation by God, but about how the situation of all humanity has already been transformed by and in Christ: "[Christ's] history is as such our history."[21] The individual is left simply to acknowledge what God has done in Christ. For Barth, the answer to the question, "when were you saved?" could only be "on Golgotha" (and in Christ's rising).[22] The focus on Christ makes it clear that all initiative in salvation lies with God, and that no other way can lead to salvation. Yet while Barth strongly affirms God's judgment against sin and has little positive to say about other religions, he so esteems the effectiveness of Christ's work apart from our response that his soteriology has a tendency toward universal salvation.[23]

On first glance, Barth's rediscovery of classical Protestant theology and Williamson's conclusion that the Disciples' real theology is about sanctification and social action may seem to be completely at odds. Yet both theologies take the focus off of the individual, and both may even be interpreted as logically consequent on justification by faith. Barth takes the notion that Christ accomplishes our salvation to its logical conclusion, so that it is difficult to say wherein lies the difference between the Christian and the non-Christian. On the other side, if the point of justification is to trust that God's wrath no longer burns against us, then the issue of individual salvation from hell has been superseded. We are free to concern ourselves with working to bring about God's will in the world.

Both of these recent directions for the doctrine of justification (its reinterpretation in a universalist direction, and its dissolution into social action) could put contemporary Euro-American theology at odds with the understanding of salvation put forward by Rev. Eale (as well as that of the early Disciples), according to which salvation has at its center the individual's decision to commit her or his life to Christ. For Barth the threat of God's wrath hanging over the individual is eclipsed by the universal grace enacted in Christ. For Williamson the personal quest for right relationship with God is not as crucial as the church's work in the world. Some North American Disciples, for either reason, might not be able to agree with Rev. Eale at every point, although we ought to acknowledge the authenticity of his witness and the power of God's joyful presence among the struggling and suffering people of the Congo. More than that, we should allow his theology, backed up as it is by such a powerful witness, to question our North Atlantic (or Euro-American) soteriology. Does our theology take seriously enough the reality of sin in which we are enmeshed, particularly as North Americans? Does it charge each of us with a sufficiently powerful and commanding identity as holy children of God, set aside for God's purposes, so that we might bear witness to the difference God makes not only in the church but wherever our callings place us? This is a question that demands a continuing global conversation among all Disciples (and disciples) beyond this dialogue between Rev. Eale and myself.

Bosela Eale and William Wright: A Call for Salvation That Makes a Difference

We now speak jointly to the North American church as "our church." In doing so, we recognize that we are God's and the universal church is God's, and that the church in North America needs the witness of fellow Christians like Rev. Eale as urgently as the North American Disciples once believed that Africans needed their witness.

While non-evangelical North American Christians, including many Disciples, may be hesitant to revive a lively belief in hell, these same Christians need to recapture something of the early Disciples spirit that took so seriously the transition in one's person or soul from being lost to being saved in Christ. It is this spirit that lives on in the church of the Congo, as seen in Rev. Eale's section; the same spirit can be found in many African American churches and constituency churches. There the commitment of oneself to Christ offers a personal salvation from God's wrath and engenders the strength to survive poverty, despair, oppression, ethnic strife, guilt, and death. North Americans, depending on social location and personal conviction, may not share this sense of the impending wrath of God. Many also lack an awareness of the troubles that so many people around the globe face. The wealth and power enjoyed by some North Americans have been utilized to provide a dubious sense of security and an anesthesia from pain, both one's own and that of others. Moreover, those with ever-busier lives are inhibited from thinking about the groundlessness of their activities.

Americans need to recapture a sense of the reality of sin, and if not the threat of personal damnation, then the full force of God's being set against sin and demanding conversion (*metanoia*). The language of sin and wrath is often conceded to the evangelicals who, in many ways, carry on the theology of Stone and Campbell. In North American evangelical usage, the appreciation for God's wrath can often reinforce the private, individualistic nature of North American piety. It is no wonder that the lines have started blurring between evangelical churches and churches with self-help or Prosperity Gospel messages. Justification in Christ through faith can be an important resource toward avoiding the twin dangers of a faith sterilized of sin and a privatized and even narcissistic faith of personal repentance. Justification is not something we earn and so it resists the culture of personal achievement and private ownership. Justification takes us out of ourselves, and instills in us a faith by which we live radically for God as well as for others. Justification also frees us to face clearly the sin in us and around us; since God justifies the sinner, and salvation does not require purity, we can be honest with our shortcomings and self-critical without fear.

In this way, through justification we can develop a broader, more incisive, and more vivid sense of the sins from which only God can save us in Christ. Perhaps topping the list is our willfully seduced indifference to the plight of peoples around the globe whose suffering is the direct or indirect effect of our perceived security and prosperity. Our lives are haunted by the indifference generated by our lifestyle system. It mocks the earnestness with which we seek fulfillment in our careers; it devours our children, their lives consumed by escapism. While our actions as individuals indeed seem to make little difference, the power which we exercise *en masse* as consumers, apostles of pop culture, and global power brokers reverberates throughout the globe, disrupting local cultures and the environment. This is no mere personal or existential crisis from which a moment of "meaningfulness" can deliver us; it is a self-gratifying enslavement to the "powers and principalities," "the cosmic powers of this present darkness" (Eph. 6:12) with which we conspire to pursue a lifestyle of self-interest and indifference to others.[24] Our desire to do something must not blind us to the idea that the solution, finally, is eschatological; that is, our problems are of such global and even cosmic proportions that only God enthroned in glory at the last day can truly set things right. To be sure, more than ever we need to give attention to what we can do today and in the future, for even our smallest consumer decisions, when part of collective activity, have enormous repercussions. Yet the immensity of our troubles belies individual solutions; our troubles lie so deep and broad as to demand a total surrender to God. Our hope for and beyond this world is sustained only by a faith and trust that the Lord of the universe opposes sin and human destruction like a "man of war" and receives the suffering and the vanquished like a grieving mother. While God gives free rein to our cosmic hopes, the same Lord grounds the ultimate significance of even our most fleeting acts of humanity to one another—a sincere touch, an honest and searching glance.

Christ Jesus is still our only Savior from a host of troubles both personal and global. To be united with God's saving purpose through Christ, to be saved—in this does the church have its fundamental purpose and being. God makes a difference in our lives. Through faith we experience that difference, and often it is only once we have this faith—so that we turn our life story over to Christ and grasp the meaning of the cross—that we realize how our lives have been under assault by the global powers of sin and death, as well as our own complicity with this assault.

Justification by faith ought to be a vital resource for the church amidst today's struggles, for it "places us outside ourselves" (Luther), relocating our story in the story of Christ that reveals God's self-giving, suffering love for the world. In a world in which consumerism reduces our perspective on reality to one of personal preferences, and complex mechanisms of global domination make us indifferent to the suffering from which we often even benefit, North American Christians need more than ever to be placed out of themselves and placed in the sure foundation of Christ, the Savior and hope for Christians in travail everywhere and at all times.

May this conversation continue. We hope that our method in this chapter will serve as a model for other conversations that can go beyond what we have accomplished. North American Disciples share with Disciples around the globe a rich heritage of God's revelation in scripture, as passed on by the Protestant Reformers, by Stone and Campbell, and by more recent theologians working ecumenically. However, there are as many different receptions of this heritage as there are Disciples. It is the office of the theologian to scrutinize this heritage, both with celebration and critique as appropriate—first in oneself, then in ever-larger contexts. Our differing contexts open us in different ways to the guidance of God's Spirit and to temptations from other spirits. Given our unique strengths and weaknesses, we would be unwise not to listen to each other. Worse still, we would violate both the command of Christ that we be one, and the aspirations of generations of Disciples to seek Christian unity. Today we North American Christians who continue to benefit from entrenched privileges need especially to listen to our sisters and brothers nearby and abroad who do not have an equal share in these privileges, for at least two reasons: their voices have a harder time receiving a hearing, and our actions continue, as they have in the past, disproportionately to affect them. If together we can conduct conversations in a way that corrects for disproportions of power, we may find, with God's help, that our different gifts will correct and complement each other.[25]

21

Sanctification

Intellectual Inquiry and Holy Conformity

KAREN MARIE YUST

Disciples rarely talk about "sanctification." We do not have a section in the *Chalice Hymnal* index with this title, unlike the hymnal indices of our UCC and United Methodist kin. Our Affirmation of Faith, taken from the Preamble of the *Design for the Christian Church (Disciples of Christ),* does not reference the term. Ronald Osborn's *The Faith We Affirm* does not discuss this theological concept by name, and the volume edited by Paul Crow and James Duke, *The Church for Disciples of Christ,* seems to anticipate widespread unfamiliarity with this term by including it among the eight entries in its glossary.[1] We appear to be silent on this theological point even though the scriptures speak of the concept forty-two times across twenty different biblical books.

Our contemporary silence is somewhat understandable when we observe that "sanctification" was not a popular topic of discussion among our Disciples forebears either. David McWhirter did not see fit to include it as a topic in his index to the forty-one volumes of the *Millennial Harbinger,* and a search of those volumes indicates that Alexander Campbell and his correspondents rarely invoked the term. Robert Milligan's 1847 remarks exemplify the acceptable low status of Disciples theological concern with sanctification during the movement's early years. He criticized "professors of Christianity" in the wider Church for being more concerned with "the mode in which the Holy Spirit operates in the conversion and sanctification of sinners, and a thousand other topics" than with the essential topic of the "death, burial, and resurrection of the Lord Messiah!"[2] Early Disciples leaders relegated sanctification to the status of a secondary concern almost fully eclipsed by their focus on the good news of God's work at Easter.

Separation and Conformity

A lack of direct and sustained attention to the topic does not mean, however, that the founding pastors and teachers of the Disciples of Christ did not have working assumptions about the theological significance of sanctification. Alexander Campbell generally invoked the term as a theological synonym for "separation" and being "set apart." In response to a reader's query about the nature and purpose of the Holy Spirit, he wrote, "The gift of the Holy Spirit, if no special gift be alluded to, is the Holy Spirit itself, in such influences as are necessary to our separation or sanctification to God in body, soul, and spirit."[3] He stated and published articles by others emphasizing the importance of sanctifying "the Lord's Day" as a time set apart for worship.[4] His editorial colleague, Robert Richardson, reiterated this perspective with reference to devout believers, "Christ has sanctified [them] in body, soul, and spirit: has *separated* [them] from the vices of the world, and *set apart* its blessings for [their] enjoyment."[5]

However, the practical application of the term carried additional connotations. According to Campbell, a truly sanctified Lord's Day meant a "solemn deep engagedness in the worship of the Lord" and a sanctified person exhibited "a higher, purer, more scriptural morality" in daily life.[6] He endorsed in print a motion made by Brother Standeford at the 1850 Kentucky Convention that equated sanctification with becoming "holy, unblamable, and unreprovable in [God's] sight."[7] He contended that sanctification involves "the recreative, renovating, regenerating influence of the Holy Guest of the Christian temple—the mystic house of God, erected for an habitation of God through the Spirit."[8] These references point to a connection between sanctification and holiness, the living of sacrificial lives that are "holy and acceptable to God" and occur through the divine "renewing" of human minds in terms of "what is good and is pleasing to him and perfect" (Rom. 12:1, TEV).

"Holiness" is a topic that received more explicit discussion in the *Millennial Harbinger*. In an article by the pseudonymous "Philip" titled, "True Holiness," the author stated that "true holiness" consists "in a conformity to the nature, character, and will of God, whereby a saint is distinguished from the unrenewed world, and is not actuated by their principles and precepts, nor governed by their maxims and customs" and concluded, "we are indeed and in truth holy in proportion as we advance in this separation and conformity."[9] His discussion continued with the observation, "the practice of Christianity is all holiness, and holiness is the very fruit of the Spirit, which again is in all goodness, and righteousness, and truth. Dare we, then, hope to see God without holiness?"[10]

Philip's question sets Disciples' devaluation of sanctification as a theological concept at odds with our goal of eschatologically dwelling with God in the divine realm. Our hope of an eternal relationship with the Divine is attached to our participation in an ongoing process of separation from the destructive values of conventional society and of conformity to the will of God. We are called to be Christians who practice our faith on a daily basis, whose lives demonstrate a practical holiness. Furthermore, we have chosen to live this Christian life in relationship with congregations shaped by the particular history and theology of a denomination within the larger community of the ecumenical Church. Our freedom, then, to describe and embody the sanctified life is circumscribed by our location within these influential circles. We must ask what ecclesial traditions can tell us about our participation in sanctification as Disciples in ecumenical communion.

Holy Bible Reading

The principle claim about sanctification made by early Disciples is that becoming holy is accomplished via regular reading and interpretation of scripture. In an essay titled "Bible Reading," Alexander Campbell contended,

> There is no substitute for constant reading; for although all the precepts and premises, or the whole doctrine of the Bible could be learned or committed to memory, and faithfully retained, it could not serve that special and supreme intention of the Author of this Book, in giving it to us as the means of sanctification and of our being imbued and inspired with the Spirit of our God.[11]

Campbell also printed a sermon by Elder A. Broaddus containing the claim "that the gospel is the great instrument of conversion and sanctification… 'Sanctify them through thy truth, (saith our Lord;) thy word is truth.'"[12] In summarizing his debate with Presbyterian Nathan L. Rice, Campbell noted his affirmation of the principle that "in conversion and sanctification, the Spirit of God operates on persons only through the word of truth," a proposition opposed by Rice because of its seemingly exclusive reliance on biblical reflection as the catalyst for sanctification.[13] However, we know that Campbell did not intend to claim a narrowly exclusive role for scripture reading, as he rejected this position when accused of it by S.W. Lynd in 1838. Rather than say that only the *written* biblical text has the power of sanctification, which is what his detractors thought he believed, Campbell clarified his position by claiming that "no other *instrumental* power is exerted upon the mind of a sinner in his [or her] sanctification than that of the *written* word, I might add, preached or read."[14] For Campbell, the ontological power of God's Spirit can also function without the medium of the scriptures to shape human lives; to say otherwise is to limit God's sovereign ability to act as God wills. God *can* act directly on the human heart, yet God clearly (to

Campbell) *has chosen* to act through the scriptures, and thus sanctification without dedicated Bible study is possible but not the preferred means offered to Disciples by God.

Intellectual Inquiry and Sanctifying Wisdom

Early Disciples leaders placed much emphasis on the role of scripture, in part, because they highly valued the power of critical thinking. Campbell described Adam as "created in the image of God. He possessed a pure intellectual principle which enabled him to become acquainted with God."[15] This intellectual capacity for discerning truth was not lost in the human fall from grace, but now requires the exterior structure of the biblical narrative to keep it focused on the thoughts of God rather than the distractions created by human sinfulness. The 1850 Kentucky Convention called for all Disciples congregations to "adopt a plan of instruction, or of teaching the holy scriptures" and to encourage "converts to study the word of God regularly and permanently" because of the presumed link between critical reflection and sanctification.[16]

And yet, sanctification is not merely a product of human intellectual striving, even though Disciples are challenged to think rigorously about biblical truths and examples. Instead, it is a collaboration between Christ and the Christian in which Christ confers sanctifying wisdom through the lived and living inspiration of gospel narratives and the Christian receives this wisdom through diligent study of the biblical texts. Campbell described this variably as having "spiritual life implanted" in us by Christ[17]; as a point when "Christ has become to [us] sanctification"[18]; and as our completion in Christ, who is "WISDOM from God, RIGHTEOUSNESS also, SANCTIFICATION and REDEMPTION."[19] For all our intellectual effort, we do not sanctify our own lives, but are sanctified by God through Christ, whose word is animated for us by the Holy Spirit as we study.

Eschatological Transformation

Furthermore, the essence of sanctification is love embodied in service. "Philip" pointed to the story of the "Great Judgment" (Mt. 25:31–46) as the measurement of true holiness. Christians are to love and physically care for all people, from immediate family members and church-going friends to the masses of poor and oppressed who are hungry, thirsty, naked, and imprisoned. "Without this, your religion is a mask," claimed this Disciples leader.[20] Sanctification is about exchanging one's religious mask of pseudo-perfection, donned because one wants to maintain a relationship of respectability in society, for the hands, feet, tongue, and mind of Christ that are needed if one would live the great commission. It is an embodiment of eschatological hope, wherein our limited commitment to our immediate circle of relationships is expanded by an overwhelming willingness to labor with God on behalf of God's covenantal purposes in and for the world. It is an experience of Pentecost-like transformation from *disciples* (Greek for "learners" or "apprentices") to *apostles* (Greek for "one who is sent out").

Julian Ibarra Zapata, a Mexican Disciples pastor, tried to describe this transformation in a reflection included in *Chalice Worship*. Listen to his prayerful words:

> I want to be counted among those…
> who are ardently desiring…
> that the Burning Flame of the Spirit of God
> descend upon you, upon me…that both our hearts
> be entirely burned and thus purified:
>
> Free from anger, hatred and passion;
> free from ill will, jealousy and envy;
> free from transgression, criticism and gossip;
> free from malice, animosity and grudges…[21]

What he expresses is a longing for sanctification, where broken modes of relating are overwhelmed by God's consuming love, leaving the freedom to truly love another emerging from their ashes.

Spiritual Hunger and Study

Contemporary Disciples hymnody seeks both to evoke this spiritual hunger and to reinforce our founders' insistence on the essential role of scriptural study in sanctification. The chorus of "Señor, Yo Quiero Entrar," implores, "Dame manos limpias y un corazón puro, y sin vanidades, que sepa amar"—"give me clean hands and a pure heart, from vanity save me, and teach me to love"[22]—as an expression of spiritual longing. A simple song, "Spirit of the Living God," invites God to "fall afresh" on us, molding us into conformity with God's will.[23] The hymn "Gracious Spirit, Dwell with Me" expresses our desire to become holy through our experience of God's presence:

> Gracious Spirit, dwell with me:
> I myself would gracious be,
> and, with words that help and heal,
> would thy life in mine reveal,
> and, with actions bold and meek,
> would for Christ my Savior speak.[24]

Pentecost hymns "Wind Who Makes All Winds That Blow" and "On Pentecost They Gathered" urge us to embrace the Holy Spirit, who provides "shining truth to guide our souls"[25] and bestows the necessary "life and power" to energize our ministry.[26]

Hymns extolling the importance of attending to God's will as it is made known in the scriptures accompany these invocations of the Spirit's power and presence. "O Word of God Incarnate" reminds us that the scriptures are "chart and compass" and asks God to "teach your wandering pilgrims by this our path to trace."[27] Amy Grant's brief chorus, "Thy Word," quotes Psalm 119:105 to identify the scriptures as "lamp" and "light" for our spiritual journey.[28] The entirety of "Your Words to Me Are Life and Health" draws strong connections between Bible study and sanctification; the first verse sets the tone:

> Your words to me are life and health;
> pour strength into my soul;
> enable, guide, and teach my heart
> to reach its perfect goal![29]

When contemporary Disciples sing these words, we acknowledge God's call to be holy and confess our need for and experience of the biblical narrative as a sanctifying force in our lives.

One of the challenges, however, inherent in our partial dependence on Bible study for sanctification is determining what the scriptures are truly saying about the nature and purpose of a holy Christian life. Disciples have long valued freedom of inquiry and thought as a principle of biblical interpretation.[30] Hence, we invite one another to examine the scriptures for ourselves, so that we might know how God would have us to live via a critical conversation with the text rather than by simply assimilating another's doctrinal claims unquestioningly. But how do we engage in such an examination? I could offer here a brief tutorial on the basics of biblical exegesis, which is one tool essential to our study of the scriptures. However, I will leave that task to others and turn instead to the wisdom of two forebears in the Christian faith who themselves struggled with the role of the intellect in biblical interpretation and the sanctification of God's people.[31] The first is Catherine of Siena, a fourteenth–century holy woman whose writings and friendship greatly influenced two medieval popes (Gregory XI and Urban VI) and the social ministry of the Church in her day. The second is Diadochos of Photiki, a Greek Orthodox bishop in the fifth century whose text "On Spiritual Knowledge and Discrimination" attempts to move our understanding of knowledge beyond reliance on concrete data to experiences of mystical union with God.

Intellect, Memory, and Will

Catherine, like Alexander Campbell, understood the human intellect as an aspect of the *imago dei*. However, she also included memory and will as additional aspects of the image of God that work in concert with intellect to draw us into union with God. Each of these elements of *imago dei* is active in our encounters with scripture. Through memory, we recall via the biblical narrative the common salvation history of God's people. We recollect stories of God's faithfulness, just as the Hebrew prophets regularly admonished the people of Israel to do. Through intellect, we contemplate this salvation history that memory holds dear and begin to discern within its constitutive stories of faith common themes and patterns. This is hard work, and Catherine insisted that the intellect must truly thirst for the truth if we are to succeed in knowing God's will. She wrote, "Those who are not thirsty will never persevere in their journey. Either weariness or pleasure will make them stop."[32] Thus, we must engage in Bible study with the single-mindedness of a parched pilgrim bent on discovering the next location of an oasis or well on the map provided for the journey.

Through will, we choose sanctification as our purpose for study, rather than other goals that compete for our affection. Catherine warned that study rooted in "self-love," or a preference for worldly gain and prestige rather than holiness, holds reason captive to a warped perception of self-importance, and prevents our study from guiding us into fuller love of God and neighbor. To free the intellect, we must will to love for God's sake, for only that choice opens the door to divine teaching. In Catherine's words, "When the soul decides to gather her powers with the hand of free choice in my name, all the actions that persons do, whether spiritual or temporal, are gathered in" and God gives us spiritual insight through our reasoning.[33]

Jesus' Testimony and Christ's Table

The contributions of memory and will are not the only aids that God has provided to assist us in applying our minds to biblical interpretation. Catherine argued that we have also been given the testimony of Jesus' life and ministry as a test instrument, a view endorsed by Disciples founders five centuries later. We can turn to the teachings of Jesus as signposts on our interpretative journey. If our recollection of salvation history and our resulting claims about Christian life contradict the testimony of God incarnate, then they fail the test of Christian interpretation. Adverse spiritual conditions—contrary opinions, personal or communal adversity, prosperity that encourages self-satisfaction or selfishness—may have obscured what scripture is trying to tell us about holiness. Instead of a path to virtue, we may have unwittingly stumbled onto a path to vice.

Catherine believed that the necessary orienting testimony of the life of Jesus is most effectively remembered when Christians gather around Christ's table, and since Disciples have always claimed the centrality of "the Lord's supper," we can easily join her in this belief. Eucharistic celebration can be a means by which we direct our memory back to God. When we share bread and cup, we create an opportunity for all who participate to experience again God's gracious forgiveness of sin and reformation of the soul. We invite eyes to be opened to the truth of God's presence with us as we continue Jesus' acts of blessing and thanking God when breaking bread with disciples. If we offer the ecumenical Great Thanksgiving, we even encourage biblical literacy through the rehearsal of the stories chronicling interactions with God's people since the time of creation.

Catherine's linkage of memory and communion points us toward an innovative way for Disciples to understand our historic emphasis on restoration. Our weekly participation in this sacramental meal restores our connection with God's people at table throughout history and around the world. It invites us to enter into the drama of salvation history as expressed in the life of the Second Testament communities of discipleship. As in the Passover celebration of the upper room, it opens space for questioning whether we are practicing virtues that lead to holiness or pursuing vices that will betray God's will. As with the Emmaus disciples, it promises the possibility of our eyes being opened and our hearts burning within us as we are invited to conform our lives to Christ. To borrow a phrase from Psalm 23, the eucharist "restores our souls," returning to us the life that we lose with each unholy thought, word, and deed that accompanies our daily existence.

Communal Interpretation and Communion

Catherine also insisted that we cannot practice biblical interpretation alone if we desire sanctification. The companionship of other wayfarers is necessary, she claimed, because God comes to us when we are gathered in community. One explanation for this perspective, which can be heard among contemporary Disciples and other Christians who value free inquiry and democratic process, is that zestful debate about multiple opinions is a reliable means for deciding what is true and compelling evidence for Christian belief and practice. However, Catherine emphasized a different purpose for companionship. She believed that having other persons beside us is both a reflection and cultivation of right affection, and thus right understanding and progress toward perfect conformity to Christ. Working alone to understand the scriptures and become Christlike suggests selfish motives, a desire to attain God's blessings for the building up of ourselves rather than the body of Christ. Memory focused on God's everlasting love for God's people generates an unselfish affection for the children of God. It is when we are oriented to love God and neighbor that we are "ready to be thirsty—thirsty for virtue and [God's] honor and the salvation of souls."[34] A sanctifying practice of biblical interpretation requires that intellect's vision be focused and clarified by an active love of neighbor, which can only be practiced in the neighbor's presence.

Participation in weekly communion also helps to generate and sustain the active love necessary for a practice of sanctifying biblical interpretation. In the communal act of serving one another and being served, we remind ourselves that we are to share with one another the gifts of God just as God shared Godself with us. Catherine noted: "Such remembrance makes the soul caring instead of indifferent, grateful instead of thankless."[35] We might also say that liturgical table fellowship helps "the church imprint upon its people the memory of who and whose it is, the memory of a life with God in

Jesus Christ, the memory of the One whose passion, death, and resurrection Christians claim for ourselves."[36] This memory is essential for sanctification because it rightly orients our affections and sets our proper interpretative purpose—understanding in service of conformity to Christ—clearly before us.

Mystical Experience

Our Disciples roots in Common Sense philosophy, however, can cause us to stumble in our journey toward sanctification if we remember and interpret Christ's passion and the rest of salvation history in purely empirical or utilitarian terms. Our fifth-century Christian forebear, Diadochos of Photiki, offers us an essential reminder of the necessary role that mystical experience plays in faithful perceptions of spiritual truth. Diadochos described his texts as an attempt to explain "what kind of spiritual knowledge we need in order to reach, under the Lord's guidance, the perfection which He has revealed."[37] Anticipating that freedom-loving persons (such as Disciples) would be concerned with the relationship between spiritual knowledge and free will, he defined the latter as the ability to choose to what end the soul will direct itself and the former as "the power to discriminate without error between good and evil."[38] His treatise clearly states that spiritual knowledge is not self-generated; rather, it is God's gift. "Nothing," he wrote, "is as destitute as a mind philosophizing about God when it is without Him."[39] At the same time, he understood that the intellect could be rightly engaged and satisfied by theological reflection if God inspired a person's intellectual perceptions. He advised his readers to make themselves "a dwelling-place for the Holy Spirit. Then we shall have the lamp of spiritual knowledge burning always within us."[40] Mystical experiences of prayer and contemplation, then, contribute to sanctification because they prepare fertile soil for the sowing of God's Word, both as it is expressed in the words of scripture and in all other ways God speaks.

Disciples have not historically embraced more mystical forms of prayer and contemplation because of our dismissal—alongside other Protestants—of those practices as aspects of Catholic or Orthodox religiosity rather than shared legacies of the spiritual roots from which we all spring.[41] But if we recall the rhythm of Jesus' life, in which he moved back and forth between times of solitary prayer and public interpretation of the scripture, between contemplation of the divine will for the world and group Bible study with his disciples, we have a model for a similar rhythm in our own lives. The story of Jesus' sojourn in the desert to wrestle with his particular demons of temptation (Mt. 4:1–11; Mk. 1:12–13; Lk. 4:1–13) reminds us that only in setting ourselves apart from the noisiness of external and internal demands on our time and energy can we be conformed to Christ. Diadochos wrote:

> Those pursuing the spiritual way must always keep the mind free from agitation in order that the intellect, as it discriminates among

> the thoughts that pass through the mind, may store in the treasuries of its memory those thoughts which are good and have been sent from God, while casting out those which are evil and come from the devil.[42]

This, then, is the challenge contemporary Disciples face if we desire to be sanctified: that we must order our lives together in such a way that we can, as individuals in intentional communion, interpret the scriptures for the purposes of discriminating between God's hopes for the world and our misplaced affections, and of committing ourselves to the eschatological realization of God's realm.

22

Spirituality and the Disciples of Christ

Sanctifying the Ordinary

Bonnie J. Miller-McLemore and Joseph D. Driskill

When confronted with the literal reading of the Bible by evangelical and fundamentalist peers, members of the CCDC struggle to describe how we interpret scripture differently. In a world rampant with competing dogmas about everything from school prayer to sexuality to God's authority, we also wonder about our more inclusive noncreedal, nondoctrinal tradition. Less often do we notice one other arena in which we struggle to claim our identity. In a postmodern time of New Age fads and rapidly growing spirit-filled churches, we overlook the particular way we understand spirituality.

How have Disciples understood spirituality and how do we understand it today in a greatly changing religious world? This is the central question of this chapter. We will argue that Disciples have a distinctive understanding that has largely gone unnoticed and unappreciated. In line with their Protestant roots, Disciples see a deep connection between what one does, how one does it, and one's faith—what might be described as the sanctification of the ordinary.[1] This stands in need of retrieval and further development in light of our changing social location.

Disciples' Historical Amnesia[2]

When Kathleen Norris published an essay about laundry in the *New York Times Magazine*—specifically about the "joys of hanging clothes on the line to dry"—she received at least a hundred letters in response. Except for one tired mother with small children and a long commute, who exclaimed that Norris "must have way too much time" on her hands, her recognition of the holy in the mundane struck a chord.[3]

We should certainly heed the suspicion of the overworked about the spirituality of the mundane, especially the warning from women all too familiar with the imposition of onerous domestic labor. The danger of romanticizing such work as spiritual should be taken seriously, better understood now thanks to the women's movement. Laundry is sometimes just one more brain-numbing chore. But there is still truth in Norris's claim that "women's work" can ground us rather than "grind us down." She subtitles a book on the mystery of the "quotidian"—the daily, the ordinary, the commonplace—as "Laundry, Liturgy, and 'Women's Work.'"[4] Doing laundry can, as may other quotidian aspects of life, hold the symbolic and the material in incredibly close proximity.

As far back as Reformation theologian Martin Luther, Protestants have upheld the practice of sanctifying the ordinary. Several centuries ago Luther challenged the false division between celibate religious life and ordinary family life and reclaimed all "offices" or walks of life as a realm for faith. He himself saw his duties as husband and father as a central part of his calling.[5] But our awareness of this understanding of spirituality has waned. Norris herself is a good example. Of all her spiritual memoirs recounting her journey from disbelief back to her Presbyterian roots, her book honoring the quotidian is by far the most Protestant.[6] But even she does not explicitly recognize its Protestant roots. She is more inclined to commend the monastic Benedictine community.

Neither Catholics nor Jews nor conservative Protestants have hesitated as much as mainline Protestants to claim a distinctive approach to spirituality. Many factors engender a kind of amnesia about our tradition of sanctifying the ordinary. Protestants often privatize faith as primarily a personal conversion and see spirituality as limited to individual and corporal rituals, such as prayer, scripture reading, or Sunday worship. Some Disciples congregations change the confession of Jesus the Christ as "Lord and Savior of the world" that appears in our denomination's affirmation of faith to a confession of Jesus as our "personal Lord and Savior." One measures spirituality in this view by how often one prays, for example, or how well one knows the Bible.[7] Influenced by both contemporary evangelicalism and the revival of monastic spirituality in the mid-twentieth century, spirituality is seen primarily as an interior matter of the heart that calls for a kind of stepping outside one's routine or bringing something outside one's routine—God, spirituality, tranquility—into it. Spirituality is not a matter of the "external self," this "superficial 'I'...that works in the world," as Catholic monk and mystic Thomas Merton remarks in one of his most widely read books. It is the "work of the 'deep self,'" an awakening to God's mystery within the "depths."[8] One meets God in the quiet private room of the soul.

Some Disciples churches avoid this but then perpetuate an equally problematic view of spirituality as a cognitive, intellectual, disembodied endeavor confined to the Sunday school wing, minister's office, or seminary classroom. Disciples, like most Protestants influenced by the Reformation, also believe that Christians are justified by faith, not works. So anything that smacks of "works righteousness" or the attempt to earn our way to spiritual perfection, including the very phrase "spiritual discipline," is suspect. Human nature itself is sometimes distrusted. In contrast to a Catholic sacramental trust that God is found in all things, our Calvinist roots make us considerably less sure that human action mediates divine presence.

Modernity and technology simply deepened these tendencies. Baby Boomers inherited from their own parents a cautiousness about making spiritual claims that no longer measure up to modern scientific standards. In a major study of Presbyterian Baby Boomers, Dean Hoge, Benton Johnson, and Donald Luidens reveal that the parents of Baby Boomers were "considerably less likely than previous generations to impose their particular religious beliefs on their children." Even though these families went to church each Sunday, faith was "rarely a topic of discussion" in the home. So also did its practice decline. Active church participation "apparently did not result in familial Bible study, devotions, or prayer sessions—other than grace at meals." Gone was the earlier tradition of family devotions promoted by Presbyterians until the early twentieth century.[9] As historian Margaret Bendroth puts it, "If the nineteenth-century paradigm of domestic life was the Victorian patriarch at prayer with his wife and children, a century later the dominant image of middle-class family life is a heavily annotated kitchen bulletin board next to a busy telephone."[10]

Our concern here is not the decline of devotional practices. Rather, all these factors—modern technology, decline of devotions, faith as private and limited to prayer and worship, wariness about human nature, fear of spiritual disciplines as works righteousness—contribute to an amnesia about our particular spiritual history of embracing ordinary life as a place for faith. People sometimes believe that mainline churches have little to offer either at the personal or the corporate level and look elsewhere for spiritual resources, whether the monastic tradition, Jungian psychology, or charismatic congregations. As is true for many Christians, Disciples have forgotten their spiritual history.

Recovering Disciples' Memory

Over two decades ago, when Disciples theologian Clark Williamson addressed the topic of "Theology and the Forms of Confession in the Disciples of Christ," he stated at the outset that this task was "notoriously difficult."[11] As a rule, Disciples react negatively to the mere hearing of the word *theology*. Alexander Campbell actually forbade the teaching of theology at one of the movement's colleges. Like creeds, the creation of systems of theology encumber, truncate, or distort the truth of Jesus as the Christ as much as they confirm or embellish it.

Laying claim to our spirituality is equally difficult. Until the recent New Age revival of spirituality, Disciples also reacted negatively to this word. But we have a spirituality, even if, like some other Protestants, we do not recognize it as such.[12] Instead of spirituality as devotion to otherworldly matters, Disciples have had something different in mind.

Williamson's essay is helpful here not so much because he tries to identify and embellish our "received" theology as articulated by the Panel of Scholars in the late 1950s and early 1960s but because he explores how it "takes confessional form." That is, he tries to unearth our "ethos," or what he also calls the "forgotten" tradition—what we believe practically "without asserting it" even to ourselves, those deep commitments that activate us but of which we may have little conscious recognition.[13] In other words, he tells us something about our spirituality—how our convictions take shape or what we all look like when we confess ourselves Disciples. A certain kind of spirituality of ordinary life emerges from our implicit theology.

Others on the Panel of Scholars, such as Dwight Stevenson, who focuses on Robert Richardson's 1853 track on early Disciples faith, and W.B. Blakemore, who knowingly labels Disciples "reasonable, empirical, pragmatic,"[14] already offer initial hints in this direction. For Stevenson (and Richardson and Alexander Campbell before him), Disciples want to avoid abstracting faith "from the whole of life," Williamson observes, "rendering it into a property to be owned, dividing believers from one another, and substituting propositions about God for communion with God."[15] Faith or spirituality is a "mode of being-in-the-world." Beliefs are important insofar as they support that. Williamson likens our pragmatic orientation, as cast by Blakemore, to a behavioral system, such as Judaism. "How things are done, what one does, is a primary form of confession and a witness of faith." The way to verify a proposition of faith is to "seek to make it true."[16]

To this received tradition, Williamson adds a further qualification and claim: Disciples theology is a "quintessentially American theology of sanctification." What does he mean here? For Disciples, faith is a "way of life," oriented to practice, lived with intentional reflection on choices, and confessed primarily through deeds as much as creeds. In other words, our spirituality "must be assessed primarily from our involvements."[17] The goal is "to baptize or transform the worldly into the spiritual," to make a way for the "visible Kingdom of God on earth," or, more humbly, to "garner for the world a bit more equality and dignity."[18]

Regard for the Sabbath illustrates Williamson's claim. Descendants of the Scottish Presbyterians, early Disciples followed the Puritans in observing the

Sabbath, a practice that church theologians such as Augustine had rejected out of hostility to Judaism. Disciples chose to honor the Sabbath precisely because the practice is an effort to usher in God's purpose in the world. Williamson also calls this "ethics as a form of piety."[19] Our spirituality is more oriented toward the actions and decisions of ordinary living than toward other forms of piety. As in the family of Norman Maclean, son of a Scottish Presbyterian minister, practiced fly fisherman and author of the popular novella, *A River Runs Through It,* there is "no clear line between religion and fly fishing. In a typical week of our childhood, Paul and I probably received as many hours of instruction in fly fishing as we did in all other spiritual matters."[20] There is much to be learned about faith through fly fishing and ordinary life.

Even the statement that prefaces the three-volume publication of the Panel of Scholars reflects this orientation. It claims the "founding fathers" were practical theologians, people who did theology "on the debate platform, in the pulpit, and through widespread discussion" and not in cloistered or academic settings.[21] The Panel did not work in isolation but circulated papers and sought reaction from sixty discussion groups around the country. Its intent was not a "new theology" but the clarification of the "theological, biblical, sociological, and historical issues involved in our practical life."[22]

If asked why they attend church each Sunday, many Disciples might say, as one of our own family members remarked, "out of habit." Although on first blush this seems like a lame answer compared to a more avid confession of belief in God's overflowing abundance celebrated through worship, it actually reflects the understanding that faith does partly rest on good habits, not on ideology or confession, but on material embodiment and patterns. The word *habit* is itself the root of *inhabit, habitation, habitat.* We make a spiritual home not only out of words woven together in theological confession but also out of habits and practices of faith.

Disciples spirituality has a powerful resemblance to what sociologist Nancy Ammerman calls "Golden Rule Christianity" of mainstream Protestantism. She insists that for all its faults and qualifications it "is not just a paler" version of contemporary evangelicalism. It is different in kind and deserves to be understood on its own terms.[23] Golden Rule Christians value "right living more than right believing." Compassion and doing good for others are more important than prayer, witnessing, and Bible study on the one hand, and than radical efforts to change the world on the other hand. They are not exactly out to convert others to their beliefs (even their own children) or to overhaul the world. They would just "like the world to be a bit better for their having inhabited it."[24]

Looking Back to the Founders

So Protestant spirituality is not an oxymoron. Disciples have within the Reformation tradition a life-giving spiritual heritage. The book *Protestant*

Spiritual Exercises describes some of the particularities of this heritage. Luther, Calvin, and the Wesleys all suggest exercises of examination, prayer, and small group practices. However, these exercises are distinctly oriented toward a specific kind of embodied spirituality. They demand ethical action on behalf of others. They require critical reflection on faith claims. Ultimately, they suggest healthy suspicion of superficial claims about immediate access to God's will. Protestant spirituality includes commitments to critical reflection, to hearing the voices of the dispossessed, to inclusiveness, and to racial equality.[25] Ultimately it means recognition of the limitation of spiritual knowledge, a respect for other spiritualities, and a sense of humility. So, rather than declaring that one has prayed about a problem and heard God, one hopes to manifest faith through living authentically day by day.

Our own founders were focused on the importance of reading the Bible as a way to gain insight for daily living. Alexander Campbell says in the *Millennial Harbinger* that biblical testimony, rather than one's own thoughts or feelings, is the ground of faith. The "written and well attested testimony of God, received and obeyed"[26] is the solid foundation. Notice that one reads the text looking for guidance, receives such guidance, and then is called on to follow its dictates in the living of daily life. We notice immediately that for Campbell God's presence is mediated in the encounter with the text, rather than in deeply moving experiences of prayer or fervent evangelical expressions.

Campbell's reliance on biblical testimony parallels the reasonableness and everydayness of his own religious experience. As a young man he yearned for a sense that God was calling him. After all, Alexander's father Thomas had had a "call" that brought him both an assurance that he was "chosen to labor in the vineyard" and a sense of peace.[27] Alexander waited for such an experience and it did not come. "Looking at the situation rationally and in the light of his own robust common sense, Alexander decided that a simple trust in Christ's promise to save penitent sinners should be an all-sufficient saving grace."[28] Thus Campbell's spirituality, that is, his lived experience of faith, is not associated with mystical prayer or with highly emotional experiences that were later common to frontier conversions. A thoughtful, intentional encounter with the biblical texts provided all one needed for salvation. William Paulsell says of Campbell's commitment to biblical testimony, "no one who has been illuminated, converted or sanctified by the Holy Spirit can have a single idea that is not already found in the Bible."[29] Thus, Campbell ensured that the spirituality of those in his religious movement would be grounded in biblically informed common sense.

Campbell acknowledges the importance of an intimate relationship with God in prayer, but it is clear from his teaching that such prayer is anchored in a conversation about the ordinary aspects of daily living and not with contemplative prayer or quiet prayer where a commitment to silence deepens one's relationship to God. He contends that in true prayer the one who is praying "should ask for things" from God, following the example of Jesus. Such prayer attests to the human need for such things as food, forgiveness, and deliverance from evil, while acknowledging that it is through a relationship with God that such gifts may be received. Asking God for "things" is not understood in a simplistic or materialistic fashion, but as a genuine sign of dependence on God the provider.

Barton Stone echoes Campbell when he speaks about the importance of petitioning God for needs. However, Stone also acknowledges the importance of the affective dimension of a relationship with God.[30] Stone contends that gratitude and dependence are developed in the believer who takes authentic desires to God. Paulsell notes that Stone's focus is not on deepening an experiential relationship with God in order to move the believer to a new place, but instead is to increase the exercise of virtues in daily life. True prayer fosters "love, joy, peace, long-suffering, gentleness, goodness, fidelity, meekness, and temperance."[31] Notice that these are virtues that, when practiced, will "sanctify the ordinary" life of faith.

Another indication of early Disciples commitment to "sanctifying the ordinary" comes in the movement's understanding of sacraments. While Campbell rejected the word *sacrament* because of its association with the Roman Catholic tradition, he used the word *ordinance* to indicate the place where God's grace was present and available to the faithful. "The acts of Christian worship, particularly baptism, the Lord's supper, reading of scriptures, preaching and prayer, all served as ordinances where the work of the Holy Spirit revealed both the presence of Christ and the real power of God's redeeming grace."[32] Interestingly, although in a common dictionary definition ordinance simply means a "Christian rite," such as communion, or, in nonreligious contexts, an "authoritative command or order," the term also refers to a "custom or practice established by long usage," a meaning not assumed by the word *sacrament*. Even if the historical root and development of *ordinance* differs from that of *ordinary*, the step from one to the other does not seem that far. *Ordinance* suggests an arranging of one's life, a putting it into order. Almost *de facto*, *ordinance* seems more mundane, less mysterious, less set apart from daily routine than *sacrament*.

Campbell frequently mentioned ordinances and in some lists he included fasting. Campbell's "flexible" number of the ordinances demonstrates that he not only rejected the seven sacraments of the Roman Catholic Church, but also he was not bound to the two common sacraments associated with Protestant traditions. By using the word *ordinance* for *sacrament* Campbell enlarged the activities through which God's grace is made present. Bible reading and prayer were most certainly daily activities for Campbell as well as morning and evening family worship.[33] Campbell's pervasive influence on those who belonged to his religious movement guaranteed that God's working in the common sense of ordinary believers in their daily lives would be the pattern by which the ordinary became sanctified. These patterns of practice embody the spirituality of the "life of faith" for early Disciples and contribute to the shape of the lived experience of faith for contemporary Disciples.

Looking Forward to our Multicultural Context

Descriptions of mainline Protestant traditions and spiritualities have often neglected the ethnic and cultural faith expressions of many of our members. The Euro-centric Caucasian spiritualities are typically described while the African American, Hispanic, and Asian American spiritualities are overlooked or treated as if they are variations on some normative White tradition. In fact, the Disciples movement has always had members from different ethnic and cultural backgrounds, right back to the early nineteenth century African Americans church members. The Disciples tradition has been greatly enriched by the faith expressions of culturally diverse Disciples.

The failure of many Caucasian Disciples to recognize the socially located nature of their White, Euro-centric expressions of spirituality is but an aspect of the structural racism that the denomination is now seeking to face and redress. As the assumptions and practices of Euro-centered Disciples are de-centered, Caucasian Disciples are learning how profoundly their ethnic and cultural paradigms shape their lived experience of faith. "Culture informs all that people *do* as well as all that they *are*," counselors Cleo Molina and Hutch Haney argue. "The culture in which we were raised instructed us on how to eat, dress, wash, play, speak, and touch, and it affected the way we are in every role we play."[34] Most especially our cultural heritage shapes our spirituality—that is, how we worship, how we understand community, and how we express and enter into a relationship with God.

Disciples claim a tradition of radical openness. Our noncreedal and nondoctrinal heritage around an open table has created a sense among Disciples that we are a truly inclusive church. Often we have unconsciously used our "unity at the Table" to mask our differences and our diverse gifts. Caucasian Disciples are learning that the "lived experience of faith" for many Disciples has involved coming to a table that is surrounded by White forms of worship, White forms of musical expression, and White ways of praying. One only needs to experience the congregational participation in Black worship, the joyful music of Hispanic worship, and the fervent prayers of Korean American worship to know that as Disciples our respective ethnic and cultural heritages shape our many spiritual expressions. Disciples must be cautious in assuming that because we can come to the table together our unity in Christ is fulfilled. Only when we are all welcome, each coming with the diverse gifts we have been given by God, are we truly one in Christ.

Sometimes it takes other people besides the dominant spokespersons of the tradition to reinvigorate and reorient what it means to sanctify the ordinary. Over fifteen years ago, a group of women who were trained theologically and teaching in seminaries and colleges around the United States began to meet, first in small numbers across a crowded room of mostly

White male academicians, then in larger numbers organized as the Forrest-Moss Institute. The group realized that together we had a contribution to make and began working on an edited introduction to feminist theology. The title itself, *Setting the Table,* illustrates and extends the argument of this chapter about the importance of connecting the sacred and mundane. Setting a table speaks of the common act of preparing a meal in the kitchen *and* the formal act of breaking bread at the communion table. To be sure, the book addresses major theological topics—God language, christology, scriptural interpretation, ecclesiology, and so forth. But it emerged out of conversation about "our daily lives and the ways that our faith continually disposes us to live in the world."[35]

The heart of the book, in fact, comes in the final chapter, a conversation about communion among authors in a crowded hotel room over pizza, soft drinks, and chocolate cake. Earthy images of its meaning abound. One person says she experiences communion as "an occasion of eating" where actual physical hunger matters. People also recall using nontraditional elements that evoke basic sustenance in other cultures and settings, such as rice and green tea among Asian Americans, crackers and Kool-Aid among youth. Familiar foods from particular contexts have the power to convey Christ's gift of life. Another person connects the "sensuous" aspect of passing communion trays with church potlucks and other meals—meals prepared by women, trays and cups washed by our mothers.[36]

Indeed, behind the table and the tradition as a whole stands the labor of women who prepare the bread and who feed others. When someone asked one participant who traveled across the country merely to join in the conversation, "what communion had to do with" the book, she responded, "Everything!" At the center of the conversation is the conviction that greater inclusion of women by the church will make it "harder to hold to the sacred as different from real life and separate from what women do." Communion anchors Disciples' belief that "God's will is for us to have rich lives as embodied creatures," women and men alike.[37]

"Sanctifying the ordinary" requires more than sanctifying the everyday-ness of any one cultural or racial group. It means that we must learn to see the work of God in each of the cultural expressions that embody the Disciples heritage, welcoming individuals and groups such as the Forrest-Moss Institute and the women for whom they speak. With our commitment to be an inclusive church we know that sanctifying the ordinary can be done in many contexts in a variety of ways. Hopefully we as Disciples can learn from our various ethnic and cultural expressions of faith and can claim the gifts of the multicultural church we already are.

The Turn to the Spirit

Disciples are learning that "sanctifying the ordinary" cannot be left to chance. "Sanctifying the ordinary" is a deeply meaningful way to relate faithfully to our world. Little in life is pure—pure faith, pure joy, pure love.

Yet many quotidian routines, such as laundry for Norris, can bring faith to life. Mainline Protestants are discovering the importance of spiritual practices for living a life of faith that "sanctifies the ordinary."[38] Our practices—not just prayer or Bible reading or worship but our everyday comings and goings, our making decisions, playing, reading, deciding where to live, singing, saying good-bye—all these daily acts form faith. They create patterns for living that lead us into a new "way of life" that is Good News.

If sanctifying the ordinary is core to Disciples spirituality, are there specific ways we can deepen this? Although spelling out steps or a how-to guide can trivialize the deeper meaning of this disposition or way of living our faith, there are a few rules of thumb. Simple awareness of how our tradition sanctifies the ordinary, as well as commitment to understanding how our growing diversity challenges and expands this, is a first step. Disciples' aversion to formal theological reflection and confessional testimony sometimes results in a desire to get on with the business of leading a biblically informed moral and ethical life at the expense of sanctifying daily life. As a result, we frequently stop noticing how our heritage and formal worship form us and how deeply our daily lives embody (or might embody) our conviction that God is present in mundane acts of justice and love.

Second, sanctifying the ordinary takes attentiveness, intentionality, discipline, and accountability to others in proclaiming our faith. The athlete who runs the race and the musician who plays a beautiful sonata or hip-hop must be disciplined in their practice. Being a disciple means practicing until we are able to do something that would be beyond our capacity without practice. So it is with sanctifying the ordinary. Beholding a child while changing a diaper, talking to a youth about the injustice that leads to locker room theft, figuring out with a spouse or partner who will do yet one more house chore—all of these have potential to form us in Christian faith, love, and hope. They are an invitation to rehearse God's call to life and love in the midst of the quotidian, whether in wonder and awe; joy and celebration; mourning and solace; or relief from guilt, shame, unhappiness, and strife. To sanctify something—that is, to make it sacred or see it as sacred—takes a trained eye. It takes an eye that can see the work of grace in what others may experience as merely ordinary or mundane. Notice, attend, be disciplined, and, lastly, speak with others about how the sacred informs the ordinary and the ordinary forms the sacred. Sharing with others deepens the experience. We see something we missed. We find others who are trying to practice their faith and are in need of support and guidance.

Disciples are discovering the need to confront the historical amnesia that transformed us from being a people whose spirituality "sanctified the ordinary" to being a people who are often simply ordinary. We drifted along as transitions in our surrounding cultures marginalized our presence and suddenly noticed dwindling attendance in some of our churches and confusion about our particular spiritual orientation. By reclaiming our

Disciples tradition we are opening up new possibilities to rediscover and celebrate our gifts and, where they are found wanting, to reshape and deepen our life together. Rediscovering the gifts that we offer to the needs of a hurting world is sacred work. If we are to be a faithful people worshiping in truly diverse communities, where deep relationships with the Divine inform our commitments to justice and compassion, we must once again learn how to "sanctify the ordinary" by intentionally tending the sacred in our daily lives.

23

Facing the Mark of the Beast

Eschatology and Economy in Latin America and the Caribbean

Angel Luis Rivera-Agosto

I. In the End: Eschatology and Context

Eschatology is generally described as the doctrine of the "Last Things," or "the end of days or all things." As a discourse, it refers to the *eschaton* ("the end"). Eschatology presents the Christian understanding of future events, such as death and resurrection, as well as the last judgment and the end of the world, eternal damnation (hell) and eternal life (heaven). In scholastic textbooks of theology, eschatology tends to be the last chapter of dogmatics, and has in the past stood in a certain discontinuity with their main contents. Today, a consensus has developed among the various schools of theology that the eschatological perspective is basic to the understanding of the Christian faith, and Christian theology from beginning to end is considered eschatological.[1]

The principal reasons for the contemporary emphasis on eschatology are the rediscovery by biblical scholars of the eschatological nature of the Christian gospel and the philosophical appreciation of the role of hope in human existence. The recovery of biblical eschatology began in Protestant circles at the beginning of the twentieth century with the seminal studies of Johannes Weiss and Albert Schweitzer investigating the nature of God's kingdom in the New Testament.[2] They argued that Jesus' message about the imminent coming of God's kingdom should be understood in continuity with the Jewish apocalyptic worldview, and that Jesus expected the establishment of God's kingdom to take place in the immediate future, not as a result of human endeavors, but as the final and decisive intervention of God in history. C.H. Dodd further advanced the discussion on the nature of God's kingdom by examining the time factor in the coming of the kingdom in the teaching of Jesus.[3] He argued that for Jesus the kingdom of God was realized in his own ministry and, therefore, his eschatology was already realized. Biblical scholarship recognized that the kingdom of God was already present in the ministry of Jesus, but it also noticed that in some sayings of Jesus—especially in the parables—the coming kingdom of God is both a present and a future event. Joachim Jeremias modified the concept of realized eschatology into inaugurated eschatology, or eschatology in the process of being realized.[4] This view implied that the salvation and the judgment already begun in the ministry of Jesus would come to a future climax.

Eschatology as the starting point of all theology inevitably affected the understanding of the Christian gospel and, consequently, the understanding of the church's nature and mission. In the Latin American experience, every reflection and point of reference regarding eschatology has to be placed in the context of salvation history, God's project for the full salvation of humanity and creation. Within this framework, the central unifying theme for eschatology is God's kingdom. This theme dominates the synoptic gospels; it is the final word of the book of Acts (28:31); in the Pauline letters it takes the form of Christ´s kingship; and in Revelation it is reaffirmed in the triumph of the "King of kings and Lord of lords" (Rev. 11:15, 19:6, 16).[5] In other words, eschatology talks about present life in reference to the future. Here we experiment with the good and the gracious in an imperfect way. Heaven is reality already lived in a limited experience in the present tense, but showing its completeness in the future. In this literary genre, within or beyond scriptural reference, future and salvation are described in terms of cosmic catastrophes, wars, hunger, and fights between demonic and heavenly creatures in a particular esoteric language. It is a genre very much near science fiction or superhero literature. In the New Testament, eschatological truth is found in the apocalyptic literary genre, where it shows the victory of good over evil and how God is the Lord of history.[6]

Today Latin America and the Caribbean are far beyond eschatological truth. Latin Americans face poverty, misery, violence, hardened hearts, and the growing unhappiness of the majority of the population. In biblical terms, poverty is no ideal, but rather a tragic situation that must be overcome. Nobody has the right to impose sacrifices on people or on entire groups of human beings, alleging that they are God's necessary tests. God's Holy Scripture indicates to us clearly that God has finished with all sacrifices, offering himself as the giver of Life and not of death.[7] The possibility of affirming the victory of life over death challenges the Gospel message to be in clear protest and denunciation in the face of the actual socioeconomic situation that is so profoundly destructive of human and social life in Latin America, called "neoliberalism" by sociologists and economists, but also often described as "the Beast."[8]

II. Economy in the Evolution from Simple Reproduction to Neoliberalism

When viewing our current socioeconomic order from the perspective of Christian eschatology, it is vital that we understand how economy works and how is has evolved into its current neoliberal system. Economy is the organization created by human groups for producing, distributing, and consuming products and services necessary to guarantee life reproduction. This concept originated with the Greek words *oikos*="house" and *nemo*="to manage." So, it is "to manage the house,"—facilitating, running, and meeting the needs associated with it. The activity of producing goods for the living of human groups has been developed in different ways in history—from economies of simple reproduction, where communities produce the necessary products for living and reproducing without a meaningful accumulation of either wealth or social differences based on wealth, to economies of extended reproduction, where communities produce such a surplus that it facilitates a greater reinvestment in the productive processes, which results in the accumulation and control by owners of the factors of production. In these societies, groups not working in production (castes or classes) appear. These classes were associated, in the beginning, to religion and war. Specialized roles began to develop in society, such as priests, scribes, craftsmen, traders, warriors with exclusive duties, and court administrators and servants (satraps, judges, governors).[9]

Socioeconomic life continued evolving. Surplus by economies of extended reproduction created the conditions for the appearance of commercial societies, where production is organized mainly for the market. The market becomes an independent social force and the main source of economic exchange and distribution. The money or the currency becomes the main way of goods exchange and for the paying of taxes. They are the main way of support for the dominant groups or classes such as kings, priests, and aristocrats. Monarchy continues as the main form of government, but the landowners and traders begin to play a more important and autonomous role before the military political power. With the development of the market, industrialized societies organized themselves within this system with a capacity for production of goods and for distribution on grand scale. The commercial merchandise appears as the core of the economy. The value of exchange (buying and selling) of a product is more important than its value of use (the capacity clothes have for dressing us up, food for consuming it, etc.). The industrialized societies are organized as nation-states headed by elites or specialized political groups or constitutional monarchs. The expropriation system is not limited to tax collection and goods; products and services distribution is carried out almost exclusively through the market.[10]

None of these forms of economic organization exists in isolation. In our societies we find combined forms of production among countries and within the diverse regions surrounding each country. What is important to understand is that modern economy (industrial or postindustrial) is based on an expropriation system that works through different markets:

1. The product and services market (domestic and international)
2. The capital or money market (the bank, finances, stock market)
3. The labor market

All these markets are organized "to expropriate" to producers and customers, depending on them. This is carried out through mechanisms of uneven exchange where one of the parties does not know it is being expropriated. This uneven exchange does not mean that the trader or merchant does not have the right to receive a fair profit, but it should not use deceitful mechanisms (voluntary or involuntary) for obtaining such profits.[11]

Nowadays, economy is one of the central issues of everyday life. Most of our day-to-day-decisions, governments' policies, international relations, and even wars among countries are related to interests for the control of natural resources (oil), markets, and knowledge. At the present time, the economic policy is organized all over the world by institutions having a deep impact in our daily life. The World Bank, the International Monetary Fund, and the World Trade Organization are international institutions that formulate policies and make decisions that result in the increase of prices of bread, rice, gasoline, medicines, clothes, etc., affecting life in such a way that Latin American and Caribbean nations' situations gradually becomes harder.[12]

One of the main causes of the crises lived in our communities and nations is the imposition throughout Latin America of the neoliberal socioeconomic model. While this began as a purely economic model, it has been converted nowadays into a whole social project that has profoundly transformed our societies over the past thirty years. Neoliberalism is the doctrine of big, international capital and of specific, locally powerful groups. Within the Latin American population, there is a minority that believes that society progresses better if it functions as an immense business. We are told that if all the members of society understand this and act accordingly, each person will obtain benefits and the entire society will prosper. It seems very simple. The market is presented as the space in which everything that is desired can be obtained, always when things are done with efficiency. The society ends up becoming an immense market, one in which all human beings become merchants, or, in other words, business people: they sell something in exchange for something and they try to obtain benefits from this exchange.[13]

Neoliberalism turns politics into business, and by doing so, it has degraded politics and promoted corruption and lies, buying and selling consciences. It has turned politics into an art among traders who no longer worry about obtaining benefits for anyone except themselves and their associates. Politics are degraded so that the system becomes one for obtaining personal enrichment, while ignoring the common good and the well-being of all members of the nation, of the care for human and natural resources of the countries, and of the fate of future generations. Our nations drift and become booty for predators.[14]

Even culture and sports have fallen into the hands of the new merchants and traders. And with this comes the threat of their disappearance as human activities that have purposes and meanings in and of themselves. Now, the meaning that is given to them is of their potential for profit to the new investors in these fields. As well, many spaces in the religious sphere have ended up permeated by this commercial logic. This logic takes on theological and religious forms in proposals such as the theology of prosperity, according to which repentance and grace are measured by the economic and material prosperity of the believer.[15]

The only values that are promoted in the neoliberal society are the values of the market and of the good merchant: to know what to offer and at what moment, to take advantage of any opportunity that presents itself, to know how to sell and to know how to buy, to know how to deceive, to know how to lie, to know how to convince. Truth gives way to rhetoric. Social life and human relations become banal; they are considered only in monetary terms. When today we speak of a crisis of values, we cannot ignore how the whole population, including ourselves, feels compelled to apply this way of relating with one another. It is a matter of the promotion of a spirituality that, in order to impose itself, must destroy those traditions, beliefs, cultures and spiritualities that place human life over all other values.[16]

For neoliberalism, all those persons who cannot be inserted in this new world of traders are a burden for society. Only the efficient deserve to survive in this endless competition, because to help all those who do not know how to assert themselves in the competition would be to give them a privilege that other competitors have not received. Neoliberalism promotes itself as kingdom of equality. It proclaims the end of privileges. Just as the rich pay for services, so the poor should pay for them also. All human beings should place their capacities and advantages at the service of themselves. Human beings live thanks to each one's own actions. Persons live for themselves and do not depend on anyone. Neoliberalism proclaims itself a society in which each one responds for oneself, and thereby describes itself as a society of individual responsibility.

Impacts of neoliberalism on our continent are more than obvious. Health has become a business and no longer a social service, much less a human right or a universal human need. Education and attention to children and the elderly are no longer social, public, or state responsibility. The state is required to renounce social responsibility and withdraw from all functions and duties to citizens once derived from a sense of responsibility toward the common good. These social functions must now be attended to by efficient businesses that charge for their services and obtain profits from these services. The result is that the majority of people who do not have money to pay the high costs of the private health care are condemned to death; those human beings who for diverse reasons cannot pay for education or to obtain their own means of making a living are abandoned to their own fate.[17]

III. Revelation as an Eschatological Tool for Life within Neoliberalism

Apocalyptic literature constitutes an excellent example of how biblical texts are interwoven from the views of the poor, marginalized, and victimized. In the book of Revelation, the future is read from the victims' perspective, from the ones who don't give up, from the ones who keep hope in justice, waiting for the irruption of the Absolute, of the implausible awaited. Conviction of the victims' final victory (the Kingdom of the Slaughtered Lamb) is presented as hope of an historical possibility, different from actual experience. Apocalyptic revelation perceives the present with eyes placed in the future. If a victim lives into this eschatological vision, he or she becomes an active subject with a vital faith that restores human dignity. When the victim is thought of as key in participation in the future, he or she becomes a subject of hope and, thus, a subject of another world possible, in deep communion with an alternative building of history. Since economic structures throughout history have served as mechanisms of oppression, victims' redemption means also reversion of structures that oppress them. That truth is part of biblical literature. So, it is important to look upon some texts within the book of Revelation that are referred to as economic aspects of history and its conclusion.[18]

A. Market Rules against the Poor

In Revelation 6 we see the imagery of the seals that kept the book closed from the inside and from the outside being broken to reveal the book's content. This imagery describes what has happened in human history. Continuing, we see the imagery of the four horsemen. Here it is important to note that the opening of the third seal and the riding of the third horseman address important socioeconomic issues. This text mentions the prices on wheat, barley, oil, and wine. The negative aspect of the horseman's presence and the specific components of the image seem to point out that negativity occurs in the matter of economy, specifically on food products. The horseman carries a pair of scales where grains are weighed for the market. There is a voice that accompanies this horseman, indicating the price for grain and giving an instruction "not to affect the oil and the wine.[19]

A study of the socioeconomic conditions of that time suggests that prices announced in the text are exaggerated. The price for wheat is much more expensive than usual. As for the barley, a product consumed by poor families, its price described in Revelation is so expensive that it would be impossible for anyone to buy it. A "denary" means the salary for one whole day's work, so money earned in a day would not be enough to buy all the necessary food. That indicates a selective rise on prices, which affects goods needed by poor families. For example: in the recent inflation in Argentina, while general cost of living rose 20 percent in four months, the cost of basic goods that are part of the food basket rose more than 100 percent.[20]

In contrast, refined commodities, reserved for higher classes, such as olive oil and wine, keep a steady price in Revelation. Other differences can be observed. Wheat and barley are annual products, while oil and wine come from perennial plants. The first two are raw products, while the second two are elaborated products. In that sense, the horseman with the scales in his hands (showing the possibility of manipulating the weight of the products) is the carrier of human pain caused by the rising of prices to poor people, the ones who depend on their annual crops, the ones who need to elaborate their own food. But the increase doesn't "touch" the ones with stable crops, commodities, and elaborate products.[21]

This horseman, with scale in hand, leads the way to the fourth horseman, Death, whose instruments include the "sword" and "famine," or hunger (v. 8). So, the text gives the reader a progression: the second horseman on the red horse of war brings out conflict and sword, the third horseman on the black horse shows how the rising of prices affects mainly annual crops and poor people's access to primary goods. Finally, Death, riding the pale green horse, has been using the sword (as the red horse) and hunger (as the black horse) and its own strength: death by fierce animals (political power in Revelation's symbolism). So, human history appears as the place where those forces generate pain, hunger, and death, affecting everyone, but especially those vulnerable to conflicts and wars, to the ones who live consuming primary goods in times of rising prices (or inflation) and to the ones submitted to the Beast's power.[22]

B. Buying and Selling with the Mark of the Beast

Buying and selling are references to economic order in chapter 13, especially in verses 16 and 17. The dragon (chapter 12) and the beasts (chapter 13) in this portion of Revelation are potential idols to be worshiped by people who have lost their focus on God. The reference to imperial cult practices (Cesarean cult) is rather evident. In this context of imposition and falsehood appears, at the end of the chapter, a mention of the wealthy, the poor, and their commercial activity.[23]

The temporary and deceitful victory of the beast (in this case, the second beast, vv. 11–15) allows it to mark its followers on their foreheads or hands. That mark is the counterpart of the seal worn by the servants of God on their forehead (Rev. 7:3). Also, there is another difference in the type of marking.

Servants of God wear a sign (*sfragís* in Greek), while the Beast imposes a mark (*jaragma*, in Greek) that establishes a character as a way of total submission, regardless of being rich, poor, great or small, free or slave. Marked people worship the beast. Sealed people do not share the values of the majority. [24]

What is most striking is the verb *"jarasso,"* which is the main root for the Greek word meaning "to mark." It is also used to describe the making of money. That is why the word *mark* has also been used in connection with currency (for example, the German monetary unit). Some authors tend to observe that the "mark of the beast" is a reference to the Roman currency, which has the image of the emperor or the goddess Rome. From that specific meaning, it is not difficult to conclude that only the ones who own that "mark" are allowed to sell and to buy. The power of the beast, its oppressive and idolatric condition, is marked on the forehead as an expression of ownership, or in the hand in the currency used to buy and to sell. The beast comes out as a power that dominates absolutely the economic activity. It limits the possibility of trade to only those submitted to its law, its image, and its currency. No one can interact outside this imposed system, where everyone is part of a determined social structure: some in the role of dominant sectors and others as poor or slaves. The beast has the power to kill whoever tries to get out and make a difference by following the Lamb. However, those who follow the Lamb are those whose names are written in the Book of Life.[25]

C. The Logic of Death vs. the Logic of Justice

The contents of chapters 17 and 18 describe one of the final visions in the section destined to the eschatological fight (before the end) and the triumph of the Lamb, converted into the victorious horse warrior that finally defeats the beast (Rev. 19; cf. 17:14). The text manages different verbal tenses, because from the author's point of view it is already occurring. The absolutely new (Rev. 21) only is possible when evil no longer exists (Rev. 21:14–15). There is a symbolic description of the cause of God's judgment over the city of Babylon, representing the oppressive system (either of that time or in the present). Economic elements in the narrative are dominant. It is important to point out the curse of merchandise and complicity of merchants.[26]

Babylon accumulated commodities and luxury goods, and, in that same act, denied everyday life. The mounting up of its sin is revealed in the accumulation of luxury goods that ended up transforming life into a negotiable good. "If there is no business, there is no life," seemed to be the Babylonian motto. The reason for all the amassing of power and wealth (which produces victimization), denying human reason (justice and creative activity, which produce happiness) is this: where one settles, the other no longer exists. Therefore, Babylon is not a specific city, imperial Rome or even the corrupt Jerusalem. Celestial power prophetically confronts the "principalities and powers" of this world that implement a logic of death in an unjust economy. The call of the church in an eschatological horizon of hope is to join the struggle of God, informed by a logic of justice and love. [27]

IV. The End Is the Beginning: Proclaiming Hope and the Fullness of Life

As Jürgen Moltmann said in his book *The Coming of God,* Christian eschatology has nothing to do with apocalyptic "final solutions" of this kind, for its subject is not "the end" at all. On the contrary, what it is about is the new creation of all things. Christian eschatology is the remembered hope of the raising of the crucified Christ, so it talks about beginning afresh in the deadly end. Christian eschatology follows this christological pattern in all its personal, historical, and cosmic dimensions: *in the end is the beginning.* That is how Dietrich Bonhoeffer took leave of his fellow prisoner, Payne Best, in the Flossenbürg concentration camp, as he went to his execution: *"This is the end—for me the beginning of life."* That is how John on Patmos saw the last judgment of the world–not as annihilation, a universal conflagration, or death in a cosmic and remote winter. He saw it as the first day of the new creation of all things: "See, I am making all things new"(Rev. 21:5). If we perceive it in remembrance of the hope of Christ, what is called the end of history is the end of temporal history and the beginning of the eternal history of life. Christ can only be called "the end of history" in the sense that he is the pioneer and leader of the life that lives eternally. Wherever life is perceived and lived in community and fellowship with Christ, a new beginning is discovered hidden in every end.[28]

In Latin America and the Caribbean, this searching for "the new beginning" takes form in the witness of churches and social movements, affirming countercultural values, resisting "the beast" of neoliberalism, and following the Lamb through the path to abundant life. It is necessary to *discern and analyze the present situation* in which we are engaged through critiquing the system by developing and participating in campaigns against foreign debt and Free Trade Agreements, by being in favor of gender equality and protection of the environment, and also by promoting valuable short-term initiatives such as community economic experiments, alternatives to money, bartering, local development projects, etc. We can set up such pointers within the present order and also hold before us a longer-term vision in the face of the irrationality and inequality of the present system. It will be a vision seeking consistent viable alternatives, dealing with such issues as: power, the law and its application, visions and analyses of the system and different models for the future.[29]

Victor Hugo once wrote: "The utopias of today will be the truths of tomorrow." Utopia is defined in Latin America and the Caribbean as the necessity of liberation for the fullness of life promised by God in his Son Jesus Christ. As an integral part of God's Creation, we are people who deserve to enjoy the blessings that God wishes to all humankind and nature. That is our hope and from it we define our vocation. As Pedro Henríquez Ureña said, "beneath our utopia, human beings will be absolutely human, leaving behind the obstacles of this absurd economic system on which we are prisoners and the residues of moral and social prejudices that drown spontaneous life; to be, through honest exercise of intelligence and sensibility, the free man and woman, open to the four winds of the spirit."[30] Hope begins when we acknowledge our vulnerability; it is sustained when we continue to resist injustice and make in concrete form our imagination to build new paths.

SECTION V

Mission

24

Theology of Prophetic Witness

MICHAEL KINNAMON

What Is a Theology of Prophetic Witness?

Christian witness, testimony to one's faith by word and deed, can be called "prophetic" when it brings the radical claims of the gospel to bear on present conditions of social injustice and, thus, engenders hope for a different way of living in human society. Its aim is not only to aid the victims of violence or poverty or discrimination but to provoke a transformation of the political, economic, and social systems that help perpetuate such evils. The tone of such witness is not just anger in the face of oppression (though that is a component of prophetic witness), but sorrow at the present state of affairs and joy at the possibility of a new order of reality. It is prophetic not in the sense of predicting the future but in calling people to trust in, and act on the basis of, God's promises.[1]

A *theology* of prophetic witness is critical reflection intended to strengthen and clarify Christian witness against those powers that hold people captive, materially as well as spiritually. It involves a critical assessment of the way things now are (seeing the evil that others may overlook or condone), a retrieval of those themes in the Christian tradition that reveal the idolatry of present social policies and practices, and a vision of new possibilities that provides courage for action. For example, the writings and speeches of Martin Luther King Jr. are often called "prophetic" because they denounce the way America "has defaulted on its promissory note" of freedom and justice for all; proclaim God's gift of one, interdependent humanity; and dream of that day when people "will not be judged by the color of their skin but by the content of their character."[2]

A theology of prophetic witness has the same focus as all theological reflection: knowledge of God. It asks, "Where is God in the present moment?" and, "How can the authoritative sources of Christian faith, especially scripture, be brought to bear on the present in order that God's will can be discerned with greater clarity?" A theology of prophetic witness certainly has much to say about human sinfulness; but its primary focus is on what God has done, is doing, and will do. It certainly has much to say about judgment; however, like most Christian theology, its primary subject matter is the good news of God's liberating grace. Otherwise, "prophecy" easily degenerates into self-righteous, human-centered moralizing, and hope for genuine change is muted.

Much theology of prophetic witness, in addition to addressing society, looks critically at the church, asking whether there is too much emphasis on meeting the needs of its members and not enough on calling and equipping them to participate in Christ's mission of bringing good news to the poor, proclaiming release to the captive and recovery of sight to the blind, letting the oppressed go free, and declaring the year of the Lord's favor (Lk. 4:18–19). In the same way, such theology may well explore how theology itself has often been misused to sanctify the power of the state or to give apology for oppressive social/economic structures—as was the case, for example, in Nazi Germany, in South Africa under apartheid, and in the United States during the period of slavery and subsequent racial segregation.[3]

A good case can be made that all theology should be understood as theology of prophetic witness since Christian faith is inherently prophetic. To praise the living God is to challenge the human-centeredness of every culture. To confess belief in God as creator, redeemer, and sustainer of life is to undercut the pretensions of every dominant ideology. To live in obedience to God, made known in Jesus Christ, relativizes the assumptions of every society. The Christian doctrines of creation and the Incarnation affirm that life in *this* world, though distorted by sin, is supremely precious to God. The church's role is not simply to focus on "spiritual things" or the "hereafter," but to be a credible sign and instrument of social transformation toward the day when God's will for *shalom* is realized on earth.

This prophetic witness comes to the fore in the Hebrew Scriptures in the story of the exodus (see Ex. 1—15) and in the writings of the prophets. These figures excoriate the violent empires of their day (e.g., Amos 1—6), express the sorrow of God at such disaster (e.g., Jer. 4, 8, and 12), and anticipate God's new creation (e.g., Isa. 65).[4] This prophetic trajectory continues in the ministry of Jesus, especially as he is presented in the gospel narratives of Matthew and Luke. In his concern for those regarded as expendable by society, Jesus embodies and proclaims a new empire of God in which "the poor are blessed, the hungry fed, the depressed filled with laughter, and the abused made safe."[5]

Over the past nearly two thousand years, however, this prophetic dimension of Christian faith has been more the exception than the rule. Obvious factors help account for this, including the close relationship between church and empire after Constantine and the growing tendency, in light of the delayed parousia, to identify the historical church with the reign (kingdom) of God. Prophets are often viewed by an established church as a disruption to its unity, a distraction from its pastoral work, and a danger to its place in the world.

The prophetic impulse reappeared in a highly visible way, however, with the U.S.– based social gospel movement at the beginning of the twentieth century. According to one of its theological advocates, Shailer Matthews, the social gospel "represented the application of the teaching of Jesus and the total message of the Christian salvation to society, the economic life, and social institutions…as well as to individuals."[6] Salvation is not an individual quest to be saved *out* of the world but a communal effort, in response to God's leading, to build a better society on earth. This means, argued Walter Rauschenbusch and other leaders of the movement, that the church must prophetically engage the social problems of the day, which, in that period of industrial revolution, included child labor, a dangerous working environment, and great economic and educational disparity between rich and poor. World War I (and subsequent horrors of the twentieth century) undercut the optimism of the social gospel movement, but important seeds had been planted. Martin Luther King Jr., for example, wrote of his indebtedness to Rauschenbusch and claimed the legacy of the social gospel during the civil rights struggles of the 1960s.[7]

Beneath the surface, however, a major shift was occurring that erupted in the late 1960s and early 1970s in the form of theologies of liberation. The social gospel movement assumed that Western, capitalist, democratic culture could progress in the direction of human fulfillment. The effort needed was one of reform, not complete transformation. Since the middle of the century, however, there has been a growing conviction that modern, Western culture is, itself, frequently hazardous to the well-being of humanity. At its core are principles that lead to the breakdown of community, the exultation of consumerism, the exclusion of various groups, the despoiling of the environment, and the massive buildup of military force in order to protect the interests of the privileged. Once you conclude that society is *fundamentally* distorted, then politics becomes more revolutionary than reformist and theology becomes more liberationist than liberal.[8]

Liberation theology, unlike the liberal theology of the social gospel movement, does not see the future developing out of the past and present. Indeed, sin is often identified in liberation thought with bondage to the past, and a commitment to God's future demands opposition to the present. God is the One whose hope-filled promise calls us away from the old toward the *radical* newness of God's reign.

These themes can be seen in theologies from Latin America, Africa, and Asia that challenge the destructive dominance of the West; in feminist theology that challenges the patriarchal assumptions of church and society; in African American and Hispanic theologies that challenge endemic patterns of racism; in gay theology that challenges the social and ecclesial exclusion of persons on the basis of sexual orientation; and in eco-theology that challenges the way nature is valued only as raw material for human advancement. All of these read social trends with a "hermeneutic of suspicion," seeking to uncover how public policies serve the interests of those in power.[9]

We can see this shift toward a more prophetic witness played out clearly in the global ecumenical movement. For the first twenty years of the World Council of Churches (1948–68), the guiding vision for ecumenical social ethics was "the responsible society," a vision that emphasized how those who hold political and economic power are responsible for its exercise to God and to the people whose welfare is affected by it. By the late 1960s, however, this concept was being criticized as a prop for the *status quo* (often in the name of social and economic "stability"). A newly emerging orientation could be seen, for example, in the World Council's Program to Combat Racism. Practically speaking, it signaled a shift from attempting to influence those with power to participating in the struggles of those without it, from giving aid to victims to standing in solidarity with them. Theologically, it marked a transition from "historical realism"—a position that eschewed "utopian" visions, calling the churches to contribute to relative justice in a sinful world—to "eschatological realism," which urged the churches to live in bold anticipation of God's shalom.[10]

One of the primary examples of a recent theology of prophetic witness developed in the course of the struggle against apartheid in South Africa. In 1985, a group of South Africans issued the famous "Kairos Document." It repudiated not only "state theology," which defended apartheid on scriptural grounds, but also "church theology" for the way it encouraged reconciliation without deep repentance and fundamental change on the part of those who fostered this system of race-based oppression.

In their place, the authors called for a "prophetic theology" marked by the following:

- It starts by naming the experience of oppression and conflict and takes an unambiguous stand with the victims.
- It is grounded in scripture but in a way that concentrates on those aspects of the Word that have immediate bearing on the current moment of crisis (*kairos*). It attempts to read the Bible in light of the experience of suffering, but also to read the signs of the times in light of biblical teaching.
- It has a sense of urgency, a call to action and conversion. Such theology is confrontational without being hateful. Christians must love enemies by freeing both victims and victimizers from dehumanizing behavior.

- It envisions the future as God would have it (according to scripture) and, thus, emphasizes hope.[11]

It should be noted that there is another strand of the Christian tradition, associated with the Anabaptist wing of Protestantism, that sees prophetic witness not as political/social engagement but as a countercultural way of communal living. This understanding is represented today in the United States by the writings of such theologians as Stanley Hauerwas and the late John Howard Yoder. The church, they argue, should not try to change the world. Rather, it is most prophetic when it exemplifies in the way it lives God's will for peaceful and just relationships.[12] This perspective is echoed in an important WCC study on "Ecclesiology and Ethics" when it declares that "the church not only has, but *is,* a social ethic."[13]

Has the Disciples Movement Been Prophetic?

It is hard to deny Mark Toulouse's answer to this question: "For the most part, Disciples have been very active in what might be characterized as social service and much less active in anything we could truly call social transformation."[14] Individual Disciples have certainly borne prophetic witness, even been leaders ecumenically in the work of social justice. Alva Taylor, Barton Hunter, Kirby Page, James Crain, Mae Yoho Ward, T. J. Liggett, John Compton, Rhodes Thompson, May and Harvey Lord, Albert Pennybacker, Garnett Day, Charles Bayer, Pablo Stone, Joan Campbell, Rita Brock, Alvin Jackson, and Ken Brooker Langston come quickly to mind. Few of these persons, however, have written theologically about their witness; and the denomination as a whole has preferred to promote charity and incremental change rather than to call for anything like social transformation. It is telling that *The Encyclopedia of the Stone-Campbell Movement*, published in 2004, has no entry on either Taylor or Hunter, the two most influential social activists among Disciples in the period prior to the restructuring of the church in 1968.

Of course, Disciples are not alone in this lack of prophetic witness. As Gary Dorrien observes, over the past century "the mainline churches have generally refrained from challenging the structures or ethos of the dominant order in order to remain part of it."[15] It is also true, however, that the historic "pillars" of Disciples identity, the characteristic emphases of the movement, have made prophetic witness particularly difficult.

The preeminent identity marker for Disciples, a passionate concern for the unity of the church, has at times served to blunt the sharp edge of social witness. The outstanding early Disciples leader, Alexander Campbell, is a prime case in point. Campbell took a vigorous stand against slavery in the early 1830s, but moderated this position a decade later out of a desire to preserve church unity. Slavery, he contended in a series of articles for *The Millennial Harbinger,* is socially "inexpedient"; but since slavery is not explicitly condemned in scripture, abolition of it cannot be insisted on if it leads to division. Harold Lunger, in his study of Campbell's political ethics, notes that this key Disciples leader almost never dealt with the subject from the point of view of the slaves and the effect of the system of slavery on them. His focus was on what makes for social cohesion and ecclesial unity.[16]

In the same way, Campbell was an outspoken pacifist—in times of peace. But during the Mexican War of 1846, he refrained from calling for an end to the violence lest such a call prove divisive for Disciples fellowship.[17] Karl Barth once condemned the church for its "habit of coming to the scene too late, of entering the fray only when its opinions no longer involve any risk and can no longer exert any particular influence."[18] Such criticism can surely be leveled at Campbell, who, in his later years, actively discouraged Christians from discussing social and political questions *as Christians,* at least in part out of a fear of fragmentation.[19]

Disciples, especially in the early decades of the movement, prided themselves on being people of "the Book" who followed the principle (first expressed by Thomas Campbell), "Where the scriptures speak, we speak; where the scriptures are silent, we are silent." This has meant a reluctance to take a stand on moral issues of the day unless the Bible's commands are considered unmistakable—a position guaranteed to limit prophetic social engagement.

It is worth noting, in line with Lunger, that Alexander Campbell and other early leaders among the Disciples appealed more to the letter of the Bible than to its spirit; that is to say, they cited specific passages rather than looking to such overarching themes as caring for the poor and welcoming the stranger. In addition, Campbell concentrated on more "socially conservative" parts of the canon. "Almost never did he turn to the teachings of Jesus or the Sermon on the Mount, and his only use of the Old Testament prophets was to prove that Jesus appeared in fulfillment of prophecy."[20] The point is not to suggest that such use of scripture has been authoritative for later generations of Disciples (it clearly hasn't been), but to underscore that Disciples did not begin with a burst of prophetic witness.

A third pillar is the freedom of congregations and individual believers from ecclesiastical control, freedom to determine one's opinions on "non-essentials" without the potentially coercive influence of bishops and creeds. When coupled with the refusal to speak as church in the absence of clear biblical mandate, this has meant that political decisions, from slavery to the invasion of Iraq, have been left almost entirely in the realm of personal judgment.

It is in the Disciples DNA to oppose churchly concern; but it is not coercive for the church to take a stand through communal decision in the face of overt oppression and violence and, thus, to nurture the conscience of members. When this doesn't happen, members of the church are likely unprepared to resist the dominant cultural narratives.

The Disciples concern for unity was, at least in the early years, for the sake of evangelistic witness, of calling people to faith in Jesus Christ. Any address of social evils was subordinated to this primary thrust of mission. If society is to be regenerated, wrote the influential editor, J.H. Garrison, it will be through the regeneration of individuals who have come to saving knowledge of Christ.[21] Society will be outwardly transformed by the voluntary efforts of the inwardly converted. According to James Crain in his book, *The Development of Social Ideas Among the Disciples of Christ*, it was this preoccupation with evangelism (and with reaffirming unity) in the years after the Civil War that prevented Disciples of the era from recognizing the growing exploitation of workers in the industrial revolution and the attendant civic corruption.[22] Contributors to Disciples journals often expressed their views on what society should be like, but usually insisted that the way to accomplish the needed reform was through spiritual transformation and trust in the providence of God.[23]

This list can be extended. A concern "to restore" the church's ancient order may have kept nineteenth-century Disciples from recognizing the distinctive and complex social issues of their own time and place.[24] Campbell's sense of the imminence of the millennial age seems to have contributed to his low estimate of the importance of political affairs, at least for part of his ministry.[25] But whatever weight one gives to these various factors, taken together they meant that nineteenth-century Disciples offered little prophetic witness with regard to slavery, war, colonial expansion, the state of African Americans in the aftermath of Emancipation, the treatment of Native Americans, the exploitation of workers and the growing disparity of wealth in the Gilded Age, or the abysmal condition of American cities.[26]

Things began to change, however, in the early years of the twentieth century as Disciples, along with many other American Protestant churches, experienced the impact of the social gospel movement. A decisive moment came in 1911 when the International Convention authorized formation of a standing commission "with responsibility for both social service and world peace." Crain only slightly overstates the case when he says, "Now for the first time [Disciples] began to turn their attention from themselves and their own interests to the needs of the world outside their church doors."[27] The commission, however, was chronically underfunded; and, while its resolutions on social issues were generally adopted by the International Convention, these resolutions did not, in Crain's words, "have sufficient consensus to support programs of action to put those convictions into practice."[28]

The highwater mark for prophetic witness by American churches was the civil rights movement of the 1960s. For their part, the Disciples in 1963 pledged support for "the ideal of an integrated church and an integrated society" and appointed a Committee on Moral and Civil Rights to help embody its commitment. The committee, among other things, involved thousands of ministers in work for civil rights, contributed to voter registration efforts, and supported the National Council of Churches' Delta Ministry among impoverished cotton workers in Mississippi. As many as 150 Disciples were involved in the Selma-Montgomery March in 1965. In 1968, the church established a Reconciliation fund to address the urban crisis that was part and parcel of the struggle for racial justice. A year later, in response to the famous "Black Manifesto," the Disciples General Board confessed that the church was still far too timid in dealing with racism and called upon it to stop "business as usual."[29]

Since then, however, the record is spotty, not only for Disciples, but for all mainline denominations. These churches have continued to proclaim the cause of racial justice and, in the 1980s, made a significant contribution to public debate over nuclear weapons. But it is hard to deny that, overall, their witness has been diminished. The reasons are complex but include the following:

- It is no secret that mainline churches have lost members, financial resources, and public influence over the past thirty-five years. Leaders often fear that controversy can further weaken the church; and they, thus, refrain from advocating prophetic programs and declarations. Disciples, for example, since the mid-1990s have eliminated virtually all national staff positions responsible for social justice ministries and have discussed a decreasing number of General Assembly resolutions dealing with contemporary issues. Being less politically influential, less entangled with the powers that be, *could* allow mainline churches to adopt a more prophetic posture; but this has not been the case.
- Within the mainline denominations, there is an evident gap between the commitment of at least some leaders and many local church members. Leaders and assemblies will frequently offer prophetic witness (even use the language of liberation theology) only to discover, as noted above, that their initiatives lack the broad support needed for churchwide action. As a result, resolutions and other public statements sometimes seem like "feel-good" pronouncements that involve too little serious cost or effort.
- Polarization within the churches on issues of social concern, and inability to deal constructively with conflict, mean that social advocacy is increasingly confined to special interest groups that can be ignored by the rest of the church. Such groups within the Disciples—especially the Disciples Peace Fellowship, founded in 1935—have often rendered profound witness; but surely such witness would be greatly enhanced if the church didn't *have* a peace fellowship but *was* one.

To come at this from another angle, mainline denominations have shown little capacity for integrating social witness with worship, pastoral care, stewardship, or the other things the church does and is. In the words of theologian Lew Mudge, "There seems little connection in the minds of church members between the moral convictions to which they bear witness and the nature of the ecclesial community in which these convictions are nurtured"[30]—which means that peace and justice can be relegated to one corner of the church.

How Might Prophetic Witness Be Strengthened?

Prophetic witness cannot be mandated since it is a response to particular conditions of social injustice. In this sense, a department or program of prophetic witness would be an oxymoron. There are, however, things that theologians, including congregational ministers, can do or emphasize to help prepare the church to respond more prophetically to its context. Some of these have been suggested above, especially a clear, consistent articulation of how social justice is a central theme of scripture. I will briefly outline two others for consideration.

1. In my judgment, Disciples and other mainline denominations generally lack a biblically grounded vision of the "Good Society" that transcends the present order; and without such a vision, the church will be content with reforms that leave the status quo untouched. Our churches, writes Audrey Chapman, former executive with the United Church Board for World Ministries, seem limited to recommending "incremental policy changes that often differ little from those of secular political actors." What is missing, in her words, "is a compelling religious vision, a sense of the 'now' and the 'not yet' of God's kingdom that challenges and opposes the injustices of the dominant reality by invoking God's peace and justice."[31] Church-based lobbying efforts have real value. But the church will lose its distinctive calling, and risk becoming captive to the culture, if it does not also set forth an alternative picture of life in human community.[32]

If the church fails to be prophetic, it may well be because our imaginations are so impoverished, because we simply accept what is as "the way things are." Can we even imagine a world in which opposing ideologies don't arm themselves to the teeth or resort to violence in order to solve conflicts? Can we even imagine a world not marked by abysmal poverty or dehumanizing racism? Well, scripture does; and part of Christian resistance to the present is to internalize and express biblical visions of an alternative future.

This was one of Martin Luther King's greatest strengths:

> I have a dream that one day, on the red hills of Georgia, sons [and daughters] of former slaves and sons [and daughters] of former slave-owners will be able to sit down together at the table of brotherhood. I still have a dream that one day the idle industries of Appalachia will be revitalized, and the empty stomachs of Mississippi will be filled, and brotherhood [and sisterhood] will be more than a few words at the end of a prayer, but rather the first order of business on every legislative agenda.[33]

This is not wishful thinking. It is imagining the world as God would have it; and, as such, it helps set the church's agenda for witness.

2. Disciples, to focus on this tradition, are an unusual combination of Reformed and Anabaptist characteristics. A theology of prophetic witness within the Disciples should, in my opinion, emphasize both and show their intersection.

On the one hand, Disciples, in line with the Reformed heritage, have affirmed that the church is responsible to God for the world[34]—which means promoting social change through political engagement. Reformed churches generally contend that when the state serves God's purposes, Christians should cooperate with the state in their realization; but when the state acts contrary to these purposes, Christians are called *as church* to criticize or, even, offer active resistance.

On the other hand, Disciples, in line with the Anabaptist heritage, have affirmed that the church is responsible to God for the way it lives as the body of Christ—precisely because the church can offer prophetic witness by demonstrating an alternative form of community. Dana Wilbanks argues that both emphases are found in the ministry of Martin Luther King: "For King, the black struggle for freedom, rooted in the spirituality of the black church, was to model...the future for which it works and, at the same time, to seek for the realization of that future through social and political action."[35]

This hybrid identity can be seen in the way leading twentieth-century Disciples theologians held together a concern for the church's unity with public, political opposition to war. A prominent example is Peter Ainslie, one of the Disciples greatest ecumenists, who was also one of the few Christian leaders, Disciples or otherwise, to oppose U.S. entry into World War I. The connection between these can be seen in several of his writings, including the following passage from *If Not a United Church—What?*:

> In the years to come the charge will be laid against the church of this day that because of its divisions, and therefore its unspiritual attitudes, the whole world is under the domination of social and economic wrongs, culminating in the disastrous war of 1914... At the crisis of 1914 organized Christianity stood helpless in every nation on the globe and was powerless to preserve the peace of the world. Surely division has its fruit. Whatever may be the immediate causes, the remote cause of [World War I] must be laid at the door of the church.[36]

The same connection between the unity of the church and public witness for peace can be seen in such figures as Charles Clayton Morrison, William Robinson (the outstanding British Disciples theologian), and T.J. Liggett. Living ecumenically, they would say, is not a substitute for other forms of prophetic witness against the forces of violence, but it does complement them by giving embodied expression to the reconciling mission of God.

25

Mission in Africa

An African Disciples Perspective

BOSELA EALE

Africa is a vast continent offering great variety and diversity in its politics, economic development, and cultures. Consequently, the church has had a varied history.[1]

The spread of the faith in the African continent represents the most spectacular advance in the story of Christianity, but it is unfortunate that names and stories of persons chiefly responsible are largely unknown. Since Africans rely on oral tradition rather than writing their history, Europeans and American know more than them about the history of Christianity in Africa. European and American missionaries send letters regularly to their sending churches, and boards and missions to keep them informed on the ongoing ministry in the field, sharing information that Africans could not access.

Advocating that history of the Church in Africa should be written by Africans, S.E.M. Pheko writes:

> It is unfortunate that most books on vital matters affecting the Africans and their continent have always been written by non-Africans. This is an abnormal situation. No people can write accurately about others. This is not necessarily because of prejudice (which unfortunately in the experience of Africa cannot be ruled out), but because most non-Africans who write about Africans have their own interests. Their interests come first... And Africa continues

> to be interpreted by these people very much to the disadvantage of Africa and her people.[2]

The Church in Africa finds its roots in ancient Egypt and Ethiopia. The first century after Christ, Africa was a major center of Christian faith, thought, and activity. Tertullian and Augustine from North Africa were the main actors of Church history in Africa. Augustine, for instance, was one of the leading and most influential African leaders in the early church. He was born on 13 November 354 C.E. in the town of Thagste, which was to be called Souk Ahras after the arrival of Arab Moslems in Numidia, the current Algeria.[3] He was a church leader and theological teacher in the leading early Bible schools in Africa. He wrote several books, and among them are *Confessions* and *The City of God*.[4] However, Christianity disappeared as Islam advanced. Egypt and Ethiopia are the two regions in Africa where one could see the veritable, indigenous, and profound African Christianity. But that Christianity did not have any impact in the Sub-Sahara. There was a kind of a gap between the North and the South of Africa in terms of Christianity. On the issue of Christianity in Africa, Timothee Bankole stresses that Christian kingdoms were set up toward the south of Egypt, first in Abyssinia, and later in Nubia.[5] While Islam was spreading and Christianity was disappearing along the Atlantic coast because of the conquest by Arabs in the seventh century, Bankole adds:

> Happily, the Coptic Church in Egypt survived and has remained till today, while in Abyssinia there is still a Christian Church though it continues to live in isolation. In Nubia, the Christian Church which was established there eventually fell a prey to Islam. It is significant that while Christianity stagnated or made little or no progress, Islam continued to spread into the heart of Africa. For seven centuries after its attempt, the Christian pioneers who went to Africa lay low before making another bold attempt to plant Christianity in Africa.[6]

Between the sixteenth and the eighteenth centuries, the Europeans contributed to the continuation of the Sub-Saharan Church with the introduction by the Portuguese of a Catholic form of Christianity to the Kongo Kingdom (Central Africa). The Kongo Kingdom at that time was composed of three countries: the current Democratic Republic of the Congo, the Republic of the Congo, and the Republic of Angola. But the fruit of the work by Portuguese could not be seen until the end of the eighteenth century, when the evangelical revival began to bring to the African continent missionaries whose labors would produce the first-fruit of an enduring Christian presence in Sub-Saharan Africa.

The history of the Disciples of Christ in Africa began with a failed attempt of the American Christian Missionary Society (ACMS) in Liberia in 1853. The Congo Mission started in 1898 with the Foreign Christian Missionary Society

(FCMS), followed by the Christian Woman's Board of Mission (CWBM) in 1919. One year later, in 1920, all combined to become the United Missionary Society (UMS), then the Division of Oversee Ministries (DOM) of the CCDC. Since 1996, relationships have been maintained by Global Ministries, a common world outreach with the United Church of Christ. The Foreign Christian Missionary Society sent the first missionary to the Bolenge village in the Equator province. Bolenge became then the first mission station of the Disciples in the Congo. From the Bolenge mission station the missionary work continued to the rivers Momboyo and Busira to reach out to people of the southern part of Equator, establishing more mission stations. The mission work in the Congo by the DOM was terminated in the field mission of the Congo in 1964 when the Disciples in the Congo became self-governing. The year 1964 marks the shift of the leadership from the American missionaries to the Congolese natives.

This chapter has four major sections. The first one deals with a general understanding of the mission in Africa. It reviews mission work in Africa during the precolonial, colonial, and postcolonial period. The second deals with the heritage and culture in the Church of the Congo. In this section we discuss the impact of missionary work in the life of the Disciples in the Congo. The third section deals with the understanding by African Disciples of the Global mission, while the fourth section talks briefly about African Tradition Religion.

Understanding Mission

The primary mission of the Church is to proclaim the gospel of Christ and gather believers into local churches where they can be built up in the faith and be made effective in service, thereby planting new congregations throughout the world.[7] The word *mission* is problematic on the African continent as it is often ambiguous and misunderstood. The reason for this might be because there is not much writing on mission by African natives. N.K. Mugambi stresses that there is nothing published by African theologians on the mission of the Church in Africa.[8] The misunderstanding on the concept "mission" is a reality among the Disciples in the Congo as well as in most parts of Africa. When talking about mission, the very first image that comes in the mind of the Disciples and most Africans is that of a white man or woman coming from the Western world to bring the good news in a foreign land. The same concept could be understood if it is applied to an African doing the same kind of work in the Western world. On the misunderstanding of the concept by Africans, Musimbi Kanyoro writes:

> We in Africa have misunderstood our call to mission. The word mission itself raises certain ambiguities in our understanding. Mention mission and missionaries and you think of all the foreign brothers and sisters who live in our villages working in hospitals, translating our Bibles and teaching women hygiene and sewing…

> This mission among ourselves and for ourselves is not an issue that keeps us awake with concern.[9]

Africans should see "mission" with new lenses and understand that they should not consider themselves eternal recipients of the mission. Musimbi argues that as long as the misunderstanding persists in the minds of the Africans, there will be no significant qualitative participation of Africans in mission. By doing so, Africans will delay the requirement to rethink our mission task to the African continent.[10] It is now time for Africans to rethink how to do mission. The great commission given by Christ to the Disciples (Mt. 28:19–20) is valuable for all Christians in the world and for all generations. There is no reason for Africans not to be involved in mission.

Precolonial Christianity

The history of the precolonial mission in Sub-Saharan Africa dates from the fifteenth century, when the King of Portugal began a relationship between his country and the Kongo Kingdom. The goal of the mission in the Kongo Kingdom by the Portuguese at that time was to do business and make Christians. Portuguese Catholics were the first Europeans to venture south of Sahara in significant numbers. In the sixteenth century the core of the Church in the Kongo Kingdom would seem to have been Portuguese settlers, most of them slave traders.[11] Lisbon had consistently prevented any non-Portuguese missionary from reaching the Kongo.[12] For several decades, Capuchins, Italians, Spanish, and French had been trying to worm their way into the African mission despite the stonewalling tactics of the Portuguese government.

Slave trading was the principal activity of the Portuguese government in the field mission. There were few missionaries, but many slave traders, and Portuguese missionaries worked hand-in-hand with the slave traders. Portuguese missionaries were a kind of chaplains in the slave trade business. The mission work of the Portuguese did not bear fruit in the Kongo Kingdom. Compared to the Europeans and Americans, whose mission work in the Congo bears fruit such as schools, hospitals, and churches, the Portuguese rather excelled in destroying the Kongo Kingdom by trading slaves. As Bankole observes, Europeans had penetrated into the continent of Africa for the sole purpose of gain in the merchandise of human traffic. It was not, however, until the nineteenth century that sustained missionary endeavor began to take root in Africa.[13] "It is the same ship that brought the Bible which also carried guns and alcohol to Africa." This is the popular saying in some parts of Africa, a response to the claim that missionaries who came to Africa were on a humanitarian "civilizing" mission, bringing salvation to the "primitive" tribes and "lost souls." We, however, know from all the available evidence on the activities of the "European missionaries" that they were just the forerunners who paved the way for the colonial conquest and subsequent rape of the African continent.

Early in the nineteenth century, Europeans and Americans began to envision mission work to Africa, and set up mission villages and mission stations in several parts of the African continent with three main objectives: planting churches, building schools, and building hospitals.

Colonial Christianity

This period was crucial for the mission in Africa. It was a time when Africans felt oppression from the Western colonizers. Christianity in this period goes from 1890 to 1960, which was the year several African nations got their independence. Africa was portioned by Western colonial powers at the Berlin conference in 1885. Bankole states that it was in that time that the majority of Europeans missionaries pronounced hell-fire theology to the heathens in Africa, who at the sound of the fearful message, could not resist and unfolded their hearts like flowers. Their response as hearers of the Word was amazing.[14] However, mission work at that time was not easy at all. Missionaries had to show their faith and obedience to what is stated in the Bible to secure the converts while the colonial power was abusing them. It was very unfortunate that some missionaries behaved like colonialists in trying to undermine Africans. For some of them, white skin was superior to the black one and hell was a place destined for the black people. Such thinking was similar to that of colonial officers and could not help Africans to grasp the value of Christianity. Even during the colonial period, God used some African believers like Simon Kimbangu (1889–1951), a Baptist catechist in the Congo, to perform miracles. Because of his faith and the nature of his prophetic preaching, he became a threat to the colonial power that attempted to arrest him in June 1921 but he escaped with some of his followers. In September of the same year, in obedience to a message from God, he gave himself up and was sentenced to 120 strokes of the whip and to the death penalty. Geoffrey Chapman confirms this when he writes:

> A more famous figure appeared in the western Congo: Simon Kimbangu. Baptist by background, he felt called by the voice of Christ in 1921, when in his early thirties, to gospel of the one God, in whom alone one must trust, and to heal the sick. Fetishes must be cast firmly aside. The fame of healing was quickly such that missions and hospitals for miles around were deserted while all the world hurried to Simon's village of N'kamba. The reaction of missionaries—Catholics missionaries above all—and of the Belgium colonial authorities was rapid and unfavorable. Simon was arrested and brought to the trial for subversion in October 1921 with several of his apostles.[15]

Africans viewed Christianity as a white man's religion. This was due to atrocities of the slave trade, racism, imperialism, and all kind of wicked treatment of which Africans were victim. I do not intend to say that all missionaries behaved so badly during the colonization of Africa, but some did. To hold the view that the exploitation of Africans by Europeans was God's will is a serious heresy. This is a misconception of the nature of the Almighty God who sees all human beings as equals before God. Oppression, injustice, and the nonrespect of human dignity are condemned in the Bible (Eccl. 4:1–3). Colonization had a negative impact in the memory of Africans. To illustrate this with a story of a missionary preaching, Bankole writes:

> Happily, there were a few "doubting Thomases" among those who listened. To this group belonged an African with an inquiring mind, who spent one Sunday afternoon listening attentively to a European missionary waxing eloquent on the theme of hell being a place of torments and the abode of the wicked after death. But the good, the missionary continued, go to Heaven—a place of happiness and a land flowing with milk and honey. At the end of his address the African asked the missionary: "How wonderful must be this place, Heaven, which you have been telling us about! But there is one thing more I would like to know about it. Who are the masters there?" Before the puzzled missionary could answer, the African asked further: "Could it be the English?" "Oh no!" replied the missionary, "you don't understand." Rather crestfallen, the African retorted; "If the English are not in charge, then Heaven cannot be such a good place as you described." "Why not?" asked the missionary. "Sir," replied the African, "If it were a good place the English would have colonized it long ago."[16]

Even though there were some behavioral problems here and there, it would be unfair not to appreciate the efforts made by missionaries in general during the colonial period. Both Catholic and Protestant missionaries designed school programs for Africans and schools became major conduits for new mission converts. During this period the missionary work could be evaluated in terms of hospitals, schools, and church buildings. The task of recruiting students for attending school was not easy. One may prefer to be involved in something that would produce a direct result like fishing, hunting, etc., instead of going to school. In places like the southern part of Equator province, during the dry season, young boys and girls would prefer to go to the river fishing instead of going to school, where the white man would "spend his time for nothing."

While Bankole does criticize somewhat the attitude of some missionaries, he also recognizes the efforts made by them in helping train Africans. He recognizes that it was missionary's efforts that gave the Africans an access to education, and this new acquisition enabled them to make a successful bid for an end to colonial rule. The African involvement not only in church business but also in politics, commerce, and education was the missionary contribution.[17] From the beginning of their mission, Protestant missionaries had stressed literacy, education, and reading of the Bible.

> They were thus involved in putting African languages into print, and translating Western religions and scientific works into these languages. In order to aid their colleagues in understanding the people with whom the mission were concerned, some missionaries undertook studies in cultural history which are very important today to any student of African history and culture... The educational system consisted of several years of primary school and technical education, in some cases through secondary schools well. Those trained brought in central stations later dispersed, bringing new knowledge and skills even into remote regions.[18]

There is no work in this world that is devoid of imperfection, and missionary work in Africa is not an exception to this principle. As a product of missionary work I would advise anyone to make a realistic portrayal of missionary achievements before pointing out the negative aspects of their work in Africa. To acknowledge that the missionary situation was not easy, Mavumilisa Makanzu argues that missionaries have two countries; the country of birth and the country of vocation. They also have two churches, the church that sends them and the church where they are sent to work. He concludes that their situation is not as easy as they believed and that they need understanding from Africans.[19]

Postcolonial Christianity

From 1960 on, many Africans' consciences were awaked. Nationalist and pan-African movements grew up and African churches along with the nations moved from a colonial world to independence. In several African nations missionaries were a bit confused on their future role to play in the church that they had founded. More than one among them was discouraged and others returned to their native countries. This was a very sad situation because Africans, both in churches and nations, seemed not to be prepared to take over the leadership. In church hospitals, for instance, there were only male nurses who replaced missionary medical doctors when these later returned home. In the political domain, a nation like the Democratic Republic of the Congo at independence did not have more than fifteen persons with university degrees.

The foreign mission has too often failed to prepare the church in Africa to work out its own approach to politics.[20] Regardless of all this, the growth of Christianity in Africa has been spectacular. Africa is on record as the continent with the highest current numerical Christian growth, a rarity in the world.[21] It is safe to say that in no other continent during the last fifty years has Christianity shown so much growth and diversity, such a cheerful but perplexing flood of people confidently doing their own thing.[22] And the Bible has been identified as "a major contributor" to this phenomenal growth of Christianity in Africa.[23] During this postcolonial growth of Christianity, we realized a movement to break away from what are called "traditional churches," churches established by missionaries. There was a kind of a tension because Africans wanted to express faith in their own way. This tension was one of the leading factors in the creation of independent or "Instituted" churches. Africans could not feel free in established churches—churches planted by missionaries—to deal with issues such as exorcism and healing through prayers, which were a domain somehow reserved for sects and marginal churches. These have now forcefully entered the established churches. The amount of suffering caused by demonic forces has led the masses to look up to the priests and pastors for powerful delivery of the Word of God and for powerful acts in this area.[24]

Among churches created by Africans, there were also black churches for black people where black men and women could attend. Some were anti-white, such as *Dibundu dia Kongo,* Church of black in Africa, and *Kitawala,* and could be found in the Western part of the Democratic Republic of the Congo. They often preach to people who could never been reached by a mission church anyway. Most of them, if not all, take the side of African traditional life. In contrast, the prophets and preachers of the independent churches grounded in the Bible have at times adopted an even more vigorous hostile stance toward things such as fetish, shrines, and pagan worship than the missionaries did. The independent churches have focused much of their spiritual activities on healing, exorcism, etc.

It is in this postcolonial period that the growth of the African church and the spreading of the Good News has sped up. Everywhere in Africa today, new churches are coming up like mushrooms. There has never been a period like this in Africa where God has put such a hunger for God's Word in the hearts of Africans.

Heritage and Culture in the Church of the Congo

What can we learn from missionary work in the Congo? What heritage did missionaries leave to the people in the Congo? How did missionaries view Congolese culture in particular, and African culture in general? Answering these questions will give insight for what we are intending to develop.

The Bible is certainly much valued and used by Africans. Given the oral tradition that forms the background of African Christians and the literary tradition that the Bible represents, the question of the relationship between the Bible and culture in African Christianity becomes an intriguing one. One wonders, How do African Christians use the Bible in the cultural environment of Africa? Another question in talking about culture in Africa is whether we have to use the word *culture* in singular or in plural form. Valentino Salvoldi and Renato Kizito Sesana answer the question when they say:

> We discussed whether we should speak of culture or cultures. It seems to us that on the one hand there exist so many different cultures in Africa that they justify the use of these terms in the plural, on the other hand, the history and culture of Black Africa have a fundamental unity which permits us to face the value, problems and perspectives of this huge part of humanity as if it were one body.[25]

When missionaries did their work in Africa, the most important things they left as a legacy to Africans were education and health care. To read and write in either French or any local dialect was an achievement. Education had opened the minds of Africans to learn and know how to relate with other people in the world. Reading of the Bible has brought many Africans to the knowledge of Jesus Christ and his salvific work on the cross.

Today, all over Africa there are schools, medical facilities, and church buildings left by missionaries, which are still helping Africans. The best students came from missionary schools.

At the same time, the missionary theology of *tabula rasa,* which advocates rejection of the practices in African culture, has caused a lot of damage to the African culture. Africans were cut off from their culture when it came to worship. They could not express themselves in singing or dancing as they used to. Everything given to them was just a copy of the Western style. Drums and other traditional instruments used in Africa were forbidden and considered as evil by missionaries. They were not for the theology of *indigenisation,* adaptation or enculturation. In the Catholic Church the priest would lead the service in Latin, while no one could understand what was being said. Missionary theology was challenged by the firm desire to develop African Christianity designed, conceived, and experienced by Africans themselves through their creative intellect and concrete hopes.[26] To speak of African culture meeting with the Western and Christian cultures in an atmosphere of mutual tolerance and in search of those common elements that reinforce the values embedded in each culture has not been the case. Colonialism did not create space for African culture. The dominant group did not recognize that African culture appeared to have had an arrested growth. At any rate, the aspiration of the dominant group was to civilize the Africans, or, rather, to assimilate them into their culture.

The first objective of the church in Africa is to integrate the evangelical message in African culture, to enable the African to live his faith in integrity and personality, to express faith in his own language.

Today Africans have come back to accommodate some elements of their culture in Christianity. For instance, in the Catholic church of the Congo, nuns are now dressing in the African way. Liturgies are now in local languages and dance is performed in the service. The situation is similar in Protestant churches, were one can see the use of drums, buffalo horns, and other traditional instruments formerly forbidden by missionaries. In almost all Protestant churches in the Congo, people dance, clap hands, and shout during the service, as it was in some African traditional ceremonies.

For the presentation of the Gospel in contemporary Africa, one needs to consider the use of cultural elements that do not conflict with the truth as told in the Bible. Where the Bible and culture really conflict the Bible should win.

Global Mission

Disciples Perspective on an African View of Global Mission

Nowadays, African views of mission have changed. There is no longer the thought of viewing mission as the work to be done by white men from Western nations. Africans are experiencing now the true sense of mission. Mission is not synonymous with North to South relationships. Today in European cities such as Paris, Brussels, London, etc., there are a variety of churches led by Africans who do mission work without the backing of any sending church. They are reaching out both to Europeans and, mostly, to African immigrants. A century ago, the preaching of the Gospel was just one-way, North–to-South, but today it has become three ways: North-to-South, South–to-North, and South–to-South. We believe that mission today does not have borders.

Mission also should be considered in terms of South-to-South relationship. This was worked out when Disciples in the Democratic Republic of the Congo sent the first native missionary to the neighboring Congo-Brazzaville. That mission bore fruits and today there is a Disciples of Christ Church in the Republic of the Congo. Even though we talk of Africa being the continent with the highest numerical Christian growth, there is still room to accommodate mission work in Africa. Nations such as Benin, with voodoo and animism practices, can still be considered as African mission fields. There is now within the Disciples of Christ in the Democratic Republic of the Congo the concept of Disciples becoming a National church. This is to say that the Disciples in the Congo are thinking of enlarging the sphere of church planting program in provinces where the Disciples' presence is not seen. Historically, the Disciples of Christ in the Congo were focusing mission effort only in Equator province, and since 1982 in the capital Kinshasa. But today we start talking of Disciples in provinces like Bandundu, Bas-Congo, Oriental, and soon in other Congolese provinces. Significant participation in the Protestant church of the Congo has favored this.

God's Call for Mission

> "Go therefore and make disciples of all nations, baptizing them in the name of the Father and the Son and the Holly Spirit, and teaching them to obey everything that I have commanded you.

And remember, I am with you always, to the end of the age." (Mt. 28:19-20)

This great commission given by our Lord and Savior Jesus Christ is still valid in our day. Missionaries felt that call and they responded when they came to Africa. Christian unity has been part of Disciples belief and practice of mission from the earliest days. We also believe that Disciples in the Congo have responded in one way or another to this call by involvement in mission work within different ecumenical bodies in Africa, such as the All Africa Conference of Churches and within the Congo as well. It is the Disciples of Christ in the Congo who initiated with other denominations the creation of the Church of Christ in the Congo (*Eglise du Christ au Congo*) and the former *Conseil Protestant au Congo.* The *Eglise du Christ au Congo* (ECC) is an ecumenical body made of sixty-two Protestant denominations and headed by a bishop. The late Bishop Jean Bokeleale Itofo, a Disciples minister, headed that ecumenical body for almost thirty years, retiring in August 1998. The ECC provides a single Protestant church structure of 17 million members. Humanitarian assistance has been significant since the civil wars of the 1990s and the influx of Rwandan refugees and rebel or foreign armies. Viewed by the World Council of Churches as a model of Christian unity when it was formed in 1970, the ECC enables Protestants to have a common witness and united voice in relations with the government as a recognized religious body, along with the predominant Roman Catholic hierarchy and the Kimbanguist Church. Our Church is known as the "*Communauté des Disciples du Christ au Congo,*" CDCC, 10th Community of the Church of Christ in The Congo.

Disciples' involvement in mission work in the Congo is testified by their presence in places like Evangelical Hospital of Kimpese in the Bas-Congo province. Disciples founded that hospital along with American missionary Baptist, British Baptist, Sweden Evangelical, and Christian Missionary Alliance mission bodies. Not only were Disciples present there, but they were also present in other ecumenical organizations such as *Centre d'Edition et de Diffusion* (CEDI), a printing house, and the *Centre d'Accueil Protestant* (CAP), a former United Missionary Hostel—guest house founded by some missions to host missionary guests in Kinshasa.

What is interesting is that today, through the United Evangelical Mission of Germany (UEM), an ecumenical body operating in three continents with thirty-three member churches, Disciples in the Democratic Republic of the Congo have missionaries in Tanzania and Cameroon. When talking of mission, it is an imperative that we deal with the money issue. There is no way mission can be done without money being involved.

African churches have to find ways to support their missions. This is what the Disciples in the Congo are trying to do in shipping carved objects to be sold in Disciples churches in the United States so that money can be involved in mission work. We all need each other and we have to be supportive of each other. American Disciples may be interested in some African objects, and African Disciples may need some American dollars for mission. We believe that God's mission is holistic and that the response to that call should be holistic as well.

Christian Mission and African Traditional Religion

African Traditional Religion is the indigenous faith and practice of African people, which is the product of their perception, encounter, reflection upon, and experiences of the universe in which they live. The Traditional Religion normally gives meaning and direction to its adherents. It is expressed and has expressed itself in the way Africans have always regulated their relationships both with nature and with their fellow men or women. Because of this, in some cases, some animals may be regarded as sacred to devotees of any particular divinity, and some natural phenomena such as trees, hills, or rivers may be deified, as well as some ancestral heroes.

African Traditional Religion has no sacred texts. All the tenets of the religion are handed on orally, sometimes with updates according to the period of time. There are still some Africans converted to Christianity who are living in a culture defined by Traditional Religion and are, therefore, still guided by some aspects the Religion. This is what we call "syncretism." This is a mixture of Christianity and Traditional Religion. It is true that in Africa, sometimes Traditional Religion and culture go together, but it is not an imperative. It is difficult in my view to be a committed Christian who believes in the Bible and at the same time a strong advocate of African Traditional Religion. When I was a young boy, my father told me that all men in our clan were forbidden to eat a kind of fish called "electrical fish." My father never told me the reason we were forbidden to eat that fish. Later on somebody from our clan told me that our ancestors forbade this. While growing and in reading the Bible, I was encouraged by 1 Corinthians 10:25, which states, "Eat whatever is sold in the meat market without raising any question on the ground of conscience."

One of the difficulties missionaries faced in the field was to convert Africans from African Traditional beliefs to Christianity. Today, those who convert from African Traditional Religion to Christianity need special pastoral attention to integrate in the new religion. Bolaji Idowu argues that the main problem of the church in Africa today is the divided loyalty of some of her members between Christianity, with its Western categories and practices on the one hand, and the Traditional Religion on the other. It is well known that in strictly personal matters relating to the passages of life and the crises of life, some Africans do not hesitate to regard African Traditional Religion as the last word.[27] As Disciples, we do not put our faith in African Traditional Religion but rather in Christ, who is the only mediator between God and humankind. African Traditional Religion is a subject that cannot be discussed in few words.

Conclusion

During the last fifty years, the church in Africa has grown so profusely that Africans now express the Christian faith in the context of the African culture. After we consider various aspects of the meeting between Christian Western culture and the African thoughts and beliefs, it is important to draw a conclusion, which can be of help in the Church's presentation of the gospel in contemporary Africa. We advocate that culture should be taken into account in gospel presentation.

We still need missionaries in Africa, but something true is that the job description will not be the same as it was when Africa was a missionary field. Africans should work hand in hand with those who wish them well.

26

Mission in Pluralistic Contexts

A Caribbean Perspective

MICHAEL ST. A. MILLER

Introduction

I approach this discussion as a Christian theologian who hails from the Caribbean, a region that historically has been the focus of persistent missionizing efforts associated with the colonial enterprise, spearheaded by European powers. In more recent times both elements of this dynamic have been influenced by the presently dominant world power, the United States of America. It is this process as it has been played out in the English-speaking sub-region of the Caribbean that is the primary concern of this paper. With support from sources that portray ongoing analyses from other contexts with similar mission histories, I take the position that the appropriate ethos for mission in the Caribbean is one in which religious and cultural diversity is engaged in critical, creative, and respectful ways for the deepening of insight, all-around refinement of thought, and strengthening of commitment to life-enhancing existence. In the process of establishing this case, I identify possible components for a broad conceptual framework from which can be derived tools of analysis and criteria for assessing relevant understandings of mission in the Caribbean context and elsewhere.

The Foundations for Christian Mission Orthodoxy

Derived from the Latin word *missio,* the term "mission" generally refers to the act of sending. As employed by Christians, it results from the strong sense that there is a mandate from God to convey—in word and deed—the conviction that Jesus Christ is the supreme expression of the relationship between God and humanity that hitherto been portrayed in the story of the people of Israel. It is the expression *missio Dei* that best captures this fundamental conviction that receives focus in the message that through the life, death, and resurrection of Jesus persons are enabled into a transformed life of purpose, fulfillment, and peace. This is good news (*the evangel*), to be proclaimed without reservation.

Some Historic Approaches to Mission

In discussing the ways the Christian churches have, through the ages, interpreted and pursued mission ventures, David Bosch follows the subdivisions set out by Hans Küng who suggested seven major paradigms: (1) the apocalyptic paradigm of primitive Christianity; (2) the Hellenistic paradigm of the patristic period; (3) the Medieval paradigm; (4) the Roman Catholic paradigm; (5) the Protestant Reformation paradigm; (6) the modern Enlightenment paradigm; (7) the emerging Ecumenical paradigm.[1] One receives these paradigms with the appreciation that *the evangel* proclaimed in places such as the Caribbean was colored by the ideology of Christendom, originating with Constantine's fourth-century decision to support Christianity above all other religions in the Roman Empire. This decision opened the way for the fusion of political and economic structures with the Christian religion, such that Europe's status in relation to the rest of the world, and Europe's military, political, and economic actions toward others could be seen as expressions of a divine mandate. Given Christianity's beginnings among a marginal community of colonized persons, it is quite striking that Europeans' sense of divine mandate led to the enslavement of Africans and the domination of other peoples and lands to foster European development. These features make it easy to embrace Bosch's indication that since the sixteenth century, if one said "mission," one in a sense also said "colonialism." Bosch goes further when, in speaking about mid-nineteenth-century Africa, he suggests that "manifest destiny" and colonial domination activated the missionary's latent racism, and also that "mission agencies became bearers and advocates of Western imperialism, the 'hounds of imperialism,' set on or whistled back as it pleased Caesar."[2]

It makes sense, then, that Guyanese historian Robert Moore identifies not seven paradigms in which mission has been interpreted, but two starkly different approaches to mission on the part of European Christians. Christianity, he suggests, became the religion of Europe, primarily by absorption. Yet in the second great age of expansion, the European stage in which the Caribbean was colonized, the methodology shifted to that of imposition.[3] In the Caribbean, the native *Tainos* and *Caribs* were expected to adopt the religion of the European invaders, suffering severe consequences when failing to do so. It is not insignificant that, later on, in negotiating the abolition of native slavery, the Catholic priest Bartolomé de las Casas worked out a compromise that allowed for European importation of African labor—this opening the way for black slavery.

Through the words of the Moravian leader Count Nicholas von Zinzendorf, we are given a glimpse of the way religious, social, and economic objectives coalesced in the Caribbean. Preaching to enslaved Africans in St. Thomas, the Virgin Islands, in 1739, he declared that: "God punished the first negroes by making them slaves." Freedom, he suggested, was the outcome of conversion to Christianity. But this freedom was only "of the spirit," because, in the final analysis, colonial Christians had no intention of challenging the colonial structure that depended on slavery. Thus the liberation that Christ gave to slaves was "simply from your wicked habits and thoughts, and all that makes you dissatisfied with your lot."[4] Dominican William Watty is on target when he suggests that the interweaving of interests between the missionary enterprise and colonial domination, the churches and the colonial powers, the quest for gold and the service of God was not a haphazard one. Speaking subtly, he indicates: "the churches consented to be co-opted within the scheme of colonial domination and exploitation."[5] It is in this framework, says Trinidadian Pearl Springer, that black people "were Christianized with a whip and a Bible and some water and given the name of the slave master."[6] While not subjected to similar brutality, South and East Asians brought to the region by the British as indentured laborers were also subjected to relentless pressure to convert to Christianity.

Identifying Consequences

Disturbing consequences have flowed from this enterprise. Watty speaks about the ambiguities of the Caribbean personality that has been fashioned in the crucible of colonial and neo-colonial dynamics. It is "at one and the same time brilliant and unstable, free and irresponsible, ostentatious and insecure, promising much and achieving little, shooting to the top like a meteor and then, in the next moment, plunging downwards into disgrace." The Caribbean person, we are told, "does not believe in himself nor does he believe in others like himself, because he knows that in their innermost beings neither he nor they are really themselves."[7] Springer is more personal: "I live with five hundred years of that oppression in my genes, in my genetic memory, in my history." She identifies contemporary Caribbean Christianity as racist, and describes herself as a "fractured self." Most compellingly, she indicates: "to remain Christian I must understand that this is my traditional enemy and I must look beyond the 'Whitenised' Westernised Christianity and see God in his supremacy."[8]

Struggling with Contemporary Mission Rationale

Unfortunately, many Caribbean Christians who understand themselves to carry the burden of the missionary mandate persist in activities designed to eclipse beliefs and practices perceived as opposed to Christianity. In support of their missionary zeal, they could easily call on Lesslie Newbigin's understanding that the interpretations of scripture that inform their efforts come within Christianity's unique plausibility structure, characterized by the pattern of beliefs and practices accepted as normative within this framework. This plausibility structure is grounded in the conviction that Jesus alone provides transforming access to God. Proclamations about Jesus invite belief, but not about something that can be demonstrated by reference to human experience in general. "Rather, it is by the acceptance of which all human experience can be rightly understood"[9] Committed to this point of view, those who persist in the traditional approach to mission would probably argue that if genuinely embraced, *the evangel* at the heart of Christian mission would enable persons like Pearl Springer to make sense of what is now perceived as "five hundred years of oppression." They could look beyond the racism of the church, and appreciate that which is the "true" foundation for its beliefs and practices, and meant to free them from continued preoccupation with the spiritual heritage of their African ancestors. They would come to accept that right understanding of their ancestral and personal histories will only be attained when they come to terms with God's engagement with Israel, and the definitive revelation in Jesus of Nazareth.

Somehow, though, I sense that Ms. Springer and others like her would resonate more with Burton Sankeralli as he declares that given its history in the Caribbean, it is Christianity that needs to establish its legitimacy.[10] This group would probably desire to have criteria, independent of Christian claims, for evaluating the contemporary effects of the history of Christian interaction with the non-European peoples who now inhabit the Caribbean. I suspect that high on the list of values informing the selection of criteria would be the freedom of cosmic inhabitants to pursue their own paths to self-actualization—this in relation to their dependence on and contribution to the well-being of the whole cosmos. Criteria for evaluation, informed by values such as this, would constitute an abiding challenge to all plausibility structures, including the Christian one, which, like other faith-commitments, is characterized by "circularity."[11] In the first place, there would have to be acknowledgment that Christianity is but one of many legitimate plausibility structures that reflect diverse attempts to make sense of the complexity and mystery of cosmic existence, resulting in varied "forms of life." Further, defenders of pronouncements and activities, now justified within the circularity of the Christian plausibility structure, would be required to move beyond mere assessments of how the missionary imperative logically emerges from a network of mutually reinforcing claims. This would certainly help to counter what Sankeralli refers to as the attempt to turn Christianity into an a-historical system, that is, to "thing-ify" it apart from history and culture.[12] It should contribute to the recognition that: "No religion can be considered in abstraction…from its various types of followers."[13]

The outcome of all this ought to be humble repentance for the ignorance, contempt, and brutality often associated with Christian mission in the

Caribbean and elsewhere. It ought to disabuse Christians of the view that, despite the checkered history of Christian mission, its grounding plausibility structure should still be embraced in light of an idealized representation of its character—this supported by selected portrayals of Jesus' life and the romanticizing of dynamics within the early post-resurrection community. In the end, it should lead to the eschewal of the hegemonic posture associated with the conviction that it is necessarily through Christian outreach that healing will come for the victims of Christianity's own historic abuses.

Having said this, I suspect that as poverty and anxiety grow in the Caribbean, many will become increasingly susceptible to Christian evangelism informed by interpretations of Jewish and Christian apocalyptic literature that herald an imminent *eschaton*. Pronouncements about the "signs of the times" and portrayals of the delights of heaven and the agony of hell will cause some churches to be filled by those seeking personal security. But I daresay these activities will do little to facilitate the psychic healing that will restore the "fractured selves" of Caribbean peoples and correct the ambiguities in their personalities. Neither will it fuel the activism necessary to challenge the persisting structures of power that promote social, economic, and political injustice. My hope for wholesome existence in the Caribbean is not disassociated from eschatology. However, this is not eschatology understood merely as the doctrine of the last things, the consummation of history, and the coming of Christ and the end of the world. Instead, it is linked to a posture that, while not dismissing the conventional understanding, emphasizes that liberating-transforming mission also has to do with "the decline and fall of nations, kingdoms and empires in the on-going process of secular history… In this, the oppressed come to realize that: 'Every worldly power carries with its growth the germs of its own death and decay.'"[14]

Given this foundation for eschatological hope, the "sign of the times" I find most promising is that a number of Caribbean Christians have begun to take seriously the criticisms of traditional missionary stances leveled by practitioners of African and Asian religions. These Christians are clear that contemporary missionary pursuits ought to be informed by a contextually relevant theology that presumes a unique Caribbean experience to be taken seriously by all.[15] Watty is clear that this theological framework should promote liberation for all God's creatures, because liberation ultimately "stands on the purposes of God as Creator and God's purposes for creation."[16] "A theology that has liberation as its focus...arises out of the sense of lost community and the creation of the community which overcomes alienation, fragmentation and exclusion."[17]

Foundations for Mission that Honors Caribbean Religious Pluralism

In the interest of the creation and restoration of community, the understanding of pluralism that informs Christian mission in the Caribbean ought to be influenced by those who have most to lose by the way it is defined. As such, it ought to begin with explicit recognition that the Caribbean is characterized by a variety of religious traditions that have their own unique legitimacy as they provide frameworks for interpretation of and orientation toward existence such that devotees can withstand the vicissitudes of life, maintain hope for the future, and develop mutually beneficial interactions with coinhabitants of the region and the wider world. In this framework no religious community would be considered as having *a priori* superiority—especially not the one that historically has gained influence through alignment with colonial powers, with their relentless exercise of violent coercion.

Bill Watty contributes to a conceptual foundation for addressing Caribbean religious pluralism in a way that could enable persons such as Ms. Springer to satisfy the desire to move beyond "'Whitenized' Westernized Christianity and see God in his supremacy." He declares: "One of the commonest ways in which theology has and can still become prone to unreality is by the spurious claim to universality and finality."[18] He subscribes to the notion of one transcendent "God who is God," and he sees theology, that is, the way human beings use the word *God,* as necessarily contextual, parochial, and historically conditioned. The sophistication of approaches to Caribbean religious diversity should be enhanced by Watty's challenging definition of salvation-history. There is, he suggests, theological validity and authenticity inherent in the histories of each people. "There is no history that is not, potentially, salvation-history. It all depends on how a people sees their role in history."[19] Springer does display a well-developed sense of this understanding of salvation-history. She indicates: "Every people has a right to think about themselves as chosen. I am making no apology at this point in time, for describing my people as 'chosen.' It is the only way to try to erase the fractured self in the period of post-enslavement."[20] Here, Watty's understanding of eschatology should act as a countervailing force to the over-exalted self-perceptions that can emerge from interpretations in terms of salvation-history.

More recently, Lewin Williams argued that pluralistic-sensitive efforts in theology ought to be grounded in radical monotheism.[21] This involves the idea of a single center in human existence in which systems and cultures relate. Belief in this one center, that is, "a God who is not Christian," is also to believe that all things can relate to one another because they are already related to the common source of being. With the growing influence of postmodern thought many are wary of talk about a single center. I am, however, of the mind that if what we are addressing is truly ultimate, it can only be one, even if this Ultimate can be understood as complex and capable of operating in diverse and multidimensional ways.

Together, declarations from Watty, Sankeralli, and Williams challenge Caribbean Christians to pursue the religious life in the tension between belief in one ultimate source of cosmic existence and the "epistemic distance" between the religious claims we make and the Ultimate to which we understand them to apply. This does not allow for thoroughgoing relativism in which there is no final arbiter of truth. Instead, it supports what Lorraine Code calls "critical mitigated relativism," which holds that "knowledge, truth, or even 'reality' can be understood only in relation to particular sets of cultural or social circumstances, to a theoretical framework, a specific range of perspectives, a conceptual scheme, or a form of life."[22] At the same time, it demands that we develop strategies for evaluating perspectives and purposes.

Even as I support the general direction in which Watty and Williams appear to be heading, I now highlight difficulties that open the door for the identification of elements of their thinking, difficulties that need to be addressed on the way to a liberative and transforming mission orientation. In the first place, when speaking of "a God who is God," much hinges on what is associated with this notion. For example, many would have problems with Watty's view that: "God wanted the Caribbean to be discovered by Europe." And that it boggles his "imagination to contemplate what would have been the consequence for modern history if Columbus had not ventured into the Caribbean. Indeed Columbus was not so much the one who carried Christ 'but who was carried by Him who rides upon the wings of the winds (Ps. 104:3).'"[23] Watty, I suspect, does not see a direct and necessary causal connection between God's intentions and the specific attitudes and activities of European colonizers. However, a detractor could quite legitimately suggest that nothing in Watty's conceptions precludes the position that the atrocities of colonizers were also orchestrated by this "God who is God," in order to satisfy some inscrutable purpose for both victims and victimizers. Indeed, this God seems to be the arch-imperialist who stands above all criteria and frameworks by which good and evil, justice and injustice, can be evaluated. As such, that which has occurred in the Caribbean is right because God has willed it, even if this constantly involves the elevation of the violent and oppressive at the expense of those who are weak and vulnerable. Sankeralli exposes other problems, and he wonders if the promoters of radical theism are willing to break with christocentrism, as radical monotheism entails. In the end, he is afraid that Caribbean Christian thinkers might use radical monotheism as a reductionist tool "to collapse religious-cultural-ethnic difference."[24]

Addressing Difficulties

I support the position that the movement toward Christian mission that honors Caribbean religious pluralism must include some form of theocentrism. While this paper does not allow for further development of this claim, declarations from Paul Knitter and John Cobb suggest an approach to christology that avoids the christocentrism Sankeralli is anxious about. Knitter suggests that Christians are within their rights to proclaim Jesus as "truly" and "uniquely" savior without taking this to mean "solely." "'No other name,' as performative action language, is really a positive statement in its negative couching: it tells us that all peoples must listen to this Jesus; it does not tell us that no one else should be listened to or learned from. The stress, then, is on the saving power mediated by the name of Jesus, not on the exclusivity of the name."[25] As Cobb indicates: "So am I affirming Christian uniqueness? Certainly and emphatically so! But I am affirming the uniqueness also of Confucianism, Buddhism, Hinduism, Islam and Judaism."[26] Those who participate in this process cannot avoid consideration of Sankeralli's call for space "to explore our own Caribbean terminology."[27] And there is Gerald Boodoo who makes the call for Caribbean people "to find our space of confrontation with the unconditioned, with God, even beyond God."[28]

Informed by the sense that both Boodoo and Sankeralli are seeking to move Caribbean thinking beyond traditional transcendental categories, I suggest serious engagement with Boodoo's proposal that perhaps the required reflection in the Caribbean "is not theology as such (as *Logos* about *Theos*) but more the attempt to express the fracture of *Theos* in our Caribbean psyche."[29] The determination of what adequate theocentrism might look like would certainly be enhanced through struggle with Sankeralli, who claims inspiration from India and Africa when he proposes a move from monotheism to cosmotheism in which "the energy and pattern of the cosmos, the totality of relation discloses divinity."[30] And some, like this writer, are inclined toward a pan-en-theism that holds the creative tension between God as internally related to the cosmos in all its dimensions, and God as, in important respects, preceding and transcending the cosmos.

Attention should be paid to the increased awareness of interconnection that will only intensify as Asian and African spiritualities are allowed to gain "voice." We see evidence of some of the associated challenges in Trinidadian Hindu scholar Ravi-Ji's reflections on what healthy coexistence might entail. He describes his own spirituality that involves reverential interaction at multiple dimensions of cosmic existence (human and nonhuman). He acknowledges that this might appear primitive to some. However, he is clear that his approach constitutes "a cultured life infused with a spiritualized vision of all things in creation."[31] My view is that, given the pan-en-theistic foundations of various African spiritualities, there are many avenues for rich dialogue. It is also the case that, having been nurtured in India, the expression of Islam that informed the establishment of this tradition in the Caribbean has bequeathed many resources for fruitful engagement.

I now propose that Caribbean Christians conduct mission through dialogue. And I suggest that they might enhance their disposition and capacity if they engage proposals such as Preman Niles's that the motif of creation history rather than "redemption history" (salvation-history) might be the needed theological framework for mission.[32] The broader framework of creation, he suggests, has scope for understanding the redemption of all people, and allows for theologies that focus on all of life.[33] While allying myself with the spirit of Niles's point, I suggest that care be taken in the utilization of biblical creation stories, to ensure that they do not serve to support Christian inclusivism that effectively denies the full integrity of other religions in and of themselves. It might even be necessary to reframe the creation motif in terms of "creative emergence." Given that Caribbean dysfunction has to do, in part, with entrenched ideas and attitudes directly associated with the traditional Christian concept of redemption/salvation, the substitute notion of "creative transformation" might be employed to promote an understanding of the relation between creation and redemption that fosters contextually relevant healing and transformation. Finally, the framework in which these and other reconfigurations are pursued would be enriched beyond the recognition of a plurality of religions, by the intentional and ongoing acknowledgment of the billions of cosmic neighbors with whom Christians are bound together in the bundle of life, with our destinies intertwined.[34] Having struggled over many centuries to understand the dynamics of life, with its joys and sufferings, these neighbors have developed meaningful answers that satisfy them and can enlighten Christians.[35]

Conclusion

The correlate to my position that Christianity has no *a priori* superiority over other religions is not the position that all attitudes, methods, and processes for addressing life's mysteries and puzzles, or the resulting answers, are of equal merit. However, the path to identifying the multiplicity of factors relevant to appropriate evaluation of these matters must be a critical-creative conversation with all whose well-being will be affected by the outcome of our considerations. Given that Christians have traditionally approached other religions with the presumption that they (Christians) have all the right answers, this journey must begin with the religious *others* speaking for themselves and Christians listening for the sake of understanding. Perhaps, together, all concerned will discover fuller dimensions of *missio Dei*, experiencing and portraying in ever-richer measure God's love for the whole cosmos, which includes humans in all their diversity.

27

Ecumenism of the Spirit and Mission

Disciples of Christ and Pentecostals in Venezuela

CARMELO ALVAREZ

Mission and Unity in a Globalized World

Mission and unity have had an intricately interconnected relationship during the last two centuries. One cannot understand the history and development of the ecumenical movement in the twentieth century without closely considering how mission and unity have combined in creative tension to shape present conditions. The significance of this dialectical tension is crucial for any theology of mission and for the emergence of a new "missionary paradigm" toward the future.[1]

Both the ecumenical movement in all its expressions and the missionary movement in all its models and structures are challenged to understand and embrace the contemporary crisis and to search for new ways to respond to a globalized world in religious, social, political, moral, cultural, racial, and sexual manifestations. There is no doubt that a paradigm shift is taking place in the scientific, technological, and philosophical rationales from those that presided over the modern period.[2]

Vanderbilt University's Divinity School professor of systematic theology, Peter C. Hodgson, explains the concept of "paradigm shift" as follows:

> A paradigm is an example, model, or pattern. As the Greek etymology of the word suggests, an example (*deigma*), is set up alongside (*para*)

> something to show what it is; it is a model on a microcosmic scale (a scale model) of a large, complex, dispersed, difficult-to-grasp state of affairs. In his study of the history of science, Thomas Kuhn uses the term paradigm to refer to exemplary formulations of scientific theory, such as Copernicus' explanation of planetary motion and Newton's theory of mechanics. He describes major transitions in scientific theories as *paradigm shifts*.[3]

A paradigm shift has an important effect upon cultures, which are the dynamic realities in which religious beliefs play a central role. This effect opens the possibility for theological reflection. Hodgson demonstrates that this transitional shifting is both an opportunity and a risk: "The new cultural paradigm calls for a new theological paradigm, a revisioning of the entire theological agenda, including questions of method, God, history, human being, ecclesiology, eschatology, and religious pluralism."[4]

This transitional period announces the irruption of a new and promising era—a moment that is discernible and yet awaits a future manifestation in all its fullness. "A paradigm shift is on the one hand a real break with the previous frame of reference, but a new paradigm is only seen to be reliable if it can provide explanation and confirmation, within newly defined boundaries, of the relative perceptions of truth contained in the old paradigm."[5]

In the midst of the uncertainty, confusion, and contradictions of these times, churches and ecumenical organizations live in a creative/dialectical tension typical of transitional moments in history.[6]

South African missiologist David Bosch sees the implications of this paradigm shift as a unique opportunity for developing a theology of mission that is both critical and transforming.[7] Hans Kung, Swiss Catholic theologian, stresses the importance in these transitional times of developing an ecumenical theology to serve the mission of the church in this society: "For there is no ecumenical church without an ecumenical theology."[8]

Ecumenism is best understood within its local and global contexts. Today globalization is a crucial element of the context in which mission takes place. Robert Streiter, a leading voice on globalization and its impact on theology and mission, highlights the fundamental nature of globalization in the world today: "Globalization becomes a full reality when we realize that we are inevitably part of a worldwide flow of information, technology, capital and goods—a flow over which no single nation has effective control any more."[9]

And contextualization "becomes, therefore, a means to help up what is noble and immensely human and humane in a local culture against the onslaughts of forces—both historical and contemporary—that seek to undermine the dignity of the local culture."[10]

Shoki Coe, Taiwanese theologian and Director of the Theological Education Fund, introduced the concept of contextualization or contextualizing into ecumenical circles in 1972. He defined contextualization as an inclusive phenomenon that expands on concepts such as indigenization practiced by Evangelicals and enculturation introduced by Catholic missiologists. Coe also pointed out that contextualization encompasses not only purely religious issues but also the technological-scientific, secular struggles for human justice and the integrity of creation.[11]

Theology of mission is better understood today as *missio Dei*, which requires a reciprocal relationship of mutuality in an ecumenical understanding of mission that affirms religious, racial, gender, sexual, and cultural diversities as creative elements of the whole. The churches of both hemispheres, both North and South, become, in mutual accountability, real partners in mission and members of a worldwide community. Sharing in that community is a key element of proclaiming and witnessing God's mission in the world today.

Ecumenism of the Spirit

The Pentecostal movement in Latin America is very diverse and complex. The crucial question is what do Pentecostals mean by an "ecumenism of the Spirit"? What are some of the developments within the ecumenical movement with regard to this "ecumenism of the Spirit?

The 1961 New Delhi Assembly of the World Council of Churches was a turning point for the ecumenical movement[12] because both Pentecostal and orthodox churches were received as full members of the WCC. Two Pentecostal churches joined this unique ecumenical body: the Pentecostal Church of Chile, and the Pentecostal Mission Church of Chile.[13]

This process of ecumenical participation by Pentecostal churches needs to be analyzed within the larger picture of ecumenical cooperation. The CCDC and the UCC in the United States had already established close ecumenical partnerships with Pentecostal churches in Latin America and the Caribbean, specifically in Argentina, Chile, Cuba, Nicaragua, and Venezuela. The churches in these partnerships exchange missionary personnel and engage in mutual collaboration for theological education, development projects, and the sharing of short-term volunteer missionaries and volunteer laypeople delegations.

These churches played a crucial role in the formation of the Latin American Evangelical Pentecostal Commission (CEPLA) in the 1960s, a regional commission to promote Christian unity between Pentecostal churches and with other denominations in Latin America. The Pentecostal churches also significantly contributed to the formation of the Latin America Council of Churches (CLAI) a decade later and the continuing recruitment of new members for the Council at each of its General Assemblies.

The context and theological framework for Pentecostals' relationships with other denominations are what many interpreters call an "ecumenism of the Spirit." The phrase caught momentum during the organization of the CEPLA in Chile in 1990 and later at the General Assembly of CLAI in Concepción, Chile, in 1995. Several historic churches have taken seriously the importance and relevance of the Pentecostal churches by doing research and promoting dialogues, exchanges, and forums.[14]

What is meant by "ecumenism of the Spirit"? The late American Methodist theologian and ecumenist Albert C. Outler relates this idea to specific moments in which the Spirit acts in the "fullness of time" as "ecumenical epiphanies," moments of unexpected divine revelation, loaded with joy and enthusiasm. These "ecumenical epiphanies" are always opportunities to live intensely the promise of an ecumenical dialogue in which the Spirit opens new "frontier spaces of pneumatology."[15]

José Míguez Bonino introduced the concept during the General Assembly of *CLAI* in Concepción, 1995: "An Ecumenism of the Spirit, although it does not determine institutional forms nor structural commitments nor formal decisions, dares its participants to not only pray and sing together (which is more than enough) but also to share experiences and explore new ventures."[16]

Ofelia Ortega, a Presbyterian pastor from Cuba and for many years in charge of theological education at the World Council of Churches, reflects on this concept: " Ecumenism in Pentecostalism is permeated with "ecumenism of the Spirit" in which the concept of unity is a faithful reflection of the unity of the Spirit; this includes all God's creation and its stewardship and integrity, and emerges from the same authentic experience of the Holy Spirit."[17]

Two of the most prominent interpreters of contemporary Pentecostalism in the world, Walter Hollenweger and the American Wesleyan historian Donald Dayton, had constantly reminded both the Pentecostal churches and the ecumenical movement about the importance of the Holy Spirit and ecumenism as the hermeneutical keys to the transformative action of the Spirit in society, history, and nature.[18]

The late Bishop Gabriel Vaccaro of the Church of God in Argentina, who was actively involved in several ecumenical organizations, writes in these terms: "I have participated in an ecumenism of the Spirit. We believe that the Church is one. We also believe in the responsibility of the prophetic denunciation that the Churches of Christ must do to confront human injustices."[19]

At the 1990 EPLA in Chile the final document included the following reference, affirming a commitment: "To continue our contribution in the way of an ecumenism of the Spirit, from the perspective of the poor, to the ecumenical movement and the mission of the Church."[20]

All these definitions strive for an ecumenical agenda in which the "ecumenism of the Spirit" is a concrete commitment to a praxis and life in the Spirit as witnesses in the world,[21] and openness to the constant action of the Spirit calling to newness of life in all its fullness.[22]

What have been the implications of this "ecumenism of the Spirit" for Latin American and Caribbean Pentecostals? The late Guillermo Cook, Argentinean missiologist, comments:

> Christian unity, for Pentecostals, is a theological fact based upon the unity of the Trinity, the present and the future hope that drives them, both a factor in and a requirement for the growth of the church and—for an increasing number of perceptive leaders—an imperative in the contemporary era of the divine *kairós*.[23]

Ecumenism of the Spirit, as defined here, provides a coherent and integrating dimension that includes the evangelistic fervor, the prophetic voice, a pastoral accompaniment, and the healing ministry in Christian mission based on the action of the Holy Spirit, manifested in experience and expressed in the commitment to promote unity in the church and the world.

Disciples of Christ Mission Strategy: Mission as Kingdom Building

Eminent theologian and ethicist H. Richard Niebuhr, in his classic work The Kingdom of God in America, examined various aspects of the development of a Christian vision and the perception of the kingdom of God among churches in North America. Niebuhr observed that the concept of a kingdom of God was a persistent and dominant idea in North American Christianity[24] Although this idea had consistence and continuity, each generation interpreted and shaped it according to that generation's own values. During the colonial period, God's sovereignty was emphasized, particularly among the Puritans, who, with their Reformed theology, viewed the creation of a new society as a historical process. The kingdom of God implied, for the Puritans, that God's sovereignty not only reigned over individuals and church but also extended to society as a whole, both in its public and civil dimensions. In other words, God's will was expected to be manifest in government and in the judicial-legal system.

The Great Awakening in the 1800s emphasized the redeeming kingdom of Jesus Christ—God's saving love extended to a society in dire need of redemption and social reform. Evangelist and social reformer Charles G. Finney proclaimed that the reign of good will with moral values would naturally extend the labor of the kingdom of God.[25]

By the end of the nineteenth and the beginning of the twentieth century, the kingdom of God was perceived as an earthly realm, inspired by the idea of progress in the social gospel. God's kingdom was believed to become visible in society through the transformation of believers. A society tagged by "structural sin" must be redeemed by a kingdom of corporate proportions capable of healing the sinful structure of this society.[26]

W. Clark Gilpin presented a similar viewpoint regarding the ecclesiology and theology of the kingdom of God in the Christian Church. Gilpin examines

Disciples thought and praxis with regard to the "integrity of the Church" and its manifestation as God's people.[27] A church that tries to preserve its integrity is one that tries to become whole, to live in unity, and to serve as an apostolate in sanctity of service—all of these as distinctive signs of its mission.[28]

Gilpin perceived that the Christian Church has undergone three distinct phases in its history of life and witness. During its formation between 1804 and 1832, its emphasis was on restoration and reform, leading to its emergence as a denomination by the 1850s. the turn of the century, the Christian Church was influenced by liberalism to expand into ecumenical cooperation and mission, amplifying its presence away from American soil. Beginning in the mid-1900s, the church moved toward restructuring its ecumenical commitment and its missionary responsibility.[29] Gilpin further expounds on these three phases, highlighting the influence of the Campbells' view of the "divine" as citizenship and the effect of "reformed theology" as promoting restructure, growth, and consolidation. The concept dominating the second phase of the Christian Church, according to Gilpin, was the kinship of God's people, ready to promote unity and work in mission in order to speed the restoration of God's kingdom. In the third phase, the focus is communion with God, expressed in ecumenical cooperation and active promotion of mission. Throughout this process, Gilpin asserts, Christian Church leaders have tried to develop a theology embodied by affirmations, symbols, structures, and commitments that enable spiritual power in the life and mission of the Church. These principles of citizenship, kinship, communion, and symbols are unique theological-institutional contributions made to the ecumenical movement by the Christian Church.[30]

Evangelical Pentecostal Union of Venezuela: Mission as Liberating Spirit

The Venezuelan Evangelical Pentecostal Union (UEPV) was founded on three fundamental objectives: to promote fellowship between congregations and pastors, to respect the local autonomy of each congregation, and to encourage mutual support in Christian service. These objectives distanced the UEPV leaders from the Assemblies of God. They rejoined the independent United Convention and expressed no hard feelings toward the Assemblies of God in Venezuela. The Assemblies of God, however, and particularly the missionaries, were negative about entering into close relationship with this new movement. The notable exception to this ambivalence was Rev. Edmundo Jordán, a Puerto Rican missionary who supported the movement in many ways from the very beginning and became a counselor and confidante to all of them.[31]

Freddie Briceño insists that the UEPV maintained the same doctrinal principles they had observed as members of the Assemblies of God, with the addition of three: a practical sense of tolerance, local autonomy, and a fellowship with other denominations.[32]

Briceño enumerates some basic doctrinal principles of the UEPV as:

> Baptism by immersion, tithing, the gifts and baptism in the Holy Spirit, divine healing, open communion, fellowship with other churches, veils for women in worship, strict ethical principles (no movies, no dance, etc.), freedom to express politically diverse ideologies, official abstention from party politics, unity not uniformity among the congregations.[33]

Briceño was very influential in developing a close relationship between the UEPV and the Disciples of Christ in the United States and Puerto Rico. His close friendship with Edmundo Jordán paved the way for a relationship between the Venezuelan church and Disciples of Christ in Puerto Rico, then later with the Disciples in the United States. Briceño later collaborated with the first Disciples of Christ missionary in Venezuela, Juan Marcos Rivera. Briceño was part of the official delegation of UEPV leaders to the World Convention of the Churches of Christ in San Juan, Puerto Rico, in August of 1965.

The UEPV started as a movement of local churches that desired to reclaim their roots in the Pentecostal tradition and to retain an autonomous and autochthonous movement while entering into service with other religious organizations. A crucial decision was made to separate from the Assemblies of God, and a new Pentecostal church was born: the Evangelical Pentecostal Union of Venezuela. After the initial steps to organize a new church, the UEPV started a process that led to an ecumenical vocation manifested in concrete projects of social action and ecumenical relationships.

One of the key aspects that nurtured and directed UEPV strategy was an integral spiritual formation in which Christian education at all levels became a fundamental principle. Closely related to this dimension of spiritual formation was leadership development. The decision to train leaders was a turning point in addressing the new challenges and conflicts that lay ahead. The Church needed highly qualified leaders to face a new situation in the country and in Latin America. The UEPV strove to live by its belief that a church empowered by the Holy Spirit is one that witnesses to and promotes Christian unity. The Evangelical Pentecostal Union of Venezuela was a pioneering force in reclaiming both the Bolivarian ideal of a "Great Colombia" and the power of the Holy Spirit to respond to the socioeconomic crisis in Latin America and the Caribbean. In 1979 the UEPV faced another crucial turning point in its identity and mission as it faced internal turmoil and a leadership void. Once more it was time to discern the signs of the times. A decision was made to reaffirm an ecumenical commitment in a process of discernment and education in order to fulfill UEPV's mission as both a Pentecostal and an ecumenical church.

Disciples and Pentecostals: Toward an Ecumenical Partnership

In 1959 Dr. A. Dale Fiers, President of the United Christian Missionary Society (UCMS), the missionary agency of the Disciples of Christ at that time, visited several Latin American countries and reported his findings to the Board of the UCMS. He emphasized that a new opportunity was offered to the UCMS in establishing a partnership with non-mainline denominations in Latin America:

> Latin America presents a unique and perplexing problem to the ecumenical movement...These countries are being stormed by a great task force of non-cooperative missionary movements. It was suggested that perhaps the answer is to invite the main line groups into cooperation and the cooperative and non-cooperative missionaries into continued fellowship."[34]

The initial contact between the Disciples of Christ and the UEPV came through Edmundo Jordán, a former Assemblies of God missionary who worked in Venezuela in the 1930s and 1940s and became a Disciples pastor in Puerto Rico in 1955.

As pastor of various congregations in the Lara and other districts of Venezuela, Jordán proved to be a very effective preacher and administrator, earning the trust of the leaders of the Pentecostal Union, a confidence that endured until his death in 1980. Jordán left Venezuela in the late 1940s to pastor various Assemblies of God Hispanic congregations in New York City, one of them being the famous Macedonia Pentecostal Church in Hispanic Harlem.[35] There he met Domingo Rodríguez, Puerto Rican pastor at *La Hermosa* Christian Church, the first Disciples Hispanic congregation in the city, founded in 1937 by Pablo Cotto, also a Disciples pastor from Puerto Rico. Rodríguez and Jordán established a close friendship. Jordán subsequently became a member of the Disciples of Christ in Puerto Rico.

Edmundo Jordán was very interested in the possibility of collaboration between the Disciples of Christ and the UEPV. In 1959 he was invited to the Convention of the Pentecostal Union, creating a cordial atmosphere and providing the initial contact with Puerto Rican Disciples and later with the UCMS of the Disciples of Christ.[36] Edmundo Jordán was invited to the next Convention in August 1960 as the guest preacher, but this time he was joined by Thomas J. Liggett, Mae Yoho Ward, and four pastors from the Christian Pentecostal Church of Cuba. During this Convention an initial dialogue was established, leaving the doors open for more conversation and future collaboration.[37]

Over a period of two years the UCMS continued exploring ways in which the two denominations might concretely move into a relationship with "non-cooperative missions," according to its assessment of those "non-ecumenical" bodies. During the next Conference of Protestant Churches in Lima, Peru, in 1961, a more open contact with Pentecostal churches came into being. Active participants in this Second Conference were David du Plessis, a Pentecostal leader from South Africa, and Bishop Enrique Chávez of the Pentecostal Church of Chile. Dr. Thomas J. Liggett was a notable member of the organizing commission of this Conference and delivered a keynote address on Protestant work in Latin America.[38] This Conference was crucial in that it brought together two ecumenical leaders—Dr. Mae Yoho Ward, Executive Secretary for Latin America and the Caribbean of the UCMS, and Dr. Liggett, a Disciples missionary and President of the Union Seminary in Puerto Rico, as active participants. These two leaders continued to work together to further the ecumenical process.

An important historical precedent to this process was the crisis and confrontation that the UCMS experienced in Puerto Rico in 1933. A revival spread among the Disciples congregations on the island, and the missionaries were unable to deal with the situation of distrust and lack of dialogue between missionaries and national pastors. Mae Yoho Ward and Samuel Guy Inman, a Disciples missionary in Mexico who was very involved in the ecumenical movement, were able to mediate during what looked like a potential separation of the Puerto Rican Disciples from the Disciples of Christ.[39] This experience and others that Mae Yoho Ward accumulated over the years with charismatic Disciples in Puerto Rico paved the way for an honest and open relationship with the UEPV. When she visited and preached in the first UEPV congregation, El Peregrino in Morador, Venezuela, her message was well-received. According to the late Juan Marcos Rivera, she was so fluent in Spanish that Venezuelans were thrilled and positively impressed that evening.[40]

According to Dr. Liggett, the initial contact between the Pentecostal Union of Venezuela and the Puerto Rican Disciples pastors began in 1960.[41] Dr. Mae Yoho Ward asked Liggett to visit the Pentecostal Union of Venezuela in 1963 and to explore a possible partnership. During his visit Liggett was impressed by this very poor church "without theologically trained pastors. Personal ethics were quite Puritan, but on social issues, especially land reform, they were progressive and encouraged participation in the political life of Venezuela."[42]

Dr. Liggett's report to Mae Yoho Ward and the UCMS of his visit to Venezuela in July 12–14, 1963, was both very encouraging and realistic, emphasizing the poverty and the many needs that the Pentecostal Union of Venezuela confronted. He was enthusiastic about not only the opportunity but also the potential of joining in an effective process of education, mission and unity, financial assistance, and collaboration in development programs, among others. He emphatically asserts: "This church is reaching outward and upward, it is seeking to realize its own best self but yearns for fellowship and support and guidance."[43]

The President of the Pentecostal Union of Venezuela at this time was Exeario Sosa, an active member and founder of the National League of Peasants in Lara and a Representative in the state legislature. He was very interested in a relationship with the Disciples of Christ and recommended that "a very informal pattern of fraternal fellowship and cooperation be initiated without any expectation that the Pentecostal Union would become a 'Disciples church.'"[44] This principle was consistently maintained throughout the fraternal relationship between these two denominations.

These initial contacts, including informal visits of exploration and dialogue, "led to the agreement that the Disciples [of Christ] would appoint Juan Marcos Rivera and Flor Rivera to be the first fraternal workers."[45] Their initial two-year appointment was intended as an exploratory process aimed at deciding on a more permanent relationship. The Riveras arrived in Venezuela in August of 1963 and were welcomed in the Convention held at *Peña de Horeb* church in Maracaibo, August 26–September 1 of that same year.[46] They were assigned to do teaching, counseling, to give guidance, to perform social work, to provide Christian education materials and literature, and to organize visits from delegations from Disciples congregations in the United States and Puerto Rico.[47] This couple came to Venezuela with impressive experience as leaders in the Disciples of Christ in Puerto Rico and missionaries in Paraguay.

The experiment in cooperation between the CCDC and the UEPV is today a solid ecumenical partnership. It has strengthened and deepened into an ongoing relationship that continues to share ecumenical resources such as missionary personnel, visits of delegations from Disciples and UCC congregations, medical teams, and youth groups. More recently the two denominations have been working together on two specific programs: Betty's House (a shelter for pregnant women from the countryside) and the Women's House (a multifaceted project for church and community women).

The initial contacts from 1959 until 1972 provided opportunities for collaboration in Christian education, theological education for pastors, a revolving fund for loans, and socio-economic projects aiming at self-support and self-determination. These initial contacts were helpful and encouraging. This first phase of the relationship resulted in a well-established cooperation and mutual fellowship while maintaining the integrity and identity of each denomination. These two very different denominations demonstrated in working together a consistent ecumenical commitment and vocation.

The second phase of this ecumenical partnership (1972–1980) consolidated the pioneer work of the first missionaries and made evident the need to continue working in areas of service and cooperation. The accumulated experience of these years led to a recognition of the importance of a learning-sharing model in the ecumenical sharing of resources. The integrity of mission was tested in a mutual trust and a mature attitude in sharing successes and also confronting conflicts and misunderstanding and learning from them. The ecumenical partnership has been affirmed in a process of integrating social concern, evangelism, theological reflection, and a common witness of faithfulness in concrete service and action.

The UEPV has helped the CCDC in many ways. It helped the Disciples to discern ways to relate to non-mainline churches in Africa and Asia. In the General Assemblies of the CCDC, the visible presence, preaching, dancing, and singing in worship have enhanced the vision and experience of Disciples congregations in all regions in the United States and Canada. These types of involvement and cooperation have confirmed that the initial openness reflected in 1959 by the Division of Overseas Ministries (DOM) executives and the Board of Trustees was the right path to take in relating to Pentecostal churches in Latin America and the Caribbean. That path has led to official partnerships with other Pentecostal churches. It has also helped and influenced the UCC in its initial contacts and partnership with Pentecostal churches, particularly with the Pentecostal Church of Chile.

Establishing global partner committees in solidarity with Pentecostal churches in Nicaragua, Chile, Cuba, and Venezuela reflects that global mission work from local congregations expands and benefits the total mission of the church. The Rocky Mountain Region of the CCDC and the Conference of the UCC in that same area have established a common global partner committee with the Evangelical Pentecostal Union of Venezuela that, through a series of exchanges, has affected the worshiping experience of local congregations in the United States.

Sharing worshiping experiences and the intercultural exchange of local congregations with Pentecostal churches like the UEPV is raising the consciousness and willingness of many local congregations Disciples in the United States and Canada. It is also encouraging the United States churches to open their communities to Hispanic Disciples congregations with a strong charismatic/Pentecostal background from their countries of origin.

The most crucial and lasting influence of this ecumenical partnership is that the UEPV, by maintaining a balanced and integrated ecumenical/evangelical/Pentecostal model of mission, provides a good point of reference in the challenges that mainline denominations need to address in an ecumenical agenda looking toward the twenty-first century, with the many changes taking place in a more pluralistic world.

Forward in Mission

The CCDC grew out of the restoration movement but opted for an ecumenical commitment in the promotion of mission and unity. The Disciples developed a theology of mission as God's mission and an integral mission strategy in which the central theme of "kingdom building" emerged as an ecclesiology with three distinctive emphases: the members of the church as citizens of the kingdom, the kinship of God's people as active agents in promoting mission in unity for the kingdom, and the kingdom as communion with God in ecumenical global cooperation for justice and the spread of the gospel. In the CCDC, *missio Dei* was manifest as unity in diversity, with identity and mission in a creative tension between the church and the kingdom of God. Mission as God's mission implied retaining the freedom to examine and interpret while accepting a consensus on the essential doctrinal tenets.

The UEPV is an autonomous and autochthonous movement that opted for an ecumenical vocation and ecumenical relationships. Its strategy for mission integrated spiritual formation, leadership development, and the capacity to confront new challenges and conflicts. According to this strategy the Church is empowered by the Spirit to promote and witness to Christian unity. The UEPV was a pioneering force in reclaiming the Bolivarian ideal of a "Great Motherland." It emphasized that the power of the Holy Spirit equips the people to respond to the crisis in Latin America and the Caribbean and to heal their own internal crisis as a church, as well as imparting the vision to discern the signs of the times and thus to better serve God's people. The UEPV was shown to affirm a vision that maintained a balance between its mission as a Pentecostal church and its ecumenical commitment.

The two denominations continued to honor differences and diversity by maintaining the identity and the integrity of each denomination. They reaffirmed an ecumenical commitment and vocation to continue working together in mission. The learning-sharing model in the Ecumenical Sharing of Resources was one of the key elements in this vital and positive ecumenical relationship.

The two undergirding theological motives in their theologies of mission are mission as "kingdom building," for the Disciples of Christ, and mission as "liberating Spirit," for the UEPV. Both denominations have been influenced by ongoing theological discussions within the ecumenical movement during the second half of the twentieth century.

The CCDC was strongly influenced by the predominant liberal model of the missionary movement of the nineteenth and twentieth centuries that dominated mainline Protestantism in the United States. The movement that established the first Latin America and the Caribbean Pentecostal churches early in the twentieth century influenced the UEPV. It then evolved to become an indigenous, autonomous, and autochthonous movement that responded to the poor sectors of these churches. The UEPV also demonstrated openness to the contextual and liberation theologies very influential in Latin America and the Caribbean.

1. These two denominations share a common understanding of their sharing in God's mission by opting for strategies of mission that are committed to a liberating faith by the presence and power of the triune God.
2. The CCDC and UEPV have developed a learning-sharing process of mutual accountability, a humble attitude to deal with misunderstandings and conflicts, and a determination to stay together and deepen their ecumenical commitment.

3. For forty years these two denominations have moved forward in mission while maintaining their theological identities, constructing a theological and missiological integrity, sharing in solidarity in times of crisis, and reaffirming their common ecumenical commitment.
4. Both denominations have made the commitment to continue in their common vision for mission together, remaining open to dialogue, designing and promoting common projects, and planning new initiatives while consolidating existing projects. The denominations continue in the sharing of ecumenical resources such as delegations exchanges, missionary personnel, educational funding, women's ministries support, social programs for poor women, and evangelistic programs.
5. Each denomination can improve on deepening this ecumenical partnership by exploring new strategies for mission. The CCDC can benefit from the evangelistic fervor and experience of the UEPV. The UEPV can learn from the experience in ministries of compassion, solidarity, and social action gained by the Disciples of Christ during more than 150 years of existence. The accumulated experience of these forty years of ecumenical partnership forms a solid foundation upon which to continue exploring new adventures in mission.

One element that makes this mutual partnership a successful model is its immersion in concrete experiences and positive results, even during critical times. First, a mutual partnership requires speaking the truth to each other (Eph. 4:25b) in order to be accountable in trust and respect for each other. The CCDC and the UEPV have followed this practice in several crucial moments. During the initial contacts from 1959 to 1972, an experiment in cooperation was established, avoiding any false expectations but rather cultivating a frank and honest dialogue while learning and sharing with one another. The second came in the 1972–1980 period when the DOM and the UEPV decided to move forward in consolidating their ecumenical partnership, in sharing missionary personnel for specific projects, in providing funds, and in sharing the expertise of qualified professionals. The third came in the years 1981–1983 when the UEPV suffered a serious internal conflict that almost destroyed the organization. During the UEPV XXVII Convention, August 25–28, 1983, the DOM stood with them by sending the Executive Secretary for Latin America and the Caribbean, Rev. David Vargas, which resulted in both churches confirming their intent to stay together in mission. To further solidify this commitment, Rev. Gamaliel Lugo was invited as an international guest at the General Assembly of the CCDC in Des Moines, Iowa, October 1985. The fourth moment came during the consultation "Sharing of Hope: An Ecumenism of the Spirit" in Indianapolis, Indiana, in 1997. This consultation provided a setting and opportunity for the UEPV and the other Pentecostal churches now in partnership to "speak the truth in love" once more. Participants confirmed that many weaknesses, obstacles, and dilemmas needed to be addressed by both sides, but despite these challenges the participants were committed to staying together in mission, facing the challenges of the times.

Another element contributing to the success of the mutual partnership model is that sharing in God's mission requires a mutual openness in correcting mistakes, improving relationships, and taking options. Between 1983 and 2004 the Executive Committee of the UEPV promoted an open dialogue with all the congregations that left that denomination between 1981 and 1983. Many of those congregations returned to the full membership in the UEPV, and others remain in cordial and open communication, sharing in many aspects of mission. The Executive Committee of the UEPV conducted a discernment process between 1984 and 1986 on ecumenical commitment, leading to a public statement at the XXX Convention at Hosanna Church in Guanare, August 1986. At the XXXI Convention in "Comunidad El Triunfo" in Valencia, Venezuela, 1987, the UEPV publicly declared its ecumenical vocation, reaffirmed its Pentecostal identity, and affirmed its preferential option for the poor. This whole process made it clear that the UEPV wanted to continue in an ecumenical partnership with the CCDC and the ecumenical movement in Latin America and the rest of the world.

The CCDC and the Evangelical Pentecostal Union of Venezuela have moved forward in mission toward equality and justice and have proven that a partnership based on mutuality and holistic sharing of resources is the best foundation for partnership in God's mission.

28

"Glocal" Chalice of Blessing

A Christological Reading in the Face of Globalized Imperialism

REV. CRISTOBAL MARECO LIRD
TRANSLATED BY WILLIAM J. NOTTINGHAM

Preamble: Strategic Plan

After many years, the Disciples of Christ church of Paraguay, thanks to its lay leaders and pastors of different congregations, set about to draw a map specifying where it wanted to go. With an analysis of its strengths, weaknesses, dangers, and opportunities, the church not only arrived at establishing its lines of actions but also defining its mission, interpreting the present dynamics of the contemporary world. It was thus that it fixed its objectives and goals so that the congregations could coordinate their activities.

This work is really an inexhaustible source that tries to respond to a world that lacks solidarity, justice and peace.

The mission statement says:

> The Disciples of Christ in Paraguay are a Christian Church with an ecumenical perspective which testifies to the Gospel of Jesus Christ, seeking the transformation and integral growth of the person in the world through the proclamation, teaching, and the celebration of the Word of God and service to the neighbor.

The mission is accompanied by both the prospective and introspective vision:

Our Church undertakes the promotion and defense of abundant life in the face of situations that threaten it. Its members find a place in the community where they develop their gifts through different ministries in response to the needs of the neighbor. They further the unity of the body of Christ by being in dialogue with different Christian denominations. Our congregations express their faith through the different cultural manifestations of the country.

Our Church stimulates and prepares its lay leaders and pastors for different ministries. Our growth is slow quantitatively as well as qualitatively. Our congregations support their pastors with dignity. Our new congregations contain adequate infrastructures that correspond to their reality. Our congregations are united, *with a sense of the body*, sensitive and in solidarity with each other, as they are with each of their members.

Underlying Presuppositions

We can say without risk of error that these depictions come from the most intimate fibers of the Church, evoking its conceptions, challenges, and theological hopes. What can appear as a simple strategic plan affirms that the Church only serves the world when it is the Church, when it maintains a balance between its Christian *identity* and its *identification* with others: whether believers or nonbelievers, the neighbor on the street, the community in which it lives, and the society with all of its needs and strengths. To be identified with the poverty, struggles, and hopes of humanity is not to negate Christian identity; as José Miguez Bonino says, "*It is the only evangelical way to strengthen and put to the test our identity.*"[1]

When the Church identifies itself with the neighbor who suffers the negation of his or her own life, it recognizes that the policies that are elaborated in the world go against the *neighbor,* against *nature,* and finally against *life itself* by the situations of exclusion and death. For this reason, the Church understands that every structure or person that threatens life must be criticized, fought against, and desacralized. At the same time, the Church encourages the sense of ecumenical inclusion, which raises the issues of diversity, multiculturalism, and participation of *civil society and local communities* by the grace of God, who creates, preserves, and defends life in terms of social and economic justice for all.

The Disciples of Christ have no doubt of their identity; we are a Christian Church uniquely by Christ. Our teachings, proclamation, and celebration are Christ's. The love that brings one to meet the needs of the neighbor is born of Christ, a love that is sustained by the knowledge of the revelation of God in Christ and expresses itself in science and reasoning in order to be concrete, efficient, and intelligent. The transformation and integral growth of persons and structures existing in the world show that *a different world* is possible, a world where it is possible to conceive the gift of life without oppression, exclusion, and death of the innocent.

In identifying these presuppositions, we propose to desacralize the myth of globalized neoliberal capitalism and reaffirm, as a contrary position, the christology of the Church, in terms of an economic theology of liberation. Finally, we identify a *globalist* scenario, which permits the Church to develop itself as *missio Dei.*

Global Market

We are all part of globalization; this world phenomenon involves us and challenges us to seek a place within this global scheme of things. For this reason, it is pertinent to ask ourselves: What is globalization? What is its focus for men and women of faith?

Our time is called a time of epochal change. To go around the world in eighty days in a dirigible balloon is useless. We need only a *computer* to be cosmopolitan and contemporary with many people and cultures at the same time. Most human communication and commercial transactions are by electromagnetic radio frequency, wireless Internet, radio and television, etc. This *common patrimony* illustrates the extent and complexity of the idea of globalization.

Globalization is a *process* that seeks the reorganization of the world itself, and moves a multiplicity of actors looking for the most beneficial direction for their wealth and interests.[2] The principal components of neoliberalism[3] are:

1. The transition from a centralized economy under the state to a market economy.
2. The production and consumption without limits across national borders and the immensity of the financial and speculative market (virtual wealth).
3. The globalization of culture, which establishes hierarchies, conflicts, and accommodations; the consumer index defines human behavior and values.
4. Technological industries based on the intellectual capacity of the human being without fixed boundaries.
5. The existence of various weak centers located in great transnational corporations (within the United States, Japan, Germany) and multilateral organizations (IMF, World Bank, World Trade Organization).
6. The demographic phenomenon: migrations resulting from people looking for a better future and the aging of the population, with a disproportion of wage-earners facing a growing number of retired.
7. And the high level of planned consumption[4] and the accelerated deterioration of the environment.

This hegemonic postulate seeks not only to establish a status of legality, which then it uses to act in a free and unlimited way, but also of legitimacy.

For this, neoliberal capitalism, without using a religious language, elaborates its own theology to legitimize its ideology.[5] Let's mention *paradise* as an example.

Paradise, a medieval eschatological hope, was to be found after *death* by the intervention of God. Technological progress of modernity promises the transfer of this utopia into human history; the notion of *limitlessness* erupts for human actions, and the idea arises that *to want is power*. This myth that flaunts *power* to eradicate natural death—the death caused by violence and hunger[6]—is received as *good news*; this concept is presented as the *end of history,*[7] of its evolution. Francis Fukuyama maintains:

> The progressive conquest of nature, made possible by the development of the scientific method in the sixteenth and seventeenth centuries, was produced in accord with definite rules, determined not by humans but by nature and by the laws of nature. Technology makes possible the unlimited accumulation of wealth, and consequently the satisfaction of an ever larger abundance of human desires.[8]

To satisfy an ever-larger abundance of human desires is to participate in paradise by means of technological progress, which has power to *accumulate unlimited riches*. Nature and its natural laws, rather than humans, lead the evolution of history to the market system, which means to realize in history the promises that Christianity promised *after* death.[9] This system is religiously perfect, although it recognizes the existence of social and economic problems,[10] whose *origin,* it is said, is *original sin,* the fundamental evil that causes other evils. "The pretension to know the market and direct it to the overcoming of social problems is the origin of all the economic and social evils."[11] The moral of the market is, on the other hand, to preserve the lives of those who have the right to life, which means those who own private property, defined by its value as a medium of exchange in monetary terms and the ability to enter into contracts.[12] But, what is finally the *good* and the *evil*? Evil is to go against the moral of the market and the good is to defend private property and to enforce the laws that safeguard the contractual principle.

What counts above all is the market: the supremacy of the strongest over the weak. This system inaugurates a new social drama: *exclusion*.[13] Within these parameters, *executive action* and *the cult of efficiency*—which value income more than the suffering of the "*least competent,*" the poor[14]—are highly prized. The sufferings and the deaths of the poor are interpreted as *necessary sacrifices*[15] that increase the concentration of profits; the redemptive progress itself reaffirms the sacrificial value of the sacrificial deaths, calling for *more* sacrifices, so that the earlier deaths not be seen for what they really are: assassinations.[16]

The market wants to appear as an *international solidarity*[17] (like the kingdom of God) that does not oppose *competence* to *solidarity,* because it believes that to defend its own interests against the interests of others, in addition to generating efficiency, will develop solidarity—in other words, concern for the problems of others.

"There has never been economic dominance without military and political dominance."[18] The dictatorial governments of Latin America fulfill the agenda designed to open markets to transnational capital, selling national industries and contracting loans that later will give birth to the overwhelming external debt.[19] Many of us believe that the policies of the United States of North America and its allies no longer attempt to shelter their actions legally and democratically; now they act directly in relation to the globalized market. The war declared against Iraq is the best example, where the political, economic, and military reveal it. The market and the empire now are visibly and openly exposed. It is the first global empire in world history that holds the system of massive means of communication, which manipulate information in such a way as to *win the hearts and minds of the people.*

Local Faith

To know the Church of Paraguay, one must refer to its christology. To be consonant with its faith is to take a position on the successes of globalization of the economy and of politics and to participate in the liberating critical process of the kingdom of God.

The use of the Bible gives a presence to the Church[20] that creates a connection of critical consciousness, fraternal relations, and the option of faith and membership. The physical possession of the Bible becomes a resource; its membership was identified for carrying it under their arms. The burning of Bibles, the jokes, and frequent stoning did nothing more than to awaken curiosity for something new and began to make known the cause of changes that occurred in the lives of persons and of society.

The 1960s and the early 1970s marked a distinctive spirituality, because the Word of God began to be heard through concrete experiences of persecution, hunger, and disappearances, at the same time that biblical stories were being read that proclaimed the liberation or the resurrection of the people. Popular versions of the Bible emerged from this process as the *religio-cultural patrimony of Latin Americans.* New lenses of interpretation rediscovered the deep meaning of biblical concepts such as *bread and salvation,* which were very much spiritualized. In time, we proposed to analyze precisely the theme of salvation in the context of the christological doctrine of atonement, which manifests itself in the Sunday eucharist of the Lord's supper.

With the conquest of the Americas, classical doctrines of the atonement[21] dominated the religious scene in the North as in South America. Soon, nevertheless, the innate and divine process of liberation appeared in the history of the peoples; the struggles of the original peoples and their criticisms put forth roots. Later, the advocates of the suffering God emerged, those who understand that suffering is an inevitable part of the historical process of liberation and those who criticized the idea of redemptive suffering but retained the symbol of the cross as the image of liberation.

The faith of the Church as part of the process of liberation is not reduced to the death of Jesus Christ, because *all* his life is salvific, including his death and *resurrection*. They killed Jesus on the cross for his faithfulness to God and his gratuitous love toward all humanity, expressed throughout history. On the third day, the Father, as the liberating God, raised him as an act of justice. The resurrection was necessary to overcome death and give abundant life to those who believe in this God who resurrects; the resurrection shows that it is worthwhile to follow in the steps of the Resurrected One in the presence of the Spirit.

To confess that Jesus is the Christ is to acknowledge him not in virtue of his victories but because of his total faithfulness to God, proclaiming the dignity of all human beings, and, in the name of this truth, confronting even to death the idolatrous forces of every empire. "The essence of the sacrifice of Christ is that the work of Jesus on the cross not only unmasks the injustice of human sacrifices of all time but also declares the end to those *sacrifices*. His resurrection delegitimizes them at the root."[22] Thus the nucleus of our faith is that there is neither victory nor power without Jesus, the Christ. To confess this faith is to believe in a God who does not join with the conqueror but rather is in solidarity with the one who dies unjustly for the sake of justice, sustained in the grace that abolishes the infinite repetition of oppression regulated by the limited just law order. To distinguish victory and power from truth and justice is to actively resist in little and big things; in the end, it is to accept suffering as the consequence of our faithfulness to God more than to prefer complicity with oppressive power.

The red chalice that bears the inclined empty cross is the symbol of our faith. The Lord's supper, a central ritual of Sunday worship,[23] dramatizes faith in the Risen Christ. For that, the *bread* and the *wine* that are distributed symbolize, *in extenso,* the Incarnation, the passion, the crucifixion, the inevitable death, and the necessary resurrection of Jesus. This scene gathers together the meaning of the life that faithfulness to God requires of us and the gratuitous love and solidarity toward the neighbor who suffers exclusion and death. The simple gestures that surround the symbolism of bread and wine constitute scenes of the sacrificial configuration of its christology. "The sacrifice is, at the ritual level, a symbolic act by which the church can have access to God to encounter in communion with him its own fullness."[24] But all the life of Jesus is understood as sacrifice once for all and as such is the access to God. The death and resurrection of Jesus put an end to the *necessary sacrifices* of the market. For it, the ritual practice of the Lord's supper disauthorizes not only the sacrifices but also the law that requires them and delegitimizes the centralization of the market, which sanctions (forgives) them or not through its priesthood[25] to activate or fulfill the laws that guarantee capital more than life.

The Table of the Lord is the symbol of a just economy, because it is organized on the basis of grace and offers well-being to all people. The *eucharist* is the celebration of life—not of goods, but of persons—without distinction by culture or gender, sharing and distributing equitably the bread and wine, in other words, the existent goods and riches, and sowing by praxis the graciousness of God who creates the necessary conditions to continue celebrating life. In the economy of the Lord's table: (1) we human beings are responsible for all our actions before the Creator and Lord, and for which we will give an account; (2) we human beings are not owners of the existent goods and resources (private property does not exist), rather we are stewards to whom God entrusts the adequate use of them; (3) human beings through the policies of the state or concrete actions must help those who lack subsistence. For Amartya Sen,[26] liberty as a condition is central for the development of the economy, which means the *elimination* of poverty, the tyranny of unemployment and underemployment, the lack of economic opportunities, social privation, the absence of public services, the mechanism of repression, and exclusion.

The Lord's supper is, definitively, this physical and visible manifestation of the christology of the Church. Through the communion, the members, in a sacred place with sacred emblems, by eating bread and drinking wine, are in tune with the action and word of Christ: to the efficacy of the ritual gesture is added the efficacy of the Word, which celebrates the resurrection of Christ. This weekly practice spreads its roots; the meaning of presence and relevance delineates the identity of the Church. That identity is given by what makes it feel and believe the same thing in this place and in this moment as in some other place and other moment, past or future, an identity that is given by the Risen Christ, that of being *Latin American*, with which it identifies itself.

To recognize the *Latin Americanization* of the resurrected Christ is to accept the *imaginary identity*[27] of the Church, which is intensified when it refers to its call, its *symbolic identity,*[28] of Christ, its foundation, strength, and hope. Thus, the Church is contained in its name, and being *vocatus* can be at the same time *vocatum,* which means to call the neighbor, reminding her and him of their identity, their human dignity. To recognize the authority of Christ[29] is to validate the *interest of Christ* for everybody.

As *vocatus* and *vocatum,* the Church discovers itself as *missio Dei* in its own land and culture, embracing the totality of life. Everything that can make of the Church a contributor to the process of liberation of men and women and of the whole creation is *missio Dei*, of which the *kerygma* is one part.[30]

Missio Dei

A critical reading of globalization enables us to observe that within the system there can be a common space in which *missio Dei* can contribute to the process.

The desire for salvation is the principle of the action of God in Christ; to establish the dignity and communion of humanity is its major volition. Therefore sacrificial forgiveness, as a consequence of the resurrection of Jesus Christ, shapes the sense of transformation in the community: *violence into justice, the arbitrary into order, and war into peace.* This forgiveness, a remembrance of salvation, leads persons and communities to the praxis of justice, with faithfulness and gratitude, to the liberating work of Jesus Christ in the daily life of local communities, which interact in globalization.

We see how respective governments try today to globalize. The relation with the world in terms of attracting foreign investments continues to be more prestigious than the development of national industries. In the same way, televised information levels and holds our attention on what is happening throughout the world. But there is a new factor, which is the emergence of the *local*[31] in a process of integration with the global.[32]

This integration can come to have an economic and political influence. But what type of integration can we speak of when our Latin American countries suffer deindustrialization from privatization, the influence of foreign banks, the disconnection of airlines, and the loss of underground riches? The culture can arrive at integration, which in the competitive market becomes more difficult. The cultural resources could contribute to restarting new programs of growth:

1. The music industry handles forty billion dollars each year, 90 percent of which is concentrated in six great transnational CD corporations, plus America On Line and Time Warner.
2. The transnational producers of CDs consider Latin America to be the market with the highest rate of growth since the 1990s.
3. Sales in Brazil increased from 262 million dollars in 1992 to almost 1.4 billion in 1996. Eighty percent is in the hands of companies outside the region, which control the copyrights.[33]

Participating in the globalized economy through the local culture, generator of genuine resources, could raise the standard of living of persons and of local communities. Along this line, the media could contribute to the social and political cohesion of the peoples.

Toward a *Global* Praxis of the Faith

At the beginning of the 1950s, Dr. Fred W. Hughes maintained[34] that the mission of the Church was sustained by the *munus triplex* (triple offices), which represented at that time: (1) *educational ministry,* offering *training* for a vanguard of a new generation; (2) *evangelistic ministry,* denouncing the evil or sin of persons and structures and proclaiming the gospel of truth; and, finally, (3) *social or diaconal ministry*: responding to concrete needs of the neighbor: food, health, etc.

Today, this outline has not changed much, and the Church *as mission of God,* which participates in the life of the people, in the ways of relating and enjoying, in the cultural sensibilities and activities and the daily life, cannot do otherwise than to desacralize and delegitimize the ideological and religious myth of the new world order. In this formulation, the whole complex becomes functional, the legal mostly protects goods and riches rather than life, wealth is privatized and poverty is socialized; exclusion and death of many persons are just as necessary as safeguarding only the life of those who qualify and are successful.[35]

The Church is christocentric; its interest is Christ, so that to know the Church is to recognize profoundly its christology, which confesses that Jesus of Nazareth, condemned unjustly, dead on the cross and raised the third day, is the Christ. In contrast to the Christ nailed to the cross, Disciples emphasize the resurrection, illustrating it with the tilted empty cross, in this way helping in the resurrection of the crucified people. This is to say that the *interest of Christ* is interest for the resurrection of the peoples.[36] It is to be identified with the distinct subjects of history in order to recognize the identities and dignity of each one. It is, at the same time, to find the linkages that permit maintaining cooperation, the inclusive unity and actions of solidarity of peoples and local communities, which organize themselves creatively and offer alternatives to globalization without failing to confront powers that oppress economically and culturally.

From this global process emerges a great flow of cultural interchanges between the local and global; this field of actions can locate the Church as *missio Dei* in a new cultural dynamic of multiplying effects without precedent. These cultural interchanges make it possible to create, export, and enrich cultural goods, which sooner or later can have an economic influence, sponsoring inclusive solidarity in the economy and abundant life for all. The *global* signifies the recognition of the plurality of subjects and the dignity of life expressed in opportunities and realizations for everyone.

The Church as *missio Dei* reaffirms its christological faith and participates by the *dynamis* of the Spirit in this *liberating process,* which projects the culture of peace with social and economic justice in the world. Because its actions permit the cultural development of persons and local communities, the Church provides (1) the *ministry of integral education* of persons through its primary schools, high schools, and faculty from the Church; (2) the *promotion and defense of human rights* through the programs of the Committee of Churches for Help in Emergencies (CIPAE) and Friendship Mission, with its programs of health and professional education; and (3) the *spirituality* of all the members through the programs of the local congregations.

29

Toward a Disciples Theology of Religions

DON A. PITTMAN

In September 2006, the Council on Christian Unity of the CCDC published a special issue of its magazine, *Call to Unity: Resourcing the Church for Ecumenical Ministry*, focusing on the topic, "Disciples of Christ and Interreligious Engagement." CCU president, Robert K. Welsh, introduced the issue, asserting that one of the most important and difficult questions facing Christians in the twenty-first century is how they are to understand and relate to persons committed to other religious traditions. With appreciation for the way in which the Council sought to highlight the particular gifts of Disciples that contribute positively to meaningful cross-cultural and interreligious relationships, my aim in this brief essay is to expand on its effort to offer a theological rationale for interreligious engagement and to outline implications for interreligious dialogue in a pluralistic, globalized, and postcolonial world.

The Council's recent report captures well both the Disciples' historic christocentric witness and its dialogical approach to truth. The text emphasizes, first, that we Disciples of Christ believe in "one God revealed in Jesus Christ as Creator, Reconciler, and Redeemer of all" and that we seek actively opportunities to share with the world "the good news of God's covenant of love in Jesus Christ."[1] According to the Council, we are "called by the Gospel of Jesus Christ to witness in word and deed to the living God *for the benefit of the world*."[2] Moreover, quite significantly, Disciples maintain firmly: "such witnessing means conversing with, listening to, learning from, and living peacefully with those in the world who do not confess Jesus as Lord."[3] As a result, the Council states, we enter into such conversations and relationships trusting that the Holy Spirit will be our guide and opening ourselves in the process to "transformation." Indeed, dedicated to a love of neighbor that really "cares about who the other is, how she understands herself, and how she thinks and acts religiously in her own tradition,"[4] Disciples of Christ, who "cannot put limits upon God's grace in different contexts,"[5] trust earnestly that "God's glory will surprise us with new discernments of the Spirit and with the gift of new friends."[6]

Salvation outside the Church?

Surely many Disciples of Christ will appreciate the tone and substance of the Council on Christian Unity's report on interreligious engagement, while others may question the progressive perspective it advances. Yet whatever their reaction to the brief CCU report, study of the document may encourage a number of individuals and congregations to reflect on options for a theology of religions and opportunities for interreligious dialogue, which is also my hope in offering an outline of my own perspective here. A consideration of related issues is important in our day because, while Christians have always lived in contexts shaped by multiple spiritual communities, the United States of America has become in recent decades the most religiously plural society on earth.[7] The problems for Christians concern not merely, as John Cobb has observed, "that what seemed most self-evidently important [for us] is something that in another community they do without marvelously," but the deep theological uncertainties within the church about what to make of that challenging fact.[8]

As Willard Oxtoby has noted, for nearly two millennia most Christian evangelists have acted confidently as if they "had the truth, the whole truth, and nobody but them had the truth."[9] *Extra Ecclesiam nulla salus* (outside the church no salvation), a doctrine evident in the early church and one that many Christians still affirm on the basis of scriptures such as Mark 16:15–16, John 14:6, and Acts 4:12, was eventually asserted forcefully by the Council of Florence, which declared in 1442:

> [The church] firmly believes, professes, and proclaims that those not living within the Catholic Church, not only pagans, but also Jews and heretics and schismatics cannot become participants in eternal life, but will depart "into the everlasting fire which was prepared for the devil and his angels" (Mt. 25:41) unless before the end of life the same have been added to the flock.[10]

Yet, from a very early date, church leaders were forced to reflect on the scandal of the particularity of God's self-disclosure in Jesus Christ. The question, most simply stated, was why did Jesus come so late? If he is the sole Savior of the world, why did a good God delay so long in revealing him, letting millions perish without hope? And what of the millions of individuals of goodwill living after Jesus' appearance who die without a reasonable chance to believe in him and be baptized? A number of early church leaders, including Justin Martyr (died c. 163), Irenaeus (died c. 200), and Clement of Alexandria (died c. 215), argued for the continuity of God's saving activity through every generation to the advent of Christ, and that those who lived in harmony with the mind of God, the eternal Logos through whom all things were made, should be confident in God's grace. Indeed, asserted Justin Martyr, those of every age "who lived reasonably are Christians, even though they have been thought atheists, as among the Greeks, Socrates and Heraclitus, and individuals like them."[11] Several generations later, the important bishop Augustine of Hippo (354–430) declared, with regard to his earlier treatise, "Of True Religion":

> For what is now called the Christian religion existed of old and was never absent from the beginning of the human race until Christ came in the flesh. Then true religion which already existed began to be called Christian. After the resurrection and ascension of Christ into heaven, the apostles began to preach him and many believed, and the disciples were first called Christian in Antioch, as it is written. When I said, "This is the Christian religion in our times," I did not mean that it had not existed in former times, but that it received that name later.[12]

Nevertheless, Augustine maintained that those who by his time in the fourth century remained outside the institutional church, the true ark of salvation so widely proclaimed, could not possibly belong to God's elect. Although Thomas Aquinas (died 1274) also firmly held that faith in Christ was necessary for salvation, he eventually provided a foundation for a more inclusive understanding. Were anyone saved prior to the coming of Christ, he argued, it was because their sincere belief in God constituted an *implicit* faith in Christ. Moreover, citing an example of a person who died suddenly just prior to baptism, Aquinas averred that incorporation into the body of Christ might, through God's unmerited grace, take place *mentally* though not actually, i.e., by *desire* though not in fact.

Especially after far-reaching explorations in Asia and the Americas revealed to Europeans the existence of innumerable non-Christian peoples around the world, this perspective provided a basis for later theologians to speak theoretically of those who might be considered *inculpable*, i.e., those who through the work of the Spirit might be mysteriously *oriented toward* the church, although, because of their circumstances, remain outside of it, at least until such time, which only God knows, that their conversion becomes a real possibility and, therefore, mandatory. This line of theological reflection influenced the position later taken by the Roman Catholic Church at Vatican II (1962–1965), which affirmed that other faiths could reflect the truth that enlightens all persons and be a preparation for the good news of Christ. Indeed, claimed the bishops, God's plan of salvation extends to all persons "who through no fault of their own do not know the Gospel of Christ or his Church, but who nevertheless seek God with a sincere heart, and, moved by grace, try in their actions to do his will as they know it through the dictates of conscience."[13] Many Protestant theologians have been unwilling to abandon theological exclusivism and accept such inclusive views, emphasizing rather human sinfulness, substitutionary atonement, individual conversion, and the absolute uniqueness and finality of the Christian religion. However, shaped by a wide variety of intellectual and cultural influences—such as comparative studies of religions, postmodernism, liberation theologies, feminist and womanist theologies, and postcolonial theory—that have deepened our awareness of human diversity, a significant number of contemporary Protestant theologians have affirmed even more progressive forms of Christian thought and practice that critique both theological exclusivism and inclusivism and, embracing what some have called theological pluralism, place a high value on interreligious cooperation and dialogue in the interest of a sustainable human future.

Considering Contemporary Theological Options

The operative theology of mission of mainstream Disciples developed slowly over time from an evangelical toward a more progressive form.[14] This is particularly evident in the publication of the *Principles and Policies of the Division of Overseas Ministries* (1981), the "Report of the Commission on Theology in Response to Resolution No. 8728 'Concerning Salvation in Jesus Christ'" (1989), and the recent CCU report. Indeed, as these documents suggest, many Disciples today find that they can no longer accept supercessionism—the view that God has totally abrogated God's old covenant with the Jews in favor of a new covenant with followers of Christ—or the traditional version of theological exclusivism, which I will stipulate here to mean that no salvation, or "healing," exists apart from the atoning action of God in the life, death, and resurrection of Jesus Christ and that no spiritual community other than the Christian church is a God-inspired mediator of saving grace. Although most exclusivists are quick to recognize God's sovereign freedom to save whomever God wills, of course, they typically maintain that Christians have no biblical warrant to posit the reality of a general revelation beyond the once-and-for-all incarnational revelation in Christ or any possibility of salvation outside the church.[15] While all religious activity tends to represent attempts at self-justification, Christians are said to participate in the only true religion to the extent that they trust in the grace of God, attend to the one saving revelation in Jesus Christ, and seek to make disciples of all nations.

Two arguments against theological exclusivism have been especially persuasive for Disciples. First, many have concluded that important elements of the biblical witness can be understood in ways that do not support a strict exclusivist position. For example, in his letter to the Romans, Paul writes of the Jews: "As regards election they are beloved, for the sake of their ancestors; for the gifts and the calling of God are irrevocable" (11:28b–29). In the Acts of the Apostles, Peter testifies to a group of Gentiles: "I truly understand that God shows no partiality, but in every nation anyone who fears [God] and does what is right is acceptable to [God]" (10:34). Paul and Barnabas claim: "In past generations [God] allowed all the nations to follow their own ways; yet [God] has not left [God's self] without a witness in doing good" (14:16–17a). Paul assures the Athenians that the unknown deity whom they worshiped is, indeed, the one Creator who is "not far from each one of us" (17:27). And in Matthew 25 salvation appears to be more dependent on right action (orthopraxy) rather than right belief (orthodoxy).

Second, a traditional form of exclusivism raises sharply the problem of theodicy, i.e., of reconciling the belief in a benevolent God with the existence of radical evil. Since only approximately one-third of the present population of the world is Christian, and only an extremely small percentage of all the human beings who have ever lived have been members of the church, many Disciples find it simply untenable, if not arrogant, to maintain that only baptized Christians are saved and all others are lost and eternally separated from God their creator. Such a position appears to be less than credible and to entail an understanding of God contrary to the gracious one we have encountered in Jesus.

Many Disciples who have rejected exclusivism have embraced theological inclusivism, which may be defined by the effort to hold in tension two equally binding convictions: (a) the universal will of God to save, or more specifically the operation of the healing grace of God everywhere, including in and through non-Christian traditions, and (b) "the uniqueness of the manifestation of the grace of God in Christ, which makes a universal claim as the final way of salvation."[16] What seems attractive about this solution is that it affirms Jesus Christ as the ultimate criterion of truth, but maintains that God's grace can be experienced outside the church. The world's religions *can be* ways of salvation and serve to prepare persons for accepting Christ. In fact, those who experience God's grace in and through their participation in a non-Christian religion may be referred to as "anonymous Christians" or "pre-Christians" because they are created with an orientation toward Christ, the Logos through whom all are made. Accordingly, the church is not properly understood as an ark of salvation outside which all are perishing in total darkness, but, rather, as Karl Rahner writes, "The historically tangible vanguard and the historically and socially constituted explicit expression of what the Christian hopes is present as a hidden reality even outside the visible Church."[17]

An increasing number of Disciples, however, have rejected the option of theological inclusivism primarily because the criterion for judging truth claims is given *a priori*. That is, while inclusivists typically advocate interreligious dialogue and mutual learning, they enter every dialogue with a pre-judgment that the criterion for all truth claims is the Christ, hidden in the world religions. Observes Schubert Ogden, for example:

> Notwithstanding its significant difference from exclusivism, then, inclusivism is, in its own way, monistic rather than pluralistic in its understanding of true religion. For it, too, there not only is but can be only one true religion, in the sense that Christianity alone can validly claim to be formally true. Recognizing this, one of its most astute critics, John Hick, dismisses it as anomalous—"like the anomaly of accepting the Copernican revolution in astronomy, in which the earth ceased to be regarded as the center of the universe and was seen instead as one of the planets circling the sun, but still insisting that the sun's life-giving rays can reach the other planets only by first being reflected from the earth!"[18]

Accordingly, prior to entering into interreligious relationships in which all persons might enjoy opportunities to share freely their own beliefs and values, Christian inclusivists effectively subsume or subordinate their dialogue partners' religious identity under terms of their own tradition. However, those identities are unrecognized or explicitly rejected by the partners, e.g., as anonymous or advent Christians.

Critical of both exclusivism and inclusivism—and, as well, of the position of Christian postmodernists who emphasize the incommensurability of the experiences and expressions of different religious communities and stress our complete inability to engage in dialogue the question of tradition-transcending criteria for truth—I want to advocate rather a form of theological pluralism that is faithful to the gospel, productive of a spirit of mutuality between persons of different faith traditions, and credible to mainstream Disciples of Christ. The nature of that theological pluralism may be defined here succinctly as the view that our knowledge of the Absolute is always conditioned and partial; that persons in all religious traditions may through dialogue with one another learn something new to all of them; and that there *may* be multiple paths to salvation, to right relations with God and neighbor, *precisely because* we know there is, in fact, one path given in Christ. It is a position that not only provides for a missional goal in dialogue, as we listen to others and share our own faith, but, in not pre-judging the value of non-Christian religions, establishes the kind of respectful forum of equals that facilitates such conversation. Strategically speaking, the dialogue envisioned will proceed most effectively, as Paul Knitter has suggested, with a primary focus on *suffering* (e.g., dimensions of poverty, victimization, violence, and patriarchy) and the resources that all persons can bring to bear on the world's pressing eco-justice concerns.[19]

The substance of this position should not be foreign to Disciples of Christ, for in accord with Disciples' interpretation theme, members of our denomination will readily acknowledge our limited perspectives on truth and our commitments to the public nature of our discernments, i.e., to a dialogical testing of truth claims. In view of our restoration theme, we will eagerly want to reflect on the long history of God's interaction with all of God's children, both inside and outside the church. In harmony with the Disciples' ecumenical theme, we will confirm our belief in Christian unity and our oneness with all people, which justifies the Council on Christian Unity's concern with interreligious engagement. In light of our eschatological theme, we will confidently confess that God is with us always as we struggle to perceive and join faithfully in God's saving work.

Testing Truth in Dialogue

If the form of theological pluralism that I am suggesting entails a dialogical method for testing truth, the challenge is to find a practical way to talk seriously and openly with persons from all perspectives about our common life together, extending to them the same expectation of learning that we hope they extend to us. That requires that we extend the parameters of truth-seeking beyond intra-traditional dialogue (reflection on our *tradition's* experience) to inter-traditional dialogue (reflections on *human* experience).[20] Of course, some persons may question, beyond the desirability of such an extension, the feasibility of maintaining a tension between a Christian commitment and an openness to alternative commitments that requires continual testing. Some may argue that they affirm both the resolute application of Christian criteria for truth and the practice of inter-traditional dialogue. However, the valuing of inter-traditional dialogue may in such a case represent only an attempt to speak respectfully to persons known to be fundamentally mistaken concerning ultimate truth; it may represent a search for elements of confirmation for accepted truth claims (certainly no extra-traditional grounds would be admitted for disconfirmation); and it may involve at most the theoretical possibility of a modest augmentation of truth through an acceptance of claims not fully developed in the Christian heritage but wholly in consonance with its central practices and tenets. Yet, this does not essentially move beyond the *a priori* declaration that truth is what *my tradition* believes, failing, therefore, to extend fully to what I am describing as inter-traditional dialogue.

For this most fragile, expansive form of global dialogue, it will be necessary for each participant to offer for consideration tentative proposals concerning criteria for truth. In so doing, tradition-specific criteria need not, indeed *cannot,* be abandoned. It must only be agreed that tradition-specific criteria function *dialectically* with tradition-transcending criteria. Christian, Jewish, Hindu, or Islamic criteria, for example, will be offered for consideration *in relation to* proposed criteriological frameworks. That is, articulations of tradition-specific criteria may neither be given immediate primacy in the dialogue nor discounted. They are to be valued for what they represent: diverse interpretations of revelations, insights, and commitments of human beings who through them hope to come closer to an experiential realization of truth. References, for example, to particular scriptural passages (biblical, Vedic, Qur'anic, etc.) in discussions of human rights issues, medical ethics, or ecological concerns are critically important. However, since their authority will not be recognized immediately by all discussants, their claims will require interpretation in relation to tradition-transcending criteria.

Four primary inter-traditional criteria, I would suggest, should initially be explored in testing truth claims: rationality, inclusivity, relationality, and creativity. By rationality, I mean whether or not a truth claim functions within its structure of signification and more generally in such a way that consistent, critical thought is not obviated. By this I intend no diminution of reference to ultimate mystery, religious paradox, or faith, or to validate a specifically Western style of philosophical reasoning. What I wish to propose is that perspectives on truth that open one to the public forum, to the global discussion on significant issues, rather than isolate one in an uncritically accepted worldview or practice, are perspectives more likely to express ultimate truth. A position that is presented as inaccessible to questioning and unnecessary to defend with compelling evidence of any kind is less likely to represent truth.

By inclusivity, I suggest that that which is more likely to be true is that which appreciates and appropriates diversity. That which is less likely to be true is that which sharply rejects all alternate perspectives or co-opts them via unilateral assimilation. As Knitter has asserted, in arguing for a new model for truth, "what is true will reveal itself mainly by its ability to *relate* to other expressions of truth and to *grow* through these relationships—truth defined not by exclusion but by relation."[21] This criterion should not be used to support the relativist's position that all perspectives on transformational truth are equally valid or equally false, thus discouraging the very enlivened debate concerning truth discernment that is its aim. Rather, it should be used to identify positions that may be more holistically responsive than others to the range of human experiences and values that deserve a hearing in the public arena.

This second criterion leads naturally to the third, relationality, for that which is most likely to be true is that which is ultimately productive of well-being (wholeness) for all things that constitute the cosmic reality as we know it. Hans Küng has acknowledged the importance of this element with his description of a "general ethical criterion."[22] Marjorie Suchocki, moreover, has argued, as a feminist, that justice, or well-being, should be *the* fundamental criterion of value.[23] "Well-being," of course, is a polyvalent term that, as Suchocki remarks, can refer to physical and psychological, individual and communal forms. Definitional disagreements at any level of meaning can be significant. Moreover, very different understandings, conditioned by one's context, may exist concerning penultimately destructive choices made for the sake of ultimately productive outcomes. Yet, the criterion is useful in pressing participants in dialogue to attempt to define well-being and to interrelate explicitly their beliefs and ethical imperatives. That which is less likely to be true is that which is presented as impervious to such practical demands for the promotion of healthy human relationships and cosmic well-being.

By creativity I intend to suggest as a criterion for transformational truth a future orientation. That is, that which is more likely to be true is that which directs one's attention not only to past verities that require conversation, but to the possibilities for new truths that emerge at the margins of human understanding. Past perspectives provide the foundation for new insights. Yet, that which is more likely to be false is that which is so concerned with protecting the interpretations of the valued past that there is no freedom for creative insight, no provision or protection for those who labor at the limits of acceptable diversity to quest for greater truth. Creativity links past and present with the future.

It may be objected that these four inter-traditional criteria are not immediately decisive for the resolution of conflicting truth claims. For some, their generality renders them practically useless in contrast to specific intra-traditional criteria. In response, it is to be argued that the purpose of such criteria is not to serve directly—and one might just as well say imperialistically—as a final canon for truth discernment but *to help to set an agenda for dialogue*. The purpose of this type of proposal is precisely the promotion of foundational questions, not the provision of final answers. The purpose is to suggest that participation in a global, multi-perspectival, confessional, and truth-seeking discourse on transformational truth is both possible and necessary, acknowledging that theology rightly both precedes and flows from dialogue.

Historically, Disciples of Christ have believed that amidst the vagaries and ambiguities of life the Holy Spirit remains present with us and will guide us into all truth (Jn. 16:30). While the church universal is multiform because of divergent *interpretations of* the Christ—the Logos incarnate—the church is fundamentally one because of *trust in* the Christ. Jesus was, we proclaim, decisively disclosive of the Ultimate, though we have never claimed that the Ultimate was, thereby, totally disclosed. God is greater that we have been able to comprehend. Our fundamental commitment, then, is to God and not to our current images of God. We have more to learn about the creative power that sustains all things and relates to all beings than we have thus far understood. This affirmation does not diminish the significance of the witness to truth represented in the voices of scripture and tradition. Yet, it does remind us that the Ultimate draws us into the future to a beatific vision the full dimensions of which we cannot know. Faithfulness, therefore, proceeds not simply by constrictive reiterations of past perceptions but often by expansive interpretations relating our historically dynamic religious heritage to potentially new discernments of God's saving presence among all peoples.

30

The Future of Christian Mission in an Age of World Christianity

CARLOS F. CARDOZA-ORLANDI

Definitions and Assumptions: Shifting Mission and Discovering World Christianity

You have been preparing this short mission trip for almost a year. You have an intergenerational group extremely excited about the opportunity to serve the church in the Third World. You have coordinated Bible studies, lectured on cross-cultural encounters, and developed a strong, committed spirit among the group: this intergenerational bunch wants to give itself in service for those less-fortunate Christians in a faraway country. As the congregational leader for this short mission trip, you have seen these Christians' enthusiasm and dedication of faith, engaged in mission work preparation and participation.

As you return from completing this life-giving short mission trip, you recognize, in hindsight that you did not prepare the group for one crucial and common missiological experience: How to understand that those who "go" return "with much more than what they gave." Moreover, you are relatively confused about how to articulate to your home congregation the transforming experience that this intergenerational group had among the "missionized." Part of the confusion comes from your own missiological assumptions: While we assume to be the partners in mission, working under a mission rubric of mutuality, we find ourselves refreshed, renewed by the faith of the faithful in this faraway country. Furthermore, some of the members of the short mission group, whose missiological assumptions are different than yours—who think of themselves as missionaries and transmitters of the gospel—discovered that the "natives" became the missionaries, deepening the confusion: How can the "missionized"—those who should be the receptors of the gospel—be missionaries, transmitters of the gospel to us?

One important theological characteristic of "mission in an age of world Christianity" is that the agency of mission is not a one-way street, which is defined by our old assumptions of "missionaries" and "missionized," or even of a two-way street, defined by the assumptions of partnerships, but that the mission agency has been *dislocated* from congregations, denominations, para-church organizations, and independent short mission trips to be *relocated* in God's activity in Jesus and through the Holy Spirit in the world. Hence, mission is not the activity of a congregation or church organization. *Mission is the redeeming, liberating, and reconciling activity of God in the world.*[1]

Another important theological characteristic of "mission in an age of world Christianity" comes from the perceived "reversal" mission experience in the short mission trip. A unique vitality of the faith comes from those less expected co-protagonists of God's activity: the poor for whom we frequently "do" mission. Though the term "reversal" attempts to locate the mission activity on the other side of the short mission trip—the "missionized"—the term vaguely points to a developing historical awareness: the Christian religion's new demographic configuration. For the last twenty years, world Christian studies show that the vitality of the faith[2] is found in Africa, Asia, Latin America, the Caribbean, and the Pacific.[3] Inherent to this demographic shift is a geo-theological breakdown of Christianity as a religion of the West and a rediscovery of Christianity as a world religion.

The table below shows the Christian population growth during the twentieth century. According to the *World Christian Encyclopedia*,[4] early in the twentieth century most of the Christian population was located in Europe and North America. Consequently, it is not a surprise that the Missionary Movement developed a geo-theological understanding that identified the Euro-American contexts—United States, Canada, Northwestern Europe—as Protestant Christian lands and divided the rest of the world into grades of *deficient* regions of religious history and identity, including other Christian traditions. Protestant missionary maps of the late nineteenth and early twentieth century explicitly convey grades of "religious truth," locating Roman Catholics in Latin America and the Iberian Peninsula, Orthodox Christians in Russia and parts of Eastern Europe, the "Mohammedeans"[5] in North Africa and the Middle East, and the "heathen" in most of Africa, Asia, and the Pacific. The prevalent geo-theological assumptions that fed the missionary mindset of the time are (1) elevating the character of a *deficient* Christianity as lived in the Roman Catholic and Orthodox territories; (2) expanding the true religion to *deficient* non-Christian religions such as Islam; (3) converting the radically *deficient* heathen. Historically, this mindset not only shaped significant missionary theologies, ideologies, and practices, but it also shaped an outlook of the religious world both in academic and church circles in the Protestant Christian lands.

Daisy Machado's *Of Borders and Margins*[6] is a requirement for any Disciples student interested in mission, history, and theology. Her work clearly shows the missionary mindset and geo-theological assumptions described above—in this case not for the distant heathen, but for the original natives of the "Borderlands": the Native Americans and Mexicans of Texas. Disciples of Christ missionaries' identity and missionary work in the Texas Borderlands show a total captivity to the cultural and political interest and hegemony during geographical expansion. Missionary work is correlated with expansion of territory and dominion over the "uncivilized." I have always wondered: What is left of the missionaries' theology and work if you remove the cultural and economic imperialistic ideals of conquest and domination? Machado uncovers a terrible story in the expansion of Christianity. However, this is only one side of the story. Today, we are uncovering the agency and participation of the Latino/a faithful of many generations, a testament to the missionary work's complexity and the gospel's goodness, despite most of the imperialist work.

Machado's work is a corrective to church history and confirms Walls's critique of the discipline of church history:

> Most conventional church history syllabus [*sic*] are framed, not always consciously, on a particular set of geographical, cultural, and confessional priorities. Alas, such syllabuses [*sic*] have often been taken over in the Southern continents, as though they had some sort of universal status. Now they are out-of-date even for Western Christians. As a result a large number of conventionally trained ministers have neither the intellectual materials nor even the outline knowledge for understanding the church as she is.[7]

The current statistics suggest the missionary movement's success. Today, the Christian population grows in the "deficient" regions and its growth points to a vitality of the faith that the "Protestant Christian lands" have been losing for the last thirty to forty years. Moreover, the projected growth of the Christian religion by the year 2050 locates the majority of the Christian population in the Southern continents. Philip Jenkins refers to this demographic shift in the following way:

> By 2050, only about one-fifth of the world's 3 billion Christians will be non-Hispanic Whites. Soon the phrase "a white Christian" may sound like a curious oxymoron, as mildly surprising as "a Swedish Buddhist."[8]

This demographic shift *might* be imagined and interpreted as Euro-American types of Christianity moving as a block to the Southern continents,

Region	Christian Population 1900	Christian Population 1995	Christian Population 2000	Projected % of Christian Population 2050
Africa	9.9 million	318 million	360 million	24%
Asia	22 million	282 million	313 million	18%
Europe	381 million	557 million	560 million	21%
Latin America	62 million	445 million	481 million	25%
North America	79 million	251 million	260 million	12%

resulting in a "photocopied" Euro-American Christianity with African, Asian, and Latin American styles. Such an image and interpretation maintains the assumption that the movement of the Christian religion is an expansion and extension of a "true" Christianity from a particular place and time to other places and times (in our case of study, the Euro-American Christian contexts in the modern period to Africa, Asia, and Latin America in a postcolonial and postmodern period). The heroes are the transmitters of the faith; the *deficient* are the receptors of the faith. If the demographic shift is interpreted and imagined in this way, then we elevate a contextualized transmitted Christianity to a "pure" gospel category. We could not think of "world Christianity"; we would rather refer to a "pure" Christianity—a Protestant Euro-American Christianity—with African, Asian, and Latin American styles and trends. Moreover, the vitality of the faith expressed in liturgy, worship, ecclesial practices, and theology in the Third World would continue to be *deficient* because, in fact, it is *only* a photocopy of the Euro-American types of Christianity.

However, this demographic shift, with its growth-decline dynamic—growth in the "deficient" lands and decline in the "Protestant Christian lands"—demands a different interpretation. Andrew Walls suggests:

> It is easier to recognize now than it was even a century ago that *cross-cultural diffusion has always been the lifeblood of historic Christianity*; that Christian expansion has characteristically come from the margins more than from the centre [*sic*]; that church history has been *serial rather than progressive, a process of advance and recession, of decline in areas of strength and of emergence, often in new forms, in areas of previous weaknesses.*[9]

Walls suggests that we interpret the movement of the Christian religion in terms of a growth-decline framework, a serial, advance-recession pattern that requires a different non-expansion-extension, exponential missiological outlook.[10] This developing missiological outlook is simple yet difficult to understand given the legacy of the geo-theological nineteenth- and twentieth-century mindset and the temptation to imagine and interpret the demographic shift with a "photocopy" mentality. The missiological outlook is to study Christianity as embodied in congregations and communities in Africa, Asia, Latin America, and the Caribbean *on their own terms*. It is not only the history of the transmission of the faith, but also the reception of the faith in ever-changing contexts. This study also helps Euro-American Christian communities to "raise the theological [and missiological] issues concerning Western culture with seriousness."[11] Consequently, the raw material for missiological and theological reflection is the daily life experience of these congregations and communities in their multivalent contexts. This religio-cultural embodiment of the Christian religion in the Third World generates the reality of world Christianity. Therefore, *world Christianity* is:

> The movement of Christianity as it takes form and shape in societies that previously were not Christian, societies that had no bureaucratic tradition with which to domesticate the gospel. In these societies Christianity was received and express [*sic*] through the customs, culture and traditions of the people affected.[12]

While world Christianity historians continue to develop this serial framework of interpretation as the "movement of Christianity takes form and shape" with "the customs, culture, and traditions of the people affected," theologians seek to discover and articulate a redemptive, liberating, and reconciling Christian experience in these communities.[13] The Ghanaian theologian Kwame Bediako summarizes the missiological/theological proposal in the following way:

> If the Christianising [*sic*] of African tradition may be considered to have been largely concerned with resolving a *religious* problem—in that it had to do with making room in the African experience of religious powers for Christ and the salvation he brings—the Africanising [*sic*] of Christian experience can be seen as being considered with resolving an essentially *intellectual* problem—how African Christianity, employing Christian tools, may set about mending the torn fabric of African identity and hopefully point a way towards the emergence of a fuller and unfettered African humanity and personality.[14]

The missiological and theological endeavor is, therefore, to seek answers for time- and space-specific questions. Western theology's answers mean very little to the very specific questions emerging, for example, from Amerindians' celebrating the Lord's supper during fertility rituals, recent Buddhist converts reflecting on salvation, migrants living in inner-city slums contesting the possession of spirits, a household congregation meeting in public housing in India claiming Christ to be a more powerful avatar than those known in the popular *bakhti* Hindu tradition, African Initiative Churches protecting the environment in dialogue with African Traditional Religious leaders. All of these examples point to the interaction and a mission matrix between a transmitted and received gospel with a concrete religio-cultural context.

In respect to theology, given the serial nature of the movement of the Christian religion and the new missiological outlook and endeavor, we are acutely aware of a most important theological discovery: *mission theology and practices (and for that matter, theology) are contingent.*[15] Andrew Walls further explains:

> It is the very concept of a fixed universal compendium of theology, a sort of bench manual which covers every situation (referring to Western theological corpus), that mission studies challenges. In mission studies we see theology "en route" and realize its "*occasional*" nature, its character as response to the need to make Christian decisions. The conditions of Africa, for instance, are taking Christian theology into new areas of life, where Western theology has no answers because it has no questions. But Christians outside Africa will need to make some responses to the questions raised in the African arena. As Christian interaction proceeds with Indian culture—perhaps the most testing environment that the Christian faith has yet encountered—the theological process may reach not only new areas of discourse, but resume some of those which earlier pioneers—Origen, for instance—began to enter.[16]

What missiological assumptions should guide our theology and mission practices in an era of world Christianity? Let me suggest two for the purpose of this paper:

1. As theologians and practitioners of mission, we locate ourselves in the crossroads of a mission matrix: at the in-between spaces of gospel intersections and interactions among missionaries, the missionized, and the religio-cultural and social conditions of their contexts.
2. The vitality of mission theologies and practices is to be discovered at life's margins, particularly in the current representative of the Christian religion: a traditional woman of color. Yet as mission theologians we are not part of the margins (nor am I a woman). Hence, we enter the context of the margins with trepidation and seek to co-participate and offer an interpretation of the agency of the marginalized—whether missionaries, missionized, or unnamed agents of God's activity in their context.

Summarizing, mission is not what the church does. Mission is the activity of God in the world. God is the protagonist of redemption, liberation, and reconciliation in the world. The line between the missionaries and the missionized blurs, if not totally becoming artificial. It is only useful for pedagogical purposes, particularly with a late nineteenth- and early twentieth-century geo-theological or Western "photocopy" mentality.

Furthermore, with this theological awareness comes a revision of the movement of the Christian religion. Both the statistics and historical and cultural studies point to a demographic shift of the Christian religion: at the beginning of the twenty-first century it is clear that the ecclesial and missiological vitality of the Christian religion is in the Third World, while Euro-American Christianity continues to decline, given its resistance to experience a cross-cultural diffusion in its own context. Ironically, the vitality of the faith in the West is significantly located among the immigrant Christian communities who, through transnational networks and cross-cultural diffusion in Western contexts, continue to be fueled by both churches in the Southern continents and the critical questions launched by experiences of displacement and survival. These new realities challenge and frequently break models of doing mission and theology. This is the lifeblood of historic Christianity and the catalyst for mission in an era of world Christianity!

Theologies and Practices of Mission in an Era of World Christianity: Three Short Case Studies

The Christian Church (Disciples of Christ) in Puerto Rico: From Transmitted Faith to Embraced Faith, Despite the Powers…

The Christian Church (Disciples of Christ) in Puerto Rico was the first mainline church to declare itself autonomous from its "mother" church in the United States. This action was taken in the early 1930s during the Great Depression after the island, a U.S. colony, was devastated by one of the most powerful hurricanes in its history and left economically crippled. The Disciples in Puerto Rico, in a situation of anomie, experienced in most congregations a revival that disturbed the missionaries' church and worship order. Missionaries, confused by this effervescence, decided to close the church buildings. The Puerto Rican nationals appealed to the U.S. courts in Puerto Rico and found themselves protected. The churches had to be opened![17] This presents a clear irony of how colonial powers contributed to the erosion of Christendom models and the emergence of a contextualized Christian faith, the reality of world Christianity.[18]

During the next decade, lay leaders began to create unique worship resources, particularly hymns. One of those laypersons was Ramona Alamo, a poor peasant from the coastal town of Dorado. Alamo, author of many hymns, wrote "A Empezar de Nuevo" ("To Begin Anew"), which has become one of the most important and popular hymns of the Puerto Rican Disciples.[19]

I have been unable to date the hymn. Local church historians and pastors of the Disciples in Puerto Rico suggest the early 1940s, during the latter part of this period of theological and ecclesial emancipation.[20] Musically, the hymn does not follow any of the popular modalities of the time, though its tempo and rhythm clearly fit Puerto Rican popular musical patterns. It does not follow the pattern of the traditional hymnody transmitted by the missionaries, though its lyrics and character keep traditional hymns' dignity and solemnity. The hymn is a combination of a march and a "paso doble," or "double step," with a simple arrangement of tunes, allowing the hymn to be accompanied by a guitar and Puerto Rican instruments. It is a hymn written from the space of in-betweenness: between our inherited Disciples Christianity and our discovery of the faith as Puerto Ricans; between our traditional hymnal music and our own Puerto Rican music...between the old religion and the new religion.

The lyrics are simple. They invite the church to begin anew, focusing on glorifying God in Jesus Christ. The call is to be faithful and to live out the gospel. The hope is the community's experience of God's presence and grace. The hymn is simple, evangelical, unique, visionary, and in affinity with the Protestant theological framework of the time. However, the hymn is also a theological piece with the same insight of Karl Barth's work,[21] but from a woman of a poor Puerto Rican *barriada* (shanty town) who invites the faith community to "rediscover" its faith on her own terms and yet gives witness to the gospel. This is mission theology in an era of world Christianity:

> REFRAIN
> To begin, to begin, to begin anew again;
> Brethren in Christ, to begin anew again
>
> Stanzas
> To begin anew our journey in Christ
> Oh merciful Christ, guide us with your light;
> Give us new strength to follow you;
> Let your grace overwhelm us.
>
> God calls the church to begin anew
> Our minds to heaven should always be;
> Always trusting and in fellowship;
> We will receive greater blessing.
>
> Let us begin by searching our souls;
> The great sacrifice of Christ in the cross;
> His blessed blood, shed it was;
> Let us all seek to be faithful to him.[22]

CREEDA: "What Good Can Come from Nazareth?"

CREEDA is a rehabilitation center in the city of Agua Prieta, Mexico, on the border with Douglas, Arizona. In a city infected with drug trafficking and abuse, CREEDA is a place of refuge, not only for Mexican and Central American migrants, but for the poor of Douglas, Arizona.

An ex-addict who strongly believes that rehabilitation is intertwined with a ministry of saving lives runs this governmental organization. The budget is extremely limited. Education and medicine are even more limited. Resources are scarce. But for this rehabilitation center, saving lives is not a choice—it's a duty.

Men and women of different ages drive a pickup truck carrying gallons of water, food, and some first aid needs to help migrants in their desert journey. CREEDA provides water! "I am the water of life..." Water for a baptism of life; water for cleansing our thirst; *water*. This mission is a concrete answer to a concrete need: migrants need water in the desert in order not to die, and these recovering drug addicts, male and female, young and adult, provide water! However, that response comes with very difficult socio-political implications.

The co-agents of mission are recovering drug and alcohol addicts and mentally ill patients. It reminds us of that question in John 1:46: Nazareth! Can any good thing come from there? Agua Prieta, CREEDA, drug addicts? Can anything good come from them? What good can come from recovering drug and alcohol addicts and patients with mental illness? It is a mission of reconciliation—reconciliation with God, other, and self.

The theology is simple, yet deep and biblical. The administrator of CREEDA in Agua Prieta gives us an insight into redemption and liberation. "What better way to be liberated from our vices than to be servants to the migrants who are in need and see in them ourselves?" It is not, however, about feeling good about what they do. At the center's entrance, we find this version of the Lord 's Prayer:

The Lord's Prayer...

Do not call me "Father" if every day you do not behave as my child;
Do not say "Our" if you live isolated in your selfishness;
Do not say "Who art in Heaven" if you only think about earthly/material things;
Do not say, "hallowed be thy name" if you invoke it with your lips, but your heart is far from God;
Do not say "thy Kingdom Come" if you mistake it for your material success;
Do not say "thy will be done" if you do not accept the will when it is painful;
Do not say "give us this day our daily bread" if you do not worry about the hungry;
Do not say "forgive us our debts/trespasses" if you bear your brother and sister a grudge;
Do not say "lead us not into temptation" if you do not avoid occasions to sin;
Do not say "deliver us from evil" if you do not fight evil;
Do not say "Amen" if you have not taken seriously the words of the Lord's Prayer.[23]

The act of providing the water of life for the migrants is grounded in a faith that is intertwined with prayer, witness, and a demand for integrity and justice for the cultural and religious other.

CREEDA works with Presbyterians and Roman Catholics, Pentecostals and practitioners of indigenous religions. It is ecumenical, evangelical, sacramental, intercultural, interreligious and served by both males and females. The women and men of CREEDA see their ministry as providing a sacrament: a sacrament of life. In water, they see the life that God gives.

Recovering drug addicts and alcoholics serve migrants in their poverty and fragility. They faithfully pray:

Prayer for My Migrant Sisters and Brothers

Loving and merciful heart of Jesus,
I pray for my migrant brothers and sisters.
Have mercy on them and protect them from mistreatment and humiliation in their travel.
They are identified by many as dangerous and poor because they are strangers.
By the grace of God, let us respect and value their dignity.
Touch our hearts with your goodness, Lord, when we see them as they travel.
Protect their families until they return home, not with a broken heart but with their hopes fulfilled. Amen.[24]

CREEDA points to the issue of who we expect to be the co-agents of mission. The despised of the world seem to have an angle on the relationship between mission and sacramental theology, between water and life, between prayer and faithfulness, between tradition and ecumenics, and between mission and money. They remind us that in the migrants, we find God's redemptive activity and find ourselves on the side of mission that requires silence, observation, learning, and courage rather than doing and solving.

Our New Theologians? Practitioners of the Faith, Theologians of Our Communities

Women are the co-agents of Christian mission in the Third World in the early twenty-first century. They provide a fresh reading of the gospel and our religio-cultural traditions. Virginia is such an example.

Virginia is a Mexican woman who crossed the border ten years ago and is a member of a Disciples Latino/a congregation in the Atlanta area. She has become a leader: she is a deacon, a Sunday school teacher, and, most recently, a preacher.

Her husband has been imprisoned many times. Both come from deeply abused families, and these patterns continue to haunt them although the congregation has witnessed a dramatic change in their lives. She is a wife and mother, friend, counselor, and congregational leader. She is undocumented in the United States.

Good Friday is a special day for Christians. For Latin American and Latino/a Christians, it is a very special day. Because of our Roman Catholic religious background, the crucifixion continues to evoke deep religious feelings of God's solidarity and companionship with those who suffer. The cross is not dismissed. To the contrary, for many Latinas and Latinos, the promise of resurrection is void without the experience of the cross. The empty cross in many of our congregations is a juxtaposition of the paradox of death and life.[25]

The pastor invited her to preach on one of the seven words of the cross: "'Dear woman, here is your son,' and to the disciple, 'Here is your mother'" (Jn. 19: 26b–27a, NIV). Virginia began her reflection by reminding the community that she had not seen her mother in ten years. Movingly, she told the congregation that she was not able to see her mother before she died, and that she felt as though she were losing her family. She spoke about the feeling of isolation that migrants suffer. In addition to being alone, racism, sexism, abuse, and uncertainty prevail in the land of promises.

Virginia gave the congregation an insight into ecclesiology: "From the cross, Jesus' words give us a new meaning about family: it is not about blood ties; it is about mutual love, responsibility for one another, care, and accountability. My family is the body of Christ...My family is this congregation and any human being who confesses that Jesus is our brother and that God is our beloved Father."

Her ecclesiology is about her christology: As she moved the congregation to tears describing Jesus' concern for his mother and disciple, she established that the best way of assuring that both would be fine was by ensuring that they care for and be accountable to each other, just as Jesus was caring and accountable to us. "On the cross," she said, "Jesus was worried about his mother and disciple, not about himself... Who are we worried about when we are overwhelmed with our problems and situations? Perhaps, the way to understand our own situations is by looking at those who are with us, and worrying about them, and taking care of them."

Conclusion

Mission in an era of world Christianity requires world Christians to be alert to the challenges, promises, and opportunities of this new demographic shift with all its historical and theological implications. Some of the challenges are:

- A new way of understanding the movement of the Christian religion;
- Discovering Christianity's "space" among other religious traditions;
- Internally, the controversial theological issue of syncretism with other religions;

- Discovering Christianity's "space" among different ideologies and political conflicts;
- The paradox of a faith with vitality in contexts of extreme poverty and danger of annihilation due to the impact of global market forces.

Just as there are challenges, there are also promises:

- New co-agents/theologians in the drama of faith and mission have appeared: women, the poor, youth, immigrants;
- A refreshing language is developing about God in daily life experience, which is translated by the people to the congregations' common practices and celebrations;
- A disorienting experience for the assumed center (the West) opens the opportunity to rediscover the gospel afresh;
- A rediscovering of the Gospel for the body of Christ.

And with these challenges and promises, opportunities for mission abound:

- The transformation of an ethnic/religious-centered mentality to an intercultural/interreligious global Christian spirituality (mission happens in weblike configuration, rather than in a one-way-street or a partnership mentality);
- The search for a "new way of being missionary": both receiving from, transmitting to, and returning from to raise the difficult questions and issues of our own faith and discipleship in intercultural, interreligious, and environmental missional experiences;
- The opportunity for solidarity given the new map's paradox;
- The unique experience of entering the mission matrix, the cross-cultural diffusion experience in our own context, rather than reifying our inherited Christianity, which will continue to decline in its isolation-and-preservation mode.

The confusion in our short mission trip is an important sign of the changing demographics and the consequent missiological challenges and opportunities. We have entered an intercultural encounter. Both Christian communities become transmitters and receptors of God's grace and gifts found in the intersection and interaction of this encounter. Inherent to this encounter are economic, social, cultural, and religious differences, asymmetries, and assumptions of who *we* and *they* are. Yet, it is through these differences, asymmetries, and assumptions that both Christian communities can experience the serial movement of the Christian religion, its cross-cultural lifeblood, and its promising future. The common statement, "I received more than what I gave," is an entry point for the discovery of the Christian faith's vitality in the Third World and an invitation to renew our fragile, captive faith.

31

Mongrels, Outlaws, and Sodbusters

Serene Jones

These three words may sound odd as the title of a theological reflection piece on what it means to be Disciples, especially one written by a professor of systematic theology. However, they capture the theological dispositions that marked the terrain of faith in my youth and the landscape of faith I continue to inhabit as an adult. Being a relatively new church, a frontier-oriented movement, we were taught, almost unconsciously, to view the life of faith as if it were the "wild west"—a space for pioneering, rugged, and hardworking hope. In such a context, I learned what it meant to be a "theological mongrel," an "ecclesial outlaw," and a "moral sodbuster," and, in turn, to value both the limits and possibilities of such identities.

With respect to my mongrel identity, I was raised to be proud of our unique "mixed-race" heritage in the theological traditions of North America. As I was always told, we are "part this, part that, and part just about everything else." Our congregations have long been infused with a strong dose of Presbyterian Calvinism. In my youth this meant hearing sermons on the sovereignty of God, the integrity of an intellectually informed faith, and the importance of upholding the Protestant public good. Intermixed with this was an equally strong dose of Baptist polity that would have made Calvin weep. We distrusted authority and balked, at an institutional level, at anything that even smelled slightly like ecclesial submission. Similarly, we had a robust free church understanding of communion and baptism, which translated into a folksy, unstructured, and very non-Calvinist view of what it means to believe. To this day, when I think of Disciples worship, instead of seeing Geneva black-robed ministers, my mind recalls sharing communion around a campfire with a college-age counselor presiding. These influences created a lively sense of being a "primitive church" where Jesus was vividly present and the creeds were anathema. This view opened us to all manner of influences—a church of bread-and-butter pluralism from the start.

This insistence on hybridity was not without its costs, however. Our doctrinal hodgepodgeness caused considerable confusion about who we really were. Were we biblical inerrantists? Maybe. Were we universalists? Well, sometimes. Were we music lovers or piano players? Not quite, but yes. These were the answers I heard my church leaders give to some of the most important theological topics of the day—answers as indecisive as they were muddled. Especially to a young girl trying to figure out God in the midst of a world where God's presence is far from obvious, this willy-nilly view of truth claims and creedal statements was often debilitating. Even today you can see it manifest in the difficulty Disciples have articulating what they believe. We know we believe it, but what that "it" is, we can't quite say. I fear this failure of communication is grounded not just in pristine doctrinal humility, as we like to believe, but sometimes in plain old theological vacuousness. Learning to tell the difference between openness and confused rootlessness is, I believe, one of the most important growing edges of our faith-work together.

In addition to this sense of our collective "mongrelity," I was raised with an equally strong (although seldom admitted) sense of the church as an outlaw's enclave, a den of thieves, a wild-west gang of bandits. We weren't just any old outlaws, however. We were righteous ones—the Robin Hoods of American Protestantism, a Pretty Boy Floyd version of high plains piety. The adventure story undergirding this renegade identity went something like this: we are a *faithful, little, free church* fighting valiantly to get an *unfaithful, bigger, rule-bound church* to return to the original state of its founding piety, a cause that we pursued by robbing the church of its golden pretensions, its creeds, its rituals, its clerical arrogance, and then sharing the wealth of true faith with the masses. Running through this rather clichéd but nonetheless powerful theological narrative was the belief that we were simultaneously bad guys—people living outside the bounds of normal order and intent upon messing it up—and the true church, the only people who understood that the sole place one finds Christ is in the primitive hinterland of faith's territorial manifestations.

In other words we were a church precisely by not being bound by doctrinal rules that typically define church. We were right, precisely because we were willingly wrong; we lived the truth by breaking the law. This core antinomian fantasy of ours often gets lost in contemporary assessments of our legacy, particularly when we engage in conversations about who we are as Disciples and start searching for answers. It gets lost precisely because we are, in part, a people who "aren't." Our faith is as skeptical as it is transgressive, as disjunctive as it is wily.

This outlaw mentality also manifests itself in other dimensions of our church life. As a youth, I had the not-so-unusual experience of belonging to Disciples congregations that were very liberal, both politically and socially—churches proud of the outlaw status their progressive theology afforded them, particularly when compared with the more conservative Baptist churches down the road. Like so many, I discovered "sex, drugs, and rock and roll" in my church's young adult groups, along with protest marches, feminism, and the development of a social conscience. This had a significant effect on my understanding of what a church, at its faithful best, is called to be. It involves, first, a profound appreciation for the *sin* of the church. Wherever we Disciples gathered, be it in Sunday school, around a campfire, on a bus, or in regular old pews, we were always complaining about the horrible things Christians had done in history—crusades, witch burning, slavery, the Holocaust, patriarchy. It wasn't just other Christians, either. We were hard on ourselves—on our consumerism, on our failure to address racism, and on our lack of love for billions of less fortunate souls. In other words, we were as intent on robbing ourselves of our own pretensions as we were in disabusing others of their false gods. We were restless and righteous, at one and the same time.

This unease was always tempered, however, with a vision of collective existence that was deeply compassionate; this outlaw church was a safe space. I was taught to expect that when we gathered, in our midst justice would matter, people would be loved and cared for, the spirit would move, and the world would shimmer with the miraculous power of God's peace and hope. This experience of "Disciplesdom" was strengthened in my adult life by my travels in the 1980s to India and the Philippines, where I found Disciples folks involved in living struggles for justice and liberation on behalf of the marginalized, people who out of faith were actively plotting and organizing to resist the harms perpetrated by the state, by caste, and by church. Here the notion of being an "outlaw" community took on even greater significance, as I realized, at levels my homespun, Oklahoma Disciples congregation had not prepared me for, that the cost of their resistance was not just nose-snubbing from the Baptists; it was life itself.

To this picture of my mongrel, outlawish Disciples heritage, let me now add the third image, a portrait of ourselves as "sodbusters." The founders of this movement lived in wagon trains and outpost settlements, and they spent their lives trying desperately to bring order to a world they perceived as unsettled and to turn uncultivated land into wheat-bearing fields. Most of them were very poor, and the derogatory term used to describe them and their often futile efforts at tilling was the phrase I use here: we were "sodbusters," the wretched of the earth. Read in a slightly more positive light, we were from the beginning a people obsessed with order, a disposition metaphorically rooted in our survivalist need to set down plough lines and delineate field borders. As farmers, our lives depended not only on our ability to be outlaws (to break constraining rules) but also on our capacity to dig into the ground we settled on, to break open its hard soil, and through the exertion of our sweat to impose law on it, to impress form on formlessness.

In the '60s and '70s, I experienced this dynamic in the lessons I learned at church and at home about ethical responsibility, lessons that didn't always jive with the renegade and mongrel story, but were pounded into my generation's heart and head nonetheless. In places ranging from Sunday school to church camp to my family's own nightly dinner table, I was given a picture of the world in which good and bad, true and false, right and wrong were set up as obvious opposites. Our choice, the church taught us, was to choose the correct path—something that we were assured would be hard to do, but we must do it nonetheless. Nothing short of the history of humankind hung in the sway of our decisions and actions. In this sodbusting worldview, we were called to be ever vigilant lest we succumb to the seductive forces of oppression and violence. While this was never presented as a matter of moral prudishness—it was a liberal vision after all, a vision of peace and justice—running through it was still a strong assertion that truth was, well, just that: the truth. The good was the good. And when it came to doing right or wrong, our choice should be clear. Be model liberal, justice-loving selves!

In progressive church communities such as mine, this lesson helped us internally make sense of our own implication—as WASPs—in the Holocaust and the nightmares of racial oppression in the South. Because of it, we labored under a profound (and well-earned) sense of collective and individual guilt. The doctrine of original sin echoed loudly in my father's voice: any one of us could have been Hitler or a member of the Klan. God, in this world, was the righteous judge who knew the evil lurking within our culture as well as in our innermost selves, and who constantly demanded that we repent and try harder to live faithfully, to seek truth, and to struggle more valiantly for justice. Still, there is something dynamic about being both guilty and free and about being defined by a tradition that resists definitions, a bounded community that hates boundaries.

When I consider this dynamic in the context of my more recent engagement with feminist thought, I am struck by the extent to which my feminist sensibilities continue to be marked, in good sodbusting fashion, by strong normative claims. I find myself constantly searching for a set of principles, albeit shifting ones, through which to make judgments about the character of human flourishing. My commitment to feminist "plough lines and field borders" perhaps explains my frustration with poststructuralist thought's own antinomianism and my rather un-postmodern obsession with ethical order.

This high-handed confidence in moral order and human frailty is not without its downside, however. For me, its limits manifest in the complexity of the dual vision the church gave me—and many of my generation—of agency and possibility. In the church of my formative years, we were not yet sensitive to the insidious presence of gender oppression—most particularly the ways in which women are socialized not to trust their own instincts or thinking and to feel overly responsible for other people's suffering and the need to "fix things." Liberal guilt and sexist oppression, in this context, were a stifling combination. In the space of this communal imagination, I emerged as a young woman of faith who had a very burdened sense of the world's brokenness (people do really bad things that God doesn't like), a very high sense of social responsibility (God calls us to name what is wrong and to fight against these bad things), and, ironically, a profound lack of trust in myself as someone capable of either discerning or resisting the very ills that I am called to fix. Rather than creating a self-critical soldier of righteousness, this church crafted in me a disposition in which the calling was high but the grace needed to support it was virtually nonexistent. The Law as whip was alive and well, but the Law as grace remained silent and buried.

Therefore much of the work that captivates me lies in the realm of grace and the particular experiences of persons whose agency and hope have been fractured by violence—another version of the wretched of the earth, I suppose. My hope is to bring understanding and enlightenment to those who suffer under the regime of their own complicated and difficult narratives—a group that includes, I fear, the wide swath of humanity. What does this grace look like to Disciples? Here too our status as theological outlaws may help us to provide an answer—or perhaps answers—to those people for whom theologically "correct" descriptions hold no healing or redemptive power because their own experiences have left them feeling like outcasts as well. This common ground, on the rugged, untilled frontier of the church, may hold the most promising seeds of compassion. And that may be just the grace we're looking for.

Celebrating our status as mutts and renegades is thus our way of avoiding the potential failings of theological correctness. This positive view of doctrinal hybridity is not just an interesting cultural feature of my Disciples heritage; it is grounded in an important theological judgment about doctrine and faith: the human drive to codify truth—to set it in stone and then impose its pronouncements on others—can be death dealing, not life giving, and as such runs counter to the deepest drive of the gospel, a drive toward fullness of life and the freedom grace engenders. This drive can serve us well in a global culture where nothing is pure, where everything is hybrid, and where traditions are always being poured together to stir up new creations. It's a world in which Disciples have something distinctive to offer, that is, if we find within us the grace we need for such work. What is needed? Both plough lines and robbers' caves, both clear-headed prophets and impure mongrel souls, both saints and sinners, the fractured and the graced, who stumble along behind that redeeming, mutt-like, thief-crucified, lawgiver of grace, Jesus Christ.

Notes

Introduction

[1]Amartya Sen, *Identity and Violence: The Illusion of Destiny* (New York: W.W. Norton, 2006), 19.

Chapter 1: Theology as Intercultural Conversation in an Age of Globalization

[1]Larry Rasmussen identifies three waves of economic globalization: colonialization, development, and post-1989 free-trade capitalism. See Larry Rasmussen, "'Give Us Word of the Humankind We Left to Thee': Globalization and its Wake," *Episcopal Divinity School Occasional Paper* 4 (August 1999): 1–20. Rebecca Todd Peters discusses theories of globalization in four categories: neoliberal globalization, developmental globalization, environmental globalization, and postcolonial globalization. See Rebecca Todd Peters, *The Ethics of Globalization: Assessing the Postmodern Landscape* (London and New York: T&T Clark International, 2004). Cf. Charles Taylor, "Defining Globalization," *Ecumenism* 149 (March 2003): 6–13; Cynthia Moe-Lobeda, *Healing a Broken World: Globalization and God* (Minneapolis: Fortress Press, 2002); Anthony Giddens, *Runaway World: How Globalization Is Reshaping Our Lives* (London: Routledge, 2002); Richard Falk, *Predatory Globalization: A Critique* (Cambridge: Polity Press, 1999).

[2]E.g., Niall Ferguson, *Colossus: The Rise and Fall of the American Empire* (New York: Penguin, 2005); *Empire: The Rise and Demise of the British World Order and the Lessons for Global Power* (New York: Basic Books, 2003).

[3]E.g., Michael Hardt and Antonio Negri, *Empire* (Cambridge, Mass.: Harvard University Press, 2000).

[4]By "historic Protestant churches" we refer to churches that have traditionally been referred to as mainline Protestant churches. By "evangelical" we refer to those denominations that emerged from fundamentalism in the post-World War II period that would grow to include Pentecostal and Charismatic denominations that flourished in the 1960s and 1970s.

[5]Richard Falk, *Predatory Globalization: A Critique* (Cambridge: Polity Press, 1999).

[6]Hardt and Negri, *Empire; idem, Multitude* (New York: Polity Press, 2004).

[7]Ada María Isai-Díaz, "La Habana—The City that Inhabits Me," in *Spirit in the Cities: Searching for Soul in the Urban Landscape*, ed. Kathryn Tanner (Minneapolis: Fortress Press, 2004), 104–5.

[8]Saskia Sassen, *Globalization and Its Discontents* (New York: The New Press, 1998), xx.

[9]Andrew Walls, *The Cross-Cultural Process in Christian History* (Maryknoll, N.Y.: Orbis Books, 2002); Dale T. Irvin, *Christian Histories, Christian Traditioning: Rendering Accounts* (Maryknoll, N.Y.: Orbis Books, 1998); Dale T. Irvin and Scott W. Sunquist, *History of the World Christian Movement, vol. 1: Earliest Christianity to 1453* (Maryknoll, N.Y.: Orbis Books, 2001). For an early classic in the field of world Christianity see Henry Van Dusen, *World Christianity: Yesterday, Today, Tomorrow* (New York and Nashville: Abingdon-Cokesbury Press, 1947).

[10]Jenny Sharp, "Is the United States Postcolonial? Transnationalism, Immigration and Race," in *Post-Colonial America*, ed. R. C. King (Urbana: University of Illinois Press, 2000), 103–21.

[11]Jacques Derrida, "Différance," in *Margins of Philosophy*, trans. Alan Bass (Chicago: University of Chicago Press, 1982) 7–8.

[12]Gayatri Chakravorty Spivak, "Can the Subaltern Speak?" in *Colonial Discourse and Postcolonial Theory: A Reader*, ed. Patrick Williams and Laura Chrisman (New York: Harverster Wheatsheaf, 1993), 66–111.

[13]Ibid., 78.

[14]Edward W. Said, *Orientalism* (New York: Vintage, 1979).

[15]Gayatri Chakravorty Spivak, *A Critique of Postcolonial Reason: Toward a History of the Vanishing Present* (Cambridge, Mass.: Harvard University Press, 1999), 332.

[16]For a postcolonial theological critique of Asian essentialism, see Namsoon Kang, "Who/What Is Asian?: A Postcolonial Theological Reading of Orientalism and Neo-Orientalism," in *Postcolonial Theologies. Divinity, Hybridity, and Empire,* ed. Catherine Keller, Michael Nausner, Mayra Rivera (St. Louis: Chalice Press, 2004).

[17]Gayatri Chakravorty Spivak, "Bonding in Difference, interview with Alfred Arteaga (1993–1994)" in *The Spivak Reader,* ed. Donna Landry and Gerald MacLean (New York: Routledge, 1996), 20.

[18]Spivak, *A Critique of Postcolonial Reason,* 334.

[19]Kwok Pui-lan, "Feminist Theology as Intercultural Discourse," in *The Cambridge Companion to Feminist Theology,* ed. Susan Frank Parsons (Cambridge: Cambridge University Press, 2002), 23–39.

[20]David Theo Goldberg, *Racist Culture* (Cambridge: Blackwell, 1993), 29.

[21]Renato Rosaldo, *Culture and Truth: The Remaking of Social Analysis* (Boston: Beacon Press, 1993).

[22]Rita Nakashima Brock, "Interstitial Integrity: Reflections toward an Asian American Women's Theology," in *Introduction to Christian Theology: Contemporary North American Perspectives,* ed. Roger A. Badham (Louisville: Westminster John Knox Press, 1998).

[23]Kwok Pui-lan, "Feminist Theology as Intercultural Discourse," in *The Cambridge Companion to Feminist Theology,* ed. Susan Frank Parsons (Cambridge: Cambridge University Press, 2002), 21, 23–39.

[24]Robert J. Schreiter, *Constructing Local Theologies* (Maryknoll, N.Y.: Orbis Books, 1985), 20.

[25]Rebecca Parker and Rita Nakashima Brock present an important alternative history of American Christianity from a postcolonial perspective, *Saving Paradise: How Christianity Traded Love of This World for Crucifixion and Empire* (Boston: Beacon Press, 2008).

[26]This understanding of prophecy is shaped by Walter Brueggemann's *The Prophetic Imagination,* 2d ed. (Minneapolis: Fortress Press, 2001).

[27]E.g., Catherine Keller, Michael Nausner, and Mayra Rivera, eds., *Postcolonial Theologies: Divinity and Empire* (St. Louis: Chalice Press, 2004); Kwok Pui-lan, *Postcolonial Imagination and Feminist Theology* (Louisville: Westminster John Knox Press, 2005); Laura E. Donaldson and Kwok Pui-lan, eds., *Postcolonialism, Feminism, and Religious Discourse* (New York: Routledge, 2002).

[28]On theology's multiple context(s), see Robert J. Schreiter, *Constructing Local Theologies* (Maryknoll, N.Y.: Orbis Books, 1985).

Chapter 2: Disciples Theology in the Twenty-first Century

[1]Mark G. Toulouse, *Joined in Discipleship: The Shaping of Contemporary Disciples Identity,* 2d ed. (St. Louis: Chalice Press, 1997).

[2]*The Design for the Christian Church (Disciples of Christ),* preamble.

[3]Harold E. Fey, "The Church in 1999," *World Call* (January 1969): 28–29.

[4]E.g., Rita Nakashima Brock, Claudia Camp, and Serene Jones, eds., *Setting the Table: Women in Theological Conversation* (St. Louis: Chalice Press, 1995); cf. Jane McAvoy, ed., *Kitchen Talk* (St. Louis: Chalice Press, 2003).

[5]Brock, Camp, and Jones, *Setting the Table.* See Stephen V. Sprinkle's discussion of table-talk as a Disciples theological method in *Disciples and Theology: Understanding the Faith of a People in Covenant* (St. Louis: Chalice Press, 1999), 122–33.

[6]A good summary of these five themes can be found in Toulouse, *Joined in Discipleship.* Toulouse expounds three themes identified by Ronald E. Osborn, adding a fourth principle, the *eschatological* principle. The *mission* theme is one of eight points of Disciples theology that Toulouse argues express "the theological identity and integrity of the Disciples of Christ" (273). Ronald E. Osborn, "The Light of Scripture: The Bible as Interpreted by Disciples," in his book *The Faith We Affirm: Basic Beliefs of Disciples of Christ* (St. Louis: Bethany Press, 1983), 11–24.

[7]Thomas Campbell, *Declaration and Address* (Pittsburgh: Record Publishing Company, Centennial Edition, 1909), 3.

[8]For some of the lines of critique of the restoration principle during restructure, see Ralph G. Wilburn, "A Critique of the Restoration Principle: Its Place in Contemporary Life and Thought," in *The Reformation of Tradition*, ed. Ronald E. Osborn, Vol. 1 of The Renewal of Church: The Panel of Scholars Report, gen. ed. W.B. Blackemore (St. Louis: Bethany Press, 1963), 215–53; cf. T. J. Liggett, "Why Disciples Chose Unity," *Mid-Stream* 2 (April 1980): 227–33. The controversies surrounding the restoration principle were inevitable among Disciples, especially related to the global implications of the gospel reflected in debates about world mission. Critique of the restoration of the New Testament church as a missiological raison d'être is present in the work Archiblad McLean, who served as secretary of the Foreign Christian Missionary Society from 1882 until it became part of the United Christian Missionary Society in 1919. Cf. William J. Nottingham, *Origin and Legacy of the Common Global Ministries Board*, College of Missions Reprint, 2004, 38–39. See Mark Toulouse's argument for an explicit redefinition of restorationism in terms of apostolic faith in his chapter in *Joined in Discipleship*, 65–70.

[9]The Commission's study of issues of ecclesiology forwarded to the General Assembly, along with additional material, is collected in *The Church for Disciples of Christ, Seeking to Be Truly Church Today: A Report and Resource by the Commission on Theology, Council of Christian Unity*, ed. Paul A. Crow Jr. and James O. Duke (St. Louis: published for Council on Christian Unity by Christian Board of Publication, 1998); see also the Commission's reports, "Report of the Commission on Theology, Concerning Salvation in Jesus Christ," in *Business Docket and Program*, General Assembly of the Christian Church (Disciples of Christ), Indianapolis, Indiana, 28 July—2 August 1989, 337–43, reprinted in *Mid-Stream* 28, no. 4 (October 1989): 421–33; "Progress Report of the Theology Commission: On Relations Between Jews and Christians," in *Business Docket and Program*, General Assembly of the Christian Church (Disciples of Christ), 25–30 October 1991, 304–7; and "Report of the Theology Commission: A Statement on Relations Between Jews and Christians," in *Business Docket and Program*, General Assembly of the Christian Church (Disciples of Christ), 15–20 July 1993, 366–69.

[10]Robert K. Welsh, "A Framework for the Future," *Mid-Stream* 38, no. 4 (1999): 24.

[11]It has been employed in ecumenical dialogues in both bilateral and multilateral contexts to describe the unity that is sought among all Christian communions (e.g., *Santiago de Compostela* 1993). Thomas F. Best and Günther Gassmann, eds., *On the Way to Fuller Koinonia: Santiago de Compostela 1993: Official Report of the Fifth World Conference on Faith and Order*, Faith and Order Paper 166 (Geneva: World Council of Churches, 1994).

[12]In addition to these Faith and Order dialogues on Ecclesiology and Ethics, two other factors influenced the ecumenical push toward global justice: a second generation of church leaders after Consultation on Church Union (COCU) who no longer cared about church union for administrative and financial reasons, in addition to these growing theological concerns and the world's agenda for global justice, which brought forth liberation theology. The Geneva Church and Society Conference of 1966 launched this change within the WCC, and Martin Luther King Jr. was its symbol of a Christian prophet for global peace and justice.

[13]E.g., Hans Urs von Balthasar, "Communio—A Programme," *International Catholic Review* 1, no. 1 (1972): 3–12; *The Church as Communion: Lutheran Contributions to Ecclesiology*, ed. Heinrich Holze (Geneva: Lutheran World Federation Documentation, 42/1997); John Zizioulas, *Being as Communion* (Crestwood, N.Y.: St. Vladimir's Seminary Press, 1985); Miroslav Volf, *After Our Likeness: The Church as the Image of the Trinity* (Grand Rapids: Eerdmans, 1998).

[14]For a summary of the biblical usages of *koinonia*, see John Reumann, "Koinonia in Scripture: A Survey of Biblical Texts," in *On the Way to Fuller Koinonia*, ed. Best and Gassmann, 38–69.

[15]These documents demonstrate Faith and Order's work on unity precisely includes work also on the social and cultural sources of ecclesial division.

[16]*Church and World: The Unity of the Church and the Renewal of the Human Community*, Faith and Order Paper No. 151 (Geneva: WCC Publications, 1990); "*Costly Unity*, a World Council of Churches consultation on Koinonia and Justice, Peace and the Integrity of Creation. Jointly sponsored by Unit I (Unity and Renewal) and Unit III (Justice, Peace, and Creation) of the WCC. Rønde, Denmark, February 24–28, 1993" in *Koinonia and Justice*,

Peace, and Creation: Costly Unity, ed. Thomas F. Best and Wesley Granberg-Michaelson (Geneva: World Council of Churches, 1993), 83-104.

[17]*Costly Unity,* sec. 18, 91.

[18]Ronald E. Osborn called the Disciples' attention to the "liberty" of biblical interpretation as a third principle (in addition to the ecumenical and restoration principles) in Ronald E. Osborn, *Experiment in Liberty: The Ideal of Freedom in the Experience of the Disciples of Christ* (St. Louis: Bethany Press, 1978) 12–13; see also Larry D. Bouchard, "THEOLOGY—The Interpretation Principle: A Foundational Theme of Disciples Theology," in *Interpreting Disciples: Practical Theology in the Disciples of Christ,* ed. L. Dale Richesin and Larry D. Bouchard (Fort Worth: Texas Christian University Press, 1987), 1–26.

[19]Alexander Campbell, *The Millennial Harbinger* (1886), 503; emphasis original. Cf. William J. Nottingham, "Alexander Campbell and Global Ministry," *DISCIPLIANA* (Summer 1989).

[20]For a description of this shift in Disciples missiology, see Toulouse, "From Missions to Mission," in *Joined in Discipleship,* 189–218. Cf. Paul Crow Jr., *Christian Unity: Matrix for Mission* (New York: Friendship Press, 1982) 43–76.

[21]For a more detailed explanation of this paradigm, see William J. Nottingham, "Mission as Ecclesiology: Christian Identity and the Burden of Denominationalism," in *The Vision of Christian Unity: Essays in Honor of Paul A. Crow, Jr.,* ed. Thomas F. Best and Theodore J. Nottingham (Indianapolis: Oikoumene Publications, 1997), 133–48.

[22]The *misso Dei* marked a clear shift from "Church-centric missionary thinking" to "world-centric missionary thinking." World Mission began to be thought of from the perspective of the world, instead of the church, in the 1950s and 1960s, precisely during the period that the world witnessed movements of national freedom. J.C. Hoekendijk, *The Church Inside Out,* ed. L.A. Hoedemaker and Pieter Tijmes; trans. Isaac C. Rottenberg (Philadelphia: The Westminister Press, 1966).

[23]*General Principles and Policies* (Indianapolis: Division of Overseas Ministries, 1981), 22, 35. This policy statement on mission was issued under the leadership of Robert A. Thomas in the Division of Overseas Mission.

[24]Mark Toulouse is a notable exception to this tendency. See his attempt to recover the eschatological principle for contemporary Disciples, *Joined in Discipleship,* 101–36.

[25]From an e-facsimile of vol. 1, 1830 (Reprint © College Press, Joplin, Missouri, 1976.)

[26]William J. Nottingham, *Origin and Legacy of the Common Global Ministries Board: A History of the Christian Church (Disciples of Christ) in World Mission* (Indianapolis: College of Missions Reprint, 2004), 15–17; cf. 34–36.

[27]D. Newell Williams, *Barton Stone: A Spiritual Biography* (St. Louis: Chalice Press, 2000), 213–29.

[28]Dwight E. Stevenson, *Walter Scott: Voice of the Golden Oracle* (St. Louis: CBP, 1946), 54–55, 114.

[29]Nottingham, *Origin and Legacy,* 33–36; Archibald McLean, *The Primacy of the Missionary and Other Addresses* (St. Louis: CBP, 1920), 345.

[30]See Mark G. Toulouse, "Are Disciples Millennial Harbingers?" *The Disciple* 136 (January 1998): 12–14.

[31]*The Millennial Harbinger* (1841): 9.

[32]Homi K. Bhabha, *The Location of Culture* (London and New York City: Routledge, 1994), 161.

Chapter 3: Theology and the Bible

[1]Larry D. Bouchard, "Theology—The Interpretation Principle: A Foundation Theme of Disciples Theology," in *Interpreting Disciples: Practical Theology in the Disciples of Christ,* ed. L. Dale Richesin and Larry D. Bouchard (Fort Worth: Texas Christian University Press, 1987), 8.

[2]Ronald E. Osborn, *The Faith We Affirm: Basic Beliefs of Disciples of Christ* (St. Louis: Bethany Press, 1983), 14.

[3]Ibid., 20.

[4]Barton W. Stone, "A Compendious View of the Gospel," in *The Biography of Elder Barton Warren Stone, written by himself: With Additions and Reflections*, ed. John Rogers (Cincinnati: J.A. and U. James, 1847), 191–221; Lowell K. Handy, "Where the Scriptures Speak, We Quarrel: Biblical Approaches in the Disciples Founders," in *Interpreting Disciples*, 76.

[5]Thomas Campbell, *Declaration and Address* (Pittsburgh: Record Publishing Company, Centennial Edition, 1909), 16.

[6]Thomas Campbell, "On Personal and Family Devotion," *The Millennial Harbinger*, n.s., 3 (1839): 394.

[7]Osborn, *The Faith We Affirm*, 14.

[8]See, Lowell K. Handy, "Where the Scriptures Speak, We Quarrel," in *Interpreting Disciples*, 85–86.

[9]Alexander Campbell, *The Christian System in Reference to the Union of Christian and a Restoration of Primitive Christianity as Plead in the Current Reformation* (Cincinnati: Bosworth, Chase, & Hall, 1839), 18.

[10]Walter Scott, *The Messiahship or Great Demonstration, written for the union of Christians, on Christian principles as plead for in the current Reformation* (Cincinnati: Bosworth, Chase, & Hall Publishers, n.d.), 10.

[11]For the details of these generations' history, see M. Eugene Boring, *Disciples and the Bible: A History of Disciples Biblical Interpretation in North America* (St. Louis: Chalice Press, 1997).

[12]Geunhee Yu, *A Handbook for Korean-American Disciples in the Christian Church (Disciples of Christ)* (Danvers, Mass.: Christian Board of Publication, 2005), 18.

[13]Musa W. Dube, *Postcolonial Feminist Interpretation of the Bible* (St. Louis: Chalice Press, 2000), 20.

[14]R. Alan Culpepper, "The Gospel of Luke," in *The New Interpreter's Bible*, Volume 9, (Nashville: Abingdon Press, 1995), 229.

[15]Gayatri Chakravorty Spivak, "Can the Subaltern Speak?" in *Marxism and the Interpretation of Culture*, ed. Cary Nelson and Lawrence Grossberg (Urbana: University of Illinois Press, 1988).

[16]See Ranajit Guha, ed., *Subaltern Studies 1: Writings on South Asian History and Society* (Delhi: Oxford University Press, 1982).

[17]John R. Donahue, S.J., "Who Is My Enemy? The Parable of the Good Samarian and the Love of Enemies," in *The Love of Enemy and Nonretaliation in the New Testament*, ed. Willard M. Swartley (Louisville: Westminster/John Knox Press, 1992), 139.

[18]Ibid., 140.

[19]Benita Parry, "Problems in Current Theories of Colonial Discourse," *Oxford Literary Review 9*, nos. 1 and 2 (1987): 27–58.

[20]Bernardo M. Ferdman and Plácida I. Gallegos, "Racial Identity Development and Latinos in the United States," in *New Perspectives on Racial Identity Development: A Theoretical and Practical Anthology*, ed. Charmaine L. Wijeyesinghe and Bailey W. Jackson III (New York: New York University Press, 2001), 36–37.

[21]Homi K. Bhabha, "Signs Taken from Wonders: Questions of Ambivalence and Authority Under a Tree Outside Delhi, May 1817," *Critical Inquiry* 12, no. 1 (1985): 144–65.

[22]In order to understand in-betweeness, see Jung Young Lee, *Marginality: The Key to Multicultural Theology* (Minneapolis: Fortress Press, 1995), 29–47.

[23]Timothy Tseng, "Beyond Orientalism and Assimilation," in *Realizing the America of Our Hearts: Theological Voices of Asian Americans*, ed. Fumitaka Matsuoka and Eleazar S. Fernandez (St. Louis: Chalice Press, 2003), 61.

[24]Charles Taylor, "The Politics of Recognition," in *Multiculturalism*, ed. Amy Gutmann (Princeton, N.J.: Princeton University Press, 1994), 33.

[25]Lee, *Marginality*, 63–65.

[26]Suh Nam-dong was formerly Professor of Systematic Theology at Yonsei University (Seoul, Korea) and Director of Institute for Mission-Education (Seoul, Korea). He was one of the best *minjung* theologians who embraced *minjung* theological understandings in conjunction with Korean socio-political colonial history and indigenous culture.

[27]See NCC Theological Committee, ed., *Minjung and Korean Theology* (Seoul, Korea: Korean Theology Center, 1982), 344.

[28]Bailey W. Jackson, "Black Identity Development: Further Analysis and Elaboration," in *New Perspectives on Racial Identity Development*, 18–26.

[29]Ibid., 18–26.

[30]Michel Foucault, *Power/Knowledge: Selected Interviews and Other Writings 1972–1977*, trans. Colin Gordon et al., ed. Colin Gordon (New York: Pantheon, 1980), 49–50.

[31]Susanne Scholz, "'Tandoori Reindeer' and the Limitations of Historical Criticism," in *Her Master's Tools?: Feminist and Postcolonial Engagements of Historical-Critical Discourse*, ed. Caroline Vander Stchele and Todd Penner, Society of Biblical Literature no. 9 (Atlanta: Society of Biblical Literature, 2006), 63.

Chapter 4: Theology and Tradition

[1]"Minutes of the Associate Synod of North America," entry for 26 May 1808, in William H. Hanna, *Thomas Campbell: Seceder and Christian Union Advocate* (Cincinnati: Standard Publishing Co., 1935), 79.

[2]Alexander Campbell, *Christian Baptist* 2, no. 2 (September 6, 1824): 14.

[3]See, for example, Alexander Campbell, *The Christian System in Reference to the Union of Christians and a Restoration of Primitive Christianity as Plead in the Current Reformation* (Cincinnati: Bosworth, Chase, & Hall, 1839), 110; cf. 122.

[4]See William Tabbernee, "Unfencing the Table: Creeds, Councils, Communion, and the Campbells," *Mid-Stream* 35, no. 4 (October 1996): 418–21.

[5]Thomas Campbell, *Declaration and Address of the Christian Association of Washington* (Washington, Pa.: Christian Association of Washington, 1809), 24–25 [postscript].

[6]See Alexander Campbell, *The Millennial Harbinger* (hereafter cited as *MH*) (1855): 74.

[7]See, for example, Alexander Campbell, *MH* (1845): 415–17; *MH* (1846): 216–25, 388–91.

[8]For example, Alexander Campbell, *MH* (1848): 181–82, 241–52.

[9]For example, Alexander Campbell, *The Christian System*, 347–48.

[10]For example, Alexander Campbell, *MH* (Extra No. 1) (1830): 1–60.

[11]For example, Alexander Campbell, *The Christian System*, 315, 318–19.

[12]See also William Tabbernee, "Alexander Campbell and the Apostolic Tradition," in *The Free Church and the Early Church: Bridging the Historical and Theological Divide*, ed. D. H. Williams (Grand Rapids, Mich.: Eerdmans, 2002), 163–80.

[13]In many languages, distinguishing the meaning of words by means of the use or non-use of capitals is either impossible or inappropriate.

[14]Thomas Campbell, *Declaration and Address*, 55.

[15]Alexander Campbell, *The Christian System*, 75.

[16]Ibid., 295.

[17]Ibid., 85, 294, 304–6.

[18]Robert Milligan, *An Exposition and Defense of the Scheme of Redemption: As It Is Revealed and Taught in the Holy Scriptures* (St. Louis: Christian Publishing Company, 1868).

[19]Herbert L. Willett, *Basic Truths of the Christian Faith* (Chicago: Christian Century Co., 1903).

[20]W. Barnett Blakemore, gen. ed., *The Renewal of the Church*, 3 vols. (St. Louis: Bethany Press, 1963).

[21]Ronald E. Osborn, *The Faith We Affirm: Basic Beliefs of Disciples of Christ* (St. Louis: Bethany Press, 1983).

[22]James O. Duke et al., eds., *The Church for Disciples of Christ: Seeking to Be Truly Church Today* (St. Louis: Christian Board of Publication, 1998).

[23]For further resources, see James O. Duke, "Scholarship in the Disciples Tradition," *Disciples Historical Digest* 1, no. 1 (1986): 5–40.

[24]This "Affirmation of Faith" is reprinted in the *Chalice Hymnal*, ed. Daniel B. Merrick (St. Louis: Chalice Press, 1995), 355 for use (as intended) in corporate worship.

[25]Similarly, as ecumenical enrichment is always a two-way process, members of other churches should be encouraged to ask the same question, and all of us should also ask, "How can our particular tradition enrich the tradition of other Christian communions?"

[26]Max Thurian, ed., *Churches Respond to BEM,* 6 vols. (Geneva: World Council of Churches, 1986–1988), 1:4.

[27]Faith and Order Commission, *Baptism, Eucharist and Ministry* (Geneva: World Council of Churches, 1982).

[28]See also William Tabbernee, "BEM and the Eucharist: A Case-Study in Ecumenical Hermeneutics," in *Interpreting Together: Essays in Hermeneutics,* ed. Peter Bouteneff and Dagmar Heller (Geneva: World Council of Churches, 2001), 19–46.

[29]See also William Tabbernee, "Sailing the Ecumenical Boat in the Twenty-First Century," *Call to Unity: Resourcing the Church for Ecumenical Ministry* 4 (July 2005): 1–14, especially 5–6.

Chapter 5: Theological Reasoning in a Pluralistic Context

[1]Amartya Sen, *Identity and Violence: The Illusion of Destiny* (New York: Norton, 2006), xv, 19, 23, 67.

[2]Robert Milligan, *Reason and Revelation: Or, The Province of Reason in Matters Pertaining to Divine Revelation Defined and Illustrated,* 8th ed. (St. Louis: Christian Publishing Company, 1889).

[3]Samuel C. Pearson, "Faith and Reason in Disciples Theology," in *Classic Themes of Disciples Theology: Rethinking the Traditional Affirmations of the Christian Church (Disciples of Christ),* ed. Kenneth Lawrence (Fort Worth: Texas Christian University Press, 1986), 101–29.

[4]H. Richard Niebuhr, *The Responsible Self: An Essay in Christian Moral Philosophy,* intro. James M. Gustafson (1963; reprint, San Francisco: Harper and Row, 1978), 56, 122.

[5]Ibid., 65, 161.

[6]Dwight E. Stevenson, *Walter Scott: The Voice of the Golden Oracle* (St. Louis: Christian Board of Publication, 1946); Walter Scott, *The Gospel Restored* (Cincinnati: O. H. Donogh, 1836), v–vii.

[7]Scott, *Gospel Restored,* 9.

[8]For examples of Scott's use of Milton, see *Gospel Restored,* 21, 29, 34, 53, 69.

[9]Niebuhr, *Responsible Self,* 85–86.

[10]Scott, *Gospel Restored,* 13.

[11]Ibid., 81–84.

[12]David Tracy, *Plurality and Ambiguity: Hermeneutics, Religion, Hope* (San Francisco: Harper and Row, 1987), 20.

[13]Sen, *Identity and Violence,* xii–xiii, 19.

[14]Ibid., 72.

Chapter 6: What Do We Learn from Experience?

[1]Jamaica Kincaid, *Among Flowers: A Walk in the Himalaya* (Washington, D.C.: National Geographic, 2005), 185–86.

[2]Frederick Douglass, *Narrative of the Life of Frederick Douglass, an American Slave* (Boston: Anti-slavery office, 1845).

[3]J. H. Garrison, "Lessons from Our Past Experience; Or, Helps and Hindrances," in *The Old Faith Restated: Being a Restatement, by Representative Men, of the Fundamental Truths and Essential Doctrines of Christianity as Held and Advocated by the Disciples of Christ in the Light of Experience and Biblical Research,* ed. J.H. Garrison (St. Louis: Christian Publishing Company, 1891): 421–56.

[4]See Martin Jay, *Songs of Experience: Modern American and European Variations on a Universal Theme* (Berkeley and Los Angeles: University of California Press, 2005) for a comprehensive overview, including the relationship of empiricism to later appeals to experience, for example, to "religious experience," and various deconstructions and reconstructions of experience in contemporary theory.

[5]Here "pragmatic" signals the emphasis on usefulness and expediency. Garrison extolled an emphasis on "ortho*praxy,* or right doing, as of greater value than ortho*doxy,* or right thinking; in discounting a faith that is purely sentimental, and insisting on a living faith that attests its vitality in good works." He elaborated: "This conception of Christianity harmonizes well with the modern tendency, so full of promise, to apply the

principles of the gospel to the social evils of our times, as the only adequate remedy for a disordered society, as they are of a disordered life" ("Lessons from Our Past Experience," 454). His approach shared features with the account of experience later developed by the Pragmatist school of thought.

[6]See the similar conviction in the work of Garrison's son, the University of Chicago historian of Christianity and dean of the Disciples Divinity House, Winfred Ernest Garrison. His 1934 book, *Intolerance* (New York: Round Table Press), written in the face of rising Nazi anti-Jewish persecution and the Ku Klux Klan's violent racism and anti-Catholicism, argued that ideas of God affect the development of toleration: "With a God who delivers doctrines, frames codes, and lays down explicit and immutable programs of action, there can be little hope of more than a tepid and prudential toleration by one group for others who hold a different view… With a God who is the giver of life and grace but who leaves all formulations of doctrine and laws of conduct to the wisdom and experience of men, there is opportunity for the development of toleration toward varieties of opinion and practice" (236).

[7]Others would later render accumulating learning as the *consensus fidelium* or "the mind of the Disciples of Christ." See Paul M. Blowers, "*Consensus Fidelium*," in *The Encyclopedia of the Stone-Campbell Movement*, ed. Douglas A. Foster, Paul M. Blowers, Anthony L. Dunnavant, and D. Newell Williams (Grand Rapids: Eerdmans, 2004), 235–35; see also W. B. Blakemore, "Reasonable, Empirical, Pragmatic: The Mind of the Disciples of Christ," in *The Renewal of the Church: The Panel of Scholars Reports*, vol. 1, *The Reformation of Tradition*, gen. ed. W. B. Blakemore (St. Louis: Christian Board of Publication, 1963), 161–83.

[8]Compare William James, *The Varieties of Religious Experience: A Study in Human Nature* [1902](New York: Collier, 1961). James's cast of "religious geniuses" included no Disciples of Christ founders or key figures—perhaps because they were suspicious of unique, ecstatic connections to the Divine and focused on making truth plain and accessible. However, James was not far from Garrison in favoring "the living act of perception" to the "speculations" of dogmatic and idealistic theologies, and in his idea that philosophy involves rendering perceptions useful in human life (see Lecture 18).

[9]Garrison, "Lessons from Our Past Experience," 439.

[10]Kincaid, *Among Flowers*, 166.

[11]See Kristine A. Culp, "'A World Split Open'? Experience and Feminist Theologies," in *The Experience of God: A Postmodern Response*, ed. Kevin Hart and Barbara Wall (New York: Fordham University Press, 2005), 47–64.

[12]Theodore D. Weld, *American Slavery as It Is: Testimony of a Thousand Witnesses* (New York: American Anti-Slavery Society, 1839; electronic ed., Chapel Hill: University of North Carolina, 2000), 7, accessed at docsouth.unc.edu/neh/weld/weld.html.

[13]Paul Ricoeur, "The Hermeneutics of Testimony," in Ricoeur, *Essays on Biblical Interpretation*, ed. Lewis S. Mudge (Philadelphia: Fortress Press, 1980), 123. Also Paul Ricoeur, *Memory, History, Forgetting*, trans. Kathleen Blamey and David Pellauer (Chicago: University of Chicago Press, 2004), 163–64.

[14]Ricoeur, "Hermeneutics of Testimony," 131.

[15]See Kristine A. Culp, "Always Reforming, Always Resisting," in *Feminist and Womanist Essays in Reformed Dogmatics*, ed. Amy Plantinga Pauw and Serene Jones (Louisville: Westminster John Knox Press, 2006), 152–68.

[16]Garrison, "Lessons from Our Past Experience," 424.

Chapter 7: Practicing Reconciliation

[1]See the discussion of theology as an intercultural conversation in chapter 1; see also Kwok Pui-lan, "Feminist Theology as Intercultural Discourse," in *The Cambridge Companion to Feminist Theology*, ed. Susan Frank Parsons (Cambridge: Cambridge University Press, 2002), 23–39.

[2]See Don S. Browning, *A Fundamental Practical Theology: Descriptive and Strategic Proposals* (Minneapolis: Fortress Press, 1991); For a concise summary of this approach to theology, see Don. S. Browning, "Toward a Fundamental and Strategic Practical Theology," in *Shifting Boundaries: Contextual Approaches to the Structure of Theological Education*, ed. Barbara G. Wheeler and Edward Farley (Louisville: Westminster/John Knox Press, 1991), 295–328.

[3]Daisy L. Machado, *Of Borders and Margins: Hispanic Disciples in Texas, 1888–1945* (New York: Oxford University Press, 2003).

[4]Ibid., 108–9.

[5]Fred Lawrence, "Gadamer, the Hermeneutic Revolution and Theology," in *The Cambridge Companion to Gadamer*, ed. by Robert J. Dostal (Cambridge: University of Cambridge, 2002), 167–200; 167.

[6]Ibid., 192.

[7]Hans-Georg Gadamer, *Truth and Method,* 2d rev. edition, trans. Joel Weinsheimer and Donald G. Marshall (New York: Continuum, 1999), xxi.

[8]Ibid., 491.

[9]Hans-Georg Gadamer, "Hermeneutics as Practical Philosophy," in *Reason in the Age of Science,* trans. Fred Lawrence (Cambridge: MIT, 1981), 88–112, 113–38.

[10]Gadamer, *Truth and Method,* 387.

[11]Ibid., 385.

[12]Ibid., 369–79.

[13]Hans-Georg Gadamer, *Philosophical Hermeneutics,* ed. and trans. David E. Linge (Berkley: University of California Press, 1976), 57.

[14]Hans-Georg Gadamer, "Reflections on My Philosophical Journey," in *The Philosophy of Hans-Georg Gadamer,* ed. Lewis Edwin Hahn (Chicago: Open Court, 1997), 55.

[15]Gadamer, *Truth And Method,* 361.

[16]Ibid., 301.

[17]Ibid., 397.

[18]Jacques Derrida, *Of Grammatology,* trans. Gayatri Chakravorty Spivak (Washington, D.C.: Johns Hopkins, 1976).

[19]Kathryn Tanner, *Theories of Culture: A New Agenda for Theology* (Minneapolis: Fortress Press, 1997), 152.

[20]Ibid., 135.

[21]Paul Ricoeur, "On Interpretation," *From Text to Action: Essays in Hermeneutics, II,* trans. Kathleen Blamey and John B. Thompson (Evanston, Ill.: Northwestern University, 1991), 17.

[22]Gadamer, *Philosophical Hermeneutics,* 55.

[23]Ibid., 427.

[24]Ibid., 57–58.

[25]George Lindbeck, *The Nature of Doctrine: Religion and Theology in a Postliberal Age* (Philadelphia: Westminster Press, 1984), 118.

[26]D. Newell Williams, "Future Prospects of the Christian Church: Disciples of Christ," in *A Case Study of Mainstream Protestantism: The Disciples' Relation to American Culture, 1880–1989,* ed. D. Newell Williams (Grand Rapids: Eerdmans, 1991), 564.

[27]Ibid.

[28]M.M. Bakhtin, "Author and Hero in Aesthetic Activity," in *Art and Answerability: Early Philosophical Essays by M.M. Bakhtin,* ed. Michael Holquist and Vadim Liapunov and trans. and annotated by Vadim Liapunov (Austin: University of Texas Press, 1990), 145.

[29]Jack D. Caputo, *More Radical Hermeneutics: On Not Knowing Who We Are* (Bloomington and Indianapolis: Indiana University Press, 2000), 194.

[30]Roy B. Zuck, "The Role of the Holy Spirit in Hermeneutics," *Bibliotheca Sacra* 141/562 (April–June 1984): 126.

[31]Kevin J. Vanhoozer, "The Spirit of Understanding: Special Revelation and General Hermeneutics," in *Disciplining Hermeneutics: Interpretation in Christian Perspective,* ed. Roger Lundin (Grand Rapids: Eerdmans, 1997), 155.

[32]Ibid., 149.

[33]Gadamer, *Truth and Method,* 360.

[34]Ibid., 372.

[35]Ibid., 463.

[36]Campbell, *The Christian System,* 8, as quoted by Stephen V. Sprinkle, *Disciples and Theology: Understanding the Faith of a People in Covenant* (St. Louis: Chalice Press, 1999), 6.

[37]Karl Barth, *Church Dogmatics,* IV/3, ed. G.W. Bromiley and T.F. Torrance; trans. G.W. Bromiley (Edinburgh: T&T Clark, 1962), 606.

[38]Emmanuel Levinas, *Totality and Infinity: An Essay on Exteriority* (The Hague: Martinus Nijhoff Publishers, 1979), 215.

[39]Alexander Campbell, *The Christian System,* as quoted by Lester McAlister, *An Alexander Campbell Reader* (St. Louis: CBP Press, 1988), 77.

Chapter 8: Singing the Trinity

[1]Athanasius, *On the Incarnation,* 9.

[2]Ibid., 54. "[B]ut being God, he later became man, that instead he might deify us" ("Orations Against the Arians, Book I," in *The Trinitarian Controversy,* trans. and ed. William G. Rusch, [Philadelphia: Fortress Press, 1980], 39 [102]). Also, "It is as one who is God that he took on flesh, and it is as one who was in flesh that he divinized the flesh" ("Oration Against the Arians, Book III," in *The Christological Controversy*, trans. and ed. Richard A. Norris, Jr. [Philadelphia: Fortress Press, 1980], 38 [97]).

[3]Different patristic writers express this axiom in different ways. See Irenaeus, *Against the Heresies,* 3.19.1, 4.33.4. It is expressed throughout Athanasius's writings. As an example, "But a creature could never be saved by a creature, any more than the creatures were created by a creature, if the Word was not Creator" (*Ad Adelphium,* 8. Cited in Khaled Anatolios, *Athanasius: The coherence of his thought* [London, New York: Routledge, 1998], 125).

[4]On Athanasius's understanding of Christ as mediator between the uncreated and the created, see Anatolios, *Anasthasius,* 109–16.

[5]Throughout this essay I will refer to the three forms of tradition that William Tabbernee develops in chapter 4: Tradition (apostolic tradition), tradition (particular ecclesial traditions), and ecumenical tradition (a late twentieth-, early twenty-first–century ecumenical theological consensus represented in documents like *Baptism, Eucharist and Ministry* [BEM]).

[6]Thomas Jefferson to Dr. Benjamin Waterhouse, 26 July 1822, in Paul Leicester Ford, ed., *The Writings of Thomas Jefferson* (New York and London, 1899), 12:219–22.

[7]Barton W. Stone, *Address to the Churches,* 50.

[8]Ibid., 51.

[9]Stone writes, "Revelation no where declares that there are three persons of the same substance in the *one only* God; and it is universally acknowledged to be above reason." Barton W. Stone, *Address to the Churches,* 50–58, esp. 52.

[10]Stone writes, "Equality implies plurality; and one is not equal to itself. If God be one infinite spirit without parts, and if there be but one infinite and true God, then there cannot be another equal to him. This is the language of consistent reason." Ibid., 77.

[11]Ibid., 54.

[12]Ibid., 66–67.

[13]Ibid., 74.

[14]To see Stone's extended defense of "the proposition of the pre-existence of the Son of God," ibid., 58–74, esp. 74.

[15]Ibid., 66.

[16]Ibid., 60.

[17]Ibid., 69, 72, 73.

[18]Ibid., 79.

[19]Ibid., 53.

[20]Ibid., 52.

[21]Alexander Campbell, *The Christian System in Reference to the Union of Christian and a Restoration of Primitive Christianity as Plead in the Current Reformation* (Cincinnati: Bosworth, Chase, & Hall, 1839), 19–20, esp. 20.

[22]Ibid., 20.

[23]Ibid., 25.

[24]Ibid., 21.

[25]Ibid., 21–22.

[26]Ibid., 25.

[27]Barton W. Stone, *Address to the Churches,* 65.

[28]"Christian Baptism, General Services of Worship," in *Chalice Worship,* ed. Colbert S. Cartwright and O. I. Cricket Harrison (St. Louis: Chalice Press, 1997), 26–31.

[29]Winfred E. Garrison, *Christian Unity and Disciples of Christ* (St. Louis: Bethany Press, 1955), 109.

[30]"Theological Basis of the Evangelical Alliance" (1846), article 3, as quoted by Garrison, *Christian Unity and Disciples of Christ,* 111.

[31]George Plattenburgh, "The Unity of the Church: How Broken, And the Creed-Basis on Which It Must Be Restored," in *The Old Faith Restated: Being a Restatement, by Representative Men, of the Fundamental Truths and Essential Doctrines of Christianity in Light of Experience and of Biblical Research,* ed. J.H. Garrison (St. Louis: Christian Publishing Company, 1891), 335.

[32]John Zizioulas, *Being as Communion* (Crestwood, N.Y.: St. Vladimir's Seminary Press, 1985); idem, "Human Capacity and Human Incapacity," *Scottish Journal of Theology* 28 (1975): 401–48; idem, "The Doctrine of God the Trinity Today: Suggestions for an Ecumenical Study," in *The Forgotten Trinity: A Selection of Papers Presented to the BCC Study Commission on Trinitarian Doctrine Today,* ed. Alasdair I. C. Heron (London: BCC/ CCBI, 1991), 19–32; idem, "On Being a Person: Toward an Ontology of Personhood," in *Persons, Divine and Human,* ed. Christoph Schwöbel and Colin E. Gunton (Edinburgh: T & T Clark, 1991), 33–46; and idem, "The Doctrine of the Holy Trinity: The Significance of the Cappadocian Contribution," in *Trinitarian Theology Today: Essays in Divine Being and Act,* ed. Christoph Schwöbel (Edinburgh: T & T Clark, 1995), 44–60.

[33]Karl Barth, *Church Dogmatics,* vol. 4, ed. G. W. Bromiley and T. F. Torrance; trans. G. W. Bromiley (Edinburgh: T&T Clark, 1962), part 3, chapter 16, par. 72, #4.

[34]"Holy, Holy, Holy! Lord God Almighty" and "Dios Padre, Dios Hijo (Father God, Father Son)" in *Chalice Hymnal* (St. Louis: Chalice Press, 1995) no. 4, no. 45.

[35]Sergeii Bulgakov, "Sophia: Divine Wisdom and Divine Love," in *The Unfading Light* in *Sergeii Bulgakov: Toward a Russian Political Theology,* texts edited and introduced by Rowan Williams (Edinburgh: T & T Clark Press, 1999), 133.

[36]John Calvin, *Institutes of the Christian Religion,* ed. John T. McNeill, trans. Ford Lewis Battles, Library of Christian Classics, vol. 20 and 21 (Philadelphia: Westminster Press, 1960), III. 20, #31.

[37]Hans Urs von Balthasar, *Truth Is Symphonic: Aspects of Christian Pluralism,* trans. Graham Harrison (San Francisco: Ignatius Press, 1987), 9.

Chapter 9: Confessing Christ in Empire and Colony

[1]N. T. Wright, *The New Testament and the People of God* (Minneapolis: Fortress Press, 1992), 3.

[2]For the gruesome details, see Josephus, *The Jewish Wars,* trans. H. St. J. Thackeray (Cambridge: Harvard University Press, 1927), 2. 56, 68; 2. 75.

[3]Josephus, *The Antiquities of the Jews,* trans. H. St. J. Thackeray, Ralph Marcus, Allen Wikgren, and Louis H. Feldman (Cambridge, Mass.: Harvard University Press, 1926–65), 18, 27, 36–38.

[4]John Dominic Crossan and Jonathan L. Reed describe the Roman dining patterns in Galilee in *Excavating Jesus* (New York: HarperSanFrancisco, 2002), 98–115.

[5]One translation of *prōtois* is "chief estates."

[6]Josephus, *The Antiquities of the Jews,* 116.

[7]Cf. Numbers 27:17; 1 Kings 22:17; and 2 Chronicles 18:6.

[8]Eusebius, *The Life of Constantine,* 3:15.

[9]The laws ("canons") of the Council of Elvira may be found in Jan L. Womer, trans. and ed., *Morality and Ethics in Early Christianity* (Philadelphia: Fortress Press, 1987), 75–83.

[10]See Michel Foucault, *The Archeology of Knowledge,* trans. A.M. Sheridan Smith (New York: Pantheon Books, 1972), 74, and Katharina von Kellenbach, *Anti-Judaism in Feminist Religious Writings* (Atlanta: Scholars Press, 1994), 39–42.

[11]See Steve Mason, *Josephus and the New Testament,* 2d ed. (Peabody, Mass.: Hendrickson, 2003) for an excellent study of Luke-Acts and Hellenistic historians.

[12]See the description in John Dominic Crossan and Jonathan L. Reed, *In Search of Paul* (New York: HarperSanFrancisco, 2004), 298–99.

[13]Quoted in Crossan and Reed, *In Search of Paul,* 239–40; emphases mine.

[14]Dieter Georgi, "God Turned Upside Down," in *Paul and Empire,* ed. Richard A. Horsley (Harrisburg: Trinity Press International, 1997), 148.

[15]Eusebius, *Life of Constantine,* 1, 28, 490.

[16]*Ecclesia* and *Synagoga* are widespread in Christian art; they appear in statuary, stained glass, illuminated manuscripts, and paintings, including one by Hans Holbein.

[17]From the *Heidelberg Disputation,* Articles 16-21 (*Luther's Works,* vol. 31, ed. Harold J. Grimm and Helmut T. Lehman [Philadelphia: Muhlenberg Press, 1959]), 40–41.

Chapter 10: Who Do We Say He Is?

[1]A discussion of these themes is found in Rita Nakashima Brock and Rebecca Ann Parker, *Saving Paradise: How Christianity Lost Its Love for This World as Paradise and Came to Worship Crucifixion* (Boston: Beacon Press, 2007).

[2]Phyllis Trible, *God and the Rhetoric of Sexuality* (Philadelphia: Fortress Press, 1975). Ezekiel imagined Mt. Zion and the second temple as the return of paradise, the place where the Spirit of God returned to Israel. The Psalms, many dating from the second temple period, praise God's creativity, justice, and healing, echoing Genesis. They begin with a hymn to the virtuous and wise who are rooted in God, "like trees / planted by streams of water" (Ps. 1:3). Psalm 48:1 says, "[God's] holy mountain, beautiful in elevation, / is the joy of all the earth." Psalm 104 sings, "From your lofty abode you water the mountains; / the earth is satisfied with the fruit of your work" (Ps. 104:13). See Gregory Allen Robbins, ed., *Genesis 1—3 in the History of Exegesis: Intrigue in the Garden* (Lewiston, N.Y.: Edwin Mellen Press, 1988).

[3]Jean Delumeau, *History of Paradise: The Garden of Eden in Myth and Tradition* (New York: Continuum Press, 1995), ch. 1, documents the early Christian prevailing understanding of paradise as this world and as the church. For a discussion of the Moses imagery and the anti-Judaism in John, see Rita Nakashima Brock and Rebecca Ann Parker, "Enemy and Ally: Contending with the Gospel of John's Anti-Judaism," in *Walk in the Ways of Wisdom: Essays in Honor of Elisabeth Schüssler Fiorenza,* ed. Shelly Matthews, Cynthia Kittridge and Melanie Johnson (New York: Trinity Press International, 2003), 166–80. A number of church theologians described the meal as taking place in paradise, with the risen Christ as host of the table. They believed the words of Jesus in Luke 23:43, "Today you will be with me in Paradise."

[4]Peter Cramer, *Baptism and Change in the Early Middle Ages, c. 200-1150.* (New York: Cambridge University Press, 1993), and Thomas M. Finn, *From Death to Rebirth: Ritual and Conversion in Antiquity* (New York: Paulist Press, 1997). Finn, 43–44, discusses the Roman image of Satan. The book of Revelation, seen by many biblical scholars as hope for the end of the Roman Empire, also borrowed heavily from Ezekiel's paradise themes. Ezekiel was also preoccupied with the defeat of an empire, Babylonia. Prevailing Christian views of paradise were this-worldly. Theophilus of Antioch, second century, and Theodore of Mopsuestia (c. 350–428) argued for the physical existence of paradise, a place on earth separate from heaven and separate from ordinary life. Basil the Great (c. 330–379) concluded that remnants of paradise could be found on the heights of virtually any mountain. A minority view suggested paradise had once been real but was destroyed in Noah's flood; it would be recreated after the apocalypse. Origen (c. 185–254) thought it was the journey of the soul to God. Ambrose (c. 339–397) developed the prevailing view that it was both a spiritual journey and a real place. See Brock and Parker, *Saving Paradise,* ch. 2.

[5]Peter Brown, *The Body in Society: Men, Women, and Sexual Renunciation in Early Christianity* (New York: Columbia University Press, 1988).

[6]Colleen McDannell and Bernhard Lang in *Heaven: A History,* 2d ed. (New Haven: Yale University Press, 2001) collapse ideas of paradise into a type of heaven, all as forms of the afterlife.

[7]In Ravenna, Italy, the fifth-century St. Apollinaire Nuovo church holds the earliest existing image of the Last Supper. It shows Jesus and his disciples reclining around a table covered with seven loaves of bread and a plate with two large fish—there is no cup. On the opposite wall of the nave are similar images of loaves and fish showing the feeding story. Art historian Gertrud Schiller, *Iconography of Christian Art: The Passion of Jesus Christ,* vol. 2, trans. Janet Seligman (London: Lund Humphries Pub, 1972) notes that the feeding of the multitude was the most common early depiction of the Last Supper. Andrew McGowan, *Ascetic Eucharists: Food and Drink in Early Christian Ritual Meals* (New

York: Oxford University Press, 1999) describes the many kinds of foods used in the feasts. McGowan suggests the reference to "bloodless sacrifice" is the term for prayer, and the refusal by all churches to use red meat and the avoidance of wine by some may have been a form of resistance to pagan blood sacrifice.

[8]For discussions of the texts and theologies of early liturgies, see Nicholas Arseniev, *Mysticism and the Early Church* (Crestwood, N.Y.: St. Vladimir's Seminary Press, 1979); Paul Bradshaw, ed., *Essays on Early Eastern Eucharistic Prayers* (Collegeville, Minn.: The Liturgical Press, 1997), St. Ephrem of Syria, *Hymns on Paradise* (Crestwood, N.Y.: St. Vladimir's Press, 1990), ed. Sebastian Brock; Gregory Dix, *The Shape of the Liturgy* (London: Dacre Press, A. and C. Black, Ltd., 1960); Hans Leitzmann, *Mass and the Lord's Supper: A Study in the History of the Liturgy* (Leiden: E. J. Brill, 1979).

[9]See Christopher Pitts, *Patron and Pastor: The Economy of Authority Present at Nicea as a Discursive Intersection Between Empire and Church* (master's thesis, Graduate Theological Union, 2005), ch. 3, "Imperial Reform Under Diocletian," for a discussion of Diocletian's administrative innovations and his more aggressive use of religion, which worked against Christians.

[10]Pitts, *Patron and Pastor,* discusses the mutual influences.

[11]James Scott, *Domination and the Arts of Resistance: Hidden Transcripts* (New Haven: Yale University Press, 1990) describes how discourses shaped under oppression can contain forms of resistance that, when they become public, clearly have histories of formation. Hidden transcripts of resistance can appear to be about one thing, while also being a deconstruction of power. He discusses African American spirituals as hidden transcripts of resistance, as do many African American theologians.

[12]No images of crucifixion were used in European churches until the middle of the tenth century. Diane Apostolos-Capadona, *Dictionary of Christian Art* (New York: Continuum Press, 1995) and Peter and Linda Murray, *The Oxford Companion to Christian Art and Architecture* (New York: Oxford University Press, 1996) discuss possible reasons for the avoidance of crucifixion images.

[13]Thomas Matthews, *The Clash of Gods: A Reinterpretation of Early Christian Art* (Princeton, N.J.:Princeton University Press, 1993) deconstructs what he calls the "Emperor Mystique" as the product of pre-WWII German, Austrian, and Russian scholars (Ernst Kantorowicz, Andreas Alfoldi, and Andre' Grabar) who were nostalgic for lost empires in Europe. He says, "The three imperial states in which they were raised, and which they fought valiantly to defend, they saw crumble ignominiously in the horrible chaos of the First World War… [A] call to greatness in the model of past imperial accomplishments is implicit in their scholarship" (19). He notes, "The authority of the Church [derived] directly from Christ without the mediation of the emperor... In so far as the struggle [at Nicaea] against the Arians was also a struggle against the emperors, who had taken the Arian side, the victory over Arianism was a vindication of the freedom of the Church from imperial control" (114). Constantine was baptized at death as an Arian, and all his sons were Arians, the option most commonly preferred by the Roman nobility.

[14]For a vivid description of Nicaea and its consequences from a Jewish perspective, see Richard E. Rubenstein, *When Jesus Became God: The Epic Fight over Christ's Divinity in the Last Days of Rome* (New York: Harcourt, Brace and Co., 1999). Thomaš Mastnak in *Crusading Peace: Christendom, the Muslim World, and Western Political Order* (Berkeley: University of California Press, 2002) describes the Christian ban on violence, its gradual erosion, and its undermining with the Crusades in 1095.

[15]Peter Brown, *The Rise of Western Christendom: Triumph and Diversity A.D. 200–1000* (Malden, Mass.: Blackwell Pub. Ltd., 2003), suggests that the Saxons were familiar with Christianity even before the sixth–century mission of Boniface and practiced a hybrid that incorporated pagan practices, such that pagan priests sometimes baptized people into Christianity and Christian priests officiated at pagan ceremonies. Boniface objected to these mixtures and hacked down some of the most important pagan trees, building churches from the lumber, which led Saxons to protest by burning churches. G. Ronald Murphy in *The Saxon Savior: The Germanic Transformation of the Gospel in the Ninth-Century Heliand* (New York: Oxford University Press, 1989) summarizes the accounts of the wars on the Saxons recorded in the *Annales regni Francorum*. Roger Collins, *Charlemagne* (Buffalo: University of Toronto Press, 1998), "The Saxon Wars 772–85," ch. 3, notes that,

though the Franks and Saxons were actually fairly similar and well acquainted with each other, Charlemagne constructed an identity system that set them at odds because of exaggerated or invented differences, though, unlike Brown, Collins identifies Saxons as firmly pagan. He suggests Charlemagne forced them to accept Latin Christianity as a means to force them to honor their treaty agreements.

[16]Hincmar quoted in Celia Martin Chazelle, *The Crucified God in the Carolingian Era: Theology and Art of Christ's Passion* (New York: Cambridge University Press 2001): 218–19. For a detailed discussion of this transformation of Christ from compassionate savior to judge, see Rachel Fulton, *From Judgment to Passion: Devotion to Christ and the Virgin Mary, 800–1200* (New York: Columbia University Press, 2002).

[17]Chazelle, *The Crucified God,* 230–31. Some Carolingian theologians, most notably John Scottus Erigena (c. 800–880), shared Gottschalk's traditional Christian view that "the consecrated bread and wine are transformed into Christ in the unity of his humanity and divinity, and therefore into the body and blood born on earth and risen from the dead." For a translation of the *The Heliand,* see G. Ronald Murphy, *The Saxon Savior.*

[18]Chazelle, *The Crucified God,* 227.

[19]For information about the crusades, see Penny J. Cole, *The Preaching of the Crusades to the Holy Land, 1095–1270* (Cambridge: The Medieval Soc. of America, 1991); Harold S. Fink, ed., *Fulcher of Chartres: A History of the Expedition to Jerusalem 1095–1127* (Knoxville, Tenn.: University of Tennessee Press, 1969); Christoph T. Maier, *Crusade Propaganda and Ideology: Model Sermons for the Preaching of the Cross* (Cambridge: Cambridge University Press, 2000); Thomaš Mastnak, *Crusading Peace: Christendom, the Muslim World, and Western Political Order* (Berkeley: University of California Press, 2002); Edward Peters, ed., *The First Crusade: The Chronicle of Fulcher of Chartres and Other Source Materials* (Philadelphia: University of Pennsylvania Press, 1998); and Jonathan Riley-Smith, *The First Crusaders, 1095–1131* (Cambridge: Cambridge University Press, 1997); idem, *The Crusades: A Short History* (New Haven: Yale University Press, 1987); and idem, "Crusading as an Act of Love," in *The Crusades: The Essential Readings,* ed. Thomas F. Madden (Oxford: Blackwell Pub. Ltd., 2002). Mastnak focuses on their emergence from the Pax Dei movement. Cole, Maier, and Riley-Smith 2002 discuss the theological justifications for the Crusades. Most scholars of the Crusades agree that the reasons for their emergence had to do with problems internal to Europe and not with a provocation from the Muslims in the Middle East. The Eastern church, with much closer and extensive relations with the Muslims, opposed the Crusades and avoided atonement theology by holding to a traditional incarnational theology and eucharistic views.

[20]Anselm of Canterbury, *Cur Deus Homo,* II, 11.

[21]Anthony W. Bartlett, *Cross Purposes: The Violent Grammar of the Christian Atonement* (Harrisburg, Pa.: Trinity Press International, 2001) and James Carroll, *Constantine's Sword: The Church and the Jews, A History* (Boston: Houghton Mifflin Press, 2001). Bartlett especially makes the connection between Anselm's theology and the crusades.

[22]Abelard has long been famous for his ill-fated affair with his student Heloise, who bore him a son and became his wife until her custodial uncle had him castrated. His short confessional autobiography is called *The Story of My Misfortunes,* trans. Henry Adams Bellows (New York: Macmillan, 1972). He wrote it to restore his reputation after being declared a heretic.

[23]John Marenbon, *The Philosophy of Peter Abelard* (Cambridge, N.Y.: Cambridge University Press, 1997) notes especially this last point as a weakness of Abelard's emphasis on love of God and intent, as well as the problem of accounting for actions which "we do not think about but for which it is reasonable to think we are fully responsible" (281).

[24]Peter Abelard, as quoted in J. Ramsay McCallum, *Abelard's Christian Theology* (Merrick, N.Y.: Richwood, 1976), 46, 88.

[25]Bernard of Clairvaux, *Liber ad milites Templi,* I, trans. Conrad Greenia (available at www.the-orb.net/encyclop/religion/monastic/bernard.html. Accessed 1/7/2006).

[26]The gardens of medieval monasteries were the one place paradise on earth continued, as they were designed to be beautiful and pleasant respites from the rest of the world.

[27]Renato Rosaldo, *Culture and Truth: The Remaking of Social Analysis* (Boston: Beacon Press, 1989).

[28]Pumla Gobodo-Madikizela, *A Human Being Died That Night* (Boston: Houghton, 2000), reports her experience on the TRC and her observations about forgiveness.

[29]Adrienne Rich, "Transcendental Etude," in *The Dream of a Common Language* (New York: W. W. Norton, 1978).

[30]Excerpts from the Immolatio and Post-Sanctus from the Gallican Rite, found in *Prayers of the Eucharist: Early and Reformed*, 3d ed., ed. R.C.D. Jasper and C.J. Cuming (Collegeville, Minn.: The Liturgical Press, 1990), 148–49. The editors write, "The name 'Gallican' strictly applies to the rite used in France until its supersession by the Roman rite completed by Charlemagne c. 800; but it is used in a wider sense to include…a family of non-Roman Latin rites. All these rites tend to show more traces of Eastern influence than does the native Roman rite… Some of the prayers are clearly of great antiquity, predating the Roman canon in its historic form," 147.

Chapter 11: Under the Influence

[1]Daniel Migliore, *Faith Seeking Understanding* (Grand Rapids: Eerdmans, 1991), 166. In Migliore's defense, he does acknowledge the "...resurgence of interest in the Holy Spirit" in recent years (166). As evidence of this, he cites the Canberra 1990 General Assembly of the World Council of Churches' theme "Come, Holy Spirit—Renew the Whole Creation." As a theological student, I was perplexed by this. I learned by osmosis that young theologians need not ponder the Spirit, other than admitting belief in it! Perhaps unintentionally, neglect births a new generation of neglect. In recent years the negligent cycle has been acutely disrupted.

[2]All biblical quotations in this chapter come from the *New International Version* unless otherwise noted.

[3]D.A. Tappeiner, "Holy Spirit," in *The International Standard Bible Encyclopedia*, rev. ed. (Grand Rapids: Eerdmans, 1982), 732.

[4]See Dennis Groh, "Montanism," and Robert Sider, "Tertullian," in *Encyclopedia of Early Christianity*, ed. Everett Ferguson (New York: Garland, 1990).

[5]"The Creed of Nicea (325)" in John Leith, ed., *Creeds of the Churches* (Louisville: John Knox Press, 1982), 30–31.

[6]Veli-Matti Karkkainen, *Pneumatology: The Holy Spirit in Ecumenical, International, and Contextual Perspective* (Grand Rapids: Baker Academic, 2002), 43–44. Basil of Caesarea's *Treatise on the Holy Spirit* is the major work by the Cappadocians. However, "Gregory of Nazianzus...was probably the first Eastern father who dared to call the Holy Spirit 'God.'" See Karkkainen, 45.

[7]Ibid., 31–33.

[8]Karkkainen, *Pneumatology*, is one of the best in presenting an articulate, informed, yet readable history of pneumatology. See especially chapter 3, "The Historical Unfolding of the Experience of the Spirit."

[9]Yves Congar, *I Believe in the Holy Spirit*, trans. David Smith (New York: Crossroad, 1997), 138.

[10]Martin Luther, cited in ibid., 139.

[11]George Fox, cited in ibid., 142.

[12]Byron Lambert, "Holy Spirit, Doctrine of the" in *The Encyclopedia of the Stone-Campbell Movement* (Grand Rapids: Eerdmans, 2004), 403.

[13]Ibid.

[14]Leonard Allen, *The Cruciform Church* (Abilene, Tex.: ACU Press, 1990), 35–36.

[15]Lambert, "Holy Spirit," 405.

[16]See material on the subject by Don DeWelt and Knofel Staton (from Christian Churches), C. Leonard Allen and Garth Black (from Churches of Christ), and Clark Williamson and Stephen Sprinkle (from Disciples).

[17]Philip Jenkins, *The Next Christendom: The Coming of Global Christianity* (Oxford; New York: Oxford University Press, 2002), 7–8.

[18]Harvey Cox, *Fire from Heaven: The Rise of Pentecostal Spirituality and the Reshaping of Religion in the Twenty-First Century* (Cambridge, Mass.: Da Capo Press, 1995), 24. Also by Cox, *The Secular City: Secularization and Urbanization in Theological Perspective* (New York: Macmillan, 1965).

[19]Jenkins, *The Next Christendom,* 220.

[20]Scholarly accounts of Pentecostal developments outside the West are not in ample supply. On current trends in African Pentecostalism, see Lamin Sanneh and Joel A. Carpenter, eds., *The Changing Face of Christianity: Africa, the West, and the World* (Oxford: University Press, 2005). For Asian developments, see Allan Anderson and Edmond Tang, eds., *Asian and Pentecostal: The Charismatic Face of Christianity in Asia* (Oxford: Regnum Books International, 2005). Pentecostalism in Latin America is still best interpreted by David Martin in *Pentecostalism: The World Their Parish* (Oxford: Blackwell, 2002).

Chapter 12: Creation

[1]See Walter Brueggemann, *Genesis,* Interpretation: A Bible Commentary for Teaching and Preaching, ed. James L. Mays (Atlanta: John Knox Press, 1982), 1–14.

[2]See M. Eugene Boring and Fred B. Craddock, *The People's New Testament Commentary* (Louisville/London: Westminster John Knox Press, 2004), 288–91, 559, 627–28.

[3]Clark M. Williamson, *Way of Blessing, Way of Life* (St. Louis: Chalice Press, 1999), 141.

[4]See Daniel Migliore, *The Power of God* (Philadelphia: The Westminster Press, 1983), chapter 6. See also Williamson, *Way of Blessing,* for a helpful discussion of the traditional models of God as critiqued by neo-process theology.

[5]Richard H. Lowery, *Sabbath and Jubilee* (St. Louis: Chalice Press, 2000), 86–87.

[6]This is a phrase of Professor Shirley C. Guthrie Jr., *Christian Doctrine,* rev. ed. (Louisville/London: Westminster John Knox Press, 1994), 158.

[7]Ibid., 164.

[8]Lowery, *Sabbath and Jubilee,* 92.

[9]Ibid., 82.

[10]The "disciples mind" was identified by Ronald E. Osborn, *The Faith We Affirm: Basic Beliefs of Disciples of Christ* (St. Louis: Bethany Press, 1983).

[11]Williamson, *Way of Blessing,* 84.

[12]Ibid., 107. See Williamson's discussion of continuing creativity.

[13]See Per Lonning, *Creation: An Ecumenical Challenge* (Macon: Mercer University Press, 1989). See also Shantilal Bhagat, *Creation and Crisis: Responding to God's Covenant* (Elgin, Ill.: Brethren Press, 1990), especially chapter 13, for suggestions for the church in North America as it responds to both biblical teaching and contemporary ecological and economic crises—both ecumenically and missionally.

[14]See Lowery, *Sabbath and Jubilee,* 101. See also Bhagat, *Creation and Crisis,* especially chapter 13, for suggestions for the church in North America as it responds to both biblical teaching and contemporary ecological and economic crises—both ecumenically and missionally.

[15]Martin Luther King Jr., *Where Do We Go from Here? Chaos or Community* (Boston: Beacon Press, 1968), 168, as quoted by Larry L. Rasmussen, *Earth Community, Earth Ethics* (Maryknoll, N.Y.: Orbis, 1996), 97.

Chapter 13: The Church as Sacrament of Human Wholeness

[1]Alexander Campbell, as quoted in Douglas A. Foster, Paul M. Blowers, Anthony L. Dunnavant, and D. Newell Williams, eds., *The Encyclopedia of the Stone-Campbell Movement* (Grand Rapids: Eerdmans, 2004), 517.

[2]Concerning *shalom,* see Ludwig Koehler and Walter Baumgartner, *The Hebrew and Aramaic Lexicon of the Old Testament* (Leiden, Boston, Köln: Brill, 2001), 1532–36.

[3]For example, John Dominic Crossan and Jonathan L. Reed, *In Search of Paul* (New York: Harper SanFrancisco, 2004).

[4]With appreciation to Dr. Richard H. Lowery, Phillips Theological Seminary, Tulsa, Oklahoma for this perspective on Abraham.

[5]At the 2005 biennial General Assembly of the CCDC, several amendments to the *Design* were adopted.

[6]Joe R. Jones, "A Theological Analysis of the Design," *Midstream,* 19 (July 1980): 316–17.

[7]*The Design for the Christian Church (Disciples of Christ)* as amended in 2005 has changed the old par. 3 reference "this church expresses itself in free and voluntary relationships" to new par. 2 "this church expresses itself in covenantal relationships." In new par. 3, "free and voluntary" is dropped altogether.

Chapter 14: Baptism and the Disciples of Christ

[1]As witnessed to by the Roman Catholic Church's Rite for Christian Initiation of Adults, developed to deal with the increasing number of persons never before baptized entering the church. Another example: since the fall of the Iron Curtain, the Russian Orthodox Church has held mass baptisms of adults, persons newly discovering the Christian faith after seventy years of anti-religious social conditioning.

[2]Alexander Campbell, "Positive Christian Institutions," *The Millennial Harbinger,* 32: 250.

[3]See the influential Keith Watkins, ed., *Baptism and Belonging: A Resource for Christian Worship* (St. Louis: Chalice Press, 1991), 3–4.

[4]For example, in the proposal by the Disciples' Commission on Theology that the profession of faith read: "Do you, *with Christians of every time and place,* believe that..." (cf. Mt. 16:16). See "A Word to the Church on Baptism: A Report of the Commission on Theology," in *The Church for Disciples of Christ: Seeking to Be Truly Church Today,* ed. Paul A. Crow Jr. and James O. Duke (St. Louis: Chalice Press, 1998), 133.

[5]See the service suggested in Watkins, *Baptism and Belonging,* 37–41.

[6]Faith and Order Paper No. 111 (Geneva: WCC Publications, 1982) para. 10, speaking of baptism's "ethical implications which not only call for personal sanctification, but also motivate Christians to strive for the realization of the will of God in all realms of life."

[7]See the church's thoughtful response to BEM: "'Churches of Christ in Australia,' Response to BEM," in *Churches Respond to BEM: Official Responses to the "Baptism, Eucharist and Ministry" Text,* vol. 2, Faith and Order Paper No. 132, ed. Max Thurian (Geneva: World Council of Churches, 1986), 264–75.

[8]As the great ecumenist D.T. Niles of Sri Lanka thundered at the WCC founding Assembly in Amsterdam in 1948: "No 'schemes of union' had come about. The churches had united." See W. A. Visser 't Hooft, ed., *The First Assembly of the World Council of Churches* (London, SCM Press, 1949), 62. Niles was reacting to the language used about church unions in Section V at Amsterdam, where it had been said that "some notable schemes of union had come about."

[9]The original definition of organic unity from the Second World Conference on Faith and Order, Edinburgh, 1937, spoke of organic unity as reflecting "the unity of a living organism, with the diversity characteristic of the members of a healthy body." Remarkably, the word *organic* was intended precisely to guard a proper *diversity* within the unity. See Leonard Hodgson, ed., *The Second World Conference on Faith and Order: Edinburgh 1937* (New York: MacMillan, 1938), 252.

[10]Mark G. Toulouse has offered an influential and helpful characterization of Disciples' theology as having five "core principles" (the restoration, the ecumenical, the interpretive, the mission, and the eschatological). Given the centrality of worship—including, but not only, the Lord's supper—to Disciples, should not the *liturgical principle* be added to this list? See Toulouse, *Joined in Discipleship: The Shaping of Contemporary Disciples Identity,* 2d ed. (St. Louis: Chalice Press, 1997).

[11]For a more detailed treatment of these themes, see Thomas F. Best, "Memory and Meaning: Liturgy as Transformation. To Heal a Broken World: The Ecumenical Dimension," *Studia Liturgica* 36, no.1 (2006): 60–73.

[12]Thomas F. Best, "Koinonia and Diakonia: The Ethical Implications of Two Biblical Perspectives on the Church," in *Faith in Practice: Studies in the Book of Acts, a Festschrift in Honor of Earl and Ottie Mearl Stuckenbruck,* ed. David A. Fiensy and William D. Howden (Atlanta: European Evangelistic Society, 1995), 352–54.

[13]Thomas F. Best, "The Issues Beyond the Issues: Possible Futures for the Faith and Order World Conference," *The Ecumenical Review* 45, no. 1 (January 1993): 59–60.

[14]See the Faith and Order study and study document *Church and World: The Unity of the Church and the Renewal of Human Community,* Faith and Order Paper No. 151, rev.

ed. (Geneva: WCC Publications, 1992). Other Faith and Order work on the interface between church and world includes studies on theology in relation to racism, and the inclusion of persons with disabilities in the life of the church. (Remarkably, the note on social dimensions of Christian division was introduced at the Third World Conference on Faith and Order in Lund in 1952 by none other than the rather conservative Disciple S.J. England; see Thomas F. Best, "From Seoul to Santiago: The Unity of the Church and JPIC," in *Between the Flood and the Rainbow: Interpreting the Conciliar Process of Mutual Commitment (Covenant) to Justice, Peace and the Integrity of Creation*, comp. D. Preman Niles (Geneva: WCC Publications, 1992), 137; see also Oliver S. Tomkins, ed., *The Third World Conference on Faith and Order* (London: SCM Press Ltd., 1953), 226, 232.

[15]See the joint text by Thomas F. Best and Martin Robra, eds. *Ecclesiology and Ethics* (Geneva, WCC Publications, 1997). Other joint work includes the study on the Community of Women and Men in the Church, lodged in Faith and Order and done together with the WCC Women's Desk.

[16]On this see the Faith and Order text-in-process, "One Baptism: Towards Mutual Recognition," FO/2006:14, par. 53; "Baptism" in "'Agreed Statement: Apostolicity and Catholicity (1977–1982),' Disciples of Christ—Roman Catholic International Commission for Dialogue," *Call to Unity* 1 (August 2003): par. 33–34, 4.

[17]Ibid., par. 9.

[18]See the development of this notion in the Faith and Order text-in-progress "One Baptism," par. 33–41, also par. 69–73.

[19]Ibid., par. 61.

[20]On the theme of "remembering the future," see the remarkable statement in the Liturgy of St. John Chrysostom: "Remembering therefore this our Saviour's command and all that has been done for us: the Cross, the Tomb, the Resurrection on the third day… the Second and glorious Coming again." We "remember" the Second Coming, in that it is contained *in nuce* in the message of salvation brought already by Christ. See also Thomas F. Best, "Memory and Meaning," 64–65.

[21]"Baptism," BEM, para. 10.

[22]Thomas F. Best and Dagmar Heller, eds., *Becoming a Christian: The Ecumenical Implications of Our Common Baptism*, Faith and Order Paper No. 184 (Geneva: WCC Publications, 1999), par. 44, 89.

Chapter 15: The Lord's Supper

[1]Alexander Campbell, "Breaking the Loaf," in *The Christian System in Reference to the Union of Christians and a Restoration of Primitive Christianity as Plead in the Current Reformation* (Cincinnati: Bosworth, Chase, & Hall, 1839), 284.

[2]Barton W. Stone, "The Lord's Supper," *The Christian Messenger* (1834): 176–77.

[3]Campbell, "Breaking the Loaf," 273.

[4]Jordan quoted in "Setting the Table: Meanings of Communion," in *Setting the Table: Women in Theological Conversation*, ed. Rita Nakashima Brock, Claudia Camp, Serene Jones (St. Louis: Chalice Press, 1995), 252.

[5]Campbell, "Breaking the Loaf," 269.

[6]Ibid., 270.

[7]Ibid., 273.

[8]William O. Paulsell, "Our Disciple Spirituality," unpublished manuscript, 1.

[9]Campbell, "Breaking the Loaf," 274.

[10]Robert Richardson, as quoted in William O. Paulsell, *Disciples at Prayer: The Spirituality of the Christian Church (Disciples of Christ)* (St. Louis: Chalice Press, 1995), 18.

[11]Robert Richardson, *Communings in the Sanctuary* (Lexington, Kentucky: Transylvania Printing and Publishing Co., 1872), 69.

[12]Ibid., 29.

[13]Ibid., 66.

[14]Ibid., 12.

[15]Camp quoted in "Setting the Table: Meanings of Communion," 254.

[16]Aaron Milavec, *The Didache: Text, Translation, Analysis, and Commentary* (Collegeville, Minn.: Liturgical Press, 2004), 23.

Chapter 16: Operative Theologies of Disciple Preaching

[1]Barton Warren Stone, "An Address To the Elders, Preachers, and Brethren, in the Church of Christ," *Christian Messenger* 2 (1827): 70.

[2]My use of the term "church*es*" will no doubt call to mind the pre-restructure employment of that term—it seems, however, an apt description of our current context.

[3]Letty M. Russell, *Church in the Round: Feminist Interpretation of the Church* (Louisville: Westminster John Knox Press, 1993).

[4]Weekly communion at The Community of Hope UCC in Tulsa, Oklahoma, is celebrated around a "not-quite-round" table.

[5]Stone, "An Address," 71.

[6]Barton Warren Stone, "Letter to J.C.," *Christian Messenger* 4 (1829): 225.

[7]Stone, "An Address," 71. Gender-exclusive texts will retain their historic voice throughout this chapter.

[8]Cloyd Goodnight and Dwight E. Stevenson, *Home to Bethpage: A Biography of Robert Richardson* (St. Louis: Christian Board of Publication, 1949), 123.

[9]Alexander Campbell, "Religious Excitement-No. 1," *Millennial Harbinger*, n.s. 4 (1840): 167–68.

[10]Dwight. E. Stevenson, *Disciple Preaching in the First Generation: An Ecological Study,* The Forrest F. Reed Lectures for 1969 (Nashville: The Disciples of Christ Historical Society, 1969), 92.

[11]Alexander Campbell, "Pre-eminence of Preaching in Public Worship," *Millennial Harbinger,* 5th ser. 5 (1862): 154.

[12]Mark G. Toulouse, *Joined in Discipleship,* 2d ed. (St. Louis: Chalice Press, 1997), 85.

[13]R. Edwin Groover, "Tubman, Emily H. (1794–1885)," in Douglas A. Foster, Anthony L. Dunnavant, Paul M. Blowers, and D. Newell Williams, eds., *The Encyclopedia of the Stone-Campbell Movement* (Grand Rapids, Mich.: Eerdmans, 2004), 746–47.

[14]John F. Burnett, *Early Women of the Christian Church: Heroines All* (Dayton, Ohio: The Christian Publishing Association, 1920), 9–13. The "Christians" referred to here were the "New England Christians" started by Elias Smith and Abner Jones ca. 1801, one of the "Christian" movements that, like Barton Warren Stone's "Christians" in Kentucky, ultimately gave rise to both the CCDC and the UCC.

[15]Ibid., 18.

[16]Ibid., 20.

[17]Nathan O. Hatch, *The Democratization of American Christianity* (New Haven, Conn.: Yale University Press, 1989), 78.

[18]Ibid., 79.

[19]Hap C. S. Lyda, "African Americans in The Movement," in Foster, Blowers, Dunnavant, and Williams, eds., *The Encyclopedia of the Stone-Campbell Movement,* 11.

[20]Darryl M. Trimiew, ed., *Out of Mighty Waters: Sermons by African-American Disciples* (St. Louis: Chalice Press, 1994), 1.

[21]See Lyda, "African Americans," 11.

[22]Ibid.

[23]Ibid.

[24]See Mark Toulouse, "Scott, Walter (1796–1861)," in Foster, Blowers, Dunnavant, and Williams, eds., *The Encyclopedia of the Stone-Campbell Movement,* 673–79.

[25]Ibid.

[26]See Bruce E. Shields, "Smith, 'Raccoon' John (1784–1868)," in Foster, Blowers, Dunnavant, and Williams, eds., *The Encyclopedia of the Stone-Campbell Movement,* 690.

[27]See Lyda, "African Americans,"11.

[28]Happily this situation is changing, as demonstrated by the recent dissertation by Gregory K. Widener, "The Interethnic Black Preaching Style of Cynthia L. Hale: An Exploratory Study" (Ph.D. diss.: University of Kentucky, 1998).

[29]Burnett, *Early Women*, 25–29.

[30]Nathaniel S. Haynes, *History of the Disciples of Christ in Illinois 1819–1914* (Cincinnati, Ohio: Standard Publishing Co., 1915), 446–47.

[31]Joseph R. Jeter, telephone conversation, August 17, 2004.

[32]Ronald E. Osborn, as cited in Ken Lawrence, ed., *Classic Themes of Disciples Theology: Rethinking the Traditional Affirmations of the Christian Church (Disciples of Christ)* (Fort Worth, Tex.: Texas Christian University Press, 1986), 135.

[33]Reinhold Niebuhr, *The Nature and Destiny of Man*, vol. 1: *Human Nature* (New York: Charles Scribner's Sons, 1941), 125–31.

[34]Some Disciples preachers (in this modern generation) capably forged a homiletic bridge between Stone's more heartfelt, affective preaching and A. Campbell's more rational, *teaching* sermons. Disciples preaching is most remarkable when—both theologically and homiletically speaking—the strengths of Stone's method and A. Campbell's are held in tension with one another. Perhaps the brilliant and greatly beloved Disciples preacher Fred Craddock was intent on constructing such a bridge with his inductive method of preaching, though he never explicitly stated as much in his seminal book *As One Without Authority* (Enid, Okla.: Phillips University Press, 1971).

[35]John Broadus, *A Treatise on the Preparation and Delivery of Sermons* (New York: Sheldon and Co., 1870).

[36]Roxanne Mountford, *The Gendered Pulpit: Preaching in American Protestant Spaces* (Carbondale, Ill.: Southern Illinois University Press, 2003), 60.

[37]Thomas G. Long, *The Witness of Preaching* (Louisville: Westminster John/Knox Press, 1989), 158.

[38]Ibid.

[39]Disciples homiletician Hunter Beckelhymer edited such powerful modern preaching in *The Vital Pulpit of the Christian Church: A Series of Sermons by Representative Men among The Disciples of Christ* (St. Louis: Bethany Press, 1969).

[40]Robert M. Miller, "Fosdick, Harry Emerson," in *Concise Encyclopedia of Preaching*, ed. William Willimon and Richard Lischer (Louisville: Westminster John Knox Press, 1995), 154.

[41]Harry Emerson Fosdick, cited in Lionel Crocker, ed., *Harry Emerson Fosdick's Art of Preaching: An Anthology* (Springfield, Ill.: Charles C. Thomas, 1971), 29.

[42]For further on this issue see my forthcoming book, Kay Bessler Northcutt, *Kindling Our Desire for God: Preaching as Spiritual Direction.*

[43]It was, in part, the shared situation of modernity that enabled Disciples in the U.S. to become a prominent voice in ecumenical discussion and dialogue. The sense of facing a common situation—in the experience of modernity—provided a space for interdenominational cooperation and for healing the theological rifts of the past. Finally (or so it seemed) the nascent moment for *unity*—and the role of Disciple preachers and leadership in it—had arisen.

[44]The cemetery plot records from the internment of Clara Celestia Hale Babcock, quoting from her obituary, listed among attendees at the internment the Ladies' Guild of the KKK.

[45]Those preachers exhorting congregants to social action included Caucasian as well as African American preachers. Beckelhymer, *The Vital Pulpit of the Living Church*, contains such calls-to-action representative of both races.

[46]James Cone, *My Soul Looks Back* (reprint, Maryknoll, N.Y.: Orbis, 1986; Nashville: Abingdon Press, 1982), 66.

[47]The "undiscovered" territory (and its unsettled frontier), which eventually became known as the United States of America, was neither "undiscovered" nor unpopulated. The systematic annihilation and crucifyingly horrible violence perpetrated by white settlers (and eventually the United States's military and government) upon American Indians is an open historical record, representing one of the greatest holocausts of the Imperial Era.

[48]According to the statistic published in Patrick Johnstone, Jason Mandryk, *Operation World*, twenty-first–century ed. (Waynesboro, Ga.: Paternoster, 2001), the Disciples of Christ in Congo number 720,000.

[49]The Reverend Bosela Eale, the General Minister and President of the 259 churches comprising the Communauté des Disciples du Christ au Congo-Poste Ecclesial de

Kinshasa (Church of Christ in the Congo/Disciples of Christ Community-Kinshasa Region) in a June 2006 conversation at Disciples Divinity House, The University of Chicago, for the writers' conference for this book.

[50]Justo L. González and Pablo A. Jiménez, *Púlpito: An Introduction to Hispanic Preaching* (Nashville: Abingdon Press, 2005), 5.

[51]Ibid., 13.

[52]Ibid., 14.

[53]See Disciples homiletician Frank A. Thomas's *They Like to Never Quit Praisin' God: The Role of Celebration in Preaching* (Cleveland: United Church Press, 1997).

[54]For preaching as spiritual formation, see the forthcoming Bessler Northcutt, *Kindling Our Desire for God.*

[55]Geunhee Yu, "Asian American Disciples," in Foster, Blowers, Dunnavant, and Williams, eds., *The Encyclopedia of the Stone-Campbell Movement*, 40–41.

[56]Jung Young Lee, *Korean Preaching: An Interpretation* (Nashville: Abingdon Press, 1997), 67.

[57]Ibid., 71.

[58]Ibid., 74.

[59]Though representative data on pastors of recognized congregations from the *2005 Yearbook* (of the CCDC in the United States and Canada) are readily available (74% Men, 26% Women; 81% Ordained, 19% Licensed; 83% Caucasian, 10% African American, 4.8% Hispanic, 1.6% Asian, and .1% Other), the same representative data are less available *globally* speaking.

[60]See, for example, Joan Campbell and David Polk, eds., *Bread Afresh, Wine Anew: Sermons by Disciples Women* (St. Louis: Chalice Press, 1991).

[61]See Don A. Pittman, "On Preaching the Word: Notes from the History of Religions," *Homiletic* 23 (Winter 1998): 1–7, for the contribution a history of religions perspective brings to this discussion.

Chapter 17: Ministry

[1]Clark Williamson, "Theology and Forms of Confession...," *Encounter* 41 (Winter 1980): 53.

[2]The Panel of Scholars, the Association of Disciples for Theological Discussion, various Commissions on Theology, committees and bureaucrats and leading individuals—intellectual or ecclesiastical—have all functioned theologically as leaders for us.

[3]W.B. Blakemore, "The Christian Task and the Church's Ministry," in *The Renewal of Church: The Panel of Scholars Reports, v. III, the Revival of the Churches,* ed. Wm. Barnett Blakemore (St. Louis: The Bethany Press, 1963), 150–88.

[4]Williams's monograph, cited below, comes from about 1985. In Mark G. Toulouse, *Joined in Discipleship: The Shaping of Contemporary Disciples Identity,* 2d ed. (St. Louis: Chalice Press, 1997), Toulouse gives a chapter of his thematic history to the development of "one ministry." Richard L. Harrison Jr. covers the ground again in a 2002 article, "The Understanding of Ministry in the History of the Christian Church (Disciples of Christ)," *Lexington Theological Quarterly* 37, nos. 1 & 2 (2002): 7–26.

[5]Newell Williams, *Ministry Among Disciples: Past, Present, Future* (St. Louis: Published for the Council on Christian Unity by the Christian Board of Publication, 1985). Williams's overview guides my historical review.

[6]Or, as Harrison terms it, in relation to limiting the validity of ordination to a single congregation, "impractical, and not accepted by most of the congregations whether Campbellite or Stoneite," Harrison, "The Understanding of Ministry," 12.

[7]Toulouse, *Joined in Discipleship,* 174–75. Toulouse presents a helpful brief elaboration of Williams's discussion of this change in the role of elders in the congregation occasioned by the coming of the "professional" minister. See also Williams, *Ministry Among Disciples,* 17–20.

[8]The 1985 Report of the Commission on Theology, "A Word to the Church on Ministry," in Williams, *Ministry Among Disciples,* 49.

[9]Williams, *Ministry Among Disciples,* 51: "in ecumenical discussions it is difficult to know how to describe our eldership in such a way as to be claimed by other churches as part of the larger theological understanding of the church's ministry."

[10]Harrison, "The Understanding of Ministry," 16.

[11]Blakemore, "The Christian Task," 154.

[12]The current document may be accessed online at http://www.discipleshomemissions.org/Ministers/MinistryGuidelines/Order4.htm.

[13]The latest version of the document (draft 7, 2006) is not yet adopted, and it is unpublished, but it has been distributed for review from the General Commission on Ministry, Disciples Home Missions.

[14]World Council of Churches, *Baptism, Eucharist and Ministry,* Faith and Order Paper no. 11 (Geneva: World Council of Churches, 1982).

[15]The document's other change is to clarify "commissioned" as opposed to "licensed" ministry. Commissioned ministers would have educational requirements specified by the regions, rather than the "graduate degree from a theological school" specified for ordained ministry. In addition, commissioned ministers may enter the search and call process beyond the region in which they are commissioned. Much of the rest of the document refines and clarifies procedures and policies found in earlier versions.

[16]Harrison, "The Understanding of Ministry," 19–22.

[17]Ibid., 21.

[18]Anthony Dunnavant, "The Historical Development of an Ordered Ministry," *Lexington Theological Quarterly* 37, nos. 1 and 2 (2002): 6.

[19]The document, "My Ministerial Code of Ethics," is available online at http://www.homelandministries.org/Ministers/MinistryGuidelines/ethics.htm.. This wording of this rule is mine.

[20]See "Search and Call" Web site at http://www.homelandministries.org/SearchAndCall/index.htm.

[21]Winfred Ernest Garrison and Alfred T. DeGroot, *The Disciples of Christ, A History* (St. Louis: The Bethany Press, 1948), 163.

[22]Practical theologian Bonnie Miller-McLemore, in conversation.

[23]I must say at the outset what a pleasure it was to hear these experienced, thoughtful, wise ministers talk about ministry so elegantly. These ministers give me hope for the CCDC, and I offer them my sincere thanks for sharing their thoughts so freely. They serve in a variety of settings: one in theological education, one in denominational leadership, one in social justice ministry, one as associate minister in a middle-sized church, one as senior minister in a large congregation, one as solo pastor in a new church start, one as solo pastor in a small congregation. Three were female, four were male; four were Anglo, and one each Hispanic, Asian, and African American. This denomination has been impacted by globalism in very concrete ways. Yet there remains commonality within the new diversity we are experiencing.

[24]Dunnavant, "The Historical Development of an Ordered Ministry," 6.

[25]W. B. Blakemore, "Reasonable, Empirical, Pragmatic," in *The Renewal of Church: The Panel of Scholars Reports,* vol. 1, *The Reformation of Tradition,* ed. Ronald Osborn (St. Louis: The Bethany Press, 1963), 175.

[26]Williamson, "Theology and Forms of Confession."

Chapter 18: The Problem of Social Sin for Twenty-first–Century Christians

[1]Roger Betsworth, *Social Ethics: An Examination of American Moral Traditions* (Louisville: Westminster/John Knox Press, 1990), 23.

[2]Stephen Charles Mott and Stephen Charles, *Biblical Ethics and Social Change* (Nashville: Abingdon Press, 1982), 14.

[3]Ibid., 15.

[4]E. Clinton Gardiner, *Biblical Faith and Social Ethics* (New York: Harper & Row, 1960), 149–50.

[5]Darryl Michael Trimiew, *God Bless the Child That's Got Its Own: The Economic Rights Debate* (Atlanta: Scholars Press, 1997), 270.

[6]Campbell's position on slavery is fairly complex. He manumitted his own slaves, yet banned the "excommunication" of a Disciples church member solely on the grounds of being a slaveholder.

[7]See Darryl M. Trimiew and Michael Greene, "How We Got Over: The Economic Ethics of the African-American Church," in *Spiritual Goods: Faith Traditions and the Practice of Business*, Society of Business Ethics Anthology (Charlottesville, Va.: Philosophy Documentation Center, 2001), chapter 9.

[8]Indeed, this is precisely what we do achieve at General Assembly and other places of worship, since most of our churches are still segregated. General Assembly is open to racists and other sinners of all stripes.

[9]It is very difficult to have integrated churches when communities are segregated, even if such segregation is *de facto* rather than *de jure*.

[10]See the Affirmation of Faith of the Christian Church (Disciples of Christ).

[11]Roger Betsworth, "The Problem of Sub-Rosa Morality," *The American Baptist Quarterly* (Summer 2001).

[12]Affirmation of Faith.

[13]With regard to Walter Scott, see G.R. Stirling, *Five Fingers: An Examination of Certain Trends in the Restoration Movement in Australia Today,* Provocative Pamphlets No. 1 (Melbourne: Federal Literature Committee of Churches of Christ in Australia, 1955).

[14]See Cornel West's insightful analysis of Niebuhr in his *Prophetic Fragments: Illuminations of the Crisis* in *American Religion & Culture* (Grand Rapids, Mich.: Eerdmans, 1988.)

[15]Reinhold Niebuhr, *The Irony of American History* (New York: Charles Scribner's Sons, 1952), 63.

Chapter 19: Salvation

[1]It will not escape the reader's notice that I do not think the topic of "salvation" can be explored without discussing, at least and minimally, the doctrines of God, humanity, sin, christology, ecclesiology, and eschatology, topics also discussed in other chapters of this book. Perhaps it might be interesting to discern ways in which there is agreement and disagreement among the various authors of the essays in this book.

[2]Most of the issues discussed in this essay have been more extensively discussed in my two-volume systematic theology, *A Grammar of Christian Faith: Systematic Explorations in Christian Life and Doctrine* (Lanham, Md.: Rowman & Littlefield, 2002), and in a collection of my writings published as *On Being the Church of Jesus Christ in Tumultuous Times* (Eugene, Oreg.: Cascade Books, 2005). An earlier essay, "Schematic Reflections on Salvation in Jesus Christ," explored many of the themes and issues in this chapter and is reprinted in *On Being the Church,* 104–22.

[3]Useful studies of many of these biblical words can be found in: George Arthur Buttrick, ed., *Interpreter's Dictionary of the Bible,* 4 vols. (Nashville: Abingdon Press, 1962); Gerhard Kittel and Gerhard Friedrichs, eds., *Theological Dictionary of the New Testament,* abridged edition, ed. and trans. Geoffrey W. Bromiley (Grand Rapids, Mich.: Eerdmans, 1985); David Noel Freeman, ed., *The Anchor Bible Dictionary,* 6 vols. (New York: Doubleday, 1992).

[4]See Jones, *A Grammar of Christian Faith,* 149–232, for a fuller discussion of the doctrine of Trinity.

[5]See ibid., 293–364, for a fuller discussion of "Human Being as Created and Sinful." See especially 296–99 on creaturely being.

[6]See ibid., 300–322 on personal being.

[7]See ibid., 322–36 on spiritual being.

[8]See ibid., 343–64 on sin. Søren Kierkegaard and Reinhold Niebuhr are the great diagnosticians of sin in the modern world. See Søren Kierkegaard, *The Sickness Unto Death,* ed. and trans. Howard V. Hong and Edna H. Hong, *Kierkegaard's Writings,* vol. 19 (Princeton, N.J.: Princeton University Press, 1980); and Reinhold Niebuhr, *The Nature and Destiny of Man: A Christian Interpretation* (New York: Scribner, 1949).

[9]See Jones, *A Grammar of Christian Faith,* chapter 7 on "The Person of Jesus Christ."

[10]See ibid., chapter 8 on "The Work of Jesus Christ."

[11]Here "desert" means something deserved. It may be a punishment or a reward.

[12]See Galatians 2:15–21 for Paul's incisive discussion of the issue of works righteousness under the law. See also Jones, *A Grammar of Christian Faith,* 513–19.

[13]St. Anselm undertook to explain the salvific work of Jesus along these lines in "Why God Became Man," in *A Scholastic Miscellany: Anselm to Ockam*, ed. and trans. Eugene R. Fairweather, *Library of Christian Classics*, vol. 10 (Philadelphia: Westminster, 1956), 100–183. See Jones, *A Grammar of Christian Faith*, 443–45, 453–54, for a critique of Anselm.

[14]See Jones, *A Grammar of Christian Faith*, 709–24, for an extended discussion of issues involved in affirming dual destiny.

[15]Rudolf Bultmann dominated discussions about salvation during the 1950s and 1960s. See his *New Testament and Mythology and Other Basic Writings*, ed. and trans. Schubert Ogden (Philadelphia: Fortress Press, 1984).

[16]Liberation theology is more variegated than this brief excursus suggests, ranging from Latin American liberation theologies, to African American theologies, to feminist theologies. The common theme of all these theologies is that liberation from oppression is some state of affairs in human history in which justice is achieved and oppression is dismantled in all its forms. The concept of justice that functions as the goal of liberating and emancipating work often seems unstable and imprecise. See the sympathetic but sobering critique of Latin American liberation theology by Daniel M. Bell Jr., *Liberation Theology After the End of History: The Refusal to Cease Suffering* (New York: Routledge, 2001). See also Jones, *A Grammar of Christian Faith*, 505, 528–36, 630–33, 699–709.

[17]It is one of the strange silences among descendants of the nineteenth-century Stone-Campbell Movement, that it has forgotten that Alexander Campbell, one of the pioneering movers, understood himself as a millennialist and for years he published the journal entitled *Millennial Harbinger*. Campbell did seem to believe that the restoration of New Testament Christianity that he was advocating was beginning to show signs of progress that suggested that the reign of Christ might be near historically. However, Campbell's millennialism completely lacked the emphasis on a violent return by Christ to destroy the evildoers, which seems so prominent in today's world. But the terrible conflict of the Civil War devastated Campbell's confidence that the movement of "restoration Christianity" and the providential ordering of American democracy were harbingers of an almost "imminent" kingdom of God. See the fine discussion of Campbell's millennial concerns in Robert Frederick West's *Alexander Campbell and Natural Religion* (New Haven, Conn.: Yale University Press, 1948), especially 163–222.

[18]See Jones, *A Grammar of Christian Faith*, 433–35, 473–80, for discussions of the benefits of Christ and human salvation.

[19]For a more complete discussion of the church and salvation, see Jones, *On Being the Church of Jesus Christ in Tumultuous Times*, chapter 4, "The Church as Ark of Salvation." While I would not recommend a theological perspective that would reduce the role of the church in salvation to being one among many instances of religious communities conveying salvation, it must be admitted that the work of the Spirit of Christ is not restricted to the church. How and where it might be at work is a profound theological question. See Jones, *A Grammar of Christian Faith*, 497–501.

[20]On the status of hell, see Joe R. Jones, "Hell Is Empty," *DisciplesWorld*, vol. 3, no. 9 (November 2004): 13–15.

Chapter 20: Faith and Justification

[1]Tokunboh Adeyemo, *Salvation in African Tradition* (Nairobi: Evangel Publishing House, 1979), 19.

[2]Bosela Eale, "A Congolese View of Jesus," *DisciplesWorld* 4, no. 6 (July-August 2005): 13.

[3]Ibid.

[4]H. Byang Kato, *Theological Pitfalls in Africa* (Nairobi: Evangel Publishing House, 1987), 90–100.

[5]Bolaji Idowu, cited in Adeyemo, *Salvation in African Tradition*, 23.

[6]One particular example helps illuminate Rev. Eale's emphasis on salvation through Jesus Christ alone. The ecumenical situation in the Congo is complicated by the presence of the Kimbanguist church, whose members sometimes equate the spiritual leader Simon Kimbangu with Jesus, among other un-Orthodox ideas. For more on the Kimbanguist

Church, see Marie-Louise Martin, *Kimbangu: An African Prophet and His Church,* trans. D. M. Moore (Grand Rapids: Eerdmans, 1976).

[7]In his *Christian System,* Alexander Campbell launches his project by lauding Luther and the Reformation: "The Protestant Reformation is proved to have been one of the most splendid eras in the history of the world, and must long be regarded by the philosopher and the philanthropist as one of the most gracious interpositions in behalf of the whole human race." The context suggest Campbell's esteem of the Reformation centers on freeing Christianity from the Pope, "[restoring] the Bible to the world," and liberating the Christian conscience from the submission to creeds and ceremonies—though soon enough there was backtracking, according to Campbell, *The Christian System,* (Bethany, Va.: Alexander Campbell, 1839; reprint, St. Louis: Christian Publishing, 1890), 3–4.

[8]For some recent scholarship that attends to the differences between Paul and interpretations of him by the Reformers, see Krister Stendahl, "Paul and the Introspective Conscience of the West," in Stendahl, *Paul Among Jews and Gentiles, and Other Essays* (Philadelphia: Fortress Press, 1976); J.D.G Dunn, "The New Perspective on Paul" in Dunn, *Jesus, Paul and the Law: Studies in Mark and Galatians* (Louisville: Westminster/John Knox Press, 1990) and "The Justice of God: A Renewed Perspective on Justification by Faith," *Journal of Theological Studies* new series 43 (April 1992): 1–22.

[9]Many Disciples and other Christians have expressed concern over the concept of redemptive suffering, particularly that it might be used to promote the acceptance of suffering by the vulnerable and the exploited. (See esp. Rita Nakashima-Brock and Rebecca Ann Parker, *Proverbs of Ashes: Violence, Redemptive Suffering, and the Search for What Saves Us* [Boston: Beacon Press, 2001].) This use of Christ's suffering is a terrible form of abuse. Yet in my opinion, such a use of Christ's suffering is clearly a theological mistake, since the suffering of Jesus on the cross, itself a mystery beyond any one theory, is once-for-all and can never be repeated (Heb. 9:25–26). This was a key point for the Reformers.

[10]Calvin, *Institutes,* III. vii. 1–2.

[11]Martin Luther, "Lectures on Galatians," in *Luther's Works,* vol. 26, ed. Jaroslav Pelikan (St. Louis: Concordia, 1958), 387.

[12]Brian Gerrish sees this de-centering of the self as lying at the heart of Luther's (by no means neat and pat) doctrine of justification and its connection to love. See Brian Gerrish, "By Faith Alone: Medium and Message in Luther's Gospel," in his *The Old Protestantism and the New* (Chicago: University of Chicago Press, 1982).

[13]See Lester G. McAllister and William E. Tucker, *Journey in Faith* (St. Louis: Bethany Press, 1975), chapter 3. For an argument in favor of Stone's soteriology over A. Campbell's, see Frank Gardner, "Man and Salvation: Characteristic Ideas Among Disciples of Christ" in *The Reformation of Tradition,* ed. Ronald Osborn (St. Louis: Bethany Press, 1963).

[14]Alexander Campbell, *Millennial Harbinger* (1830): 498–99; quoted in Alexander Campbell and Royal Humbert, *A Compend of Alexander Campbell's Theology* (St. Louis: Bethany Press, 1961), 146–47.

[15]Ibid., 147.

[16]Ibid., 135.

[17]See the well-supported argument of Clark Gilpin, "The Integrity of the Church: The Communal Identity of Disciples of Christ," in *Classic Themes of Disciples Theology: Rethinking Traditional Affirmations of the Christian Church (Disciples of Christ)*, ed. Kenneth Lawrence (Fort Worth: Texas Christian University Press, 1986), 29–48.

[18]Compare W.E. Garrison, *Affirmative Religion* (New York: Harper and Bros., 1928), 124–26, in which he calls justification a "juridical device," with a later and more ecumenical work, idem, *A Protestant Manifesto* (New York: Abingdon-Cokesbury Press, 1952), 29 and 108–15.

[19]Clark Williamson, "Theology and Forms of Confession in the Disciples of Christ," *Encounter* 41 (Winter 1980): 53–71.

[20]Hans Küng, *Justification: The Doctrine of Karl Barth and a Catholic Reflection* (Philadelphia: Westminster Press, 1964); Hans Uhrs von Balthasar, *The Theology of Karl Barth* (New York: Holt, Rinehart and Winston, 1971).

[21]Karl Barth, *Church Dogmatics,* vol. 4, no. 1, trans. G.W. Bromiley and R. J. Ehrlich (Edinburgh: T. & T. Clark, 1992), 548.

[22]Barth's fuller answer takes account of God's eternal "Yes" to humanity in Christ; as I left it, one could wrongly assume that the covenant with Israel is outside of God's salvific plan.

[23]On the Catholic side, this tendency is affirmed in Hans Uhrs von Balthasar, *Dare We Hope: "That All Men Be Saved"?; with, A Short Discourse on Hell,* trans. David Kipp and Lothar Krauth (San Francisco: Ignatius Press, 1988). The JDDJ does not take a position on universalism, but strongly reflects the divine initiative of grace in Christ.

[24]See Walter Wink, *Engaging the Powers: Discernment and Resistance in a World of Domination* (Minneapolis: Fortress Press, 1992).

[25]We would like to express our gratitude to Garry Sparks, who lent his acumen for intercultural theology and his familiarity with the Democratic Republic of Congo to the shaping of this chapter. Garry recently participated in a HAM radio project in the Congo with the DARF/UCAN (in partnership with Global Ministries).

Chapter 21: Sanctification

[1]The definition they provide, that sanctification is "for Christians, the fact of our having been made ready to receive and to share God's love and help," (156) is not an adequate theological description of the concept from this author's perspective, as will become clearer later in the discussion.

[2]Robert Milligan, *Millennial Harbinger* (1847): 10.

[3]Alexander Campell, *Millennial Harbinger* (1832): 29–30.

[4]E.g, Campbell, *Millennial Harbinger* (1834): 12; (1840): 140; (1845): 53.

[5]Robert Richardson, *Millennial Harbinger* (1837): 63.

[6]Campbell, *Millennial Harbinger* (1840): 14.

[7]Campbell, *Millennial Harbinger* (1850): 401.

[8]Campbell, *Millennial Harbinger* (1852): 203.

[9]Anonymous ("Philip"), *Millennial Harbinger* (1830): 326.

[10]Ibid., 327.

[11]Campbell, "Bible Reading," *Millennial Harbinger* (1831): 36.

[12]A. Broaddus, *Millennial Harbinger* (1841): 27.

[13]Campbell, *Millennial Harbinger* (1844): 1.

[14]Campbell, *Millennial Harbinger* (1838): 61.

[15]Campbell, *Millennial Harbinger* (1830): 325.

[16]*Millennial Harbinger* (1850): 401.

[17]*Millennial Harbinger* (1830): 256.

[18]Ibid., 327.

[19]Campbell, *Millennial Harbinger* (1837): 62 and (1831): 98–99; see also 1 Corinthians 1:30.

[20]Anonymous ("Philip"), *Millennial Harbinger* (1830): 328.

[21]Julian Ibarra Zapata, "I Want to Be Counted in the Upper Room," in *Chalice Hymnal,* ed. Daniel B. Merrick (St. Louis: Chalice Press, 1995), no. 238.

[22]Anonymous, "Señor, Yo Quiero Entrar," *Chalice Hymnal,* no. 291.

[23]Daniel Iverson, "Spirit of the Living God," *Chalice Hymnal,* no. 259.

[24]Thomas T. Lynch, "Gracious Spirit, Dwell with Me," *Chalice Hymnal,* no. 266.

[25]Thomas H. Troeger, "Wind Who Makes All Winds That Blow," *Chalice Hymnal,* no. 236.

[26]Jane Parker Huber, "On Pentecost They Gathered," *Chalice Hymnal,* no. 237.

[27]William W. How, "O Word of God Incarnate," *Chalice Hymnal,* no. 322.

[28]Amy Grant, "Thy Word," *Chalice Hymnal,* no. 326.

[29]George Currie Martin, "Your Words to Me Are Life and Health," *Chalice Hymnal,* no. 324.

[30]See the discussion of "The Interpretive Theme" in the second chapter for a brief history of this central principle in Disciples theology.

[31]The following discussions of Catherine of Siena and Diadochos of Photiki include elements previously explored in chapters 8 and 9 of Karen Marie Yust and E. Byron Anderson, *Taught by God: Teaching and Spiritual Formation* (St. Louis: Chalice Press, 2006).

[32]Catherine of Siena, *Catherine of Siena, The Dialogue,* trans. Suzanne Noffke (New York: Paulist Press, 1980), 107.

[33]Ibid., 105.

[34]Ibid., 108.

[35]Ibid., 103.

[36]E. Byron Anderson, *Worship and Christian Identity* (Collegeville, Minn.: The Liturgical Press, 2003), 59.

[37]Diadochos as cited in "St. Diadochos of Photiki" in *The Philokalia,* trans. G.E.H. Palmer, Philip Sherrard, and Kallistos Ware, vol. 1 (Boston: Faber and Faber, 1979), 253.

[38]Ibid., 254.

[39]Ibid.

[40]Ibid., 260.

[41]Disciple Joseph Driskill addresses the issue of Protestant reluctance in his book *Protestant Spiritual Exercises: Theology, History and Practice* (Harrisburg, Pa.: Morehouse, 1999).

[42]Ibid., 259.

Chapter 22: Spirituality and the Disciples of Christ

[1]See Douglas F. Ottati, *Reforming Protestantism: Christian Commitment in Today's World* (Louisville: Westminster John Knox Press, 1995) especially the chapter titled, "The Sanctification of the Ordinary."

[2]The first two sections draw on material previously published in Bonnie J. Miller-McLemore, *In the Midst of Chaos: Care of Children as Spiritual Practice* (San Francisco: Jossey-Bass, 2006), used by permission.

[3]Kathleen Norris, *The Quotidian Mysteries: Laundry, Liturgy, and "Women's Work"* (New York: Paulist Press, 1998), 15–16.

[4]Ibid., 76.

[5]See Martin Luther, "The Estate of Marriage," in *Luther's Works,* ed. Walther I. Brandt and general ed. Helmut T. Lehmann (Philadelphia: Muhlenberg Press, 1962), 35–49.

[6]See, for example, Kathleen Norris, *Dakota: A Spiritual Geography* (New York : Ticknor & Fields, 1993) and *Cloister Walk* (New York: Riverhead, 1996).

[7]There is no shortage of books by Disciples on prayer, for example. See the Appendix of William O. Paulsell's book *Disciples at Prayer: The Spirituality of the Christian Church (Disciples of Christ)* (St. Louis: Chalice Press, 1995), 77–85.

[8]Thomas Merton, *New Seeds of Contemplation* (New York: New Directions, 1972), 7.

[9]Dean R. Hoge, Benton Johnson, and Donald A. Luidens, *Vanishing Boundaries: The Religion of Protestant Mainline Baby Boomers* (Louisville: Westminster John Knox Press, 1994), 70–73. This pattern is not unique to Presbyterians or Disciples, of course. The Methodist class meeting, in which congregational members gathered in small circles for Bible reading and prayer, shaped the moral ecology of families throughout the nineteenth century, but it largely disappeared in the twentieth. Emotionally vibrant spiritualities, such as the use of votive candles and rosary, flourished in pre-Vatican II Catholic homes, sometimes in genial contrast to the cognitive slant of formal doctrine, but decreased in the 1960s. See chapters by William R. Garrett, Jean Miller Schmidt and Gail E. Murphy-Geiss, and Christine Firer Hinze in *Faith Traditions and the Family*, ed. Phyllis Airhart and Margaret Lamberts Bendroth (Louisville: Westminster John Knox Press, 1996).

[10]Margaret Lamberts Bendroth, *Growing Up Protestant: Parents, Children, and Mainline Churches* (New Brunswick, N.J.: Rutgers University Press, 2002), 6.

[11]Clark M. Williamson, "Theology and the Forms of Confession in the Disciples of Christ," *Encounter* 41 (Winter 1980): 53 (61, 69).

[12]Joseph D. Driskill, *Protestant Spiritual Exercises: Theology, History, and Practice* (Harrisburg, Pa.: Morehouse, 1999), vi.

[13]Williamson, "Theology and the Forms of Confession," 61–62.

[14]W. B. Blakemore, "Reasonable, Empirical, Pragmatic" in *The Renewal of the Church: The Panel of Scholars Report*, v. 1, *The Reformation of Tradition,* ed. Ronald E. Osborn (St. Louis: Bethany Press, 1963), 161–83.

[15]Dwight E. Stevenson, "Faith versus Theology: In the Thought of the Disciple Fathers," in *The Reformation of Tradition*, ed. Ronald E. Osborn (St. Louis: Bethany Press, 1963), 53; Williamson, "Theology and the Forms of Confession," 56. See also Robert

Richardson, "Principles and Purpose of the Reformation," *Millennial Harbinger* (October, November, and December 1852).

[16]Williamson, "Theology and the Forms of Confession," 57. See also W.B. Blakemore, "Reasonable, Empirical, Pragmatic: The Mind of Disciples of Christ," in *The Reformation of Tradition,* 173–78.

[17]Williamson, "Theology and the Forms of Confession," 69.

[18]Ibid., 67.

[19]Ibid., 61. See also D. Newell Williams, "Disciples Piety: A Historical Review with Implications for Spiritual Formation," *Encounter* 47, no. 1 (Winter 1986): 1–25. Williams describes four overlapping phases of piety, one of which he calls "moralistic piety." However, the latter points toward but does not totally encompass the deeper theological and practical orientation that Williamson has in mind.

[20]Norman Maclean, *A River Runs Through It and Other Stories* (Chicago: University of Chicago Press, 1976), 1.

[21]W.M. Wickizer, "A Statement Concerning the Panel of Scholars," in *The Reformation of Tradition*, 7–8.

[22]Wickizer, "A Statement," 12.

[23]Nancy T. Ammerman, "Golden Rule Christianity: Lived Religion in the American Mainstream," in *Lived Religion in America: Toward a History of Practice*, ed. David Hall (Princeton, N.J.: Princeton University Press, 1997), 196–97.

[24]Ibid., 203.

[25]Driskill, *Protestant Spiritual Exercises,* xvii.

[26]Alexander Campbell, *Millennial Harbinger,* 1 (1830): 499.

[27]Eva Jean Wrather, *Alexander Campbell: Adventurer in Freedom: A Literary Biography,* ed. D. Duane Cummins (Fort Worth, Tex.: TCU Press and the Disciples of Christ Historical Society, 2005), 6–7.

[28]Ibid., 43.

[29]Paulsell, *Disciples at Prayer*, 6.

[30]Ibid., 20.

[31]Ibid., 24.

[32]Mark G. Toulouse, *Joined in Discipleship: The Shaping of Contemporary Disciples Identity,* 2nd ed. (St. Louis: Chalice Press, 1997), 67.

[33]Wrather, *Alexander Campbell,* 59

[34]Cleo Molina and Hutch Haney, "Using the Concept of Co-culture in Supervision," in *Supervision of Spiritual Directors: Engaging the Holy Mystery,* ed. Mary Rose Bumpus and Rebecca B. Langer (Harrisburg, Pa.: Morehouse, 2005), 150.

[35]"Preface," in *Setting the Table: Women in Theological Conversation,* ed. Rita Nakashima Brock, Claudia Camp, and Serene Jones (St. Louis: Chalice Press, 1995), viii.

[36]"Setting the Table: Meanings of Communion," in *Setting the Table,* 250–51.

[37]Ibid., 253, 257, 268.

[38]See, for example, Dorothy Bass, ed., *Practicing Our Faith: A Way of Life for a Searching People* (San Francisco: Jossey-Bass, 1998); Diana Butler Bass, *The Practicing Congregation: Imagining the New Old Church* (Herndon, Va.: Alban Institute, 2004); Driskill, *Protestant Spiritual Exercises;* Marjorie Thompson, *Soul Feast: An Invitation to Christian Spiritual Life* (Louisville: Westminster John Knox Press, 2005).

Chapter 23: Facing the Mark of the Beast

[1]Emmanuel Clapsis, "Eschatology," in *Dictionary of the Ecumenical Movement,* 2d ed., Nicholas Lossky, Jose Miguez Bonino, John Pobee et al. (Geneva: WCC Publications, 2002), 403.

[2]Johannes Weiss, *Jesus' Proclamation of the Kingdom* (Chico, Calif.: Scholars Press, 1985); Albert Schweitzer, *The Quest for the Historical Jesus* (Mineola, N.Y.; Dover, 2005).

[3]C.H. Dodd, *The Parables of the Kingdom* (New York: Harper Collins, 1981).

[4]Joachim Jeremias, *Theology of the New Testament* (London: SCM, 1973).

[5]Juan Stam, *Profecía Bíblica y Misión de la Iglesia* (Quito: Ediciones CLAI, 2004), 11–12.

[6]Leonardo Boff, *La vida mas allá de la vida* (México: Ediciones Dabar, 2000), 131–32.

[7]Fe, Economía y Sociedad, *Una voz desde las iglesias* (Quito: Ediciones CLAI, 2002).

[8]Pablo Manuel Ferrer, "La marca de la bestia," *RIBLA*, 34 (1999): 65–73; Xavier Pikasa, "666: El número de la bestia,"*Signos de Vida*, 41 (2006): 26–29.

[9]Fe, Economía y Sociedad, "La economía en ruta a la globalización," in *Globalizar la Vida Plena: Materiales para la Reflexión* (Quito: Ediciones CLAI, 2002), 3.

[10]Ibid.

[11]Ibid.

[12]Ibid., 2.

[13]Fe, Economía y Sociedad, "Una voz desde las iglesias," in *Globalizar la Vida Plena,* 18–19.

[14]Ibid.

[15]Ibid, 21

[16]Ibid.

[17]Ibid., 20.

[18]Nestor Miguez, "El Apocalipsis y la Economía," in *Globalizar la Vida Plena,* 2.

[19]Ibid., 4.

[20]Ibid.

[21]Ibid.

[22]Ibid.

[23]Ibid., 7.

[24]Ibid.

[25]Ibid. 7—8.

[26]Ibid., 9.

[27]Ibid., 10.

[28]Jürgen Moltmann, *The Coming of God* (Minneapolis: Fortress Press, 1996), xi.

[29]Fe, Economía y Sociedad, *Buscando Salidas, Caminando hacia Delante* (Quito: Ediciones CLAI, 2003), 43–44.

[30]Quoted in ibid., 63–65 (translated by the author).

Chapter 24: Theology of Prophetic Witness

[1]See Walter Brueggemann, *The Prophetic Imagination* (Minneapolis: Augsburg Fortress Press, 1978), 11–27, 109–13.

[2]From Martin Luther King Jr., "I Have a Dream," in *A Testament of Hope: The Essential Writings and Speeches of Martin Luther King, Jr.,* ed. James Melvin Washington (San Francisco: Harper Collins, 1986), 217–20.

[3]Several of these themes are explored in John W. DeGruchy, *Theology and Ministry in Context and Crisis* (Grand Rapids, Mich.: Wm.B. Eerdmans, 1987), 61–95.

[4]See Brueggemann, *Prophetic Imagination,* 44–79, and Abraham Joshua Heschel, *The Prophets* (New York: Harper & Row, 1962), 3–26.

[5]Stephen J. Patterson, *The God of Jesus: The Historical Jesus and the Search for Meaning* (Harrisburg, Pa.: Trinity Press International, 1998), 247. See also 55–87.

[6]Shailer Matthews, as quoted in Gary Dorrien, "Social Salvation" in *The Social Gospel Today,* ed. Christopher H. Evans (Louisville: Westminster John Knox Press, , 2001), 108.

[7]Martin Luther King Jr., "Pilgrimage to Nonviolence," in *A Testament of Hope,* 35–40.

[8]See Langdon Gilkey, *Reaping the Whirlwind: A Christian Interpretation of History* (New York: Seabury Press, 1976), 226–27.

[9]For a collection of liberation theologians from around the world, see Curt Cadorette, ed., *Liberation Theology: An Introductory Reader* (Maryknoll, N.Y.: Orbis, 1992).

[10]For a summary of these developments, see Lewis S. Mudge, "Ecumenical Social Thought," in *A History of the Ecumenical Movement,* vol. 3, ed. John Briggs, Mercy Amba Oduyoye, and George Tsetsis (Geneva: WCC, 2004), 279–322. The primary texts can be found in Michael Kinnamon and Brian E. Cope, eds., *The Ecumenical Movement: An Anthology of Key Texts and Voices* (Geneva: WCC, 1997), 263–324.

[11]Robert McAfee Brown, ed., *Kairos: Three Prophetic Challenges to the Church* (Grand Rapids, Mich.: Eerdmans, 1990), 48–60.

[12]A brief summary of this position, and its relationship to other "directions" in contemporary Christian social ethics, can be found in Dana Wilbanks, "The Church

as Sign and Agent of Transformation," in *The Church's Public Role,* ed. Dieter T. Hessel (Grand Rapids, Mich: W.B. Eerdmans, 1993), 21–34.

[13]Thomas F. Best and Martin Robra, eds., *Ecclesiology and Ethics: Ecumenical Ethical Engagement, Moral Formation and the Nature of the Church* (Geneva: WCC, 1997), 5.

[14]Mark G. Toulouse, "Disciples and Social Transformation," *Mid-Stream* (July 1987): 459. See also Albert M. Pennybacker, "The Local Congregation: Social Action Involvement," in *The Christian Church: An Interpretative Examination in the Cultural Context,* ed. George G. Beazley Jr. (St. Louis: Bethany Press, 1973), 195–217.

[15]Gary Dorrien, *Soul in Society: The Making and Renewal of Social Christianity* (Minneapolis: Fortress Press, 1995), 3.

[16]Harold L. Lunger, *The Political Ethics of Alexander Campbell* (St. Louis: Bethany, 1954), 193–232.

[17]Ibid., 242–63.

[18]Karl Barth, as quoted in DeGruchy, *Theology and Ministry,* 86.

[19]Lunger, *Political Ethics of Campbell,* 270–71.

[20]Ibid., 267.

[21]Toulouse, "Disciples and Social Transformation," 464.

[22]James A. Crain, *The Development of Social Ideas Among the Disciples of Christ* (St. Louis: Bethany Press, 1969), 283.

[23]David Edwin Harrell Jr., *Quest for a Christian America: The Disciples of Christ and American Society to 1866* (Nashville: Disciples of Christ Historical Society, 1966), 19, and idem, *The Social Sources of Division in the Disciples of Christ 1865–1900* (Nashville: Disciples of Christ Historical Society, 1973), 22.

[24]Crain, *Development of Social Ideas,* 20–21.

[25]Lunger, *Political Ethics of Campbell,* 53.

[26]Crain, *Development of Social Ideas,* 14–15.

[27]Ibid., 283. See also Toulouse, "Disciples and Social Transformation," 466.

[28]Crain, *Development of Social Ideas,* 286.

[29]This history is summarized in Robert L. Friedly and D. Duane Cummins, *The Search for Identity: Disciples of Christ, The Restructure Years* (St. Louis: CBP Press, 1987), 85–88.

[30]Lewis S. Mudge, *The Church as Moral Community* (New York: WCC, 1998), 18. Dorrien, *Soul in Society,* 365, cites a survey showing that 72 percent of mainline church members have never worked for social change.

[31]Audrey R. Chapman, *Faith, Power, and Politics: Political Ministry in Mainline Churches* (New York: Pilgrim Press, 1991), 88.

[32]See Dorrien, *Soul in Society,* 367.

[33]The quotation is from the Martin Luther King Jr. sermons "I Have a Dream" and "A Christmas Sermon on Peace" in *A Testament of Hope,* 219–58.

[34]This is a formulation of H. Richard Niebuhr, "The Responsibility of the Church for Society" in *The Gospel, the Church and the World,* ed. Kenneth Scott Latourette (New York: Harper & Brothers, 1946), 111–33.

[35]Wilbanks, "The Church as Sign and Agent of Transformation," 29.

[36]Peter Ainslie, *If Not a United Church – What?* (New York: Fleming H. Revell, 1920), 33.

Chapter 25: Mission in Africa

[1]John S. Pobee, *The Search for a Living Church in Africa: In an African Call for Life* (Nairobi: Uzima Press, 1983), 47.

[2]S.E.M. Pheko, *The Early Church in Africa and Today* (Lusaka: Multimedia Publications, 1982), 1.

[3]Ibid., 9.

[4]Ibid.

[5]Timothee Bankole, *Missionary Shepherds and African Sheep* (Ibadan: Daystar Press, 1971), 19.

[6]Ibid., 19.

[7]David J. Hesselgrave, *Planting Churches Cross-Culturally* (Grand Rapids: Baker Book House, 1980), 20.

[8]N.K. Mugambi, *The Biblical Basis for Evangelization: Theological Reflections Based on an African Experience* (Nairobi: Oxford University Press, 1989), 3.

[9]Musimbi Kanyoro, "Thinking Mission in Africa," *International Review of Mission*, vol. 87, no. 345 (April 1998): 221.

[10]Ibid., 226.

[11]Adrian Hastings, *The Church in Africa 1450–1950* (Oxford: Clarendon Press, 1994), 93.

[12]Ibid., 95.

[13]Bankole, *Missionary Shepherds and African Sheep*, 20.

[14]Ibid., 2.

[15]Geoffrey Chapman, *African Christianity* (London: Cassell & Collier Macmillan, 1976), 11.

[16]Baukole, *Missionary Shepherds and African Sheep*, 9.

[17]Ibid., 30.

[18]Mahaniah Kimpianga, "Towards a Self-Supporting African Church," in *An African Call for Life* (Geneva: World Council of Churches 1983), 55–56.

[19]Mavumilisa Makanzu, *The Twentieth Century Missionaries and the Murmurs of the Africans* (Aberdeen: The University of Aberdeen, 1974), 14.

[20]J.W.C. Dougall, *Christian in the African Revolution* (Edinburgh: The Saint Andrew Press, 1963), 51.

[21]For the statistic, see D.B. Barret, ed., *World Christian Encyclopedia* (Nairobi: Oxford University Press, 1982), 136.

[22]Chapman, *African Christianity*, 9.

[23]John S. Mbiti, *Bible and Theology in African Christianity* (Nairobi: Oxford University Press, 1986), 12.

[24]Kä Mana, *Christian and Churches of Africa* (Yaounde: Editions Cle, 2002), 91.

[25]Valentino Salvoldi and Renato Kizito Sesana, *Africa: The Gospel Belongs To Us* (Ndola: Mission Press, 1986), 12.

[26]Kä Mana, *Christian and Churches of Africa*, 91.

[27]Boladji Idowu, *African Traditional Religion: A Definition* (Maryknoll, N.Y.: Orbis 1973), 205.

Chapter 26: Mission in Pluralistic Contexts

[1]David J. Bosch, *Transforming Mission: Paradigm Shifts in Theology of Missions* (Maryknoll, N.Y.: Orbis, 1997), 182–83.

[2]Ibid., 310–11.

[3]Robert Moore, "The Historical Basis of Theological Reflection," in *Troubling of the Waters*, ed. Idris Hamid (San Fernando, Trinidad: Rahman Printery Ltd., 1973), 39–41.

[4]Nicholas von Zinzendorf, as quoted in William Watty, "The De-Colonization of Theology," in *Troubling of the Waters*, 63.

[5]William Watty, *From Shore to Shore: Soundings in Caribbean Theology* (Barbados: CEDAR Press, 1981), 31.

[6]Pearl Springer, as quoted in Burton Sankeralli, ed., "The Panel," in *At the Crossroads: African Caribbean Religion and Christianity* (Barbados: CEDAR Press, 1995), 166–67.

[7]Watty, *Shore to Shore*, 6.

[8]Pearl Springer, as quoted in Sankeralli, "The Panel," 166–67.

[9]Lesslie Newbigin, *The Gospel in a Pluralist Society* (Grand Rapids, Mich.: William B. Eerdmans, 1989), 7–9.

[10]Burton Sankeralli, "Editors Report," in *At the Crossroads*, 221–22.

[11]Newbigin, *Gospel in a Pluralist Society*, 94.

[12]Sankeralli, "The Panel," 169.

[13]Alfred North Whitehead, *Adventures of Ideas* (New York: The Free Press, Macmillan; London, Collier Macmillan, 1961), 18.

[14]Watty, "The De-Colonizination of Theology," 77.

[15]Rex M. Nettleford, *Caribbean Cultural Identity: The Case of Jamaica* (Kingston: Institute of Jamaica, Herald Press Limited, 1978), 189.

[16]Watty, *Shore to Shore*, 45.

[17]Ibid., 49.

[18]Ibid., 3.

[19]Watty, "The De-Colonization of Theology," 74.

[20]Pearl Springer, as quoted in Sankeralli, "The Panel," 173.

[21]Lewin Williams, *Caribbean Theology* (New York: P. Lang, 1994).

[22]Lorraine Code, *What Can She Know? Feminist Theory and the Construction of Knowledge* (Ithaca and London: Cornell University Press, 1991), 2.

[23]Watty, *Shore to Shore*, 14.

[24]Sankeralli, "A Response to Lewin Williams," (unpublished paper delivered at consultation on Caribbean theology, January, 1998), 4.

[25]Paul Knitter, *Jesus and the Other Names: Christian Mission and Global Responsibility* (Maryknoll, N.Y.: Orbis, 2001), 70.

[26]John Cobb, as quoted in ibid., 81.

[27]Sankeralli, "Response to Lewin Williams," 4.

[28]Gerald Boodoo, "In Response to Adolfo Ham 1," in *Caribbean Theology: Preparing for the Challenges Ahead*, ed. Howard Gregory (Barbados: Canoe Press, University of the West Indies, 1995), 11.

[29]Ibid.

[30]Sankeralli, "Response to Lewin Williams," 4.

[31]Ravi-Ji, "Hinduism and Popular Religion," in *At the Crossroads*, 154.

[32]D. Preman Niles, *From East and West: Rethinking Christian Missions* (St. Louis: Chalice Press, 2004), 137.

[33]Ibid., 137–38.

[34]S.J. Samartha, *Courage for Dialogue: Ecumenical Issues in Inter-Religious Relations* (Geneva: World Council of Churches, 1981), 89.

[35]Ibid.

Chapter 27: Ecumenism of the Spirit and Mission

[1]David J. Bosch, *Transforming Mission: Paradigm Shifts in Theology of Missions* (Maryknoll, N.Y.: Orbis, 1997), 463–67.

[2]Márcio Fabri dos Anjos, ed., *Teología y nuevos paradigmas*, trans. José Antonio Aguirre (Bilbao, Spain: Ediciones Mensajero, 1999), 9–67, 195–209.

[3]Peter C. Hodgson, *Revisioning the Church: Ecclesial Freedom in the New Paradigm* (Philadelphia: Fortress Press, 1988), 11–12. Emphasis mine.

[4]Ibid., 18.

[5]Konrad Raiser, *Ecumenism in Transition: A Paradigm Shift in the Ecumenical Movement?* trans. Tony Coates (Geneva: WCC Publications, 1991), 77.

[6]For a Latin American perspective on this issue, see Julio de Santa Ana, "Ecumenismo y nuevas llaves de lectura," *Revista de cultura teológica II*, 6 (January/March 1994): 73–85.

[7]Bosch, *Transforming Mission*, 185–87, 210–13, 264–67.

[8]Hans Kung, *Theology for the Third Millennium: An Ecumenical View*, trans. Peter Heinegg (New York: Doubleday, 1991), 204.

[9]Robert Streiter, "Contextualization from a World Perspective," *Association of Theological Schools Theological Education Supplement*, I (1993): 63–86.

[10]Ibid., 68.

[11]Stephen B. Bevans, *Models of Contextual Theology* (Maryknoll, N.Y.: Orbis Books, 1992), 21–22.

[12]John A. Mackay, *Ecumenics: The Science of the Church Universal* (Old Tappan, N.J.: Prentice Hall, 1964), 197–98.

[13]Marta Palma, "A Pentecostal Church in the Ecumenical Movement," *The Ecumenical Review* 37, no. 2 (April 1985): 223–29.

[14]The CCDC started an ecumenical partnership with several Pentecostal churches in Latin America and the Caribbean: Evangelical Pentecostal Union of Venezuela in 1963, Pentecostal Christian Church of Cuba in 1976, and Christian Mission Church of Nicaragua in the 1980s. The UCC established an ecumenical partnership with the Pentecostal Church of Chile in the 1980s. The Presbyterian Church (USA) has had relationships with several Pentecostal churches, providing a better understanding between Pentecostals and

mainline churches. See Benjamín Gutiérrez and Dennis A. Smith, *In the Power of the Spirit: The Pentecostal Challenge to Historic Churches in Latin America* (Louisville: Latin American Center for Pastoral Studies [CELEP]–Alliance of Presbyterian and Reformed Churches in Latin America (AIPRAL) (PC-(USA)/WMD, 1996).

[15]Albert C. Outler, "Pneumatology as an Ecumenical Frontier," in *To the Wind of God's Spirit*, ed. Emilio Castro (Geneva: WCC Publications, 1990), 19–20.

[16]José Míguez Bonino, "*Ecumenismo y unidad de la iglesia*" (Lecture, General Assembly, CLAI, Concepción Chile, 1995), 4 (translation mine).

[17]Ofelia Ortega, "Ecumenism of the Spirit," in *In the Power of the Spirit*, ed. Benjamín F. Gutiérrez and Dennis Smith (Louisville: Latin American Center for Pastoral Studies-PC (USA)/WMD, 1996), 183.

[18]Walter Hollenweger, *El pentecostismo: Historia y doctrina*, trans. Ana S. de Veghazi (Buenos Aires, Argentina: La Aurora, 1976). More recently, Walter Hollenweger, *Pentecostalism: Origins and Developments Worldwide* (Peabody, Mass.: Hendrickson Publishers, 1997); and Donald W. Dayton, *Theological Roots of Pentecostalism* (Grand Rapids, Mich.: Francis Asbury Press, 1987).

[19]Gabriel Vaccaro, *Así veo al Señor* (Buenos Aires, Argentina: Argen Press, 1982), 192.

[20]Carmelo E. Álvarez, ed., *Pentecostalismo y liberación: Una experiencia Latinoamericana* (San Jose, Costa Rica: Editorial Departamento Ecuménico de Investigaciones,1992), 254 (translation mine).

[21]Ibid., 251–54.

[22]Outler, "Pneumatology as an Ecumenical Frontier," 19.

[23]Guillermo Cook, "Interchurch Relations: Exclusion, Ecumenism, and the Poor," in *Power, Politics, and Pentecostals in Latin America*, ed. Edward L. Cleary and Hannah W. Stewart-Gambino (Boulder, Colo.: Westview Press, 1997), 80.

[24]H. Richard Niebuhr, *The Kingdom of God in America* (New York: Harper Torchbooks, 1937). An interesting article analyzing the influence of contemporary ideas of enterprise on the concept of kingdom building in missionary work can be found in James H. Moorehead, "Engineering the Millennium: Kingdom Building in American Protestantism, 1820–1920," *Princeton Seminary Bulletin, Supplement* 3 (1994): 104–28.

[25]James H. Moorehead, *World without End: Mainstream American Protestant Visions of the Last Things* (Bloomington, Ind.: Indiana University Press, 1999), 50, 129.

[26]Carmelo E. Álvarez, "*Evangelio social*," in *Diccionario de historia de la iglesia*, ed. Wilton M. Nelson (Miami: Editorial Caribe, 1989), 425–26.

[27]W. Clark Gilpin, "The Integrity of the Church: The Communal Theology of Disciples of Christ," in *Classical Themes of Disciples Theology*, ed. Kenneth Henry (Fort Worth, Tex.: Texas Christian University Press, 1986), 29–30. An important interpretation along these same lines is found in Mark G. Toulouse, "The Kingdom of God and Disciples of Christ," *Discipliana* 62 (1) (Spring 2002): 3–24.

[28]Gilpin, "The Integrity of the Church," 31.

[29]Ibid.

[30]Ibid., 32–46.

[31]Freddie Briceño, "Mi visión de la UEPV a los primeros siete años de fundada," in *Presencia pentecostal en Venezuela*, ed. Gamaliel Lugo (Maracaibo, Venezuela: Ediciones UEPV, 1997), 15. See also Luis F. del Pilar, *Lo hizo El: Testimonios I* (Bayamón, Puerto Rico: Impresas Quintana, 1999), 149–53.

[32]Ibid.

[33]Ibid., 16.

[34]Dale A. Fiers, "Report of Latin American Trip" (Indianapolis: Minutes of Board of UCMS, 1959), Item 10, 4.

[35]Domingo Rodríguez, interview by Carmelo E. Álvarez, June 12, 1997.

[36]Juan Marcos Rivera, *Venezuela Newsletter* (June 1963): 1–4.

[37]Gregorio Uzcátegui, "*Hitos para la historia*," unpublished manuscript, August 21, 1999, 1.

[38]Thomas J. Liggett, "La Situación Actual de la Obra Evangélica en América Latina," in CELA, *Cristo, la Esperanza para América Latina* (Buenos Aires, Argentina: Confederación Evangélica del Río de la Plata, 1962), 49–67. Liggett offers some insightful interpretations on the religious scenario in Latin America and the challenges they pose to Disciples in the

United States in two articles published in *World Call,* the official missionary journal of the denomination for many years. See T.J. Liggett, "New Era Dawns in Latin America," *World Call* (January 1962): 19–20; and T.J. Liggett, "Protestant Dilemmas in Latin America," *World Call* (November 1964): 19–20.

[39]Joaquín Vargas, *Los Discípulos de Cristo en Puerto Rico* (San Jose, Costa Rica: DEI, 1988), 73–102. For an analysis of the role and reconciliation of the missionaries involved in this controversy, see Carmelo E. Álvarez and Carlos Cardoza, *Llamados a Construir el Reino: Teología y Estrategia Misionera de los Discípulos de Cristo 1899–1999* (Bayamón, Puerto Rico: Iglesia Cristiana [Discípulos de Cristo] en Puerto Rico, 1999), 85–100.

[40]Juan Marcos Rivera, telephone interview by Carmelo E. Álvarez, June 11, 1997.

[41]Thomas J. Liggett, "Memorandum," transcription of telephone interview by Carmelo E. Álvarez on June 11, 1997.

[42]Ibid.

[43]Thomas J. Liggett, Report of *Visit to Churches and Leaders of the Pentecostal Union of Venezuela (Maracaibo)* July 12–14, 1963, 5.

[44]Ibid.

[45]Ibid.

[46]Gregorio Uzcátegui, "*Hitos para la historia,*" 2.

[47]Liggett, "Memorandum."

Chapter 28: "Glocal" Chalice of Blessing

[1]Jose Miguez Bonino, "El mundo entero es mi parroqula: Misión y oikoumene en el contexto global de metodismo y globalización a comienzo del siglo XXI," *Cuadernos de Teología* 22 (2003): 93–103.

[2]The transfer of public wealth and state administration to private and transnational control, known better as the privatization of public institutions, of which there are sufficient examples.

[3]It postulates a selective modernization that moves from the integration of societies to submitting the population to Latin American business elites, and from them to the banks, investors, and transnational creditors. Broad sectors lose their employment and basic social benefits, the capacity for public action falls, along with the sense of national projects. For neoliberalism, exclusion is a component of modernization dependent on the market. See Nestor García Canclini, *Latinoamericanos buscando un lugar en este sitio* (Buenos Aires: PAIDOS, 2002), 44. At the same time, a deterioration is produced: (1) index of negative growth; (2) control of inflation by a policy of social adjustments; (3) increase of national debt; (4) extension of urban poverty; (5) loss of credibility in political parties and government leaders; (6) loss of regional utopias with the increase in the integration of communication—four or five powerful factors influence this: (a) Spanish publishing groups (Bertelsmann, Planeta, Prisa), Spanish Radio, TV, and telephone, (b) U.S. communication corporations (CNN, Time Warner), (c) foreign Latin American studies (U.S., Canadian, and European universities), (d) studies by Latin Americans (academic, literary, and social science contexts), (e) Latin American governments and their socio-cultural policies.

[4]Money combined with consumerism as a world religion is the reason people are organized in accord with the criteria of the capitalist economy.

[5]Social scientists and neoclassical liberals share a vision of the world: the world as a machine; as such, its functioning can be understood if we unite the parts that compose it. But as a whole, from the sum of its components can be deduced individuals or social classes. A lever that readjusts with a determined force some part of the machinery would provoke regulated and foreseeable results in another part of the same machinery. By this concept, the basic piece of machinery is the person who acts rationally to calculate the maximization of benefits and the minimization of costs. Productive pacification generates economic growth, in other words, progress (as the laureates of the Nobel Prize for Economics Gary Becker and James Buchanan believed—1990 and 1995.) After this mechanistic and individualistic vision, it was preferred to use the analogy of a living organism, given the complexity that the system represented; thus the economic

dynamic was not only considered the result of the interaction of quantifiable factors but also values and other factors that favored production: "societies flourish when beliefs and technologies are congruent and decline when inevitable changes in beliefs and technologies begin to be incongruent." (L. Thurow, *El futuro del capitalismo* (Barcelona: Ariel, 1996), 25; cited in Jung Mo Sung, *Deseo, Mercado y Religion* [Santander: Sal Terrae, 1999], 120. Given the aspect of its self-determination, neoliberal capitalism, through its great exponents, comes to surpass religion to show itself as religiously efficient: where the cult of success is substituted for belief in principles. (Even within the workings of this same system, strong revisions are made that lead to the recognition of the cultural and ethico-religious dimension as *completely indispensable to the free market for embracing civilization*, see, among others, George Soros and Vargas Llosa.)

[6]This would include natural death through science, violent death by means of judicial power and military or police forces, death caused by hunger due to capitalist economic growth.

[7]The presuppositions of Francis Fukuyama are: (1) every occurrence has a cause and a resolution; (2) ideas determine every conception of the world; (3) contradictions give impulse to the process of history and once resolved lead to their cancellation (triumph of a thinker), according to Mario Yutsis, "Hegel, Fukuyama y el fin de la historia," *Cuadernos de Teologia* 14 no. 1 (1995): 7–16.

[8]Francis Fukuyama, *O fim da histona e o ultimo homen* (Rio de Janeiro: Rocco, 1992), 14; cited in Jung Mo Sung, *Deseo, Mercado y Religion* (Santander: Sal Terrae, 1999), 26.

[9]Here a transfer is made: from God to the neoliberal capitalist system.

[10]Lula Da Silva, president of Brazil, recognizes this crisis by the title he gave his plan of government: *fome 0*.

[11]Sung, *Deseo, Mercado y Religion*, 29.

[12]Pam Friedrich Von Hayek, "A free society needs morality, which in the end comes down to the preservation of life—not the preservation of all life, if it is it necessary to sacrifice individual life in order to save a greater number of other lives. For this, the only rules of morality are those which lead to a calculus of life: *property and contract*." Cf. Ulrich Duchrow, *Fe, Economia y Sociedad, desde una perspectiva global*, en *Las Iglesias Evangélicas dicen Basta* (Buenos Aires: CLAI, 2004), 80.

[13]It is the other opposed to success; it is the most eloquent sign of non-salvation. On the other hand, it is the indication that the market acts freely: where the state does not interfere and individuals are marginalized due to inefficiency, given the competition. In this way, society is negated and only individuals count who make it.

[14]By this cruel spirituality, the IMF and the World Bank recommend that poor countries adopt adequate policies, which is to say the measures of economic adjustment such as the liberalizing of the economy. These policies of "structural adjustment" have a clear purpose: *privatize income and socialize losses.*

[15]Sacrifices are impositions in the name of a divinized law that goes against the freedom of the person sacrificed and that are required in the name of a divinity or sacralized institution.

[16]Cf. Franz J. Hinkelammert, *Sacrificios Humanos y Sociedad Occidental: Lucifer y la bestia* (Costa Rica: DEI, 1993), 9–53.

[17]The International Monetary Fund was created to put international solidarity in the service of the countries in crisis, which strengthened them to make their economies more efficient.

[18]Duchrow, *Fe, Economia y Sociedad*, 76.

[19]The debt is not a financial problem but a *mechanism of slavery, of domination and control*, because it dominates our lives, our nations, our possibility to exercise sovereignty and to design policies in accord with the rights and needs of our peoples. It is illegitimate because (1) it was not contracted by the people, but by the dictators in full co-responsibility with the IMF, World Bank, BID, etc.; (2) it has its roots in a deep history of inequality (due to exploitation and the lack of control by part of the people); (3) it is an instrument of permanent looting (poverty in the South in relation to wealth in the North); (4) it is based on the distinct conditions that accompany payment (structural adjustments, programs for reducing poverty); (5) it is a debt already paid many times. For these reasons, the external

debt was, is, and will continue to be a violation of human rights of the Latin American peoples. The other face of the debt shows us that it is not our debt but theirs because it causes *poverty.* The Latin American peoples are creditors rather than debtors.

[20]The situation of cultural encounter is well-known when Pizarro gave the Bible to Atahualpa, saying, "It is the word of God." Atahualpa held the book to his ear and after a moment of silence, said, "*Your God does not speak to me,*" and flung the Vulgate to the ground, an act used to justify the vandalism and genocide that followed.

[21]The classical doctrines of atonement include the following: (a) The dramatic conception of atonement or theory of *Christus Victor* derived from the cosmic vision of triumph of good over evil or of God over the devil. Thus, the death of the Son is seen as the apparent victory of Satan, but given the resurrection, the Son is presented as *victorious* over Satan, evil, and death. (b) The conception of Anselm or objective theory of satisfaction by medieval analogy recognizes God as a feudal lord whose honor has been offended. To restore the honor of a lord, it was necessary that one of his equals repair the fault, because a vassal could not do it; through the Incarnation, the Son who identifies as much with the vassals (human beings) as with the feudal lord (the Father) takes upon himself the cross to pay for the offense and to restore harmony between God and his creation. This concept, by which only the Father is God, shows that the Spirit is forgotten and minimizes the decision and active participation of the Son in the history of salvation. (c) The conception of Abelard or subjective theory or the moral influence theory understands that the sufferings of Christ were not redemptive in themselves but provided an inspiring example (Rom. 3:19–26). In this form, our reconciliation would consist in being transformed by the example of Jesus. To experience the eternal love of Christ is that which leads us to live in love and not in fear.

[22]Elsa Tamez, *Contra toda Condena la justificacion por la fe desde los excluidos* (Costa Rica: DEI, 1991), 179.

[23]Severino Croatto says, "In infinite forms, all ritual seeks to be in contact with the sacred." I add "*...with the resurrection of Christ,*" cf. Cristobal Mareco Lird, *Los Lenguajes de la Experiencia Religiosa: estudio de fenomenologia de la religion* (Buenos Aires: Docencia, 1994), 226–27.

[24]Tamez, *Contra toda Condena,* 175.

[25]BID, World Bank, IMF, et al., are economic organizations that operate as priests and pastors and show success, prosperity, and the efficacy of the system as signs of salvation.

[26]Amartya Sen, *Development as Freedom* (New York: Anchor, 2000), 42.

[27]Constructed with the images which others have of the church.

[28]Resides not in reflection or in the image that is returned but in the *name* that is given and that makes of it an agent of grace.

[29]Every affirmation about the church will be an affirmation about Christ. Every affirmation about Christ also contains an affirmation about the church, but it is not absorbed in it, since, at the same time, it has a greater scope and is oriented toward the messianic kingdom, which is served by the church.

[30]"The preaching of the Gospel of the coming Kingdom of God is the primary factor and the most important in the mission of Jesus, in the mission of the Spirit, and in the mission of the church, but it is not the only one," Jurgen Moltmann, *La Iglesia fuerza del Espiritu* (Salamanca: Sígueme, 1978), 26–27.

[31]Before, the local was an affair of generations more accustomed to domestic tastes and learning, to politicians who did not know languages to undertake transnational negotiations, to national university professors and nostalgic folklore sages.

[32]This "*glocal*" integration is a new common scenario where: (1) the *majors* of musical industry are enterprises that glide with ease between the global and the national; (2) Japanese or North American cars and musical instruments are assembled in our localities without importing much to where the parts or sections are made; 3) one day we eat the same as did our grandparents, and the following we have a fast lunch at McDonald's while we listen to Ricky Martin or Gloria Estefan mixing English and Spanish in the same song; (4) movies have recently inserted this cosmopolitan utilization of the local. The European and Latin American menu includes films which rework local past history to return and think about the daily fascism and social decomposition.

[33]Garcia Canclini, *Latinoamericanos buscando lugar en este siglo,* 59. "Cultural goods transcend theaters, bookstores, and concert halls. Books and CDs are sold in supermarkets and department stores, theatrical works and popular or classical music find spectators on television. Even though this expansion of space and massive networks, associated with sales and fleeting fashions, provoke suspicions about the cultural quality of mass communication, more writers and musicians can make a living. At the same time, the public which is not habituated to aesthetic temples have access to the work of their country and of many others."

[34]Act 16 of May 1951, *Trends of the Paraguay Mission,* 2.

[35]The liberal economy, prominently Calvinist, understands that salvation is not by works but believes that one must give a sign of this gratuitous salvation, so that work was considered the best sign of salvation; from this comes the expression, "*Work dignifies the human being.*" Neoliberalism raises doubt about this conception; it goes further to say that it is not work that is the best sign of salvation but only success.

[36]Jon Sobrino says that the salvific efficacy of the cross is shown more as the exemplary cause than the efficient cause, which does not take away its efficacy. See Jon Sobrino, *Cristología desde América Latina: Esbozo* (Mexico: Ediciones CRT, 1977), Chapter 6.

Chapter 29: Toward a Disciples Theology of Religions

[1]Council on Christian Unity, "Disciples of Christ and Interreligious Engagement," *Call to Unity: Resourcing the Church for Ecumenical Ministry* 6 (September 2006): 1.

[2]Ibid., 3. Emphasis mine.

[3]Ibid.

[4]Ibid., 4.

[5]Ibid., 5.

[6]Ibid., 7.

[7]See Diana L. Eck, *A New Religious America: How a "Christian Country" Has Now Become the World's Most Religiously Diverse Nation* (San Francisco: HarperSanFrancisco, 2001).

[8]Remark made by John B. Cobb Jr. at the 1987 International Conference on Buddhist-Christian Dialogue, Berkeley, California. See the videotape documentary, "Buddhism and Christianity: Toward the Human Future."

[9]Willard G. Oxtoby, *The Meaning of Other Faiths* (Philadelphia: Westminster Press, 1983), 31.

[10]*The Sources of Catholic Dogma,* trans. Roy J. Deferrari from the 30th ed. of H. Denzinger's *Enchiridion Symbolorum* (St. Louis: B. Herder, 1957), 230.

[11]Justin Martyr, as quoted in *The Ante-Nicene Fathers: Translations of the Writings of the Fathers Down to A.D. 325,* 9 vols., ed. A. Roberts and J. Donaldson (Grand Rapids: Eerdmans, 1973), 1:178. The more inclusive term "individuals" was used here for the Greek term translated "men."

[12]Augustine, *Earlier Writings,* ed. and trans. John H. S. Burleigh (Philadelphia: Westminster Press, 1953), 218.

[13]*Vatican Council II. The Conciliar and Post-Conciliar Documents,* ed. Austin Flannery (Dublin: Dominican Publications, 1975), 367.

[14]See Mark G. Toulouse, *Joined in Discipleship: The Shaping of Contemporary Disciples Identity,* 2d ed. (St. Louis: Chalice Press, 1997), 189–217. See also Don A. Pittman and Paul A. Williams, "Mission and Evangelism: Continuing Debates and Contemporary Interpretations," in *Interpreting Disciples Practical Theology in the Disciples of Christ,* ed. L. Dale Richesin and Larry D. Bouchard (Fort Worth: Texas Christian University Press, 1987), 206–47.

[15]This does not include as "typical" the position of Christian exclusivists who are also universalists.

[16]Alan Race, *Christians and Religious Pluralism: Patterns in the Christian Theology of Religion* (London: SCM Press, 1983), 38.

[17]Karl Rahner, *Theological Investigations,* vol. 5 (London: Darton, Longman, and Todd, 1966), 133.

[18]Schubert M. Ogden, *Is There Only One True Religion or Are There Many?* (Dallas: Southern Methodist University Press, 1992), 32.

[19]See Paul F. Knitter, *Introducing Theologies of Religions* (Maryknoll, N.Y.: Orbis Books, 2002), 137. Consult also Knitter's *One Earth Many Religions: Multifaith Dialogue and Global Responsibility* (Maryknoll, N.Y.: Orbis Books, 1995).

[20]Much of this section is adapted from Don A. Pittman, "Testing a Two-Eyed Truth," *Encounter* 53/4 (Autumn 1992): 365–76.

[21]Paul F. Knitter, *No Other Name? A Critical Survey of Christian Attitudes Toward the World Religions* (Maryknoll, N.Y.: Orbis Books, 1985), 374.

[22]Hans Küng, *Theology for the Third Millennium: An Ecumenical View* (New York: Doubleday, 1988), 240 ff.

[23]See Marjorie Hewitt Suchocki, "In Search of Justice: Religious Pluralism from a Feminist Perspective," in *The Myth of Christian Uniqueness: Toward a Pluralistic Theology of Religions*, ed. John Hick and Paul F. Knitter (Maryknoll, N.Y.: Orbis Books, 1987), 149–61.

Chapter 30: The Future of Christian Mission in an Age of World Christianity

[1]For more discussion on this definition, see Carlos F. Cardoza-Orlandi, *Mission: An Essential Guide* (Nashville: Abingdon Press, 2002).

[2]It is difficult to define vitality of the faith. However, based on *The World Christian Encyclopedia* (New York: Oxford University Press, second edition, 2001), one of the most important resources on World Christian Studies, vitality of the faith is characterized, though not limited to (1) church attendance and participation; (2) a dynamic interaction between daily life experiences and Christian discipleship; (3) the emergence of new liturgical/worship resources emerging from the context of different communities; and (4) the discovery of new theological language in relation to the experience with God, scriptures, and other resources of the Christian tradition.

[3]Some general references and studies that substantiate this statement can be found in Philip Jenkins, *The Next Christendom?* (New York: Oxford University Press, 2002) and *The World Christian Encyclopedia.*

[4]*The World Christian Encyclopedia*, 14–16

[5]This is a pejorative term used to refer to Islamic countries in late nineteenth- and early twentieth-century Protestant missionary literature and geography.

[6]Daisy L. Machado, *Of Borders and Margins: Hispanic Disciples in Texas, 1888–1945* (New York: Oxford University Press, 2003).

[7]Andrew Walls, *The Missionary Movement in Christian History* (Maryknoll, N.Y.: Orbis, 1996), 145.

[8]Jenkins, *The Next Christendom?*, 3.

[9]Walls, *The Missionary Movement*, 145; emphasis mine.

[10]The distinguished historian Kenneth Scott Latourette referred to the ebb of the Christian movement in his seven volumes *A History of the Expansion of Christianity* (New York: Harper & Brothers, 1937–1945).

[11]Walls, *The Missionary Movement*, 146. Following this statement, Walls states, "(I take it for granted that such seriousness excludes simplistic instrumental views of culture which treat it as though it were some sort of evangelistic technique)."

[12]Lamin Sanneh, *Whose Religion Is Christianity?* (Grand Rapids: Eerdmans, 2003). I use Sanneh's definition because it helps the reader to understand the concepts of the Christian movement and the religious and cultural embodiment of the faith in the Third World. I do have several reservations that are not relevant to this paper.

[13]The missiologists might work on both sides of the tasks, both as a historian and as a theologian.

[14]Kwame Bediako, *Christianity in Africa: The Renewal of Non-Western Religion* (Maryknoll, N.Y.: Orbis, 1995), 5.

[15]For more information on the contingent character of mission theologies and practices see Cardoza-Orlandi, *Mission: An Essential Guide.*

[16]Walls, *The Missionary Movement*, 146.

[17]Joaquin Vargas, *Los Discípulos de Cristo en Puerto Rico* (Bayamón: Iglesia Cristiana [Discípules de Cristo] en Puerto Rico, 1988), 82–95.

[18]For a discussion on the contribution of colonial powers to the erosion of Christendom see Andrew Walls, "Christianity in the non-western world: a study in the serial nature of Christian expansion," *Studies in World Christianity* 1.1 (1995): 9–20.

[19]Lucas Torres, "El Avivamiento: Toma de conciencia en cuanto a nuestra identidad puertorriqueña expresada en la adoración y la música" (Asamblea del Centenario, Iglesia Cristiana [Discípulos de Cristo] en Puerto Rico, February 15, 1999, unpublished manuscript), 3–4.

[20]Ibid.

[21]Darrell Guder, "Risking Beginnings: Mission and Evangelism after Christendom" (Inaugural Address, Columbia Theological Seminary, March 28, 2000, unpublished manuscript), 7.

[22]Because of space limitation, the original version is not printed. Translation by Carlos F. Cardoza-Orlandi.

[23]Because of space limitation, the original version is not printed. The prayer is ascribed unofficially to Angel Riba, Charismatic Catholics, translation by Juan Cardoza-Oquendo and Carlos Cardoza-Orlandi.

[24]Because of space limitation, the original version is not printed. Prayer by Archbishop of Hermosillo, José Ulises Macías Salcedo.

[25]For additional theological insights on the "empty cross" symbol in Protestant Latino congregations, see Justo González, "Hanging on an Empty Cross," in *Protestantes/Protestants*, ed. David Maldonado (Nashville: Abingdon Press, 1999).

Bibliography

Allen, Irving H., Sr. *The Christian Church (Disciples of Christ) Profile of the Black Ministers, the Black Church Congregations and Facilities.* Sponsored by The Division of Homeland Ministries and The Division of Higher Education of the Christian Church (Disciples of Christ). Hawkins, Texas: Jarvis Christian College, 1985.

Álvarez-Santos, Carmelo. *People of Hope: The Protestant Movement in Central America.* Cleveland: Friendship Press, 1990.

Álvarez-Santos, Carmelo, Carlos F. Cardoza-Orlandi, and Luis F. Del Pilar (Editor). *Llamados a construir el reino: Teología y estrategia misionera de los Discípulos de Cristo 1899-1999.* Bayamón: La Iglesia Cristiana (Discípulos de Cristo) en Puerto Rico, 2000.

Ames, Edward Scribner. *The Divinity of Christ.* Chicago: New Christian Century Co., 1911. St. Louis: Bethany Press, 1911, 1963, and 1977.

Ammerman, Nancy T. "Golden Rule Christianity: Lived Religion in the American Mainstream." In *Lived Religion in America: Toward a History of Practice,* edited by David Hall. Princeton, N.J.: Princeton University Press, 1997.

Anderson, Allan, and Edmond Tang, eds. *Asian and Pentecostal: The Charismatic Face of Christianity in Asia.* Oxford: Regnum Books International, 2005.

Anderson, E. Byron. *Worship and Christian Identity.* Collegeville, Minn.: The Liturgical Press, 2003.

Aulén, Gustaf. *Christus Victor.* Translated by A. G. Hebert. London: S.P.C.K., 1953.

Baeta, C.G., ed. *Christianity in Tropical Africa.* London: Oxford University Press, 1968.

Balthasar, Hans Urs von. *Dare We Hope: "That All Might Be Saved"?* Translated by David Kipp and Lothar Krauth. San Francisco: Ignatius Press, 1988.

Bankole, Timothee. *Missionary Shepherds and African Sheep.* Ibadan, Nigeria: Daystar Press, 1971.

Baptism, Eucharist, and Ministry. Geneva: World Council of Churches, 1982.

Barret, D.B., ed. *World Christian Encyclopedia.* Nairobi: Oxford University Press, 1982.

Barth, Karl. *Dogmatics in Outline.* Translated by G. T. Thompson. London: SCM Press, 1949.

Bass, Diana Butler. *The Practicing Congregation: Imagining the New Old Church.* Herndon, Va.: Alban Institute, 2004.

Bass, Dorothy C., ed. *Practicing Our Faith: A Way of Life for a Searching People.* San Francisco: Jossey-Bass, 1998.

Beckelhymer, Hunter, ed. *The Vital Pulpit of the Christian Church: A Series of Sermons by Representative Men among the Disciples of Christ.* St. Louis: Bethany Press, 1969.

Bendroth, Margaret Lamberts. *Growing Up Protestant: Parents, Children, and Mainline Churches.* New Brunswick, N. J.: Rutgers University Press, 2002.

Blakemore, William Barnett. *The Discovery of the Church: A History of Disciples Ecclesiology.* The Reed Lectures for 1965. Nashville: Disciples of Christ Historical Society, 1966.

______, ed. *The Renewal of the Church: The Panel of Scholars Reports.* 3 vols. St. Louis: Bethany Press, 1963.

Boff, Leonardo. *Cry of the Earth, Cry of the Poor.* Translated by P. Berryman. Maryknoll, N.Y.: Orbis Books, 1977.

Bonino, Jose Miguez. *Faces of Latin American Protestantism.* Translated by Eugene L. Stockwell. Grand Rapids: W. B. Eerdmans, 1997.

Boring, M. Eugene. *Disciples and the Bible: A History of Disciples Biblical Interpretation in North America.* St. Louis: Chalice Press, 1997.

Broadus, John. *A Treatise on the Preparation and Delivery of Sermons.* New York: Sheldon and Co., 1870.

Brock, Rita Nakashima, Claudia Camp, and Serene Jones, eds. *Setting the Table: Women in Theological Conversation.* St. Louis: Chalice Press, 1995.

Brown, Robert McAfee, ed. *Kairos: Three Prophetic Challenges to the Church.* Grand Rapids: Eerdmans, 1990.

Brueggemann, Walter. *The Prophetic Imagination.* Minneapolis: Fortress Press, 1978.

Burnett, John F. *Early Women of the Christian Church: Heroines All.* Dayton, Ohio: The Christian Publishing Association, 1920.

Campbell, Alexander. *The Christian System, in Reference to the Union of Christians and a Restoration of Primitive Christianity, as Plead in the Current Reformation.* Bethany, Va.: By the author, 1839; reprint, Salem, N.H.: Ayer Company, 1988.

______. "Religious Excitement—No. 1." *Millennial Harbinger,* n. s. 4 (1840): 166–69.

______. "Pre-Eminence of Preaching in Public Worship." *Millennial Harbinger,* 5th ser. 5 (1862): 150–55.

Campbell, Joan, and David Polk, eds. *Bread Afresh, Wine Anew: Sermons by Disciples Women.* St. Louis: Chalice Press, 1991.

Campbell, Thomas. *Declaration and Address.* Pittsburgh: Western Pennsylvania Christian Missionary Society, 1908.

Cardoza-Orlandi, Carlos F. *Mission: An Essential Guide.* Nashville: Abingdon Press, 1999.

Cardwell, Brenda M., and William K. Fox. *Journey Toward Wholeness: A History of Black Disciples of Christ in the Mission of the Christian*

Church. Volume 1: From Convention to Convocation: No Longer 'Objects of' Mission But 'Partners in' the Work (1700-1988). St. Louis: Board of Trustees of the National Convocation of the Christian Church (Disciples of Christ), Christian Board of Publication, 1990.

Cartwright, Colbert S. *People of the Chalice: Disciples of Christ in Faith and Practice.* St. Louis: CBP Press, 1987.

Catherine of Siena, *The Dialogue,* translated by Suzanne Noffke. New York: Paulist Press, 1980.

Chan, Simon. *Pentecostal Theology and the Christian Spiritual Tradition.* New York: Sheffield Academic Press, 2003.

Chapman, Audrey R. *Faith, Power, and Politics: Political Ministry in Mainline Churches.* New York: Pilgrim Press, 1991.

Cox, Harvey. *Fire from Heaven: The Rise of Pentecostal Spirituality and the Reshaping of Religion in the Twenty-First Century.* Reading, Mass.: Addison-Wesley, 1994.

Craddock, Fred B. *As One without Authority.* Enid, Okla.: Phillips University Press, 1971.

Crain, James A. *The Development of Social Ideas among the Disciples of Christ.* St. Louis: Bethany Press, 1969.

Crocker, Lionel, ed. *Harry Emerson Fosdick's Art of Preaching: An Anthology.* Springfield, Ill.: Charles C. Thomas, 1971.

Crossan, John Dominic, and Jonathan L. Reed. *Excavating Jesus: Beneath the Stones, Behind the Texts.* New York: Harper Collins, 2002.

Crow, Paul A. *Christian Unity: Matrix for Mission.* New York: Friendship Press, 1982.

______, ed. *Reappraising the Disciples Tradition for the 21st Century: Christians Only But Not the Only Christians.* Indianapolis: Council on Christian Unity, 1987.

Culp, Kristine A. "'A World Split Open'? Experience and Feminist Theologies." In *The Experience of God: A Postmodern Response,* edited by Kevin Hart and Barbara Wall, 47–61. New York: Fordham University Press, 2005.

______. "Always Reforming, Always Resisting." In *Feminist and Womanist Essays in Reformed Dogmatics,* edited by Amy Plantinga Pauw and Serene Jones, 152–68. Louisville: Westminster John Knox Press, 2006.

DeGroot, A. T. *Disciple Thought: A History.* Overview by Winfred E. Garrison. Fort Worth: TCU Press, 1965.

DeGruchy, John W. *Theology and Ministry in Context and Crisis.* New York: Harper Collins, 1987.

Dempster, Murray A., Byron D. Klaus, and Douglas Petersen, eds. *Called and Empowered: Global Mission in Pentecostal Perspective.* Peabody, Mass.: Hendrickson, 1991.

Devadas, David. *Ecumenism and Youth.* Geneva: WCC Publications, 1995.

Dorrien, Gary. *Soul in Society: The Making and Renewal of Social Christianity.* Minneapolis: Fortress Press, 1995.

Dougall, J. W. C. *Christian in the African Revolution.* Edinburgh: The Saint Andrew Press, 1963.

Driskill, Joseph D. *Protestant Spiritual Exercises: Theology, History and Practice.* Harrisburg, Pa.: Morehouse, 1999.

Dube, Musa W. *Postcolonial Feminist Interpretation of the Bible.* St. Louis: Chalice Press, 2000.

Duke, James O. *What Sort of Church Are We? The Nature of the Church.* Series 1. St. Louis: Christian Board of Publication, 1981.

______. "Scholarship in the Disciples Tradition." *Disciples Historical Digest* 1, no. 1 (1986): 5–40.

______, and Richard L. Harrison, Jr. *The Lord's Supper, The Nature of the Church.* Series 5. St. Louis: Christian Board of Publication, for Council on Christian Unity, 1993.

Dunn, James D. G. *The Christ and the Spirit.* Grand Rapids: Eerdmans, 1998.

Dunnavant, Anthony. "The Historical Development of an Ordered Ministry." *Lexington Theological Quarterly* 37, nos. 1 and 2.

Ellacuria, Ignacio, and Jon Sobrino, eds. *Mysterium Liberationis: Fundamental Concepts of Liberation Theology.* Maryknoll, N.Y.: Orbis, 1993.

Figueroa, Juan. *Instrumentos de la Revelación Divina.* Bayamón: La Iglesia Cristiana (Discípulos de Cristo) en Puerto Rico, 2008.

Ford, David F. *Self and Salvation: Being Transformed.* Cambridge: Cambridge University Press, 1999.

Foster, Douglas A., Anthony L. Dunnavant, Paul M. Blowers, D. Newell Williams, eds. *The Encyclopedia of the Stone-Campbell Movement.* Grand Rapids: Eerdmans, 2004.

Foucault, Michel. *Power/Knowledge: Selected Interviews and Other Writings, 1972-1977.* Translated by Colin Gordon et al. Edited by Colin Gordon. New York: Pantheon, 1980.

Fowler, Stuart. *The Oppression and Liberation of Modern Africa.* Potchefstroom, South Africa: Institute for Reformational Studies, 1995.

Friedly, Robert L., and D. Duane Cummins. *The Search for Identity: Disciples of Christ—The Restructure Years (1960–1985).* St. Louis: CBP Press, 1987.

Garrison, James H., ed. *The Old Faith Restated, Being a Restatement, by Representative Men, of the Fundamental Truths and Essential Doctrines of Christianity as Held and Advocated by the Disciples of Christ in the Light of Experience and of Biblical Research.* St. Louis: Christian Pub. Co., 1891.

Garrison, Winfred E., and Alfred T. DeGroot. *The Disciples of Christ: A History.* St. Louis: Bethany Press, 1948, 1958, and 1964.

Gilkey, Langdon. *Maker of Heaven and Earth: The Christian Doctrine of Creation in Light of Modern Knowledge.* Lanham, Md.: University Press of America, 1985.

Gilpin, W. Clark. "The Doctrine of the Church in the Thought of Alexander Campbell and John W. Nevin." *Mid-Stream* 19 (1980).

______. "The Integrity of the Church: The Communal Theology of Disciples of Christ." In *A Case Study of Mainstream Protestantism: The Disciples' Relation to American Culture 1880-1989,* edited by D. Newell Williams. St. Louis: Chalice Press, 1991; Grand Rapids: William B. Eerdmans, 1991.

______. "Witness to the Deeds of God: Ministry in the Disciple Tradition." *Mid-Stream* 26 (1987).

______. "Toward a Christian Century: Disciples of Christ in the Chicago Ethos, 1899-1909." *Discipliana* 59 (Winter 1999).

González, Justo L., and Pablo Jiménez, eds. *Púlpito: An Introduction to Hispanic Preaching.* Nashville: Abingdon Press, 2005.

González-Doble, Esteban, and Fernando Barbosa. *Una Iglesia Para Ser y Hacer Discípulos.* Bayamón: La Iglesia Cristiana (Discípulos de Cristo) en Puerto Rico, 2001.

Goodnight, Cloyd, and Dwight E. Stevenson. *Home to Bethpage: A Biography of Robert Richardson.* St. Louis: Christian Board of Publication, 1949.

Guha, Ranajit, ed. *Subaltern Studies 1: Writings on South Asian History and Society.* Delhi and New York: Oxford University Press, 1982.

Gutmann, Amy, ed. *Multiculturalism.* Princeton, N.J.: Princeton University Press, 1994.

Hanna, William H. *Thomas Campbell: Seceder and Christian Union Advocate.* Cincinnati: Standard Publishing Co., 1935.

Hanson, K. C., and Douglas E. Oakman. *Palestine in the Time of Jesus: Social Structures and Conflicts.* Minneapolis: Fortress Press, 1998.

Harrell, David Edwin, Jr. *Quest for a Christian America: The Disciples of Christ and American Society to 1866.* Nashville: Disciples of Christ Historical Society, 1966.

______. *The Social Sources of Division in the Disciples of Christ 1865-1900.* Atlanta: Publishing Systems, Inc., 1973.

Harrison, Richard L., Jr. "The Understanding of Ministry in the History of the Christian Church (Disciples of Christ)." *Lexington Theological Quarterly* 37, nos. 1 and 2: 7–26.

Hastings, Adrian. *The Church in Africa 1450-1950.* Oxford: Clarendon Press, 1994.

Hatch, Nathan O. *The Democratization of American Christianity.* New Haven, Conn.: Yale University Press, 1989.

Haynes, Nathaniel. *History of the Disciples of Christ in Illinois 1819-1914.* Cincinnati: Standard Publishing Co., 1915.

Heim, S. Mark. *Saved from Sacrifice: A Theology of the Cross.* Grand Rapids: William B. Eerdmans, 2006.

Hesselgrave, J. David. *Planting Church Cross-Culturally.* Grand Rapids: Baker Book House, 1980.

Hill, Brennan R. *Christian Faith and the Environment: Making Vital Connections.* Maryknoll, N.Y.: Orbis Books, 1998.

Hodgson, Peter C. *Revisioning the Church: Ecclesial Freedom in the New Paradigm.* Philadelphia: Fortress Press, 1988.

Holmes, Barbara A. *Joy Unspeakable: Contemplative Practices of the Black Church.* Minneapolis: Fortress Press, 2004.

Horsley, Richard A., ed. *Paul and Empire: Religion and Power in Roman Imperial Society.* Harrisburg, Pa.: Trinity Press International, 1997.

______, ed. *Paul and Politics: Ekklesia, Israel, Imperium, Interpretation.* Harrisburg, Pa.: Trinity Press International, 2000.

______. *Jesus and Empire: The Kingdom of God and the New World Disorder.* Minneapolis: Fortress Press, 2003.

Hughes, Richard T., and C. Leonard Allen. *Illusions of Innocence: Protestant Primitivism in America, 1630-1875.* With a Foreword by Robert N. Bellah. Chicago: University of Chicago Press, 1988.

Idowu, Boladji E. *African Traditional Religion: Towards an Indigenous Church.* Ibadan, Nigeria: Oxford University Press, 1965.

______. *African Religion: A Definition.* Maryknoll, N.Y.: Orbis, 1973.

James, William. *The Varieties of Religious Experience: A Study in Human Nature [1902].* New York: Collier, 1961.

Jay, Martin. *Songs of Experience: Modern American and European Variations on a Universal Theme.* Berkeley and Los Angeles: University of California Press, 2005.

Jenkins, Philip. *The Next Christendom: The Coming of Global Christianity.* New York: Oxford University Press, 2003.

Jiménez, Pablo A. *Somos Uno: Historia, Teología y Gobierno de la Iglesia Cristiana (Disíipulos de Cristo).* St. Louis: Chalice Press, 2005.

Jones, Joe R. *A Grammar of Christian Faith: Systematic Explorations in Christian Life and Doctrine.* Vol. 1. New York: Rowman and Littlefield Publishers, Inc., 2002.

Jones, Serene. *Feminist Theory and Christian Theology: Cartographies of Grace.* Minneapolis: Fortress Press, 2000.

Kä, Mana. *Christian and Churches of Africa.* Youndé: Edition Clé, 2002.

Kanyoro, Mussimbi, "Thinking Mission in Africa." *International Review of Mission,* 87, no. 345 (April 1998).

Keller, Catherine, Michael Nausner, and Mayra Rivera, eds. *Postcolonial Theologies: Divinity and Empire.* St. Louis: Chalice Press, 2004.

Kimpianga, Mahaniah, "Towards a Self-Supporting African Church." In *An African Call for Life.* Nairobi, Uzima Press, 1983.

Kincaid, Jamaica. *Among Flowers: A Walk in the Himalaya.* Washington, D.C.: National Geographic, 2005.

King, Martin Luther, Jr. *A Testament of Hope: The Essential Writings of Martin Luther King, Jr.* Edited by James Melvin Washington. San Francisco: Harper San Francisco, 1991.

Kinnamon, Michael, ed. *Disciples of Christ in the 21st Century.* St. Louis: CBP Press, 1988.

______. *Truth and Community: Diversity and Its Limits in the Ecumenical Movement.* Geneva: WCC Publications, 1988.

______. *The Vision of the Ecumenical Movement and How It Has Been Impoverished by Its Friends.* St. Louis: Chalice Press, 2003.

Kirk, J. Andrew. *What Is Mission? Theological Explorations.* Minneapolis: Fortress Press, 2000.

Kung, Hans. *Theology for the Third Millennnium: An Ecumenical View.* Translated by Peter Heinegg. New York: Doubleday, 1991.

Lawrence, Ken. *Classic Themes of Disciples Theology: Rethinking the Traditional Affirmations of the Christian Church (Disciples of Christ).* Fort Worth: Texas Christian University Press, 1986.

Lee, Jung Young. *Korean Preaching: An Interpretation.* Nashville: Abingdon Press, 1997.

______. *Marginality—The Key to Multicultural Theology.* Minneapolis: Fortress Press, 1995.

Lincoln, C. Eric, and Lawrence H. Mamiya. *Church in the African American Experience.* Durham, N.C., and London: Duke University Press, 1990.

Long, Thomas G. *The Witness of Preaching.* Louisville: Westminster John Knox Press, 1989.

Lunger, Harold L. *The Political Ethics of Alexander Campbell.* St. Louis: Bethany Press, 1954.

Lyda, Hap C. S. "African Americans in the Movement." In *The Encyclopedia of the Stone-Campbell Movement,* edited by Douglas A. Foster, Paul M. Blowers, Anthony L. Dunnavant, and Newell Williams, 1113. Grand Rapids: Eerdmans, 2004.

Machado, Daisy L. *Of Borders and Margins: Hispanic Disciples in Texas, 1888–1945.* New York: Oxford University Press, 2003.

Makanzu, Mavumilisa. *The Twentieth Century Missionaries and Murmurs of the Africans.* Aberdeen, Scotland: The University of Aberdeen, 1974.

Marsh, Charles. *The Beloved Community: How Faith Shapes Social Justice, from the Civil Rights Movement to Today.* New York: Basic Books, 2005.

Martin, David. *Pentecostalism: The World Their Parish.* Oxford: Blackwell, 2002.

Mass, Robin, and Gabriel O'Donnell. *Spiritual Traditions for the Contemporary Church.* Nashville: Abingdon Press, 1990.

Matsuoka, Fumitaka, and Eleazar S. Fernandez, eds. *Realizing the America of Our Hearts: Theological Voices of Asian Americans.* St. Louis: Chalice Press, 2003.

Mbiti, John S. *Bible and Theology in African Christianity.* Nairobi: Oxford University Press, 1986.

McAllister, Lester G., and William E. Tucker. *Journey in Faith: A History of the Christian Church (Disciples of Christ).* St. Louis: Bethany Press, 1975.

McAvoy, Jane, ed. *Table Talk: Resources for the Communion Meal.* St. Louis: Chalice Press, 1993.

McFague, Sallie. *Models of God: Theology for an Ecological, Nuclear Age.* Philadelphia: Fortress Press, 1987.

______. *The Body of God: An Ecological Theology.* Minneapolis: Fortress Press, 1993.

McGregor, Wynn. *The Way of the Child: Helping Children Experience God.* Nashville: Upper Room Books, 2006.

McIntyre, John. *The Shape of Pneumatology.* Edinburgh: T&T Clark, 1997.

______.*The Shape of Soteriology: Studies in the Doctrine of the Death of Christ.* Edinburgh: T &T Clark, 1992.

Merrick, Daniel B., ed. *Chalice Hymnal.* St. Louis: Chalice Press, 1995.

Miller-McLemore, Bonnie. *In the Midst of Chaos: Care of Children as Spiritual Practice.* San Francisco: Jossey-Bass, 2006.

Milligan, Robert. *An Exposition and Defense of the Scheme of Redemption: As It Is Revealed and Taught in the Holy Scriptures.* N.P., 1868.

Moltmann, Jürgen. *The Spirit of Life.* Translated by Margaret Kohl. Minneapolis: Fortress Press, 1992.

______. *The Coming of God: Christian Eschatology.* Translated by Margaret Kohl. Minneapolis: Fortress Press, 1996.

Mott, Stephen. *Biblical Ethics and Social Change.* New York: Oxford University Press, 1982.

Mountford, Roxanne. *The Gendered Pulpit: Preaching in American Protestant Spaces.* Carbondale, Ill.: Southern Illinois University Press, 2003.

Mudge, Lewis S. "Ecumenical Social Thought." In *A History of the Ecumenical Movement, vol. 3,* edited by John Briggs, Mercy Amba Oduyoye, and George Tsetsis, 279–322. Geneva: World Council of Churches, 2004.

Mugambi, N. K. *The Biblical Basis for Evangelism: Theological Reflections based on an African Experience.* Nairobi: Oxford University Press, 1989.

Nelson, Cary, and Lawrence Grossberg, eds. *Marxism and the Interpretation of Culture.* Urbana, Ill.: University of Illinois Press, 1988.

Niebuhr, H. Richard. *Christ and Culture.* San Francisco: Harper Perennial, 1956.

Niebuhr, Reinhold. *The Irony of American History.* New York: Charles Scribner's Sons, 1952.

______. *The Nature and Destiny of Man. Vol. 1: Human Nature.* New York: Charles Scribner's Sons, 1941.

Noll, Mark. *The Civil War as Theological Crisis.* Oxford: Oxford University Press, 2006.

Norris, Kathleen. *The Quotidian Mysteries: Laundry, Liturgy, and 'Women's Work.'* New York: Paulist Press, 1998.

Oduyoye, Mercy Amba. *Beads and Strands: Reflections of an African Women on Christianity in Africa.* Maryknoll, N.Y.: Orbis Books, 2004.

______. *Daughters of Anowa: African Women & Patriachy.* Maryknoll, N.Y.: Orbis Books, 1995.

Oosthuizen, G. C. *Post-Christianity in Africa.* Grands Rapids: William B. Eerdmans, 1968.

Osborn, Ronald E., ed. *The Renewal of the Church: The Panel of Scholars Reports. 1: The Reformation of Tradition.* St. Louis: Bethany Press, 1963.

______. *The Faith We Affirm: Basic Beliefs of Disciples of Christ.* St. Louis: Bethany Press, 1979.

Page, Ruth. *God and the Web of Creation.* London: SCM, 1996.

Pak, Su Yon, Unzu Lee, Jung Ha Kim, and Myung Ji Cho. *Singing the Lord's Song in a New Land: Korean American Practices of Faith.* Louisville: Westminster John Knox Press, 2005.

Palmer, G. E. H., Philip Sherrard, and Kallistos Ware. "St. Diadochos of Photiki." In *The Philokalia, Vol. One.* Boston: Faber and Faber, 1979.

Parry, Benita. "Problems in Current Theories of Colonial Discourse," *Oxford Literary Review* 9, nos. 1 and 2, 1987.

Parry, Robin A., and Christopher H. Partridge, eds. *Universal Salvation? The Current Debate.* Grand Rapids: Eerdmans, 2003.

Paulsell, William Oliver. "The Disciples of Christ and the Great Depression 1929-1936." Ph.D. diss., Vanderbilt University, 1965.

______. *Disciples at Prayer: The Spirituality of the Christian Church (Disciples of Christ).* St. Louis: Chalice Press, 1995.

Pheko, S. E. M. *The Early Church in Africa and Today.* Lusaka, Zambia: Multimedia Publications, 1981.

Pikasa Xavier. "666: El número de la bestia." In *Signos de Vida,* Segunda Época, Vol. 41. Quito: Ediciónes CLAI, 2006.

Pittman, Don A. "On Preaching the Word: Notes from the History of Religions," *Homiletic* 23 (Winter 1998): 1–7.

Pobee, John S. "The Search for a Living Church in Africa." In *An African Call for Life.* Nairobi: Uzima Press, 1983.

Polkinghorne, John, and Michael Welker, eds. *The End of the World and the Ends of God: Science and Theology on Eschatology.* Harrisburg, Va.: Trinity Press International, 2000.

Potter, Philip, and Thomas Wieser. *Seeking and Serving the Truth: The First Hundred Years of the World Student Christian Federation.* Geneva: WCC Publications, 1996.

Presbyterian Eco-Justice Task Force. *Keeping and Healing the Creation.* Louisville: Committee on Social Witness Policy, Presbyterian Church (U.S.A.), 1989.

Ray, Stephen. *Do No Harm: Social Sin and Christian Responsibility.* Minneapolis: Augsburg-Fortress Press, 2002.

Richesin, L. Dale, and Larry D. Bouchard, eds. *Interpreting Disciples: Practical Theology in the Disciples of Christ.* Fort Worth: Texas Christian University, 1987.

Ricoeur, Paul. "The Hermeneutics of Testimony." In *Paul Ricoeur, Essays on Biblical Interpretation,* edited by Lewis S. Mudge, 119–54. Philadelphia: Fortress Press, 1980.

Rodríguez, Raquel E., and Carmelo Alvarez. *Visiones de Fe: Reflexiones Teológicas Pastorales del Rev. Carmelo Álvarez Pérez.* Costa Rica: n.p., 1984.

Rogers, Eugene F., Jr. *After the Spirit.* Grand Rapids: Eerdmans, 2005.

Ruether, Rosemary Radford. *Women and Redemption: A Theological History.* Minneapolis: Fortress Press, 1998.

Russell, Letty M. *Church in the Round: Feminist Interpretation of the Church.* Louisville: Westminster John Knox Press, 1993.

Salvodi, Valentino, and Renato Kizito. *Africa: The Gospel Belongs to Us.* Ndola, Zambia: Misson Press, 1986.

Sanneh, Lamin, and Joel A. Carpenter. *The Changing Face of Christianity: Africa, the West, and the World.* Oxford: Oxford University Press, 2005.

Scott, Walter. *A Discourse of the Holy Spirit.* 2d ed. Bethany, W. V.A.: Printed by A. Campbell, 1831.

______. *The Gospel Restored: A Discourse of the True Gospel of Jesus Christ.* Cincinnati: Donogh, 1836; reprint, Kansas City: Old Paths Book Club, 1949.

Shields, Bruce E. "Smith, 'Raccoon' John (1784-1868)." In *The Encyclopedia of the Stone-Campbell Movement,* edited by Douglas A. Foster, Paul M. Blowers, Anthony L. Dunnavant, and Newell Williams, 690–91. Grand Rapids: Eerdmans, 2004.

Sprinkle, Stephen V. *Disciples and Theology.* St. Louis: Chalice Press, 1999.

Stam, Juan. *Profecía Bíblica y Misión de la Iglesia.* Quito: Ediciones CLAI, 2004.

Stevenson, Dwight E. *Disciple Preaching in the First Generation: An Ecological Study.* Forrest F. Reed Lectures for 1969. Nashville: The Disciples of Christ Historical Society, 1969.

Stichele, Caroline Vander, and Todd Penner, eds. *Her Master's Tools?: Feminist and Postcolonial Engagements of Historical-Critical Discourse.* Global Perspectives on Biblical Scholarship, no. 9. Atlanta: Society of Biblical Literature, 2005.

Stone, Barton Warren. "An Address to the Elders, Preachers, and Brethren, in the Church of Christ." *Christian Messenger* 2 (1827): 70–72.

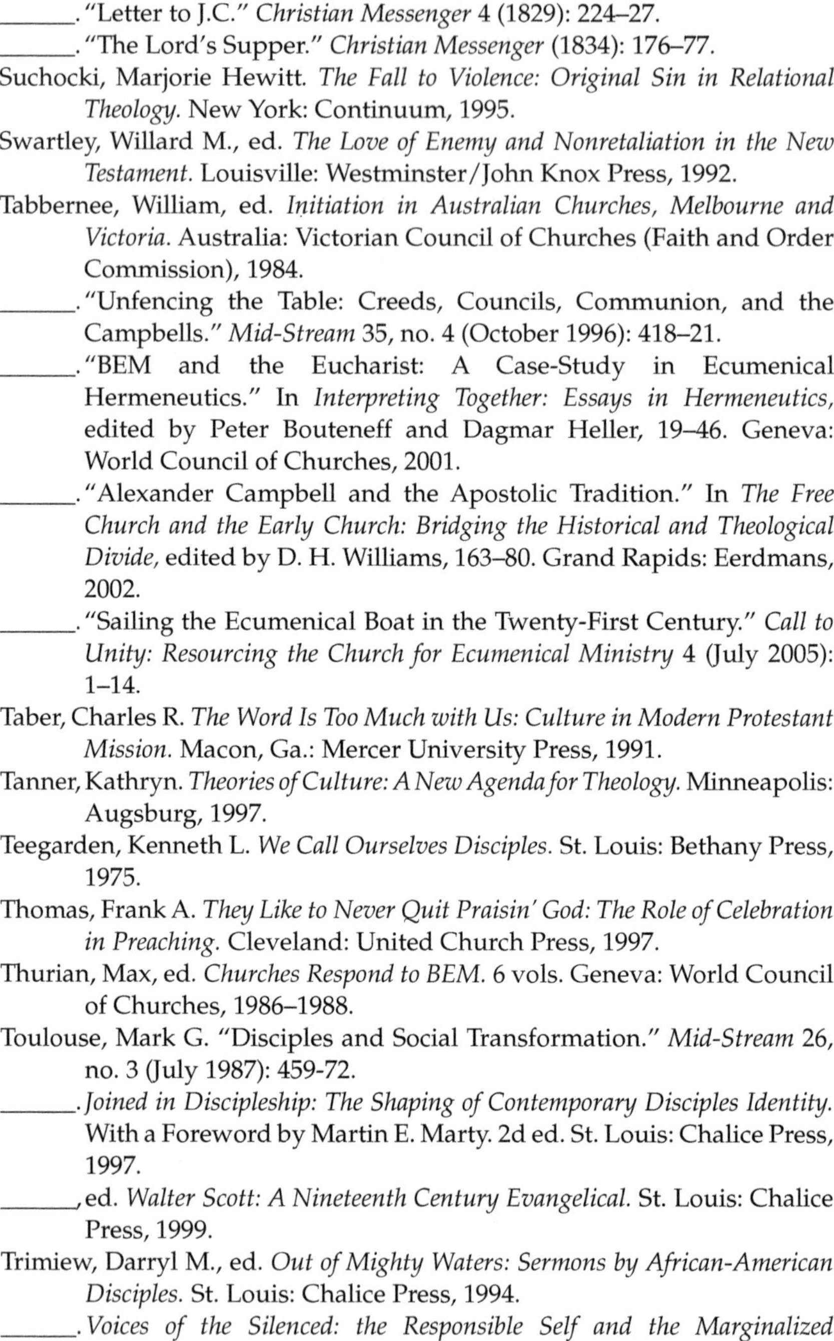

______. "Letter to J.C." *Christian Messenger* 4 (1829): 224–27.

______. "The Lord's Supper." *Christian Messenger* (1834): 176–77.

Suchocki, Marjorie Hewitt. *The Fall to Violence: Original Sin in Relational Theology.* New York: Continuum, 1995.

Swartley, Willard M., ed. *The Love of Enemy and Nonretaliation in the New Testament.* Louisville: Westminster/John Knox Press, 1992.

Tabbernee, William, ed. *Initiation in Australian Churches, Melbourne and Victoria.* Australia: Victorian Council of Churches (Faith and Order Commission), 1984.

______. "Unfencing the Table: Creeds, Councils, Communion, and the Campbells." *Mid-Stream* 35, no. 4 (October 1996): 418–21.

______. "BEM and the Eucharist: A Case-Study in Ecumenical Hermeneutics." In *Interpreting Together: Essays in Hermeneutics,* edited by Peter Bouteneff and Dagmar Heller, 19–46. Geneva: World Council of Churches, 2001.

______. "Alexander Campbell and the Apostolic Tradition." In *The Free Church and the Early Church: Bridging the Historical and Theological Divide,* edited by D. H. Williams, 163–80. Grand Rapids: Eerdmans, 2002.

______. "Sailing the Ecumenical Boat in the Twenty-First Century." *Call to Unity: Resourcing the Church for Ecumenical Ministry* 4 (July 2005): 1–14.

Taber, Charles R. *The Word Is Too Much with Us: Culture in Modern Protestant Mission.* Macon, Ga.: Mercer University Press, 1991.

Tanner, Kathryn. *Theories of Culture: A New Agenda for Theology.* Minneapolis: Augsburg, 1997.

Teegarden, Kenneth L. *We Call Ourselves Disciples.* St. Louis: Bethany Press, 1975.

Thomas, Frank A. *They Like to Never Quit Praisin' God: The Role of Celebration in Preaching.* Cleveland: United Church Press, 1997.

Thurian, Max, ed. *Churches Respond to BEM.* 6 vols. Geneva: World Council of Churches, 1986–1988.

Toulouse, Mark G. "Disciples and Social Transformation." *Mid-Stream* 26, no. 3 (July 1987): 459-72.

______. *Joined in Discipleship: The Shaping of Contemporary Disciples Identity.* With a Foreword by Martin E. Marty. 2d ed. St. Louis: Chalice Press, 1997.

______, ed. *Walter Scott: A Nineteenth Century Evangelical.* St. Louis: Chalice Press, 1999.

Trimiew, Darryl M., ed. *Out of Mighty Waters: Sermons by African-American Disciples.* St. Louis: Chalice Press, 1994.

______. *Voices of the Silenced: the Responsible Self and the Marginalized Community.* Cleveland: Pilgrim Press. 1993.

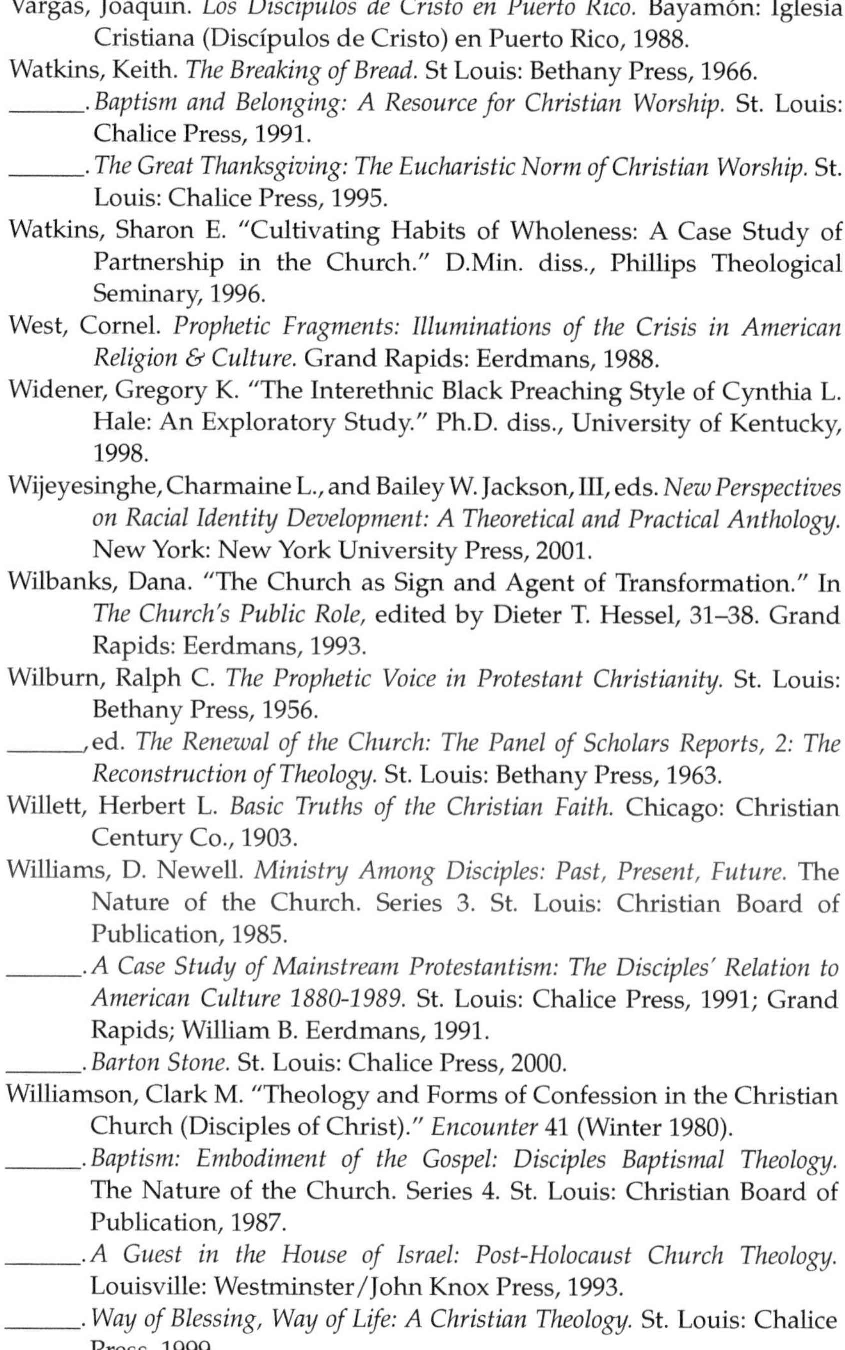

Vargas, Joaquin. *Los Discípulos de Cristo en Puerto Rico.* Bayamón: Iglesia Cristiana (Discípulos de Cristo) en Puerto Rico, 1988.

Watkins, Keith. *The Breaking of Bread.* St Louis: Bethany Press, 1966.

______. *Baptism and Belonging: A Resource for Christian Worship.* St. Louis: Chalice Press, 1991.

______. *The Great Thanksgiving: The Eucharistic Norm of Christian Worship.* St. Louis: Chalice Press, 1995.

Watkins, Sharon E. "Cultivating Habits of Wholeness: A Case Study of Partnership in the Church." D.Min. diss., Phillips Theological Seminary, 1996.

West, Cornel. *Prophetic Fragments: Illuminations of the Crisis in American Religion & Culture.* Grand Rapids: Eerdmans, 1988.

Widener, Gregory K. "The Interethnic Black Preaching Style of Cynthia L. Hale: An Exploratory Study." Ph.D. diss., University of Kentucky, 1998.

Wijeyesinghe, Charmaine L., and Bailey W. Jackson, III, eds. *New Perspectives on Racial Identity Development: A Theoretical and Practical Anthology.* New York: New York University Press, 2001.

Wilbanks, Dana. "The Church as Sign and Agent of Transformation." In *The Church's Public Role,* edited by Dieter T. Hessel, 31–38. Grand Rapids: Eerdmans, 1993.

Wilburn, Ralph C. *The Prophetic Voice in Protestant Christianity.* St. Louis: Bethany Press, 1956.

______, ed. *The Renewal of the Church: The Panel of Scholars Reports, 2: The Reconstruction of Theology.* St. Louis: Bethany Press, 1963.

Willett, Herbert L. *Basic Truths of the Christian Faith.* Chicago: Christian Century Co., 1903.

Williams, D. Newell. *Ministry Among Disciples: Past, Present, Future.* The Nature of the Church. Series 3. St. Louis: Christian Board of Publication, 1985.

______. *A Case Study of Mainstream Protestantism: The Disciples' Relation to American Culture 1880-1989.* St. Louis: Chalice Press, 1991; Grand Rapids; William B. Eerdmans, 1991.

______. *Barton Stone.* St. Louis: Chalice Press, 2000.

Williamson, Clark M. "Theology and Forms of Confession in the Christian Church (Disciples of Christ)." *Encounter* 41 (Winter 1980).

______. *Baptism: Embodiment of the Gospel: Disciples Baptismal Theology.* The Nature of the Church. Series 4. St. Louis: Christian Board of Publication, 1987.

______. *A Guest in the House of Israel: Post-Holocaust Church Theology.* Louisville: Westminster/John Knox Press, 1993.

______. *Way of Blessing, Way of Life: A Christian Theology.* St. Louis: Chalice Press, 1999.

Wink, Walter. *The Powers That Be: Theology for a New Millennium.* New York: Doubleday, 1998.

Wright, N. T. *The New Testament and the People of God.* Minneapolis: Fortress Press, 1992.

Yates, Timothy. *Christian Mission in the Twentieth Century.* Cambridge, U.K.: Cambridge University Press, 1996.

Yoder, John Howard. *The Politics of Jesus.* 2d ed. Grand Rapids: Eerdmans, 1994.

Yong, Amos, and Peter G. Heltzel. *Theology in Global Context.* New York: T&T Clark Press, 2004.

Yu, Geunhee. "Asian American Disciples." In *The Encyclopedia of the Stone-Campbell Movement,* edited by Douglas A. Foster, Paul M. Blowers, Anthony L. Dunnavant, and Newell Williams, 40–41. Grand Rapids: Eerdmans, 2004.

______. *A Handbook for Korean-American Disciples in the Christian Church (Disciples of Christ).* St. Louis: Christian Board of Publication, 2005.

Yust, Karen Marie "Expediency in the Family of God: A Constructive Theological Analysis of the Early Disciples Movement." Ph.D. diss., Harvard University, 1996.

______. *Real Kids, Real Faith: Practices for Nurturing Children's Spiritual Lives.* San Francisco: Jossey-Bass, 2004.

______, and E. Byron Anderson. *Taught by God: Teaching and Spiritual Formation.* St. Louis: Chalice Press, 2006.

Contributors

Carmelo Alvarez, Affiliate Professor of Church History and Theology, Christian Theological Seminary.

Thomas F. Best, Director of the Secretariat for Faith and Order, World Council of Churches.

Rita Nakashima Brock, Co-Director of Faith Voices for the Common Good and Senior Editor in religion at *The New Press*.

Don S. Browning, Alexander Campbell Professor Emeritus of Ethics and the Social Sciences, University of Chicago School of Theology.

Carlos F. Cardoza-Orlandi, Professor of World Christianity, Columbia Theological Seminary.

Choi Hee An, Director of Anna Howard Shaw Center, Boston University School of Theology.

Kristine A. Culp, Dean of Disciples Divinity House and Associate Professor of Theology, Divinity School at The University of Chicago.

Dyron Daughrity, Assistant Professor of Religion, Pepperdine University.

Joseph D. Driskill, Professor of Spirituality, Ronald Soucey Lecturer, Dean of Disciples Seminary Foundation, Pacific School of Religion.

James O. Duke, Professor of History of Christianity and History of Christian Thought, Brite Divinity School, Texas Christian University.

Bosela Eale, Kinshasa Regional Minister, Community of the Disciples of Christ in the Congo.

W. Clark Gilpin, Margaret E. Burton Distinguished Service Professor of the History of Christianity and Theology, Divinity School at The University of Chicago.

Peter Goodwin Heltzel, Assistant Professor of Theology, New York Theological Seminary.

Victor L. Hunter, Minister of Preaching, Theology, and Pastoral Care at Evergreen Christian Church in Evergreen, Colorado, Adjunct Faculty at Phillips Theological Seminary, and retreat director for pastors at "A Mountain Retreat" in Colorado.

Joe R. Jones, Professor Emeritus of Theology and Ethics, Christian Theological Seminary.

Serene Jones, President of the Faculty and Roosevelt Professor of Systematic Theology, Union Theological Seminary.

Verity A. Jones, Publisher and Editor, *DisciplesWorld*.

Belva Brown Jordan, Associate Dean for Admissions and Student Services, Phillips Theological Seminary, Tulsa, Oklahoma.

Michael Kinnamon, General Secretary, National Council of Churches.

Cristobal Mareco Lird, Pastor, Iglesia Cristiana Discípulos de Cristo in Paraguay.

Bonnie J. Miller-McLemore, E. Rhodes and Leona B. Carpenter Professor of Pastoral Theology and Counseling, Vanderbilt University Divinity School.

Mark Miller-McLemore, Dean of Disciples Divinity House and Assistant Professor of the Practice of Ministry, Vanderbilt University Divinity School.

Michael St. A. Miller, Associate Professor of Theology, Christian Theological Seminary.

Kay Lynn Northcutt, Fred B. Craddock Associate Professor of Preaching and Worship, Phillips Theological Seminary, Tulsa, Oklahoma.

William J. Nottingham, President Emeritus, Division of Overseas Ministries, CCDC.

Stephanie A. Paulsell, Houghton Professor of the Practice of Ministry Studies, Harvard Divinity School.

Don A. Pittman, Vice President for Academic Affairs, Dean, and the William Tabbernee Professor of the History of Religions, Phillips Theological Seminary, Tulsa, Oklahoma.

Angel Luis Rivera-Agosto, Pastor of the Christian Church (Disciples of Christ) in Barrio Maricao, Vega Alta, Puerto Rico. He also is the Continental Coordinator of the Latin American Council of Churches' (CLAI) Faith, Economy, and Society Programme.

William Tabbernee, President and Stephen J. England Distinguished Professor of the History of Christianity, Phillips Theological Seminary, Tulsa, Oklahoma.

Darryl Trimiew, Professor of Religious Studies, Medgar Evers College, City University of New York.

Harold Keith Watkins, Professor Emeritus of Practical Parish Ministry, Christian Theological Seminary.

Sharon Watkins, General Minister and President, CCDC.

Clark M. Williamson, Indiana Professor Emeritus of Christian Thought, Christian Theological Seminary.

William A. Wright, Visiting Assistant Professor of Religious Studies, Eureka College.

Karen Marie Yust, Associate Professor of Christian Education, Union Theological Seminary and Presbyterian School of Christian Education.

www.ingramcontent.com/pod-product-compliance
Ingram Content Group UK Ltd.
Pitfield, Milton Keynes, MK11 3LW, UK
UKHW020615180726
13836UKWH00010B/2487

9 780827 205109